THE ANCIENT TRACK

THE ANCIENT TRACK

The Complete Poetical Works of
H. P. Lovecraft

Edited by S. T. Joshi

Hippocampus Press

New York

CONTENTS

5

CONTENTS

Contents

CONTENTS

INTRODUCTION

This new edition of *The Ancient Track* is substantially revised from the first edition of 2001: some small errors in the poems have been corrected, several poems and fragments that have come to light in recent years have been added, along with two appendices, and the notes have been thoroughly overhauled and augmented. It can now safely be said that this volume includes all known poems by H. P. Lovecraft in existence, including untitled or fragmentary poems found in letters and other documents. This is not the place for an analysis of Lovecraft's poetic work; instead, I wish here merely to explain some features of this edition.

I have chosen to segregate Lovecraft's poetry in various categories distinguished by subject-matter; within each category, the poems are arranged in chronological order by date of writing, so far as that can be established; undated poems are placed at the end of each section. Those who wish to read Lovecraft's poetry in absolute chronological order can do so by consulting the "Chronology of Lovecraft's Poems" at the rear of the volume. Many poems could conceivably have been placed in several different categories, and it is merely a matter of judgment that they have been placed in one or the other.

The first category, "Juvenilia," contains all extant poems written by Lovecraft between 1897 and 1905.

The second category, "Fantasy and Horror," features the poems for which Lovecraft is best known. Aside from poems that actually relate a weird or horrific scenario, I have also included poems that perhaps only tangentially deal with the weird, e.g. Lovecraft's tributes to Lord Dunsany, Clark Ashton Smith, and Virgil Finlay.

The largest category in this volume is "Occasional Verse," which includes poems on general topics. The great majority of these poems were written between 1914 and 1920, the period of Lovecraft's heaviest concentration on verse-writing.

Lovecraft's satirical poems form a distinct branch of his output and are gathered in the fourth category. Included in this section are such things as his *Ad Criticos* cycle (1913–14), as well as the poems in the parodic amateur journal *Tosh Bosh*.

Lovecraft's many poems on the seasons or months of the year, or on topographical landmarks (mostly rural locales in New England), are gathered in a fifth category. Of these poems, only a few written in the later 1920s can claim any substantial merit.

A wide array of poems specifically focusing on amateur affairs are included in the sixth category. In reality, the great majority of Lovecraft's poems were written during the period of his first extensive involvement in amateur journalism (1914–22), so that in a sense all his poems of this period could be included here; similarly, poems in the "Occasional Verse" section frequently discuss many individuals with whom Lovecraft had become acquainted in the amateur movement. But the poems in this section deal with quite specific events in the amateur world and merit segregation in their own section. Included here are Lovecraft's many birthday tributes to the aged amateur poet Jonathan E. Hoag.

Lovecraft's poems on politics and society form the seventh category. It is of interest that most of these poems were written during World War I; indeed, the last of them dates only to 1919. It should be noted that several of the poems in the "Satire" section are also on political topics.

In the section of "Personal" poems are included those verses dealing either with Lovecraft's own character or with close family members. The lengthy "Epistle" to Maurice W. Moe is, in its first half, a reminiscence of the year 1904 and, in its second half, a verse response to Moe's previous letter to Lovecraft.

Lovecraft's only play, *Alfredo,* is included in the ninth section, and is followed by a section of fragments.

I have added two appendices to this edition. The first includes the several poems that Lovecraft revised for other writers. There are probably many more such items; for example, Lovecraft admitted to revising much of the verse of the Rev. David Van Bush from about 1920 onward. The poems included here are those for which definitive documentary evidence or strong internal evidence exists as to Lovecraft's involvement.

Appendix 2 includes works by other writers that have a direct bearing on some of Lovecraft's own poems or revisions of poems. Included here are poems by Horace, Ovid, and others that Lovecraft translated; poems that inspired some of Lovecraft's poems, or to which he responded with poems of his own; and the originals (where extant) of poems that he revised.

In my notes I have listed the manuscript sources (if any) on which the texts are based, as well as the first appearances in print of the poems. I have also attempted to provide some background on the writing of the poems and on some of their more interesting features. In this new edition, I have considerably expanded the notes to include elucidations of specific historical, literary, and other references contained in them. References to terms from Graeco-Roman mythology have not been explained, as these terms can readily be found in reference works or online sources. In recent years there has been considerable commentary on Lovecraft's poems, and I have cited a number of perspicacious articles by such scholars as Donald R. Burleson, David E. Schultz, and Robert H. Waugh. An index of titles and first lines (compiled by David E. Schultz) concludes the volume.

In this edition, the previously unavailable poem "An American to Mother England" (discovered by Sean McLachlan) has been included, along with

"Dirge of the Doomed," "To the Recipient of This Volume," and several untitled or fragmentary poems, most of them found in letters.

Lovecraft's poetry must be regarded as a far lesser facet of his literary output than his fiction, essays, and letters, but it merits collection precisely because it is an important ancillary to these other bodies of his work. Prior to the publication of *The Ancient Track* in 2001, Lovecraft's poetry had been scattered in several different volumes whose textual accuracy was not always exemplary, while several poems remained uncollected. This collected edition of Lovecraft's verse is not likely to affect his literary standing to any significant degree, but it may yield some insights into the man and his work that have heretofore remained obscure. A few of his poems, at least, have substantial merits of their own that deserve recognition.

I am grateful to Martin Andersson, David Haden, Juha-Matti Rajala, and David E. Schultz for assistance in the preparation of the text and notes to this new edition.

—S. T. JOSHI

Seattle, Washington
February 2013

I. JUVENILIA: 1897–1905

The Poem of Ulysses, or The Odyssey

The nighte was darke! O readers, Hark!
And see Ulysses' fleet!
From trumpets sound back homeward bound
He hopes his spouse to greet.
Long he hath fought, put Troy to naught   5
And levelled down it's walls.
But Neptune's wrath obstructs his path
And into snares he falls.
After a storme that did much harme
He comes upon an isle   10
Where men do roam, forgetting home,
And lotos doth beguile.
From these mean snares his men he tears
And puts them on the ships.
No leave he grants, and lotos plants   15
Must no more touch their lips.
And now he comes to Cyclops homes
Foul giants all are they.
Each hath 1 eye, and hard they ply
Great Vulcan to obey.   20
A cyclop's cave the wandrers brave
And find much milk & cheese
But as they eat, foul death they meet
For them doth Cyclops seize.
Each livelong day the Cyclops prey   25
Is two most noble Greeks
Ulysses brave he plans to save
And quick escape he seeks.
By crafty ruse he can confuse
The stupid giant's mind   30
Puts out his eye with dreadful cry
And leaves the wretch behind.
Now next he finds the king of winds
Great Æolus's home
The windy king to him doth bring   35
Wind-bags to help him roam.
He now remains in fair domains
In Circes palace grand.
His men do change in fashion strange
To beasts at her command.   40

But Mercury did set him free
From witcheries like this
Unhappy he his men to see
Engaged in swinish bliss.
He drew his sword and spake harsh word   45
To Circe standing there
"My men set free", in wrath quoth he
"Thy damage quick repair"!!!
Then all the herd at her brief word
Become like men once more   50
Her magic beat, she gives all treat
Within her palace door.
And now Ulysses starts in bliss
The Syrens for to pass
No sound his crew's sharp ears imbues   55
For they are stop-ped fast.
Now Scylla's necks menace his decks
Charybdis threats his ships
Six men are lost—O! dreadful cost
But he through danger slips.   60
At last from waves no ship he saves
But on Calypsos isle
He drifts ashore and more & more
He tarries for a while.
At Jove's command he's sent to land   65
To seek his patient wife,
But his raft breaks, and now he takes
His life from Neptune's strife.
He quickly lands on Scheria's strands
And goes unto the king.   70
He tells his tale, all hold wassail;
An ancient bard doth sing.
Now does he roam unto his home
Where suitors woo his spouse
In beggar's rags himself he drags   75
Unknown into his house
His arrows flew at that vile crew
Who sought to win his bride
Now all are killed and he is filled
With great & happy pride.   80
His swineherd first, then his old nurse
Do recognise him well

Then does he see Penelope
With whom in peace he'll dwell.
Until black death doth stop his breath   85
And take him from the earth;
He'll ne'er roam far from Ithaca,
The island of his birth—

Ovid's Metamorphoses

Introduction

I tell of forms transmuted into new;
And since, ye Gods, these deeds were wrought by you,
Smile on my task, and lead my ceaseless lay
From Earth's beginning to the present day.

The Creation of the World

Ere sea & lands, & cov'ring sky were made,   5
Crude Nature one amorphous face display'd;
Chaos, 'twas call'd, a raw unfinish'd mass
Of ill-join'd seeds, congested in one place.
No Titan sun yet shew'd the world his light,
Nor did fair Phoebe mend her crescent bright;   10
No balanc'd Earth th' enclosing vapours bore,
And Amphitrite's arms reach'd not the shore.
Where there was land, were also sea & air;
Weak was the Earth, & naught would Ocean bear;
The atmosphere no rays of light could keep,   15
And warring matter form'd one shapeless heap.
Heat fought with cold; the moist opposed the dry;
Soft things with hard sustained the enmity;
Imponderable clouds display'd their hate
Toward things more solid, & possessing weight.   20
This strife kind Nature & a God subdu'd;
Cut land from heav'n, from land the surging flood;
Distill'd the liquid sky, the aether rare,
From denser vapours, and the humid air.
Which done, the things from Chaos late unwound   25
Were in a more harmonious order bound:
The weightless empyrean first was rais'd,
And in the citadel of heaven blaz'd.
Second in lightness, air took second place,

25

And flow'red, contented in the middle space,   30
Whilst heavier earth the heavier atoms drew,
And, self-compress'd, a rigid solid grew.
Sunk to the depths, upon the strands thus made,
The girdling waters of the Ocean play'd.
When thus the God, whoe'er he may have been,   35
Cut sep'rate members from his wild demesne,
The first, lest some unequal part be there,
Rounded the earth, and shap'd it to a sphere.
Then bade the wind-swell'd channels to surround
The solid shares of the encircl'd ground.   40
Swamps, lakes, and founts he added to the rest;
Descending streams 'twixt sloping banks he prest.
In divers parts, in divers ways they flow;
Suck'd in by earth, some lose themselves below,
Whilst others the expanded Ocean reach;   45
Disdain their banks, and beat the distant beach.
At his command the spacious plains extend;
The grassy vales to various depths descend;
The leaves o'erspread the woods with verdant dye,
And stony mountains rise to meet the sky.   50
As the high heav'n by circling zones are cleft,
Two on the right, as many on the left,
Between which pairs a fifth more ardent lies,
So is the earth the mirror of the skies.
Th' encompass'd solid, by the great god's care,   55
Bears just such regions as the heavens bear.
With deadly heat the middle district glows;
The two extremes lie frozen 'neath the snows;
'Twixt fire & ice the temp'rate zones extend,
Where heat & cold in just proportion blend.   60
O'er these impends an airy canopy,
Which heavier is than fire as earth than sea.
In air's dominion, by divine command,
The fleecy clouds & foggy vapours stand;
Thunders terrific to the mortal mind;   65
The flashing lightning, & the frigid wind.
But Earth's creator gave not these to bear
Conflicting sway, & rule the passive air;
Hard though it be, to shield the world from gales,
(Such strife betwixt the brother blasts prevails)   70
Each wind 's forbid, save from his own domain,

To blow the breeze, or hurl the hurricane.
Thus forc'd & bridled, Eurus now recedes
Toward Nabathaea & the Persian meads;
Where bright Aurora spreads her rosy blaze,   75
And massive mountains meet the morning rays.
From Evening shores, that warm in sunset's beams,
Mild Zephyrus breathes out his airy streams;
While Scythia's steppes, where shines the seven-starr'd Plough,
Beneath the might of dreadful Boreas bow;   80
The rainy Auster, in the cloudy south,
Destroys alike the sunlight & the drouth:
And o'er all these is plac'd the liquid sky,
Which hath no earthy dregs, nor gravity.

The Creation of Man

All sep'rate things were hardly thus dispos'd   85
When myriad stars, by Chaos long enclos'd,
Burst from their bondage, & began to light
The heav'n's whole vault, & cheer the sombre night.
And now, lest any part should vacant be
Of animals in just variety,   90
The constellations, & the forms divine,
Possess the aether, & with splendour shine.
The rolling ocean, & the rippling stream,
With sportive schools of slipp'ry fishes teem.
On solid Earth, ferocious beasts appear   95
Whilst feather'd flocks fly through the mobile air.
Yet one more race Creation still requir'd;
Of holier sort, with nobler spirit fir'd:
To dominate all else in Nature's plan,
Was form'd that last & greatest king—Man.   100
Perchance the fabricator of all things,
The mighty source whence mundane order springs,
From lofty elements, or sacred seed,
Made mortal creatures to supply the need;
Or else the ground, new-made & torn from heav'n,   105
Yet keeping fragments of celestial leav'n,
Jäpetus' great son, Prometheus, took,
Blent it with water from a running brook,
And deftly copy'd in the dampen'd clay,
Th' immortal Gods, that all Creation sway.   110

27

Though animals of less exalted birth,
With drooping glances eye the lowly earth,
The man is bid to lift his lofty face;
Enjoy the blue, & view the starry space.
Terrestrial matter, rough & undefin'd,   115
Thus chang'd, gave rise to stately humankind.

H. Lovecraft's Attempted Journey betwixt Providence & Fall River on the N.Y.N.H. & H.R.R.

Long, long ago, in prehistoric times
Began the subject of these ill-form'd rhymes,
When some craz'd mind, which engines did disdain,
Conceiv'd a plan for an electric train.
Which like a street-car should by trolley run;   5
But heark! my reader, for my tale's begun:

———

After the usual delay of years
Fraught with vain hopes & melancholy fears,
Which ever doth in Providence attend
All plans which seek to alter or amend,   10
We see the old N.Y.N.H. & H.
Bring this idea within its grasping reach
And seek to banish smoke and sable soot
By using lightning on the Bristol route.
No more the trains shall enter Fox Point station;   15
The crowded streets shall be the destination
Of these new cars, by Osgood Bradley built,
With motors new, and fresh in paint & gilt—
One winter's morn, when all man kind did shiver,
I took a train, directed toward Fall-River.   20
Well up in front a seat by chance I chose,
Then settled down, prepar'd for calm repose.
That noble string of freshly painted coaches
The foot of College Hill with speed approaches,
When all at once I'm waken'd with surprise;   25
From off the track my cumbrous chariot flies,
And giving forth a longing hungry roar
Attacks the front of Leonard's Groc'ry store!
With thund'rous crash, the portal is destroy'd
But all the strength of train-men is employed   30
To set on rails the now dethronèd car

28

Which soon is done, with jack & iron bar.
Again we're off, and headed down South Main;
Our speed increases and our spirits gain,
When suddenly a junction meets our view   35
And each car seeks its own way to pursue.
The motor-car inclines toward Wickenden;
The humble trailer seeks South-Main, and then,
Upon its side the rearmost partner slips;
The motor-car in dizzy fashion tips.   40
At last the o'erturn'd trailer's left behind;
Whilst in its mate are all its load confin'd.
A smart conductor, clad in uniform,
Seeks fares from those who have surviv'd the storm.
Quoth one old man, "Take what ye will from me",   45
"But in my damage suit I'll take from thee"!
And now the train essays the hill to climb,
The motors groan, and swiftly flies the time.
At Brook-Street's switch the two trucks disagree
The front goes on, the rear aims diff'rently,   50
And though Fall River is the promis'd shore
This stubborn truck seeks Brook-Street to explore.
By firm yet gentle care we're set aright
And once more try to wing our upward flight.
Just at the summit, as we're slipping back   55
We're tow'd to safety by a one-horse hack.
Soon on an ancient bridge our course is laid
(This bridge was in the middle ages made)
Beneath our weight it gives uncanny groans,
We groan no less from jarr'd & aching bones.   60
Dry land attain'd, we turn a sharp-laid curve
With little hope our safety to preserve.
The monstrous car our bodies threats to mangle,
For this strange curve resembles a right angle.
And now the railway track is in our sight,   65
But adverse fortune once more stays our flight.
For if the railway's wires we would use,
Another trolley-wheel our crew must choose,
And here the Union Railroad Company,
In favour of New-Haven men must flee.   70
After a long and enervating wait,
We start once more, and only six hours late.
The railway track in comfort and with speed
Receives the wheels of our electric steed.

At Riverside the loafers ope their eyes;   75
At Crescent Park the vulgar rabble cries.
The Drownville rustics in confusion gape;
Nor can we Nayatt's wond'ring gaze escape.
But as we near the streets of Barrington
Our coach grows cold, and starts to slowing down.   80
Soon it is still'd, and after one brief hour
We're told that Warren's ceas'd to give us pow'r.
Frigid we rest, 'till later in the day
A locomotive bears us on our way.
We soon reach Warren, but are stall'd again   85
By some mishap to a far distant train
Which lies inert on single track ahead,
With crippled motors, and the wires dead.
But now a ray of hope pervades my mind:
I leave the car, and in the twilight find   90
A willing yokel with an ox-drawn cart
Who when with most of my spare change I part,
Consents to take me where I wish to go,
If I demur not at his progress slow.
At dawn we cross Slade's Ferry and my guide   95
Bids me farewell and 'gins his homeward ride.
Worn and fatigu'd, I seek a good hotel
Wherein I rest my body for a spell.

Next day *by boat* safe homeward I return'd,
And as I 'gan these lines, by chance I learn'd   100
That my staunch train, which I at Warren left
Was now no more of all its pow'r bereft
For though at first for old Fall-River bound
An ancient farmer heard the raucous sound
Of its triumphant, all-rejoicing whistle;   105
Safe home at last, the car had enter'd—BRISTOL!

Poemata Minora, Volume II

Ode to Selene or Diana

Immortal Moon, in maiden splendour shine.
Dispense thy beams, divine *Latona's* child.
Thy silver rays all grosser things refine,
And hide harsh truth in sweet illusion mild.

In thy soft light, the city of unrest 5
That stands so squalid in thy brother's glare
Throws off its habit, and in silence blest
Becomes a vision, sparkling bright and fair.

The modern world, with all it's care & pain,
The smoky streets, the hideous clanging mills, 10
Fade 'neath thy beams, *Selene* and again
We dream like shepherds on *Chaldæa's* hills.

Take heed, *Diana,* of my humble plea.
Convey me where my happiness may last.
Draw me against the tide of time's rough sea 15
And let my spirit rest amid the past.

To the Old Pagan Religion

Olympian Gods! How can I let ye go
And pin my faith to this new *Christian* creed?
Can I resign the deities I know
For him who on a cross for man did bleed?

How in my weakness can my hopes depend 5
On one lone God, though mighty be his pow'r?
Why can *Jove's* host no more assistance lend,
To soothe my pains, and cheer my troubled hour?

Are there no Dryads on these wooded mounts
O'er which I oft in desolation roam? 10
Are there no Naiads in these crystal founts?
Nor Nereids upon the Ocean foam?

Fast spreads the new; the older faith declines.
The name of *Christ* resounds upon the air.
But my wrack'd soul in solitude repines 15
And gives the Gods their last-receivèd pray'r.

On the Ruin of Rome

Low dost thou lie, O *Rome,* neath the foot of the *Teuton*
Slaves are thy men, and bent to the will of thy conqueror:
Whither hath gone, great city, the race that gave law to all nations,
Subdu'd the east and the west, and made them bow down to thy consuls.
Knew not defeat, but gave it to all who attack'd thee? 5

31

Dead! and replac'd by these wretches who cower in confusion
Dead! They who gave us this empire to guard and to live in
Rome, thou didst fall from thy pow'r with the proud race that made thee,
And we, base *Italians,* enjoy'd what we could not have builded.

To Pan

Seated in a woodland glen
By a shallow reedy stream
Once I fell a-musing, when
I was lull'd into a dream.

From the brook a shape arose   5
Half a man and half a goat.
Hoofs it had instead of toes
And a beard adorn'd its throat

On a seat of rustic reeds
Sweetly play'd this hybrid man   10
Naught car'd I for earthly needs,
For I knew that this was *Pan*

Nymphs & Satyrs gather'd 'round
To enjoy the lively sound.

All too soon I woke in pain   15
And return'd to haunts of men.
But in rural vales I'd fain
Live and hear *Pan's* pipes again.

On the Vanity of Human Ambition

Apollo, chasing *Daphne,* gain'd his prize
But lo! she turn'd to wood before his eyes.
More modern swains at golden prizes aim,
And ever strive some worldly thing to claim.
Yet 'tis the same as in *Apollo's* case,   5
For, once attain'd, the purest gold seems base.
All that men seek 's unworthy of the quest,
Yet seek they will, and never pause for rest.
True bliss, methinks, a man can only find
In virtuous life, & cultivated mind.   10

C. S. A.: 1861–1865

To the Starry Cross of the SOUTH

When first this warlike Banner was unfurl'd
A noble cause was born into the World;
No purer Flag hath e'er defy'd the Wind
Proclaiming high the Rights of Human kind.
The cruel YANKEE, midst ignoble Fight,   5
Stood aw'd, or fled in Panick at the Sight;
And though the South by Treachery's o'erthrown,
The Mem'ry of past Valour ne'er is gone:
Midst Ruin vast, and overwhelming Loss,
All Southrons true revere the STARRY CROSS!   10

De Triumpho Naturae

The Triumph of Nature over Northern Ignorance

Lines Dedicated to William Benjamin Smith, Tulane University, La.
Author of "The Colour Line" a Brief in Behalf of the Unborn.

The Northern bigot, with false zeal inflam'd,
The virtues of the Afric race proclaim'd;
Declar'd the blacks his brothers and his peers,
And at their slav'ry shed fraternal tears;
Distorted for his cause the Holy Word,   5
And deem'd himself commanded by the Lord
To draw his sword, whate'er the cost might be,
And set the sons of Aethiopia free.
First with the South in battle he engag'd;
And four hard years an impious warfare wag'd,   10
Then, deaf to Nature, and to God's decree,
He gave the blacks their fatal liberty.
The halls where Southern justice once had reign'd
He now with horrid negro rites profan'd.
Among the free in cursèd mock'ry sate   15
The grinning Aethiop, conscious of his state.
But reckless folly can no further run;
The will of Nature must in Time be done.
The savage black, the ape-resembling beast,
Hath held too long his Saturnalian feast.   20

From out the land, by act of far'way Heav'n,
To ling'ring death his numbers shall be driv'n.
Against God's will the Yankee freed the slave
And in the act consign'd him to the grave.

II. FANTASY AND HORROR

To the Late John H. Fowler, Esq.

Author of Poems of the Supernatural

Farewell, skill'd Fowler, whose weird numbers glow'd
With native genius by the Gods bestow'd;
Whose moving pen th' unbody'd shades inspir'd,
Whilst we, too crude to imitate, admir'd.
Thou haunting poet of the haunted wood,   5
How rapt have we o'er thy bright pages stood!
How oft with thee to heights supernal soar'd,
Or by thy aid uncanny depths explor'd!
Thine were the secrets of the gloomy glen,
Where wraiths, wind-wafted, kept their distant den;   10
Where sighing spirits move the listless leaves,
And owlets nest on ruin'd castles' eaves:
Forgotten fancies fill'd thy fairy field,
Nor would thy spell, save with thy body, yield!
Thy lustrous line with soul spontaneous grew,   15
Nor labour'd art nor pedant's polish knew:
For measur'd cadence throbb'd the tuneful tide,
And what we shape, to thee the Muse supply'd.
With what high fortitude did thy refrain
Deny the burden of thy earthly pain!   20
Th' afflicted flesh, by force of courage borne,
Remain'd for others, but not for thee, to mourn.
Tho' now thy eyes are clos'd in ceaseless rest,
Thy mem'ry by thy living work is blest;
Life's ills are vanish'd, but thy honour'd name   25
Lingers in state, and knows a grateful fame:
Th' eternal bard, whom changing ages scan,
Defies destruction, and survives the man.
So live, sweet spirit, to awake the heart,
And with thy song responding bliss impart: 30
Sing as of yore, with tuneful notes that shew
The grace of Waller, and the depth of Poe.
Scarce death is thine, whose soul but sought that land
Of fair enchantment painted by thy hand!

The Unknown

A seething sky—
    A mottled moon—
Waves surging high—
    Storm's raving rune;

Wild clouds a-reel—   5
    Wild winds a-shout—
Black vapours steal
    In ghastly rout.

Thro' rift is shot
    The moon's wan grace—   10
But *God! That blot*
    Upon its face!

The Poe-et's Nightmare

A Fable

    Luxus tumultus semper causa est.

Lucullus Languish, student of the skies,
And connoisseur of rarebits and mince pies,
A bard by choice, a grocer's clerk by trade
(Grown pessimist thro' honours long delay'd),
A secret yearning bore, that he might shine   5
In breathing numbers, and in song divine.
Each day his fountain pen was wont to drop
An ode or dirge or two about the shop,
Yet naught could strike the chord within his heart
That throbb'd for poesy, and cry'd for art.   10
Each eve he sought his bashful Muse to wake
With overdoses of ice-cream and cake;
But tho' th' ambitious youth a dreamer grew,
Th' Aonian Nymph declin'd to come to view.
Sometimes at dusk he scour'd the heav'ns afar,   15
Searching for raptures in the evening star;
One night he strove to catch a tale untold
In crystal deeps—but only caught a cold.
So pin'd Lucullus with his lofty woe,
Till one drear day he bought a set of Poe: 20
Charm'd with the cheerful horrors there display'd,

He vow'd with gloom to woo the Heav'nly Maid.
Of Auber's tarn and Yaanek's slope he dreams,
And weaves an hundred Ravens in his schemes.
Not far from our young hero's peaceful home   25
Lies the fair grove wherein he loves to roam.
Tho' but a stunted copse in vacant lot,
He dubs it Tempe, and adores the spot;
When shallow puddles dot the wooded plain,
And brim o'er muddy banks with muddy rain,   30
He calls them limpid pools or poison pools
(Depending on which bard his fancy rules).
'Tis here he comes with Heliconian fire
On Sundays when he smites the Attic lyre;
And here one afternoon he brought his gloom,   35
Resolv'd to chant a poet's lay of doom.
Roget's Thesaurus, and a book of rhymes,
Provide the rungs whereon his spirit climbs:
With this grave retinue he trod the grove
And pray'd the Fauns he might a Poe-et prove.   40
But sad to tell, ere Pegasus flew high,
The not unrelish'd supper hour drew nigh;
Our tuneful swain th' imperious call attends,
And soon above the groaning table bends.
Tho' it were too prosaic to relate   45
Th' exact particulars of what he ate
(Such long-drawn lists the hasty reader skips,
Like Homer's well-known catalogue of ships),
This much we swear: that as adjournment near'd,
A monstrous lot of cake had disappear'd!   50
Soon to his chamber the young bard repairs,
And courts soft Somnus with sweet Lydian airs;
Thro' open casement scans the star-strown deep,
And 'neath Orion's beams sinks off to sleep.
Now start from airy dell the elfin train   55
That dance each midnight o'er the sleeping plain,
To bless the just, or cast a warning spell
On those who dine not wisely, but too well.
First Deacon Smith they plague, whose nasal glow
Comes from what Holmes hath call'd "Elixir Pro";   60
Group'd round the couch his visage they deride,
Whilst thro' his dreams unnumber'd serpents glide.
Next troop the little folk into the room

Where snores our young Endymion, swath'd in gloom:
A smile lights up his boyish face, whilst he 65
Dreams of the moon—or what he ate at tea.
The chieftain elf th' unconscious youth surveys,
And on his form a strange enchantment lays:
Those lips, that lately thrill'd with frosted cake,
Uneasy sounds in slumbrous fashion make; 70
At length their owner's fancies they rehearse,
And lisp this awesome Poe-em in blank verse:

Aletheia Phrikodes

Omnia risus et omnia pulvis et omnia nihil.

Daemoniac clouds, up-pil'd in chasmy reach
Of soundless heav'n, smother'd the brooding night;
Nor came the wonted whisp'rings of the swamp, 75
Nor voice of autumn wind along the moor,
Nor mutter'd noises of th' insomnious grove
Whose black recesses never saw the sun.
Within that grove a hideous hollow lies,
Half bare of trees; a pool in centre lurks 80
That none dares sound; a tarn of murky face
(Tho' naught can prove its hue, since light of day,
Affrighted, shuns the forest-shadow'd banks).
Hard by, a yawning hillside grotto breathes,
From deeps unvisited, a dull, dank air 85
That sears the leaves on certain stunted trees
Which stand about, clawing the spectral gloom
With evil boughs. To this accursed dell
Come woodland creatures, seldom to depart:
Once I beheld, upon a crumbling stone 90
Set altar-like before the cave, a thing
I saw not clearly, yet from glimpsing fled.
In this half-dusk I meditate alone
At many a weary noontide, when without
A world forgets me in its sun-blest mirth. 95
Here howl by night the werewolves, and the souls
Of those that knew me well in other days.
Yet on this night the grove spake not to me;
Nor spake the swamp, nor wind along the moor,
Nor moan'd the wind about the lonely eaves 100
Of the bleak, haunted pile wherein I lay.

I was afraid to sleep, or quench the spark
Of the low-burning taper by my couch.
I was afraid when thro' the vaulted space
Of the old tow'r, the clock-ticks died away   105
Into a silence so profound and chill
That my teeth chatter'd—giving yet no sound.
Then flicker'd low the light, and all dissolv'd,
Leaving me floating in the hellish grasp
Of body'd blackness, from whose beating wings   110
Came ghoulish blasts of charnel-scented mist.
Things vague, unseen, unfashion'd, and unnam'd
Jostled each other in the seething void
That gap'd, chaotic, downward to a sea
Of speechless horror, foul with writhing thoughts.   115
All this I felt, and felt the mocking eyes
Of the curs'd universe upon my soul;
Yet naught I saw nor heard, till flash'd a beam
Of lurid lustre thro' the rotting heav'ns,
Playing on scenes I labour'd not to see.   120
Methought the nameless tarn, alight at last,
Reflected shapes, and more reveal'd within
Those shocking depths than e'er were seen before;
Methought from out the cave a daemon train,
Grinning and smirking, reel'd in fiendish rout;   125
Bearing within their reeking paws a load
Of carrion viands for an impious feast.
Methought the stunted trees with hungry arms
Grop'd greedily for things I dare not name;
The while a stifling, wraith-like noisomeness   130
Fill'd all the dale, and spoke a larger life
Of uncorporeal hideousness awake
In the half-sentient wholeness of the spot.
Now glow'd the ground, and tarn, and cave, and trees,
And moving forms, and things not spoken of,   135
With such a phosphorescence as men glimpse
In the putrescent thickets of the swamp
Where logs decaying lie, and rankness reigns.
Methought a fire-mist drap'd with lucent fold
The well-remember'd features of the grove,   140
Whilst whirling ether bore in eddying streams
The hot, unfinish'd stuff of nascent worlds
Hither and thither thro' infinities

Of light and darkness, strangely intermix'd;
Wherein all entity had consciousness,   145
Without th' accustom'd outward shape of life.
Of these swift-circling currents was my soul,
Free from the flesh, a true constituent part;
Nor felt I less myself, for want of form.
Then clear'd the mist, and o'er a star-strown scene,   150
Divine and measureless, I gaz'd in awe.
Alone in space, I view'd a feeble fleck
Of silvern light, marking the narrow ken
Which mortals call the boundless universe.
On ev'ry side, each as a tiny star,   155
Shone more creations, vaster than our own,
And teeming with unnumber'd forms of life;
Tho' we as life would recognise it not,
Being bound to earthy thoughts of human mould.
As on a moonless night the Milky Way   160
In solid sheen displays its countless orbs
To weak terrestrial eyes, each orb a sun;
So beam'd the prospect on my wond'ring soul:
A spangled curtain, rich with twinkling gems,
Yet each a mighty universe of suns.   165
But as I gaz'd, I sens'd a spirit voice
In speech didactic, tho' no voice it was,
Save as it carried thought. It bade me mark
That all the universes in my view
Form'd but an atom in infinity;   170
Whose reaches pass the ether-laden realms
Of heat and light, extending to far fields
Where flourish worlds invisible and vague,
Fill'd with strange wisdom and uncanny life,
And yet beyond; to myriad spheres of light,   175
To spheres of darkness, to abysmal voids
That know the pulses of disorder'd force.
Big with these musings, I survey'd the surge
Of boundless being, yet I us'd not eyes,
For spirit leans not on the props of sense.   180
The docent presence swell'd my strength of soul;
All things I knew, but knew with mind alone.
Time's endless vista spread before my thought
With its vast pageant of unceasing change
And sempiternal strife of force and will;   185

I saw the ages flow in stately stream
Past rise and fall of universe and life;
I saw the birth of suns and worlds, their death,
Their transmutation into limpid flame,
Their second birth and second death, their course 190
Perpetual thro' the aeons' termless flight,
Never the same, yet born again to serve
The varying purpose of omnipotence.
And whilst I watch'd, I knew each second's space
Was greater than the lifetime of our world. 195
Then turn'd my musings to that speck of dust
Whereon my form corporeal took its rise;
That speck, born but a second, which must die
In one brief second more; that fragile earth;
That crude experiment; that cosmic sport 200
Which holds our proud, aspiring race of mites
And mortal vermin; those presuming mites
Whom ignorance with empty pomp adorns,
And misinstructs in specious dignity;
Those mites who, reas'ning outward, vaunt themselves 205
As the chief work of Nature, and enjoy
In fatuous fancy the particular care
Of all her mystic, super-regnant pow'r.
And as I strove to vision the sad sphere
Which lurk'd, lost in ethereal vortices, 210
Methought my soul, tun'd to the infinite,
Refus'd to glimpse that poor atomic blight;
That misbegotten accident of space;
That globe of insignificance, whereon
(My guide celestial told me) dwells no part 215
Of empyrean virtue, but where breed
The coarse corruptions of divine disease;
The fest'ring ailments of infinity;
The morbid matter by itself call'd man:
Such matter (said my guide) as oft breaks forth 220
On broad Creation's fabric, to annoy
For a brief instant, ere assuaging death
Heal up the malady its birth provok'd.
Sicken'd, I turn'd my heavy thoughts away.
Then spake th' ethereal guide with mocking mien, 225
Upbraiding me for searching after Truth;
Visiting on my mind the searing scorn

Of mind superior; laughing at the woe
Which rent the vital essence of my soul.
Methought he brought remembrance of the time 230
When from my fellows to the grove I stray'd,
In solitude and dusk to meditate
On things forbidden, and to pierce the veil
Of seeming good and seeming beauteousness
That covers o'er the tragedy of Truth, 235
Helping mankind forget his sorry lot,
And raising Hope where Truth would crush it down.
He spake, and as he ceas'd, methought the flames
Of fuming Heav'n resolv'd in torments dire;
Whirling in maelstroms of rebellious might, 240
Yet ever bound by laws I fathom'd not.
Cycles and epicycles, of such girth
That each a cosmos seem'd, dazzled my gaze
Till all a wild phantasmal glow became.
Now burst athwart the fulgent formlessness 245
A rift of purer sheen, a sight supernal,
Broader than all the void conceiv'd by man,
Yet narrow here. A glimpse of heav'ns beyond;
Of weird creations so remote and great
That ev'n my guide assum'd a tone of awe. 250
Borne on the wings of stark immensity,
A touch of rhythm celestial reach'd my soul;
Thrilling me more with horror than with joy.
Again the spirit mock'd my human pangs,
And deep revil'd me for presumptuous thoughts: 255
Yet changing now his mien, he bade me scan
The wid'ning rift that clave the walls of space;
He bade me search it for the ultimate;
He bade me find the Truth I sought so long;
He bade me brave th' unutterable Thing, 260
The final Truth of moving entity.
All this he bade and offer'd—but my soul,
Clinging to life, fled without aim or knowledge,
Shrieking in silence thro' the gibbering deeps.

Thus shriek'd the young Lucullus, as he fled 265
Thro' gibbering deeps—and tumbled out of bed;
Within the room the morning sunshine gleams,
Whilst the poor youth recalls his troubled dreams.

He feels his aching limbs, whose woeful pain
Informs his soul his body lives again,   270
And thanks his stars—or cosmoses—or such
That he survives the noxious nightmare's clutch.
Thrill'd with the music of th' eternal spheres
(Or is it the alarm-clock that he hears?),
He vows to all the Pantheon, high and low,   275
No more to feed on cake, or pie, or Poe.
And now his gloomy spirits seem to rise,
As he the world beholds with clearer eyes;
The cup he thought too full of dregs to quaff
Affords him wine enough to raise a laugh.   280
(All this is metaphor—you must not think
Our late Endymion prone to stronger drink!)
With brighter visage and with lighter heart,
He turns his fancies to the grocer's mart;
And strange to say, at last he seems to find   285
His daily duties worthy of his mind.
Since Truth prov'd such a high and dang'rous goal,
Our bard seeks one less trying to his soul:
With deep-drawn breath he flouts his dreary woes,
And a good clerk from a bad poet grows!   290
Now close attend my lay, ye scribbling crew
That bay the moon in numbers strange and new;
That madly for the spark celestial bawl
In metres short or long, or none at all:
Curb your rash force, in numbers or at tea,   295
Nor overzealous for high fancies be;
Reflect, ere ye the draught Pierian take,
What worthy clerks or plumbers ye might make;
Wax not too frenzied in the leaping line
That neither sense nor measure can confine,   300
Lest ye, like young Lucullus Languish, groan
Beneath Poe-etic nightmares of your own!

The Rutted Road

Bleak autumn mists send down their chilly load,
    A raven shivers as he flutters by;
Thro' lonely pasture winds the Rutted Road
    Where bord'ring elms loom bare against the sky.

Those deep-sunk tracks, which dumbly point ahead   5
    O'er travell'd sands that stretch to Vision's rim,
Wake hidden thoughts—a longing half a dread—
    Till Fancy pauses at the prospect dim.

Descending shadows bid me haste along
    The ancient ruts so many knew before;   10
A cricket mocks me with his mirthless song—
    I fear the path—I fain would see no more.

Yet here, with ox-drawn cart, each thoughtless swain
    His course pursu'd, nor left the common way;
Can I, superior to the rustic train,   15
    On brighter by-roads find the dawning day?

With questing look I scan the dark'ning moor;
    Perchance o'er yonder mound all blessings wait;
But still the Rutted Road's resistless lure
    Constrains my progress to the Path of Fate.   20

So must I grope between the brooding trees
    Where those before me found the mystic night;
I travel onward, past the wither'd leas—
    But what, beyond the bend, awaits my sight?

Do fairer lands than this invite my feet?   25
    Will Fate on me her choicest boons bestow?
What lies ahead, my weary soul to greet?
    Why is it that I do not wish to know?

Nemesis

    Thro' the ghoul-guarded gateways of slumber,
        Past the wan-moon'd abysses of night,
    I have liv'd o'er my lives without number,
        I have sounded all things with my sight;
And I struggle and shriek ere the daybreak, being driven to madness with fright.   5

    I have whirl'd with the earth at the dawning,
        When the sky was a vaporous flame,
    I have seen the dark universe yawning,
        Where the black planets roll without aim;
Where they roll in their horror unheeded, without knowledge or lustre or name.   10

I have drifted o'er seas without ending,
    Under sinister grey-clouded skies
That the many-fork'd lightning is rending,
    That resound with hysterical cries;
With the moans of invisible daemons that out of the green waters rise.   15

I have plung'd like a deer thro' the arches
    Of the hoary primordial grove,
Where the oaks feel the presence that marches
    And stalks on where no spirit dares rove;
And I flee from a thing that surrounds me, and leers thro' dead branches above. 20

I have stumbled by cave-riddled mountains
    That rise barren and bleak from the plain,
I have drunk of the frog-foetid fountains
    That ooze down to the marsh and the main;
And in hot cursed tarns I have seen things I care not to gaze on again.   25

I have scann'd the vast ivy-clad palace,
    I have trod its untenanted hall,
Where the moon writhing up from the valleys
    Shews the tapestried things on the wall;
Strange figures discordantly woven, which I cannot endure to recall.   30

I have peer'd from the casement in wonder
    At the mouldering meadows around,
At the many-roof'd village laid under
    The curse of a grave-girdled ground;
And from rows of white urn-carven marble I listen intently for sound.   35

I have haunted the tombs of the ages,
    I have flown on the pinions of fear
Where the smoke-belching Erebus rages,
    Where the jokulls loom snow-clad and drear;
And in realms where the sun of the desert consumes what it never can cheer. 40

I was old when the Pharaohs first mounted
    The jewel-deck'd throne by the Nile;
I was old in those epochs uncounted
    When I, and I only, was vile;
And Man, yet untainted and happy, dwelt in bliss on the far Arctic isle.   45

Oh, great was the sin of my spirit,
    And great is the reach of its doom;
Not the pity of Heaven can cheer it,

Nor can respite be found in the tomb;
Down the infinite aeons come beating the wings of unmerciful gloom.   50

Thro' the ghoul-guarded gateways of slumber,
Past the wan-moon'd abysses of night,
I have liv'd o'er my lives without number,
I have sounded all things with my sight;
And I struggle and shriek ere the daybreak, being driven to madness with fright.   55

Astrophobos

In the midnight heavens burning
    Thro' ethereal deeps afar,
Once I watch'd with restless yearning
    An alluring, aureate star;
Ev'ry eye aloft returning,   5
    Gleaming nigh the Arctic car.

Mystic waves of beauty blended
    With the gorgeous golden rays;
Phantasies of bliss descended
    In a myrrh'd Elysian haze;   10
And in lyre-born chords extended
    Harmonies of Lydian lays.

There (thought I) lie scenes of pleasure,
    Where the free and blessed dwell,
And each moment bears a treasure   15
    Freighted with a lotus-spell,
And there floats a liquid measure
    From the lute of Israfel.

There (I told myself) were shining
    Worlds of happiness unknown,   20
Peace and Innocence entwining
    By the Crowned Virtue's throne;
Men of light, their thoughts refining
    Purer, fairer, than our own.

Thus I mus'd, when o'er the vision   25
    Crept a red delirious change;
Hope dissolving to derision,
    Beauty to distortion strange;

48

Hymnic chords in weird collision,
    Spectral sights in endless range.   30

Crimson burn'd the star of sadness
    As behind the beams I peer'd;
All was woe that seem'd but gladness
    Ere my gaze with truth was sear'd;
Cacodaemons, mir'd with madness,   35
    Thro' the fever'd flick'ring leer'd.

Now I know the fiendish fable
    That the golden glitter bore;
Now I shun the spangled sable
    That I watch'd and lov'd before;   40
But the horror, set and stable,
    Haunts my soul for evermore.

Psychopompos: A Tale in Rhyme

    I am He who howls in the night;
        I am He who moans in the snow;
    I am He who hath never seen light;
        I am He who mounts from below.

    My car is the car of Death;   5
        My wings are the wings of dread;
    My breath is the north wind's breath;
        My prey are the cold and the dead.

In old Auvergne, when schools were poor and few,
And peasants fancy'd what they scarcely knew,   10
When lords and gentry shunn'd their Monarch's throne
For solitary castles of their own,
There dwelt a man of rank, whose fortress stood
In the hush'd twilight of a hoary wood.
De Blois his name; his lineage high and vast,   15
A proud memorial of an honour'd past;
But curious swains would whisper now and then
That Sieur De Blois was not as other men.
In person dark and lean, with glossy hair,
And gleaming teeth that he would often bare,   20
With piercing eye, and stealthy roving glance,
And tongue that clipt the soft, sweet speech of France;
The Sieur was little lov'd and seldom seen,

49

So close he kept within his own demesne.
The castle servants, few, discreet, and old,   25
Full many a tale of strangeness might have told;
But bow'd with years, they rarely left the door
Wherein their sires and grandsires serv'd before.
Thus gossip rose, as gossip rises best,
When mystery imparts a keener zest;   30
Seclusion oft the poison tongue attracts,
And scandal prospers on a dearth of facts.
'Twas said, the Sieur had more than once been spy'd
Alone at midnight by the river's side,
With aspect so uncouth, and gaze so strange,   35
That rustics cross'd themselves to see the change;
Yet none, when press'd, could clearly say or know
Just what it was, or why they trembled so.
De Blois, as rumour whisper'd, fear'd to pray,
Nor us'd his chapel on the Sabbath day;   40
Howe'er this may have been, 'twas known at least
His household had no chaplain, monk, or priest.
But if the Master liv'd in dubious fame,
Twice fear'd and hated was his noble Dame;
As dark as he, in features wild and proud,   45
And with a weird supernal grace endow'd,
The haughty mistress scorn'd the rural train
Who sought to learn her source, but sought in vain.
Old women call'd her eyes too bright by half,
And nervous children shiver'd at her laugh;   50
Richard, the dwarf (whose word had little weight),
Vow'd she was like a serpent in her gait,
Whilst ancient Pierre (the aged often err)
Laid all her husband's mystery to her.
Still more absurd were those odd mutter'd things   55
That calumny to curious list'ners brings;
Those subtle slanders, told with downcast face,
And muffled voice—those tales no man may trace;
Tales that the faith of old wives can command,
Tho' always heard at sixth or seventh hand.   60
Thus village legend darkly would imply
That Dame De Blois possess'd an evil eye;
Or going further, furtively suggest
A lurking spark of sorcery in her breast;
Old Mère Allard (herself half witch) once said   65

The lady's glance work'd strangely on the dead.
So liv'd the pair, like many another two
That shun the crowd, and shrink from public view.
They scorn'd the doubts by ev'ry peasant shewn,
And ask'd but one thing—to be let alone!   70

'Twas Candlemas, the dreariest time of year,
With fall long gone, and spring too far to cheer,
When little Jean, the bailiff's son and heir,
Fell sick and threw the doctors in despair.
A child so stout and strong that few would think   75
An hour might carry him to death's dark brink,
Yet pale he lay, tho' hidden was the cause,
And Galens search'd in vain thro' Nature's laws.
But stricken sadness could not quite suppress
The roving thought, or wrinkled grandam's guess: 80
Tho' spoke by stealth, 'twas known to half a score
That Dame De Blois rode by the day before;
She had (they said) with glances weird and wild
Paus'd by the gate to view the prattling child,
Nor did they like the smile which seem'd to trace   85
New lines of evil on her proud, dark face.
These things they whisper'd, when the mother's cry
Told of the end—the gentle soul gone by;
In genuine grief the kindly watcher wept,
Whilst the lov'd babe with saints and angels slept.   90
The village priest his simple rites went thro',
And good Michel nail'd up the box of yew;
Around the corpse the holy candles burn'd,
The mourners sighed, the parents dumbly yearn'd.
Then one by one each sought his humble bed,   95
And left the lonely mother with her dead.
Late in the night it was, when o'er the vale
The storm-king swept with pandemoniac gale;
Deep pil'd the cruel snow, yet strange to tell,
The lightning sputter'd while the white flakes fell;   100
A hideous presence seem'd abroad to steal,
And terror sounded in the thunder's peal.
Within the house of grief the tapers glow'd
Whilst the poor mother bow'd beneath her load;
Her salty eyes too tired now to weep,   105
Too pain'd to see, too sad to close in sleep.

The clock struck three, above the tempest heard,
When something near the lifeless infant stirr'd;
Some slipp'ry thing, that flopp'd in awkward way,
And climb'd the table where the coffin lay;   110
With scaly convolutions strove to find
The cold, still clay that death had left behind.
The nodding mother hears—starts broad awake—
Empower'd to reason, yet too stunn'd to shake;
The pois'nous thing she sees, and nimbly foils   115
The ghoulish purpose of the quiv'ring coils:
With ready axe the serpent's head she cleaves,
And thrills with savage triumph whilst she grieves.
The injur'd reptile hissing glides from sight,
And hides its cloven carcass in the night.   120

The weeks slipp'd by, and gossip's tongue began
To call the Sieur De Blois an alter'd man;
With curious mien he oft would pace along
The village street, and eye the gaping throng.
Yet whilst he shew'd himself as ne'er before,   125
His wild-eyed lady was observ'd no more.
In course of time, 'twas scarce thought odd or ill
That he his ears with village lore should fill;
Nor was the town with special rumour rife
When he sought out the bailiff and his wife: 130
Their tale of sorrow, with its ghastly end,
Was told, indeed, by ev'ry wond'ring friend.
The Sieur heard all, and low'ring rode away,
Nor was he seen again for many a day.

When vernal sunshine shed its cheering glow,   135
And genial zephyrs blew away the snow,
To frighten'd swains a horror was reveal'd
In the damp herbage of a melting field.
There (half preserv'd by winter's frigid bed)
Lay the dark Dame De Blois, untimely dead;   140
By some assassin's stroke most foully slain,
Her shapely brow and temples cleft in twain.
Reluctant hands the dismal burden bore
To the stone arches of the husband's door,
Where silent serfs the ghastly thing receiv'd,   145
Trembling with fright, but less amaz'd than griev'd;
The Sieur his dame beheld with blazing eyes,

52

And shook with anger, more than with surprise.
(At least 'tis thus the stupid peasants told
Their wide-mouth'd wives when they the tale unroll'd.)   150
The village wonder'd why De Blois had kept
His spouse's loss unmention'd and unwept,
Nor were there lacking sland'rous tongues to claim
That the dark master was himself to blame.
But village talk could scarcely hope to solve   155
A crime so deep, and thus the months revolve:
The rural train repeat the gruesome tale,
And gape and marvel more than they bewail.

Swift flew the sun, and winter once again
With icy talons gripp'd the frigid plain.   160
December brought its store of Christmas cheer,
And grateful peasants hail'd the op'ning year;
But by the hearth as Candlemas drew nigh,
The whisp'ring ancients spoke of things gone by.
Few had forgot the dark demoniac lore   165
Of things that came the Candlemas before,
And many a crone intently eyed the house
Where dwelt the sadden'd bailiff and his spouse.
At last the day arriv'd, the sky o'erspread
With dark'ning messengers and clouds of lead;   170
Each neighb'ring grove Aeolian warnings sigh'd,
And thick'ning terrors broadcast seem'd to bide.
The good folk, tho' they knew not why, would run
Swift past the bailiff's door, the scene to shun;
Within the house the grieving couple wept,   175
And mourn'd the child who now forever slept.
On rush'd the dusk in doubly hideous form,
Borne on the pinions of the gath'ring storm;
Unusual murmurs fill'd the rainless wind,
And hast'ning trav'llers fear'd to glance behind.   180
Mad o'er the hills the daemon tempest tore;
The rising river lash'd the troubled shore;
Black thro' the night the awful storm-god prowl'd,
And froze the list'ners' life-blood as he howl'd;
Gigantic trees like supple rushes sway'd,   185
Whilst for his home the trembling cotter pray'd.
Now falls a sudden lull amidst the gale;
With less'ning force the circling currents wail;

Far down the stream that laves the neighb'ring mead
Burst a new ululation, wildly key'd;   190
The peasant train a frantic mien assume,
And huddle closer in the spectral gloom:
To each strain'd ear the truth too well is known,
For that dread sound can come from wolves alone!
The rustics close attend, when ere they think,   195
A lupine army swarms the river's brink;
From out the waters leap a howling train
That rend the air, and scatter o'er the plain:
With flaming orbs the frothing creatures fly,
And chant with hellish voice their hungry cry.   200
First of the pack a mighty monster leaps
With fearless tread, and martial order keeps;
Th' attendant wolves his yelping tones obey,
And form in columns for the coming fray:
No frighten'd swain they harm, but silent bound   205
With a fix'd purpose o'er the frozen ground.
Straight course the monsters thro' the village street,
Unholy vigour in their flying feet;
Thro' half-shut blinds the shelter'd peasants peer,
And wax in wonder as they lose in fear.   210
Th' excited pack at last their goal perceive,
And the vex'd air with deaf'ning clamour cleave;
The churls, astonish'd, watch th' unnatural herd
Flock round a cottage at the leader's word:
Quick spreads the fearsome fact, by rumour blown,   215
That the doom'd cottage is the bailiff's own!
Round and around the howling daemons glide,
Whilst the fierce leader scales the vine-clad side;
The frantic wind its horrid wail renews,
And mutters madly thro' the lifeless yews.   220
In the frail house the bailiff calmly waits
The rav'ning horde, and trusts th' impartial Fates,
But the wan wife revives with curious mien
Another monster and an older scene;
Amidst th' increasing wind that rocks the walls,   225
The dame to him the serpent's deed recalls:
Then as a nameless thought fills both their minds,
The bare-fang'd leader crashes thro' the blinds.
Across the room, with murd'rous fury rife,
Leaps the mad wolf, and seizes on the wife;   230

With strange intent he drags his shrieking prey
Close to the spot where once the coffin lay.
Wilder and wilder roars the mounting gale
That sweeps the hills and hurtles thro' the vale;
The ill-made cottage shakes, the pack without   235
Dance with new fury in demoniac rout.
Quick as his thought, the valiant bailiff stands
Above the wolf, a weapon in his hands;
The ready axe that serv'd a year before,
Now serves as well to slay one monster more.   240
The creature drops inert, with shatter'd head,
Full on the floor, and silent as the dead;
The rescu'd wife recalls the dire alarms,
And faints from terror in her husband's arms.
But as he holds her, all the cottage quakes,   245
And with full force the titan tempest breaks:
Down crash the walls, and o'er their shrinking forms
Burst the mad revels of the storm of storms.
Th' encircling wolves advance with ghastly pace,
Hunger and murder in each gleaming face,   250
But as they close, from out the hideous night
Flashes a bolt of unexpected light:
The vivid scene to ev'ry eye appears,
And peasants shiver with returning fears.
Above the wreck the scatheless chimney stays,   255
Its outline glimm'ring in the fitful rays,
Whilst o'er the hearth still hangs the household shrine,
The Saviour's image and the Cross divine!
Round the blest spot a lambent radiance glows,
And shields the cotters from their stealthy foes: 260
Each monstrous creature marks the wondrous glare,
Drops, fades, and vanishes in empty air!
The village train with startled eyes adore,
And count their beads in rev'rence o'er and o'er.
Now fades the light, and dies the raging blast,   265
The hour of dread and reign of horror past.
Pallid and bruis'd, from out his toppled walls
The panting bailiff with his good wife crawls:
Kind hands attend them, whilst o'er all the town
A strange sweet peace of spirit settles down.   270
Wonder and fear are still'd in soothing sleep,
As thro' the breaking clouds the moon rays peep.

55

Here paus'd the prattling grandam in her speech,
Confus'd with age, the tale half out of reach;
The list'ning guest, impatient for a clue,   275
Fears 'tis not one tale, but a blend of two;
He fain would know how far'd the widow'd lord
Whose eerie ways th' initial theme afford,
And marvels that the crone so quick should slight
His fate, to babble of the wolf-wrack'd night.   280
The old wife, press'd, for greater clearness strives,
Nods wisely, and her scatter'd wits revives;
Yet strangely lingers on her latter tale
Of wolf and bailiff, miracle and gale.
When (quoth the crone) the dawn's bright radiance bath'd   285
Th' eventful scene, so late in terror swath'd,
The chatt'ring churls that sought the ruin'd cot
Found a new marvel in the gruesome spot.
From fallen walls a trail of gory red,
As of the stricken wolf, erratic led;   290
O'er road and mead the new-dript crimson wound,
Till lost amidst the neighb'ring swampy ground:
With wonder unappeas'd the peasants burn'd,
For what the quicksand takes is ne'er return'd.

Once more the grandam, with a knowing eye,   295
Stops in her tale, to watch a hawk soar by;
The weary list'ner, baffled, seeks anew
For some plain statement, or enlight'ning clue.
Th' indulgent crone attends the puzzled plea,
Yet strangely mutters o'er the mystery.   300
The Sieur? Ah, yes—that morning all in vain
His shaking servants scour'd the frozen plain;
No man had seen him since he rode away
In silence on the dark preceding day.
His horse, wild-eyed with some unusual fright,   305
Came wand'ring from the river-bank that night.
His hunting-hound, that mourn'd with piteous woe,
Howl'd by the quicksand swamp, his grief to shew.
The village folk thought much, but utter'd less;
The servants' search wore out in emptiness: 310
For Sieur De Blois (the old wife's tale is o'er)
Was lost to mortal sight for evermore.

The Eidolon

'Twas at a nameless hour of night
When fancies in delirious flight
About the silent sleeper reel
And thro' his mindless visions steal;
When flesh upon its earthly bed   5
Sprawls corpse-like and untenanted—
Vacant of soul, which freely flies
Thro' worlds unknown to waking eyes.
The horned moon above the spire
With ghastly grace was crawling high'r,   10
And in the pallid struggling beams
Grinn'd memories of ancient dreams.
Aloft in heav'n each starry sign
Flicker'd fantastic and malign,
Whilst voices from the gaping deep   15
Bade me assuage my woes in sleep.
This scene, one night in chill November,
I shall thro' many a year remember.
Beneath another moon I espy'd
A bleak and barren countryside,   20
Where spectral shadows darkly crept
O'er moorland mounds where dead things slept.
The beck'ning moonlight wanly play'd
On forms unusual and ill-made,
Aërial forms from strange dominions,   25
Hither and thither borne on pinions
That flutter'd as in fev'rish quest
Of some far land of light and rest.
In this dark throng my sight could trace
Beings from all ethereal space;   30
A sentient chaos gather'd here
From ev'ry immemorial sphere,
Yet of one mind, with ardour rife
To find the Eidolon call'd *Life*.
The murky moon, a daemon eye   35
Drunkenly winking in the sky,
Flew on and on above the plain
And drew my spirit in its train.
I saw a mountain, coronate
With cities populous and great,   40
Whose habitants, a mighty number,

Lay hid in deep nocturnal slumber,
So that the moon for long dim hours
Leer'd on lone streets and silent tow'rs.
Fair beyond words the mountain stood,   45
Its base encircled by a wood;
Adown its side a brooklet bright
Ran dancing in the spectral light.
Each city that adorn'd its crest
Seem'd anxious to outvie the rest,   50
For carven columns, domes, and fanes
Gleam'd rich and lovely o'er the plains.
And now the moon in heav'n stood still
As if no more foreboding ill,
Whereat the throngs aërial knew   55
That *Life* at last was in their view;
That the fair mount each gaz'd upon
Was *Life*, the long-sought Eidolon!
But lo! what rays the scene illume
As dawn intrudes upon the gloom?   60
The East is hideous with the flare
Of blood-hued light—a garish glare—
While ghastly grey the mountain stands,
The terror of the neighb'ring lands.
The cursed wood of twisted trees   65
Waves awful talons in the breeze,
And down the slope the oozing stream
Reflects the day with shocking gleam.
Aloft the light of knowledge crawls,
Staining the crumbling city walls   70
Thro' which in troops ungainly squirm
The foetid lizard and the worm.
White leprous marble in the light
Shews sculptures that repel and fright,
And many a temple hints the sin   75
And blasphemy that reign within.
"O Pow'rs of Light and Space and Aidenn,
Is *Life* with such foul horrors laden?
Pray hide no more the wondrous plan,
But shew the living glory—Man!"   80
Now on the streets the houses spew
A loathsome pestilence, a crew
Of things I cannot, dare not name,

So vile their form, so black their shame.
And in the sky the leering sun   85
Laughs at the havock he hath done,
Nor pities the vague forms that flee
Back to the Night eternally.
"O Moonlit, Mound-mark'd Moor of *Death,*
Renew thy reign! Thy lethal breath   90
Is balm elysian to the soul
That sees the light and knows the whole."
I sought to join the winged train
That plung'd into the dusk again,
But Horror, eating at my mind,   95
Held my poor falt'ring steps behind.
In dreams I fain would flee the day—
Too late, for I have lost the way!

A Cycle of Verse

Oceanus

Sometimes I stand upon the shore
Where ocean vaults their effluence pour,
And troubled waters sigh and shriek
Of secrets that they dare not speak.
From nameless valleys far below,   5
And hills and plains no man may know,
The mystic swells and sullen surges
Hint like accursed thaumaturges
A thousand horrors, big with awe,
That long-forgotten ages saw.   10
O salt, salt winds, that bleakly sweep
Across the barren heaving deep:
O wild, wan waves, that call to mind
The chaos Earth hath left behind:
Of you I ask one thing alone—   15
Leave, leave your ancient lore unknown!

Clouds

Of late I climb'd a lonely height
And watch'd the moon-streak'd clouds in flight,
Whose forms fantastic reel'd and whirl'd
Like genii of a spectral world.

Thin cirri veil'd the silv'ry dome   5
And waver'd like the ocean foam,
While shapes of darker, heavier kind
Scudded before a daemon wind.
Methought the churning vapours took
Now and anon a fearsome look,   10
As if amidst the fog and blur
March'd figures known and sinister.
From west to east the things advanc'd—
A mocking train that leap'd and danc'd
Like Bacchanals with joined hands   15
In endless file thro' airy lands.
Aërial mutt'rings, dimly heard,
The comfort of my spirit stirr'd
With hideous thoughts, that bade me screen
My sight from the portentous scene.   20
"Yon fleeing mists," the murmurs said,
"Are ghosts of hopes, deny'd and dead."

Mother Earth

One night I wander'd down the bank
Of a deep valley, hush'd and dank,
Whose stagnant air possess'd a taint
And chill that made me sick and faint.
The frequent trees on ev'ry hand   5
Loom'd like a ghastly goblin band,
And branches 'gainst the narrowing sky
Took shapes I fear'd—I knew not why.
Deeper I plung'd, and seem'd to grope
For some lost thing as joy or hope,   10
Yet found, for all my searchings there,
Naught save the phantoms of despair.
The walls contracted as I went
Still farther in my mad descent,
Till soon, of moon and stars bereft,   15
I crouch'd within a rocky cleft
So deep and ancient that the stone
Breath'd things primordial and unknown.
My hands, exploring, strove to trace
The features of the valley's face,   20
When midst the gloom they seem'd to find

60

An outline frightful to my mind.
Not any shape my straining eyes,
Could they have seen, might recognise;
For what I touch'd bespoke a day   25
Too old for man's fugacious sway.
The clinging lichens moist and hoary
Forbade me read the antique story;
But hidden water, trickling low,
Whisper'd the tales I should not know.   30
"Mortal, ephemeral and bold,
In mercy keep what I have told,
Yet think sometimes of what hath been,
And sights these crumbling rocks have seen;
Of sentience old ere thy weak brood   35
Appear'd in lesser magnitude,
And living things that yet survive,
Tho' not to human ken alive.
I AM THE VOICE OF MOTHER EARTH,
FROM WHENCE ALL HORRORS HAVE THEIR BIRTH."   40

Despair

O'er the midnight moorlands crying,
Thro' the cypress forests sighing,
In the night-wind madly flying,
    Hellish forms with streaming hair;
In the barren branches creaking,   5
By the stagnant swamp-pools speaking,
Past the shore-cliffs ever shrieking;
    Damn'd daemons of despair.

Once, I think I half remember,
Ere the grey skies of November   10
Quench'd my youth's aspiring ember,
    Liv'd there such a thing as bliss;
Skies that now are dark were beaming,
Gold and azure, splendid seeming
Till I learn'd it all was dreaming—   15
    Deadly drowsiness of Dis.

But the stream of Time, swift flowing,
Brings the torment of half-knowing—
Dimly rushing, blindly going

61

Past the never-trodden lea;   20
And the voyager, repining,
Sees the grisly death-fires shining,
Hears the wicked petrel's whining
    As he helpless drifts to sea.

Evil wings in ether beating;   25
Vultures at the spirit eating;
Things unseen forever fleeting
    Black against the leering sky.
Ghastly shades of bygone gladness,
Clawing fiends of future sadness,   30
Mingle in a cloud of madness
    Ever on the soul to lie.

Thus the living, lone and sobbing,
In the throes of anguish throbbing,
With the loathsome Furies robbing   35
    Night and noon of peace and rest.
But beyond the groans and grating
Of abhorrent Life, is waiting
Sweet Oblivion, culminating
    All the years of fruitless quest.   40

Revelation

In a vale of light and laughter,
    Smiling 'neath the friendly sun,
Where fulfilment follow'd after
    Ev'ry hope or dream begun;
Where an Aidenn, gay and glorious,   5
    Beckon'd down the winsome way;
There my soul, o'er pain victorious,
    Laugh'd and linger'd—yesterday.

Green and narrow was my valley,
    Temper'd with a verdant shade;   10
Sun-deck'd brooklets musically
    Sparkled thro' each gorgeous glade;
And at night the stars serenely
    Glow'd betwixt the boughs o'erhead,
While Astarte, calm and queenly,   15
    Floods of fairy radiance shed.

There amid the tinted bowers,
    Raptur'd with the opiate spell
Of the grasses, ferns, and flowers,
    Poppy, phlox, and pimpernel,   20
Long I lay, entranc'd and dreaming,
    Pleas'd with Nature's bounteous store,
Till I mark'd the shaded gleaming
    Of the sky, and yearn'd for more.

Eagerly the branches tearing,   25
    Clear'd I all the space above,
Till the bolder gaze, high faring,
    Scann'd the naked skies of Jove;
Deeps unguess'd now shone before me,
    Splendid beam'd the solar car;   30
Wings of fervid fancy bore me
    Out beyond the farthest star.

Reaching, grasping, wishing, longing
    For the pageant brought to sight,
Vain I watch'd the gold orbs thronging   35
    Round celestial poles of light.
Madly on a moonbeam ladder
    Heav'n's abyss I sought to scale,
Ever wiser, ever sadder,
    As the fruitless task would fail.   40

Then, with futile striving sated,
    Veer'd my soul to earth again,
Well content that I was fated
    For a fair, yet low domain;
Pleasing thoughts of glad tomorrows,   45
    Like the blissful moments past,
Lull'd to rest my transient sorrows,
    Still'd my godless greed at last.

But my downward glance, returning,
    Shrank in fright from what it spy'd;   50
Slopes in hideous torment burning,
    Terror in the brooklet's ride;
For the dell, of shade denuded
    By my desecrating hand,
'Neath the bare sky blaz'd and brooded   55
    As a lost, accursed land.

The House

'Tis a grove-circled dwelling
    Set close to a hill,
Where the branches are telling
    Strange legends of ill;
Over timbers so old   5
    That they breathe of the dead,
Crawl the vines, green and cold,
    By strange nourishment fed;
And no man knows the juices they suck from the depths of their dank slimy bed.

In the gardens are growing   10
    Tall blossoms and fair,
Each pallid bloom throwing
    Perfume on the air;
But the afternoon sun
    With its red slanting rays   15
Makes the picture loom dun
    On the curious gaze,
And above the sweet scent of the blossoms rise odours of numberless days.

The rank grasses are waving
    On terrace and lawn,   20
Dim memories sav'ring
    Of things that have gone;
The stones of the walks
    Are encrusted and wet,
And a strange spirit stalks   25
    When the red sun has set,
And the soul of the watcher is fill'd with faint pictures he fain would forget.

It was in the hot Junetime
    I stood by that scene,
When the gold rays of noontime   30
    Beat bright on the green.
But I shiver'd with cold,
    Groping feebly for light,
As a picture unroll'd—
    And my age-spanning sight   35
Saw the time I had been there before flash like fulgury out of the night.

The City

It was golden and splendid,
 That City of light;
A vision suspended
 In deeps of the night;
A region of wonder and glory, whose temples were marble and white. 5

I remember the season
 It dawn'd on my gaze;
The mad time of unreason,
 The brain-numbing days
When Winter, white-sheeted and ghastly, stalks onward to torture and craze. 10

More lovely than Zion
 It shone in the sky,
When the beams of Orion
 Beclouded my eye,
Bringing sleep that was fill'd with dim mem'ries of moments obscure and
 gone by. 15

Its mansions were stately
 With carvings made fair,
Each rising sedately
 On terraces rare,
And the gardens were fragrant and bright with strange miracles blossoming
 there. 20

The avenues lur'd me
 With vistas sublime;
Tall arches assur'd me
 That once on a time
I had wander'd in rapture beneath them, and bask'd in the Halcyon clime. 25

On the plazas were standing
 A sculptur'd array;
Long-bearded, commanding,
 Grave men in their day—
But one stood dismantled and broken, its bearded face batter'd away. 30

In that city effulgent
 No mortal I saw;
But my fancy, indulgent
 To memory's law,
Linger'd long on the forms in the plazas, and eyed their stone features with awe. 35

I fann'd the faint ember
    That glow'd in my mind,
And strove to remember
    The aeons behind;
To rove thro' infinity freely, and visit the past unconfin'd.   40

Then the horrible warning
    Upon my soul sped
Like the ominous morning
    That rises in red,
And in panic I flew from the knowledge of terrors forgotten and dead.   45

To Edward John Moreton Drax Plunkett, Eighteenth Baron Dunsany

As when the sun above a dusky wold
Springs into sight, and turns the gloom to gold,
Lights with his magic beams the dew-deck'd bow'rs,
And wakes to life the gay responsive flow'rs;
So now o'er realms where dark'ning dulness lies,   5
In solar state see shining *Plunkett* rise!
Monarch of Fancy! whose ethereal mind
Mounts fairy peaks, and leaves the throng behind;
Whose soul untainted bursts the bounds of space,
And leads to regions of supernal grace;   10
Can any praise thee with too strong a tone,
Who in this age of folly gleam'st alone?
Thy quill, *Dunsany,* with an art divine
Recalls the gods to each deserted shrine;
From mystic air a novel pantheon makes,   15
And with new spirits fills the meads and brakes;
With thee we wander thro' primeval bow'rs,
For thou hast brought earth's childhood back, and ours!
How leaps the soul, with sudden bliss increas'd,
When led by thee to lands beyond the East!   20
Sick of this sphere, in crime and conflict old,
We yearn for wonders distant and untold;
O'er Homer's page a second time we pore,
And rack our brains for gleams of infant lore:
But all in vain—for valiant tho' we strive   25
No common means those pictures can revive.
Then dawns *Dunsany* with celestial light,
And fulgent visions break upon our sight:

His barque enchanted each sad spirit bears
To shores of gold, beyond the reach of cares.   30
No earthly trammels now our thoughts may chain;
For childhood's fancy hath come back again!
What glitt'ring worlds now wait our eager eyes!
What roads untrodden beckon thro' the skies!
Wonders on wonders line the gorgeous ways,   35
And glorious vistas greet the ravish'd gaze;
Mountains of clouds, castles of crystal dreams,
Ethereal cities and Elysian streams;
Temples of blue, where myriad stars adore
Forgotten gods of aeons gone before!   40
Such are thine arts, *Dunsany*, such thy skill,
That scarce terrestrial seems thy moving quill;
Can man, and man alone, successful draw
Such scenes of wonder and domains of awe?
Our hearts, enraptur'd, fix thy mind's abode   45
In high *Pegāna;* hail thee as a god;
And sure, can aught more high or godlike be
Than such a fancy as resides in thee?
Delighted Pan a friend and peer perceives
As thy sweet music stirs the sylvan leaves;   50
The Nine, transported, bless thy golden lyre,
Approve thy fancy, and applaud thy fire;
Whilst Jove himself assumes a brother's tone,
And vows thy pantheon equal to his own.
Dunsany, may thy days be glad and long;   55
Replete with visions, and atune with song;
May thy rare notes increasing millions cheer,
Thy name beloved, and thy mem'ry dear!
'Tis thou who hast in hours of dulness brought
New charms of language, and new gems of thought;   60
Hast with a poet's grace enrich'd the earth
With aureate dreams as noble as thy birth.
Grateful we name thee, bright with fix'd renown,
The fairest jewel in *Hibernia's* crown.

Bells

I hear the bells from yon imposing tow'r;
    The bells of Yuletide o'er a troubled night;
Pealing with mock'ry in a dismal hour
    Upon a world upheav'd with greed and fright.

Their mellow tones on myriad roofs resound;   5
    A million restless souls attend the chime;
Yet falls their message on a stony ground—
    Their spirit slaughter'd with the sword of Time.

Why ring in counterfeit of happy years
    When calm and quiet rul'd the placid plain?   10
Why with familiar strains arouse the tears
    Of those who ne'er may know content again?

How well I knew ye once—so long ago—
    When slept the ancient village on the slope;
Then rang your accents o'er the starlit snow   15
    In gladness, peace, and sempiternal hope.

In fancy yet I view the modest spire;
    The peaked roof, cast dark against the moon;
The Gothic windows, glowing with a fire
    That lent enchantment to the brazen tune.   20

Lovely each snow-drap'd hedge beneath the beams
    That added silver to the silver there;
Graceful each col, each lane, and all the streams,
    And glad the spirit of the pine-ting'd air.

A simple creed the rural swains profess'd,   25
    In simple bliss among the hills they dwelt;
Their hearts were light, their honest souls at rest;
    Cheer'd with the joys by reas'ning mortals felt.

But on the scene a hideous blight intrudes;
    A lurid nimbus hovers o'er the land;   30
Daemoniac shapes low'r black above the woods,
    And by each door malignant shadows stand.

The jester Time stalks darkly thro' the mead;
    Beneath his tread contentment dies away.
Hearts that were light with causeless anguish bleed,   35
    And restless souls proclaim his evil sway.

Conflict and change beset the tott'ring world;
    Wild thoughts and fancies fill the common mind;
Confusion on a senile race is hurl'd,
    And crime and folly wander unconfin'd.   40

I hear the bells—the mocking, cursed bells
    That wake dim memories to haunt and chill;
Ringing and ringing o'er a thousand hells—
    Fiends of the Night—why can ye not be still?

The Nightmare Lake

There is a lake in distant Zan,
Beyond the wonted haunts of man,
Where broods alone in hideous state
A spirit dead and desolate;
A spirit ancient and unholy,   5
Heavy with fearsome melancholy,
Which from the waters dull and dense
Draws vapours curst with pestilence.
Around the banks, a mire of clay,
Sprawl things offensive in decay,   10
And curious birds that reach that shore
Are seen by mortals nevermore.
Here shines by day the searing sun
On glassy wastes beheld by none,
And here by night pale moonbeams flow   15
Into the deeps that yawn below.
In nightmares only is it told
What scenes beneath those beams unfold;
What scenes, too old for human sight,
Lie sunken there in endless night;   20
For in those depths there only pace
The shadows of a voiceless race.
One midnight, redolent of ill,
I saw that lake, asleep and still;
While in the lurid sky there rode   25
A gibbous moon that glow'd and glow'd.
I saw the stretching marshy shore,
And the foul things those marshes bore:
Lizards and snakes convuls'd and dying;
Ravens and vampires putrefying;   30
All these, and hov'ring o'er the dead,
Necrophagi that on them fed.
And as the dreadful moon climb'd high,
Fright'ning the stars from out the sky,
I saw the lake's dull water glow   35

69

Till sunken things appear'd below.
There shone, unnumber'd fathoms down,
The tow'rs of a forgotten town;
The tarnish'd domes and mossy walls;
Weed-tangled spires and empty halls;   40
Deserted fanes and vaults of dread,
And streets of gold uncoveted.
These I beheld, and saw beside
A horde of shapeless shadows glide;
A noxious horde which to my glance   45
Seem'd moving in a hideous dance
Round slimy sepulchres, that lay
Beside a never-travell'd way.
Straight from those tombs a heaving rose
That vex'd the waters' dull repose,   50
While lethal shades of upper space
Howl'd at the moon's sardonic face.
Then sank the lake within its bed,
Suck'd down to caverns of the dead,
Till from the reeking, new-stript earth   55
Curl'd foetid fumes of noisome birth.
About the city, nigh uncover'd,
The monstrous dancing shadows hover'd,
When lo! there oped with sudden stir
The portal of each sepulchre!   60
No ear may learn, no tongue may tell
What nameless horror then befell.
I see that lake—that moon agrin—
That city and the *things* within—
Waking, I pray that on that shore   65
The nightmare lake may sink *no more!*

On Reading Lord Dunsany's *Book of Wonder*

The hours of night unheeded fly,
    And in the grate the embers fade;
Vast shadows one by one pass by
    In silent daemon cavalcade.

But still the magic volume holds   5
    The raptur'd eye in realms apart,
And fulgent sorcery enfolds
    The willing mind and eager heart.

The lonely room no more is there—
    For to the sight in pomp appear   10
Temples and cities pois'd in air,
    And blazing glories—sphere on sphere.

To a Dreamer

I scan thy features, calm and white
Beneath the single taper's light;
Thy dark-fring'd lids, behind whose screen
Are eyes that view not earth's demesne.

And as I look, I fain would know   5
The paths whereon thy dream-steps go;
The spectral realms that thou canst see
With eyes veil'd from the world and me.

For I have likewise gaz'd in sleep
On things my mem'ry scarce can keep,   10
And from half-knowing long to spy
Again the scenes before thine eye.

I, too, have known the peaks of Thok;
The vales of Pnath, where dream-shapes flock;
The vaults of Zin—and well I trow   15
Why thou demand'st that taper's glow.

But what is this that subtly slips
Over thy face and bearded lips?
What fear distracts thy mind and heart,
That drops must from thy forehead start?   20

Old visions wake—thine op'ning eyes
Gleam black with clouds of other skies,
And as from some daemoniac sight
I flee into the haunted night.

With a Copy of Wilde's Fairy Tales

Madam, in whom benignant gods have join'd
The gifts of fancy, melody, and mind;
Whose kindly guidance first enrich'd my sight
With great DUNSANY'S Heliconian light:
Pray take from one so deeply in thy debt   5
These jewell'd thoughts, by master artist set;

For sure (except for PLUNKETT'S dreams alone)
The dreams of WILDE are nearest to thine own.
Here wilt thou find, in pleasing order fix'd,
A host of golden fantasies unmix'd;   10
Tales that the dust of modern life dispel,
And take us back to fairyland to dwell.
May each quaint story, told with magic pow'r,
Speed the still moments of some leisure hour;
To rural shades a keener beauty add,   15
Or help to make thy winter fireside glad.
Yet slight indeed the trivial gift must seem,
If measur'd by the giver's firm esteem!

[On *The Thing in the Woods* by Harper Williams]

BELKNAP, accept from Theobald's spectral Claw
These haunting Chapters of daemoniack Awe;
Such nightmare Yarns we both have often writ,
With goblin Whispers, and an Hint of IT,
Till sure, we're like to think all Terror's grown   5
A sort of private Product of our own!
Lest, then, our Pride our sober Sense mislead,
And make us copyright each hellish Deed,
'Tis ours to see what ghastly Flames can blaze
From Spooks and Ghouls that other Wizards raise!   10

The Cats

Babels of blocks to the high heavens tow'ring,
    Flumes of futility swirling below;
Poisonous fungi in brick and stone flow'ring,
    Lanterns that shudder and death-lights that glow.

Black monstrous bridges across oily rivers,   5
    Cobwebs of cable by nameless things spun;
Catacomb deeps whose dank chaos delivers
    Streams of live foetor, that rots in the sun.

Colour and splendour, disease and decaying,
    Shrieking and ringing and scrambling insane,   10
Rabbles exotic to stranger-gods praying,
    Jumbles of odour that stifle the brain.

Legions of cats from the alleys nocturnal,
    Howling and lean in the glare of the moon,

72

Screaming the future with mouthings infernal,   15
    Yelling the burden of Pluto's red rune.

Tall tow'rs and pyramids ivy'd and crumbling,
    Bats that swoop low in the weed-cumber'd streets;
Bleak broken bridges o'er rivers whose rumbling
    Joins with no voice as the thick tide retreats.   20

Belfries that blackly against the moon totter,
    Caverns whose mouths are by mosses effac'd,
And living to answer the wind and the water,
    Only the lean cats that howl in the waste!

Primavera

There is wonder on land and billow,
    And a strangeness in bough and vein,
For the brook or the budded willow
    Feel the Presence walking again.
It has come in the olden fashion,   5
    As the tritest of lutes have sung,
But it carries the olden passion
    That can never be aught but young.

There are whispers from groves auroral
    To blood half-afraid to hear,   10
While the evening star's faint choral
    Is an ecstasy touch'd with fear.
And at night where the hill-wraiths rally
    Glows the far Walpurgis flame,
Which the lonely swain in the valley   15
    Beholds, tho' he dare not name.

And in every wild breeze falling
    Out of spaces beyond the sky,
There are ancient voices calling
    To regions remote and high;   20
To the gardens of elfin glory
    That lie o'er the purple seas,
And mansions of dream and story
    From childhood memories.

I am call'd where the still dawns glitter   25
    On pastures and furrow'd crests,
And the thrush and the wood-lark twitter

Low over their brookside nests;
Where the smoke of the cottage hovers,
 And the elm-buds promise their shade,   30
And a carpet of new green covers
 The floor of the forest glade.

I am call'd where the vales are dreaming
 In golden, celestial light,
With the gables of castles gleaming,   35
 And village roofs steep and bright;
With distant spires set slimly
 Over tangles of twining boughs,
And a ribbon of river seen dimly
 Thro' fields that the farmer ploughs.   40

I am call'd where a twilight ocean
 Laps the piers of an ancient town,
And dream-ships in ghostly motion
 Ride at anchor up and down;
Where sea-lanes narrow and bending   45
 Climb steep thro' the fragrant gloom
Of chimneys and gambrels blending
 With orchard branches in bloom.

And when o'er the waves enchanted
 The moon and the stars appear,   50
I am haunted—haunted—haunted
 By dreams of a mystic year;
Of a year long lost in the dawning,
 When the planets were vague and pale,
And the chasms of space were yawning   55
 To vistas that fade and fail.

I am haunted by recollections
 Of lands that were not of earth,
Of places where mad perfections
 In horror were brought to birth;   60
Where pylons of onyx mounted
 To heavens with fire embower'd,
And turrets and domes uncounted
 O'er the terrac'd torrents tower'd.

I am call'd to these reachless regions   65
 In tones that are old and known,

By a chorus of phantom legions
    That must have been once my own——
But the spell is a charm swift fleeting,
    And the earth has a potent thrall,   70
So I never have known the freeing,
    Or heeded the springtime's call.

Festival

    There is snow on the ground,
        And the valleys are cold,
    And a midnight profound
        Blackly squats o'er the wold;
But a light on the hilltops half-seen hints of feastings unhallow'd and old.   5

    There is death in the clouds,
        There is fear in the night,
    For the dead in their shrouds
        Hail the sun's turning flight,
And chant wild in the woods as they dance round a Yule-altar fungous
    and white.   10

    To no gale of earth's kind
        Sways the forest of oak,
    Where the sick boughs entwin'd
        By mad mistletoes choke,
For these pow'rs are the pow'rs of the dark, from the graves of the lost
    Druid folk.   15

    And mayst thou to such deeds
        Be an abbot and priest,
    Singing cannibal greeds
        At each devil-wrought feast,
And to all the incredulous world shewing dimly the sign of the beast.   20

Hallowe'en in a Suburb

The steeples are white in the wild moonlight,
    And the trees have a silver glare;
Past the chimneys high see the vampires fly,
    And the harpies of the upper air,
        That flutter and laugh and stare.   5

For the village dead to the moon outspread
    Never shone in the sunset's gleam,

But grew out of the deep that the dead years keep
    Where the rivers of madness stream
      Down the gulfs to a pit of dream.   10

A chill wind weaves thro' the rows of sheaves
    In the meadows that shimmer pale,
And comes to twine where the headstones shine
    And the ghouls of the churchyard wail
      For the harvests that fly and fail.   15

Not a breath of the strange grey gods of change
    That tore from the past its own
Can quicken this hour, when a spectral pow'r
    Spreads deep o'er the cosmic throne
      And looses the vast unknown.   20

So here again stretch the vale and plain
    That moons long-forgotten saw,
And the dead leap gay in the pallid ray,
    Sprung out of the tomb's black maw
      To shake all the world with awe.   25

And all that the morn shall greet forlorn,
    The ugliness and the pest
Of rows where thick rise the stone and brick,
    Shall some day be with the rest,
      And brood with the shades unblest.   30

Then wild in the dark let the lemurs bark,
    And the leprous spires ascend;
For new and old alike in the fold
    Of horror and death are penn'd,
      For the hounds of Time to rend.   35

[On Ambrose Bierce]

Immortal Bierce a World of Colour calls
To those Disciples whom his Work enthralls;
Yet strange enough, to each one is display'd
A sep'rate Aura, and a diff'rent Shade!
Loveman sees blue, Long spies a greenish Taint,   5
Till the vext Critick knows not what to paint—
So with due Caution, lest I be not right,
I'll set old Ambrose down in black and white!

The Wood

They cut it down, and where the pitch-black aisles
    Of forest night had hid eternal things,
They scal'd the sky with tow'rs and marble piles
    To make a city for their revellings.

White and amazing to the lands around   5
    That wondrous wealth of domes and turrets rose;
Crystal and ivory, sublimely crown'd
    With pinnacles that bore unmelting snows.

And through its halls the pipe and sistrum rang,
    While wine and riot brought their scarlet stains;   10
Never a voice of elder marvels sang,
    Nor any eye call'd up the hills and plains.

Thus down the years, till on one purple night
    A drunken minstrel in his careless verse
Spoke the vile words that should not see the light,   15
    And stirr'd the shadows of an ancient curse.

Forests may fall, but not the dusk they shield;
    So on the spot where that proud city stood,
The shuddering dawn no single stone reveal'd,
    But fled the blackness of a primal wood.   20

The Outpost

When evening cools the yellow stream,
    And shadow stalks the jungle's ways,
    Zimbabwe's palace flares ablaze
For the great King who fears to dream.

For he alone of all mankind   5
    Waded the swamp that serpents shun;
    And struggling toward the setting sun,
Came on the veldt that lies behind.

No other eyes had ventured there
    Since eyes were lent for human sight—   10
    But there, as sunset turned to night,
He found the Elder Secret's lair.

Strange turrets rose beyond the plain,
    And walls and bastions spread around

The distant domes that fouled the ground   15
Like leprous fungi after rain.

A grudging moon writhed up to shine
    Past leagues where life can have no home;
    And paling far-off tower and dome,
Shewed each unwindowed and malign.   20

Then he who in his boyhood ran
    Through vine-hung ruins free from fear,
    Trembled at what he saw—for here
Was no dead, ruined seat of man.

Inhuman shapes, half-seen, half-guessed,   25
    Half solid and half ether-spawned,
    Seethed down from starless voids that yawned
In heav'n, to these blank walls of pest.

And voidward from that pest-mad zone
    Amorphous hordes seethed darkly back,   30
    Their dim claws laden with the wrack
Of things that men have dreamed and known.

The ancient Fishers from Outside—
    Were there not tales the high-priest told,
    Of how they found the worlds of old,   35
And took what pelf their fancy spied?

Their hidden, dread-ringed outposts brood
    Upon a million worlds of space;
    Abhorred by every living race,
Yet scatheless in their solitude.   40

Sweating with fright, the watcher crept
    Back to the swamp that serpents shun,
    So that he lay, by rise of sun,
Safe in the palace where he slept.

None saw him leave, or come at dawn,   45
    Nor does his flesh bear any mark
    Of what he met in that curst dark—
Yet from his sleep all peace has gone.

When evening cools the yellow stream,
    And shadow stalks the jungle's ways,   50

Zimbabwe's palace flares ablaze
For a great King who fears to dream.

The Ancient Track

There was no hand to hold me back
That night I found the ancient track
Over the hill, and strained to see
The fields that teased my memory.
This tree, that wall—I knew them well,   5
And all the roofs and orchards fell
Familiarly upon my mind
As from a past not far behind.
I knew what shadows would be cast
When the late moon came up at last   10
From back of Zaman's Hill, and how
The vale would shine three hours from now.
And when the path grew steep and high,
And seemed to end against the sky,
I had no fear of what might rest   15
Beyond that silhouetted crest.
Straight on I walked, while all the night
Grew pale with phosphorescent light,
And wall and farmhouse gable glowed
Unearthly by the climbing road.   20
There was the milestone that I knew—
"Two miles to Dunwich"—now the view
Of distant spire and roofs would dawn
With ten more upward paces gone. . . .

There was no hand to hold me back   25
That night I found the ancient track,
And reached the crest to see outspread
A valley of the lost and dead:
And over Zaman's Hill the horn
Of a malignant moon was born,   30
To light the weeds and vines that grew
On ruined walls I never knew.
The fox-fire glowed in field and bog,
And unknown waters spewed a fog
Whose curling talons mocked the thought   35
That I had ever known this spot.
Too well I saw from the mad scene

79

That my loved past had never been—
Nor was I now upon the trail
Descending to that long-dead vale.   40
Around was fog—ahead, the spray
Of star-streams in the Milky Way. . . .
There was no hand to hold me back
That night I found the ancient track.

The Messenger

To Bertrand K. Hart, Esq.

The thing, he said, would come that night at three
From the old churchyard on the hill below;
But crouching by an oak fire's wholesome glow,
I tried to tell myself it could not be.
Surely, I mused, it was a pleasantry   5
Devised by one who did not truly know
The Elder Sign, bequeathed from long ago,
That sets the fumbling forms of darkness free.

He had not meant it—no—but still I lit
Another lamp as starry Leo climbed   10
Out of the Seekonk, and a steeple chimed
Three—and the firelight faded, bit by bit.
Then at the door that cautious rattling came—
And the mad truth devoured me like a flame!

Fungi from Yuggoth

I. The Book

The place was dark and dusty and half-lost
In tangles of old alleys near the quays,
Reeking of strange things brought in from the seas,
And with queer curls of fog that west winds tossed.
Small lozenge panes, obscured by smoke and frost,   5
Just shewed the books, in piles like twisted trees,
Rotting from floor to roof—congeries
Of crumbling elder lore at little cost.

I entered, charmed, and from a cobwebbed heap
Took up the nearest tome and thumbed it through,   10

Trembling at curious words that seemed to keep
Some secret, monstrous if one only knew.
Then, looking for some seller old in craft,
I could find nothing but a voice that laughed.

II. Pursuit

I held the book beneath my coat, at pains
To hide the thing from sight in such a place;
Hurrying through the ancient harbour lanes
With often-turning head and nervous pace.
Dull, furtive windows in old tottering brick   5
Peered at me oddly as I hastened by,
And thinking what they sheltered, I grew sick
For a redeeming glimpse of clean blue sky.

No one had seen me take the thing—but still
A blank laugh echoed in my whirling head,   10
And I could guess what nighted worlds of ill
Lurked in that volume I had coveted.
The way grew strange—the walls alike and madding—
And far behind me, unseen feet were padding.

III. The Key

I do not know what windings in the waste
Of those strange sea-lanes brought me home once more,
But on my porch I trembled, white with haste
To get inside and bolt the heavy door.
I had the book that told the hidden way   5
Across the void and through the space-hung screens
That hold the undimensioned worlds at bay,
And keep lost aeons to their own demesnes.

At last the key was mine to those vague visions
Of sunset spires and twilight woods that brood   10
Dim in the gulfs beyond this earth's precisions,
Lurking as memories of infinitude.
The key was mine, but as I sat there mumbling,
The attic window shook with a faint fumbling.

IV. Recognition

The day had come again, when as a child
I saw—just once—that hollow of old oaks,
Grey with a ground-mist that enfolds and chokes
The slinking shapes which madness has defiled.
It was the same—an herbage rank and wild   5
Clings round an altar whose carved sign invokes
That Nameless One to whom a thousand smokes
Rose, aeons gone, from unclean towers up-piled.

I saw the body spread on that dank stone,
And knew those things which feasted were not men;   10
I knew this strange, grey world was not my own,
But Yuggoth, past the starry voids—and then
The body shrieked at me with a dead cry,
And all too late I knew that it was I!

V. Homecoming

The daemon said that he would take me home
To the pale, shadowy land I half recalled
As a high place of stair and terrace, walled
With marble balustrades that sky-winds comb,
While miles below a maze of dome on dome   5
And tower on tower beside a sea lies sprawled.
Once more, he told me, I would stand enthralled
On those old heights, and hear the far-off foam.

All this he promised, and through sunset's gate
He swept me, past the lapping lakes of flame,   10
And red-gold thrones of gods without a name
Who shriek in fear at some impending fate.
Then a black gulf with sea-sounds in the night:
"Here was your home," he mocked, "when you had sight!"

VI. The Lamp

We found the lamp inside those hollow cliffs
Whose chiselled sign no priest in Thebes could read,
And from whose caverns frightened hieroglyphs
Warned every living creature of earth's breed.
No more was there—just that one brazen bowl   5
With traces of a curious oil within;

82

Fretted with some obscurely patterned scroll,
And symbols hinting vaguely of strange sin.

Little the fears of forty centuries meant
To us as we bore off our slender spoil,   10
And when we scanned it in our darkened tent
We struck a match to test the ancient oil.
It blazed—great God! . . . But the vast shapes we saw
In that mad flash have seared our lives with awe.

VII. *Zaman's Hill*

The great hill hung close over the old town,
A precipice against the main street's end;
Green, tall, and wooded, looking darkly down
Upon the steeple at the highway bend.
Two hundred years the whispers had been heard   5
About what happened on the man-shunned slope—
Tales of an oddly mangled deer or bird,
Or of lost boys whose kin had ceased to hope.

One day the mail-man found no village there,
Nor were its folk or houses seen again;   10
People came out from Aylesbury to stare—
Yet they all told the mail-man it was plain
That he was mad for saying he had spied
The great hill's gluttonous eyes, and jaws stretched wide.

VIII. *The Port*

Ten miles from Arkham I had struck the trail
That rides the cliff-edge over Boynton Beach,
And hoped that just at sunset I could reach
The crest that looks on Innsmouth in the vale.
Far out at sea was a retreating sail,   5
White as hard years of ancient winds could bleach,
But evil with some portent beyond speech,
So that I did not wave my hand or hail.

Sails out of Innsmouth! echoing old renown
Of long-dead times. But now a too-swift night   10
Is closing in, and I have reached the height
Whence I so often scan the distant town.
The spires and roofs are there—but look! The gloom
Sinks on dark lanes, as lightless as the tomb!

83

IX. *The Courtyard*

It was the city I had known before;
The ancient, leprous town where mongrel throngs
Chant to strange gods, and beat unhallowed gongs
In crypts beneath foul alleys near the shore.
The rotting, fish-eyed houses leered at me   5
From where they leaned, drunk and half-animate,
As edging through the filth I passed the gate
To the black courtyard where the man would be.

The dark walls closed me in, and loud I cursed
That ever I had come to such a den,   10
When suddenly a score of windows burst
Into wild light, and swarmed with dancing men:
Mad, soundless revels of the dragging dead—
And not a corpse had either hands or head!

X. *The Pigeon-Flyers*

They took me slumming, where gaunt walls of brick
Bulge outward with a viscous stored-up evil,
And twisted faces, thronging foul and thick,
Wink messages to alien god and devil.
A million fires were blazing in the streets,   5
And from flat roofs a furtive few would fly
Bedraggled birds into the yawning sky
While hidden drums droned on with measured beats.

I knew those fires were brewing monstrous things,
And that those birds of space had been *Outside*—   10
I guessed to what dark planet's crypts they plied,
And what they brought from Thog beneath their wings.
The others laughed—till struck too mute to speak
By what they glimpsed in one bird's evil beak.

XI. *The Well*

Farmer Seth Atwood was past eighty when
He tried to sink that deep well by his door,
With only Eb to help him bore and bore.
We laughed, and hoped he'd soon be sane again.
And yet, instead, young Eb went crazy, too,   5
So that they shipped him to the county farm.

Seth bricked the well-mouth up as tight as glue—
Then hacked an artery in his gnarled left arm.

After the funeral we felt bound to get
Out to that well and rip the bricks away,   10
But all we saw were iron hand-holds set
Down a black hole deeper than we could say.
And yet we put the bricks back—for we found
The hole too deep for any line to sound.

XII. The Howler

They told me not to take the Briggs' Hill path
That used to be the highroad through to Zoar,
For Goody Watkins, hanged in seventeen-four,
Had left a certain monstrous aftermath.
Yet when I disobeyed, and had in view   5
The vine-hung cottage by the great rock slope,
I could not think of elms or hempen rope,
But wondered why the house still seemed so new.

Stopping a while to watch the fading day,
I heard faint howls, as from a room upstairs,   10
When through the ivied panes one sunset ray
Struck in, and caught the howler unawares.
I glimpsed—and ran in frenzy from the place,
And from a four-pawed thing with human face.

XIII. Hesperia

The winter sunset, flaming beyond spires
And chimneys half-detached from this dull sphere,
Opens great gates to some forgotten year
Of elder splendours and divine desires.
Expectant wonders burn in those rich fires,   5
Adventure-fraught, and not untinged with fear;
A row of sphinxes where the way leads clear
Toward walls and turrets quivering to far lyres.

It is the land where beauty's meaning flowers;
Where every unplaced memory has a source;   10
Where the great river Time begins its course
Down the vast void in starlit streams of hours.
Dreams bring us close—but ancient lore repeats
That human tread has never soiled these streets.

XIV. Star-Winds

It is a certain hour of twilight glooms,
Mostly in autumn, when the star-wind pours
Down hilltop streets, deserted out-of-doors,
But shewing early lamplight from snug rooms.
The dead leaves rush in strange, fantastic twists,   5
And chimney-smoke whirls round with alien grace,
Heeding geometries of outer space,
While Fomalhaut peers in through southward mists.

This is the hour when moonstruck poets know
What fungi sprout in Yuggoth, and what scents   10
And tints of flowers fill Nithon's continents,
Such as in no poor earthly garden blow.
Yet for each dream these winds to us convey,
A dozen more of ours they sweep away!

XV. Antarktos

Deep in my dream the great bird whispered queerly
Of the black cone amid the polar waste;
Pushing above the ice-sheet lone and drearly,
By storm-crazed aeons battered and defaced.
Hither no living earth-shapes take their courses,   5
And only pale auroras and faint suns
Glow on that pitted rock, whose primal sources
Are guessed at dimly by the Elder Ones.

If men should glimpse it, they would merely wonder
What tricky mound of Nature's build they spied;   10
But the bird told of vaster parts, that under
The mile-deep ice-shroud crouch and brood and bide.
God help the dreamer whose mad visions shew
Those dead eyes set in crystal gulfs below!

XVI. The Window

The house was old, with tangled wings outthrown,
Of which no one could ever half keep track,
And in a small room somewhat near the back
Was an odd window sealed with ancient stone.
There, in a dream-plagued childhood, quite alone   5
I used to go, where night reigned vague and black;

Parting the cobwebs with a curious lack
Of fear, and with a wonder each time grown.

One later day I brought the masons there
To find what view my dim forbears had shunned,   10
But as they pierced the stone, a rush of air
Burst from the alien voids that yawned beyond.
They fled—but I peered through and found unrolled
All the wild worlds of which my dreams had told.

XVII. A Memory

There were great steppes, and rocky table-lands
Stretching half-limitless in starlit night,
With alien campfires shedding feeble light
On beasts with tinkling bells, in shaggy bands.
Far to the south the plain sloped low and wide   5
To a dark zigzag line of wall that lay
Like a huge python of some primal day
Which endless time had chilled and petrified.

I shivered oddly in the cold, thin air,
And wondered where I was and how I came,   10
When a cloaked form against the campfire's glare
Rose and approached, and called me by my name.
Staring at that dead face beneath the hood,
I ceased to hope—because I understood.

XVIII. The Gardens of Yin

Beyond that wall, whose ancient masonry
Reached almost to the sky in moss-thick towers,
There would be terraced gardens, rich with flowers,
And flutter of bird and butterfly and bee.
There would be walks, and bridges arching over   5
Warm lotos-pools reflecting temple eaves,
And cherry-trees with delicate boughs and leaves
Against a pink sky where the herons hover.

All would be there, for had not old dreams flung
Open the gate to that stone-lanterned maze   10
Where drowsy streams spin out their winding ways,
Trailed by green vines from bending branches hung?
I hurried—but when the wall rose, grim and great,
I found there was no longer any gate.

87

XIX. The Bells

Year after year I heard that faint, far ringing
Of deep-toned bells on the black midnight wind;
Peals from no steeple I could ever find,
But strange, as if across some great void winging.
I searched my dreams and memories for a clue,   5
And thought of all the chimes my visions carried;
Of quiet Innsmouth, where the white gulls tarried
Around an ancient spire that once I knew.

Always perplexed I heard those far notes falling,
Till one March night the bleak rain splashing cold   10
Beckoned me back through gateways of recalling
To elder towers where the mad clappers tolled.
They tolled—but from the sunless tides that pour
Through sunken valleys on the sea's dead floor.

XX. Night-Gaunts

Out of what crypt they crawl, I cannot tell,
But every night I see the rubbery things,
Black, horned, and slender, with membraneous wings,
And tails that bear the bifid barb of hell.
They come in legions on the north wind's swell,   5
With obscene clutch that titillates and stings,
Snatching me off on monstrous voyagings
To grey worlds hidden deep in nightmare's well.

Over the jagged peaks of Thok they sweep,
Heedless of all the cries I try to make,   10
And down the nether pits to that foul lake
Where the puffed shoggoths splash in doubtful sleep.
But oh! If only they would make some sound,
Or wear a face where faces should be found!

XXI. Nyarlathotep

And at the last from inner Egypt came
The strange dark One to whom the fellahs bowed;
Silent and lean and cryptically proud,
And wrapped in fabrics red as sunset flame.
Throngs pressed around, frantic for his commands,   5
But leaving, could not tell what they had heard;

While through the nations spread the awestruck word
That wild beasts followed him and licked his hands.

Soon from the sea a noxious birth began;
Forgotten lands with weedy spires of gold;   10
The ground was cleft, and mad auroras rolled
Down on the quaking citadels of man.
Then, crushing what he chanced to mould in play,
The idiot Chaos blew Earth's dust away.

XXII. Azathoth

Out in the mindless void the daemon bore me,
Past the bright clusters of dimensioned space,
Till neither time nor matter stretched before me,
But only Chaos, without form or place.
Here the vast Lord of All in darkness muttered   5
Things he had dreamed but could not understand,
While near him shapeless bat-things flopped and fluttered
In idiot vortices that ray-streams fanned.

They danced insanely to the high, thin whining
Of a cracked flute clutched in a monstrous paw,   10
Whence flow the aimless waves whose chance combining
Gives each frail cosmos its eternal law.
"I am His Messenger," the daemon said,
As in contempt he struck his Master's head.

XXIII. Mirage

I do not know if ever it existed—
That lost world floating dimly on Time's stream—
And yet I see it often, violet-misted,
And shimmering at the back of some vague dream.
There were strange towers and curious lapping rivers,   5
Labyrinths of wonder, and low vaults of light,
And bough-crossed skies of flame, like that which quivers
Wistfully just before a winter's night.

Great moors led off to sedgy shores unpeopled,
Where vast birds wheeled, while on a windswept hill   10
There was a village, ancient and white-steepled,
With evening chimes for which I listen still.
I do not know what land it is—or dare
Ask when or why I was, or will be, there.

89

XXIV. The Canal

Somewhere in dream there is an evil place
Where tall, deserted buildings crowd along
A deep, black, narrow channel, reeking strong
Of frightful things whence oily currents race.
Lanes with old walls half meeting overhead   5
Wind off to streets one may or may not know,
And feeble moonlight sheds a spectral glow
Over long rows of windows, dark and dead.

There are no footfalls, and the one soft sound
Is of the oily water as it glides   10
Under stone bridges, and along the sides
Of its deep flume, to some vague ocean bound.
None lives to tell when that stream washed away
Its dream-lost region from the world of clay.

XXV. St. Toad's

"Beware St. Toad's cracked chimes!" I heard him scream
As I plunged into those mad lanes that wind
In labyrinths obscure and undefined
South of the river where old centuries dream.
He was a furtive figure, bent and ragged,   5
And in a flash had staggered out of sight,
So still I burrowed onward in the night
Toward where more roof-lines rose, malign and jagged.

No guide-book told of what was lurking here—
But now I heard another old man shriek: 10
"Beware St. Toad's cracked chimes!" And growing weak,
I paused, when a third greybeard croaked in fear:
"Beware St. Toad's cracked chimes!" Aghast, I fled—
Till suddenly that black spire loomed ahead.

XXVI. The Familiars

John Whateley lived about a mile from town,
Up where the hills began to huddle thick;
We never thought his wits were very quick,
Seeing the way he let his farm run down.
He used to waste his time on some queer books   5
He'd found around the attic of his place,

90

Till funny lines got creased into his face,
And folks all said they didn't like his looks.

When he began those night-howls we declared
He'd better be locked up away from harm,   10
So three men from the Aylesbury town farm
Went for him—but came back alone and scared.
They'd found him talking to two crouching things
That at their step flew off on great black wings.

XXVII. The Elder Pharos

From Leng, where rocky peaks climb bleak and bare
Under cold stars obscure to human sight,
There shoots at dusk a single beam of light
Whose far blue rays make shepherds whine in prayer.
They say (though none has been there) that it comes   5
Out of a pharos in a tower of stone,
Where the last Elder One lives on alone,
Talking to Chaos with the beat of drums.

The Thing, they whisper, wears a silken mask
Of yellow, whose queer folds appear to hide   10
A face not of this earth, though none dares ask
Just what those features are, which bulge inside.
Many, in man's first youth, sought out that glow,
But what they found, no one will ever know.

XXVIII. Expectancy

I cannot tell why some things hold for me
A sense of unplumbed marvels to befall,
Or of a rift in the horizon's wall
Opening to worlds where only gods can be.
There is a breathless, vague expectancy,   5
As of vast ancient pomps I half recall,
Or wild adventures, uncorporeal,
Ecstasy-fraught, and as a day-dream free.

It is in sunsets and strange city spires,
Old villages and woods and misty downs,   10
South winds, the sea, low hills, and lighted towns,
Old gardens, half-heard songs, and the moon's fires.
But though its lure alone makes life worth living,
None gains or guesses what it hints at giving.

XXIX. Nostalgia

Once every year, in autumn's wistful glow,
The birds fly out over an ocean waste,
Calling and chattering in a joyous haste
To reach some land their inner memories know.
Great terraced gardens where bright blossoms blow,   5
And lines of mangoes luscious to the taste,
And temple-groves with branches interlaced
Over cool paths—all these their vague dreams shew.

They search the sea for marks of their old shore—
For the tall city, white and turreted—   10
But only empty waters stretch ahead,
So that at last they turn away once more.
Yet sunken deep where alien polyps throng,
The old towers miss their lost, remembered song.

XXX. Background

I never can be tied to raw, new things,
For I first saw the light in an old town,
Where from my window huddled roofs sloped down
To a quaint harbour rich with visionings.
Streets with carved doorways where the sunset beams   5
Flooded old fanlights and small window-panes,
And Georgian steeples topped with gilded vanes—
These were the sights that shaped my childhood dreams.

Such treasures, left from times of cautious leaven,
Cannot but loose the hold of flimsier wraiths   10
That flit with shifting ways and muddled faiths
Across the changeless walls of earth and heaven.
They cut the moment's thongs and leave me free
To stand alone before eternity.

XXXI. The Dweller

It had been old when Babylon was new;
None knows how long it slept beneath that mound,
Where in the end our questing shovels found
Its granite blocks and brought it back to view.
There were vast pavements and foundation-walls,   5
And crumbling slabs and statues, carved to shew

Fantastic beings of some long ago
Past anything the world of man recalls.

And then we saw those stone steps leading down
Through a choked gate of graven dolomite   10
To some black haven of eternal night
Where elder signs and primal secrets frown.
We cleared a path—but raced in mad retreat
When from below we heard those clumping feet.

XXXII. *Alienation*

His solid flesh had never been away,
For each dawn found him in his usual place,
But every night his spirit loved to race
Through gulfs and worlds remote from common day.
He had seen Yaddith, yet retained his mind,   5
And come back safely from the Ghooric zone,
When one still night across curved space was thrown
That beckoning piping from the voids behind.

He waked that morning as an older man,
And nothing since has looked the same to him.   10
Objects around float nebulous and dim—
False, phantom trifles of some vaster plan.
His folk and friends are now an alien throng
To which he struggles vainly to belong.

XXXIII. *Harbour Whistles*

Over old roofs and past decaying spires
The harbour whistles chant all through the night;
Throats from strange ports, and beaches far and white,
And fabulous oceans, ranged in motley choirs.
Each to the other alien and unknown,   5
Yet all, by some obscurely focussed force
From brooding gulfs beyond the Zodiac's course,
Fused into one mysterious cosmic drone.

Through shadowy dreams they send a marching line
Of still more shadowy shapes and hints and views;   10
Echoes from outer voids, and subtle clues
To things which they themselves cannot define.
And always in that chorus, faintly blent,
We catch some notes no earth-ship ever sent.

93

XXXIV. Recapture

The way led down a dark, half-wooded heath
Where moss-grey boulders humped above the mould,
And curious drops, disquieting and cold,
Sprayed up from unseen streams in gulfs beneath.
There was no wind, nor any trace of sound   5
In puzzling shrub, or alien-featured tree,
Nor any view before—till suddenly,
Straight in my path, I saw a monstrous mound.

Half to the sky those steep sides loomed upspread,
Rank-grassed, and cluttered by a crumbling flight   10
Of lava stairs that scaled the fear-topped height
In steps too vast for any human tread.
I shrieked—and *knew* what primal star and year
Had sucked me back from man's dream-transient sphere!

XXXV. Evening Star

I saw it from that hidden, silent place
Where the old wood half shuts the meadow in.
It shone through all the sunset's glories—thin
At first, but with a slowly brightening face.
Night came, and that lone beacon, amber-hued,   5
Beat on my sight as never it did of old;
The evening star—but grown a thousandfold
More haunting in this hush and solitude.

It traced strange pictures on the quivering air—
Half-memories that had always filled my eyes—   10
Vast towers and gardens; curious seas and skies
Of some dim life—I never could tell where.
But now I knew that through the cosmic dome
Those rays were calling from my far, lost home.

XXXVI. Continuity

There is in certain ancient things a trace
Of some dim essence—more than form or weight;
A tenuous aether, indeterminate,
Yet linked with all the laws of time and space.
A faint, veiled sign of continuities   5
That outward eyes can never quite descry;

94

Of locked dimensions harbouring years gone by,
And out of reach except for hidden keys.

It moves me most when slanting sunbeams glow
On old farm buildings set against a hill,   10
And paint with life the shapes which linger still
From centuries less a dream than this we know.
In that strange light I feel I am not far
From the fixt mass whose sides the ages are.

Bouts Rimés

Beyond Zimbabwe

The drums of the jungle in ecstasy boom,
And summon the chosen to torture and doom;
The quivering throngs wait expectant and sad,
While the shrieks of the priest echo drunkenly mad.
Round the altars are tributes of barley and cream,   5
And the acolytes stagger in opiate dream.
It is thus that the Shadow grows mighty and whole,
As it feeds on the body and sucks at the soul.

The White Elephant

Dim in the past from primal chaos rose
That form with mottled cloak and scaly hose
Who bade the lesser ghouls to earn their bread,
Perform dread rites, and echo what he said.
They bred the leprous tree and poison flower   5
And pressed dim aeons into one black hour.
Wherefore we pray, as pious pagans must,
To the white beast he shaped from fungous dust.

In a Sequester'd Providence Churchyard Where Once Poe Walk'd

Eternal brood the shadows on this ground,
Dreaming of centuries that have gone before;
Great elms rise solemnly by slab and mound,
Arch'd high above a hidden world of yore.
Round all the scene a light of memory plays,   5

And dead leaves whisper of departed days,
Longing for sights and sounds that are no more.

Lonely and sad, a spectre glides along
Aisles where of old his living footsteps fell;
No common glance discerns him, tho' his song   10
Peals down thro' time with a mysterious spell:
Only the few who sorcery's secret know
Espy amidst these tombs the shade of Poe.

To Mr. Finlay, upon His Drawing for
Mr. Bloch's Tale, "The Faceless God"

In dim abysses pulse the shapes of night,
    Hungry and hideous, with strange mitres crown'd;
Black pinions beating in fantastic flight
    From orb to orb thro' sunless void profound.
None dares to name the cosmos whence they course,   5
    Or guess the look on each amorphous face,
Or speak the words that with resistless force
    Would draw them from the hells of outer space.

Yet here upon a page our frighten'd glance
    Finds monstrous forms no human eye should see;   10
Hints of those blasphemies whose countenance
    Spreads death and madness thro' infinity.
What limner he who braves black gulfs alone
And lives to make their alien horrors known?

To Clark Ashton Smith, Esq., upon
His Phantastick Tales, Verses, Pictures, and Sculptures

A time-black tower against dim banks of cloud;
    Around its base the pathless, pressing wood.
Shadow and silence, moss and mould, enshroud
    Grey, age-fell'd slabs that once as cromlechs stood.
No fall of foot, no song of bird awakes   5
    The lethal aisles of sempiternal night,
Tho' oft with stir of wings the dense air shakes,
    As in the tower there glows a pallid light.

For here, apart, dwells one whose hands have wrought
    Strange eidola that chill the world with fear;   10

Whose graven runes in tones of dread have taught
    What things beyond the star-gulfs lurk and leer.
Dark Lord of Averoigne—whose windows stare
On pits of dream no other gaze could bear!

Nathicana

It was in the pale gardens of Zaïs,
The mist-shrouded gardens of Zaïs,
Where blossoms the white nephalotë,
The redolent herald of midnight.
There slumber the still lakes of crystal,   5
And streamlets that flow without murm'ring;
Smooth streamlets from caverns of Kathos
Where brood the calm spirits of twilight.
And over the lakes and the streamlets
Are bridges of pure alabaster,   10
White bridges all cunningly carven
With figures of fairies and daemons.
Here glimmer strange suns and strange planets,
And strange is the crescent Banapis
That sets 'yond the ivy-grown ramparts   15
Where thickens the dust of the evening.
Here fall the white vapours of Yabon;
And here in the swirl of the vapours
I saw the divine Nathicana;
The garlanded, white Nathicana;   20
The slender, black-hair'd Nathicana;
The sloe-ey'd, red-lipp'd Nathicana;
The silver-voic'd, sweet Nathicana;
The pale-rob'd, belov'd Nathicana.
And ever was she my belovèd,   25
From ages when Time was unfashion'd;
From days when the stars were not fashion'd
Nor any thing fashion'd but Yabon.
And here dwelt we ever and ever,
The innocent children of Zaïs,   30
At peace in the paths and the arbours,
White-crown'd with the blest nephalotë.
How oft would we float in the twilight
O'er flow'r-cover'd pastures and hillsides
All white with the lowly astalthon;   35
The lowly yet lovely astalthon,

And dream in a world made of dreaming
The dreams that are fairer than Aidenn;
Bright dreams that are truer than reason!
So dream'd and so lov'd we thro' ages,   40
Till came the curs'd season of Dzannin;
The daemon-damn'd season of Dzannin;
When red shone the suns and the planets,
And red gleam'd the crescent Banapis,
And red fell the vapours of Yabon.   45
Then redden'd the blossoms and streamlets,
And lakes that lay under the bridges,
And even the calm alabaster
Glow'd pink with uncanny reflections
Till all the carv'd fairies and daemons   50
Leer'd redly from backgrounds of shadow.
Now redden'd my vision, and madly
I strove to peer thro' the dense curtain
And glimpse the divine Nathicana;
The pure, ever-pale Nathicana;   55
The lov'd, the unchang'd Nathicana.
But vortex on vortex of madness
Beclouded my labouring vision;
My damnable, reddening vision
That built a new world for my seeing;   60
A new world of redness and darkness,
A horrible coma call'd living.
So now in this coma call'd living
I view the bright phantoms of beauty;
The false, hollow phantoms of beauty   65
That cloak all the evils of Dzannin.
I view them with infinite longing,
So like do they seem to my lov'd one;
So shapely and fair like my lov'd one;
Yet foul from their eyes shines their evil;   70
Their cruel and pitiless evil,
More evil than Thaphron or Latgoz,
Twice ill for its gorgeous concealment.
And only in slumbers of midnight
Appears the lost maid Nathicana,   75
The pallid, the pure Nathicana,
Who fades at the glance of the dreamer.
Again and again do I seek her;
I woo with deep draughts of Plathotis,

Deep draughts brew'd in wine of Astarte   80
And strengthen'd with tears of long weeping.
I yearn for the gardens of Zaïs;
The lovely lost gardens of Zaïs
Where blossoms the white nephalotë,
The redolent herald of midnight.   85
The last potent draught I am brewing;
A draught that the daemons delight in;
A draught that will banish the redness;
The horrible coma call'd living.
Soon, soon, if I fail not in brewing,   90
The redness and madness will vanish,
And deep in the worm-peopled darkness
Will rot the base chains that have bound me.
Once more shall the gardens of Zaïs
Dawn white on my long-tortur'd vision,   95
And there midst the vapours of Yabon
Will stand the divine Nathicana;
The deathless, restor'd Nathicana
Whose like is not met with in living.

III. OCCASIONAL VERSE

The Members of the Men's Club of the First Universalist Church of Providence, R.I., to Its President, About to Leave for Florida on Account of His Health

Since your physician and the hostile fates
Withdraw you from your fond associates,
A host of Universalists lament
The loss of their departing president;
A loyal club, when southward you have gone,   5
The founder and executive will mourn.
The club's foundations by your hands were laid;
Beneath your rule its guiding laws were made;
Your efforts caus'd the social band to gain
The pow'r at once to teach and entertain.   10
With careful thought, its policy you fix'd,
The grave and gay in just proportion mix'd;
Nor let its frequent meetings know a dearth
Of lofty learning, or diverting mirth.
Why should we not regret that you must go,   15
Since we to you our club's existence owe?
Why should we not, whilst you are absent, burn
With hot impatience for your swift return,
And wait the day when you'll again abide
Within our midst, and o'er the club preside?   20

Meanwhile, amongst the oranges and palms,
Remote from Boreal winter's icy harms,
The sunny air of Florida will lend
A genial glow, and all your ills amend.
'Neath southern skies you'll gain redoubled strength,   25
And overflow with vigour, till at length,
Your health renew'd, you seek the northern strand
And meet the welcome of your native land.

To Mr. Terhune, on His Historical Fiction

Editor, Argosy:
Since showy scribblers can with greater ease
The feelings than the understanding please,
Our modern tales lose all their forceful grace,
And sense is smother'd in a soft embrace.
Th' ambitious authors play the scholar's part,   5

And, sans the substance, ape the air of art.
Yet, head and shoulders o'er the Grub-street crew
Tow'rs tried Terhune, to old traditions true;
Who now his undiminish'd skill displays
Like Milton in the Restoration days.   10
Hail! thou whose works are erudite yet plain,
With pow'r at once to teach and entertain.
In truest taste are all thy subjects fix'd;
The grave and gay in just proportion mix'd.
Beneath the spell of thy harmonious words,   15
The ages live, and Clio's self applauds.
Contain'd in dull descriptive tomes alone,
The glorious past, till by Terhune made known,
A phantom panorama seem'd to be,
Remote from life and hid in history.   20
The daring Smith, who sought Virginia's shore,
To living flesh but small resemblance bore,
Whilst our own revolution look'd as far
Behind our times, as e'en the Trojan war.
Brave Washington, tho' wide diffus'd his fame,   25
Seem'd scarce so much a human as a name,
And grasping Bonaparte, by greed undone,
Sat like an ogre on a spectral throne.
Yet thou, Terhune, reviv'st each ancient scene;
Who reads thy tales back thro' the years hath been.   30
The living past unfolds and meets our eyes,
Stript of its dulness and pedantic guise.
The deadly guns of Bunker Hill we hear;
The cruel snows of Valley Forge appear,
And distant ages, bath'd in stronger light,   35
Enchain our gaze, and charm our ling'ring sight.
By thy skill'd art and lucid phrases led,
Historic ground with swelling mien we tread,
For what man lives, but that his fancy glows
Where virtue dwelt, and freedom first arose?   40
The true American, with proper pride,
Sees how his fathers liv'd and fought and dy'd.
Our weaker spirits catch the noble rage,
And feel the valour of a sterner age.
But why continue? Sure, my wretched verse   45
Too feeble is, such subjects to rehearse.
To stay time's fleeting is the priceless boon
Lent by the graphic pages of Terhune!

To Mr. Munroe, on His Instructive and Entertaining Account of Switzerland

Display'd by dull descriptive maps alone,
Helvetia's realm, till thro' your pages known,
A strange and distant country was to me,
Not of the world, but of geography.
The snow-crown'd Alps, along whose slipp'ry sides　　　　　5
In slow descent the giant glacier glides,
Where regal Rhine and rushing Rhone are born;
Where tow'r the Simplon and the Matterhorn,
From me seem'd sever'd by as great a space
As Tycho, on the moon's unchanging face.　　　　　　　10
The blue Geneva, and the clean Lucerne,
Look'd less like lakes, than lessons laid to learn;
While Bernard's hospice, of immortal fame,
Was scarce so much a convent as a name.
Mere markings on the geographic sphere　　　　　　　15
Did Zurich and the beauteous Berne appear,
Nor any part impress'd itself more true
Upon my mind, than some fictitious view.
Yet your descriptions animate the scene;
Who reads your words, to Switzerland hath been.　　　　20
Th' untravell'd student, close within his doors,
The lofty peak and crystal lake explores.
The living land unfolds, and stands apart
From dry delineations on the chart.
The mountain torrent's sprightly song we hear;　　　　25
We breathe the bracing Alpine atmosphere;
And waters sparkling in the sun's bright rays,
Revive our spirits, and enchain our gaze.
By your skill'd art and lucid phrases led,
Historic streets with rev'rent mien we tread;　　　　　30
For what man lives, whose bosom fails to swell
Where faith and freedom unmolested dwell?
The pious Protestant with proper pride
Beholds the town where Calvin preach'd and dy'd;
Whilst learned minds of Clio's noble clan　　　　　　35
Delight in Gibbon's lov'd retreat—Lausanne.
But why continue? Such a theme as this
Will turn a sturdy Saxon to a Swiss!
Travel, avaunt! At home, abroad we go,
Borne by the graphic chapters of Munroe!　　　　　　40

105

Regner Lodbrog's Epicedium

With our swords have we contended!
Come but new to Gothland's shore
For the killing of the serpent
We have gain'd from Thor (   )
(   )   5
From this deed they call me man
Because I have transfix'd the adder:
Shaggy breeches from that slaughter.
(   )
I have thrust a spear into the serpent   10
With metal brighter (   )

With our swords have we contended!
But a youth was I when eastward,
In the channel of Oreon,
With our foemen's gore in torrents   15
We the (   ) and wolves delighted;
And the yellow-footed buzzard.
There the harden'd steel resounded
On the high-wrought hostile helmets.
One vast wound was all the ocean   20
And the hungry raven waded
Searching for its carrion food
Deep in dead men's thick'ning blood.

With our swords have we contended!
Ere two score of years we counted   25
High we bore our glist'ning lances
Wide we heard our fame and praises.
In the east before the harbour
(Barons eight we overcame;)
We the rav'ning eagle glutted;   30
Dripping wounds fill'd up the ocean.
Weary of the hopeless fray,
All the host dissolv'd away.

With our swords have we contended!
When the Vistula we enter'd   35
With our ships in battle order
We unto the hall of Woden
Sent the bold Helsingian foemen.
Then the sword-points bit in fury;

All the billows turn'd to life-blood   40
Earth with streaming gore was crimson'd;
Reeking sword with ringing note
Shields divided; armour smote.

(*With our swords have we contended!*)
(None had fallen on that day   )   45
(Till on his ship Heraudus fell:)
(Than him before no braver baron   )
Cleft the sea with ships of battle;
Never after him was chieftain
Lighter hearted in the fighting.   50

With our swords have we contended!
Now the host flung down their bucklers;
Flying spears tore heroes' bosoms
Swords on Scarfian rocks were striking.
Gory was his shield in slaughter   55
Till the royal Rafno perish'd.
Sweat from weary brows and pale
Trickled down the suits of mail.

With our swords have we contended!
Copious booty had the ravens   60
Round about th' Indirian islands,
In that single day of action,
(One in many deaths was little.   )
(The rising sun grew bright on spears   )
In the forms of prostrate warrior-men.   65
Arrows from their bows ejected;
(Weapons roared on Lano's plain.   )
(Long the virgin mourned that slaughter)

To an Accomplished Young Gentlewoman on Her Birthday, Decr. 2, 1914

Dear Madam (laugh not at the formal way
Of one who celebrates your natal day):
Receive the tribute of a stilted bard,
Rememb'ring not his style, but his regard.
Increasing joy, and added talent true,   5
Each bright auspicious birthday brings to you;

May they grow many, yet appear but few!

To the Recipient of This Volume

Congenial Cole, I pray thee condescend
To take this off'ring of a distant friend.
Within these year-worn pages canst thou find
A feast of culture for the eager mind.
Here shine the precepts of a statelier age,   5
To mould the line, and smooth th' unpolished page.
With study'd grace the sentence to adorn,
And rise to images sublimely drawn.
E'en now the Muse's choicest gifts are thine:
How, then, will glow thy labour'd, polish'd line!   10
Son of the plains! May thy Pierian flights
Sustain thee upward to Parnassus' heights!

On Receiving a Picture of Swans

With pensive grace the melancholy Swan
Mourns o'er the tomb of luckless Phaëton;
On grassy banks the weeping poplars wave,
And guard with tender care the wat'ry grave.
Would that I might, should I too proudly claim   5
An Heav'nly parent, or a Godlike fame,
When flown too high, and dash'd to depths below,
Receive such tribute as a Cygnus' woe!
The faithful bird, that dumbly floats along,
Sighs all the deeper for his want of song.   10

To Charlie of the Comics

(With profuse Apologies to Rheinhart Kleiner, Esq., Poet-Laureate and
Author of "To Mary of the Movies".)

You trip and tumble o'er the sheet
That holds your life-like image.
You shuffle your prodigious feet
Thro' love-scene, chase, or scrimmage.
As gazing on each comic act   5
I stare at your perfection,
I find it hard to face the fact
That you're a mere projection.

I've seen you as an artist rare,
With brush and paint-smear'd palette;   10

108

I've seen you fan the empty air
With ill-intention'd mallet.
I've watch'd you woo a winsome fay
(You must a dream to her be),
But ne'er have caught you in a play   15
Without that cane and derby!

Dear lad, I trust your happiness
May be like that you give us,
And since ripe years the mirthful bless,
That you may long outlive us.   20
May you the smiles of Fortune see,
Nor know what want of cash is;
And may your times of trouble be
As short as your moustaches!

I'd like to meet you, Charles, old chap,   25
Tho' vast the space dividing;
Yet I must merely sit and clap
At your fantastic gliding.
But tho' you're far away, we know,
You still have pow'r to rouse us: 30
Your films can pack a picture-show
That's roomy as your trousers!

On the Cowboys of the West

In Whom Is Embodied the Nature-Worshipping Spirit of Classical Antiquity

Dedicated to Ira A. Cole

Far from the throng, upon the western plain,
Earth's wondrous childhood comes to life again.
A godlike race in primal glory roam,
Who claim no spot but Nature for their home.
Unspoil'd by art, or philosophic lore,   5
They read in rocks, or hear in rivers' roar
Th' unchanging tales that charm'd the Grecian ear,
And trace the Gods in heav'n's nocturnal sphere.
In their wild song, that o'er the prairie rings,
The soul of Orpheus, or Orion, sings;   10
In their quick strife, of careless passion bred,
We spy the shades of Greek and Trojan dead.

From ev'ry cliff, to their poetic eyes,
Some tokens of divinity arise;
That which to us the musty volumes give,   15
They study not; but know, and feel, and live!

To Samuel Loveman, Esquire, on His Poetry and Drama, Writ in the Elizabethan Style

So like in name, in art so much the less,
Let Lovecraft lines to Loveman's Muse address:
How blest art thou, who thro' thy pow'r of song
Beside Pierus' sacred fount belong.
Son of Apollo; lov'd of all the Nine;   5
The gifts of Orpheus in thy verses shine.
With purest words of Shakespeare's golden age,
Thou cheer'st alike the study and the stage.
Unspotted Beauty moves thy magic style
As rare adornments on each other pile.   10
In thee no taint of modern times is seen;
Thy purling numbers are a rill serene:
Devoid of filth, they sparkle as they flow,
And with each turn of thought the deeper grow.
In subtle Fancy's swift, ethereal flight,   15
What other poet can attain thy height?
Thy soaring line shakes off the bonds of earth,
And Saturn's reign in thee hath second birth.

The Bookstall

An Epistle to Rheinhart Kleiner, Esq., Poet-Laureate

Congenial KLEINER, whose broad brow sustains
The bays that prove the sweetness of thy strains:
To rougher rhymes than thine an audience lend,
And take th' admiring tribute of a friend.
What shall I say? Must I in pain rehearse   5
The deadly dulness of a modern verse,
Or prate of Whitman, whose Boeotian bawl
Can scarce be justly labell'd verse at all?
Alas! such themes no charms for me afford,
Nor can I scan them happy and unbor'd.   10
Pox on the rogues that writ these lifeless lays!
My fancy beckons me to nobler days!

Say, waking Muse, where ages best unfold,
And tales of times forgotten most are told;
Where weary pedants, dryer than the dust,   15
Like some lov'd incense scent their letter'd must;
Where crumbling tomes upon the groaning shelves
Cast their lost centuries about ourselves.
Mine be the pleasure of the grimy stand
Where age-old volumes sleep on ev'ry hand.   20
Mine be the joy to live in Thought's demesne
The bygone hours of volumes thick and lean;
With Wittie's aid to count the Zodiac host,
Or hunt with Johnson for the Cock-Lane Ghost.
O'er Mather's prosy page, half dreaming, pore,   25
Or follow Hawkesworth to the distant shore.
Ye old familiar friends whom ages bless,
How oft ye greet me in a diff'rent dress!
Watch shining Maro, who on ev'ry side
Adorns the dingy walls with Roman pride.   30
Untouch'd or English'd; French or Leipzig made,
The lustrous lines of Virgil pierce the shade.
O Mantuan Lamp! what bard before or since
Can such a wealth of polish'd force evince?
Thus the quick question, but the answer lies   35
Where yonder rotting Homer meets our eyes.
The blind, the bearded bard before us burns,
And thrills our temples with his tragic turns.
Of Ilion's siege each time as new we hear,
While shrewd Ulysses charms the eager ear.   40
These share we all, yet what affection twines
About obscurer, less remember'd lines!
Each knows his fav'rites, and in fancy claims
For boon companions those forgotten names.
Would ye read Lucan? Start ye then and go   45
Where Lucan gains Britannic garb from Rowe.
Full many a Grecian lyrist smiles or grieves
To English tunes thro' Elton's quarto leaves.
Or if our own originals you'd see,
Go smell the drugs in Garth's Dispensary!   50
What shades scholastic thro' the twilight flit
Where Knapton's sagging folios loosely sit!
The skull-capp'd dealer, crouching on his stool,
O'er the vague past can claim a wizard's rule:

On his seam'd face the myriad wrinkles play,   55
And subtly link him to the yesterday.
Rise, Stanhope, rise! Thy macaroni train
Dance in the beams that pierce the dusty pane.
Hail! sportive Rochester, bestir thy feet,
And mince in fancy o'er the cobbled street!   60
House after house appear in gabled rows,
And the dim room Old London's spirit shews!
Upon the floor, in Sol's enfeebled blaze,
The coal-black puss with youthful ardour plays;
Yet what more ancient symbol may we scan   65
Than puss, the age-long satellite of Man?
Egyptian days a feline worship knew,
And Roman consuls heard the plaintive mew:
The glossy mite can win a scholar's glance,
Whilst sages pause to watch a kitten prance.   70
Outside the creaking door a nation boils,
And Progress crushes Learning in its coils.
The blessed Past in mad confusion fades,
And Commerce blasts Retirement's quiet shades.
Unnumber'd noises, in demoniac choir,   75
Wake the curs'd Pit, and stir the seething fire.
A million passengers, in hast'ning heat,
Jostle their fellows, and disturb the street.
From their coarse lips barbaric tones diffuse,
To shock the sense, and affront the Muse.   80
Decadent day! that Culture must return
To cloister'd cell, and Men, secluded, learn.
O! for the days when I would idly dream
In grassy meads by Seekonk's swelling stream;
When leafy groves adorn'd the rising hill,   85
And in the copse the feather'd train would trill.
When fragrant zephyrs fann'd the summer green,
And stars, undimm'd, lit winter's snowy scene.
Then flow'd the verse spontaneous from the heart,
That now demands the student's labour'd art.   90
Then pour'd Creation's blessings on us all,
Which now we strain from books in dingy stall.
Yet let us bless the bookstall whilst it stays;
That, too, may soon be part of other days!

Content

An Epistle to RHEINHART KLEINER, Esq.,
Poet-Laureate, and Author of "Another Endless Day".

> Beatus ille qui procul negotiis,
>   Ut prisca gens mortalium,
> Paterna rura bubus exercet suis.
>   —HORACE.

KLEINER! in whose quick pulses wildly beat
The youth's ambition, and the lyrist's heat,
Whose questing spirit scorns our lowly flights,
And dares the heavens for sublimer heights:
If passion's force will grant an hour's relief,   5
Attend a calmer song, nor nurse thy grief.
What is true bliss? Must mortals ever yearn
For stars beyond their reach, and vainly burn;
Must suff'ring man, impatient, seek to scale
Forbidden steeps, where sharper pangs prevail?   10
Alas for him who chafes at soothing ease,
And cries for fever'd joys and pains to please:
They please a moment, but the pleasure flies,
And the rack'd soul, a prey to passion, dies.
Away, false lures! and let my spirit roam   15
O'er sweet Arcadia, and the rural home;
Let my sad heart with no new sorrow bleed,
But rest content in Morven's mossy mead.
Wild thoughts and vain ambitions circle near,
Whilst I, at peace, the abbey chimings hear.   20
Loud shakes the surge of Life's unquiet sea,
Yet smooth the stream that laves the rustic lea.
Let others feel the world's destroying thrill,
As 'midst the kine I haunt the verdant hill.
Rise, radiant sun! to light the grassy glades,   25
Whose charms I view from grateful beechen shades;
O'er spire and peak diffuse th' expanding gleam
That gilds the grove, and sparkles on the stream.
Awake! ye sylphs of Flora's gorgeous train,
To scent the fields, and deck the rising main.   30
Soar, feather'd flock, and carol o'er the scene,
To cheer the lonely watcher on the green.

Sweet is the song the morning meadow bears,
And with the darkness fade ambitious cares:
Above the abbey tow'r the rays ascend,   35
As light and peace in matchless beauty blend.
Why should I sigh for realms of toil and stress,
When now I bask in Nature's loveliness?
What thoughts so great, that they must needs expand
Beyond the hills that bound this fragrant land?   40
These friendly hills my infant vision knew,
And in the shelt'ring vale from birth I grew.
Yon distant spires Ambition's limit shew,
For who, here born, could farther wish to go?
When sky-blest evening soothes the world and me,   45
Are moon and stars more distant from my lea?
No urban glare my sight of heav'n obscures,
And orbs undimm'd rise o'er the neighb'ring moors.
What priceless boon may spreading Fame impart,
When village dignity hath cheer'd the heart?   50
The little group that hug the tavern fire
To air their wisdom, and salute their squire,
Far kinder are, than all the courtly throng
That flatter Kings, and shield their faults in song!
And in the end; what if no man adore   55
My senseless ashes 'neath Westminster's floor?
May not my weary frame, at Life's dim night,
Sleep where my childhood first enjoy'd the light?
Rest were the sweeter in the sacred shade
Of that dear fane where all my fathers pray'd;   60
Ancestral spirits bless the air around,
And hallow'd mem'ries fill the gentle ground.
So stay, belov'd Content! nor let my soul
In fretful passion seek a farther goal.
Apollo, chasing Daphne, gain'd his prize,   65
But lo! she turn'd to wood before his eyes!
Our earthly prizes, tho' as hotly sought,
Prove just as fleeting, and decay to naught.
Enduring bliss a man may only find
In virtuous living, and contented mind.   70

The Smile

Ride, si sapis.

Attend! ye tearful train, whose sombre stare
Clouds the bright noon, and chills the summer air;
Whose fretful fancy, torn by transient woes,
Prolongs the pain, nor grateful sweetness knows:
Of trivial shadow born, your doleful mien   5
Creates a million shades where one had been!
At dawn, when soft Aurora wakes the wold,
In curtain'd room poor Maestus' frown behold:
Depress'd with grief for his rejected rhymes,
He spurns the soothing pleasures of the times;   10
Courts the dark midnight, and reviles the ray
Of cheering sunshine that proclaims the day.
The verdant vale, with orient beams aglow,
Affronts his mood, and stimulates his woe,
And the fair meadow, gay with floral grace,   15
But carves new furrows on his furrow'd face!
The joys of Nature for her sons design'd,
Perturb the more his barren, brooding mind;
He scorns the countless boons the hours provide
Whilst weeping o'er the one small boon deny'd!   20
Astir at last, and pacing down the road,
Sour Maestus still retains his gloomy load;
At friendly blossoms casts an angry look,
And mutters curses at the murm'ring brook.
Beside yon cottage gate a childish throng   25
Enjoy the day in sport and happy song:
By one black glance the sulker mars their glee,
Incens'd that they should blithe or blissful be!
With sneering snarl he gains the village green,
And flings an insult at the peaceful scene: 30
The smiling faces by each humble door
Perceive his morbid mood and smile no more.
The neighb'ring copse, where bird-born warbling floats,
Provokes poor Maestus with the tuneful notes:
The light-wing'd choristers their song suspend,   35
And flee the foe who fears to be their friend.
Thus stalks the mourner, whose distressful eye
Darkens the sun, and veils th' unclouded sky;
Seeks out the weeds amidst the garden flow'rs,

115

In crystal starlight spies the coming show'rs;   40
Foul calumny with avid ardour learns,
And in each virtue hidden ill discerns!
His hand no help, his heart no kindness bears,
Nor strives he to relieve a brother's cares:
His own sick soul, with melancholy low,   45
Cares not how many others suffer so.
Mankind he shuns, possess'd by hatred dim,
And Man repays the debt by shunning him!

    Mark now bright Laetus, who at breaking day
Delights to watch the climbing sunbeams play: 50
Pleas'd with the glow and grateful for the sight,
He casts away the ills of yesternight;
With smiling grace th' auspicious morning greets,
And prints his smile on ev'ry face he meets.
For him the mead with greener splendour spreads,   55
And flow'rs bloom brighter from their dewy beds;
With milder breath the matin zephyr stirs
The lowland maples and the mountain firs;
The brook with added joy its chorus chants,
While shapelier fronds bedeck the fringing plants.   60
At Laetus' tread behold the infant train,
Distress'd by Maestus, all their joy regain:
Around the cottage door in gladness vie,
And bless their smiling squire with laughing eye.
The village throng his sprightly step attend,   65
For ev'ry wight knows Laetus as his friend:
His beaming glance, by kindly heart endow'd,
Reflected shines from all the circling crowd.
Nor with indiff'rence is that glance endow'd
Upon his fellows in the travell'd road: 70
Solicitude his gen'rous mien pervades,
And, duke or churl, each suff'ring soul he aids.
Deaf to ill rumour, keen to good report,
His lenient judgment is the village court;
The countryside in his forgiving ear   75
Their sorrows pour, for comfort and for cheer:
The cares of all his soothing arts beguile,
And from his own, they learn a gen'ral smile!

    Hark! From the copse returning carols ring,
As blithesome birds the smiling Laetus sing;   80

The chirping chords o'er elm and oak resound,
To bless the vale, and thrill the rising mound.
Above th' adjacent moor a cloud ascends,
And thunder now the rustic quiet rends:
But while poor Maestus shakes in doleful fright,   85
Laetus rejoices in the flashing light:
Th' Olympian Jove behind the thunder sees,
And hails the show'r that slakes the thirsty trees.
Within a glen, whose leaf-thatch'd roof allows
A grateful refuge 'neath the bending boughs,   90
In common quest of shelter from the rain,
Behold a random meeting of the twain!
The angry Maestus shakes his dripping cloak,
And curses even the protecting oak;
Observes his soggy hat with with'ring look;   95
Eyes the damp powder on his wet peruke;
But as the fretful fool all things reviles,
His happier brother meets his gaze—and smiles!
Thrice-potent smile! whose glad, pervasive pow'r
Lights up the gloom, and cheers the rainy hour;   100
The darkest mood dispels, and from the mind
Wafts the sad image like a summer wind!
Unhappy Maestus sees, and o'er his face
The grief-drawn lines unwonted patterns trace;
The tight-prest lips relax; the curling sneer   105
Attempts to form, yet seems to disappear;
The brows to hold their frown in vain essay,
And glaring eyeballs lose their baleful ray.
Again kind Laetus, with his cheerful glance,
In friendly fashion makes a new advance;   110
With offer'd aid, his hand in greeting lends,
While o'er his lips a brighter smile extends.
Maestus, perplex'd, a sadden'd accent tries,
But ere his sob is born, the sadness dies:
Half struggling to the end, he pants awhile,   115
Then bursts in laughter—conquer'd by the SMILE.

Inspiration

One fragrant morn, when Spring was young,
    I roam'd the glen in eager quest,
Hoping with careful eye among
    The grass to find the violet's nest;
But not a leaf or bud seem'd sprung   5
    Up from the couch of wintry rest:
And yet, when all my greedy search was o'er,
By chance I spy'd the flow'r I miss'd before!

One night, within my chamber pent,
    I strove my fancies to enchain   10
In breathing numbers, and to vent
    Some portion of my bliss and pain;
But strife of soul my musings rent—
    The sluggish pencil mov'd in vain:
Yet out upon the mead the starlight brought   15
The long-wish'd song, unbidden and unsought!

Respite

Thro' well-kept arbours fruitlessly I stray'd
    In quest of respite from the causeless woes
That throng the weary spirit, and invade
    The mind too seldom dreamless with repose.

Not neat-hedg'd path, nor garden's radiant grace,   5
    Nor crystal fountain playing o'er the green,
Could cheer my heart, or from my soul efface
    The tragedy of things that might have been.

The orchard boughs, bedeck'd with flow'rs of spring,
    The verdant lawns, with skilful labour shorn,   10
To me no joy nor grateful thrill could bring;
    In tears I came, and linger'd but to mourn.

One day, in idleness, my footsteps found
    The weed-chok'd slope that leads to sylvan deeps
Where leafy carpets clothe th' untrodden ground,   15
    And Nature, unadorn'd, her palace keeps.

'Twas here, in regions to mankind unknown,
    Where swamp and brake benignant spirits hide,

I stood at last, with Nature's God alone,
    And gain'd the respite that the world deny'd.   20

Brotherhood

In prideful scorn I watch'd the farmer stride
    With step uncouth o'er road and mossy lane;
How could I help but distantly deride
    The churlish, callous'd, coarse-clad country swain?

Upon his lips a mumbled ballad stirr'd   5
    The evening air with dull cacophony;
In cold contempt, I shudder'd as I heard,
    And held myself no kin to such as he.

But as he leap'd the stile and gain'd the field
    Where star-fac'd blossoms twinkled thro' the hay,   10
His lumb'ring footfalls oftentimes would yield,
    To spare the flow'rs that bloom'd along the way.

And while I gaz'd, my spirit swell'd apace;
    With the crude swain I own'd the human tie;
The tend'rest impulse of a noble race   15
    Had prov'd the boor a finer man than I!

Lines on Graduation from the R.I. Hospital's School of Nurses

To Be Spoken by the Author's Sister

As all-engulfing Time, in ceaseless flow,
Destroys the bonds that student comrades know;
Those bonds of friendship, whose endearing pow'r
Casts a sad shadow o'er the parting hour;
We fondly pause, reluctant to disperse,   5
And three short years of pleasing toil rehearse.
With what just pride our rising ranks we scan;
The foes of suff'ring, and the friends of man!
With what half-regal consciousness we feel
Our magic pow'r to succour and to heal!   10
Let others vaunt a valiant warrior's name,
And thro' destruction seek immortal fame;
Our gentler band reject the art of strife,
Nor deem it nobler to bring death, than life:

119

What martial bays or honours could surpass   15
The well-earn'd laurels of our little class?
Together striving in a glorious cause,
How oft have we survey'd Hygeia's laws;
How oft in studious ardour search'd the page
Where Aesculapian art informs the age;   20
How oft with care unselfish borne the strain
Of weary vigils by the couch of pain;
How oft, besides, have we with joy endur'd
Ills of our own, that others might be cur'd!
In such pursuits our mutual friendship gave   25
A double fervour to assist and save;
Our cordial ties the dreariest labour eas'd,
Till nothing was so hard, but that it pleas'd:
Congenial amity so warmly throve,
That work must needs a social pleasure prove!   30
With true delight we view th' attractive scene,
Where Galen's shade assumes a milder mien.
As now we part, possess'd by mem'ries sweet,
We would we might our student hours repeat;
Yet duty bids us with imperious tone   35
Attend the future, and push on alone!
'Tis ours to give an ailing race our skill,
And spread new vigour thro' persistent ill;
Be first to cool the suff'rer's febrile breath,
And last to leave the gloomy bed of death;   40
Bring cheer where cheer was never brought before,
Brave the dark squalor of the pauper's door;
The wand'ring mind with soothing words to calm,
And o'er distress diffuse a tender balm;
To nurse the sick with more than human care,   45
And, uncomplaining, ev'ry burden bear:
Good without end for slight reward bestow,
And prove the angels of a world of woe!
These dignities the future holds in store:
Could we, indeed, be crown'd or honour'd more?   50
The prologue's done—the play of life succeeds;
Our graver years respond to graver needs;
Yet shall we never in the wider sphere
Forget the happy days we linger'd here.
'Tis here that learning shap'd the course of youth,   55
And set our footsteps on the path of truth;

With kindly force our high ideals fix'd,
And art and practice in due measure mix'd:
'Tis here, from each companion's earnest face,
We drank our deepest draughts of friendship's grace: 60
And here our dearest thoughts must ever cling,
Whate'er of wealth or fame the years may bring!

Fact and Fancy

How dull the wretch, whose philosophic mind
Disdains the pleasures of fantastic kind;
Whose prosy thoughts the joys of life exclude,
And wreck the solace of the poet's mood!
Young Zeno, practic'd in the Stoic's art,   5
Rejects the language of the glowing heart;
Dissolves sweet Nature to a mess of laws;
Condemns th' effect whilst looking for the cause;
Freezes poor Ovid in an ic'd review,
And sneers because his fables are untrue!   10
In search of Truth the hopeful zealot goes,
But all the sadder turns, the more he knows!
Stay! vandal sophist, whose deep lore would blast
The graceful legends of the story'd past;
Whose tongue in censure flays th' embellish'd page,   15
And scolds the comforts of a dreary age:
Would'st strip the foliage from the vital bough
Till all men grow as wisely dull as thou?
Happy the man whose fresh, untainted eye
Discerns a Pantheon in the spangled sky;   20
Finds Sylphs and Dryads in the waving trees,
And spies soft Notus in the southern breeze;
For whom the stream a cheering carol sings,
While reedy music by the fountain rings;
To whom the waves a Nereid tale confide   25
Till friendly presence fills the rising tide.
Happy is he, who void of learning's woes,
Th' ethereal life of body'd Nature knows:
I scorn the sage that tells me it but seems,
And flout his gravity in sunlit dreams!   30

Percival Lowell

1855–1916

So near liv'd LOWELL to the shining skies,
    In crystal air with upward-soaring sight,
That he must needs a little farther rise,
    And dwell among his cherish'd orbs of light.

His soul to Heav'n enduring kinship own'd,   5
    Pure with the grace of high ethereal thought;
Celestial spheres a grateful love inton'd,
    And friendly stars his closer presence sought.

Upon the earth our strains threnetic mourn
    With poignant sorrow his untimely loss;   10
But he, thro' realms of glad refulgence borne,
    Adds a new brilliance to the Southern Cross!

Prologue to "Fragments from an Hour of Inspiration" by Jonathan E. Hoag

The western sun, whose warm, rubescent rays
Touch the green slope with soul-awak'ning blaze,
A thoughtful bard reveals, whose polish'd flights
Spring from the scene on Dillon's pleasing heights.
An ancient boulder is the poet's seat,   5
A verdant vista fronts the blest retreat;
From distant banks there comes th' elusive gleam
That speaks the Hudson's silent, stately stream.
Here, ere the birth of man, a granite train
In speechless splendour rul'd the rising main;   10
In later days an Indian horde decreed
The varying fortunes of the fragrant mead.
Here Dutchmen trod, till Albion's stronger sway
Carv'd out the nation that we know today;
'Twas here th' insurgent swain his King defy'd,   15
And rural rebels broke Burgoyne's bold pride.
Such is the scene, with shades historic rife,
That *Hoag*, in numbers, gives eternal life!

Earth and Sky

When the rude shepherd, thro' the starlit night,
　　Watch'd o'er his flocks beside Chaldaean streams,
His eager eyes, with unexplain'd delight,
　　Turn'd upward to the thousand friendly beams
That mark'd his seasons, and in beauty bright　　　　　　　5
　　Took fancy'd shapes, and pictur'd out his dreams.
In grateful awe the simple watcher pray'd,
And from each star a worshipp'd godhead made.

With what true pleasure must the swain have view'd
　　Arcturus, climbing o'er the hills in spring;　　　　　10
Soft summer gems of ev'ry magnitude,
　　And blazing skies that winter evenings bring,
When great Orion's rays, with cheer indued,
　　Rob the inclement winds of half their sting.
He could not help but deem the wondrous show　　　　　15
A boon design'd for suff'ring earth below.

When infant Science taught us first to trace
　　The sun and moon and planets thro' the skies,
To count the almost countless orbs of space,
　　And mark them as they set, or south, or rise,　　　　20
And chart the boundless blue's bespangled face,
　　Guessing the changeless laws by which it flies,
Our groping minds perceiv'd the order'd plan,
And sought to learn of Heav'n's effect on man.

Alas! how long did man essay to read　　　　　　　　　25
　　His doubtful future in the circling spheres!
His chain'd conceptions could not oft exceed
　　A little sky to guide his hopes and fears;
And all Creation's glory he would heed
　　But to predict his own inglorious years.　　　　　　30
Deluded days, when astronomic fame
Could wreathe the temples of a Nostradame!

Triumphant Truth! What marvels are reveal'd
　　When thy vast precepts penetrate the mind.
Stupendous space, by Ignorance conceal'd,　　　　　　35
　　Expands, and shews Creation unconfin'd,
Yet that Creation—all the starry field—
　　May be but one of billions scarce divin'd.

123

Infinitude! Upon thy endless sea,
What paltry waifs are mortals such as we!   40

To M. W. M.

Behold the labourer, who builds the walls
That soon shall shine as Learning's sacred halls;
A man so apt at ev'ry art and trade,
He might well govern what his hands have made!

Lines on the 25th. Anniversary of the *Providence Evening News,* 1892–1917

As some staunch citizen of wit and worth
In manhood's prime surveys his life from birth;
Casts o'er the changing scene a backward glance,
Content to mark the well-spent years' advance;
Our patriot page tonight the past reviews,   5
Pleas'd with the bays that justly crown THE NEWS:
Exulting columns each bright year revive,
And proudly cry, "THE NEWS is twenty-five!"
Who but with satisfaction must commend
The right's bold champion, and the people's friend?   10
First in the fray to guard the public weal,
And first to mirror what the public feel;
To homes a teacher, and to all a guide,
Alert to serve mankind on Virtue's side:
Its voice by factions and by mobs unsway'd,   15
Unfetter'd by the chains that gold hath made:
No man too humble to partake its smile,
And none too learned to approve its style;
Uncurb'd in thought, devoted to the free,
The chosen mouthpiece of Democracy.   20
Scornful the pow'r of servile fear to own,
It bows to Justice, and to that alone!
Let vaunting rivals seek with proud intent
To shape a war, or mould a government;
Stir the slow currents of patrician hate,   25
And slight the people to exalt the state.
Let baser minds debauch the yellow page
With maudlin filth and half-seditious rage,
Or daub those mirthless shocks to sense and eye—
"Cartoons" that look like naught in earth or sky;   30

124

Our modest sheet the wiser plan pursues,
And gives the reader what it is—THE NEWS!
Auspicious Clio! whose unfading scroll
Preserves the past, and keeps the record whole,
Who twines with myrtle those deserving brows   35
That hold the spark which genuine worth endows;
Retrace the road of time, and shew again
THE NEWS, like Pallas, born from HEATON'S brain;
Recall th' ensuing years and wider plan,
As the young daily led Progression's van;   40
With loving care its rising path display;
Point out the boons it strow'd along the way;
Tell how its pages, with precision writ,
Increas'd in service as they grew in wit;
Nor fail the genius of the whole to crown,   45
But grant the stateliest wreath of all to BROWN!
Such is the past and present; here the tale
Falls to the Sibyl since the Muses fail:
What new Cumaean, in prediction bold,
Shall tell of half the future ages hold;   50
Of greener laurels for good deeds well done,
And lasting fame by rigid Justice won?
If brave Integrity commands the field,
What will not soon to such pure pages yield?
What rival is with equal care design'd   55
To serve the race, and lift the gen'ral mind?
A monarch's might the potent press commands,
And might means arrogance in common hands;
Rare is that pen, unlur'd by fame or pelf,
Which moves unsullied, close to Virtue's self.   60
But this THE NEWS can claim, and with it reach
The public vision, to advise and teach;
Whilst in each part of life the precepts fall
With aptness and amenity to all.
The grateful town with cordial warmth reveres   65
The time-tried friend of five-and-twenty years,
And fondly hopes, that as in ages past,
Each fruitful twelvemonth may outrank the last!

To the Nurses of the Red Cross

Where martial splendour sinks to gruesome gloom,
And pride of conquest turns to dread of doom;

125

Where order'd ranks in maim'd confusion lie
Till stench and suff'ring shock the pitying sky;
Where bestial figures sprawl, that once were man,   5
And vermin finish what the shells began;
'Tis there you shine, a heav'n-descended train,
To ease the anguish and to purge the pain.
Oh, for a lyre that might express in song
A tribute worthy of your saintly throng!   10
Oh, for a pen whose Attic skill might trace
The deathless glories of your gentle race!
But what mere mortal justly could record
Your Christ-like labour, and your scant reward?
The warrior, moulded of a stouter clay,   15
In song and jest awaits the fatal day;
Fir'd with excitement, to his fate resign'd,
No fears distract, nor sights unnerve his mind.
His miry trench with stoic calm he bears,
Nor counts disease or death among his cares;   20
His surging ranks, resistless as machines,
March on, and grow accustom'd to the scenes.
Such are our heroes, honour'd, lov'd, and sung
Where'er the folds of Freedom's flag are flung:
If theirs be valour, unafraid and true,   25
What may we say, intrepid fair, of you?
You, whose frail lives a tender care hath bless'd;
Whose fine-wrought fancies ill hath ne'er oppress'd;
Whose shielded youth no cruel strife hath known;
O'er whose calm seas no vexing gales have blown.   30
What courage spurs you, that with such glad haste
You quit your ease for Europe's war-torn waste?
'Tis yours the fields of slaughter to assuage,
And scatter mercy o'er the realms of rage;
Relieve the dying hero's burning drouth,   35
And drag the wounded from the cannon's mouth;
Toil where the bombs in wild profusion soar,
Where shrapnel shrieks and lethal vapours pour;
Sustain each horror of the martial state,
Nor fear to meet the soldier's darkest fate;   40
All this is yours, and yours alone from choice—
Can fitting praise be sung by mortal voice?
Ye nymphs of Helicon! immortal Nine,
Contrive a song of nobler key than mine!

Such heights of spirit needs must gain their praise   45
From godlike singers and Aonian lays:
Our lowlier band the heav'nly splendour see,
But stand abash'd before divinity!
We can but dumbly scan th' undaunted fair
Who brave the shell-scarr'd plain and noisome air;   50
We can but pause, and rev'rently admire
The valiant train, whom no fierce hopes inspire:
From maids like these, perchance our fathers drew
Britannia's fabled features, dear to view;
Or proud Columbia's form, that rules the West,   55
Or gracious Liberty, by millions blest.
This all may swear, that ev'ry fearless face
Glows brightly with a more than mortal grace;
That ev'ry heart with holy purpose burns;
That ev'ry soul for sacred service yearns: 60
Reign, lofty spirits, o'er the lab'ring lands
Where Saxons face the foe with new-clasp'd hands!

To the Arcadian

As Grub-Street hacks their reputations raise
Thro' wretched prologues hung to worthy plays;
Like parasites cling round a mighty name,
And draw their glory from another's fame,
The rhymester here with borrow'd lustre shines,   5
And palms Boeotian with ARCADIAN lines!
Friends of the Nine! What praise can be too strong
To suit the graces of a JORDAN'S song?
Lives there a critick who unmov'd can read
The airy chronicles of Morven's Mead?   10
Sound upon sound, beauty on beauty floats,
And pleasing fancies deck the warbling notes.
How rare the bard whose faultless taste commands
The untainted glamour of Arcadian lands;
Whose native skill a sordid world disdains,   15
And flouts reality in sanguine strains!
Let timid Codrus tediously indite
The twice-told precepts of the Stagirite,
Or like a pedant on Pindaricks cry
To yawning readers how to live or die.   20
Let love-sick Bavius of his Chloris rage,
And sing the fair at half-a-crown per page.

127

Let maudlin Maevius, mad with lyrick heat,
Dissect his soul and publish his conceit:
Their lumb'ring lays adorn the dust-clad shelf,   25
Whilst we, in JORDAN'S lines, find beauty's self!

Laeta; a Lament

Respectfully Dedicated to Rheinhart Kleiner, Esq.

With Compliments of the Author

How sad droop the willows by Zulal's fair side,
Where so lately I stray'd with my raven-hair'd bride:
Ev'ry light-floating lily, each flow'r on the shore,
Folds in sorrow since Laeta can see them no more!

Oh, blest were the days when in childhood and hope   5
With my Laeta I rov'd o'er the blossom-clad slope,
Plucking white meadow-daisies and ferns by the stream,
As we laugh'd at the ripples that twinkle and gleam.

Not a bloom deck'd the mead that could rival in grace
The dear innocent charms of my Laeta's fair face;   10
Not a thrush thrill'd the grove with a carol so choice
As the silvery strains of my Laeta's sweet voice.

The shy Nymphs of the woodland, the fount and the plain,
Strove to equal her beauty, but strove all in vain;
Yet no envy they bore her, while fruitless they strove,   15
For so pure was my Laeta, they could only love!

When the warm breath of Auster play'd soft o'er the flow'rs,
And young Zephyrus rustled the gay scented bow'rs,
Ev'ry breeze seem'd to pause as it drew near the fair,
Too much aw'd at her sweetness to tumble her hair.   20

How fond were our dreams on the day when we stood
In the ivy-grown temple beside the dark wood;
When our pledges we seal'd at the sanctify'd shrine,
And I knew that my Laeta forever was mine!

How blissful our thoughts when the wild autumn came,   25
And the forests with scarlet and gold were aflame;
Yet how heavy my heart when I first felt the fear
That my starry-eyed Laeta would fade with the year!

The pastures were sere and the heavens were grey
When I laid my lov'd Laeta forever away,   30
And the river-god pity'd, as weeping I pac'd,
Mingling hot bitter tears with his cold frozen waste.

Now the flow'rs have return'd, but they bloom not so sweet
As in days when they blossom'd round Laeta's dear feet;
And the willows complain to the answering hill,   35
And the thrushes that once were so happy are still.

The green meadows and groves in their loneliness pine,
Whilst the Dryads no more in their madrigals join,
The breeze once so joyous now murmurs and sighs,
And blows soft o'er the spot where my lov'd Laeta lies.   40

So pensive I roam o'er the desolate lawn
Where we wander'd and lov'd in the days that are gone,
And I yearn for the autumn, when Zulal's blue tide
Shall sing low by my grave at the lov'd Laeta's side.

To Mr. Kleiner, on Receiving from Him the Poetical Works of Addison, Gay, and Somerville

Since the cold Muses, heedless of my mood,
Deny me pow'r to sing my gratitude;
These limping lines, in grace and genius slight,
Must feebly hint the warmth I yearn to write!
KLEINER! whose gift, and greeting nobly penn'd,   5
Reveal the brilliant bard and gen'rous friend;
Whose taste and judgment so acutely find
The very book to suit a Georgian mind;
Condemn me not, if dull thanks I deliver,
Or poring o'er the gift, neglect the giver!   10
Happy the day that prompted you to dare
The dingy bookstall's subterraneous air;
The shadowy cave, within whose depths are mass'd
The ling'ring relics of a lustrous past:
Where drowse the ancients, free from modern strife,   15
That crusty pedants fain would wake to life!
As kindly souls an orphan'd waif remove
From publick refuge to paternal love,
So have you now a lonely volume sent
Where, warmly welcom'd, it will find content: 20

Midst kindred tomes in new importance rest,
With studious care and constant reading blest.
What mem'ries haunt the retrospective brain
That views once more the bright Augustan train!
See peerless ADDISON, whose virtuous quill   25
Refin'd the town, and purg'd the times of ill.
Whilst clumsy Puritans, with heavy rage,
But injur'd when they meant to help the age,
Our bland SPECTATOR ply'd a lighter art,
And with his humour cleans'd the gen'ral heart.   30
Vice thrives on preaching; feeds on melancholy—
He who would cure, must laugh it off as folly!
Turn now to Gay, whose sprightly thoughts embrace
A fund of fancy and a world of grace;
In whom simplicity and art, combin'd,   35
Shap'd the bright virtues of an active mind.
With him we tread the town, or roam the lawn;
Or are with beasts in fabled converse drawn;
At Lincoln's Inn Fields clap his tuneful play
Till Nicolini flings his mask away.   40
The Dean we fear; the Guardian we approve;
Pope we admire—but simple Gay we love!
Attend, ye rural groves, and hear the praise
Of honest Somerville's Arcadian lays.
Scorn not his theme, nor slight his rustic fires,   45
But hail the laureate of our country 'squires:
Honour to them, whose deeds our pride provoke;
Who form Britannia's dauntless heart of oak!
Thrice blessed books, whose fav'ring pow'r permits
Our stupid age to scan the ancient wits;   50
From crystal springs a purer nectar draw,
And led by sages, learn each time-try'd law;
Keep from the past a few remaining gleams
Of Will's and Button's Heliconian beams,
Nor sink too deeply in the quicksand snares   55
Of modern manners and affected airs!
KLEINER, to your kind thoughtfulness I owe
This bright addition to the genial glow;
This golden guide to pastures rare and new,
Where classick beauties greet the grateful view.   60
Can I my pen with decent ardour lift
To sing in fitting strains so choice a gift?

Pleasure more keen one thing could bring alone—
A new-imprinted book of *Kleiner's* own!

A Pastoral Tragedy of Appleton, Wisconsin

Young Strephon for his Chloë sigh'd
    In accents warm but vain;
Th' Hibernian nymph his suit deny'd,
    Nor melted at his pain.

But one day from an Eastern scene   5
    Fair (?) Hecatissa came;
She ey'd the swain with fav'ring mien,
    And felt the Paphian flame.

No answ'ring flame the youth display'd;
    He scorn'd her doubtful charms,   10
And still implor'd th' Hibernian maid
    To seek his outstretch'd arms.

Thus Strephon, both unlov'd and lov'd,
    Both pleading and refusing,
Plann'd, that to passion might be mov'd   15
    The maiden of his choosing.

With seeming scorn he ceas'd his sighs,
    And careless turn'd away;
Then courted with dissembling eyes
    The maid from Boston Bay.   20

The willing fair (?) his wooing heard;
    With bliss his suit receiv'd;
Bright Chloë, list'ning, notes each word,
    With jealous longing griev'd.

At length the nymph for Strephon frets,   25
    And mourns the lonely lack;
In tears her frigid course regrets,
    And yearns to win him back.

One kindly glance the fair one sends,
    And Strephon's at her side;   30
In grief poor Hecatissa bends—
    Forsaken ere a bride!

And on that joyous nuptial morn
    When Strephon wed the fair,
A hooded figure, wan, forlorn,   35
    Stole thro' the dewy air.

Down to the dam the sad one went,
    Pray'd Heaven to forgive her,
Then leap'd with desperate intent
    Into the swift Fox River!   40

P.S. The river-god her face espy'd,
    And felt a sudden pain—
Declin'd to claim her as his bride,
    And cast her back again!

Damon and Delia, a Pastoral

Dedicated to Consul Hasting, Esq.

Young Damon, blest with wit and art,
    In vain for lovely Delia pin'd;
The rosy god that pierc'd his heart
    His tongue perversely seem'd to bind.

At length the timid swain essay'd   5
    A random word in casual tone,
And kindled in the conscious maid
    A smile responsive to his own.

But jealous Daphne, mov'd with spleen,
    In public mock'd th' enamour'd pair,   10
And with derision came between
    Poor Damon and his smiling fair.

With pride the youthful sage withdrew,
    And hid the passion in his breast;
Proud Delia feign'd indiff'rence, too,   15
    Whilst each in secret mourn'd the jest.

In wit the lover cloak'd his woe,
    His language sharp, that once was sweet;
Cooler the fair one seem'd to grow,
    Repell'd by what she thought conceit.   20

Damon her alter'd mien perceiv'd,
    And lov'd her more for her disdain;
Hid all his learning as he griev'd,
    Resolv'd her sympathy to gain.

Mark now the metamorphosis   25
    That turns a scholar to a clown;
With rueful jest he courts his miss,
    And tries to laugh away her frown.

One day the village beaux and belles
    Far'd forth at dawn in festive mood,   30
To view the verdant rural dells,
    And wander thro' the neighb'ring wood.

Two serving men a basket bore,
    Replete with dainties for a feast;
Each nymph and swain a bright smile wore,   35
    Their joy by Nature's charms increas'd.

O'er grassy plain and flow'ring slope
    The sportive train, delighted, danc'd;
Inspir'd by vigour, youth, and hope,
    And by the pleasing scene entranc'd.   40

How blest the groves and leafy bow'rs;
    How cool the shade of ev'ry nook;
How green the moss, how gay the flow'rs;
    How sweet the music of the brook!

Amid the feasters Damon mov'd,   45
    A cloud of sadness o'er his face;
Whilst near at hand was she he lov'd,
    Delightful in her artless grace.

The youth, with love grown pale and thin,
    Walk'd shyly lest he seem absurd;   50
For studious swains oft raise a grin
    Amongst the fair, by deed and word.

But tho' he felt a lover's fear,
    And strove his Delia to ignore,
His steps, unguided, drew him near   55
    The nymph he could not but adore.

With downcast glance and muffled sigh,
    Th' embarrass'd swain his fair address'd;
The maiden murmur'd a reply,
    As slow they stray'd from all the rest.   60

No well-form'd thought the pair propell'd;
    No settled goal allur'd their feet;
But close in Paphian bondage held,
    They stumbled on a snug retreat.

Gay was the floor, where daisies white   65
    And violets blue reliev'd the green;
The roof with bloss'ming vines was bright,
    And twining myrtles deck'd the green.

Here sat the lovers, shy and still,
    Scarce knowing they were hand in hand;   70
As from beyond a shelt'ring hill
    Flew soft a gentle feather'd band.

Down to a bough close by the pair,
    Secluded, yet within their view,
There flutter'd thro' the fragrant air   75
    Two woodland doves of snowy hue.

With tender mien each creature spoke
    Its simple tale of sylvan love;
Their cooing notes the echoes woke,
    And Cupid govern'd all the grove.   80

The bashful Damon nothing said,
    But ardent eyed the melting maid;
Delia, growing kinder, hung her head,
    And bless'd the blush-concealing shade.

At last the conscious maiden's glance   85
    To meet her timid Damon's try'd;
Compell'd to make the first advance,
    Since fear his tongue so fast had ty'd.

"Damon," she whisper'd, "see how these
    Sagacious birds their hearts reveal   90
Within sequester'd bow'rs at ease
    Where no sour Daphne's jest may steal!

"No foolish pride their speech restrains;
    No cold conceit their ardour chills:
Content they haunt the groves and plains,   95
    And tell their passion to the hills.

"If the rude pair on yonder tree
    To such rational bliss incline,
What course is worthy such as we,
    Or suits a wit as keen as thine?"   100

The list'ning swain, transported, heard,
    Half doubtful to believe his ears;
Intent he hung on ev'ry word,
    Fill'd with delight, yet close to tears.

His nimble wit the words explain'd,   105
    Yet had her speech been more obscure,
The meaning he might well have gain'd
    From those dark eyes, so fond and pure.

Young Damon doffs his bashfulness,
    And in his arms his Delia folds;   110
Affection glows in each caress,
    Requited by the nymph he holds.

Thus gain'd the pair that lasting joy
    Which soon was seal'd by wedlock's rite;
Which naught may weaken or destroy,   115
    And which the years but make more bright.

Ye nymphs and swains, a moral take
    From Damon and his comely bride:
Let no proud whim your young hearts break,
    But look to Nature as your guide.   120

To Delia, Avoiding Damon

The old Bard *Tityrus* addresseth a Beautiful Perverse Nymph
on behalf of his young Amorous Friend *Damon,* ending with a
Threat of Satire if the Maid prove not kind to the youth.

Wherefore, cruel nymph, dost fly
When thy Damon draweth nigh?
O'er the plain thy timid feet
Trip in fawn-like coy retreat;

Raven tresses stream behind,   5
Toss'd and tumbled in the wind.
Eyes of azure, bright and clear,
Shine with mingled scorn and fear:
Foolish maid, thy haste forego—
Why should Damon fright thee so?   10
Fear'st thou he pursues to slay,
Like some sylvan beast of prey;
Deem'st thou he would track thee down
Like some low-born rural clown?
Stupid fair! observe the grace   15
Glowing in yon manly face;
Tender features that proclaim
Lofty thoughts and noble name:
Mark each sigh that speaks the truth—
Canst thou still distrust the youth?   20
Thus did Peneus' daughter run
From the young god of the sun,
Losing all the joys of love
As a laurel of the grove.
Tell me, girl, wouldst rather be   25
Happy bride or listless tree?
Ponder long on Daphne's fate,
Lest thou rue thy choice too late.
Wilful child, why hold thy charms
From thy Damon's ardent arms?   30
When the part is not o'erplay'd,
Shyness well becomes a maid;
Yet I fear it is with thee
But a cloak for cruelty;
Art thou so unkind and vain   35
That thou sport'st with Damon's pain?
Shame upon thee, if thou art
Such a nymph without a heart!
Why not spare a glance or kiss—
Would it bankrupt thee in bliss?   40
Anaxarete the fair
Drove her Iphis to despair;
Scorn'd and mock'd, in death he found
Blissful balm to heal his wound:
Yet he perish'd not alone,   45
For the maid was turn'd to stone!

Wouldst thou, girl, tread o'er her path,
Tempting Venus' rightful wrath?
Senseless creature! thus to scorn
One to wit and glory born;   50
Future times with proud acclaim
Shall revere thy Damon's name:
If thou prove not his, thy lot
Bleak shall be—thy name forgot!
Cease thy flight, unreas'ning one,   55
Let the genial rites be done;
Take a lesson from the past—
Atalanta wed at last!
Raven locks with myrtle bind,
Learn to favour and be kind!   60
For the sea-born goddess send;
Bid the fervid boy attend,
Whilst each Grace, with loosen'd zone,
Hails the feasting as her own.
Damon shall, with gen'rous pride,   65
Sing the virtues of his bride,
Shaming in his tuneful fire
Old Amphion's golden lyre.
Such awaits thee, winsome miss,
If thou wilt accept the bliss!   70
But shouldst thou still cruel prove,
And reject the proffer'd love,
Think not that the Gods will smile
On thy vanity and guile.
Damon will to Lycë turn,   75
And for Lycë only burn,
Whilst my Muse, young Damon's friend,
Shall her spleen in satire spend.
If thou pain'st at the tender youth,
Do not look to me for ruth: 80
Nymph, beware! be not too bold—
Mind Archilochus of old!

Hellas

Lov'd land of light! from whose elysian shore
The dawning beams of thought and freedom pour;
Whose lucent soul, to earthwide splendour grown,
Deathless survives, and blazes in our own;

137

What voice remains, since all of thine are still,   5
To chant thy glories with becoming skill?
Greece! Who unmov'd can hear thy magic name
When wit and art thy parent pow'r proclaim;
When truth and beauty boast an Attic birth,
And Grecian graces glad th' applauding earth?   10
Naught may we read, but Greece illumes the way;
No chisell'd marble but affirms thy sway;
Bright Nature's self to lovelier heights can rise,
When view'd thro' Hellas' mythologic eyes;
Yet vain are praises, since we take from thee   15
All that we are, and all we hope to be!

Ambition

On crimson'd plains the deadly missiles dart,
    And surging legions to destruction pour;
Above the strife, unconscious and apart,
    The skylark sings as blithely as before.

Beneath the wave the loathsome thing of steel   5
    Lurks coward-like to claim its helpless prey;
Round and about the ancient billows reel,
    As vast and blue as on earth's primal day.

From tott'ring thrones the trembling tyrants crawl;
    Ecstatic crowds a new-born age acclaim;   10
In quiet groves the with'ring oak-leaves fall,
    And seasons roll eternally the same.

Thus in its little hour a mortal brood
    Affects to mould a cosmos by its deeds;
The while Creation's mighty magnitude   15
    Whirls on thro' changeless Time, nor hears nor heeds!

To Alfred Galpin, Esq.

President of the United Amateur Press Association, on His Nineteenth
Birthday, November 8, 1920.

Ye Mysian nymphs, reward the poet's pains,
And smile propitious on his humble strains;
For you, above the Nine, can best befriend
The bard whose lines to tender youth are penn'd:

Let your fond vision thro' the ages run,   5
And see, in GALPIN, Hylas' self outdone!
GALPIN, I pause, unknowing what to think
When I behold thee pois'd on manhood's brink:
Thy mind already of the world of men,
Tho' on this day thou thou turn'st but nine and ten;   10
I may but cry, admiring as I see,
That all the Muses join their gifts in thee!
Not so divine Arion play'd of yore,
Nor Aristotle writ his learned lore;
With feebler sense Lucretius shew'd the course   15
Of whirling atoms and ethereal force;
Ruder Aratus sang the vaulted skies,
And Seneca appears but half as wise:
Peer of the best, in polish, art, and truth,
Thou lead'st them all in life's prime blessing—youth!   20
Is't true, indeed, that thou so short a time
Hast known the air of our terrestrial clime?
Art thou not rather some experienc'd sage
Who hast like Aeson lost thy hoary age?
This none may say, for in thy soul appear   25
Youth's virtue, yet the wit of many a year.
Scarce nobler seem'd the Latmian swain whose grace
Could raise a glow on Dian's placid face;
Jove, seeing thee, from Ganymede would turn;
And Cyprus' queen her lov'd Adonis spurn;   30
The gifts that in each fabled stripling shine
Turn into truth, and in thyself combine!
With what fond envy must the age-dimm'd eye
Behold young genius as it soars on high!
Our lives, too long in antique courses run,   35
Bow to the glory which hath just begun.
Could any age afford as well as ours
A worthy field for youth's aspiring pow'rs?
Afar and near the ancient order shakes,
And Liberty from rusted fetters breaks: 40
We who have liv'd, cling dully to the dead,
Whilst younger leaders guide the world ahead!
In this fair train, that rise on ev'ry hand,
Foremost of all can gifted GALPIN stand;
Young as the youngest, brilliant as the best,   45
Thy lightning brain was made to lead the rest.

'Tis thine to combat ev'ry ling'ring wrong;
To help the feeble, and subdue the strong:
Stand forth, bold youth, within whose bosom bright
The Past's grave lore, and Future's force, unite!   50

To the Eighth of November

(Joint Birthday of Master Alfred Galpin, Jr. (1901), and
Mistress Margaret Abraham (1902), of Appleton, Wisconsin.)

Eventful day, whose magic pow'r hath sent
Two fulgent minds to light our continent!
First of the twain see radiant PHOEBUS rise,
Next wise MINERVA quit her native skies:
Both, by the will of Jove, design'd to reign   5
O'er APPLETON, and all th' Hesperian plain;
To raise the dying Muses; calm the soul;
Teach falt'ring poesy again to roll;
Cast from decaying prose a baneful spell,
And shew the world the art of writing well.   10
Bright day of days, a thankful earth proclaims
The splendour of thy children's noble names:
A genuine praise, devoid of ev'ry sham,
Attends a GALPIN and an ABRAHAM!

Damon: A Monody

Sacred to the Memory of the Late Alfred Galpin, Junior.

Warm vernal Zephyrs fan the budding Grove
    Where Dryad throngs the waking PAN adore;
But the fair Train with pensive Bearing move,
    Since their lov'd idol, DAMON, is no more!

How lately did those antient Aisles resound   5
    With the sweet Musick of young DAMON'S Lay!
The Plains are hush'd—bleak desolated Ground—
    Since the bright ardent Stripling went away.

Lone pine the Nymphs that doted on his Face;
    No salter tears for PHAETON were shed;   10
The mountain Fauns recall his pleasing Grace,
    And own a Rival, now that he is dead.

140

In classic Shades TIBALDUS wipes his Eyes,
    That once could scorn to own a furtive Tear;
While sacred MOCRATES deserted sighs,   15
    And both lament that DAMON is not here!

The HELICONIAN Meadows vainly grieve
    At Notes unanswer'd and at Songs unsung;
As wise Men falter, fated to believe
    Ye w. k. Saying—'that the Good die young'!   25

Hylas and Myrrha: A Tale

Dedicated to Edward Softly, Esq.

Thro' Dorian meads, where countless beauties bide,
A gentle river pours its crystal tide;
Pensive but sweet the singing currents flow,
While in each wave surpassing graces shew.
In this broad flood a tow'ring rock is seen,   5
Remote alike from either bank of green;
Around its base caressing ripples move,
And murmur with the dulcet tones of love.
Here the white dove, by Cyprus' goddess bless'd,
With tender skill constructs its lofty nest;   10
Whilst on the stony summit proudly stands
A temple, looking o'er the stream-cleft lands.
Sometimes at night upon the river banks
A howling throng appear, in eager ranks;
Of feline form, their voices yet contain   15
A conscious throb, and more than beast-like strain.
Their longing glance the rocky islet seeks,
While ev'ry howl a baffled wish bespeaks;
At the cold stone their eyes enamour'd gleam,
And tongues revile the intervening stream.   20
Each spring there come from all the lands around
A virgin train, to tread the sacred ground.
In many a boat they reach the templed isle,
To pray for Cytheraea's fav'ring smile;
And there 'tis said the Paphian Queen imparts   25
A balm that heals their love-distracted hearts.
Hither one day, by vagrant fancy brought,
I wander'd, half-dissolv'd in curious thought.
The silver stream shone beautiful and bright;
The island rock gleam'd lovely to my sight;   30

141

On flow'ring banks, and many a pansy'd steep,
Lay dreaming swains, at ease amidst their sheep.
The eldest of the band, whose beard of snow
Belied his black eyes' reminiscent glow,
My question heard, and in quaint words unroll'd   35
The local legend, kept from days of old.

Long years ago, in these sequester'd shades,
Dwelt Myrrha, loveliest of the rustic maids;
No neighb'ring fair an equal grace possess'd,
And ev'n the nymphs inferior gifts confess'd.   40
Blue were her eyes; gold ringlets deck'd her head;
Rose-hued her cheeks, her lips of deeper red;
Unrivall'd features vied with height of soul,
And ev'ry charm of manner crown'd the whole.
But tho' no other maid such charms could own,   45
On beauty's peak the fair stood not alone;
For in a bow'r that nestled on the lawn
Liv'd the young Hylas, radiant as the dawn.
What words can paint, what tongue describe in truth
The fulgent graces of the tender youth?   50
A head Praxiteles might ne'er excel;
A form whose poise no poet half could tell;
Brown sparkling eyes in face of marble gleam'd;
Brown curling locks in rich profusion stream'd;
Such lips Apollo might in vain desire,   55
And over all shone wisdom's gen'rous fire.
This stripling, rich in beauty and in art,
Own'd the fond Myrrha's young confiding heart;
No noon seem'd bright, no azure sky seem'd clear
To Myrrha, save when Hylas linger'd near.   60
His lucent smile was trusting Myrrha's sun,
And when he frown'd, she felt the day was done;
In his brown eyes her sole Elysium lay,
While in his arms she dream'd the hours away.
How oft the pair would tread the spangled green,   65
And praise the rapture of the rural scene!
Thro' fragrant groves their blissful way they took,
Or paus'd to watch the windings of the brook;
Now and again their wand'ring forms would rest
On some acclivous slope, with daisies dress'd,   70
And here the lovely youth, with tender care,

Would weave a chaplet for his Myrrha's hair.
Alas, that such blest innocence must know
The pangs of malice, and the hand of woe!
But while the ardent twain their loves reveal'd,   75
Invidious echoes fill'd the floral field.
Enrag'd to see a mortal maid enjoy
Such heav'nly pleasure, and so fair a boy,
The jealous Oreads of the hillside bow'rs
Conferr'd, and summon'd all their evil pow'rs.   80
Chief of the band malignant Phimua stood,
The proudest nymph in all the hilly wood;
Her had young Hylas oft in days gone by
Repuls'd and scorn'd, as Myrrha's form drew nigh.
Now spurr'd to action, she her minions leads,   85
And evil presence haunts the rolling meads.
'Twas on a roseate morning in genial June,
When op'ning buds forecast a cloudless noon,
The tender Hylas, some small wish deny'd,
Roam'd in a transient pet from Myrrha's side.   90
Up a green slope the pouting stripling stray'd
(The while half-frantic for the absent maid),
When sudden from a secret grotto came
Rejected Phimua, warm with am'rous flame.
Ere he could flee, the nymph had seized his hand,   95
And call'd about her all the ardent band;
The more he struggled, tighter did they hold,
With love inflam'd, and with great numbers bold:
At length his feeble efforts died away,
And wretched Hylas own'd the Oreads' sway.   100
These tidings soon to lonely Myrrha flew,
And blanch'd her crimson cheeks to ashen hue;
Morn, noon, and night beside the brook she mourn'd,
With streaming eyes, and tresses unadorn'd.
Succeeding months increasing anguish brought,   105
Till grief and pain possess'd her ev'ry thought;
Her ceaseless tears the rising brooklet bore
In mounting tides that lav'd the pensive shore,
And one bleak day a new-swell'd stream alone
Mark'd the sad spot that Myrrha once had known.   110

High in the hills the hapless youth remain'd,
Lov'd but unloving, by the Oreads chain'd;

While passing time but magnify'd his pain
To see the treasur'd Myrrha once again.
One night when all of Phimua's train were deep   115
In the blank folds of wine-imparted sleep,
The boy, impatient of his hated lot,
Fled from the precincts of the hillside grot.
Down darkling slopes his hast'ning course he took,
Eager for Myrrha and the well-lov'd brook,   120
When a snapp'd twig that lurk'd along the route
Awak'd his captors, and arous'd pursuit.
From cave to copse swift pour'd the Oread throng,
On the hot chase by frenzy borne along,
Whilst Hylas pray'd for wings, that he might soar   125
To Myrrha's side, and see the nymphs no more.
On far'd the fleet pursuers and pursu'd,
O'er moonlit glade, and thro' the shady wood,
Till Hylas, nearly spent, now breath'd the air
Of lower meads, where flow'd his alter'd fair.   130
The conscious flood the strange procession spies,
And waves of wonder on her surface rise;
Her lover's flight she notes with joyous mind,
Yet dreads the throng that press him hard behind.
On, on, the runners race, till Hylas sees   135
The new-swoln stream, and marks the grassy leas;
With many a cry the panting nymphs essay
To reach the boy, and bear the prize away;
But Hylas now the unknown river braves,
And plunges headlong in the friendly waves.   140
On to the shore bold Phimua's band advance,
Intent to follow thro' the stream's expanse,
When Venus from the sky observes the sight,
And casts her magic on the troubled night.
Unwonted peace now fills the swaying groves,   145
And not a form on the broad champaign moves.
The nymphs, arrested in their eager chase,
Stand chang'd, and stript of all their former grace;
The beauteous train to furry felines shrink,
And hover baffled by the river's brink!   150
Meanwhile the youth, within th' embracing stream,
Senses his Myrrha in the pale moon's gleam;
The flood, responsive, seeks with wat'ry flow
Some fond caress, or mark of love to shew.

Again the Paphian Queen her pow'r displays,   155
And on the scene a kind enchantment lays;
For as young Hylas nears the middle tides
A creeping change o'er all his figure glides:
He slackens, stops, then settles with a smile—
Transform'd forever to a rocky isle!   160
Thus rest the lovers thro' eternal time,
While Nature blesses all the genial clime;
Her constant waves his faithful form caress,
And he survives in all his loveliness.
Atop his brow a fane of Venus stands,   165
Where pray the virgins of the neighb'ring lands,
And Myrrha's tides on distant banks restrain
The feline hordes that still the youth would gain.——

Here ceas'd the shepherd, as the blazing day
In gold and purple twilight died away.   170
The deep'ning sky a starry host reveal'd,
And the young moon shone bright o'er flood and field.
I glanc'd about, entranc'd by all I view'd,
Then sought my homeward path thro' shadowy wood.

John Oldham: A Defence

Written with every conceivable apology to Rheinhart Kleiner, Esquire.

Whilst modern wits with scorn may rage
O'er honest Oldham's rugged page;
May vow his Muse was weak and pale,
His rhyming harsh, his humour stale;
May censure with a knowing leer   5
The failings of a pioneer,
And dulness ev'ry bard must own
In Oldham damn, in self condone;
I sometimes think, had he not dy'd,
Old John might shew another side: 10
For what could not the poet say
Of things these witlings scrawl today?

Myrrha and Strephon

While zephyrs aestival among the blooms
    Of Vulpes' tinted margin idly play,
And from far austral meads the strange perfumes

Of lands unknown exert exotic sway,
Upon the bank, beneath a willow's shade,   5
Pensive each noon reclines a beauteous maid.

So fair a nymph was never seen before;
    Venus hides close, averse to be compar'd;
The rural throng her myriad charms adore,
    And by each Faun the ecstasy is shar'd: 10
The gentle Naiads from their coverts peep,
To ape her graces as she lies asleep.

Yet this blest maid, whom mortals Myrrha call,
    One blessing lacks, and mourns with tearful eye;
For the young swain, who to her heart is all,   15
    Keeps cold and distant, being aw'd and shy:
That beauty which should bring him to her feet,
Dazzles his gaze, and frights him to retreat!

Narcissus' self no colder mien preserv'd
    Than lovely Strephon, tenderest of boys;   20
Full many an Echo, lonely and unnerv'd,
    Pleads all in vain to share his simple joys:
But the fair lad ignores them as they pray,
And startled by their pleading, runs away.

One moment he on fair-hair'd Myrrha smil'd—   25
    A favour to no other damsel giv'n—
As if by such surpassing grace beguil'd
    To grant the bearer one small glimpse of heav'n;
And sure, sweet Myrrha should his best love win,
Since both in beauty are so close akin!   30

But when the nymph his leaving sought to stay,
    And spake of walks in many a distant grove,
The stripling's cheek, like light Aurora's ray,
    Told of his inexperience with love:
Full coy was he, nor wishful to be taught   35
The doubts and pains wherewith all passion's fraught.

"Why dost thou hold me?" with alarm he cries;
    "Wouldst steal my heart but for an idle jest?
Wouldst chain my spirit with thine azure eyes,
    Then leave me lone, unloved, and unblest?   40

I fear thy kindness, nymph, since in thy pride
Thou win'st so many, but to cast aside!"

In vain doth Myrrha vow her changeless love,
    And call on Eros to attest her word;
Her tearful prayer to Strephon naught can prove,   45
    Who hath of other swains so often heard:
Of Aegon, Lycidas, and Polydore,
Whom Myrrha once did love, but loves no more.

Thus Myrrha, pining for the bashful swain
    Of whose caress she by past flames is cheated,   50
Is left alone upon the flow'ring plain,
    Fulgent with beauty, yet in love defeated:
And as she sighs to Naiads on the lea,
She bids them tread the paths of constancy!

Wisdom

The 28th or "Gold-Miner's" Chapter of Job, paraphrased from a literal
translation of the original Hebrew text, supplied by Dr. S. Hall Young.

In stretching veins the glitt'ring silver lies;
Gold hath its place, and glads the miner's eyes;
Tellural ores vast ferreous wealth disclose,
While from scorch'd rocks the molten copper flows.
Boldly the miner sets an end to night,   5
And drags the stones of darkness up to sight;
In lonely realms he probes th' untrodden land,
And swings down shafts of subterraneous sand.
Here from the soil springs many a useful herb,
Whilst igneous flames the lower crust disturb;   10
Here gravel beds refulgent sapphires hold,
And here the searcher wins his store of gold.
Here paths extend, to bird and beast unknown,
Where the skill'd delver tunnels thro' the stone;
With potent force he blasts the mighty hills,   15
And carves among the rocks his sluicing rills;
With glance discerning each bright treasure spies;
Dams up the streams, and bares their hidden prize.
But tho' on earth such pleasing boons abound,
Where shall pure Wisdom's greater gifts be found?   20
The price of Wisdom can no mortal tell,

Nor in the land of living does it dwell;
"'Tis not in me," affirms the shadowy cave;
"'Tis not with me," replies the lashing wave;
Nor gold nor silver can the treasure buy—   25
In vain with Ophir's choicest wealth we try—
Onyx and sapphire form too coarse a stuff;
Gold with its crystal quartz is not enough;
In no rich jewels can the cost be paid;
Coral and diamond fruitless are display'd;   30
Ev'n the red ruby with its lambent glow,
For priceless Wisdom is a price too low:
The Aethiopian topaz is but earth,
And Wisdom tow'rs o'er gold of purest worth.
Whence, then, comes Wisdom? What its mystic lair;   35
Hid from the living, and the fowls of air?
Death and destruction have a rumour heard,
But speak obscurely with uncertain word.
God, God it is, who knows the glorious whole;
Whose voice alone the secret can unroll;   40
For His high glance surveys the bounds of land,
And ev'ry deep by heav'n's bright circle spann'd.
When he the weight of wind and water found,
The tempest order'd, and the lightning bound;
Then did He see and search, and then proclaim   45
The truth supreme, that He alone could frame:
"Behold," He cries unto the mortal throng,
"This is the Wisdom ye have sought so long:
To reverence the Lord, and leave the paths of wrong!"

Birthday Lines to Margfred Galbraham

All hail, ye infant wonders from on high,
Whose advent cheer'd the grey November sky;
Whose soaring minds together cast renown
On wide Wisconsin, and your native town!
Praise to the Nine, who thus benignant place   5
Two souls so mighty in so small a space:
A year apart, you shed your common ray
On one blest city, and one lucky day!

Tryout's Lament for the Vanished Spider

Dear humble friend in labour and in play,
Say to what region thou hast fled away!
Week after week thy busy life was spent
Within these classic walls in calm content.
Thy noble patience, like the Muse's beams,   5
Inspir'd my efforts, and adorn'd my themes;
Till I had grown to hold thee as a guide,
To all my hopes and ventures close ally'd.
How well my thoughts thy talents could engage!
How shone thy magic on the *Tryout's* page!   10
Tho' calm thy manner, and thy speeches brief,
Well might I call thee Editor-in-Chief!
Shall any say thy place was slight or low,
Or doubt the lustre of thy heav'nly glow?
Let such consider with observant eye   15
The annals of the myriad years gone by.
A spider 'twas that rescu'd Islam's head
When from the foe within a cave he fled;
Nor can proud Scotia venture to despise
The lowly beast that help'd her monarch rise.   20
Ev'n the curs'd Hun must speak with bated breath
Of him who sav'd old Frederick from death.
In short, we find the spider thron'd in state;
Friend of the Nine, and guardian of the great!
But thou, tried comrade of my busy hours—   25
Whither hast crept with all thy magic pow'rs?
Hath some strange vision of thy spider-brain
Mov'd thee to quit our sordid sphere of pain?
Warm was thy home, and well-arrang'd thy lair;
Thy meat and drink supply'd with tender care;   30
Were juicy flies too few and far between,
Or was aught lacking in the kerosene?
Sadly I view thy vacant dwelling-place—
Thou transient trav'ller of an ancient race!
Would that I might, with Fancy's curious pow'r,   35
Trace thy meanderings to thy hidden bow'r;
Mark ev'ry secret step, and see thee stand
A sceptred potentate of spider-land!
What wonders unsuspected may exist
In those far provinces of web and mist!   40
Gossamer castles with their moats of dew;

149

And fairy palaces too small to view;
Or is thine Empire of a darker kind—
Some bury'd spot the world hath left behind?
Own'st thou some temple, where thy strands embrace   45
The crumbling substance of a Pharaoh's face,
Or some black crypt beneath the shifting sand
Where a forgotten city us'd to stand?
In Tyre and Carthage, Babylon and Ur,
Luxor and Karnak, do thy legions stir;   50
For thee and such as thou the world was made—
Thy reign commences when our own's decay'd.
Down immemorial steps, to man unknown,
Thy spinning tribes drape many a gilded throne;
Ram-headed gods; objects too dark to name,   55
Altars that bore of old an impious flame,
Wing'd shadowy lions wrought of rock and brass,
And all the treasures despots can amass—
These thy dominions, vanish'd wand'ring one
Who lately bask'd 'neath *Haverhill's* bright sun!   60
But whilst I mourn, or thro' my fancy grope,
Within my heart bestirs a thrill of hope;
For bounteous Pan, who rules the vernal wold,
Can oft restore the blessings lost of old:
Content I'll wait, and trust that he will bring   65
My faithful spider with returning Spring!

Cindy: Scrub-Lady in a State Street Skyscraper

Black of face and white of tooth,
Cindy's soul has lost its youth.
Strangely heedless of the crowd,
O'er her mop forever bow'd:
Eyes may roll and lips may grin,   5
But there's something dead within!

Brow serene—resign'd to Fate—
Some three hundred pounds in weight—
Cindy wields a cynic's broom,
Thinking not of hope or doom.   10
For the world she cares no more—
She has seen it all before!

Cindy's always dress'd in red,
With a kerchief round her head.
What may blight the damsel so?   15
Watermelon, work, or woe?
Tho' her days may placid be,
Glad I am, that I'm not she!

The Voice

On distant hills the murmur first is heard,
Faint as the pipings of a snow-chill'd bird;
Down melting slopes soft echoes bear the cry
To vales and woods that yet enmantled lie.
At night the stars with milder lustre shine,   5
And thro' the deeps convey th' auspicious sign;
From all the land a mystic vapour springs,
While by the op'ning rill a presence sings;
Majestic trees unspoken calls avow,
And subtle juices fill each tingling bough: 10
Heaven and earth attend the rising lay,
And own, in Pan, a greater pow'r than they.

 Poor timid souls, who tediously have said
From pen and pulpit, "Mighty Pan is dead!"
Dull'd with the darkness of a mystic creed,   15
They see the truth, but seeing fail to read.
For them in vain the vernal breezes stir;
Northward in vain the feather'd wand'rers whir;
Deaf with their doctrines, blind with their belief,
Amid such joys they whine in pious grief.   20
But yesterday within a willow'd dell
I heard the fauns their precious secrets tell;
In melting streams I saw the naiads wake,
And spy'd a satyr in the budding brake.
Sweet at the dusk, beneath young moonbeams dim,   25
All the wild scene inton'd a pagan hymn;
The mountains sang, as from their snowy shrouds
They sprang in loveliness to greet the clouds;
The plains responded, as they cast aside
The graceless garments of the wintertide.   30
Groves sway'd in music, and the dryad throng
Join'd with the bubbling fountain's liquid song;
While far away the never-silent sea

Added the notes it learn'd in Arcady.
But hark! o'er ev'ry voice that softly blends, 35
A deeper note, a wilder hymn, ascends.
Westward from shores where broken columns lie,
A call of antique beauty rides the sky:
"O thou whose soul th' eternal past recalls,
Whose eyes can pierce the present's sombre walls, 40
Rememb'rest still the prophecy of old
That annual rings in syrinx-tones of gold—
Rememb'rest thou the promise of the morn,
The swelling tide of ecstasies reborn?
Once more Maenalian winds shall fan thy cheek, 45
And sea-borne voices from Arcadia speak;
Once more thine eyes upon the wat'ry plain
Shall glimpse old Nereus and his green-hair'd train;
Thee once again upon the sylvan steep
An Oread band shall gently sing to sleep; 50
And to thy sight, where ferny forest lies,
Fair forms thro' immemorial years shall rise."

    The accents ceas'd—and as I glanc'd around,
I drank the odours of the spongy ground;
From peak and vale mysterious sounds convey'd 55
Some potent message to the deep'ning shade;
The sinking moon unusual shadows threw,
And formless beings rov'd the spangled blue;
On ev'ry hand strange mem'ries fill'd the air—
I look'd for landmarks, and they were not there. 60
Yon outrag'd hill, by stack and chimney crown'd,
Loom'd from the past, a grassy virgin mound;
And by the stream where noisy paddles turn,
I saw a bearded god with flowing urn.
From raptur'd eyes the veil of ages fell; 65
Again I view'd the old familiar dell,
While round my form a saltant, shadowy choir
Sang of great Pan, and beauty's smould'ring fire.
List'ning, I learn'd each long-forgotten truth
Of gods and men, and sempiternal youth; 70
And cry'd with joy to know that man's mad day
Is brief, whilst Pan shall never pass away!

On a Grecian Colonnade in a Park

From the green shore the gleaming marble tow'rs
    Against the dusk and verdure of the trees;
Beyond, there rise the odours of rare flow'rs
    To swell the fragrance of the Eastern breeze.

That breeze, which o'er Hymettus' slopes hath play'd,   5
    Finds beauty here, like that it fondled there;
And to these scenes, in classic semblance made,
    Adds the old magic of the Grecian air.

In the calm twilight, as the hushed wood
    Darkens in mystery, obscure and deep,   10
Forgotten shadows come to dream and brood,
    Wak'd for a moment from Elysian sleep.

The dim past beckons thro' the marble gate,
    Stately and silent, distant and divine,
While the still pool reflects a duplicate   15
    Within its depths—a shadowy ocean shrine.

Once in the gloom beyond that porch of white
    I heard a murmur of ethereal sound,
And seem'd to see, as by some eerie light,
    A shimm'ring band, with woodland myrtles crown'd.   20

The waters, too, a strange enchantment breath'd,
    And old, old thoughts rose spectral from the grave;
I saw Leucothea, in damp blossoms wreath'd,
    And young Palaemon from his coral cave.

That shrine of white, deep in the glassy mere,   25
    Upon my soul a charm resistless cast;
The dark gate lur'd, as to my straining ear
    Came voices, calling from the cherish'd past.

And now at eve there lingers in my soul
    The haunting mem'ry of that placid scene;   30
While in my dreams I strain to reach a goal
    Where Glaucus waits me, clad in kelpy green.

The portal calls; beyond that wat'ry door
    Lies all the bliss my heart hath ever known;
The past is there—yet I stand on the shore   35
    In the cold present, alien and alone.

So as pale forms by sunken altars praise
    Deserted gods of years remote and blest,
I, too, shall tread again those ancient ways,
    And in the templed deeps sink down to rest.   40

The Dream

Respectfully Dedicated to Master Consul Hasting

As t'other night young Damon lay
A-dreaming o'er his studious day,
To his lone couch there stole with grace
The likeness of his Delia's face.
Above his raptur'd eyes it hung,   5
And round his heart a magic flung;
Till all the gifts of heav'n seem'd blent
In one fair figure's slight extent.
The nymph (tho' fair enough in truth)
Shone doubly to the spellbound youth,   10
For in her childish look there gleam'd
A score of charms he only dream'd.
Who shall with fitting pencil draw
The vision that young Damon saw?
The task is sure beyond my skill,   15
Whose nights such visions never fill!
Fancy a visage young and fair,
With ev'ry goddess' mingled air;
A lip that envious Graces lack,
And matchless eyes of lustrous black.   20
Tresses of silk, as dark in hue
As summer midnights sweet with dew,
And a slim form whose robes of white
Trail'd by like clouds of filmy light.
This Damon saw, and as he gaz'd,   25
His love to ardent lustre blaz'd;
The bending nymph he dumbly view'd,
And bless'd the pleasing solitude.
Closer the lovely phantom came,
As brighter burn'd the stripling's flame;   30
Till ere her kind intent was known,
The vision's lips had touch'd his own!
In bliss the conscious youth essay'd
To clasp the form his dream had made;

But such rude haste all spells must break,   35
So Damon started broad awake.
"Delia!" he cry'd, "return, return,
To quench the fires that in me burn!"
But empty space repeats his cries,
And only mem'ry fills his eyes.   40
Transported thus, young Damon swore
His nymph in virtue to adore:
With sounding oath he vow'd that ne'er
To well-known sports would he repair.
Charisius' banquets, rich with wine,   45
He vow'd for ever to resign;
The games, the dice, the friendly cup,
All these forthwith he must give up.
Sustain'd by vows, he sought the street,
Nor could a saint more vows repeat!   50
That evening as he call'd to mind
The virtues of the day behind;
The solemn rigour of his tread,
The wines untouch'd, the jests unsaid,
Young Damon sought to pass the time,   55
Now grown so dull, by scribbling rhyme.
With hard-push'd quill he strove to tell
Of comely Delia's magic spell;
Of love, and youth, and such affairs
As bards concoct to kill their cares.   60
But sad to say, 'twas soon made clear
That verse was not his proper sphere;
Tho' great the pains a bard may take,
Fine dreams will oft poor dactyls make!
The hour grew late, but still the swain   65
To write his thoughts essay'd in vain;
When sudden all his virtues new
Burst in a curse and fled from view.
Cry'd he, "How vast a dunce am I
To put my solid pleasures by!   70
If dreams my soul to good impel,
I'll dream my virtuous life as well!"

On Receiving a Portraiture of Mrs. Berkeley, yᵉ Poetess

As Phoebus in some ancient shutter'd room
Bursts golden, and dispels the brooding gloom,
Drives ev'ry shadow to its lair uncouth,
And with bright beams revives forgotten youth;
So 'mid the centuried shades of Time's retreat   5
See radiant BERKELEY rise in counterfeit!
A score of ghosts, dim dreaming thro' the night,
Start sudden at the unaccustom'd light;
From dusty frames the white-wigg'd rhymers stare
In quaint confusion as they hail the fair.   10
Here *Goldsmith* gapes, half-doubting as he views,
Whether he sees a goddess or a Muse;
Waller close by, a jealous look puts on,
To see his *Saccharissa* thus outshone,
Whilst *Pope* inquires if in this sight there gleam   15
Indeed a poet, or a poet's theme!
But now another bard insistent call;
Blest *Hellas'* train, each from his pedestal;
See *Venus* and *Minerva* spiteful vie
To have the new arrival settled nigh.   20
Graces and *Muses* in contending songs
Advance the merits of their rival throngs,
Till *Jove* rebukes them with a thund'rous oath
For claiming one who is ally'd to both!
Now speaks that leader who with light divine   25
O'er all the pantheon can in splendour shine;
The *Delian* god, to art and beauty bred,
Who wears the laurel on his golden head:
"Cease, trifling nymphs, as equals to protest
To one whose gifts so much excel your best;   30
Tho' outward form the fair indeed would place
Within the ranks of Venus' comely race,
Yon shapely head so great an art contains
That *Pallas'* self must own inferior strains.
If one fair object be a thing to shrine   35
In marble fanes, and worship as divine,
How may we judge the mind whose magic pow'r
Creates new worlds of beauty ev'ry hour?
As *Venus* fair, but as *Athena* wise,
New honours wait a BERKELEY in the skies;   40
Blest with vast beauties that are hers alone,

156

She claims from us a new exalted throne.
Let none dispute her place, but let her shine
Impartial o'er the *Graces* and the *Nine!*"
He ceas'd, and all the heav'nly train obey'd,   45
Whilst the new deity dispers'd the shade.
The grave old bards around the study hung
Straighten their wigs, and labour to seem young.
Author and god alike acclaim her might,
And sculptur'd fauns approve the pleasing sight: 50
So the whole throng the novel wonder bless—
At once a poem and a poetess!

To a Youth

(Dedicated to Master Alfred Galpin, Jun.)

Learned boy, upon whose brow
    Sits the green Thessalian bay,
Heir to youthful joys that now
    Bloom along the fragrant way:
Pluck thy garlands with a care   5
    For the winter days ahead;
Laurels canst thou gaily wear
    When the roses all are dead!

Dryads chase thy tripping feet,
    Muses love thine eager eyes;   10
Keep thou as the Dryads sweet,
    Grow thou as the Muses wise.
Beauties round thy pathway wind,
    Virtues round thy forehead dart;
Sip the beauties for thy mind,   15
    Clasp the virtues to thy heart.

Youth is but a swift caress,
    Age is long and cold and drear;
Feast thy sight on loveliness
    In the springtide of thy year.   20
Flow'rs and dreams beside thee lie,
    Gather wisely what will last;
Flow'rs will wither bye and bye,
    Dreams will keep for thee the past!

So adown the blossomy road   25
    Wander lightly, wander free;
It will not again be trod,
    Gentle traveller, by thee.
Joys are fleeting—mourn not deep—
    Mem'ries for the future store;   30
Then, unfearing, sink to sleep,
    Blest and dreamless evermore!

On the Return of Maurice Winter Moe, Esq., to the Pedagogical Profession

As when some prodigal, whose erring tread
Thro' realms remote and deserts drear hath led,
Turns in his course, and mindful of his home
Forbears at last the barren moors to roam,
See sparkling MOE, long wand'ring o'er the plain,   5
Reform, and turn a pedagogue again!
Hail to the chief! by fav'ring heav'n design'd
To guide with matchless art th' expanding mind;
Grac'd with each gift benignant Muses bear,
And form'd to mould the young with tender care.   10
He, with Aonia's brightest, happiest ray,
Can rule with mirth, and alter work to play;
The dullest mind with studious purpose light
And fan to genius what was merely bright.
Beneath his reign the schoolroom cobwebs fade,   15
Whilst fair content dispels the dismal shade;
The letter'd past no more in dulness lurks,
For classic bards spring living from their works!
Here Chaucer from his tales approving smiles,
There tuneful Pope the light-wing'd hour beguiles;   20
Avon's sweet swan a friend and neighbour grows,
And Goldsmith glitters in his verse and prose.
Nor is blest MOE made only to succeed
In teaching how to think and how to read;
His subtle pow'rs the charms of art diffuse,   25
Till each disciple feels the heav'nly Muse:
They read and burn—then at his mild command
New authors rise to grace th' admiring land!
Thus radiant genius lights the teacher's throne,
And kindles aptitude to match his own;   30
A raptur'd class attend their leader's nod,

And kindly smiles replace the birchen rod.
Ave! A throng in ecstasy acclaim
The child of wisdom, and applaud his name;
On green Parnassus rings the joyful cry,   35
Whilst blue-eyed Pallas echoes it on high;
Delighted dryads from Arcadian bow'rs
Awake to strow his homeward path with flow'rs;
The world entire their grateful homage shew,
And crown with laurels lov'd, returning MOE!   40

To Mr. Galpin,

Upon His 20th. Birthday, November 8, 1921

Around thy door tonight there floats
    The half-heard sound of distant song,
As if to thee in antique notes
    There caroll'd some aërial throng.

Upon thy sill I seem to see   5
    The twining bay and myrtle creep,
Harmonious with the melody
    That lulls thine hours of cryptic sleep.

The autumn breeze his chill resigns,
    And for a moment bears the scent   10
Of groves Nysaean, and the vines
    That once with Phrygian grapes were bent.

And from those realms above thy head
    Where thou, perchance, in dreams art found,
The aether trembles at the tread   15
    Of airy maids, with laurel crown'd.

Adown the moonbeams' misty road
    The nymphs celestial dance their way,
Each bent beneath her aureate load
    Of gifts to deck thy natal day.   20

The twentieth time that choir appears;
    The twentieth time the breeze is sweet;
And gods that mark thy growing years
    Lay new-made talents at thy feet.

159

They who of old with regnant care   25
    Spread beauty from Olympus' throne,
Combine to grace thy comely hair
    With coronals to match their own.

Thy ruddy lips with wine they stain,
    And honey from Hymettus' hives;   30
And breathe in thee a pure refrain
    To tell the glory of their lives.

Thine ivory brow they gird with light,
    And in thy hyacinth-eyes implant
The luminous and celestial sight   35
    Of poet, sage, and hierophant.

Thy golden voice they teach anew
    To spread Athena's sacred fame,
And thy young hand with pow'r endew
    To write in words of limpid flame.   40

Thy name with tender sound they breathe,
    And bid thee make it doubly great;
And whilst thy sleeping head they wreathe,
    They summon all the boons of Fate.

So as thou wakest, gentle boy,   45
    Be thine the care their will to heed;
Nor ever thy bright art alloy
    With transient whim or venal greed.

Thy heart's pure grace with kindness hold;
    Thine eye's clear flame with virtue fan;   50
Nor let thy fancy be less bold
    To sound the depths of Nature's plan.

Endymion's kin and Phoebus' son;
    Bless'd with such gifts as few may know;
May thy life prosper as begun,   55
    With art's rare scent and wisdom's glow!

Sir Thomas Tryout

Died Nov. 15, 1921

To the venerable cat of a quaint gentleman in His Majesty's Province of ye
Massachusetts-Bay, who publishes an amateur magazine call'd *The Tryout*.

The autumn hearth is strangely cold
    Despite the leaping flame,
And all the cheer that shone of old
    Seems lessen'd, dull'd, and tame.

For on the rug where lately doz'd   5
    A small and furry form,
An empty space is now disclos'd,
    That no mere blaze can warm.

The frosty plain and woodland walk
    In equal sadness sigh   10
For one who may no longer stalk
    With sylvan hunter's eye.

And if as olden Grecians tell,
    Amidst the thickets deep
A host of fauns and dryads dwell,   15
    I know that they must weep.

Must weep when autumn twilight brings
    Its mem'ries quaint to view,
Of all the little playful things
    That TOM was wont to do.   20

So tho' the busy world may pass
    With ne'er a tearful sign
The tiny mound of struggling grass
    Beneath the garden vine,

There's many an eye that fills tonight,   25
    And many a pensive strain
That sounds for him who stole from sight
    In the November rain.

No sage can trace his soul's advance,
    Or say it lives at all,   30
For Death against our curious glance
    Has rear'd a mighty wall.

Yet tender Fancy fain would stray
    To fair Hesperian bow'rs,
Where TOM may always purr and play   35
    Amidst the sun and flow'rs.

To Damon

(Alfred Galpin, Jun.)

Upon His Coming of Age, Nov. 8, 1922

Damon, I pause, perplex'd to own
A Muse too dull and feeble grown
To greet with just applause a day
So bright with Hope's auspicious ray;
As when at court some booby squire   5
But stammers when he would admire:
My falt'ring lines erratic run
While tun'd to hail thee twenty-one!
Untainted boy! whose agile brain
So quick outstrips the vulgar train;   10
Whose sprightly wit and able sense
With heavy shams so well dispense!
For thee no moments gone to waste
On vapid dreams and doubtful taste,
On myths that ev'ry fact denies   15
And beauties meant for common eyes;
Thy mind, for noble reason cast,
Surveys and sifts the teeming past;
Selects the good for brilliant use
With what the present can produce,   20
And joins the whole, as fits a sage,
To visions of the future age!
How loves th' admiring eye to trace
Thy progress in the gradual race;
To mark thy spirit's rising pow'r   25
From prattling childhood's careless hour!
Thine infant words, of learned kind,
With joy I oft recall to mind:
The pretty jest, the swift conceit,
The turn of satire, sharp and fleet;   30
The marshall'd facts, a num'rous store,
And fancy's well-assorted lore,
All this profuse, and neatly knit
To worldly wisdom's priceless wit!
So young and wise! Yet as thy years   35
Increase, still greater sense appears.
I still can see thy growing days,

162

Illum'd with art's expanding blaze;
Thy wid'ning vision, ever bright
With beams of philosophic light;   40
Thy reason, vaster far than mine,
Proportion'd to a proud design;
And pride itself—imperious gift—
Above the mob thy soul to lift!
So now thou stand'st so quickly grown   45
To manhood's high and dizzy throne;
Can I believe it, who so late
Observ'd thee still in boyhood's state?
Use well, young sage, thy new domains,
Nor scorn thy fellows' cruder pains;   50
Let that deep wisdom which can shew
The emptiness of what we know,
Teach thee to flout all things of earth
Save kindness, honour, taste, and worth.
Thine older days in bliss enjoy—   55
Let please the man what pleas'd the boy—
Nor fail to own that o'er the rest
Contentment stands to make thee blest.
Be mild, tho' learn'd, nor needless fret
At all the cares about thee set;   60
The world is fix'd, nor can thy will
Abate or cure a single ill;
'Tis wisdom's part to mould the mind
To bear each varying woe we find:
Do what thou canst with even thought,   65
But shun the snares vain hopes have wrought;
Let simple pleasures bless thy soul,
And gentle manners prove thy goal;
Adopt the sense the past can bring,
But ne'er to outworn fetters cling;   70
Accept the new if it can please
Without the loss of truth or ease,
Yet spurn that novelty whose lure
Is brief, and never can endure.
Let the mob's mouthings pass thee by,   75
Whose inner soul tow'rs lone and high;
Yet mock them gently, since they form
But mindless eddies in the storm.
Fix thine abode—a peaceful spot—

In fancy's vari-colour'd grot,   80
Where with a thought thou canst possess
Castles and gardens limitless;
Ethereal groves and flow'ring plains,
And faery music's moving strains;
Realms that no vulgar eye may see,   85
Nor vulgar greed subtract from thee!
DAMON, thy pathway now must reach
Just as thy guideless sense may teach;
Thou stand'st mature, empow'r'd to choose
The road to tread, the arts to use.   90
And as I mark the milestone pass'd
Rememb'ring how thy mind is cast,
I smile content, well pleas'd to know
That wisdom prompts thee how to go!

To Rheinhart Kleiner, Esq.,

Upon His Town Fables and Elegies

'Tis hard, I vow, that Fashion's crowded pit
Should clap a prayer for his want of wit,
Yet such we find whene'er our glance surveys
Our modern critics, and the bards they praise.
Zoilus declares no verses to be good   5
Which by the public can be understood,
Whilst babbling Macer puffs with pomp profound
Him who least shews the world we see around.
Oh, for a tongue to speak in calm defence
Of just perspective and untwisted sense!   10
Oh, for a hand to fit the laurel bough
On the sane slopes of some well-balanc'd brow!
Oh, for a time when art may have its due
For painting what it sees, unwarp'd and true!
Perchance some future age, with clearer sight,   15
May dawn to set our addled judgment right;
To melt the clouds, and shed a fav'ring glow
On quills that scintillate, whate'er they shew:
Then may we spy the solid worth that gleams
In easy numbers and familiar themes;   20
Worth that our biass'd eyes have vainly sought
Beyond the tumid realms of inward thought.

'Tis then, when sense may guide our growing taste,
And prove our depths but emptiness and waste,
That decent wreaths and proper fame shall crown   25
The bard of wit, and singer of the town.

Your stanzas, KLEINER, shine with flawless grace,
And a light world with fluent lightness trace;
For you no stupid groves, remote and drear,
Without the play's and coffee-house's cheer;   30
No idle pastures of the languid Muse,
Where not a fop his powder'd course pursues;
Bright as the lamps that gild your well-lov'd streets,
Your verse parades, adorning all it treats!
Who shall contend that rural themes surpass   35
The talk of towns, and Fashion's bevell'd glass?
What nymph or faun could wake a nobler strain
Than the pert belles and beaux of Drury-Lane;
What sylvan bow'r excite a warmer spark
Than the trim windings of St. James's Park?   40
And what fam'd castle furnish more delight
Than any theatre we haunt at night?
Yours, then, skill'd KLEINER, to record in song
The godlike pleasures of the polish'd throng;
The little stratagems, shifts, hates, and greeds   45
In which the buck and idol find their needs;
Ombre and basset, and the puppet-show,
The opera's tinsel, and the tie-wig's snow;
Lap-dog and link-boy, journeyman and jade;
Mob, Mohock, madness, and the masquerade.   50
What fields are here, where epic pens may range
Round Vauxhall-Gardens, and the New-Exchange!
What more could Homer (but for blindness) ask,
Than yonder party-patch or vizard-masque?
Swords, canes, and buckles; curls and flounces vie   55
To prompt an Iliad or an Odyssey!
And you, blest bard, have kept in crystal rhyme
These gay memorials of the town and time;
In your brisk line see Chartres rise again,
And with its revels shock the sober train;   60
See Nash, at Bath and Tunbridge, wield his sway,
And on our careless joys an order lay;
See each smooth trifle—in the cosmic plan

As grave and weighty as the fate of man!
For you have learnt the hollowness of all,   65
And match an Adam's with a tucker's fall!
Let none maintain, that truer life is found
In some Arcadia's dreary distant ground:
Chaos rules all, and no distinction keeps
Betwixt the place which stirs, and that which sleeps.   70
'Tis yours to draw that living, flowing Styx
Where chairs and coaches, lords and beggars mix;
Where in one seething, glitt'ring, pois'nous tide
Our mortal vermin wriggle side by side;
Life here prevails, as thro' the surface breaks   75
That tawdry force, which man's chief nature makes.
KLEINER, we hail you! Laureate of the town;
First of your order, ripe for high renown;
May purer taste increasing honours give,
And crown you Cham whilst yet you write and live.   80
Your tuneful lines the greater value prove
Of routs in town, o'er vigils in the grove;
And subtly change, with wizard's art divine,
A slough of folly to a sea of wine!

Chloris and Damon

Inscrib'd to the Author's Grandson, Consul Hasting, Esq.

Trim CHLORIS was a nymph of parts,
Divinely skill'd in Music's arts,
    And with a sparkling eye;
Wrapt up in grave harmonic chants,
She spurn'd the awkward shy gallants   5
    Who at her door would sigh.

Thus thron'd with vestal equipage,
A very Pallas of our age,
    The learned fair abode;
Surrounded by a docile band,   10
She with a kind impartial hand
    Her gifts of mind bestow'd.

But one day to her cool retreat—
The frigid Nine's exalted seat—
    Unrivall'd DAMON came;   15

He spoke, and as his young lips shed
A wiser lore than seers have said,
    She own'd pert Cupid's flame.

No nobler youth the world hath had
To cheer the realms that else were sad,   20
    Than tender DAMON'S self.
Our tall and slender boy combin'd
Adonis' grace and Plato's mind—
    Sublime and godlike elf!

See now young CHLORIS' eye dilate   25
With tenderness she scarce can state,
    And melt upon the youth!
Within her raven hair she twines
Fresh-gather'd leaves and fragrant vines;
    A lovesick maid in truth!   30

Yet DAMON'S heart, to passion steel'd
By stubborn nymphs who would not yield,
    No kind response essays;
Alas! the boy recalls to mind
When rose-cheek'd Delia was unkind,   35
    And Lycë scorn'd his praise!

So as the weeks unfruitful pass,
Poor CHLORIS fades before her glass
    Whilst DAMON cons his lore.
One hapless nymph reaps all the woe   40
Her fickle sex were wont to sow
    In cruel days before.

Take warning, then, ye belles of pride,
Who conquer but to cast aside,
    And sport with Cupid's darts;   45
Against yourselves the god will turn,
Till you that gnawing anguish learn
    Which vex'd your victims' hearts!

To Endymion

(Frank Belknap Long, Jun.)

Upon His Coming of Age, April 27, 1923

Rise, friendly moon, thy beams to cast
On tender genius, grown at last;
And glorify with argent ray
ENDYMION, twenty-one today!
Ethereal child! how brief a span   5
Hath serv'd to change thee to a man!
But yesterday thine infant mind
Caught dreams of wonder from the wind,
Soar'd with the clouds of roseal skies
Where the lone white flamingo flies,   10
And sail'd the perfum'd austral sea
That laps the strand of Arcady.
Such dreams the youthful poet light
With flames irradiately bright,
And such—by kind Selene's will—   15
Immortal Boy, possess thee still!
Mine, then, the task to hail this hour
With praise of no new coming pow'r;
But joying that the hosts divine
Should leave what was already thine.   20
ENDYMION! kept by favours rare
For ever young, for ever fair;
Fann'd by the breeze on Latmos' crest
In ceaseless innocence and rest!
Thy world a thousand spells can boast   25
Which to our duller realms are lost;
A thousand colours delicate,
And songs that unknown birds create;
A thousand vistas, rang'd serene
In many a mystic moonlit scene;   30
Prospects and peaks that are not giv'n
The light of sun or moon or heav'n—
Great ships of gold, wing'd monsters dire,
And strange sea-caves of liquid fire.
Keep then thy youth—be ever young   35
As when thy first sweet notes were sung,
Nor let the years corrode the gleam

168

Of each fresh amethystine dream.
For thee no common view expands
O'er the grey waste of earthly lands;   40
No common passions seethe along
The crystal aether of the song:
'Tis thine to paint with brush of flame
Spheres hyaline and void of name.
Blest child, may all thy thoughts of youth   45
Incline thee still to ways of truth;
To stainless fancy, rich and kind,
Simplicity that calms the mind,
Virtue unstudy'd, reason bold,
Courage thine own proud place to hold,   50
Ripe scholarship the Muse to wake,
And beauty for its own pure sake.
Best-lov'd of Phoebe! As I scan
The future days that call thee man,
A path of silver light I see;   55
Unbroken toward eternity.
On that bright path thine elfin feet
Can never falter or retreat,
But must trip on till Time shall bring
The Aidenns of thy visioning!   60

To Mr. Baldwin, upon Receiving a Picture of Him in a Rural Bower

What radiant features here confront my sight,
With genius and contentment jointly bright?
Like story'd Bacchus 'mid his vines at ease,
See gifted BALDWIN, lyre attun'd to please.
Not Tityrus, resting in his beechen shades,   5
With softer numbers woo'd the rural maids;
For sure, no scene but this cou'd hope to raise
Such moving smiles, and win such verdant bays.
Nymphs from the neighb'ring coverts coyly peep,
Whilst friendly satyrs to the musick leap;   10
And ev'ry faun that haunts the groves around
Stands mute and smiling, ravisht with the sound!

Damon and Lycë

Where bright Cephissus murm'ring flows
    Beside the templed Academe,
Proud Lycë reign'd with cheeks of rose,
    And eyes that sham'd the sparkling stream.

A pleasing glance the fair possesst,   5
    And hair that wav'd in nice array;
The trim small foot, the snowy breast,
    All charms confirm'd her conscious sway.

But not to honest dreams of love
    Her liquorish fancy oft inclin'd,   10
For with a heart dispos'd to rove,
    She look'd for joys of briefer kind.

No sage too grave, no youth too good,
    Her greedy melting look to gain;
She lur'd, and left in changeful mood,   15
    Unheeding all th' inflicted pain.

Wise Agathon had borne her lust,
    And broken Straton knew her fire;
Scholars and saints crush'd down to dust
    To slake her goatish quick desire.   20

So tho' her ruthless acts she hid
    In specious cant of sentiment,
Erinys reckon'd what she did,
    And not her words of smooth intent.

'Twas thus when to these garden shades   25
    Young DAMON bent his easy course;
Slim idol of th' assembled maids,
    And master of all wisdom's force.

'Twere trite to paint the mingled charms
    That set the boy above the crowd;   30
The godlike height, the muscled arms,
    The noble features, fair and proud.

Such graces every poet limns
    Who to Apollo tunes his song,
And such a mind wakes all the hymns   35
    That to Athena's praise belong.

Hot Lycë look'd, and burst to flame,
    Enraptur'd with the grace she saw;
Nor did she stay her brutish aim
    To blast the mind that rous'd her awe.   40

Forthwith, her lovers half-dismiss'd,
    The fickle wench her plan matur'd;
And with pretended shyness kiss'd
    The budding boy she wou'd have lur'd.

Alas for fickle shameless sport!   45
    Not yet have all the gods forborne
To offer wisdom's safe resort
    To lambs they fain wou'd save unshorn.

For comely DAMON'S boyish face
    A sharpen'd cynick brain conceal'd,   50
So that in but a little space
    He saw each base design reveal'd.

Each false-drawn sigh he smiling heard,
    And feign'd to answer ev'ry kiss;
Yet still with cunning art deferr'd   55
    The moment of expected bliss.

Amongst the garden's learned few
    Was Nea, sweet ancestral friend,
Whose father DAMON'S father knew
    In ties of fealty without end.   60

To this pure maid he spoke betimes,
    And told what she already guess'd;
Still more knew she of Lycë's crimes,
    Nor was she slow to name the rest.

Now DAMON, nerv'd to pay at last   65
    This swine-soul'd Circe for the woe
She had on all her lovers cast,
    Resolv'd upon a mortal blow.

Down on bright DAMON'S Chian farm
    Liv'd Glaber, young but dull of soul,   70
Who mirror'd DAMON'S outward charm
    But lack'd the fire that crown'd the whole.

A shrill-voic'd slave, whose mother's eyes
    Young DAMON'S kin had lov'd to praise;
Whom art had made a greater prize   75
    By methods known to ancient days.

This beauteous lad sharp DAMON brought
    To share his villa on the plain;
And sure, they seem'd in one mould wrought,
    Tho' Glaber had an idiot's brain.   80

Kept close conceal'd, the idiot slave
    On DAMON'S banquet-leavings far'd;
Or sav'ry scraps that Nea gave,
    For she alone the secret shar'd.

Then one soft evening Lycë's arms   85
    About young DAMON slyly crept,
And he agreed to sing her charms
    That very night before he slept.

His dog he chain'd far from the gate,
    And just ajar he set his door;   90
Then, leaving Glaber couch'd in state,
    His Nea to the priest he bore.

Ionian bards have sweetly told
    The joys his after life contain'd,
For fifty precious years unroll'd   95
    Where love with him and Nea reign'd.

A sourer Muse in whisper'd tone
    Recounts the fate that Lycë knew,
But Dian smiles upon her throne
    To see a trollop get her due.   100

Poor Glaber's face was scratch'd and torn
    When he his kindly master found,
Whilst Lycë fretted all forlorn,
    Her pride destroy'd with such a wound.

And when she sought Leucadia's cliff,   105
    With Sapphic death to purge her sin,
'Tis said an hundred lovers' grief
    Was temper'd with a wry-fac'd grin.

[On the Pyramids]

There was an old geezer from Gizeh,
Who used to take everything ihzeh;
    When the big sandstorm came,
    He would squat just the same,
And declare it was pleasantly brihzeh!   5

[Stanzas on Samarkand]

Too long the jangling of the Muse run mad
    Hath vext the air of our decaying land—
Turned to the golden past, we quit Bagdad,
    And take the Golden Road to Samarkand.

Frantick with rumours of eternal night,   5
    And bury'd lore that none may understand,
We leave behind the realms of pitch and fright,
    And take the Golden Road to Samarkand!

Reality, the King of Idiot Gods,
    Fumbles his puppets with a palsy'd hand: 10
Come leave him as he paws his whining clods,
    And take the Golden Road to Samarkand!

Each distant mountain glows with faery grace,
    The flame-lit lakelet laps the level strand;
Lur'd by dim vistas beck'ning out of space,   15
    We take the Golden Road to Samarkand!

[On Rheinhart Kleiner Being Hit by an Automobile]

Mechanick Force the gentle Poet feels,
And Genius sinks beneath insensate Wheels;
Unfeeling Matter, careless of its Way,
Rides down the Light that sheds PIERIA'S Ray.
But lo! from ev'ry Grove and Fountain run   5
Consoling Nymphs with healing Orison.
So whilst the dull Destroyer hides in Shame,
The Bard triumphant shines with brighter Flame!

To Samuel Loveman Esq.

Upon Adorning His Room for His Birthday

Tonight, blest Minstrel, we are gather'd here
To hail the rarest day in all the year,
For on the calendar 'tis writ in state
That thou this moment turnest thirty-eight!
And we, whose hearts so great a debt reveal   5
For ecstasies thy lute hath made us feel,
Must seize this hour in concert to declare
The praise we proffer, and the love we bear!
Loveman, 'tis not for us to make the strain
Of termless pleasure and ethereal pain,   10
Of towers chryselephantine, and of seas
Where lotos winds croon fragrant mysteries;
Not ours to murmur in the Naxian night
Of broken columns, ivy'd, vein'd, and white,
Or mourn that slender, silent Bacchanal   15
That waits the dawn in vaults that none recall:
Ours but to listen, and with ravisht ears
Display our rapture or release our tears;
To pause attentive at the Attick sound,
And see our Minstrel fitly hail'd and crown'd!   20
So here, bright brother, we have sought to shew
The vast esteem our mingled souls bestow:
Each trivial gift a load of fondness bears,
Which ev'ry wight in equal measure shares:
Scorn not their crudeness, for we see too well   25
How ill they match thine art's high miracle—
But know how keen our longing to express
Some echo of thy Muse's loveliness!

To Saml Loveman Esq.

With a Belated Present of Some Stationery

Attend, good Sir, on this belated day
An echo of our recent roundelay:
The gang, intent to chain thee by their side,
Each home-like instrument would fain provide;
Hence here behold those trivial odds and ends   5
Whereon a poet's peace so much depends;

Things that the soaring bard forgets to buy,
Tho' art insists he have them hov'ring nigh.
Pray use them oft, and let them prove the key
To set thy mounting muse at liberty;   10
Let each smooth sheet reflect with heighten'd grace
Those spreading glories that thy windows face,
And let each pen and pencil rise to fame
As the bright torch of an immortal flame.
Such, then, the gift—we scarcely need repeat   15
Th' esteem that brings it to thine airy seat.
We wish 'twere more, but circumstance hath cast
Our purses slender, tho' our blessings vast.
So must we sign, whose notions thus would light
Anew the spark of the Hermaphrodite.   20
With all good wishes—cheerful but not ribald,
Admiring Belknap and his Grandpa Theobald!

To George Kirk, Esq.,

Upon His Entertaining a Company in His New-Decorated Chambers

Gay, gen'rous host whose faultless taste is shewn
Each day in volumes bought for worth alone,
On this bright evening in thy freshen'd nest
Receive the praise of those who love thee best!
Graceful the walls that now enclose thee round,   5
Eternal beauty hovering profound,
With classick urn and graven image join'd
In one vast whole to please the tasteful mind.
Light touches here, and bits of colour there
Lend pleasing charms, and animate the air;   10
And not a prospect but impels the eye,
Rejoicing, to confess its majesty.
Drest thus in style, these scenes must needs distil
Keen lively judgment from thy fluent quill;
In style piquant of thee a critick mould   15
Refin'd in manner, but in matter bold—
King of them all, inform'd and agile-soul'd!

My Favourite Character

About this season 'tis a smart proceeding
    In mild aesthetick groups and letter'd places
To choose a fav'rite from one's daily reading,
    Explaining brightly one's selective basis;
But sure, whate'er I say can only hurt me,   5
For fac'd with such a test, my wits desert me!

I'm told that certain tastes are e'er in fashion—
    Safe, tame, and classic, e'en tho' somewhat shopworn;
A choice thus order'd ne'er will be a rash one,
    Suiting those thoughts and standards on the top worn—   10
Esmond, D. Copperfield, or Hiawatha,
Or anything from some nice high-school author.

A few gay souls affect with scorn to question
    The proper pref'rences of milder mortals,
And with much pride display a tough digestion   15
    For such spic'd themes as lurk behind lockt portals:
Jurgen, Clerk Nicholas, Boccaccio's misses,
And sundry things of Joyce's, from *Ulysses*.

But if sincerity be not outmoded
    In this degen'rate day of muddled meaning,   20
Much may be said for those whose hearts are loaded
    With figures of a lowlier mood and leaning—
Boyhood's own idols, whom the sages hear not—
Frank Merriwell, Nick Carter, and Fred Fearnot!

Then, too, 'tis hard just now to dodge the moderns,   25
    Our cubists, sharply to tomorrow dated;
Aesthetes of model 1930—odd ones
    Whose palates with all thought and grace are sated:
Trust them to give some shapeless freak a trial,
From T. S. Eliot or last April's *Dial!*   30

Now as for me, I am no man of learning
    To know just what I like and why I like it;
Letters and hist'ry set my poor head turning
    Till not a choice can permanently strike it!
My fav'rite? Fie on printed information—   35
I'll frankly hand myself the nomination!

[On the Double-R Coffee House]

Amid the tap-room's reeking air
    Where smoky clouds the candles choke,
The choicest wit is said to flare,
    And art to shed its daily cloak.

Here may free souls forget the grind   5
    Of busy hour and bustling crowd,
And sparkling brightly mind to mind
    Display their inmost dreams aloud.

The sober stalls inspiring loom,
    The temper'd lights a spell diffuse,   10
Till in the dingy panell'd room
    Flames up—they say—the deathless Muse.

Each teeming corner echoes strong
    With merriment of source unplac'd,
As o'er their coffee ling'ring long   15
    Loaf cohorts of the vacant-fac'd.

The platitudes of yesterday
    Between their coughs the mob repeat,
Or sated with the mental play
    Each lounges listless in his seat.   20

And so they puff and sip and brood
    With faces blank or saturnine;
Studies in emptiness and mood,
    These patterns of a world divine.

Midst them I sit with smoke-try'd eyes,   25
    Intent no flash of wit to miss;
Basking 'neath gay Bohemian skies,
    And grateful for a shrine like this!

[To Frank Belknap Long on His Birthday]

Belknap, how quick does time again
Draw forth the tributary strain,
And move Old Age afresh to greet
The milestone pass'd by youthful feet!
Have I thy birthday rightly heard—   5
Is this indeed thy twenty-third?

177

Sure, infant genius swift is nurs'd
To manhood's prime, in wisdom vers'd!
But tho' thy mind be thus mature,
Let boyish fancy linger pure,   10
Nor with each mounting natal day
Cast innocence and grace away;
Coarseness reject, corruption spurn,
From subtle sophists proudly turn,
And keep, intact in every part,   15
The wonder of a Virgin Heart!

A Year Off

Had I a year to idle thro',
    With cash to waste and no restriction,
I'd plan a programme to outdo
    The wildest feats of travel fiction.

On steamship guides I'd slake my thirst,   5
    And railway maps would make me wiser—
America consider'd first
    To please the local advertiser.

O'er England and the Continent
    I'd chart a course to shame the sages,   10
In each cathedral town intent
    To catch the colour of the ages.

Paris and Rome I would not miss;
    Without the Rhine I'd be no planner,
For one must make a jaunt like this   15
    A Grand Tour in the ancient manner!

But Europe is a trifle trite,
    So I would spare no pains in learning
How best to scan in casual flight
    The East, where sheiks and sands are burning.   20

I'd look up ferries on the Nile,
    And 'bus fares for the trip to Mecca;
Have chemists test in proper style
    The drinking-fountain of Rebecca.

The route of ev'ry Tigris barge   25
    I'd note, and find how much they'd ask us;

What good hotels in Bagdad charge,
    And yellow taxis in Damascus.

And I would surely have on hand
    The folders of that great excursion,   30
The Golden Road to Samarcand,
    Thro' Bahai bow'rs and gardens Persian.

Beyond, the Pullman rates I'd get
    For Kiao-chan and Yokohama,
Arranging passage thro' Thibet   35
    To dally with the Dalai Lama.

In tropic isles I'd plan to stay
    Till South Sea melodies would bore me,
And for the North Pole book a day,
    Where only Peary went before me.   40

Thus might I scheme—till in the end
    The year would slip away unheeded,
My money safe with me to spend,
    And the wild outing scarcely needed!

To an Infant

They have captured and chained you, my brother, from Aidenne beyond
    the blue,
The Fates and the vast All-Mother, to laugh at an hour or two.
They have envied your wings dilated, beating heedless of age or clime,
So they snared you and cast you weighted into dungeons of space and time.
And now as you newly languish in the quivering bonds called flesh,   5
Unknowing as yet the anguish and gall of the long-felt mesh,
They smile as they find you comely, and gloat on their ancient power
To twist you and drive you dumbly for the sport of a listless hour.
They have given you joy but to take it, and youth but to snatch it away,
They have made you a will but to break it, and hope but to lead you astray; 10
They have bound you to objects inutile, and senses that shut out the light,
That themselves, who are bitter and futile, may laugh as you grope in their
    sight.
But you, if you will, can cheat them, and join in the mocking mirth,
For you have that to defeat them which could not be chained at birth:
Though your heart they have trussed and tethered, and your soul they
    have stricken drear,   15

179

Yet a spark from your dreams has weathered all the whirlwinds that swept
    you here.
It has slipt by the onyx portal that holds you to earthly things,
From the crystalline gulfs immortal, that sounded once to your wings.
It will flame through the mists of morning and lighten the hours of your
    youth,
Till the blaze of its bright adorning will banish the clouds of truth.   20
But foster it well, young dreamer, lest the covetous Great Ones call
On Time, the malign Arch-Schemer, to gather it into his thrall;
For dreams, as they are most precious, are most fragile of all we prize,
And the power of earth that enmesh us would sear them out of our eyes;
Would marshal the years to slay them, and summon the flesh to teach   25
Our hardening brains to betray them, and drive them beyond our reach.
They are all that we have to save us from the sport of the Ruthless Ones,
These dreams that the cosmos gave us in the void past the farthest suns;
They are freedom and light surviving as a flicker in cells of ill,
As against the Dark Gods' contriving we must harbour and guard them still.   30
So may you, in whose eyes serenely so much of the old lore shines,
Grow valiant, and battle keenly the envious Gods' designs;
Dissolve when they seek to bind you; fling worlds at their clanking chain;
That never their noose may find you, and never their whim restrain.
Weave magic against their weaving, dream out of their sly duress,   35
Till the prisons of their deceiving shall crumble to nothingness.
Mock back when they storm your reason, and hold you from all you crave,
For your body alone they seize on—no dream can be made a slave.
Deride all their empty offers, and sneer at their specious lure,
Enriching your fancy's coffers with gold that is always pure.   40
Your dreams are yourself, so tend them as all that preserves you free;
With all of your strength defend them, nor grant to the years a fee;
Let never a daemon buy them with pleasures that flash and fade,
Nor sophistry's tongue defy them, nor dogma diffuse its shade.
For these are your own, my brother, and hold in their boundless sweep   45
The wings that the Gods would smother, and the key to your native deep!

To George Willard Kirk, Gent., of Chelsea-Village, in New-York, upon His Birthday, Novr. 25, 1925

Watchman, attend! What feast is this which lights
The village street that should be dark o' nights?
Say, what strange rapture brings ecstatick fires
Where rural CHELSEA rears its peaceful spires?
Unwonted streamers deck the antique walls,   5

And o'er the green, confetti mounts and falls:
Scholar and cit as one resign their work,
And shout in mingled joy, "Long flourish KIRK!"
Health to the sage whose natal night we sing;
Whose praises loud from ev'ry trumpet ring;   10
Health to the sage, who has with skilful pains
Led learning back to CHELSEA'S verdant lanes.
Each loyal cotter beams with brimming eye,
And studious swains promote the minstrelsy:
For KIRK'S Egyptian art, with spells of yore,   15
Lights once again the long-quencht lamp of MOORE!

How long ago that pleasing minstrel sung
The Yuletide lines alive on ev'ry tongue:
"Night Before Christmas", which our fancies took
From lips maternal, or the picture-book!   20
These spacious acres form'd our MOORE'S domain
Ere CHELSEA'S rows of brick involv'd the plain;
But as the village proud and prosp'rous grew,
The Muse for want of nourishment withdrew:
Southward to GREENWICH she her footsteps train'd,   25
Where, tho' scarce worshipt, she was shrewdly feign'd.
Thus pass'd the years, when lo! auspicious Fate
Our CHELSEA spies, and mourns her lost estate;
Scours the broad West for some heroick hand
To throne Apollo in a twice-born land,   30
And finds skill'd KIRK, of letter'd knights the head,
By AKRON mother'd, and by CLEVELAND bred!
See now the conqu'ror stride with shining lance,
Boeotia trembling at his bold advance;
See frighten'd Dulness in far caverns hide,   35
Whilst fleeing Vanity discards her pride:
Grim lines of sombre mansions smile anew,
And vanisht splendour climbs once more to view;
Learning, long exil'd, claims her ancient seat,
And led by KIRK, troops stately up the street!   40
His mellow tomes, to all the town display'd,
The scholar's treasure, and the Muses' aid,
Gleam in the windows, while his festive door
Welcomes a throng that knew not books before.
But not content with what the great have writ,   45
Vivacious KIRK must needs have living wit:
Like Will's or Button's must his threshold glow

181

With the sage sermon and the quick *bon-mot:*
Wise in his time, he draws from meads around
Bright courtly balladists, and bards profound;   50
Poets and pedants, scholiasts and seers,
Midst whom he sits, the first among his peers!
Reviving CHELSEA heeds, and from her shores
The grateful birthday paean lively pours:
Each ancient wharf, where restless vessels ride,   55
Responsive sings, and tells the roving tide.
Sequester'd quads, where piety is nurst,
Wake from their hymns, and into tributes burst,
Whilst envious GREENWICH o'er the southern fields
With envy sighs, and all her laurels yields.   60

KIRK, may thy life be happy, wise, and long,
With learning blest, and bright with Delian song;
May Virtue be no stranger, and may joy
Perpetual reign, and all thy care employ.
Few are thy years as yet, but as they fly,   65
May genial mem'ry gild the hours gone by,
Till all about thee shine with waxing ray,
And doubled treasures greet each natal day!

[On *Old Grimes* by Albert Gorton Greene]

Old Theobald for an elder scene
    This garish age is dropping;
The verses are by Albert Greene,
    Cuts by Augustus Hoppin.

His gratitude no common song   5
    With fitting grace may sound;
The book, tho' musty, still is strong,
    And very well rebound.

To lovelier scenes it leads his feet,
    By Seekonk's shady hill;   10
For fixing up the leaves to neat
    There must be quite a bill.

Thus ceasing, lest with soaring aims
    His thankful throat shall burst;
He vows that Horton well reclaims   15
    What Rider publish'd first.

182

In Memoriam: Oscar Incoul Verelst of Manhattan

1920–1926

Damn'd be this harsh mechanick Age
    That whirls us fast and faster,
And swallows with Sabazian Rage
    Nine Lives in one Disaster.

I take my Quill with sadden'd Thought,   5
    Tho' falt'ringly I do it;
And, having curst the Juggernaut,
    Inscribe: OSCARVS FVIT!

The Return

The sun with brighter beams on high
    Lights up the Merrimack's swift rill,
And village bells in chorus cry,
    "TRYOUT is back in Haverhill!"

The friendly roofs and steeples ring   5
    With echoes of the cordial strain,
For one who from long voyaging
    Today is welcom'd home again.

Familiar hills his feet invite,
    And conscious streets his presence tell,   10
Pleas'd with the fond, remember'd sight
    Of him who loves their windings well.

In neighb'ring forests, glades, and meads,
    The sprightly fauns their brother hail,
And Pan awaits 'mid lakeside reeds   15
    His long-miss'd step, with rod and pail.

The orchards bend with grateful fruits,
    And autumn boughs resplendent blaze;
While the late autumn gorgeous shoots
    Thro' sunset-fir'd October haze.   20

Hail to our TRYOUT'S nimble tread!
    Hail to his song of clanking steel,
As the neat page so fondly read
    Anew his busy hours reveal!

May joy inspire the hearthside flame   25
    That lights its master's form once more,
And peace a full dominion claim
    Round the snug walls and cottage door.

Back to his own! There let him bask
    Long in the scenes he holds so dear;   30
Blest with whate'er his soul may ask
    To fill each happy, home-like year!

Hedone

Catullus from his Sirmian bow'r
    The world of fancy thrust away,
And drunken in the moonlit hour,
    Midst roses with his Lesbia lay.

For him in vain dead cities dream'd,   5
    And isles of wonder starr'd the sea;
Blind while the Roman eagles gleam'd,
    Deaf to the songs of victory.

And as the days of dalliance sped,
    And moons and roses came and went,   10
The lips of Lesbia comforted
    A heart with present bliss content.

But month by month and year by year
    Before the moon a shadow grew,
And roses, shrivelling and sere,   15
    Fell blighted by a poison dew.

Those lips so tempting once to him
    Now drool'd repulsive in his sight,
Whilst o'er the ivory cheek and limb
    Spread age and vice, a livid blight.   20

Weary of love he turn'd at last
    To once-scorn'd dreams in late desire,
But found his deaden'd soul bound fast
    To foetid flesh and charnel fire.

So frantick thro' the Sirmian dusk   25
    Catullus flees in endless pain,
As ghostly winds of rose and musk
    Recall his idle hours in vain.

And at his heels there seems to prowl
    A dogging shape with matted hair,   30
Whose burning breath, obscene and foul,
    Pours horror on the midnight air.

But in the Mantuan moonlight still
    The golden fancies sparkling lie,
Whilst wonder hovers on the hill   35
    In forms too old and pure to die.

Proud o'er the plain the eagles press,
    And glory crowns the Palatine,
For godlike dreams the dreamer bliss
    With festive joys of source divine!   40

To Miss Beryl Hoyt

Upon Her First Birthday—February 21, 1927

What dreams, sprung fresh from dawning skies,
Shine sweet behind those wond'ring eyes?
    What tales untold?
For still about thee wistful clings
Some echo of celestial things—   5
    Just one year old!

And as thy radiant days progress,
May all those dreams of loveliness
    Leave gifts of grace
To mould thy deeds in later time,   10
While glints of happiness sublime
    Light up thy face!

Dirge of the Doomed

Dulce et decorum est pro basilica mori

Still dream the placid ancient ways
    That once your footsteps knew,
Tho' with uncertain, number'd days
    The courthouse greets our view.

Behold a chart of all the change   5
    Men hereabouts would fix—

New pinnacles and belfries strange . . .
    But no 256!

A sadden'd twilight drap'd the shore
    Not so many bygone evens   10
When in the dark of Adams' store
    I met your partner Stevens.

(I'd come for milk, be sure to grant—
    And not for bootleg gin;
I was a-dining with my aunt*,   15
    And helping cart things in!)

We talk'd, we mourn'd, yet overhead
    Still lower'd the pall of doom;
For Adams' last fond hope is dead—
    Across the street, no room!   20

Eheu! *Sic transit*—as they cry
    On many a tardy 'bus;
'Tis sad to see a mem'ry die—
    A shrine be shatter'd thus!

But hope pervades the pious dream,   25
    For just below the hill
Safe nestling by the perfumed stream
    Our Jacques is with us still!

* Mrs. Gamwell, who lives at the Handicraft Club in the old Beckwith
mansion at College & Benefit.

To a Sophisticated Young Gentleman,

Presented by His Grandfather with a Volume of Contemporary Literature

Ingenious Age once more essays to find
A proper gift for youth's sophistick mind,
Well tho' he know how bootless 'tis to send
Aught that his own old head can comprehend.
Perplext, the Grandsire scours the stalls to chuse   5
Some spawn of Chaos and the bedlam Muse;
Some complex fruit of multiple dimensions,
With modern outlines and remote pretensions,
Which, scorning Euclid and the pedant race,
Revolts from Time, and flings a sneer at Space;   10

Of wit and beauty keeps discreetly chary,
And forfeits sense to be contemporary.
What best can suit so deep a disillusion,
And cater to such civilis'd confusion?
Whose pen indeed the wrought-steel crown deserves   15
As Cham of cubes, and Arbiter of curves?
For sure, 'twere vain on normal art to lean
In youth's jazz'd world of concrete and machine!
Gods of the Waste Land! say what monster new
Shou'd grace a shelf by *Benda* or *Luleu?*   20
What best befits a bookcase carv'd to ape
An airplane's angles or a subway's shape?
Subtle the style that fits our motor nation,
Smooth as a *Ford,* prim as a filling-station,
Mass'd and severe as yonder office tow'r,   25
Short in its wave-length, statick in its pow'r;
High as the crown of *Mencken's* scornful hat,
Objective as a *Times-Square* Automat;
Devoid of pomp as *Woolworth's* or *McCrory's,*
And cerebral as *Vogue* or *Snappy Stories;*   30
Mature as moonshine booze, and free of bunk
As the frank perfume of the candid skunk;
Gay as a billboard, ardent as the graphick
And muddled as a stream of Broadway traffick;
Firm as a gangster or a stick-up man,   35
Ironick as an old tomato-can,
As radio loud, as movies democratick,
Symbolick as a Greenwich Village attick;
Bright as the tungsten of a *Wrigley* "ad",
And settled as the latest sideburn fad—   40
Thus the deep lines that may alone express
Our whirling epoch in its rightful dress!
But who, mid our embarrassment of riches,
Wears the true laureate's four-plus flannel breeches?
See in what throngs th' ambitious candidate   45
Crashes and storms—and sometimes gets—the gate!
Here *Joyce* appears with Odysseys demure,
His prose a junk-pile, and his mind a sewer;
Hard on his heels the *Hechtick* hero hurtles,
With rose-tipt beak, and twin'd with *Paphian* myrtles.   50
Wise Eliot stalks in state—no friend of cant he—
And stores a cosmos in a triple "Shantih";

187

Cursing all caps, the comely *Cummings* comes,
And *Lindsay* pounds his syncopated drums;
With fun and folklore struts romantick *Cabell*,   55
Chalking his half-hid smut behind the stable;
Stein formless foams, and chants the tender button,
Whilst *Arlen's* wisecracks knowing saps may glut on.
Cubist and futurist combine to shew
Sublimer heights in *Kreymborg* and *Cocteau*;   60
The shade of *Huysmans* reddens prose and rhyme,
And fiction soars in *Burke* and *Bodenheim*.
Assist, ye brazen Nymphs of *Montparnassus*,
To chuse a chief from the bold hordes that gas us:
Say what pied knight of these assorted lots   65
Outshines with broken lines or rows or dots?
Tell aged Ignorance what seer to pick
As symbol of a world gone lunatick.
Count them all o'er, and find a name to lead
A dizzy universe of nameless speed.   70
How shall we do it? Simple as the day!—
Listen intent whilst modern criticks bray.
Weigh the wild clamour, and proclaim as proudest
The jumbled scribe whose name is heard the loudest.
Him we elect, and to the heights promote   75
As King Sophisticate by true straw vote.
His words alone we hold supremely fit
To feast a flaming youth of modern wit.
Hark! One—two—three!—the long-ear'd herd decide
On a vague ghost to be their aesthete-guide: 80
Hail to the chief their phrensy'd plaudits boost—
And take, Young Man, a tome by MARCEL PROUST!

Veteropinguis Redivivus

1. *Veteropinguis Redivivus: A Poem*

Let the sad cypress and the yew
'Neath bays and myrtle sink from view,
    And to oblivion fly;
For lying Rumour's pow'r is riv'n,
As from a mythic grave is giv'n   5
    A form too tough to die.

An ear or nose, by Nature's law,
The fates of warfare well may chaw;
    What oak's too strong to bend?
But not so easy does the fire   10
Of ninefold feline life expire,
    And in dull embers end!

Hail to the rustick batter'd form
That stoutly weathers ev'ry storm
    And howls triumphant still!   15
Tho' yet unskill'd in elder ways,
And alien to the chimney's maze,
    Thou spurnst the clutch of ill!

Long may the placid twelvemonths glide
With thee a-trotting by our side,   20
    Terror of neighb'ring rats!
May Time preserve thee hale and old,
Thy fur and heart alike of gold—
    Dean of the Pack—Old Fats!

2.

Our sadden'd orbs o'erflow with pensive brine,
    And linger on the vacant hearthside space,
For gentle Pettie, seiz'd with a decline,
    Will nevermore display his polisht grace.

That golden soul, too delicate for earth,   5
    Mourn'd for old Printer's counsel, calm and wise;
And sick'ning at the unaccustom'd dearth,
    Follow'd his lov'd preceptor to the skies.

3.

Underneath this ferreous bowl
Lyes the matron we extol;
Pettie's sister, Marcelle's mother.
Death, ere thou hast kill'd another
Wise and good as this lost kit,   5
Time will pause a Little Bit.

4.

Donald, since last you met my aged eyes
It seems you have increas'd somewhat in size:
What alien sire can thus have summon'd up
A tow'ring monster from a sportive pup?
Once I'd have said, a china-shatt'ring Taurus—   5
But now, I swear it was a brontosaurus!

5.

A health to the train that unflagging uphold
The traditions bequeath'd by Bubastis of old:
Old Fats—in whose roughness lies many a charm;
And the Prince whose proud ermine no clawing can harm;
Lithe Tardee, the scourge of each mouse-hole and glade;   5
Marcelle, whom a thousand bold Toms serenade;
And last but not hindmost there floats on the tide
Light, oöphagous Corky, the future's young pride!

6.

To this calm spot where many a slab and urn
    Attests the shortness of our mortal span,
For pensive meditation I return,
    Pond'ring the woes of Heav'n's terrestrial plan.

On ev'ry hand memorial blossoms bloom,   5
    But sadder than the saddest of them all
Is one press'd petal from a distant tomb,
    That can old PRINTER'S lov'd grey form recall.

7.

STITCHIE, tho' eye and ear
    For you be going under,
May this but keep you clear
    Of vexing flash and thunder!

With worth that flouts decay,   5
    Tho' sight and sound be jaded,
You face the close of day—
    A gentleman unfaded!

8.

Suspitious Souls with Pride are wont to tell
How quick they can a Rodent's Presence smell;
Yet if the scamp'ring Train be swift and small,
'Tis easie not to glimpse the Rogues at all.
In Printer's Day, when Act was quick as Thought,   5
How few the Mice that cou'd survive uncaught!
Our languid Age displays a lesser Skill,
And the brown Nibblers vex our Cheese at will!
But here and there, where western Rivers pour,
Young Heads preserve their Sires' forgotten Lore;   10
Catch the old Scent, and trap for future Time
The brood that burrows deep in doubtful Rhyme.

To a Young Poet in Dunedin

You haunt the lonely strand where herons hide,
    And palm-framed sunsets open gates of flame;
Where marble moonbeams bridge the lapping tide
    To westward shores of dream without a name.

Here, in a haze of half-remembering,   5
    You catch faint sounds from that far, fabled beach.
The world is changed—your task henceforth to sing
    Dim, beckoning wonders you could never reach.

[Metrical Example]

Sun shining cheerily,
Rain falling drearily,
    Noontide or night:
All are the same to him—
Only a name to him—   5
    Sunder'd from sight.

Chaos and clarity,
Likeness, disparity,
    Fine and uncouth:
Mix themselves hazily   10
When we lag lazily
    Sunder'd from truth.

191

The Odes of Horace: Book III, ix

A Dialogue betwixt Horace and Lydia

(Translated by a Gentleman of New-England)

Horace
Whilst I was pleasing to your Taste,
Nor likelier Youths your Neck embrac'd,
I liv'd more happy on Love's Throne
Than *Persia's* Monarch on his own.

Lydia
Whilst you did for no other burn,   5
Nor *Lydia's* Charms for *Chloë's* spurn,
I flourish'd with a lofty Name,
And envy'd not great *Ilia's* Fame.

Horace
To Thracian *Chloë*, skill'd in Song
And on the Lyre, I now belong.   10
For her I wou'd not fear to die,
Wou'd Death, in Payment, pass her by.

Lydia
Now *Calaïs* kindles my Desire,
With Torch alight with equal Fire;
For him the Tomb I twice cou'd dare,   15
Wou'd Death the graceful Youth but spare!

Horace
What if old Love at last be woke
To bind us in its mem'ry'd Yoke?
If golden *Chloë* reign no more,
And *Lydia* face an open'd Door?   20

Lydia
Tho' he the brightest Star outbeam,
Whilst you with Froth and Choler teem,
With you my Days I'd willing spend,
And glad with you wou'd greet the End.

Gaudeamus

Come hither, my lads, with your tankards of ale,
And drink to the present before it shall fail;
Pile each on your platter a mountain of beef,
For 'tis eating and drinking that bring us relief:
     So fill up your glass,   5
     For life will soon pass;
When you're dead ye'll ne'er drink to your king or your lass!

Anacreon had a red nose, so they say;
But what's a red nose if ye're happy and gay?
Gad split me! I'd rather be red whilst I'm here,   10
Than white as a lily—and dead half a year!
     So Betty, my miss,
     Come give me a kiss;
In hell there's no innkeeper's daughter like this!

Young Harry, propp'd up just as straight as he's able,   15
Will soon lose his wig and slip under the table;
But fill up your goblets and pass 'em around—
Better under the table than under the ground!
     So revel and chaff
     As ye thirstily quaff;
Under six feet of dirt 'tis less easy to laugh!   20

The fiend strike me blue! I'm scarce able to walk,
And damn me if I can stand upright or talk!
Here, landlord, bid Betty to summon a chair;
I'll try home for a while, for my wife is not there!
     So lend me a hand;   25
     I'm not able to stand,
But I'm gay whilst I linger on top of the land!

The Greatest Law

by C. Raymond and Ludwig von Theobald

Arise, ye swains! for fair Aurora's light
Shews the wild geese in scurrying matin flight;
In shifting ranks their silent course they take,
And for the valley marshlands quit the lake:
Tho' loose they fly, in various modes arrang'd,   5
Their eyes are steady, and their goal unchang'd.

Thus in brute instinct Nature shews her law;
Excites our wonder, and compels our awe.
But hark! from yonder grove the pleasing peal
Of redbreasts, winging to their morning meal;   10
In softer tones the lusty bluejay chants,
While maple shades the bobbing grackle haunts:
From neighb'ring wall the bluebird's carol rings,
And in the mead the lark rejoicing sings.
Forests and fields attend the welcome strain,   15
And hail the advent of the feather'd train;
Swift pour the airy legions from the shores
Where Mexique's Bay its genial currents pours:
In waves unnotic'd throng the tuneful band,
To glad the soul, and cheer the Northern strand,   20
Obedient to the sway of Jove's all-pow'rful hand.
Alive with song the gentle bluebird floats;
The hermit thrush disdains melodious notes;
None marks their solid course, but as they come,
Each gains a greeting to his Northern home.   25
Now drip the maples with their vernal juice,
While growing thorns their swelling buds unloose;
On grassy slopes the furry coils untwine,
Where soon hepatica's white blooms will shine.
Almighty Pan! whose vast unchanging will   30
Clothes the green wildwood and enrobes the hill,
How calm the workings of thy great decrees!
How still thy magic o'er the flow'ry leas!
No march of feet, or sound of timbrel shakes
The sylvan scene, or stirs the drowsy brakes: 35
In songful peace the law resistless moves,
And pleases while it rules the meadows and the groves.

Part II. Why Trees Are Tall—by Ward Phillips

Attend! Attend! ye dreaming Dryad throng!
Bend your green boughs, and mark the rising song!
Awake, ye Naiads, feel the vernal thrill,   40
And from each fount increase the crystal rill!
O'er rolling plains let rural Fauns disport,
While Pan, their King, holds universal court:
All Nature's choir, with ever-youthful voice,
Proclaims the spring, and bids the world rejoice.   45

'Twas at this joyful time that o'er the wold
Roam'd a sad swain, oppress'd with grief untold;
Damon his name, who found his Delia cold.
Six feet and one the slender stripling tow'rs,
Bends o'er the trees, and stoops to glimpse the bow'rs;   50
A comely youth, in wit and learning great,
Skill'd in each art, and master of debate—
Yet pensive now, since Eros' cruel dart
Had pierc'd his own, but not his Delia's, heart.
Th' unhappy youth his burning misery   55
In sonnets carv'd on many a hoary tree;
Till ev'ry bird, and ev'ry rustling wind
Could read the tale—"My Delia is unkind!"
It chanc'd one noon, that on a woodland steep
The heavy-lidded shepherd dropt to sleep;   60
Worn out with weeping, he in dreams implor'd
His cruel Delia for a gentle word;
Till mov'd beyond his wont, he spake aloud
The fruitless plaint, while still in slumber bow'd.
Now at this sound the pitying trees are mov'd,   65
For well they know young Damon's fate unlov'd:
Carv'd on their bark the woeful truth appears,
And their deep roots are damp with Damon's tears.
From out each trunk the patron Dryad starts,
And all behold the youth who touch'd their hearts;   70
Around his slumbrous form in throngs they press,
To mark his grief, and praise his loveliness.
"Sisters, behold!" the grave Ptelea cry'd,
"The lovely victim of a Delia's pride!
"So fair a stripling should not pine alone—   75
"I vow, I'll make the tender boy mine own!"
Scarce had she spoke, when winsome Phegia's voice
Oppos'd the speaker, and denounc'd the choice;
"It is not meet," the rival nymph declar'd,
"That with thy age his tender youth be pair'd;   80
"I, I alone, deserve a wife's estate;
"A bright companion, and a fitting mate!"
But as they quarrel, other nymphs exclaim
In rising tones, and utter Damon's name:
The blooming Drusa owns a loving fire,   85
And sad Aegeira swells the amorous choir;
Sphendamnia with Oesua now contends,
And female strife the forest quiet rends.

"He's mine!" each screams, and seeks to clutch the prize,
  Yet fails to clasp the idol of her eyes;   90
"He's mine!" Aloft the echoing cry proceeds,
  And frets the Fauns that roam the upland meads.
The youth, awaked, the beauteous train beholds,
  Whilst ev'ry nymph her arms about him folds.
He sees—he screams—ungentle to the fair   95
  When he perceives his Delia is not there—
But all too late; for in a frenzy'd mood
  The Dryads hold him in their native wood.
Each swears to keep him, and as lawful pelf
  Labours in vain to draw him to herself;   100
Till the mad band, their strength diversely bent,
  Grasp but sad fragments, by the tussle rent.
Thus Thracia's savage matrons wildly tore
  The pensive Orpheus on swift Hebrus' shore.
Ptelea gains his head, so lately deck'd   105
  With twining myrtle, and vast intellect;
Young Phegia wins an arm, whose pendent hand
  The magic quill of genius could command.
All mourn alike, throughout the sighing grove,
  The hapless object of their common love;—   110
When lo! on high supernal rays diffuse,
  And shew Apollo with each wrathful Muse:
Down from Parnassus swoop the angry train
  T' avenge their fav'rite—but they swoop in vain.
For the quick Dryads, as they view the sky,   115
  Back to their shelt'ring trees in terror fly.
The mangled swain they with themselves enclose,
  And where he roam'd, an empty forest grows.
In genuine tears stand Phoebus and the Nine;
  Like mortals in their grief, but in their wrath divine. 120

Meanwhile young Damon's friends, in lonely quest,
  Search for the tender lad they lov'd the best.
"Damon!" In vain the aged Theobald cries!
"Damon!" Oft wipes wise Mocrates his eyes.
No sign, no word, the vanish'd youth conveys,   125
  Tho' each sad comrade for a letter prays;
And anguish'd poets sing their grief in Dorick lays.

But one bright day, within the heart of spring,
  The sorrowing Theobald went a-wandering;

With eyes intent upon the heav'ns above,   130
In grief he trod each w. k. mead and grove,
Till suddenly his elevated glance
Observ'd a most unusual circumstance!
What may this mean—that ev'ry tree in sight
Shou'd rise to more than twice its wonted height?   135
What novel influence sways the Dryad throng
That trees shou'd grow so lanky and so long?
Thus mus'd the bard, till thro' the tow'ring trees
Spread a low sound, as of a passing breeze;
Old Theobald pauses, and with straining ears   140
A tale of wonder from the branches hears.
"In this tall grove," low sigh'd the leafy train,
"Behold the Damon thou hast sought in vain!
"By Dryads captur'd, and by Dryads torn,
"In hoary trees my spirit is reborn;   145
"My body, lost, has yet this pow'r alone—
"To give the trees dimensions like its own:
"So mark thou well; henceforth shall woods arise
"Whose verdant branches touch the airy skies.
"My soul survives, altho' my frame be dead,   150
"And turn'd to wood—so like my Delia's head!"
Thus paus'd the prison'd youth, and nevermore
His accents bless'd the Appletonian shore.
E'er must his spirit own the Dryad thrall,
And trees grow graceful, Galpinesque, and tall!

[Sonnet Study]

A

Sonnets are sighs, breathed beautiful and brief
From spirits sobered by their weight of dreams;
Figures in jade whose perfection gleams
A tortured thought too luminous for grief,
Shaped with that ecstasy which brings relief   5
And rest, distilled from woe's encircling streams.
Solemn and high the poet's chosen themes,
Their stray tones gathered to a stately sheaf.

Not mine to mould such Tuscan symphonies,
Wherein each note must sound the singer's mood;   10
Octave advance and sestet retrogress
In subtler turns than common vision sees;

197

Dulness stands lost in an enchanted wood
Pathless to eyes untouched by loveliness.

B
The subtle mind in subtle tones can speak,
    Nor trip in paths Italianate;
Finding the door for which his wishes seek
    In the slow sonnet which made Petrarch great.

Such ordered shadings, drawn with grave intent,   5
    A thousand charms of musing bring to light,
As brooding dusk reveals in his descent
    The countless day-enshrouded orbs of night.

But we, of plainer, hardier metal wrought,
    A straighter path demand, whose hedge and goal   10
May suit the Saxon's undivided thought,
    And guide his changeless impulse, warm and whole:

Summing his message in one final shout
That speaks his mind and drowns all wavering out.

Verses Designed to Be Sent by a Friend of the Author to His Brother-in-Law on New-Year's Day

Respected Smith, to mark the fleeting time,
Munroe salutes you in fraternal rhyme.
An infant year again the old o'erthrows;
Another twelvemonth meets its certain close.
May all your troubles, with the parting year   5
Depart as well; as surely disappear;
And may the new, with all-pervading peace,
Delight your heart, and ev'ry joy increase.

[To a Cat]

Last of an elder race, whose treasur'd lore
    No younger hierophant deserv'd to share!
May Fortune grant thee, on a sunnier shore,
    Eternal hours exempt from worldly care.

May heav'nly ladders bear thee from this earth,   5
    Up hidden flues to realms of endless day,
Where bliss shall crown thy time-attested worth
    In fields of catnip rich with rodent prey.

IV. Satire

Providence in 2000 A.D.

(It is announced in the *Providence Journal* that the Italians desire
to alter the name of Atwell's Avenue to "Columbus Avenue".)

For years I'd sav'd my few and hard-earn'd pence
To cross the seas and visit Providence,
For tho' by birth an Englishman am I,
My forbears dwelt in undersiz'd R.I.
Until, prest hard by foreign immigrations,   5
Oblig'd they were to leave the old Plantations,
And seek a life of quiet and repose
On British soil, whence our fam'ly rose.

When on my trip I ventur'd to embark,
I stepp'd aboard a swift and pond'rous ark   10
Which swimm'd the waves, and in a single day
Attain'd its port in Narragansett Bay.
I left the ship, and with astonish'd eyes
Survey'd a city fill'd with foreign cries.
No word of discourse could I understand,   15
For English was unknown throughout the land.
I went ashore at Sao Miguel's Cape,
Where cluster'd men of ev'ry hue and shape.
They say, this place as "Fox Point" once was known,
But negro Bravas have that name o'erthrown.   20
Upon a shaky street-car, north I flew,
Swift borne along O'Murphy's Avenue.
Long, long ago, this street was call'd "South Main",
But such plain titles Erin's sons disdain.
At Goldstein's Court I quit the lumb'ring car,   25
And trod the pave that once was "Market Square".
At the east end, close by a tow'ring hill,
There stands the ruin of a brick-built pile:
The ancient "Board of Trade", the people say,
Left from the times before the Hebrew's sway.   30
Across a bridge, where fragrant waters run,
I shap'd my journey toward the setting sun.
A curving junction first engag'd my gaze;
My guide-book calls it "Finklestein's Cross-ways",
But in a note historical 'tis said,   35
That the old English nam'd the spot "Turk's Head".

A few yards south, I saw a building old;
A stone Post Office, waiting to be sold.
My course now lay along a narrow street,
Up which I tramp'd with sore and weary feet.   40
Its name is Svenson's Lane, for by the Swede
"Westminster Street" was alter'd thus to read.
I next climb'd on a car northwestward bound,
And soon 'mid swarthy men myself I found
On La Collina Federale's brow,   45
Near Il Passagio di Colombo.
I then return'd and rode directly north;
On rusty rails the car humm'd o'er the earth.
Loud near my seat a man in scorn decry'd
An easy plan for reaching the East Side.   50
Thro' New Jerusalem we swiftly pass'd,
Beheld the wealth that Israel amass'd.
And quick arriv'd within New Dublin Town,
A city large from small "Pawtucket" grown.
From there I wander'd toward Nouvelle Paris,   55
Which, in the past, "Woonsocket" us'd to be
Before the Gaul from Canada pour'd in
To swell the fact'ries, and increase their din.
Soon I return'd to Providence, and then
Went west to beard the Polack in his den.   60
At what was once call'd "Olneyville" I saw
A street sign painted: Wsjzxypq$?&%$ ladislaw.
With terror struck, I sought the wharf once more,
But as my steamboat's whistle 'gan to roar,
A shrivell'd form, half crouching 'twixt the freight,   65
Seiz'd on my arm, and halted short my gait.
"Who art thou, Sirrah?" I in wonder cry'd;
"A monstrous prodigy," the fellow sigh'd:
"Last of my kind, a lone unhappy man,
My name is Smith! I'm an American!"   70

Fragment on Whitman

Behold great *Whitman*, whose licentious line
Delights the rake, and warms the souls of swine;
Whose fever'd fancy shuns the measur'd pace,
And copies Ovid's filth without his grace.
In his rough brain a genius might have grown,   5
Had he not sought to play the brute alone;

202

But void of shame, he let his wit run wild,
And liv'd and wrote as Adam's bestial child.
Averse to culture, strange to humankind,
He never knew the pleasures of the mind.   10
Scorning the pure, the delicate, the clean,
His joys were sordid, and his morals mean.
Thro' his gross thoughts a native vigour ran,
From which he deem'd himself the perfect man:
But want of decency his rank decreas'd,   15
And sunk him to the level of the beast.
Would that his Muse had dy'd before her birth,
Nor spread such foul corruption o'er the earth.

[On Robert Browning]

Thy lyrics, gifted Browning, charm the ear,
And ev'ry mark of classic polish bear.
With subtle raptures they enchain the heart;
To soul and mind a mystic thrill impart:
Yet would their rhythmic magic be more keen,   5
If we could but discover what they mean!

Ad Criticos

Liber Primus

What vig'rous protests now assail my eyes?
See Jackson's satellites in anger rise!
His ardent readers, steep'd in tales of love,
Sincere devotion to their leader prove;
In brave defence of sickly gallantry,   5
They damn the critic, and beleauger me.
Ingenious Russell, I forgive the slur,
Since in such clever lines your sneers occur.
Your verse, with true Pierian heat inflam'd,
Should be at some more worthy object aim'd.   10
Think not, good rhymester, that I sought to shew
In my late letter merely what I know,
Nor that I labour'd, with my humble quill,
To bend the universe to suit my will.
My aim, forsooth, was but to do my best   15
To free these pages from an am'rous pest.
With no false hopes did I so strongly plead;

203

Small chance had I, unaided, to succeed.
Of Russell's rhymes thus briefly I dispose,
And next consider Crean's perspicuous prose.   20
Forbear, kind sir, to think my plaint was made,
That I my store of language might parade:
In truth, my words are not beyond the reach
Of him who understands the English speech;
But Crean, I fear, by reading Jackson long,   25
Hath lost the pow'r to read his mother tongue.
Yet hark! I face another diatribe;
My critic says, I am a luckless scribe.
Dismiss the charge! From that disgrace I'm free;
No line of fiction e'er was writ by me!   30
So much for Crean, but ere my song I end,
I porze, Fonetik Bennett too Kummend.
His rugged wit hath such a solid worth,
'Tis not amiss to doubt his rustic birth,
And guess he toils, his protests to prepare,   35
Safe seated in an editorial chair,
From whence he hurls deceptive ridicule
'Gainst all who fight soft Jackson and his school.
Scrawl on, sweet Jackson, raise the lover's leer;
'Tis plain, you please the fallen public ear.   40
As once in Charles the Second's vulgar age,
Gross Wycherley and Dryden soil'd the stage;
So now again erotic themes prevail,
However loud the sterner souls bewail.
Pure fiction wanes, and baser writings rise—   45
But cease, my Muse! No more I'll criticise.

Liber Secundus

Still louder bawl the bold Boeotian band,
And seize their arms at sentiment's command:
The lovers' legion, martially array'd,
To tender Jackson brings its eager aid.
Their acid quills, fresh pluck'd from Cupid's wing,   5
At me the Myrmidons of Venus fling.
Intrepid Saunders heads the hostile horde,
And hurls with deadly skill the poison'd word;
Help'd on by books, both sacred and profane,
He seeks to shine in the satiric strain.   10

Peace! Oklahoman, cease my words to rate:
"Jacksonian", "Jacksonine", "Josh Billings-gate"
Claim no existence but as satire's tools;
Owe no allegiance to linguistic rules,
Whilst as for "Hanoverian", take care   15
Lest as a faulty scholar you appear;
Too much upon your lexicon you lean,
For *proper names* in such are seldom seen.
As studious Saunders, like the kangaroo,
Jumps in a hansom, and is lost to view,   20
Laconic Bonner takes the leader's place,
And throws his modest "classic" in my face.
Now fairer forms from out the ranks emerge;
The Amazons in reckless fury charge.
Good Madam Loop, like Crean of Syracuse,   25
Protests unkindly 'gainst the words I use:
Whoe'er this lady's firm esteem would seek,
In monosyllables must ever speak.
The North and West have now their rancour spent,
And Old Virginia joins the tournament.   30
Here once a nobler JACKSON wag'd his wars,
And died a hero in a glorious cause.
Lost is the cause, but deathless STONEWALL'S fame.
Alas, that lesser men should bear his name!
But down, my Muse, to present actions skip;   35
And meet th' attack of Mistress Blankenship.
The maid of Richmond, with romantic mind,
Considers my opinions most unkind;
And finds in Jackson's tales of love intense
A charming sweetness; beauteous innocence.   40
What fascination! Ah! what loveliness—
Save us, ye Gods, from such a nauseous mess!
Exactitude the fair one hardly heeds,
Since she "erratic" for "erotic" reads,
But unimportant 'tis, for by my troth,   45
Jackson's erratic and erotic both!
How vain the task such champions to oppose;
Fred's fond battalion ev'ry moment grows.
Naught can I do, save here and now to close.

Liber Tertius

What skill'd replies can modest letters bring!
My waspish foes in metric manner sting:
Before my face in rage they buzz along,
And beat their wings in Heliconian song.
Russell, like Butler, seeks to school the times   5
In four-foot verse bestrown with double rhymes.
He lights on me, and stings with careless courage,
As if I were the Hudibras of our age.
For answ'ring sneers I vainly search my mind;
No blemish in his numbers can I find.   10
And yet, methinks, he still mistakes my aim,
When I 'gainst dull erotic tales declaim.
To aid his cause, he points with logic's art
At Boz, and Cooper, Avon's bard, and Scott:
"Behold," he cries, "thro' classic pages move   15
The sweet delusions of idyllic love."
Russell, 'tis true. Give proper love its own,
But let us not be fed on love alone!
Now, heav'nly Muse, thy latest pupil see,
As Saunders bares his soul in poetry.   20
To grave heroics does his taste incline;
His verse is modell'd after Pope's (or mine).
A worthy measure, worthily employ'd;
By no false accent is the ear annoy'd.
The wit is biting, and the language pure;   25
The sense, like Browning's, is a bit obscure:
The thoughts in most ingenious cloaks are wrapp'd;
The metaphors, tho' somewhat mix'd, are apt.
Thy pen, brave Saunders, from a ploughshare made,
Writes deadly words, and strikes us all afraid.   30
Beneath thy verse we guilty wretches cower;
Detested Lovecraft, and fierce Isenhour.
Stay, conqu'ring scribe, thou hast no need to fly,
When in the dust thy foemen prostrate lie.
But what shrill shoutings now offend my ear?   35
Methinks, some rough and raucous Rahs I hear.
No brutal force my new opponent lacks;
He bluntly yells, I should receive the axe!
Ungentle headsman, spare a death so mean;
I vastly should prefer the guillotine.   40

The calmer, kinder Forrest next succeeds,
And mercy for unhappy Jackson pleads.
The plea is granted, for the war is o'er;
The crusty bachelor will rant no more.
Still may he rage, but never shall he pen it;   45
That task he leaves to honest Master Bennett.

Liber Quartus

Russell again! This time he tries to damn
His daz'd opponent with an epigram.
He shuns politeness in his spleenful scrawl,
And swears my stock of learning is but small.
In well-turn'd lines, with sickly venom writ,   5
He counts my failings to display his wit.
Yet for one fault, let Russell bear the curse:
'Tis he that led the fighters into verse!
Russell, retire, as clever Cummings comes,
Who brilliant quips in jingling measure hums.   10
His tuneful nonsense charms the list'ning ear,
While wondrous merits in his pun appear:
He gains distinction and eternal fame,
From neatly playing on a hated name.
A third now seeks his rugged rhymes to wield,   15
And fierce fantastic Forster fills the field.
His searing satires no false arts adorn;
His learned lines the rules of metre scorn.
In true trochaic rage the bard begins,
When, lo! an odd iambus intervenes.   20
Some eight lines down, he strikes the ballad form,
But soon a dactyl swells the shapeless swarm:
The fifteenth line assumes heroic length,
And stands apart in solitary strength.
As for the rest, what man among us knows   25
If it be verse, or merely rhyming prose?
On Forster's sense, I waste but little care,
For why discuss a thing that is not there?
Jackson's forgot, but still the mob delight
To vent in venom'd verse their random spite: 30
Without a leader, and without a cause,
They force on me these long defensive wars.
Methinks, when scribes thus bitterly contend,
The Editor alone the fray can end.

Frustra Praemunitus

As Jackson once again explodes,
And one more Pint of Mush unloads,
Good Russell shakes with Apprehension
Lest Lovecraft give it his Attention,
And take the Novel as Excuse   5
For forty Lines of fresh Abuse.
Yet why should Russell hate and fear
To see his Foeman's Rhymes appear?
'Tis true, the Screeds are monstrous drastic;
The Humour weak; the Style bombastic: 10
But what of that? The Stuff affords
Chance to retort in witty Words.
However dull be Lovecraft's Letter,
'Tis useful to provoke a better.
Russell, as now you reign in State,   15
The *Argosy's* crown'd Laureate,
Reflect, that but for me alone,
To Log-Book Fame you'd be unknown;
You seize your Pen and wait with Fright
What I of "Winged Feet" may write.   20
Ready to sneer, but loath to see,
You watch for the "Calamity".
Yet after all, in vain you dread;
I'll not condemn what I've not read!

N.B. I'll now leave Russell Style,   25
And scribble in my own awhile.

De Scriptore Mulieroso

Russell affirms that he who does not care
To read forever of the fickle Fair,
Must needs have gain'd his Coldness and his Sense
From cruel Maids and sad Experience.
Who strikes at Jackson (rhymes the Bard) reveals   5
The Stings of scorn'd Affection that he feels:
And Authors shew their Sorrow or Delight
In Prose and Verse when of the Sex they write.
Now if from Writings we their Loves may guess,
Jackson, I'll swear, a Harem must possess!   10

On a Modern Lothario

By some strange spell, upon the virgin heart
Lothario, or Griffin, plies his art;
A dozen faces must he daily see
Red with the blush of maiden modesty.
No bashful scruples can his zeal restrain;   5
Each hour he strives new conquests to attain;
Yet, one attain'd, for countless more he burns,
Surveys the field, and to the chase returns.
To his seductive lips the willing fair
Offer their own, and love eternal swear.   10
Now, from what cause hath all his magic grown?
Easy to find: He's kiss'd the —— ——!

The End of the Jackson War

Indulgent sir, pray spare an inch or two,
And print the carping critics' joint adieu.
So long it is since we began the fray
That readers swear we've filched your Log away!
Forgive, we beg, the sinners that presume   5
To fill with venomed verse such precious room.
Inflamed by war, and in a martial rage,
We held a while the centre of the stage
Till, blinded by each other's furious fire,
We battled on, forgetting to retire.   10
But fiercest feuds draw sometimes to their ends,
And ancient foemen live to meet as friends:
So do we now, conjoin'd in lasting peace,
Lay down our pens, and mutual slander cease.
What sound is this? 'Tis but a joyous yell   15
From thankful thousands, as we say farewell.

Gryphus in Asinum Mutatus;

or, How a Griffin Became an Ass

(After the Manner of Ovid's Metamorphoses)

NOTE: The Griffin, or Gryphon, is according to Smith's Classical Dictionary "a fabulous animal, with the body of a lion and the head and wings of an eagle, dwelling in the Rhipaean mountains, between the Hyperboreans and the one-eyed Arimaspians, and guarding the gold of the North. The Arimaspians mounted on horseback, and attempted to steal the gold, and hence arose the hostility between the horse and the Griffin. The belief in Griffins came from the East, where they are mentioned among the fabulous animals which guarded the gold of India."
Milton, in the second book of *Paradise Lost*, thus refers to the Griffin:

> As when a Griffin through the wilderness,
> With wingèd course, o'er hill and moory dale
> Pursues the Arimaspian, who by stealth
> Hath from his wakeful custody purloin'd
> His guarded gold.

We shall now see how this noble beast sunk to the Blarney, or North Carolinian species.

The frightful Griffins (so the legends tell)
Amid the far Rhipaean mountains dwell.
Perch'd on the peaks, eternal watch they hold,
And guard their hoards of Hyperborean gold.
In vain the one-eyed Arimaspian tries   5
With mounted might to seize the glitt'ring prize:
For Griffins' forms are made from monstrous things,
The lion's trunk; the eagle's head and wings:
What thief with hopes of vict'ry can oppose
In greedy conflict such ferocious foes?   10

Yet one there was who tho' of rugged race
Aspir'd to hold a softer, sweeter place.
With liquid glance the silly creature eyed
The lissome nymphs that rang'd the mountainside.
No thought of strength nor martial deeds he took,   15
And never strove but for a melting look.
His brothers fought, whilst he would lounge at ease
Amidst a group of sweet Oreades;
He train'd his cruel claws to pick the lyre,

210

And burnt with Eros', not with Ares' fire.   20
In his fair speech such smooth persuasion lay
That ev'ry doubt and fear he drove away.
Th' enchanted nymphs his hideous mien ignor'd,
And, mad with love, for one kind word implor'd.

'Twas on a cloudless day, that o'er the plain   25
Rov'd great Diana with her virgin train.
The arrows flew, the silver bow was bent;
And each fair nymph was on the sport intent.
Northward the pack pursu'd the fleeing deer;
The sounds of hunting reach'd the Griffin's ear: 30
Down on the plain he saw the eager chase
And mark'd the beauty of the goddess' face.
Long did he look, and with the looking came
A sudden thought he scarcely dar'd to name.
Why could not he, of ev'ry maid the pet,   35
Enmesh Diana's self in Cupid's net?
Not even she who loath'd the thought of love
Could long unkind to such a lover prove!
His warlike kin, who scorn'd his am'rous life,
Would scorn no more, once Dian were his wife!   40
With these wild dreams, and eager for the fair,
On his broad wings he rose into the air.
Round and above the huntress-queen he flew,
And with each look his foolish passion grew.
Now does he sink to seize the prey divine,   45
His eagle eyes with greedy lustre shine;
But as he nears, by some auspicious chance,
The goddess spies him in an upward glance.
The leering look his foul intent reveals,
And the chaste maid Olympian anger feels.   50
As once Actaeon suffer'd from her hate,
So now the Griffin meets his proper fate;
For as she glares, his shape begins to fade,
And strange new features are in him display'd.
The eagle's gleam hath vanish'd from his eyes,   55
And on his head two monstrous ears arise.
To shaggy grey is chang'd his tawny hide,
With hoofs for claws upon his feet supply'd.
The flapping wings from off his shoulders pass,
And down he falls, transmuted to an ass.   60

The Power of Wine: A Satire

Spes donare novas largus, amaraque
Curarum eluere efficax.
—Horace.

Hail! gift of Bacchus; red, delicious Wine,
To raise the soul, and ev'ry thought refine;
What blissful transports can thy pow'r impart,
And fill us with Anacreontic Art!
Unhappy man above the beast was plac'd; 5
Stript of his joys, and with mere Reason grac'd:
Sweet Wine alone his pleasures can restore;
Let him but quaff, and he's a beast once more!
Say, good Silenus, how the grape inspires
The bashful bard, and fans poetic fires. 10
The halting quill, inflam'd to vinous rage,
With alcoholic fancies fills the page;
Convivial poets have no need for sense,
If they be gen'rous to their audience!
What sapient speeches fill the tavern hall, 15
Where smoke and spirits rouse the minds of all!
Here church and state their proper functions learn,
And patriotic hearts their brightest burn.
Yon hoary sage, supported by the bar,
Shews how the Germans should conduct the war, 20
Whilst others near him teach with brains aglow
The only way to conquer Mexico.
Behold the singer, who with trembling notes
Upon his home and loving parents dotes.
Benignant Wine can all his sorrows quench, 25
And he forgets his home is the park bench.
Another glass from teasing mem'ry saves
Of grieving parents sent to early graves.
Drink deep, thou pauper, and forget with glee
The ailing wife, and starving family! 30
Forget their sorrows in the hour's delight;
To kill the reason is thy vested right.
Down with thee, base Reformer! to disturb
Our happy state, and all our spirits curb.
Tyrannic fool! seek not to interfere 35
With pers'nal liberty, and lawful cheer.
Reflect, ye fathers, how the fluid speeds

Your sturdy sons to bold and manly deeds.
The youthful Tom, with Dionysiac might,
Waylaid and robb'd an aged Jew last night, 40
Whilst reeling Dick, with Bacchic ire possess'd,
Shot down his best beloved friend in jest.
How great the pow'r of Wine to beautify
The manly form, and please th' exacting eye!
What graceful steps the polish'd drunkard knows! 45
How sweetly can he in the road repose!
The flaming face, the gently leering stare,
Bespatter'd clothing, and disorder'd hair,
The od'rous breath, and incoherent voice,
All charm our fancy, and increase our joys. 50
The sparkling Wine, display'd on gentle boards,
A just example to the poor affords:
What man so destitute he cannot gain
A blissful glass to elevate his brain?
Since pride, as proverbs say, precedes a fall, 55
In Wine we find the greatest boon of all.
By no man let its wonders be deny'd,
But here behold the deadliest foe to pride:
The needy Prince a whining beggar turns,
To ease the thirst that all his body burns. 60
Come, all ye Bacchanalian train, and sing
The bliss that Wine to fever'd brains can bring.
Rehearse the pleasing forms that oft appear
To him who knows the grape for many a year.
Observe, Sir Drunkard, in the growing gloom, 65
The nameless things that fill thy shadow'd room:
How bright those eyes with fearful lustre shine!
How smooth these coils about thy limbs entwine!
Rejoice, Silenus! for thy lengthen'd spree
Hath form'd these beauteous comrades just for thee! 70
Hosts of the Darkness, join our merry throng!
Satan, arise, and pass the cup along!
Laugh, brethren, laugh! for in each flowing bowl
Our band infernal gains a human soul.
Shriek with delight, and writhe in ghoulish mirth; 75
With ev'ry draught another sin hath birth;
Beat your black wings, and prance with cloven feet;
With hideous rites the friends of Chaos greet!
Minions of Hell, your fiendish tones combine,
And chant in chorus of the Pow'r of Wine! 80

213

The Simple Speller's Tale

(Translated into English)

When first among the amateurs I fell,
I blush'd in shame because I could not spell.
Tho' skill'd in numbers, and at ease in prose,
My letters I could never well dispose.
Thoughts came abundant, language was the same;   5
Yet none the less I scarce could spell my name!
The kindly printer (with an eye for trade)
A clumsy care for all my work display'd:
Indiff'rent as I was, I us'd his art
Till critics cry'd, "My printer should be shot!"   10
Thus boldly censur'd, I began to seek
A means to thwart the rude reviewers' clique:
My fever'd eye in rage I cast around,
When all at once the wish'd-for plan I found.
It happen'd on a summer's holiday,   15
That past a madhouse gate I took my way.
Within that bedlam was a sage confin'd,
Who had from too much study lost his mind.
Now strolling out, in watchful keeper's care,
With childish sounds the madman fill'd the air.   20
Still dreaming of his letter's days of yore,
His ravings on remember'd subjects bore:
Dim came the thoughts of what he us'd to teach,
And he began to curse our English speech.
"Aha!" quoth he, "the men that made our tongue   25
Were arrant rogues, and I shall have them hung.
For long-establish'd customs what care we?
Come, let us tear down etymology.
Let spelling fly, and naught but sound remain;
The world is mad, and I alone am sane!"   30
Thus rav'd the sage; inventing, as he walk'd,
A hundred ways to spell our words as talk'd.
He simplify'd until his fancy bred
A system quite as simple as his head.
In scholarship disastrous change he wrought,   35
And alter'd, as he went, for want of thought.
But I, attentive, heard with joyful ear
The wild distortions, and perversions queer.

Why could not I defend my ill-spell'd page
In progress' name, and with reformer's rage?   40
With hope renew'd, I hasten'd home to write,
And passing wondrous was my work that night;
For classic purity I sought no more,
But strove to make worse blunders than before.
O fickle fortune! In a week my name   45
From scholars' praise attain'd immortal fame,
Whilst other scribes with vague orthography
Seiz'd on the clever ruse, and copy'd me.
Today in ev'ry Skateville Amateur
Amorphous letters pass as language pure,   50
And when some pompous pedant dares to raise
A voice remonstrant 'gainst our foolish ways,
We never fail the apt retort to give,
But damn him as a blind CONSERVATIVE.

Yet why on us your angry hand or wrath use?   55
We do but ape Professor B———— M————!

[On Slang]

Slang is the life of speech, the critics say,
And stript of slang, our tongue would pass away.
If this be so, how well the amateur
Takes care that English ever shall endure!

Ye Ballade of Patrick von Flynn

Or, The Hibernio-German-American England-Hater

"Germanis ipsis Germaniores"

Attind ye all me wonthrous tale, an' Oi will tell to you,
Of how an honest Oirishman into a Proosian grew.
'Twas nigh on twinty year' ago Oi lift me native bog
To seek in these majestic States a place to earn me grog.
Sure, wurrk was aisy found fur me, fer Oi'm a clever man;   5
Oi earnt so much Oi soon cud buy me whiskey by the can.
Wid half a dozen other Micks, a merry, dhrinkin' crew,
Oi used to hang around shebeens an' currse Ould England blue!
Jist why Oi hate the Englishmen, Oi don't remimber quoite,
But Jimmy Dugan's grand-dad says they've ne'er used Oireland roight.   10

Sure all they iver done fer us was civilise our land,
An' we've no use fer sober laws, but all fer fraydom shtand!
How glad will be the fateful day whin England last draws breath,
An' good Ould Oireland shall be free—to dhrink hersilf ter death!
Now comes the cruel, cruel warr, wid Germans runnin' loose. 15
Sure, here's the toime to make a shtir, an' give some more abuse!
Us Oirish have no love fer Dutch, but side wid Germany
Because she hates Ould England most as fiendishly as we!
We know der Kaiser'd treat us wurrse thin England iver done,
But sure, if we used England roight we'd lose our sweetest fun! 20
There's somethin' in the Oirish hearrt thot niver bows to rules;
At jooty's call we tache our sons sedition in the schools.
Last night the Germans hereabouts all gather'd in a hall,
Wid German flags above the stage, an' Kaisers on the wall.
Oi don't know what they wanted, but so far as Oi could see, 25
They mere hoched der Kaiser and enjoin'd "noothrality".
They all denounc'd the President an' currs'd the Yankee laws
Fer bein' too un-noothral loike to hilp the German cause.
Thin they shtarted afther England, an' me hearrt bate quick wid proide
As about "foul British perfidy" they babbled an' they lied. 30
Oi thought we Oirish cud invint the rankest Billingsgate,
But wonthrous arre the fishy yarrns thim Dutchmen kin relate!
Me frinds what had come wid me was so mov'd wid martial ire,
They cluster'd round the rusty shtove to argue an' perspire.
Oi grew so pathriotic thot I tuk me hat in hand 35
An' shouted "Hoch der Kaiser, und das dear ould Vaterland!"
Bedad, we'll lick thim Britishers within a fortnight sharrp,
An' jine on one thriumphant flag the aigle an' the harrp!
Thin all began to fraternise; McNulty and von Bohn—
O'Donovan and Munsterberg, von Bulow an' Malone. 40
In Bacchic bonds our pact we seal'd; in harrmony serayne
We sang at once "Die Wacht am Rhein" an' "Wearin' av the Grane".
Ould von der Goltz pick'd up a brogue; in Dutch young Dooley sang;
Mid Prussian an' Hibernian shtrains the ancient rafthers rang!
Now all at once a magic seem'd to creep into me bones— 45
Me whiskey-mellow'd Oirish voice burst forth in Prussian tones!
Oi felt a sthrange sinsation, and in fancy seem'd to see
Instad of dear ould Shannon's banks, the gently rippling Spree—
No, not the Spree ye think Oi mane, but that which softly flows
Through glorious Deutschland's grassy leas, where warr an' kultur grows. 50
Ochone! Ochone! Where am Oi now? What conflict am Oi in?
Do Oi belong in Dublin town or back in Ould Berlin?

A week ago me son was borrn; his christ'nin's not far off;
Oi wonther will I call him Mike, or Friedrich Wilhelm Hoff?
'Tis hard indade fer one loike me to know jist where he's at;   55
Oi wonder if me name is Hans or if it shtill is Pat?
But let me bore ye all no more; the proper course is clear:
Oi'll slanther England all Oi dare, an' rayson niver hear.
A loyal "noothral" Oi shall be in all me wurrds an' worrk,
An' niver shpake excipt to praise the Dutchman an' the Turrk!   60

The Isaacsonio-Mortoniad

Composed in a Major Key

"Arma virosque cano."

Wake, Heav'nly Muse! to hear the tuneless yell
Of Infidelity and Israel:
Mortonian mists th' embattled field befog,
Whilst Carlo barks from shelt'ring synagogue.
Beware, *Conservative,* the hostile two;   5
The learned atheist and the vengeful Jew.
With frothing mouth and fact-destroying lance,
Observe the radicals in pomp advance.
Their thoughts, their speech, and e'en their press are free
(For folly oft appears as liberty).   10
With Whitman's word their soaring sails they fire,
And cast upon the foe their native mire.
Impetuous Isaacson, in roaring rage,
Mixes the marks of ev'ry previous age.
The quaint Dan Chaucer and the good Queen Bess,   15
To his blind hate an equal age confess,
While heedless Raleigh nods to Handel's chords,
As Lovelace, from his prison-cell, applauds;
Melodious Herrick's ghost, with boundless scope,
Lives on and wears the periwig of Pope.   20
Nurs'd thus in Chaos, it were vain to dream
That captious Charles could pen a scholar's theme;
His sneering "Honi soit qui mal y pense"
He fathers on the cynic court of France!
Yet let us not at his crude scribbling smile,   25
When he but boasts of his unfashion'd style;
He laughs at learning, and leads on the day

217

When scholarship will earn the name of play!
Drunk with his freedom, worldly he indites,
And now "abeisance" for "obeisance" writes!   30
Since art and letters have no pow'r to please,
In politics his nerves he seeks to ease:
Here is his Oriental fancy daz'd,
With din a thousand demagogues have rais'd.
Amid the noise the loudest shrieks he heeds,   35
And gobbles, hook and line, the rabble's creeds.
"All men are equal! Let us have no kings!"
(How tritely thus the well-worn sentence rings.)
"All races are alike! Despite their hues
Raise hook-nos'd octaroons and woolly Jews!   40
Let Afric ape with Aryan combine,
And sink the white man in a mongrel line!"
Thus the mad Isaacson, whose rabid pace
Would plunge a mighty nation in disgrace.
His empty freedom and his negro lore   45
He seeks to lay at fair Columbia's door;
But let him not our dignity degrade:
Columbia was by sturdy Saxons made!
Whilst the brave Semite loud of freedom cants,
Against this freedom he, forgetful, rants: 50
Eternal licence for himself he pleads,
Yet seeks restraint for his opponents' deeds;
With the same force that at oppression rails,
He'd bar *The Jeffersonian* from the mails!
When outrag'd Georgia from the law breaks free,   55
And hangs some murd'rer from a friendly tree,
Should not our hero with his praises fill
The echoing air, and sing the people's will?
Blush, sweet Consistency! Judaea's child,
With hot hysteria, waxes monstrous wild;   60
Apes Don Quixote with his fuming mind,
Whilst Goodwin, like poor Sancho, rides behind.
One vile assassin and his proper fate,
To Isaacson can damn a sovereign state!
But tho' with fury fill'd, his valour shrinks,   65
When on the sterner side of life he thinks.
However natural, whate'er their cause,
With sobbing sigh he mourns the wicked wars.
Careless of honour, void of saving sense,

He begs the land to banish its defence: 70
Like Christian saint to turn the other cheek,
And injuries from bolder neighbours seek.
Too proud to fight, he hopes for war to cease,
And welcomes insult as the price of peace!
From peace to luxury the step is slight,   75
And Venus reigns when Mars withdraws his might.
Thus the soft Isaacson, to war oppos'd,
Finds wondrous charms in Paphian lines disclos'd;
Tho' duly shock'd by riotous Vanbrugh,
He reads the artful Whitman thro' and thro';   80
And when the sober try his taste to cure,
He shouts that vice, if unasham'd, is pure!
When crafty Whitman admiration draws
With loftier flights, and rugged, conscious flaws,
The willing Charles dilates his eager throat,   85
And swallows at a gulp each faulty note:
He thrives on discord, and the witless lay
To him grows great if form be cast away.
Thus did old Walt the force of folly see,
And gilded brazen trash with novelty!   90
So vanish, Isaacson! Declaim no more,
But turn thy fancy to rabbinic lore.
Sound now the trumpets, and awake the drums,
For matchless Morton in his chariot comes!
The Dean of Darkness, wrecker of the church,   95
Crowing with scorn from his exalted perch!
Great Antichrist! The friend of Reason's rule,
Who looks for reason in the churlish fool;
Who fondly dreams a rabble can be sway'd
By fine abstractions saints have disobey'd!   100
But search not Morton for the vulgar fault,
Nor scan his page for awkward phrase or halt:
Whate'er your talent, and howe'er you feel,
He forms a foeman worthy of your steel.
His steps, tho' wild, a subtle charm attends,   105
And art to him unnumber'd graces lends.
When he insults, his polish soothes the pain,
And victims, undisturb'd, as friends remain.
Thus privileged, great Morton's force is spent
On those who favour, while they still dissent.   110
He lauds the negro, and the negro shines

As long as we sit rapt o'er Morton's lines;
When the stern rays of Truth our minds awake,
We weep that such a sage should e'er mistake.
So venerated Morton rules the skies,   115
And pleases when he means to patronise!
Shall we complain when such a pen appears
To shake our doctrines or excite our fears?
Shall Morton's thunder rouse vindictive ire,
Or shall we smile, uninjur'd, and admire?   120
Thus from the window, undisturb'd and warm,
We safely view the grandeur of the storm:
The raging blast, sent earthward to destroy,
Is watch'd and study'd with artistic joy.
Loud-thund'ring Morton, shaking land and sea,   125
Parts Socialism from raging anarchy.
In dumb discretion we his word admit;
One's but the brink; the other is the pit!
If such dark regions tyranny could own,
Well might they seat King Morton on their throne!   130
And now farewell! With unconfounded mien
We watch the mighty atheist quit the scene.
Soon will his shafts to other targets fly,
As some evangelist attracts his eye.
Tho' like a bull at us he plunges one day,   135
Tomorrow he'll be goring Billy Sunday!

Unda; or, The Bride of the Sea

A Dull, Dark, Drear, Dactylic Delirium in Sixteen Silly, Senseless,
Sickly Stanzas

Respectfully Dedicated with Permission to MAURICE WINTER MOE, Esq.

> "Ego, canis, lunam cano."
> —Maevius Bavianus.

Black loom the crags of the uplands behind me;
Dark are the sands of the far-stretching shore.
Dim are the pathways and rocks that remind me
Sadly of years in the lost nevermore.

Soft laps the ocean on wave-polish'd boulder;   5
Sweet is the sound and familiar to me.

220

Here, with her head gently bent on my shoulder,
Walk'd I with Unda, the Bride of the Sea.

Bright was the morn of my youth when I met her,
Sweet as the breeze that blew in o'er the brine.   10
Swift was I captur'd in Love's strongest fetter,
Glad to be hers, and she glad to be mine.

Never a question ask'd I whence she wander'd,
Never a question ask'd she of my birth:
Happy as children, we thought not nor ponder'd,   15
Glad with the bounty of ocean and earth.

Once when the moonlight play'd soft 'mid the billows,
High on the cliff o'er the waters we stood.
Bound was her hair with a garland of willows,
Pluck'd by the fount in the bird-haunted wood.   20

Strangely she gaz'd on the surges beneath her,
Charm'd by the sound, or entranc'd by the light.
Then did the waves a wild aspect bequeath her,
Stern as the ocean and weird as the night.

Coldly she left me, astonish'd and weeping,   25
Standing alone 'mid the regions she bless'd:
Down, ever downward, half gliding, half creeping,
Stole the sweet Unda in oceanward quest.

Calm grew the sea, and tumultuous beating
Turn'd to a ripple, as Unda the fair   30
Trod the wet sands in affectionate greeting,
Beckon'd to me, and no longer was there!

Long did I pace by the banks where she vanish'd:
High climb'd the moon, and descended again.
Grey broke the dawn till the sad night was banish'd,   35
Still ach'd my soul with its infinite pain.

All the wide world have I search'd for my darling,
Scour'd the far deserts and sail'd distant seas.
Once on the wave while the tempest was snarling,
Flash'd a fair face that brought quiet and ease.   40

Ever in restlessness onward I stumble,
Seeking and pining, scarce heeding my way.

Now have I stray'd where the wide waters rumble,
Back to the scene of the lost yesterday.

Lo! the red moon from the ocean's low hazes   45
Rises in ominous grandeur to view.
Strange is its face as my tortur'd eye gazes
O'er the vast reaches of sparkle and blue.

Straight from the moon to the shore where I'm sighing
Grows a bright bridge, made of wavelets and beams.   50
Frail may it be, yet how simple the trying;
Wand'ring from earth to the orb of sweet dreams.

What is yon face in the moonlight appearing;
Have I at last found the maiden that fled?
Out on the beam-bridge my footsteps are nearing   55
Her whose sweet beckoning hastens my tread.

Currents surround me, and drowsily swaying,
Far on the moon-path I seek the sweet face.
Eagerly hasting, half panting, half praying,
Forward I reach for the vision of grace.   60

Murmuring waters about me are closing,
Soft the sweet vision advances to me:
Done are my trials; my heart is reposing
Safe with my Unda, the Bride of the Sea.

Epilogue

As the rash fool, a prey of Unda's art,   65
Drowns thro' the passion of his fever'd heart,
So are our youth, inflam'd by tempters fair,
Bereft of reason and the manly air.
How sad the sight of Strephon's virile grace
Turn'd to confusion at his Chloë's face,   70
And e'er Pelides, dear to Grecian eyes,
Sulking for loss of his thrice-cherish'd prize.
Brothers, attend! If cares too sharply vex,
Gain rest by shunning the destructive sex!

[On "Unda; or, The Bride of the Sea"]

Gentle Maurice, if thy longing be sated,
If my sad stanzas appeal to thy taste,

Let me at once as a poet be rated:
Then to heroics again I may haste.

Gems from *In a Minor Key*

(With Remarks by *The Conservative*)

"—mentally unpalatable, even as are the words of George Sylvester Vierick
to the great (no kidding) English People."
                    W. H. Goodwin.

No kidding, Goodwin, you with wisdom say
That England likes not George Sylvester's way:
The honest truth poor Vierick ne'er could speak,
And Britons hate a liar and a sneak!

"—Germans, and all *persecuted* peoples."
                    Charles D. Isaacson.

Heav'n help the Prussian, fragile and oppress'd,   5
Whose injur'd feelings lacerate his breast.
O Cruel World! this peaceful creature spare,
That he may ravage land, and sea, and air!

"We will not fight. We will not march to war."
                    Charles D. Isaacson.

Horatius at the bridge intrepid stands,
A branch of olive in his gentle hands.   10
Th' Etruscan host draws near, and with *pride*
The manly hero bows and steps aside!

The State of Poetry

"Non bene junctarum discordia semina rerum."
                    —Ovid.

Attend, ye modern bards, who dimly shine
As worthy scions of Mac Flecknoe's line!
Tho' scarce on Heliconian heights to gleam,
To one still clumsier ye supply a theme:
As meagre stalk from sterile garden climbs,   5
So springs my trash from your Boeotian rhymes.
In state establish'd on the Dunce's throne,
Hear infant Codrus with the colic moan.
His dreary wail no hint of sense conveys,

But critics hide their ignorance in praise.   10
Hard by the King, the pale-fac'd Raucus stands,
A ream of witless ballads in his hands.
Metre forgot, he screams his sickly song
In quatrains part too short and part too long.
But ere he stops, Agrestis fills the air   15
With dainty accents, and illusions rare.
How might we praise the lines so soft and sweet,
Were they not lame in their poetic feet!
Just as the reader's heart bursts into flame,
The fire is quenched by rhyming "gain" with "name",   20
And ecstasy becomes no easy task
When fields of "grass" in Sol's bright radiance "bask"!
To Durus now our keen attention turns,
Whose rugged page with manly passion burns.
Would that his apt expressions did not lie   25
Where syllable and tone must go awry;
A lesser sentiment we needs must feel
If "re-al" love be mispronounced as "reel";
While far from his loose line we long to roam,
When stately "po-em" masquerades as "pome"!   30
Next Hodiernus with his lyre appears,
And glads the modern critic's Midas-ears.
Upon his shelves neglected classics rest,
Whilst he reads Kipling, and proclaims him best.
The well-turn'd verse, the choice, harmonious phrase,   35
Are foreign to his new, corrupted ways.
Form is an error, elegance a crime,
To him who courts the plaudits of the time.
Ablest is he who can in rhyming reach
The lofty coarseness of a Cockney's speech.   40
No name we give to yon degen'rate swine
That apes the filthy Whitman's vulgar line.
The stamm'ring sound, the tainted atmosphere,
The blank confusion, and the prospect drear,
So much repel the mind of decent grade,   45
That author's lost 'mid Chaos he hath made!
Mark now Mundanus, who with sordid mind
Dwells on our joys and ills of meaner kind.
For him no grassy slopes of Tempe wait,
Nor does his Muse Arcadian bliss relate: 50
Strephon and Chloë, all the splendid train,

Excite his wrath, and summon his disdain.
Saturnian days no thought of his engage,
But all the world's to him an Iron Age.
His earthy fancy never mounts the sky, 55
But draws its source from kennel, barn, and sty.
No sylvan scenes, nor reed-fring'd brooks in June,
But mills, and mines, and shops inspire his tune.
Almighty Dulness! see the empire rise,
The pure to stain, the strong to paralyse: 60
Destructive Commerce! thy all-blighting pow'rs
Pollute our lines, and crush Thought's fairest flow'rs.
Can Art survive in a degraded age
When none but boors and cynics hold the stage?
When verse ideal brings the vulgar smile, 65
And honest words are slighted for the vile?
He who would light again the poet's fire
Must straight to some secluded spot retire;
Where, pond'ring on the happier days of yore,
His fancy may the ancient times restore; 70
Where, as of old, kind Nature's voice is heard,
To raise the mind, and prompt the written word.
There may we find the Golden Age anew,
Where thoughts are simple, and our dreamings true;
In such blest scenes we may rehearse again 75
The classic grandeur of Eliza's reign,
In Shakespeare's fashion move the anxious heart,
Or charm the woodland nymphs with Jonson's art.
But let me cease! No such expanding hope
Can stir my pencil from the style of Pope; 80
The sounding line, which neither breaks nor halts,
Is needful to conceal my graver faults!

The Magazine Poet

The modern bard restrains poetic rage,
To fit his couplets to a quarter-page.
Who now regards his skill, or taste, or strength,
When verse is writ and printed for its length?
His soaring sentiment he needs must pinch, 5
And sing his Amaryllis by the inch.
The art is easy when the artist tries
Not for Parnassus, but alone for size.
He wastes no care on polish, wit, or grace,

Who rhymes to fill an idle bit of space.   10
None heeds his worth; his listless lines are bought
Because some favour'd story is too short.
No critic's sneer his honest ire incites,
For none, forsooth, peruses what he writes!

My Lost Love

Respectfully Dedicated to Maurice Winter Moe, Esq., With Compliments of
the Author.

I.
When the evening shadows come
Then my fancies they do roam
Round the dear old rustic cottage by the lane,
Where in days that are no more
Liv'd the maid I did adore,   5
Liv'd my own beloved sweetheart, darling Jane!

(Chorus)
O my dearest, sweetest pride,
Thou couldst never be my bride,
For the angels snatch'd you up one summer day;
Yet my heart is ever true,   10
And I love you yes I do,
And I'll mourn for you until I pine away!
I—pine—a—way— (by 1st Tenor).

II.
'Twas a twilight hour divine
When you promis'd to be mine,   15
And above our heads the little birds did sing;
But they never sing no more
As in happy days before,
For them dear old wedding bells did never ring!

III.
It is now all horrid gloom   20
Where the pretty flow'rs did bloom,
And my sweetest little blossom of them all
Was too quickly call'd above
Nevermore to be my love,
Tho' I long for her each day as leaves do fall!   25

IV.
As my grief is getting worse
I express my woes in verse,
With the hope that many more may read and see;
For I'm lonely all the time,
And when you have read my rhyme,   30
In my mis'ry I will sure have companee!
Have—com—pa—nee— (by 2nd Bass).

The Beauties of Peace

An Epistle to Henry F. Thomas, Esq., Author of "A Prayer for Peace and
Justice" in The Evening News for June 23, 1916.

"Iniquissimam pacem justissimo bello antefero."

Harmonious THOMAS, whose pacific pen
Stabs with reproach a world of wicked men;
Whose patriot soul a Nation's honour spurns,
And for mankind in Quaker passion burns:
Thy Muse, high soaring on her dove-like wings,   5
In dulcet strain sweet Ignominy sings!
With what bold zeal thy soft-spun rhymes relate
The virtues of the unresisting State!
How thrills the heart to hear thy voice decry
The impious fools that for their country die!   10
Abstain, thrice-sinful hand! who rashly dare
Defend your homes, or for defence prepare:
'Tis wrong, I vow, to curb the foeman's rage,
When Arbitration rules th' enlighten'd age!
Let blood-mad Villa drench the Texan plain;   15
Let sly Carranza ev'ry right profane;
To savage hordes a cordial hand extend,
And greet th' invader as a welcome friend:
What tho' he slew your brothers yesternight?
We must be pious—and 'tis wrong to fight!   20
While friends and kinsmen perish in the strife,
'Tis ours to arbitrate them back to life!
Should some rude enemy our hand refuse,
And scorning Peace, continued warfare choose,
Our duty's plain; surrender must ensue;   25
For tho' he sin, we'll not be sinful, too!
Rejoice, ye Cherubim of realms above!

Strike your blest lyres, and chant fraternal love!
Tho' foes engulf, and tyrant hands enslave,
We shun at least a hero's shameful grave;   30
Kind Heav'n preserve our soft, submissive race
From fearless manhood—the supreme disgrace!
As rough, unrighteous creatures boldly fall
In martial order at their country's call,
With noisy rifles arm'd, to march away   35
And bear our Starry Banner to the fray;
The peaceful tear-drop trickles in its course,
Distress'd that men should thus descend to force!
Man's Brotherhood! O glorious tie to own,
That binds us to the one-arm'd Obregon;   40
To mongrel Villa, and the whisker'd lie
Who prates of laws, which all his horde defy:
With friends like these, 'twere harsh and overnice
To balk at petty human sacrifice!
How crude and brutal was the ancient creed   45
That call'd for satisfaction, deed for deed!
Revenge most horrid! 'Twas distressing—quite—
And, worst of all, 'twas monstrous impolite!
But thou, wise doubting THOMAS, wouldst destroy
Th' unpolish'd manners that our sense annoy;   50
The dreadful code at which we wince and faint;
The painful pride that shocks the sinless saint;
At thy command we turn the other cheek,
And injuries from bolder neighbours seek:
Too proud to fight, we pray for war to cease,   55
And welcome insult as the price of peace.
Descend! ye Fairies of Titania's train,
To smile on Ford's and Bryan's spotless reign;
Prattle with glee, ye happy infant throng,
For to your world great THOMAS' words belong.   60
Let us be joyful, and 'mid flow'rs of June
In grateful groves our peaceful pipes entune:
Secure are we, for War's distracting roar
Could ne'er resound on Seekonk's park-lin'd shore!
To thee, enlight'ning THOMAS, we convey   65
The cultur'd greeting of a cultur'd day.
Thy matchless verse War's emptiness reveals,
And fans the fire each gentle patriot feels;
Exalts high Reason to her proper throne,

And leads us on to glories yet unknown: 70
With lofty spirit and discerning mind,
Thou know'st all things—excepting humankind!

Epitaph on yͤ Letterr Rrr. . . . . . .

Dearr readerr, pause—and shed a tearr,
Forr one that ly'th interred herrre.
Poorr Masterr Rrr scant welcome found
On sterrn New-England's rocky ground;
Sorre spurrn'd on Earrth, and torrn with woes,
In burial soon he gain'd repose.
Today we hearr the roll no more,
Save that of ocean on the shorre!

The Dead Bookworm

Good Morning, Winewell! Heard the news?
(Have a cigar—the sort I use!)
Yes—it's old Bookworm—queerish chap—
He's dropped off for his final nap!
I hadn't seen him for a year—   5
But then, you know, he was *so* queer!
A Temperance crank—confounded ass!
He frown'd upon the social glass.
And such a bore! 'Twas scarcely strange
He rather dropped out of our range.   10
Books—Books—and Books—week in, week out!
He'd nothing else to talk about.
They sometimes said his health had failed him—
I thought 'twas laziness that ailed him!
He wrote—they tell me—quite a bit;   15
I knew he had a caustic wit,
But hardly thought 'twould ever do
For literary stuff—did you?
I guess the stuff was pretty raw—
'Twas in no books I ever saw!   20
Remember when he was a lad?
A queerer chum we never had!
He'd not a thought akin to ours—
But shewed off his precocious powers.
I always said—though as a friend—   25
He'd some day come to a bad end!

229

That fellow never seemed to thrive—
I guess he was but half alive.
Now that he's gone, I wish I might
Not thus have let him drop from sight—   30
But pshaw! he cared for reading only,
And couldn't have been very lonely!
Well, now it's over! (Hello, Jack!
Enjoy your trip? I'm glad you're back!)
Yes—Bookworm's dead—what's that? Go slow!   35
Thought he was dead a year ago?
No—it just happened. (Have a match?
These lucifers *are* hard to scratch!)
I hate a death! And—Oh, the deuce!
That fellow always was no use!   40
Seen my new racer? It's a winner!
I'm going home to dress for dinner!

Ad Balneum

Hail! little sea, in whose bright waters shine
The myriad graces of the boundless brine;
Whose shallow calms and rippling surges bear
Th' eternal sway of Neptune's curule chair:
Thy kindly pow'r a grateful race confess,   5
And count thy virtues next to godliness;
Blest be thy waves, by no rude breezes blown,
To Britons sacred, and to Jews unknown!
How oft have I, in childhood's blissful day,
Drawn o'er thy face my tiny fleets at play!   10
See bold Ulysses plough the Grecian main,
And Nelson at Trafalgar die again;
See Pompey's triremes break the corsair's pride,
And Northern Vikings brave the Arctic tide.
Fancy can trace within thy meagre bound   15
The storied deep, that girds our planet round!
What noble mem'ries thy white banks awake
Of Roman might that made creation quake!
Thy marble ancestors, by Tiber's stream
In tribute to Imperial bounty gleam: 20
Where'er a Caesar's wisdom rul'd the land,
In east or west, the stately thermae stand!
Say, lucid lake, what sylphs and fairies dwell
Beneath the crystal magic of thy spell?

Art as a fount in blest Arcadian mead   25
Where naiad throngs the sylvan syrinx heed,
Or dost thou bow to Triton's wider rule,
And hold an ocean in thy placid pool?
Do little nereids, suited to thy size,
(Too small to glimpse with our crude mortal eyes)   30
Sport thro' thy waves, and ev'ry crest adorn,
Upon the backs of tiny dolphins borne?
Imagination fain would find in thee
The charm, and lure, and glory of the sea!
How swells thy breast when on thy porcelain bed   35
Descending cloudbursts their mad fury shed!
How whirls thy tide when thro' thy punctur'd floor
The angry waters in a maelstrom pour!
Then dost thou lie—a dry, deserted thing
For Gods to mourn, and third-rate bards to sing!   40

[On Kelso the Poet]

Poor Kelso the poet, defending his verse,
Forbids us to laugh, since we're like to write worse.
Sure, 'tis horribly rough, and unmanly as well,
To sneer at a bard whom you cannot excel!
But I'm thinking, myself, that although I am told   5
That my rhyming is bad, and my manner be old,
It would hardly be difficult, dull tho' I be,
To prove I'm not quite such a bungler as he.
So in spite of his warning, I must, for a while,
Give vent to my feelings by cracking a smile!   10

Futurist Art

The skill'd Apelles, by his Prince decreed
To paint with living line the panting steed,
Employ'd in vain each trick and study'd grace,
The likeness of the charger's foam to trace.
At length, in pique, his dripping brush he flung   5
Against the canvas horse before him hung—
When lo! by chance there spatter'd o'er each part
The painted lather that defy'd his art!
Thus the wild cubists of a later age
With freakish toil their fancies seek to cage,   10
Tho' their poor daubings all would nobler be
Should they splash paint as aimlessly as he!

The Nymph's Reply to the Modern Business Man

With Apologies to W. Raleigh, Esq. See *Tryout* for October, 1916.

If all the world and love were young,
And I had ne'er before been "stung",
I might enough a dullard prove
To live with thee and be thy love.

But promis'd "autos", Love's rewards,   5
Turn out too often to be Fords;
And tho' you vaunt your splendid yacht—
'Tis but a rowboat, like as not!

Your silks and sapphires rouse my heart,
But I can penetrate your art—   10
My seventh husband fool'd my taste
With shoddy silks and stones of paste!

I like your talk of home and touring;
They savour of a love enduring;
But others have said things like that—   15
And led me to a Harlem flat!

So, dear, tho' were your pledges true
I should delight to dwell with you;
I still must as a widow rove,
Nor live with thee, nor be thy love!   20

The Poet of Passion

Pray observe the soft poet with amorous quill
    Waste full half of a sheet on vague inspiration.
Do not fancy him drunk or imagine him ill
    If he wails by the hour of his heart's desolation:
        'Tis but part of his trade   5
        To go mad o'er a maid
On whose beautiful face his eyes ne'er hath laid—
    And the fond ardent passion that loudly resounds
    May tomorrow in Grub Street bring two or three pounds!

On the Death of a Rhyming Critic

My Muse attempts a doleful rune:
Poor MACER Sunday afternoon
Resign'd the cares of earthly strife,
And reach'd his last eternal life!
A curious fellow in his time, 5
Fond of old books and prone to rhyme—
A scribbling pedant, of the sort
That scorn the age, and write for sport.
A little wit he sometimes had,
But half of what he wrote was bad; 10
In metre he was very fair;
Of rhetoric he had his share—
But of the past so much he'd prate,
That he was always out of date!
He lean'd to mythologic matters, 15
And sang of Gods and Nymphs and Satyrs,
Till so unvary'd grew his art,
You could not tell his works apart!
The modern ear he'd often pain
With rantings in heroic strain: 20
And when the town would call them witty,
'Twas mostly out of friendly pity.
Tho' much by ancient notions marr'd,
He was a fairly clever bard;
His numbers smooth enough would roll, 25
But after all—he had no soul!
His pen was ever keen to fight
For manly virtue and the right—
But somehow he was rather weak;
Instead of slang he quoted Greek! 30
He serv'd his purpose—to correct
Each rising poet's crude defect,
And yet—he ne'er made life the sweeter,
For all he knew was rhyme and metre.
His even verses will be miss'd— 35
Tho' he was quite an egotist!
Of all his views I can't approve,
But still, I mourn with tears of love.
My grief is deep—since half past three
I've worked upon an elegy, 40
Yet cannot seem to get it done

233

In time to reach the *Morning Sun!*
The polish must my care engage,
For I am promis'd the first page!
Yes, he is gone! I feel the sorrow—   45
The fun'ral will be held tomorrow—
My broadcloth suit I'm having press'd
To go and see him laid to rest.
God speed his soul! I trust he'll rove
In peace 'mid Seraphim above—   50
And by the way, tho' I've been told
He had but little wealth in gold,
I wonder what his heirs will do
With all his books—they were not few!
In truth, I know of two or three   55
That could be nobly us'd by me!
So many strugglers he befriended,
That rougher bards on him depended:
His death will still more pens than his—
I wonder where the fellow is!   60
He's in a better land—or worse—
(I wonder who'll revise my verse?)
He never left a stanza slack—
But I could hardly wish him back.
Tears for his loss do freely flow—   65
Yet after all, 'tis better so!

To the Incomparable Clorinda

You ask for verse—yet who cou'd justly write
When dazzled by your beauty's radiant light?
What line so smooth, but 'twou'd seem harsh and weak
Beside the velvet softness of your cheek?
My ill-scrawl'd words can win no greater praise   5
Than having drawn the glory of your gaze;
And much I fear, 'twill seem too rash in me
To rise from mere Olympian themes to thee!
                (Very confidential P.S.)
With this, Clorinda, must thou rest content:
'Twou'd be no better, *even if 'twere meant!*   10

To Saccharissa, Fairest of Her Sex

When Nature fix'd the lamps of space
    To gild the plain and light the blue,
She made three orbs of diff'ring grace—
    The silver Moon, the Sun, and You.

The lesser two she plac'd aloft   5
    As Guardians of the Night and Day;
But You she left, whose magick soft
    Rules *both* with sweet resistless sway!

To Rhodoclia—Peerless among Maidens

Were the blue of the sea and the blue of the skies
Half as sweet and as pure as the blue of your eyes;
Were the scent of the fields, and the flow'r-laden air
Half as potent and rich as your dear golden hair

         { nut-brown
          raven
          silver
         crimson }

Then the world were an Heaven, and mine were the bliss   5
To write verses forever as freely as this!

To Belinda, Favourite of the Graces

Nymph, whose glance demure and kind
    Turns the darkest hour to joy;
In whose witching face are join'd
    Venus and the Paphian Boy;
Take this tribute, tho' my hand   5
    Ne'er could pen a tribute meet.
Labour done at thy command,
    Howe'er fruitless, still is sweet!

To Heliodora—Sister of Cytheraea

When Paris made his fateful choice
    According to his duty,
To Venus with unfalt'ring voice
    He gave the prize of beauty;
Her godlike sisters, hard to please,   5
Grew piqued, and turn'd his enemies.

* * *

Now were that prize bestow'd today
    Poor Paris needs must tremble;
For greater ills wou'd haunt his way,
    Cou'd he not well dissemble: 10
For *ev'ry* god his foe wou'd be,
Since Beauty's prize belongs to *Thee!*

To Mistress Sophia Simple, Queen of the Cinema

Before our sight your mobile face
    Depicts your joys or woes distracting;
We marvel at your winsome grace—
    And wish you'd learn the art of acting!

Your eyes, we vow, surpass the stars;   5
    Your mouth is like the bow of Cupid;
Your rose-ting'd cheeks no wrinkle mars—
    Yet why are you so sweetly stupid?

The hero views you with delight,
    To win your hand forever working;   10
We pity him—the witless wight—
    To fall a victim to your smirking!

And yet, why should we wail in rhyme
    Because so crudely you dissemble?
We can't expect, for one small dime,   15
    To see a Woffington or Kemble!

The Introduction

To Maurice Winter Moe, Esq.

Wise Doctor Moe prescribeth
    That I should change my Rhyming;
So let him, pray, peruse each Lay,
    None with the Other chiming.

As for my lov'd Heroicks,   5
    Destroy 'em if you can, Sir!
These silly Strains and wild Refrains
    Are but your Victim's Answer.

My Wit is not so polish'd
    That I can suit all Measures; 10
What I have wrought hath less of Thought
    Than idle rhythmic Pleasures.

Yon roughly chisell'd Stanzas,
    Compos'd thro' your Advices,
Court not the Heart nor follow Art, 15
    But seek Commercial Prices.

But who can capture Favour
    With Ballades he despiseth?
'Tis true I ape each Poet's Shape,
    Yet naught but Trash ariseth. 20

Now close to Precept have I
    Adher'd to well-worn Matter;
Whene'er I write I seek the Trite,
    And sing but idle Chatter.

But since you say the Papers 25
    Wish most for common Musing,
Tho' Classics quake my Lyre I take,
    Each modern Measure using!

Epilogue

Whene'er distracted by a light Refrain,
I needs must catch my old Heroick Strain. 30
As Charles' Return chang'd Gloom to gay Relief,
So shall I soothe my modern metric Grief;
And like a Patient, dos'd with Castor-Oil,
Who seeks with later Sweets the Taste to foil,
Straightway must I my outrag'd Muse appease, 35
And in Heroicks take my hard-earn'd Ease!

Grace

With Unstinted Apologies to the Author of "Ruth"

In the dim light of the unrustled grove,
    Amidst the silence of approaching night,
I saw thee standing, as thro' boughs above
    Filter'd the pencils of the dying light.

Grace! I had thought thou wert by far too proud,   5
    Too harden'd to the world and all its pain,
To pause so wistfully, with fair head bow'd,
    Forgetting all thy coldness and disdain.

But in that instant all my doubts and fears
    Were swept away as on the evening breeze,   10
When I beheld thee, not indeed in tears,
    But rack'd and shaken with a mighty *sneeze!*

To Col. Linkaby Didd:

Guardian of Democracy

While struggling Factions press their rival claims,
And Envy's tongue our CAESAR'S rule defames;
Whilst lab'ring Virtue pants beneath the weight
Of savage greed, and a divided state,
High o'er the servile crowd see DIDD arise,   5
To summon exil'd Justice from the skies!
All Hail, Illustrious DIDD! whose honest quill
Hath serv'd us long, and ably serves us still;
Whose lofty mind, from fear and folly free,
Shews us the path to Peace and Liberty: 10
'Tis thine to guide us thro' the fev'rish fight,
And lead us to O'SHAUNESSY and Right!
Freemen, behold! Our civil fabric stands
The bright ideal of the neighb'ring lands;
Firm at the head Imperial CAESAR holds   15
Enlighten'd pow'r, and all his people moulds;
Obedient Senates bless the learned reign,
And yield their judgment to their monarch's brain:
The honest commons, aw'd at peril's brink,
Waive with delight the tedious right to think!   20
Democracy! thou guardian of the just,
That bend'st the stubborn thinker to the dust;
Thou sweet contemner of the vengeful fray
Which but for thee will sweep the Goth away!
Hail to thy courage, CAESAR, who wouldst dare   25
The guns to muzzle, and the foe to spare:
Thy theoretic will bids hatred cease,
And without Victory would bring us Peace!
Peace! Lovely Peace! Best blessing to befall!

(I wonder why we went to war at all?)   30
What tho' the Cain-mark'd Goth unpunish'd go
If we but banish warfare's wicked woe?
Let bygones rest—the past is thro' and done—
Brothers, embrace the dear repentant Hun!
But whilst our fluent CAESAR types his notes,   35
'Tis ours to aid his strategy with votes;
Subjects, attend! A mighty monarch pleads
Your suffrage to endorse his regal deeds:
Disloyal he who ventures to debate
A sov'reign's course—for CAESAR IS THE STATE!   40
CAESAR, whose soul with equal fire abhors
Ignoble conflict, and mixt metaphors!
Behold O'SHAUNESSY, in pomp array'd,
Intent to bear his royal master aid:
The people's champion and the Kingdom's pride,   45
With whom all Right and Wisdom are ally'd.
'Tis he that sav'd our state when warfare's cloud
Hung in the sky, and ev'ry head was bow'd:
His was the hand that gave our legions gold—
(At least, by him the legend thus is told—)   50
And his the strength that from the money'd clan
Seiz'd ill-got wealth to feed the working-man.
Thrice Virtuous *George*, who hath the blended good
Of *Fox,* the *Gracchi, Cade,* and *Robin Hood!*
Such is the man our loyal plebs would send   55
To join the Conscript Fathers as their friend;
A sage whose worth a mighty throng attest—
By *Tammany* enshrin'd among the best!
Yet there is one (I blush with decent shame
To utter so Republican a name)   60
Who dares, like *Cato,* ev'ry King defy,
And seek the Freedom of an age gone by:
How canst thou, COLT, so rashly mock at Fate,
And vie with CAESAR'S chosen candidate?
COLT! Who can name the dark unnumber'd crimes   65
Thou hast inflicted on the dismal times?
Was it not thou whose false and cruel lips
Deny'd the Goth a payment for his ships?
Fie, hateful traitor; modern Catiline!
A people's wrath, and Kaiser's curse, are thine!   70
O Foe to Labour, whose inhuman mood

Oppos'd the saintly railway brotherhood;
Couldst thou not hear a suff'ring people's plea,
Nor spoil fair Blackmail of her sanctity?
When CAESAR, last in arms, to battle flew,   75
Wert thou to him and to his minions true?
Stand forth, betrayer, while thy censures ring—
Thou held'st thy country greater than thy King!
These crimes, indeed, each docile subject knows;
But what new horrors doth our DIDD disclose!   80
From Nooseneck's peak unwonted wisdom pours,
And revelation sounds on Seekonk's shores.
How boils our loyal blood as we behold
The page of sin and treachery unroll'd;
Unending evils strike our anguish'd eyes,   85
As deeds Republican to sight arise.
'Twas COLT that struck the hapless Belgian down;
COLT, who has sought a world's Imperial crown;
LE BARON COLT, who stretch'd a greedy hand
To clutch the Serbian and the Russian land.   90
COLT, whose deep plot the lurking U-boats led,
And doom'd each vessel to an ocean bed;
And COLT, who (worse than all his deeds before)
Seduc'd our peaceful nation into war!
But if his crimes against the world be great,   95
What hath his party heap'd upon our State?
King Philip's war, Moshassuck's od'rous rill,
The Cove (which Democrats were forc'd to fill),
The Union Station, ugly to the gaze,
Prepayment cars—the bane of summer days,   100
The late Grand Trunk (whose brief career was done
Almost before its young life was begun)—
In fact, all pests reveal his workmanship,
From old Sam Gorton down to Spanish Grippe!
Would not these vile atrocities be hid   105
In darksome silence, but for valiant DIDD?
His voice alone convincing proof conveys,
And lifts O'SHAUNESSY to publick praise:
(For GEORGE, with modesty, hath well conceal'd
Th' unnumber'd virtues by our DIDD reveal'd.)   110
A civick crown to him who thus hath shewn
So many truths, to all the world unknown!
Would that I might possess, to deck my song,
The grace of Pope, or Edward Leland Strong;

My humbler genius must attempt in vain   115
To sing our heroes in a fitting strain.
But skill'd or not, my subject lends me fire
To court the Muses and excite the lyre;
Say what you will, it is not wasted ink
That lauds O'SHAUNESSY and Colonel "LINK".   120

Amissa Minerva

"Humano capiti cervicem pictor equinam
  Jungere si velit, et varias inducere plumas
  Undique collatis membris, ut turpiter atrum
  Desinat in piscem mulier formosa superne;
  Spectatum admissi risum teneatis amici?"
                        —Horace, *Ars Poetica.*

In ancient times, when bards without pretence
Knelt down to beauty, and deferr'd to sense,
Bright Nature glow'd in well-selected dress,
And pleas'd us with a double loveliness.
'Twas then great Homer warm'd the list'ning heart,   5
And gentle Maro cheer'd the soul with art:
Then Horace made the laws of writing known,
And what he preach'd attended in his own;
With care reflected, and with wisdom taught
Each turn of poesy and rule of thought.   10
In various fashions various authors writ,
Yet none but strove for melody and wit;
Dulness was eas'd, and worth sublimely grac'd,
With even numbers, and harmonious taste.
Succeeding times an equal genius bore,   15
Yet the skill'd bard attends the rules of yore;
Unchang'd they reign, tho' novel themes abound,
Their goal exalted, and their spirit sound.
Thus lofty Shakespeare struck the living lyre,
And Milton sang with scarce inferior fire;   20
Thus facile Pope our modern tongue refin'd,
And Horace's to Homer's talents join'd:
Thus Thomson the revolving year review'd,
And shew'd the changing charms of wold and wood;
Thus gentle Goldsmith and the dismal Dean   25
With classic ease serv'd up their smiles or spleen.
Cowper's sad Muse enervate art display'd,
And Wordsworth's prattle pain'd the Heav'nly Maid;

241

Yet thro' it all the poet throng she led,
Beauty and truth still beaming bright ahead.   30
Immortal Keats th' Olympian impulse knew,
And hapless Poe kept Helicon in view.
Sweet Tennyson melodic murmurs roll'd,
And shining Swinburne felt the flame of old:
So from on high the noble notes we hear,   35
When hark! they fade—they pause—they disappear!

Engulfing folly! Spawn of febrile earth!
Destructive monster of unnatural birth!
Aonia weeps as thy foul dictates sway
The public fancy and the poet's lay.   40
True art, like Nature, variously glows,
And ev'ry side in gen'rous measure shews;
Surveys the scene with calm appraising eye,
And sings its choicest features as they lie.
No odd perspective lends eccentric tone,   45
Nor aimless musing takes its flight alone;
The idle fancy and the vagrant mind,
In science, not in art, their province find.
Artistic souls the earthly picture scan;
Paint what hath shone to centuries of man;   50
Psychology the mental wand'rer views,
And Aesculapius claims him, not the Muse!
Yet see on ev'ry hand the antic train
That swarm uncheck'd, and gibber o'er the plain.
Here Librist, Cubist, Spectrist forms arise;   55
With foetid vapours cloud the crystal skies;
Or led by transient madness, rend the air
With shrieks of bliss and whinings of despair.
Exempt from wit, each dullard pours his ink
In odes to bathtubs, or the kitchen sink;   60
Bent on effect, they search their souls for themes,
And spout disease, or colic-troubled dreams.
See to what depths a Lowell can descend;
How Masters can his guideless force expend;
Hear morbid Gould inflict a limping tune,   65
Or striving Sandburg bay the suff'ring moon.
Distress'd we watch the clownish chorus chant
Unmeaning nonsense and abhorrent cant;
When thro' the gloom some reason is diffus'd,
We mourn to think of so much sense unus'd!   70

Undying Pallas, whose all-pow'rful rule
Exalts the artist and condemns the fool,
Whose gentle will made Grecian genius shine,
And gave to Rome her majesty divine,
Pardon the erring race which bade thee fly   75
So lately to thine own Olympian sky:
Descend once more to these celestial meads,
To kindle art, and ease our mortal needs.
Instruct each bard in bright forgotten truth,
And from his follies save aspiring youth;   80
Unfold again the heav'n-imparted code
That shapes the lyric, pastoral, and ode.
Pierian skill a second time confer
On feeble man, so prone to sink and err,
And with kind patience teach his race anew   85
To choose the good, the beautiful, the true.
These boons, Athena, in thy mercy send
To bless the few who still would call thee friend;
The faithful few who with threnetic lays
Implore thy succour, and diffuse thy praise: 90
Offspring of Jove, may thy forgiving care
Reward our smoking altars and our pray'r!

[On Prohibition]

The fateful night hath come at last—
    The demon Rum is dying;
The Tappa Tappa Keg is past—
    And thirsty swains are sighing.

Monody on the Late King Alcohol

Thro' Naxian groves the doleful dirge resounds,
And echoes sad on Nysa's distant bounds;
A with'ring wreath Lyaeus' brow entwines,
While grapes hang listless from the anxious vines;
Whence the sharp grief that bows each ivy'd head?   5
The Maenads answer—"*Alcohol* is dead!"
Lamented King! stern foe to ev'ry care,
Friend of the weak, and bright'ner of despair;
Whose godlike pow'r, the legacy of Jove,
To heights of wit the leanest mind could move: 10
Without the aid of thy divine pretence,

243

How may poor Dulness masquerade as sense?
Those throngs that once at many a tavern bar
Solv'd the hard knots of statecraft near and far,
In sorrow languish by the wat'ry bier   15
Of him who gave them all their sapient cheer:
Alone they mourn their absent show of brain,
Reveal'd as clowns of Folly's thoughtless train!
Equal the tribute which those weepers pay
Who haunt the clubroom and the cabaret;   20
Each genial pleasure, once so bright to view,
Appears in raiment of less roseate hue:
Less are the jokes, the nonsense, and the laughter—
And less the headaches of the morning after!
Saddest of all that cluster round the tomb   25
(Three sister Fiends of Cithaeronian gloom),
See Crime, Pain, Poverty, the ether rend
With howls Sabazian at their master's end.
Vice, Vileness, Violence, in chorus pray
And fret aloud at their diminish'd sway: 30
While skulking Licence wails in pensive key,
No more allow'd the dress of Liberty.
Mark yonder thyrsus of the ruddy god
Lose all its leaves, and turn a useful rod;
Behold Silenus throw his wine-skin down,   35
And sober seek to win a new renown:
Dark are the times for Evil's wide domain
When to such might grows tyrant Virtue's reign!
Thou, *Alcohol,* wert Darkness' friend indeed,
And mourning Satyrs sound the dismal reed;   40
Taygetus repeats the gen'ral woe,
Whilst Charon grumbles in the gulf below:
Alas! they cry, that to so dire an end
The once almighty monarch should descend!

The Pensive Swain

Dedicated to P. M., Esq.

Where Auster with his am'rous breath
    Ruffles the warm Sicilian air,
See Daphnis on the sun-drap'd heath
    Sigh for a distant, unknown fair.

No rural nymph of neighb'ring grove   5
    His pensive longing can appease,
But (whilst his flocks neglected rove)
    He wanly scans the sparkling seas.

Why, asks the ploughman as he spies
    The moonstruck youth upon the shore,   10
Doth Daphnis thus with wat'ry eyes
    Look hungrily the billows o'er?

Are not the maids by Acis' streams,
    Or by the reedy Cyane,
Fair as the phantom of his dreams,   15
    Or fit for such a swain as he?

The sage attends with smiling face,
    Amus'd young Daphnis' plight to note,
And vows that ne'er can present grace
    Match charms imagin'd and remote!   20

To Phillis

(With humblest possible apologies to Randolph St. John, Gent.)

Ah, Phillis, had I but bestow'd the art
Upon my verses, that I vainly gave
To fond designs and schemes to win your heart,
And tributes that abas'd me as your slave;
If that fine fervour that I freely pour'd   5
In suppliance at your feet had liv'd in rhyme,
And the soft warmth wherewith my soul ador'd
Been sav'd in numbers for applauding Time;
Had all th' affection, spent on you alone,
Provok'd my fancy to poetic flights: 10
Fill'd my rapt brain with passions not my own,
And wafted me to dizzy lyric heights;
The scanty laurels of this feeble quill,
Believe me, kid, would sure be scantier still!

The Poet's Rash Excuse

As the fond doting swain essays
To chant his latest charmer's praise
He twists the ancient songs and stories
To fit his own beloved Doris!

245

He sings the winning lyric lore   5
That gentle Waller sang before,
And whispers soft the selfsame word
To Doris, that Corinna heard!

When chid for triteness, he'll aver
The stuff is only true of her—   10
But he'll recall that vow with sorrow
When he courts Phillis on the morrow!

On Religion

Would that we all might innocently dream
In primal bliss by Lethe's flow'ry stream;
'Neath fancy's glow a fairy world survey,
Nor glimpse, beyond, the with'ring light of day;
Drink from the perfum'd tide a pleasing draught,   5
And breathe the scent that lotos'd zephyrs waft,
While others, not so blest, lift tearful eyes
To the bleak cycle of the godless skies!
O Truth! What ills attend thy grisly train!
What griefs and sorrows share thy frigid reign!   10
From curtain'd deeps thy claws the curtains tear,
And mortals weep to find but vacant air.
On ev'ry side the treasur'd idols fade,
Visions of mist our own poor wishes made;
Here cherish'd Justice, with the heavens, falls,   15
Whilst Immortality no more enthralls;
Right, wrong, and purpose, tales of future bliss,
All vanish mocking in the vast abyss;
Hope, effort, fame, to empty chaos tend—
Atoms on atoms, reeling without end!   20
How dream'd our fathers, to whose minds unvex'd
Came no disturbing light, no learned text!
Happy in ignorance, they seem'd to see
O'er all their lives a guiding Deity:
His little world encompass'd ev'ry thought,   25
And blessings flow'd from what their fancy wrought.
So, thou whose mind in kindly myth retires,
Spurning the beck'ning flame of Reason's fires,
Dream while thou mayest, with the heart of youth,
Nor seek the curst, revealing glare of Truth: 30
From boundless space thy searching eyes remove,
And of gay poppies weave thy God of Love!

The Pathetick History of Sir Wilful Wildrake

Dedicated to the Rt. Hon. Rheinhart Kleiner, Gent.

In elder Days, when ruttish Rips
Were always pardon'd for their Slips;
When CHARLES (as if to set the Pace)
With Doxies swell'd our British Race,
There liv'd a Rake of antient Name   5
Whose Sires had known a martial Fame;
But who, indiff'rent to the Sword,
Fought softer Fights, and gayly whor'd.
This Brat, of rampant Squire begot,
Was sure design'd for Lecher's Lot: 10
At Birth he had a roving Eye
That winkt at Wenches passing by,
And ere he cou'd in Speech converse
He got a Bastard on his Nurse.
When ten the Boy had known with Pride   15
Each Trollop of the Countryside,
And pass'd, so ably did he whore 'em,
The old *Jus Trium Librorum!*
His Father, liking not to see
So swift a Growth of Peasantry   20
(Or yet a Rival quite so bold as he),
Ere long the little Satyr sent
To travel on the Continent;
But many a Tale his Tutor told
That prov'd the Stripling still more bold.   25
He charm'd the *easie* Gallick Jades,
And Bitches of *Italia's* Shades—
God help us all if Years ahead
Our Sons must fight the Troops he bred!
(Myself, I think it downright Treason   30
To wench abroad in any Season.)
But in due Time young WILDRAKE came
Back to our Isle to vaunt his Fame,
And gain the Prize our King design'd
For Merit of a gallant Kind.   35
Behold him now at ev'ry Ball
That frets the Peace of Windsor Hall;
A Maccaronie of Renown
With ev'ry Baggage of the Town;

247

Bold with the Trulls, and quick to boast   40
Of Vict'ries o'er each reigning Toast,
Nor slow to hint he hath been rash
With Lady *Blank,* or Countess *Dash!*
One idle Day a Nymph he knew
Prov'd pleasing to the Royal View,   45
Whereat our crafty riggish Imp
To serve his Fortune turn'd a Pimp:
The Fray was won—the Maiden blighted—
And WILL, to pay his Virtue, knighted.
(I need but add, the Drab was made   50
A Duchess, grand in red Brocade.)
Whene'er some pious Fool wou'd snivel
That such damn'd Raking pleas'd the Devil,
Our love-lockt Goat wou'd wink in Scorn
And vow that he for this was born;   55
For sure, the only Joy he knew
Was of the *Cyprian* and the Stew,
Whilst he wou'd rather far be dead
Than out of some loose Mopsy's Bed.
Of Husbands WILL was much in Awe,   60
And smil'd the more, the less he saw;
But *Cupid* oft will craft provide,
So WILDRAKE early learn'd to hide.
Now all went well, till one sad Day
WILL'S Nose beam'd out with redder Ray,   65
And powder'd Leeches cry'd that sure
He must depart to take the Cure.
Not once but often did they force
The rake-hell Blade to change his Course,
Yet spyte of all the poor Wretch grows   70
Pain'd, pox'd, and putrid with his Woes.
The years as well their Tribute claim,
They seam his Face and bend his Frame,
Till ere his Mind his State can see,
He finds no Joy in Venerie.   75
The Ladies flee as he draws near,
And ev'ry Strumpet costs him dear.
And what is worse, each bawdy Fling
No Spark of Pleasure now can bring.
Bred up to live on Lust alone,   80
A Courtier by *Priapus'* Throne,
He sees ahead a weary Waste

Whose Bliss he never learn'd to taste.
"Alas!" he whines, "had I but thought
Of what vast Ills by Love are wrought!   85
Had I but train'd my mind to glimpse
Some Goal above my Whores and Pimps!
Fifty and feeble, I must crave
And ogle vainly to my Grave,
Whilst even then (if Crones err not)   90
My itching Ghost will haunt the Spot!"
But one last Joy our WILDRAKE learns,
The while in pox'd old Age he burns;
For tho' the Flame of Love be low,
In Godliness new Beauties grow.   95
The Rake, his genial Ardour spent,
Turns pious, proud, and penitent;
Dons sober grey; trys Church each Week
To doze, or hear the Parson speak;
Too old to whore, the Rip grows chaste,   100
And damns the Bliss he once embrac'd.
Resolv'd to wed, he seeks a Maid
Of Age and Chancres unafraid;
An ugly Chit, tho' young and sound,
And bred on her ancestral Ground;   105
Nor (save for Errours with a Groom)
Devoid of Dian's virgin Bloom.
With this sweet Nymph the Rake essays
In rustick Peace to end his Days;
Trades Bawdry for a Patriot's Fire,   110
And turns a stolid country Squire.
Three infant Forms the Household bless,
Entrancing in their Loveliness;
An idiot Girl, a weakling Boy,
And one small Saint, the Mother's Joy,   115
Whose Groom-like Looks his lover's Sire annoy.
So ends poor WILL, whom Parents praise
For prudish Tongue and virtuous Ways;
First to reprove a lick'rish Air,
And first to stone the erring Fair.   120
'Tis he that rails with righteous Zest
At Modern Nymphs in Style undress'd
With shrinking Petticoat and naked Breast.
His Merits all the Country fill,

And Heirs adore him for his Will; 125
No one (aloud) can think with Ease
That Death so good a Man will seize.
Nagg'd, cuckolded by doltish Wife,
The Hypocrite concludes his Life;
Once hot for *Cupid's* Pleasures only 130
He pines—dull, rotten, lewd, and lonely!

Medusa: A Portrait

TO THE HON. IDA COCHRAN HAUGHTON, VISCOUNTESS
      WOODBY————

MY LADY:—

    I shou'd be but a Cheater, and unworthy of the poetick Art, were I not to acknowledge to you by this Dedication the Indebtedness I bear you. For 'tis plain that I may my self claim but partial Credit for a Picture which, without so illustrious a Model, wou'd never have been drawn with any Sort of Fidelity. Truly, the Satirist desiring to shew certain Traits of Mind, wou'd be hard put to it, had he not before him some Sort of living Example; and I am in Candour forc'd to concede, that of the Qualities I here seek to pourtray, no human Being cou'd display so great and flourishing an Abundance as your self. I shall ever count it a Piece of the greatest good Fortune, if my Satire proceed, that your Hatred of me mov'd you to slander and vilify me behind my Back; for lacking that Provocation I shou'd have neither had the Temerity to expose your Failings, nor possest so compleat a Fund of Lies and Calumnies from which to draw a Picture of such Venom as I never thought before to exist upon Earth.

    Conscious, therefore, of my Debt, I will commend this unpretentious Effort to your well-known Graciousness, and beg leave to subscribe my self,
      MY LADY,
        Your Ladyship's most obedient,
          most devoted, humble servant,
          THEOBALDUS SENECTISSIMUS, ARMIGER.

Soak'd in her noxious venom, puff'd with gall,
Like some fat toad see dull MEDUSA sprawl;
Foul with her spleen, repugnant to the sight,
She crudely whines amidst eternal night.
From wit and sense by slothful brain debarr'd, 5
And with the chains of age and sourness scarr'd,
Her half-liv'd life one hateful wish reveals:
To give to others all the pain she feels!
Unschool'd in youth, unchasten'd by the years,
Grotesque with ignorance, absurd with fears; 10

Shunn'd for her ugly face and fretful mind,
She crawls alone, at war with all mankind.
In her black heart no love or kindness dwells,
But hate that shocks, and malice that repels;
Her narrow thoughts an equal vileness shew,   15
For there but envy and suspicion grow.
Blind to the truth, by jealous passion fann'd,
She slanders all she cannot understand,
And with loose tongue the sinner and the saint
Alike befouls in one inclusive taint.   20
Slow to see goodness, quick to smell a fault,
She scours the earth for victims to assault;
With what strain'd words she doles her lagging praise!
With what glad force her instant hatreds blaze!
Sluggish of wit, her loathsome bulk attests   25
One spark alone—a rage that never rests!
But not content to be an open fool,
Or candid knave, she seeks to cheat by rule;
Her want of sense in quoted saws she cloaks,
And with trite pelf a double laugh provokes,   30
Whilst all her cruelty must candour seem,
Tho' doubly evil for the stratagem.
So lurks MEDUSA, scourge of all around,
With hate, spleen, vanity, and dulness bound.
Anxious the wretch that courts her tardy smile,   35
And hapless he that knows her sneers and guile;
For since her envy flays all greater minds,
In ev'ry one alive a foe she finds—
Save for a little band of kindred sort,
In torpor mighty, but in wisdom short.   40
Void of all humour but the sly grimace,
She sees a challenge in each smiling face,
And spreads with twofold zeal her net malign,
Since she as injur'd innocence may shine.
From such a pest what rescue may we gain?   45
What spell may crush her hypocritic strain?
Her human form (perchance 'twas human once)
Forbids us smother the offending dunce;
Besides, we hesitate to smother such
A reptile thing, repellent to the touch.   50
A musket-ball but little harm could do
Where there's no brain or heart to hurtle thro',

251

So still the monster heaves and puffs and rolls,
The toothless tearer of a thousand souls!
So must she fume, insatiate, sour, and wild;   55
Deaf, stupid, blear'd; by ev'ry tongue revil'd:
So must we wait, till Heav'n the curse revokes,
And the swoln snake in her own poison chokes!

Simplicity: A Poem

Whilst the town-Muse with fever'd accents bays,
Chok'd by the times, and mov'd to hectick lays;
Whilst learn'd Confusion, weighing on the mind,
Turns ev'ry head to thoughts of jumbled kind;
Whilst weary'd singers hide in sapient fear   5
The thrill of joy at what the past held dear,
See o'er the rural mead, serene and bright,
A radiant god who puts the clouds to flight!
Simplicity! blest Nature's first ally;
Child of the balmy groves and lucent sky;   10
Friend of the breezes and the vernal rain,
And of each early flow'r that decks the plain;
Spirit benign, that gleams in ev'ry glade,
And smiles assuring from the leafy shade;
Kin of the Oreads on the craggy mounts;   15
Kin of the nymphs that haunt the grotto founts;
God of the vale, the thicket, and the slope,
And last kind guardian of declining Hope!

Thus sings the bard whose gaze in wisdom leaves
The scene where sad Sophistication grieves;   20
Who scans the truth that shows at calm content,
And hoards the wonder worldlier men have spent;
Laughs at the poison letter'd sorc'rers brew,
Nor pants for pleasures that he never knew.
For him the gay reviving spring unfolds   25
Perennial beauties o'er the fragrant wolds;
His ear alone the feather'd wand'rers please
With tales of faery worlds beyond the seas;
His favour'd eye in ev'ry wind may trace
Ethereal spirits of celestial grace;   30
And he, unspoil'd, may childlike bask again
Beneath the beams of Saturn's golden reign.
Mark yonder rise, o'er whose smooth em'rald crest

252

Trips sprightly Maia, in white blossoms drest;
Her verdant wand the air with perfume fills,   35
Tips the warm boughs, and paints the conscious hills;
Lights up the matin fields with crystal dew,
And gilds the sunset's airy cliffs anew;
Her sportive train to ev'ry scene impart
Unwonted spells, and cheer the languid heart;   40
Dancing and song enchant the world around,
Till Pan makes joyous at the pleasing sound.
In noontide stillness, when no urban eye
May chill the bliss or mar the revelry,
Simplicity descries on ev'ry hand   45
The prancing presence of the antique band:
Here laurell'd Muses all their arts rehearse,
And ivy'd Bacchus waves his budding thyrse;
Here myrtled Venus spreads her genial fire,
Whilst aureate Phoebus sounds the festive lyre;   50
Here, here alone, those lavish gifts are flung
To those whose fancy stays for ever young.
Behold yon hamlet, blest with mellow years,
That bosom'd in the oaky vale appears;
Here urban eyes* a stupid life discern;   55
And urban minds** unwholesome secrets learn;
But wise *Simplicity*, with fresher gaze,
Refines the whole, and sifts the brighter rays;
Spurns the dull thoughts that darkly flit between,
And as a picture*** glories in the scene: 60
Spires mixt with verdure; walls with ivy fair;
Calm leafy ways—a prospect rich and rare.
Simplicity! Chief boon of suff'ring man!
First of the blessings in th' eternal plan!
May thy glad mantle ever shield my form   65
From the dread terrors of the circling storm.
With thee beside me, may I tranquil rest
Close to benignant Nature's soothing breast;
Nor ever spy, too keen of wit or soul,
The lurking hemlock in the flow'r-wreath'd bowl!   70

* Sinclair Lewis, Esq.
** Sherwood Anderson, Esq.
*** Schopenhauer hath observ'd, that the world is beautiful as an object.

Plaster-All

(Apologies to "Pastorale" of Mr. Crane in the *Dial.*)

1

    I, who live
In the fourth dimension
On the third story
Of a not-unfashionable house
In a fashionable neighbourhood,   5
With pictures of Bill Sommer hung on the wall,
And an occasional one by myself—
That one, the woman's uplifted face, for instance—
My best, I think,
A miraculous stroke,   10
Unthinkingly executed;
But Willy Lescaze liked it. . . .
Lescaze . . . smearing the butter on one's bread
With the supreme unction
Of a third-rate director   15
Of a fourth-rate playhouse,
Discoursing the pros and cons of art,
Somewhere in a bookshop in the Taylor Arcade,
Smiling to the ladies with bobbed hair
And occasionally to the gentlemen—   20
How I hate that type!
Hate it—hate it,
With the consistance of a hard substance,
Despising a piece of fluidity!

2

    Yes, I know   25
Most of the *Spittle Review* crowd,
But something,
Money, no doubt,
Drew me to Cleveland,
To the home of Crane's Candies,   30
Mary Garden Chocolates,
And Laukhuff's Bookshop.
Here it was,
That in the light of an interpreter,

Soon I met and succeeded   35
In surrounding myself
With a few of the Intelligentsia
That Cleveland affords,
Loveman, Sommer, Lescaze, Hatfield, Guenther. . . .
But Loveman   40
Left the fold early—pity, yes!
I might have made much of him,
In spite of his Hebraism,
Which (sibilantly whispered)
I did not recognize,   45
Even on my mother's hearsay—
But there was much of the rebel,
Inborn and instinctive,
(As in all Jews)
In Loveman,   50
And so, after a perfectly wild argument
With him one lovely night, late July,
With the syringas in full blossom
On 115th Street,
We parted   55
To meet no more—at least as friends.

                                3

        And so,
Realizing, after all,
As I did, and so many before me,
Maxwell Bodenheim, T. S. Eliot, Margaret Anderson, Sherwood Anderson
        (No relations!), James Joyce, Ezra Pound,   60
And how many others,
Even less than myself,
That what it all amounts to,
In life, as in literature—
Is form.   65
Not emotion, not poetry, not beauty,
But the hard, visible outline.
Dave Gordon
(I can hardly control myself when I think of him!)
Asserted to Loveman,   70
Which in a fit of epilepsy, apoplexy or delirium,
Loveman seconded;

That my work—my own—my own,
Was a shade of T. S. Eliot's, who was a shade
Of Jules Laforgue!   75
Ridiculous! Stupid! Ridiculous!
Men of genius
Are all derivative.
Shakspere, for instance,
Has even as much influenced   80
Internally as externally,
T. S. Eliot.

                              4

         The wind wails
Around the corner of Euclid and 115th St.,
The trees shiver   85
Like brass, or cymbals of some such metal,
It rains and then it ceases,
But I, seated on my Aztec carpets,
And playing Debussy
On the wheezy Victrola,   90
(What Rhythms! What Rhythms!)
Conjure for myself
An entire world,
Made of myself, by myself, for myself!
Knowing myself   95
To be myself.

To Zara

(Inscribed to Miss Sarah Longhurst)

By Edgar A. Poe (?)

I looked upon thee yesternight
Beneath the drops of yellow light
That fell from out a poppy moon
Like notes of some far opiate tune.
I looked and sighed, I knew not why,   5
As when a condor flutters by,
And thought the moonbeams on thy face
Timid to seek thy resting-place.
O sacred spot! Memorial bower!

Unsuited to the mocking hour   10
When winds of myrrh from Tempë's lake
Stir soft, yet stir thee not awake!
Thy clear brow, Zara, rests so fair
I cannot think death lingers there;
Thy lip as from thy blood is red,   15
Nor hints of ichors of the dead:
Canst thou, whom love so late consumed,
Lie prey to worms—dissolved, entombed?
And he, whose name suffused thy cheek
With ecstasies thou couldst not speak;   20
Will he in fancy hold thee ever
Fair as thou art, decaying never,
And dreaming, on thine eyelids press
A tribute to thy loveliness?
Or will his fancy rove beneath   25
The carven urn and chiselled wreath,
Where still—so still—the shroud shall drape
Grotesque, liquescent turns of shape?
No, Zara, no! Such beauty reigns
Immortal in immortal fanes;   30
Radiant for ever, ever laden
With beams of uncorrupted Aidenn,
And naught that slumbers here tonight
Can perish from a lover's sight.
Where'er thy soul, where'er thy clay   35
May rise to hail another day,
Thy second soul, thy beauty's flame,
The songs of passionate lutes shall claim;
Pale, lovely ghost—so young, so fair,
To flutter in sepulchral air—   40
To flutter where the taper dies
Amidst a mourner's choking sighs!

Waste Paper

A Poem of Profound Insignificance

Πάντα γέλωσ καὶ πάντα κόνισ καὶ πάντα τὸ μηεδέν

Out of the reaches of illimitable night
The blazing planet grew, and forc'd to life
Unending cycles of progressive strife

257

And strange mutations of undying light
And boresome books, than hell's own self more trite   5
And thoughts repeated and become a blight,
And cheap rum-hounds with moonshine hootch made tight,
And quite contrite to see the flight of fright so bright
I used to ride my bicycle in the night
With a dandy acetylene lantern that cost $3.00   10
In the evening, by the moonlight, you can hear those darkies singing
Meet me tonight in dreamland . . . BAH
I used to sit on the stairs of the house where I was born
After we left it but before it was sold
And play on a zobo with two other boys.   15
We called ourselves the Blackstone Military Band
Won't you come home, Bill Bailey, won't you come home?
In the spring of the year, in the silver rain
When petal by petal the blossoms fall
And the mocking birds call   20
And the whippoorwill sings, Marguerite.
The first cinema show in our town opened in 1906
At the old Olympic, which was then call'd Park,
And moving beams shot weirdly thro' the dark
And spit tobacco seldom hit the mark.   25
Have you read Dickens' *American Notes?*
My great-great-grandfather was born in a white house
Under green trees in the country
And he used to believe in religion and the weather.
"Shantih, shantih, shantih" . . . *Shanty House*   30
Was the name of a novel by I forget whom
Published serially in the *All-Story Weekly*
Before it was a weekly. Advt.
Disillusion is wonderful, I've been told,
And I take quinine to stop a cold   35
But it makes my ears ring . . . always ring . . .
Always ringing in my ears . . .
It is the ghost of the Jew I murdered that Christmas day
Because he played "Three O'Clock in the Morning" in the flat above me.
Three O'Clock in the morning, I've danc'd the whole night through,   40
Dancing on the graves in the graveyard
Where life is buried; life and beauty
Life and art and love and duty
Ah, there, sweet cutie.
Stung!   45

Out of the night that covers me
Black as the pit from pole to pole
I never quote things straight except by accident.
Sophistication! Sophistication!
You are the idol of our nation   50
Each fellow has
Fallen for jazz
And we'll give the past a merry razz
Thro' the ghoul-guarded gateways of slumber
And fellow-guestship with the glutless worm.   55
Next stop is 57th St.—57th St. the next stop.
Achilles' wrath, to Greece the direful spring,
And the Governor-General of Canada is Lord Byng
Whose ancestor was shot or hung,
I forget which, the good die young.   60
Here's to your ripe old age,
Copyright, 1847, by Joseph Miller,
Entered according to act of Congress
In the office of the librarian of Congress
America was discovered in 1492   65
This way out.
No, lady, you gotta change at Washington St. to the Everett train.
Out in the rain on the elevated
Crafted, sated, all mismated.
Twelve seats on this bench,   70
How quaint.
In a shady nook, beside a brook, two lovers stroll along.
Express to Park Ave., Car Following.
No, we had it cleaned with the sand blast.
I know it ought to be torn down.   75
Before the bar of a saloon there stood a reckless crew,
When one said to another, "Jack, this message came for you."
"It may be from a sweetheart, boys," said someone in the crowd,
And here the words are missing . . . but Jack cried out aloud:
        "It's only a message from home, sweet home,   80
             From loved ones down on the farm
         Fond wife and mother, sister and brother. . . ."
         Bootleggers all and you're another
 In the shade of the old apple tree
'Neath the old cherry tree sweet Marie   85
The Conchologist's First Book
By Edgar Allan Poe

Stubbed his toe
On a broken brick that didn't shew
Or a banana peel   90
In the fifth reel
By George Creel
It is to laugh
And quaff
It makes you stout and hale,   95
And all my days I'll sing the praise
Of Ivory Soap
Have you a little T. S. Eliot in your home?
The stag at eve had drunk his fill
The thirsty hart look'd up the hill   100
And craned his neck just as a feeler
To advertise the Double-Dealer.
William Congreve was a gentleman
O art what sins are committed in thy name
For tawdry fame and fleeting flame   105
And everything, ain't dat a shame?
Mah Creole Belle, ah lubs yo' well;
Aroun' mah heart you hab cast a spell
But I can't learn to spell pseudocracy
Because there ain't no such word.   110
And I says to Lizzie, if Joe was my feller
I'd teach him to go to dances with that
Rat, bat, cat, hat, flat, plat, fat
Fry the fat, fat the fry
You'll be a drug-store by and by.   115
Get the hook!
Above the lines of brooding hills
Rose spires that reeked of nameless ills,
And ghastly shone upon the sight
In ev'ry flash of lurid light   120
To be continued.
No smoking.
Smoking on four rear seats.
Fare will return to 5¢ after August 1st
Except outside the Cleveland city limits.   125
In the ghoul-haunted woodland of Weir
Stranger pause to shed a tear;
Henry Fielding wrote *Tom Jones*.
And cursed be he that moves my bones.

Good night, good night, the stars are bright   130
I saw the Leonard-Tendler fight
Farewell, farewell, O go to hell.
Nobody home
In the shantih.

[On a Politician]

Nova, Nova,
Second Grover!
Pass the hat
Fer a Dimmy-crat!
He's no rover,   5
Brooklyn all over—
Nova, Nova,
We want Nova!
Vote for Nova
An' live in clover—   10
Butcher, beggar,
Barber, bootlegger;
Don't weaken or soften,
Vote early and often!

[On a Room for Rent]

At size and light
   I'll cavil not;
But here's MY fight—
   ARE THOSE ROOMS HOT?

[On J. F. Roy Erford]

See fumbling ERFORD in confusion flit,
And mask with Billingsgate his want of wit;
Loud oe'r the rest in raucous falsehood bray,
Whilst grinning foes applaud the antick fray.
Health to his goose, whose mind and quill combine   5
To wake our mirth, and kill his dull design:
Thrice-gen'rous clown, whose prattle works alone
Against his purpose, to promote our own!

Lines upon the Magnates of the Pulp

In former times our letter'd brethren sought
To starve their bodies while they fed their thought;
Unaw'd by wealth, unbought by luxury,
They own'd their brains, and scorn'd the slaver's fee.
Poor, modest, proud, they held the princely pen,   5
Masters and peers, and conscious gentlemen;
And who, unbow'd, would not their place prefer
To the rich tradesman's—harness'd, fawning cur?
But Time, the Goth, each pleasing virtue blights
As his curst legions storm our guarded heights;   10
Behold! where bards free musick once outpour'd,
A crowd of lackeys cringe around their lord;
From gold-stain'd pockets beg their tawdry doles,
And stuff their bellies as they sell their souls.
What shall they write? 'Tis not for them to say—   15
King Mob will give them orders for the day!
Scrawling what's bid, they woo the unwash'd throng
In chap-book prose, and loud illiterate song;
Themselves in boasting, not in art, express,
And reckon worth in terms of gainfulness.   20
See! see! where once the honest dreamer try'd
To scale the slopes of loveliness and pride,
To cast off earth, and reach th' ethereal mead
High o'er the sloughs where waddling porkers feed,
Our newer band opposing objects find,   25
And lose the freeman's in the miser's mind.
'Tis theirs to shine in tests of haggling skill,
Their bulging purses, not their heads, to fill;
To drown their yearnings and their freeman's bent
In sticky swamps of servile excrement.   30
Hail to the carcass, fed, tho' bound in chains;
Pox on your dreamer's or your poet's pains!
We drink to flesh in one black Stygian gulp,
And sink our spirits in a grave of PULP!

Dead Passion's Flame

A Poem by Blank Frailty

Ah, Passion, like a voice—that buds!
With many thorns . . . that sharply stick:
Recalls to me the longing of our bloods . . .
And—makes my wearied heart requick! . . . .

Arcadia

By Head Balledup

O give me the life of the village,
    Uninhibited, free, and sweet;
The place where the arts all flourish,
    Grove Court and Christopher Street.

I am sick of the old conventions,   5
    And critics who will not praise,
So sing ho for the open spaces,
    And aesthetes with kindly ways.

Here every bard is a genius,
    And artists are Raphaels,   10
And above the roofs of Patchin Place
    The Muse of Talent dwells.

Lullaby for the Dionne Quintuplets

——————————————————
——————————————————
——————————————————
——————————————————

              —Giambattista della Sforza

The Decline and Fall of a Man of the World

Young Damon was a model son,
    With wit and art aglow,
Till he partook in curious fun
    Of C_2H_6O.

His active senses, quickly pleas'd,   5
    As speedily were cloy'd;
And soon, that they might more be eas'd,
    He try'd an alkaloid.

$C_{10}H_{14}$ and N_2
    The stripling first inhal'd,   10
But outrag'd Nature takes her due,
    And worse desires prevail'd.

$C_{17}H_{19}N$
    $O_3 + H_2O$
The hapless youth took now and then,   15
    And knew De Quincey's woe.

But still his tortur'd brain-cells whirl'd
    With cosmic retribution,
So one dark night he quit this world
    With KCN solution!   20

HIC. IACET. DAMON. INFELIX.

[Epigrams]

On a Poem for Children, Writ by J. M. W.

Thy fancy, WIDDOWS, was by Heav'n design'd
To please the babe, and soothe the infant mind:
Why, then, must thou to graver regions flit,
And shew Maturity thy want of wit?

On ——'s Gaining in Weight

If grape-nuts and cream can make Mrs. M——
Gain the mountainous bulk of an hundred and two,
What wou'd be the effect ('tis too vast to be thought on)
Of a similar diet on good Mrs. H——n???

Lines on a Dull Writer Having Insomnia

The sleepless scribbler grows more tedious yet,
And gives to others what he cannot get!

On a Pathetick Poem, by J. M. W.

Tears, idle Tears, bedew my anxious eye,
For WIDDOWS makes me laugh until I cry!

Idle Lines on a Poetick Dunce

When Dulness on her gilded throne
    The realms of song survey'd,
She chose three bards to be her own,
    Three fools of diff'ring grade:
Tho' SELLE and BUSH both stood the test,   5
'Twas WIDDOWS that she lov'd the best.

On the Habit of Letter-Writing

Save BUSH alone, there is no fool too dense
To pass (on paper) for a man of sense!

Life's Mystery

Life! Ah, Life!
What may this fluorescent pageant mean?
Who can the evanescent object glean?
He that is dead is the key to Life—
Gone is the symbol, deep is the grave!   5

Man is a breath, and Life is the fire;
Birth is death, and silence the choir.
Wrest from the aeons the heart of gold!
Tear from the fabric the threads that are old!
Life! Ah, Life!   10
            —L. Phillips Howard

On Mr. L. Phillips Howard's Profound Poem Entitled "Life's Mystery"

These lines profound expressly were design'd
To please the deep poetic modern mind.
Herein no tawdry metric art appears,
Nor does the meaning roughly stain our ears.
With true chaotic grace the formless rhymes   5
Stagger along, and suit the cultur'd times.
Should some chance word a sweeter sound present,

Frown not too harshly on the accident;
And if one trace of utter sense be there,
Forgive the poet for his want of care.   10

On an Accomplished Young Linguist

Proficient Paul hath so much Language got,
That he appears a very Polyglot.
Latin and *Greek* he talks with equal Ease,
And daily reads ten Pages of *Chinese;*
Translates a *Russian* Sentence at a Glance,   5
And revels in the fluent Tongue of *France.*
He thinks in *Sanscrit, Arabic,* and Such,
And writes his Notes in *Hebrew* and *High-Dutch.*
In sweet *Italian* sings a soft Refrain,
And greets us in the stately Speech of *Spain.*   10
In fine, to him consummately is known
Each Language, dead or living, but his own.

"The Poetical Punch" Pushed from His Pedestal

Uxurious Punch, inspir'd by Judy's charms,
His frigid foe with raving rhyme alarms.
As Cupid's clerk he heads the lover's class,
And slyly puffs the lauded tales of Cass.
He laughs to scorn the sober man's disgust,   5
And brands the honest critic as unjust!
'Tis strange, thinks he, to heed the years of *Mars;*
For as on earth, so up amongst the stars,
The ruddy war-god fails his mind to please,
And thoughts of *Venus* fill his hours of ease.   10
Ironic fancies thro' his musings run;
He calls his old opponent "Solomon":
No doubt he marks the diff'rence in their lives,
Comparing them in wisdom, not in wives.
He wonders how his enemy endures   15
The wanton waltzing of barbaric boors;
The shameful steps that all decorum lack;
The capers copy'd from the Afric black.
The answer's brief: when virtues thus unbend
No pow'r can force the critic to attend.   20

The Road to Ruin

Young Cyril stuck to model ways,
    Devoid of evil thirst,
Till came the dull and arid days
    Beginning July first.

Then at a festive spread, design'd   5
    To watch poor Bacchus go,
He first partook with curious mind
    of C_2H_6O.

Single Stanza Version

'Twas at a Junetime spread, design'd
    To watch poor Bacchus go,
That CYRIL first with curious mind
    Took C_2H_6O.

Sors Poetae

Who wields his pen a living to provide,
Must cast the precepts of the Nine aside;
Forget the purest phrases that he knows,
And sink himself in unharmonious prose.
'Tis true, your lines may reach the public's eye,   5
But how much bread will public reading buy?
E'en tho' the Times contain his latest ode,
Whitechapel is the Grub Street hack's abode.
Jackson, with nonsense, can the substance get
To keep him cloth'd and lodg'd and out of debt;   10
Whilst better men, with fifty times his skill,
Are thrust in Newgate for a tailor's bill;
No plot so stale, no levity so strain'd,
But that an idle guinea may be gain'd.
Yet let the bard his labour'd lines display,   15
And courtesy ends when he demands his pay.
"Have done," the printer cries, "with these fine airs;
Thou 'rt lucky to be shewn, not kick'd, downstairs!"

V. SEASONAL AND TOPOGRAPHICAL

Quinsnicket Park

> "... at latis otia fundis
> Speluncae vivique lacus; at frigida Tempe
> Mugitusque boum mollesque sub arbore somni
> Non absunt."
>
> Virg. *Georg.* lib. ii.

Ye sylvan Dryads! turn the harass'd mind
From talk of towns to themes of rural kind;
Amidst decadent sights a spot disclose
Where ancient woodlands give their blest repose;
Where clement Time hath spar'd his alt'ring hand, 5
And left unchang'd our own ancestral land.
Quinsnicket! haven of the weary'd heart;
Close to the busy town yet far apart:
Whose azure lakes and verdant pastures blend,
And as one fair harmonious whole extend; 10
Whose shady glens the years dissolve away,
And lead us backward to a happier day.
Enchanting hour! when first the trav'ller scales
Th' encircling hills, and wanders down the vales.
'Tis Spring; the buds deck ev'ry forest bough, 15
While honest rustics labour with the plough.
Among the trees the feather'd songsters cheer
The vernal scene, and hail th' increasing year.
Yon tiny torrent, fed by swollen springs,
Leaps in the sun, and o'er the mountain sings; 20
Thro' fields below, the streamlet flows along
With greater amplitude, but less of song;
At length the force of thankless toil to feel,
And strain incessant at the whirling wheel.
Thus with mankind, the sweetest days are first; 25
From youthful lips the songs spontaneous burst:
Maturer years a graver aspect give,
And men become more wretched as they live.
Away, Reality! and let us roam
Quinsnicket's realm—Imagination's home. 30
Let us ascend the gently rising mound,
And from its summit view the country round.
What city of the blest is that which lies
Far to the south, half hidden from our eyes;

Whose gold-pav'd avenues astound our gaze;   35
Whose spires and domes reflect the morning rays?
Bewitching distance! by thy aid alone
The sordid town to splendour thus hath grown.
Would that I might display in nobler rhyme
Quinsnicket's beauties in the summer time!   40
As sun-burn'd farmers gather in the hay,
In sylvan shades we shun the heat of day.
Charm'd by the fragrance of the leafy bow'r,
Within the glen we pass the noontide hour.
On ev'ry side the rugged slopes arise,   45
And verdure shields us from the blazing skies.
In yonder reedy pool we half expect
Some timid Nymph or Satyr to detect:
Our raptur'd eyes for fleeing Naiads scan,
And ears are strain'd to hear the pipes of Pan.   50
The rushing waterfall its music lends;
Creation smiles, and ev'ry joy attends.
Autumnal days their sweetest boons bestow
Where cool Quinsnicket greets the milder glow.
The harvest field, with order'd rows of sheaves,   55
Vies with the forest and its tinted leaves.
The wild ravine an added grandeur gains,
And brooklets swell with equinoctial rains.
Yon rocky bluff, above the water's side,
Defies the ages with primeval pride.   60
Of those stern heights, to ev'ry tempest turn'd,
How oft the Indian's council flame hath burn'd!
How oft his tribe have grateful shelter found
Betwixt the cloven rocks that stand around.
Imagination brings once more to view   65
The squatting chief and braves of copper hue:
The sober look, the pipe pass'd to and fro;
The reckless war-dance to the tom-tom's blow.
How little hath the silent landscape chang'd
Since dusky warriors o'er the forest rang'd!   70
In neighb'ring meadows all unalter'd stand
The ancient dwellings of an ancient land.
No modern finger yet hath dar'd to mar
These quaint reminders of an age afar.
Behold yon stone-built mansion by the road;   75
Of stately outline—gentry's own abode.

272

What powder'd beaux have dwelt within its walls!
What revelry hath cheer'd its spacious halls!
Alone it stands, each trav'ller to remind
Of brighter, happier ages left behind.   80
Midst fruitful orchards, by Pomona blest,
The simple cots of old New-England rest;
By stone protected on the forest end
From flaming darts that lurking braves might send.
In massive chimney, hearth, and vine-clad side,   85
The signs of long-departed years abide.
What rugged men have trod these sagging floors!
What pious bliss hath reign'd within these doors!
Contented households here have held their sway;
Would that they fill'd our spacious land today!   90
A Boreal blast the suff'ring country chills,
And Winter next invades Quinsnicket's hills.
Yet what can Winter's beauty better shew
Than fields and forests clad in virgin snow?
The bending boughs a diamond wealth amass,   95
Whilst lakes and streams are turn'd to crystal glass.
Night soon steals on, and from the gorgeous sky
A thousand blazing beacons cheer the eye.
High in the south Orion lends his beams;
Th' adjacent Bull with rival radiance gleams.   100
Above the ice-clad trees see Sirius shine,
And Leda's heav'nly twins their light combine.
Straight overhead behold Capella's rays,
And glitt'ring Perseus with his golden blaze.
In dazzled towns such sights are left unseen   105
To save their splendour for the wild demesne.
Hail! fair Quinsnicket, fair thro' all the year;
Where ev'ry season's blessings most appear:
Remnant of old New-England's brighter age,
To cheer our spirits, and our grief assuage.   110
No modern menace here our joy can blast:
Who sees Quinsnicket sees the beauteous past!

New England

When the January tempest sweeps across the barren hill,
And life itself can scarce withstand the marrow-piercing chill,
When the snows drift o'er the pastures and choke the dreary dell,
Then the cold New England country seems a sort of frozen hell.

When the sky's nocturnal splendour mocks the frigid earth below,   5
And Orion and the Dog-Star in the sterile silence glow,
When not all the fires in heaven can the winter's cold dispel,
Then we eye the cruel stars in vain, and call the land a hell.

When the mad, malignant billows rage along the rocky coast,
And the ship with ice-clad rigging in the ocean storm is toss'd;   10
Then the anxious seaport cottagers look on the treach'rous swell,
And, thinking of the absent, call the savage clime a hell.

But when the North awakes in spring, and white gives way to green,
And crystal brooks begin to flow, and flow'rs bedeck the scene;
When rushes fringe the placid pool and leaflets shade the dell,   15
Then we revel in the welcome warmth, without a thought of hell.

March

Let other bards with nobler talents sing
The beauties of the mild, maturer spring.
My rustic Muse on bleaker times must dwell,
When Earth, but new-escap'd from winter's spell,
Uncloth'd, unshelter'd, unadorn'd, is seen;   5
Stript of white robes, nor yet array'd in green.
Hard blows the breeze, but with a warmer force.
The melting ground, the brimming watercourse,
The wak'ning air, the birds' returning flight,
The longer sunshine, and the shorter night,   10
Arcturus' beams, and Corvus' glitt'ring rays,
Diffuse a promise of the genial days.
Yon muddy remnant of the winter snow
Shrinks humbly in the equinoctial glow,
Whilst in the fields precocious grass-blades peep   15
Above the earth so lately wrapt in sleep.
What sweet, elusive odour fills the soil,
To rouse the farmer to his yearly toil!
Tho' thick the clouds, and bare the maple bough,
With what gay song he guides the cumbrous plough!   20
In him there stirs, like sap within the tree,
The joyous call to new activity:
The outward scene, however dull and drear,
Takes on a splendour from the inward cheer.
Prophetic month! Would that I might rehearse   25
Thy hidden beauties in sublimer verse:

Thy glorious youth, thy vigour all unspent,
Thy stirring winds, of spring and winter blent.
Summer brings blessings of enervate kind;
Thy joys, O March, are ecstasies of mind.   30
In June we revel in the bees' soft hum,
But March exalts us with the bliss to come!

A Mississippi Autumn

Being the Much Appreciated Prose-Poetical Conclusion of Mrs. Renshaw's
Letter of October the 1st, Done into Regular Heroic Couplets

The genial summer hours, so lately flown,
Still haunt the mind, a precious mem'ry grown;
But whilst we ponder on accomplish'd deeds,
The season 'neath the lash of autumn bleeds.
See now the teeming field and fruitful vine   5
Their bounteous care for grateful man resign,
While o'er the radiant summer's less'ning breath
Spread azure mists; the robes of coming death.
And mourning groves in altered aspect weep
And wait in splendour for the wintry sleep: 10
Where once was verdure, leaves of brazen hue
Succeed the gold and red that come to view.
The dying flow'rs excite a pitying tear,
And man laments the swift-revolving year.
The striving soul, in mystic madness bound,   15
Renews the harvest of the annual round,
And finds in summer's death and winter's birth
A sign of promise for the lab'ring earth.
Late-ling'ring summer from the eastern sky
With treasures came, nor coldly pass'd us by.   20
The fragrant roses, and the feather'd train,
The loving laughter of the moon-struck swain,
Each as a blessed boon the summer gave,
That now, unburden'd, seeks its western grave.
Rose-petals for a few; thorns for the rest: 25
For some the bird-song; most, the empty nest.
Some hail the end with welcome and relief,
Some cling with tears of unavailing grief.
Some with a glad content the season speed;
And some with sorrow scan the fading weed.   30

Where late the rainbow blossoms lin'd the path,
Behold the pallor of the aftermath:
Expiring summer, with its genial rays,
Draws the last breath in autumn's gorgeous blaze.
How rich a shroud the pensive autumn weaves,   35
With fox grape purple, maple's tinted leaves,
The crimson dogwood and the sassafrass,
The gums and goldenrod will grace the mass.
Chrysanthemums will crowd the op'ning door,
And view the season soon to be no more;   40
Whilst the wild clematis, in sacred state,
Will clasp its throat; a rosary of fate.
Like holy candles, dimly burning by,
The tow'ring reeds will watch the summer die,
And fragrant lavender, like incense rare,   45
Will lend its sweetness to the sighing air.
Earth gains the rest that frosty breezes bring,
And still'd in slumber, waits the sun of spring.

A Rural Summer Eve

Approach! ye length'ning shades that streak the green,
To cool the breeze, and ease the torrid scene.
Let Phoebus now with ruddy beams retire,
Whilst purple hills conceal the sinking fire.
The painted west a gorgeous glow displays,   5
As kindly clouds set off the evening rays;
O'er field and wood the pleasing veil descends,
And day with dusk in one calm twilight blends.
The glen behind, where dreamy dryads dance,
Feels first the shadow of the night's advance: 10
Black are its depths, where placid pools before
Reflect the sunset from the western shore.
Save Philomel alone, the feather'd train
Cease their sweet songs, nor cheer the homeward swain;
But in the pool the green Hypsiboas leads   15
His deeper choir amongst the bending reeds:
Perch'd on the lily-pads the frogs entune
Their raucous lay, and hail the rising moon.
Unnumber'd insects lend their supple throats,
And with soft chords supply orchestral notes.   20
High o'er the noblest of the circling pines,
The night's first star in single splendour shines;

276

Each shade successive still another brings,
Till Heaven's bright sphere a silent paean sings.
Low o'er the south the dread Antares crawls;   25
While northward from the heights Callisto falls.
Altair and Vega o'er the meadows glow,
And bright Arcturus swells the spangled show.
Far as the vision grasps, thro' vale and field,
The folding flow'rs to dewy portions yield;   30
Whilst all the land an alter'd aspect gains,
As mounting moonbeams gild the grassy plains.
Wak'd by the rays, bewitch'd by gentle gleams,
In tones responsive sing the sparkling streams.
From out the waters rise a naiad throng   35
That view the scene, and join the sacred song.
As now reflected stars adorn the lake,
So wink the fireflies in the humid brake;
While Fancy traces in the fitful light
The torches of the fauns that dance by night.   40
Hark! from the oak the waking Nocturne cries,
And wings his hooting course across the skies.
With strident voice he swells the vesper tune,
And darkly flits against the soaring moon.
Benignant Night! whose gentle joys allay   45
The carking cares that fill the dazzling day:
Whose milder scenes the weary mortal bless,
And sordid Truth in sweet Illusion dress.
All sight and sounds of Nature, here combin'd,
Enchant the soul, and rouse the thoughtful mind;   50
Calm the sad spirit, and with Peace invest
The troubled heart that seeks relief and rest.
Here as in nobler days we freely scan
The sacred universe, unspoil'd by Man.
With rev'rent eye the wondrous whole we see,   55
For all contains, and forms, Divinity!

Brumalia

O'er the bleak, barren hills see the storm-clouds impending,
    Where lately the herds of Alexis were rang'd;
On the sere, stricken mead see the tempest descending,
    And white fleecy flocks for the snow-drifts exchang'd.
By the deep frozen fountain the poor Naiads languish,   5
    Their chaplets of wild-flow'rs all wither'd and dead;

In the grove, drooping Dryads complain of their anguish,
    Whilst bare, wind-blown boughs plead their cause overhead.

But mourn not, ye Nymphs, at the winds of December,
    Nor weep thou, Alexis, at Winter's brief pain;   10
For Flora and Ceres earth's children remember,
    And Phoebus his car turneth northward again.

So deck your fair temples with evergreen garlands,
    And bid the great Yule-log refulgently blaze:
Tho' cold is the world, thro' the high vaulted star-lands   15
    Come tokens of sunshine and sweet summer days!

On Receiving a Picture of the Marshes at Ipswich

High o'er the fen the shielding verdure shoots,
And hides the marshy rankness at the roots;
The passing glance a waving plain beholds,
Nor marks the wat'ry waste the green enfolds:
Thus pleasing prospects charm the distant eye,   5
But fade and tarnish as the gaze draws nigh;
Thus sceptred pomp, magnificently bright,
Turns gross and tawdry to the closer sight.
Judge not the world by wealth of outward show,
But test the firmness of the soil below!   10

A Garden

There's an ancient, ancient garden that I see sometimes in dreams,
Where the very Maytime sunlight plays and glows with spectral gleams;
Where the gaudy-tinted blossoms seem to wither into grey,
And the crumbling walls and pillars waken thoughts of yesterday.
There are vines in nooks and crannies, and there's moss about the pool,
And the tangled weedy thicket chokes the arbour dark and cool:
In the silent sunken pathways springs an herbage sparse and spare,
While the musty scent of dead things dulls the fragance of the air.
There is not a living creature in the lonely space around,
And the hedge-encompass'd quiet never echoes to a sound.
As I walk, and wait, and listen, I will often seek to find
When it was I knew that garden in an age long left behind;
I will oft conjure a vision of a day that is no more,
As I gaze upon the grey, grey scenes I feel I knew before.
Then a sadness settles o'er me, and a tremor seems to start:
For I know the flow'rs are shrivell'd hopes—the garden is my heart!

April

Hertha, awake! discard thy snowy sheen,
And greet the dews that drape the sprouting green;
Let sun and show'r revive the sleeping plain,
Whilst April leaflets deck the grove again.
Feel the soft zephyr, that at glow of dawn   5
Plays in delight o'er crocus-spangled lawn;
Behold the blossoms that adorn each bow'r,
And breathe the perfume of the op'ning flow'r;
Imbibe the rapture, and with joy attend
The feather'd choir whose notes harmonic blend.   10
Rejoice, ye Fauns that roam the shaded hill!
Rejoice, ye Nymphs that haunt the sylvan rill!
Eternal Pan a rustic garland weaves,
And leaps, goat-footed, 'neath the tender leaves.
Deep in the hollow, where the willow springs,   15
The crystal Arethusa softly sings;
Around her banks in modest grace are set
The purple petals of the violet:
'Tis here the gentle Dryads pause to drink,
And pluck their chaplets by the flow'r-fring'd brink;   20
'Tis here the swain, stretch'd on the bord'ring sod,
Learns to love Nature, and love Nature's God!

Upon the slope that fronts the noontide sun
The sportive flocks and supple eanlings run;
With lissome gambols please the shepherd's eye,   25
And feel the ardour of the smiling sky:
In golden wealth beneath their prancing feet
Lie the fair forms of daffodillies sweet;
Whose rising fragrance, delicate and rare,
Gives potent magic to the vernal air.   30
See the trim orchard, whose all-cov'ring green
Is fleck'd with white, as blossoms burst between;
Before our gaze upon the branches grow
Ethereal drifts of aromatic snow!
As the warm sap the grateful tree ascends,   35
So to mankind new life its vigour lends:
Our weary race their winter burdens shed,
And young once more, look blithesomely ahead!
Behold the blue, where Sol's Hesperian rays
Dispute the azure with a redd'ning blaze;   40

279

Where golden Venus, bright Olympian spark,
Relieves the shadows of the creeping dark.
O'er western slopes with feeble beams expire
The fading embers of Brumalian fire,
Whilst far aloft, in gem-bespangled space,   45
Majestic Leo glows with warmer grace.
Young, like the year, Diana's silver car
Hangs crescent in pellucid deep afar;
And hills and woods, responsive to the sight,
Gleam fairy-like in tender, timid light.   50

Eternal Nature! whose undying pow'r
Wakes to new beauty in the springtime hour;
Whose April skies, enjoin'd by changeless truth,
Arouse the meadows to resurgent youth;
Thro' frost-curs'd vortices of Scythian strife   55
Thou bring'st the blessed vernal boon of Life!

On Receiving a Picture of yᵉ Towne of Templeton, in the Colonie of Massachusetts-Bay, with Mount Monadnock, in New-Hampshire, Shewn in the Distance

In Peace beneath the crystal summer Skies,
Behold the Spires of *Templeton* arise;
Around the Green the grove-deck'd Mead expands,
Whilst vary'd Blossoms tint the smiling Lands.
Pleas'd with the Beauties of the blest Domain,   5
No *Goldsmith* long could mourn sweet *Auburn's* Plain;
The rural Grace *Old England* lov'd to view
Here blooms again, transplanted to the New!
The rip'ning Corn along the furrow'd Leas
Nods in Content, and dances in the Breeze;   10
In stately Elm and stout-limb'd Oak combine
To paint the Prasises of *New-England's* Line.
Can ancient Bliss from such a Scene depart,
Or dull Decadence pain the pensive Heart?
Can with'ring Change ancestral Shades o'erride,   15
And aliens live where sturdy *Saxons* died?
May fav'ring Fate a kindly Respite lend,
And keep the Vale untainted to the End!
Look to the North! where grand *Monadnock's* Height
Enchains the Fancy, and rewards the Sight;   20

Such rock-ribb'd Hills our own *New-England* gave
To mould her Sons as rugged and as brave.
Ancient *Monadnock!* silent, pine-girt Hill,
Whose Majesty could move a *Whittier's* Quill;
Whose distant Brow the humbler Pen excites;   25
Whose purpled Slope the raptur'd Gaze invites;
Stand thou, Great Sentinel, tho' Nations fall—
In thee *New-England* triumphs over all!

Autumn

Arcadian Goddess! whose fond pleasing reign
Enchants the forest and delights the plain;
O'er vernal scenes a gentle magic pours,
And glads the flow'rs that bloom on summer shores:
To days less bright thy potent charm extend,   5
Nor scorn the sad Vertumnus as thy friend.
As Phoebus falters with declining light,
Half conquer'd by th' encroaching hosts of night;
His genial rays by chilling blasts subdu'd
To suit the season's melancholy mood;   10
As skies once blue grow desolate and drear,
And with'ring meads proclaim th' expiring year;
As fallen blossoms strow the frost-struck ground,
While birdless groves lament the absent sound;
Thy pow'rs, Arcadian Muse, dispel the woe,   15
And thro' the gloom unnumber'd beauties shew!
Behold the fields, by kindly Pales blest,
In regal robes of yellowing herbage drest;
Mark how the rustic train, with chorus'd tune,
Reap the rich produce 'neath the harvest moon.   20
Each bending stalk some buxom Chloë cleaves;
And honest Damon binds the swelling sheaves.
Happy their lot, whom no gay town can spoil;
Pleas'd with their rural shades and simple toil!
What world-worn Sybarite, tho' far he roam,   25
Can find an happier scene than harvest-home?
Here nymphs and swains, whose mingled accents praise
The bounteous goddess of the golden maize,
With harmless mirth their useful cares divide,
And husk the gen'rous fruitage by their side.   30
The teeming orchard and the laden vine
Declare the rule of pow'rs no less benign:

Pomona's blessing crowns the fertile trees,
And vineyards yield to Liber's mild decrees.
On yonder wooded hill, where nimbly rove   35
The sylvan Pan, and spirits of the grove,
A faery spell the graceful scene transmutes,
And dazzling splendour o'er the verdure shoots:
Each hamadryad sheds her wreath of old,
To don fresh garlands, gay with red and gold.   40
With lib'ral hand, they fling their gaudy store
Of pleasing pigments round the forest floor.
Hark to the music of the hunter's horn,
That wakes the meadows and salutes the morn!
Look whilst the pack their panting prey pursue,   45
And lead afield the mounted retinue:
The sharper winds our spirits but restore;
Excite the chase, and whet us on the more!
When o'er the marsh the hunter's moon appears,
And silver light the bleak October cheers,   50
Th' inclement winds in rapture we defy,
Charm'd with the glories of the crystal sky.
Aloft in space the shimm'ring Pleiads shew
Their dainty beams to frosty realms below,
Whilst huge Orion, climbing o'er the lea,   55
Dilates the soul with wond'ring ecstasy.
Capella and Aldebaran unite
To dwarf the Heav'nly Twins' inferior light;
And all the vault with growing glow essays
To mend the loss of Phoebus' warmer rays.   60
Resplendent Autumn! whose prismatic veil
Drapes the sad earth, and hides the coming gale;
In sumptuous state the dying year adorns,
And cheers the grieving watchers whilst it warns.
As gorgeous gleams the fading day attend,   65
And vary'd hues in sunset lustre blend,
So now the season, drawing to its last,
Outvies the calmer radiance of the past.
Like the bright butterfly, whose glorious hour
Speaks but the end of life and earthly pow'r,   70
The tinted valley and the spangled hill
Blaze for awhile—then languish cold and still.
'Tis thine, Arcadian Muse, the heart to raise
With pleasing fancies and auspicious lays;

282

Amidst a frigid world 'tis thine to sing   75
Th' unbroken promise of returning spring:
Close to the hearth by Autumn rigours bound,
We hear the song, and bless the annual round.

Sunset

The cloudless day is richer at its close;
    A golden glory settles on the lea;
Soft, stealing shadows hint of cool repose
    To mellowing landscape, and to calming sea.

And in that nobler, gentler, lovelier light,   5
    The soul to sweeter, loftier bliss inclines;
Freed from the noonday glare, the favour'd sight
    Increasing grace in earth and sky divines.

But ere the purest radiance crowns the green,
    Or fairest lustre fills th' expectant grove,   10
The twilight thickens, and the fleeting scene
    Leaves but a hallow'd memory of love!

Old Christmas

    "Caput apri defero,
      Reddens laudes domino."

Ye modern throng, whose tinsel joys reveal
The strain'd and labour'd ecstasies you feel;
Whose empty pastimes hold a spurious bliss,
And feebly copy brighter days than this:
Your clumsy games suspend, and pause to hear   5
Of genuine mirth, and ancient Christmas cheer!
Would that some Druid, wise in mystic lore,
Might waft me backward to the scenes of yore;
Midst happier years my wand'ring soul detain,
And let me dwell in ANNA'S virtuous reign;   10
Warm in the honest glow of pure content,
And share the boons of rustic merriment.
Awake, Pierian Muse! and call to view
The snow-clad groves and plains my grandsires knew;
Bring back the winding road and neat-clipt hedge   15
That primly skirts the forest's shadowy edge:
Revive the picture, and adroitly weave

283

O'er all the subtle spell of Christmas Eve!
Hark to the merry strains of Yuletide song
As the full coach to Norfolk flies along;   20
Its ample room scarce able to confine
The home-bound crowd whose voices gaily join;
See the stout driver, whose rubescent face
Grows redder at each wayside stopping-place,
And the flush'd passengers, their cheeks aglow   25
With the cold air and gently stirring snow.
Behold yon sturdy lads in height of glee,
From classics, rod, and master's precept free;
Read in each laughing face and manly smile
The future glories of BRITANNIA'S Isle!   30
Swift whir the wheels, and smartly snaps the whip;
The swaying coach assumes a livelier clip;
Down the long road in majesty we fly,
An hundred cots and hamlets sweeping by;
Whilst now and then a rural wain we sight,   35
High pil'd with holly for the festive night.
Up the steep slope our cumbrous chariot creaks,
Attains the crest, and lowlier meadows seeks;
Before our gaze the steepled town expands,
And grateful eyes survey th' extended lands: 40
Thro' melting clouds the frosty moonlight gleams,
And gilds the picture with bewitching beams;
O'er spire and roof the genial radiance steals,
And ev'ry grove the pleasing magic feels.
Now rolls the coach thro' many a cobbled street,   45
Where well-stock'd shops the thrifty buyer greet;
A gaping crew our rattling course attend,
And urchins hail the driver as their friend.
The tavern gate at length our flight concludes,
Where varied solace suits our sev'ral moods;   50
Apicius in the spacious kitchen spies
The hams and bacon that delight his eyes,
And stout Lucullus seeks the sweet relief
Of hot plum-pudding, musty ale, and beef.
Th' important coachman struts in pompous pride,   55
Whilst four fresh horses to the coach are tied;
The trav'llers take their places one by one,
And the long journey is once more begun.
Brief is our ride, ere thro' the bord'ring trees
The watchful eye a lighted window sees;   60

Our travels done, the lumb'ring coach we leave,
And the lodge-gates our weary forms receive:
Here Granny Goodwife to an infant train
Repeats her oft-told legends once again;
Tells of the sheeted vision at the Hall,   65
And how the spectre scales the garden wall.
The wither'd crone with joy our footstep hears,
And greets her former charge with genuine tears:
Dear wrinkled ancient—faithful nurse of yore,
Who nurs'd ourselves, and nurs'd our sire before!   70
The bliss of Home! what heav'nly raptures vie
With the sweet joys that in our birthplace lie?
Each stone and timber hallow'd by the past,
Where countless generations breath'd their last;
No inch of ground in all those acres wide   75
But bears a symbol of ancestral pride:
In park and mansion, wall and hedge we trace
The mystic aura of our honour'd race.
Along the well-kept walks we quickly tread,
And seek the lights of home that gleam ahead;   80
About our feet a canine legion bark,
That know their master even in the dark.
The full-orb'd moon, with intermittent rays,
About the lawns and terrac'd gardens plays;
On the white paths unusual shadows throws,   85
And makes a fairy landscape as it glows.
Now opens wide the door, from whence there floats
A merry discord from unnumber'd throats;
'Tis Christmas Eve, and all the household join
In revels fitting to our ancient line: 90
Master and servant each glad rite go thro',
And the old Saturnalian pledge renew;
The servile throng in boist'rous games disport,
While the staid guests to milder joys resort.
Bright Christmas candles the vast hall illume,   95
And sprigs of holly deck each spacious room:
The mistletoe in splendour is display'd,
To tempt the swain, and trap th' unwary maid;
But over all the rest in stately fame,
See the great Yule-Log with its fulgent flame!   100
The lordly log a mighty heat exhales,
And o'er the chill of winter air prevails;

285

Gives an eternal promise of the spring
That Sol, turn'd back, to Northern climes will bring.
The solstice day our pagan fathers kept,   105
And hail'd the turning sun whilst Nature slept;
Their simple fanes with evergreen entwin'd,
To fix the coming days of warmth in mind:
Succeeding years elaborate forms impose,
And the plain feast to Saturnalia grows;   110
But tho' the throng the Roman god adore,
The ancient customs linger as before.
An age still newer blends the heathen glee
With the glad rites of Christ's Nativity;
Yet firm thro' ev'ry change of outward show,   115
We keep th' ancestral feast of long ago!
Fair as the glow that from the Yule-Log spreads,
Is the warm welcome ev'ry feaster sheds:
With patriarchal grace the Squire imparts
A genial mirth, and lights the coldest hearts;   120
On the mix'd crowd a family blessing lays,
And wakes the Christmas cheer of former days:
Here sport a merry train of young and old;
Aunts, uncles, cousins, kindred shy and bold;
The ample supper ev'ry care dispels,   125
And each glad guest in happy concord dwells.
With Yuletide songs the time-blest roof awakes,
While the grey harper into music breaks;
Feasting and joy the spacious mansion fill,
Nor dares intrude one jarring note of ill.   130
Upon the oaken floor the children find
Ecstatic bliss in toys of ev'ry kind;
Less simple gifts the elder throng reward,
But all partake the season's blest accord.
Now comes the dance, wherein each airy school   135
Of jigs and capers claims alternate rule:
The honest Squire leads forth his gentle spouse,
And with a rigadoon excites the house;
Mol Pately, and the homely Country Dance,
Vie with the latest tripping steps from France;   140
Terpsichore, amaz'd, the scene observes,
And flees the unfamiliar dips and curves;
Yet more of honest joy therein resides,
Than in cold London's stateliest turns and glides!

286

The dancing o'er, we climb the broad oak stair,   145
And seek the bedside with an evening pray'r;
On the still night in sacred chorus floats
The waits' sweet harmony, in faint-borne notes:
Such choirs, methinks, remind the grateful earth
Of herald angels at our Saviour's birth!   150
Thus lull'd with liquid song, divinely blest,
On Christmas Eve we softly sink to rest.
Hail to the Holy Morn! when joy and peace
Reign o'er the land, and ev'ry boon increase;
A golden sun th' encircling park awakes,   155
And gaily glitters on the ice-bound lakes.
Each frosted lawn and whiten'd terrace gleams
With glowing splendour in the rising beams,
While silver chimes from gorgeous spires proclaim
To list'ning meads the great Messiah's fame.   160
In fam'ly chapel we devoutly hear
The virtuous Squire read forth the word of cheer;
Then to the morning meal and daily walk,
Where innocence enjoys its harmless talk;
In order'd gardens we at ease converse,   165
And the fond bliss of Christmastide rehearse.
Now sounds the bell from that proud steepled fane
Wherein the parson holds benignant reign;
Down the long slope with rev'rent steps we go,
And meet the peasants from the town below: 170
Each rural clown his Sunday raiment wears,
And ev'ry face a smile of greeting bears.
Behold the churchyard, where in silence lie
The honest villagers of days gone by:
From such brave blood great ENGLAND rose of yore—   175
God grant the future may produce us more!
Within the church a fervent sermon rings,
And the full choir a pious anthem sings;
The rural choristers chant loud and strong,
And have in spirit what they lack in song.   180
The black-gown'd chaplain, modest of his wit,
Reads the wise precepts other parsons writ:
No laurels for himself he seeks to gain,
But gives his flock the best his books contain.
The service done, our genial Squire extends   185
An invitation to his humble friends;

Up to the Hall in many an awkward group,
The gaping swains and happy ploughmen troop:
Beneath the master's roof they take the feast
That richly waits the lowliest and the least;   190
With merry pastimes stir the quiet air,
And bless their patron for the lib'ral fare.
'Twas thus the Romans at this season gave
Saturnalian licence to the serf and slave:
Our British race the ancient gift improve,   195
And treat the peasant with paternal love.
Assist, gay gastronomic Muse, whilst I
In noble strains sing pork and Christmas pie!
What quill like mine can more than half afford
A proper notion of the Yuletide board?   200
Quick to the hall a num'rous crowd pour in
At the sharp summons of the rolling-pin;
Saucers and flagons, cups and many a plate,
In festive eagerness the spread await:
Th' impatient throng half grudge the pious space   205
That the good Squire consumes in saying grace,
And from each throat a grateful sigh is drawn,
As the Boar's Head in majesty comes on.
The stout grey butler pompously sustains
The silver plate, and shews officious pains: 210
One on each side, two sober menials bear
Refulgent dips with ceremonious care,
With rosemary the platter is bedeck'd,
Whilst harpers' chords increase the glad effect:
The ready crowd an Oxford song repeat,   215
And laud in ancient style the roasted meat;
The college Latin, pleasing to recite,
Improves the feast, and whets the appetite.
But not alone the stately Boar is plac'd
To please the palate and reward the taste;   220
Huge sirloin mountains dot the damask field,
And peacock pies a haunting odour yield:
Puddings and gravies, sauces, roasts, and stews,
Enchant the diner, and defy the Muse!
Now comes the servant band with brush and tray   225
To clear the remnants of the feast away;
Upon the board the Wassail Bowl is laid,
Fill'd with a nectar by old precepts made:

To each the silver dish is pass'd around,
Whilst merry wassail songs aloft resound;   230
In ancient fashion ev'ry guest partakes,
And the rich wine unwonted brilliance wakes—
Alas! that man should ever be so prone
To seek a Bacchic humour not his own!
Quips, jests, and stories now untrammell'd start;   235
And harmless gossip plays a pleasing part;
Legends and anecdotes appear in state,
And grow the larger as they circulate:
Ev'n the staid parson drops his sober mien,
And joins the others in the jovial scene.   240
But mad hilarity at length subsides,
And prattling youth its sweeter joys provides;
The hall is clear'd, and all the infant throng
Conduct their pastimes with diverting song.
Unreason's Abbot full dominion claims,   245
And leads the children in their ancient games.
Quaint murmurs thro' the spacious house parade,
And former times in costume are display'd;
Old Father Christmas dances hand in hand
With some odd Indian of the western land;   250
Turks jostle Roundheads, all the mimic train
Obey the laws of Saturn's festive reign.
Gay Drury-Lane such acting ne'er beheld,
And Covent-Garden's masques are here excell'd:
Frolick and fun in laughing pantomime   255
Surpass description, and confound our rhyme!
The evening shades touch many a tired head
As the young rompers breathless climb to bed;
Our older band in fireside comfort sit,
And tell our tales, or try our shafts of wit: 260
O'er all the company a peace descends,
Whilst the great log its cheering radiance lends.
To ev'ry mind there comes a thankful thought
For the rich blessings that the day hath brought,
And many a scoffer, bred in London air,   265
Midst this calm scene sends up a silent pray'r.
Here virtue rules, and each contented swain
Enjoys the bliss of his paternal plain;
A life like this benignant Heav'n design'd
To lift the soul, and soothe the fretful mind: 270

Why must our modern wits in scorn refuse
These rural realms their sires were proud to choose?
Above the frozen grove the moon appears,
And tender light the quiet garden cheers;
The winding walks, the fountain, and the green   275
Take on the semblance of a fairy scene:
Light dancing o'er the sod, an elfin crew
In fond imagination come to view;
And friendly pines in rhythmic measures sway,
Their patron nymphs responsive to the play.   280
All the soft picture seems alive with grace,
And peopled with a sweet ethereal race:
Thro' the still air bewitching spirits glide,
And spread the sorcery of Christmastide!
Must I awake to find these visions flown,   285
The past long dead, and happiness unknown?
Have honest merriment and rural cheer
Gone with the fleeting snows of yesteryear?
Unhappy age! whose joys so ill contrast
With the spontaneous pleasures of the past;   290
Wherein our languid youth to gloom resort,
And listless children must be taught their sport:
Whose arts the stamp of waning pow'r confess,
And hide their weakness in eccentric dress;
Canst thou not see thy many woes proceed   295
From false ambition, commerce, haste, and greed?
Wise is the man who spurns the seething times,
Nor madly up the hill of Plutus climbs;
Rests on his own hereditary soil,
Remote from care or avaricious broil: 300
His father's place assumes, and keeps his name
On the calm records of agrestic fame.
For such an one the field of learning waits,
And art attends his hospitable gates;
'Tis his to feed the flame of sense and wit   305
And ancient lore to future times transmit;
Preserve the good his grandsires prov'd before,
And drive the wolf of dulness from the door;
Each Gothic novelty with skill attack,
And bring the grace of former ages back.   310
Ye hoary groves! whose many-centuried oaks
The wistful bard with longing lyre invokes,

290

Look down once more in your imperial state
On such a race as made Old ENGLAND great!
View once again the hearty rural Squire 315
Whose lib'ral soul contain'd a gen'rous fire;
Whose mild dominion sway'd the peasant band,
And spread contentment thro' the grateful land:
Such, and such only, can the past revive,
And keep our well-lov'd Christmas joys alive; 320
Meanwhile the Muse, in reminiscent strain,
Forgets the years, and sings those joys again!

A Summer Sunset and Evening

In the metre (though perchance not the manner) of the *Poly-Olbion*
of MIKE DRAYTON, ESQ.

The ruddy sun sinks down beyond the purple hill,
And all the painted west an hundred colours fill.
The bars of dark'ning cloud that streak the flaming sky
Set off the splendid scene and please the watching eye.
The shadow'd glen behind foretastes the coming night; 5
The placid pool before reflects the fading light.
The harmonies of birds are hushed with the eve,
But straight the insect choirs the still of dusk relieve.
Sweet are the summer chords the little host entune,
Whilst frogs in lily'd pools salute the rising moon. 10
Above yon tow'ring pine peeps out a single ray,
The first of Heav'n's bright host to speed departing day.
And ev'ry shade that falls another starlet brings,
Till all the sphere above a silent anthem sings.
In pastures that extend to realms beyond our view, 15
The folding flow'rets nod, made drowsy by the dew.
And all the scene about an alter'd aspect gains,
As moonbeams gild the brook and wake responding strains.
Now in the humid brake the fitful firefly's gleam
Winks like the mirror'd star in lake and placid stream. 20
From branches arching o'er the hooting owl awakes,
And glimps'd against the moon his stately flight betakes.
All sights and sounds are blent to rouse the thoughtful mind,
And who that looks and hears adores not all combin'd?
The pageant of the night with rev'rent eye we see, 25
For Deity's in all, and all in Deity!

Epilogue

Behold kind Nature in her sweetest mood,
When neither day nor solar glare intrude.
What man so dull he faileth to receive
The darker beauties of the summer eve?   30
Egad! 'tis dull my ardour to confine
To Alexandrine pace, and Drayton's line.
Alone in fair Quinsnicket's wood by night,
I fain would follow Thomson's smoother flight!

A Winter Wish

(A Pseudo-Poetical Disaster Occasioned by the Recent Spell of Cold Weather.)

Ye wintry gusts, that round my casement blow,
And pile in drifts the pallid daemon snow;
Ye cruel frosts, that numb with poison breath
A suff'ring world, and serve the will of death:
How well could I (did Fortune but permit)   5
Your terrors vanquish, and your arts outwit!
Grant me, ye gods, a dome of crystal glass,
Whose size the Pantheon's tenfold might surpass,
Thro' whose clear surface sun and stars might blaze,
While safe within glow artificial rays: 10
Let this my garden and my cot confine,
Free from the chilling air and blast malign;
Here let me dwell, and in December sing
Midst balmy zephyrs of eternal spring!
What fond delights, what sweet Arcadian grace,   15
Could such a spot within its bounds embrace!
Thro' mossy meads a limpid stream might run,
Its ripples sparkling in the noonday sun;
Its length reduc'd to many a pleasing part
By tiny waterfalls, contriv'd with art;   20
Along the banks the supple reeds asway,
And nimble trout within the waves at play.
A floral train the rolling green might bear,
And birds unnumber'd glad the genial air;
To their soft notes a bubbling fountain lend   25
Euphonious chords whilst nodding groves attend.
On azure lakes, where stirs a gentle tide,
The fleecy swans in majesty might glide;

292

Abundant lilies deck each little sea,
And fragrant herbage rise along the lea.   30
On terrac'd lawns, that mount with order'd skill,
Unusual flow'rs the well-plac'd urns might fill;
Sequester'd nooks the weary swain invite,
And curious bow'rs admit a verdant light.
A summer-house, in Grecian likeness made,   35
Might well afford a classic marble shade;
Corinthian columns the white roof uphold,
And match th' acanthus sprouting from the mould.
Here might the studious mind at ease expand,
Nor feel the woes that fret a wintry land: 40
Here might the Muse, protected from the storm,
In endless spring melodious couplets form;
Graces and Nymphs, a fair ethereal train,
With Fauns and Satyrs sport along the plain;
Whilst reedy Pan, and all the Naiad crew,   45
In shady founts and brooklets come to view.
Endymion here might in contentment dream
Beneath his lov'd Diana's crescent gleam;
And Meliboeus nurse his tender goats,
Or sound the rustic pipe with lovelier notes;   50
Thyrsis and Damon, Corydon the blest,
Might here their songs repeat with keener zest;
And Strephon for his Chloë's golden hair
A brighter wreath of meadow-flow'rs prepare.
Damoetas, grey with years, his youth once more   55
In such a realm of springtime might restore;
Nor could one mortal, nymph, or faun, or god,
Resist the charms of this enchanted sod.
But see—alas—the pleasing picture fades—
And icy fields displace the vernal shades!   60
Th' idyllic scene, too quickly left behind,
Proves but a fleeting phantom of the mind:
Yet when, indeed, does life reward or please
With truer things than visions such as these?
Our struggling years too little bliss could own   65
Were they confin'd to genuine joys alone:
'Tis Fancy's province to enlarge the cheer,
And fill our days with musings doubly dear;
With Doric lay the bleakest ills remove,
And bear us to the Heliconian grove: 70

Tho' changing seasons o'er the mead may roll,
Spring reigns perpetual in the smiling soul!

Ver Rusticum

"Candidus auratis aperit cum cornibus annum
    Taurus, et adverso cedens Canis occidit astro."
                                        —VIRGIL.

Ye bare-branch'd groves, and herbage dank and cold,
Ye matted leaves, and vapour-breathing mould;
Ye dripping heav'ns, that weep for Nature's pain,
And mourn detested Winter's boreal reign:
Hark to the note that thrills the languid air,   5
And bids exhausted Earth discard her care!
Pan, drunk with Autumn grapes, and stretch'd at length
Upon the plain, a thing of slumb'ring strength,
Feels the returning sun; and as a beam
His curtain'd eye creeps o'er, and breaks his dream,   10
Turns in his leafy blanket, eyes the mead,
And stirs to sound once more the sylvan reed.
Delighted Nature hears, and from each vale
A faery band the genial season hail;
Join in the dance, and o'er the eager trees   15
Lay sweet enchantment; while from Western seas
Mild Zephyrus attends the call, and strows
The greening vale with flow'rs of various hues.
Borne on soft Auster's warm aërial tide,
The feather'd race in gay-plum'd grandeur ride;   20
With gladsome carolling delight the plains,
And sing eternal youth in moving strains.
Fresh with the nectar of the melting hills,
The cool sequester'd fountain pours its rills;
Swift flow the streamlets from the reed-grown urn,   25
Raising along the marge the timid fern,
Whisp'ring of joy to primrose-haunted shades,
And gaily gleaming thro' the forest glades.
O'er the damp wold Apollo's shafts descend
In golden show'rs, that mercifully rend   30
The Python chill of Winter, whose dread pow'r
So lately coil'd about the budding bow'r.
Meanwhile his rays inspire the grateful peak,
Soothe the green valleys, and the woods bedeck;

294

Gild all creation with a vernal light   35
That blends with each glad scent and sound and sight.
Now shine the hills, and valleys stretch'd between,
And willow-fringed brooks, and groves of green;
Whilst in yon hollow 'twixt the shelt'ring crests,
The dear familiar hamlet calmly rests: 40
In each bright roof and glitt'ring spire we trace
A heighten'd charm, and more than usual grace.
Now wind the verdant lanes, grass-carpeted,
Where with their flocks the sprightly shepherds tread,
Thence bound for sunny uplands, there to lie   45
At ease beneath the azure April sky:
O'er flow'ry slopes the nibbling lambkins play,
While the young shepherds dream the hours away.
Now bloom the hedges, and the rolling mead
Where placid kine in tinkling comfort feed;   50
Now wake the fields, whose earthly face must know
The useful plough, and bounteous harvests grow.
Ungrateful Man! who can such boons despise,
Nor view the rural realm with raptur'd eyes!
How dull the bard who flouts a pastoral theme,   55
And scans his soul for some obscurer dream,
Neglects the world for things he ne'er can see,
And scorns the splendour of simplicity!
Vain is his lay, whose narrow fancy clings
To urban trifles, and unnatural things;   60
Glows with false flame, and morbidly repeats
Impassion'd nothings and chaotic heats:
To sylvan scenes the fav'ring Nine belong,
And smile their sweetest on the shepherd's song!
So let me seek for Beauty in the dawn   65
Of April days, or on the dew-deck'd lawn
That sleeps beneath Arcturus' evening light,
Or in the watches of the vernal night.
Let the fond lyre each verdurous bow'r explore,
And sing the Nereids of the quiet shore;   70
The languorous Dryads, and the Satyrs fleet,
And bearded Pan, who leaps with cloven feet;
And nymphs and clowns that chant Arcadian strains
At twilight thro' the farmers' teeming plains.
Let me for Beauty seek far from the strife   75
Of with'ring commerce, and congested life,

295

Where primal Nature wakes spontaneous fire,
And golden fancies rouse the living lyre.
No walls but hills the poet's shrine must own;
No roof besides the vernal sky alone;   80
No altar-flame but Phoebus, or the blaze
Of his pale sister's soft nocturnal rays;
No tapers but the stars must light the fane;
No incense must the sacred air sustain
But that which rises from th' unfolding woods,   85
And flow'ring banks, and spangled solitudes,
No hymnic strains but those of singing birds,
Or rippling brooks, or gently lowing herds,
Or pensive croonings of the fragrant breeze
In the tall rushes and Aeolian trees.   90
So the young poet, at the close of day,
Sang from the pansied slope whereon he lay,
His eyes fix'd on the prospect wide around,
Of nodding groves, and cowslip-cover'd ground,
And glinting streams, red with the sunset fires,   95
And cottage roofs, and slender village spires,
And verdant hillocks, gaily blossoming
With the sweet tokens of the early spring:
He paus'd, enraptur'd by the vernal view,
Then in sublimer strains burst forth anew!   100

A June Afternoon

A quiv'ring haze the verdant meadow vests;
    Calm sleep the valley and the sun-clad height;
Beyond the hill the ancient hamlet rests,
    Each spire and roof aglow with golden light.

A drowsy hum, as of contented bees   5
    In distant hives, pervades the balmy air;
O'er slope and plain the barely stirring breeze
    Wafts from the South a perfume mild and rare.

The wooded hollow, where late violets grow,
    Spreads like an ocean of inviting green;   10
Thro' whisp'ring aisles the filter'd sunbeams flow
    O'er brook and pathway, soften'd and serene.

In rural bow'rs the op'ning roses blush,
    Whilst pale syringas strow their fragrant blooms;

Thickets are vocal with a tuneful thrush,   15
    And all the grove a mellow charm assumes.

Delightful scene! The soul in rapture mounts,
    And magic lights the blissful afternoon;
Above long years of care our fancy counts
    One precious moment of Elysian June!   20

The Spirit of Summer

Aërial Nymph, whose jocund sway
Can melt our vexing cares away,
Whose winsome train the valleys bless
With perfume, warmth, and loveliness;
From fulgent skies once more appear,   5
To spread thy annual gifts of cheer.
Let nimble Naiads cease their sport,
And gather wild-flow'rs for thy court,
While graceful Sylphs, admiring, lend
Their praises as thy feet descend.   10
How mild the zephyrs from afar
Fan with sweet breath thy gliding car;
How soft the Fauns of yonder grove,
Pleas'd with the sight, affirm their love!
Nature, rejoicing, hails thy reign,   15
And pleasure fills the grateful plain.
Now trip the agile hours in haste,
With new delights and comforts grac'd;
Tho' yesterday no bliss could give,
Today 'tis joyous just to live!   20
The bright'ning mind of genius glows
In warmer verse and livelier prose;
And o'er the dull terrestrial throng
Disports a breeze of Teian song.
The aureate sun, whose soothing rays   25
Pour languor thro' the noontide haze,
To each green bow'r a charm imparts,
And gilds them with enchanting arts.
Here may the pensive swain, at rest,
Behold, in robes of fancy drest,   30
The fays of air and sea and land,
Link'd in a sprightly saraband;
Old Pan, his brow with myrtles bound,

297

Young Satyrs, leaping o'er the ground,
Shy Oreads lur'd from distant hills   35
By melodies of reedy rills,
Ethereal Dryads from the wood,
And river-gods in festive mood,
All fir'd with Corybantian glee
To dance, aërial Nymph, for thee!   40
Gay Goddess, may thy bounteous will
Diffuse more lasting treasures still;
Nor suffer these glad scenes alone
To form the province of thy throne;
'Tis thine in ev'ry heart to plant   45
Thy bliss, a true inhabitant,
That thro' far drearier days than thine,
The soul of summer still may shine!

August

Come, mellow month, whose full-blown charms
    O'er mead and wood diffuse their grace;
Whose ardour all the valley warms,
    And glads the grateful mountain's face.

The waving corn in yonder field,   5
    Delighted, owns thy genial ray;
Whilst clover'd plains adoring yield
    The frankincense of new-mown hay.

The sky a lovelier blue puts on;
    The sun thro' Virgo proudly rides;   10
The lark sings sweeter at the dawn;
    The stream with purer crystal glides.

The grove with tropic plenty flow'rs,
    And Summer reigns in regal state;
Precious the boon of earlier hours,   15
    Yet now doth each one culminate.

To youthful bards the Spring I give;
    To sighing swains the June divine;
But I midst riper joys would live,
    And choose the August days as mine!   20

Spring

Paraphrased from the Prose of Clifford Raymond, Esq., in the *Chicago Tribune*.

Arise, ye swains! for fair Aurora's light
Shews the wild geese in scurrying matin flight;
In shifting ranks their silent course they take,
And for the valley marshland quit the lake:
Tho' loose they fly, in various modes arrang'd,   5
Their eyes are steady, and their goal unchang'd.
Thus in brute instinct Nature shews her law;
Excites our wonder, and compels our awe.
But hark! from yonder grove the pleasing peal
Of redbreasts, winging to their morning meal;   10
In softer tones the lusty bluejay chaunts,
While maple shades the bobbing grackle haunts:
From neighb'ring wall the bluebird's carol rings,
And in the mead the lark rejoicing sings.
Forests and fields attend the welcome strain,   15
And hail the advent of the feather'd train;
Swift flock the airy legions from the shores
Where Mexique's Bay its genial current pours:
In waves unnotic'd throng the tuneful band,
To glad the soul, and cheer the Northern strand,   20
Obedient to the sway of Jove's all-pow'rful hand.
Alive with song the gentle bluebird floats;
The hermit thrush disdains melodious notes;
None marks their solid course, but as they come,
Each gains a greeting to his Northern home.   25
Now drip the maples with their vernal juice,
While growing thorns their swelling buds unloose;
On grassy slopes the furry coils untwine
Where soon hepatica's white blooms will shine.
Almighty Pan! whose vast unchanging will   30
Clothes the green wildwood and enrobes the hill,
How calm the workings of thy great decrees!
How still thy magic o'er the flow'ring leas!
No march of feet, or sound of timbrel shakes
The sylvan scene, or stirs the drowsy brakes: 35
In songful peace the law resistless moves,
And pleases while it rules the meads and groves.

April Dawn

I love to watch the meadow-lands awake
  Beneath the breezes of an April dawn,
When o'er the stone-wall'd hill the sunbeams break,
  And tremble on the tender-tufted lawn.

When vernal tints of earth and heaven fuse 5
  Into one placid mist of morning light,
And the still landscape's intermingled hues
  Paint the high crests, and make the valleys bright.

The red-gold sun, reluctant to ascend,
  Lingers a moment o'er the velvet mound; 10
Mead, grove, and garden their faint fragrance blend,
  And matin skylarks thrill with crystal sound.

The fresh-turn'd furrows, damp with dew and haze,
  Breathe out a message of resurgent life;
Each shrub and tree receives increasing rays, 15
  And splendid shines, with joy and vigour rife.

Say you a barren vista strikes the eye;
  That no wild grace adorns the rolling green?
Say you that here unlovely pastures lie,
  And awkward cottage-roofs impair the scene? 20

Not so the sentient poet-glance can see
  The gentle glory of the sun-gilt slope;
A million Aprils from eternity
  Gleam in this one, and sing a world's fair hope!

January

In bleach'd, forbidding robes array'd,
  Stern January treads the wold,
Within his icy hand a blade
  Of lethal might—the cruel cold.

Vainly the sun with slanting beams 5
  Attempts the tyrant god to slay;
The naked boughs and frozen streams
  Feel still the rigours of his sway.

But when the twilight shades descend,
    And heav'n unveils before our sight,   10
There shines a promise of the end
    In visions of celestial light!

October

Low sighs the wind that frets the wither'd leaves
    And sends them flutt'ring to the greying ground;
A hunter's moon gleams thro' the silent sheaves
    That loom like ghosts of vanish'd joys around.

A nameless chill falls on the hoary wood   5
    Which yesterday such verdant charms could boast,
And mounds and moors in desolation brood,
    Unpeopled save by sadness' spectral host.

At golden noon the dying sun can still
    Some semblance of the former bliss impart;   10
But when the twilight creeps from yonder hill,
    The shadow, length'ning, strikes the restless heart.

The airy throngs whose carols we have known,
    From coming winter flee on nimble wings;
They pipe farewell, then leave us still and lone,   15
    Unhappiest of the earth's deserted things.

The transient splendour of each aging leaf
    Bids us dismiss our woe in hopeful cheer;
The world, it cries, finds spring beyond the grief—
    But the heart whispers, "Shall I, too, be here?"   20

Christmas

The cottage hearth beams warm and bright,
    The candles gaily glow;
The stars emit a kinder light
    Above the drifted snow.

Down from the sky a magic steals   5
    To glad the passing year,
And belfries shake with joyous peals
    For Christmastide is here!

[On Marblehead]

What wonders now engag'd my ravisht sight,
Mellow and magick in the golden light?
Behold on ev'ry hand the rocky steeps
O'er which the vivid verdure splendid creeps:
Ahead rise bold a train of spectral trees   5
Whose branches whisper in the evening breeze,
Whilst to the east, o'er crags of sombre dye,
A purple ocean joins th' aethereal sky.
Here flit the myriad sails, a snowy band,
And here the stately stone-built beacons stand;   10
Close to the shoar, and pleasing to the gaze,
Fair verdant islands strow the wat'ry ways.
But lo! new marvels gild the ancient air
As o'er the road our eager footsteps fare;
See yonder meadow fring'd with hoary oaks   15
Whose guardian shade a Druid spell invokes,
And where at night a firefly throng recall
Forgotten years, and witchcraft's ghoulish pall.
Here at the bend, where, salt and shallow, reach
A cove's dim waters on a mossy beach,   20
Behold that gloomy mansion, set about
By titan tree-trunks in daemoniac rout.
Smother'd with shocking ivy, still it rears
Uncanny walls, and counts two hundred years.
Stranger to sun, immerse'd in humid shade,   25
With willows like vast octopi array'd,
It leers perpetual from the deeps of time,
And mirrors gulphs down which no man may climb.
Upward and on—thus runs our pleasing course,
Each novel turning lovelier than its source;   30
Meads, groves, and steeps successive charm the soul,
And hint at ev'ry bend a brighter goal.
Ecce! Eureka! What is this that dawns
From the still crest, across the sloping lawns?
What faery glimmer of celestial seas,   35
And crystal spires that rise from distant leas?
Can a meer earth such beauteous sights contain;
Such marvels deck the dull terrestrial main?
'Tis sunset's magic, 'neath whose kindly spell
All things are true, and all high wonders dwell: 40
Thus Salem Harbour greets congenial skies,

While Salem's towers and steeples distant rise.
Entrancing sight! The eye can scarce withdraw
From such a prospect of irradiate awe!
Dim fall the vesper shades, and far behind   45
The lights of Marblehead of home remind.
Now for the vale, where shadows eldritch wait
To mock the trav'ller with their hints of fate;
The dark'ning skies a thousand stars disclose,
While the lone cotters seek their calm repose.   50
Again the narrow streets and terrac'd hills,
Where Georgian mem'ry each keen spirit fills;
Black are the winding ways, save for yon gleam
Of fanlight, or yon chequer'd windows beam—
O'er all the town the past unchanging broods,   55
And Time trips lightly in his mildest moods!

[On a Scene in Rural Rhode Island]

Far as the Eye can see, behold outspread
The serried Hills that own no Traveller's Tread;
Dome beyond Dome, and on each flaming Side
The hanging Forests in their virgin Pride.
Here dips a Vale, and here a Mead extends,   5
Whilst thro' the piny Strath a Brooklet bends:
Yon farther Slopes to violet Æther fade,
And sunset Splendour gilds the nearer Glade:
Rude Walls of Stone in pleasing Zig-zag run
Where well-plac'd Trees salute the parting Sun;   10
Vext with the Arts that puny Men proclaim,
Nature speaks once, and puts them all to Shame!

Providence

Where bay and river tranquil blend,
    And leafy hillsides rise,
The spires of Providence ascend
    Against the ancient skies.

Here centuried domes of shining gold   5
    Salute the morning's glare,
While slanting gables, odd and old,
    Are scatter'd here and there.

And in the narrow winding ways
    That climb o'er slope and crest,   10
The magic of forgotten days
    May still be found to rest.

A fanlight's gleam, a knocker's blow,
    A glimpse of Georgian brick—
The sights and sounds of long ago   15
    Where fancies cluster thick.

A flight of steps with iron rail,
    A belfry looming tall,
A slender steeple, carv'd and pale,
    A moss-grown garden wall.   20

A hidden churchyard's crumbling proofs
    Of man's mortality,
A rotting wharf where gambrel roofs
    Keep watch above the sea.

Square and parade, whose walls have tower'd   25
    Full fifteen decades long
By cobbled ways 'mid trees embower'd,
    And slighted by the throng.

Stone bridges spanning languid streams,
    Houses perch'd on the hill,   30
And courts where mysteries and dreams
    The brooding spirit fill.

Steep alley steps by vines conceal'd,
    Where small-pan'd windows glow
At twilight on the bit of field   35
    That chance has left below.

My Providence! What airy hosts
    Turn still thy gilded vanes;
What winds of elf that with grey ghosts
    People thine ancient lanes!   40

The chimes of evening as of old
    Above thy valleys sound,
While thy stern fathers 'neath the mould
    Make blest thy sacred ground.

Thou dream'st beside the waters there,   45
    Unchang'd by cruel years;
A spirit from an age more fair
    That shines behind our tears.

Thy twinkling lights each night I see,
    Tho' time and space divide;   50
For thou art of the soul of me,
    And always at my side!

Solstice

Where steel and stone invade the sky
    And alien millions throng,
Yuletide recalls the hours gone by
    Like some remember'd song.

Again New-England's frosty breeze   5
    The exile's vision clears,
And thro' a mist of memories
    The ancient town appears.

The steepled village by the bay
    Whose twisting lanes are white;   10
Whose cottage candles twinkling play
    On snows of Christmas night.

The rolling fields, the hoary oaks,
    The road meand'ring lone
By streams that stern December chokes,   15
    And walls of tumbled stone.

The scent of pines, the scent of pines!
    And starlight on the hill—
The farmhouse roof where Sirius shines
    When dusk is young and still!   20

Tonight I am at home again,
    Far from that fleshly tent
Which breathes and walks and knows the pain
    Of scenes for me unmeant.

I am at home, beside my soul   25
    In that dear seaport street

Which from the first to life's last goal
    Must be its changeless seat.

And, TRYOUT, now a strong command
    I waft thro' stretching skies,   30
Bidding my dull and distant hand
    Express these thoughts that rise!

October

Mellow-fac'd, with eyes of faery, wistful clad in tinted leaves,
See the brown October tarry by the golden rows of sheaves;
Oak and acorn in his garland, fruit and wineskin in his hands,
Mystic pilgrim from a far land down the road to farther lands.

Softly treading, gently breathing, casting spells on wood and wold,   5
Vines with purple clusters wreathing, witching boughs to red and gold;
Bearing sicklemen their pleasure when the harvest toil is o'er,
And the autumn's garner'd treasure lies within the festive door.

Bearing dreams to all who listen as he sounds his elfin horn
Where the crystal vapours glisten past the farther hills at morn;   10
Where the sunset hovers playing on the teeming cottage yard
Till the cryptic night comes straying in a mitre tall and starr'd.

Dreams elusive and uncertain, fleeting as the dying year,
Glimpses from behind the curtain, half to cherish, half to fear;
Memories that charm and beckon, vanish'd scene and vanish'd face,   15
Phantoms past the world we reckon, reaching from the wells of space.

Mounting as with necromancy, welcome visions hold the sight;
Bygone fields assail the fancy, radiant in a golden light.
Ancient lanes lead cool and bending past remember'd farms and byres,
Where the curling smoke ascending tells of happy autumn fires.   20

I can catch the flaming riot of the oaks and elms I know,
And the breathless ruddy quiet of the sunset's spectral glow;
And the farmhouse chimney peeping thro' the scarlet maple shade,
And the gorgeous fruits of reaping by the door in order laid.

Greens that red and yellow dapple, tints that match the blazing sky;   25
Swelling pumpkin, rosy apple, cluster'd grapes of Tyrian dye;
And behind the orchard reaching where the rolling meadows bide,
I can see the corn-shocks bleaching and the stubble stretching wide.

Skies alive with southward winging, ravens perch'd on sheaf and stack,
Groves with eager trumpets ringing as the quarry flees the pack;   30
Swains with nuts and fagots plodding homeward to the twilight garth,
Soon to cluster, warm and nodding, round their cider and their hearth.

Notes of village bells are soaring, peaceful in their vesper tune,
As an eerie light comes pouring from the rising hunter's moon;
Wild above the wooded mountains, weirdly shining on the streams,   35
Yellow floods from haunted fountains, witches dancing in the beams.

Half-seen sights from outer distance, half-heard sounds from outer spheres,
Beat with goblin-born insistence on the spirit's eyes and ears.
Thoughts half-thought and yearnings sober, formless as the atuumn smoke,
These thy gifts, obscure October, these the symbols of thy yoke.   40

Mellow-fac'd, with eyes of faery, wistful clad in tinted leaves,
See the brown October tarry by the golden rows of sheaves;
Oak and acorn in his garland, fruit and wineskin in his hands,
Mystic pilgrim from a far land down the road to farther lands.

[On Newport, Rhode Island]

Where the bright Blue assaults the chaulk-white Strand,
The beetling, ledge-lin'd Cliffs titanick stand;
Here verdant Fields in sunny Calm extend,
Whilst the low Waves agreeable Echoes lend.
On yonder Knoll an Abbey Tow'r is spy'd,   5
And pastur'd Kine survey the rising Tide;
O'er all the Hush of rustick Virtue glows,
And antient Mem'ry grants the Soul repose.

Where now the Idler scales the craggy Ground,
Philosophy in Triumph once was found;   10
For each grey Rock above the Blue upthrown
A *Berkeley's* Feet and *Berkeley's* Thoughts hath known!
Beneath yon hanging Peak's petrifick Shade
An *Alciphron* in all its Parts was made,
And ev'ry Path some ling'ring Trace contains   15
Of the great Clerick's wise melodious Strains:
Wou'd that my sterile Muse might here ignite
With some residual Spark of that vast Light!

The East India Brick Row

(Old Warehouses in South-Water Street, Providence, Threatened with
Demolition in the Name of Aesthetic "Progress", 1929)

It is so long they have been standing there—
    Red brick, slant roofs, above the harbour's edge;
Chimneys against a fragment of salt air,
    And a green hill ascending ledge by ledge.

They fit the place so well—as much a part   5
    As hill or sky. They almost seem to be
Growths of that Nature, wiser than all art,
    Which gives us flowers and mountains and the sea.

No one remembers when they did not shew
    The dawn's bright ingots like an open chest,   10
Or when, near dusk, they were not there to glow
    With hinted wonders from a fire-lashed west.

They are the sills that hold the lights of home;
    The links that join us to the years before;
They are the haven of old questing wraiths that roam   15
    Down long, dim aisles to a familiar shore.

They store the charm that years build, cell by cell
    Like coral, from our lives, our past, our land;
Beauty that dreamers know and cherish well,
    But hard eyes slight, too dulled to understand.   20

Symbols of old New-England thoughts and ways—
    They are the forms that beauty must unfold
Here, where a gayer pomp would vainly blaze
    For want of bonds with what our memories hold.

Sometimes at night the stir of wharves and slips   25
    Comes faint and distant from another day,
And the old brick is barred with masts of ships
    That crowd as ghosts along the ancient bay.

Bales from Bermuda, towers of Malay teak;
    Satins and spices from the Yangtse's mouth;   30
Lapping of waters, and the half-heard creak
    Of ropes and spars that sway against the south.

And from behind, the murmur of old streets,
    And curious lanes that climb the steepled hill;
Peals from old belfries—till the day defeats   35
    Phantom and dream, and the faint sounds are still.

It does not seem they ever can be gone;
    Or that the hill's old spires could ever trace
Such haunting shapes across a winter's dawn
    Without that setting for their slender grace.   40

So if at last a callous age must tear
    These jewels from the old town's quiet dress,
I think the harbour streets will always wear
    A puzzled look of wistful emptiness.

And strangers, staring spaciously along   45
    An ordered green that ponderous pylons frame,
Will always stop to wonder what is wrong,
    And miss some vital thing they cannot name.

On an Unspoil'd Rural Prospect

    ". . . et in terram guttae cecidere calentes,
      Vernat humus, floresque et mollia pabula surgunt."
          —Ovid. *Metam.* vii, 283–4

How tranquil spread these sloping meads
    That glow as evening gilds the west,
And verdant from the river's reeds
    Ascend to join the beech-crown'd crest!

Yon bosky vale, where lily'd streams   5
    Glide on to shadowy glens unknown,
Seems drowsing with the ling'ring dreams
    Of ages happier than our own.

For here the breeze with soften'd strain
    Salutes a scene of changeless grace,   10
And spring on spring returns again
    As to a lov'd, remember'd place.

These oaks and elms seem echoing still
    To pipes that bygone shepherds play'd,
As resting on this selfsame hill   15
    They grateful scann'd the neighb'ring shade.

309

Notes that cou'd please the naiad band,
    And charm the dryads of the wood,
Sound low once more along the land
    When twilight looms on solitude.   20

The winding walls, that vines enfold,
    The mossy roofs beyond the mere,
Shine ancient, as the sunset's gold
    Recalls each long-departed year.

Here the encumb'ring weight of age   25
    Its bitterest force a while resigns,
For sylvan spells reverse the page,
    And bare the long-hid earlier lines.

In aureate floods o'er grove and field
    The verdant aeons sing from sight,   30
Till time and death, dissolving, yield
    A breath's eternity of light!

Saturnalia

From Morven's Mead to Arcady
    Let bays the temple columns twine,
Whilst wreathèd throngs relax in glee,
    And tapers thro' the darkness shine:

For ev'ry frosty star above   5
    Prophetick spreads its twinkling beams,
To cheer the dismal wintry grove
    With golden show'rs of vernal dreams.

[Christmas Greetings]

1. [To Samuel Loveman]

At ease behind thy lofty casement,
    Charm'd magick, op'ning on the foam
Of perilous seas wherein have placement
    The faery spire and island dome,
Accept these maund'rings, dull and charmless,   5
    Such as old men in dotage whine;
Assur'd that they at least are harmless,
    Pat to the season, and benign!

2. [To Eugene B. Kuntz et al.]

May good St. Nick, like as a bird of night,
Bring thee rich blessings in his annual flight;
Long by thy chimney rest his pond'rous pack,
And leave with lessen'd weight upon his back!

3. [To ?]

In wishing Christmas joys for you,
I don't know where to stop, that's true;
But sure, to stop were useless pains,
Since not a bound my wish restrains!

4. [To Anne Tillery Renshaw]

Madam, accept a halting lay
That fain would cheer thy Christmas Day;
But fancy not the bard's good will
Is as uncertain as his quill!
  —From the Copy-Reviser

5. [To Sarah Susan Lovecraft]

May these dull verses for thy Christmastide
An added ray of cheerfulness provide,
For tho' in art they take an humble place,
Their message is not measur'd by their grace.
As on this day of cold the turning sun
Hath in the sky his northward course begun,
So may this season's trials hold for thee
The latent fount of bright futurity!
  —Yr aff. son & obt Servt., H.P.L.

6. [To M. P. K.]

Since heathen creeds a *Christmas* wish prevent,
A card *Brumalian* speaks my good intent;
For know ye, that this season held its cheer
Long ere it grew to saints and Christians dear.
  —M. Lollius Paganus

7. *A Brumalian Wish* [To Maurice W. Moe]

 From the damnable shadows of madness,
  From the corpse-rotten hollow of Weir,
 Comes a horrible message of gladness,

5

And a ghost-guided poem of cheer—
And a gloom-spouting pupil of Poe sends the pleasantest wish of the year!   5

    May the ghouls of the neighbouring regions,
        And the cursèd necrophagous *things,*
    Lay aside their dark habits in legions,
        For the bliss that Brumalia brings—
And may Druids innum'rable bless thee, as they dance on the moor's fairy-rings!   10

    So, Galba, may pleasures attend thee
        Thro' all thy bright glorious days;
    May the world and the mighty commend thee,
        And the cosmos resound with thy praise—
And may all future ages be brilliant with the light of thine intellect's rays!   15
—Edward John Ambrose Bierce Theobald

8. [To Lillian D. Clark]

Tribute, like Charity, begins at home,
Nor will this first-writ message farther roam;
In vain the westward postman bears his pack—
For each o'erflowing Christmas wish comes back!

9. [To James F. Morton, Samuel Loveman, and Annie E. P. Gamwell]

As Saturnalian garlands wreathe
    The pillars of each pagan door,
Let one unalter'd Roman breathe
    His annual Yuletide wish once more!

10. [To Albert A. Sandusky]

Hot dawg, ol' cell-mate—may the day be
Grief's funeral for one rough baby!
Fly o'er the gas Yule's twin red banners,
And Santa'll fill 'em with bananas!

11. [To Charles A. A. Parker]

There was an old geezer nam'd THEOBALD,
Who'd rather have dropped in than scribbled;
    But his roll ebb'd too low—
    For 'twas all outbound flow
Whilst inbound the jack only dribbled!   5

12. [To Rheinhart Kleiner and Jonathan E. Hoag]

Once more Boeotia in presumption scrawls
A flatt'ring message to Aonian halls,
And hopes the Bard, in retrospective vein,
May live the old remember'd days again!

13. [To Frank Belknap Long]

Whilst you invade with prattling joy
    The chrome-blue swamp oneiroscopick,
And like a multivalent boy
    Divagate some bidextrous topick;
Whilst, as I say, you thus amuse   5
    A modern mind with Eliot leanings,
Pray laugh not if your Grandpa choose
    A simpler rhyme, and one with meanings.

We old folks know, of course, the world
    Is but a chaos frail and vicious;   10
A very rubbish-vortex, hurl'd
    In shapes delusive and capricious;
But split me, Child, if we can mend
    Our stale empirick imperfection,
Or keep from making outlines blend   15
    The way they do before dissection!

And so tonight with pen in hand
    To wish the blessings of the season,
I'm curst if I can well command
    The mode in analytick reason!   20
I can't take Santa Claus apart,
    In shreds denigrate with strabismus,
So, Child, I'll quit the quest of art,
    And wish an Old Man's Merry Christmas!

14. [To W. Paul Cook]

O'er frosty meads my humble couplets roll
To greet in song the world's most gen'rous soul;
This lib'ral day from thee was sure design'd,
Since 'tis so plain a pattern of thy mind!

15. [To C. W. Smith]

As now the Yuletide hours appear,
And firesides beam with festive cheer,
May no blest hearth at evening shine,
TRYOUT, with warmer glow than thine!

16. [To ?]

Illustrious Monarch, in whose lofty mind
The scholar and executive are join'd,
See round the throne thy docile subjects kneel
To speak this wish, that all united feel:
"May each bright moment of thy holidays   5
Glow with the warmth of joy's unhinder'd blaze!"

17. [To Rheinhart Kleiner]

St. John, accept 'mid winter's blast
A pictur'd mem'ry of the past;
July his image sends to cheer
Your Christmas and your coming year.

18. [To ?]

In these dull lines regards I give—
Conserver from Conservative;
But conservation does not fill
My mind when dealing out good will!

19. [To Verna McGeoch]

Tho' late I vow'd no more to rhyme,
    The Yuletide season wakes my quill;
So to a fairer, flowing clime
    An ice-bound scribbler sends good will.

20. [To Philip B. McDonald?]

Plotinus, tho' thy mystic mind
    Soars high o'er the atomic world,
Scorn not the wishes, bright and kind,
    At thee by T. LUCRETIUS hurl'd!

21. [To Mary Faye Durr]

Behold a wretch with scanty credit,—
An editor who does not edit—

But if thou seek'st a knave to hiss,
Change cars—he lives in Elroy, Wis.!

22. [To W. Paul Cook]

That Yuletide came from Saturn's annual feast,
Is claim'd by ev'ry pompous sciolist;
The gen'rous attitude, they say, is drawn
From lib'ral Roman virtues, past and gone:
What rot to fool each shallow-pated ass—   5
For Christmas was set up in Athol, Mass.!

23. [To John Milton Samples]

May Yuletide lend its genial ray
To ease the burdens of the way;
And with its pow'r at last restore
The CLARION'S peal to Georgia's shore.

24. [To Arthur Goodenough]

Bright Tityrus of the mountains green,
    Who sweetly pip'st in beechen shades,
Let Christmas find thy blest demesne
    The haunt of all th' Aonian maids.

From frozen steeps in song proclaim   5
    The sleeping Pan, and let them ring
With Flora's and Apollo's name,
    Prophetic of the verdant spring.

25. [To C. W. Smith]

May Nymphs and Graces ever bless
    Thy home, and keep thy pathway bright,
Cheering each day with happiness
    And sending joyous dreams each night.

May TRYOUT flourish as of yore,   5
    And THOMAS free from snares remain;
And long by thy congenial door
    May Pleasure pause with all her train!

26. [To Jonathan E. Hoag]

As garlands on each happy door
Proclaim the Christmas feast once more,

Let THEOBALD send his deep regard
To SCRIBA, Muse-befriended bard.
May the New Year auspicious hold   5
Fresh honours added to the old;
And may there beam, thro' Fortune's art,
An AVALON within thy heart!

27. [To L. Evelyn Schump]

May Yuletide bless the town of snow
    Where Mormons lead their tangled lives;
And may the light of promise glow
    On each grave cit and all his wives.

28. [To Rheinhart Kleiner, Alice M. Hamlet, and Eugene B. Kuntz]

In Yuletide verse I'd fain convey
Thoughts from a bard of yesterday;
Yet deem no wish that I repeat,
Like my dull rhyming, obsolete!

29. [To Laurie A. Sawyer]

As Christmas snows (as yet a poet's trope)
Call back one's bygone days of youth and hope,
Four metrick lines I send—they're quite enough—
Tho' once I fancy'd I could write the stuff!

30. [To Tat (Edith Miniter's cat)]

As once *Hortensia,* mythical and bright,
A sparkish COLE to couplets could incite;
So thou, Sir *Tatt,* with less fictitious grace,
Inspir'st a lover of thy furry race!

31. *Theobaldian Hibernation* [To Edith Miniter]

See in his cell the lonely Hermit sit,
    Whilst the gay world its festival is keeping;
Fantastick figures in his visions flit—
    Forgotten dust, thro' many an aeon sleeping:
But lo! he stirs—and on a Lydian breeze   5
Wafts his grave message down the centuries!

32. [To Winifred Virginia Jackson]

Inferior worth here hails with limping song
The new-crown'd Monarch of Aonia's throng;
And sends in couplets weak and paralytick,
The Yuletide greetings of a crusty critick!

33. [To D. R.]

In these dull lines, deserving of no praise,
Old age to infancy a tribute pays;
And hopes that time to you may kindly give
Unfading youth, but boundless years to live!

34. [To Annie E. P. Gamwell]

This deathless epick hath not far to go,
And its round trip is mostly made for show;
Yet it conveys good will no less sincere
For Saturnalia and the coming year!

35. [To Lillian D. Clark and C. W. Smith]

As Saturnalian days draw near
To mark the climax of the year,
And green-drap'd temples glimmer bright
With waxen tapers' sacred light;
As Phoebus draws his heav'nly rein   5
And turns his coursers north again,
I trust that you may richly share
In ev'ry boon the gods prepare!

36. [To Alfred Galpin, Myrta Alice Little, Winifred Jackson, and Verna McGeoch]

Tho' Christmas to the stupid pious throng,
These are the hours of Saturn's pagan song;
When in the greens that hang on ev'ry door
We see the spring that lies so far before.

37. [To Annie E. P. Gamwell]

Tho' short the course my humble note must run,
In warm good-will 'tis not to be outdone:
May this bright day and Saturnalian mirth
Improve your fortunes, and reward your worth!

38. [To Lillian D. Clark]

My trifling lines, in wit too feebly dumb,
Arrive anon exactly whence they come!
But tho' their circling bounds be monstrous small,
They hold good wishes with no bounds at all!

39. [To Lillian McMullen and Jonathan E. Hoag]

To poetry's home the bard would fain convey
The brightest wishes of a festal day;
Yet fears they'll seem, so lowly is the giver,
Coals to Newcastle; water to the river!

40. [To Rheinhart Kleiner]

To shades Aonian I address my song,
Where dreams the noblest of the poet-throng;
And makes my fondest Yuletide wishes known
In couplets *he* wou'd be asham'd to own.

41. [To W. Paul Cook]

May Yule to thee all blessings swift impart,
Artist, and patron of each soaring art;
Long live thy house, and may the future know
Athol as nucleus of the Muses' glow:
Let foremost stand, for ornament and use,   5
Thy tasteful volumes, and thy bright *Recluse!*

42. [To James F. Morton]

From mines celestial Santa digs a gem
To deck your proud Museum's diadem;
A common stone, yet worthy of a place
In some dark alcove, or inferior case:
'Tis Christmas cheer—swell'd livelier and greater   5
By him who bears it to a sage Curator!

43. [To C. W. Smith]

Enclos'd you'll find, if nothing fly astray,
Cheer for a bright New-England Christmas day;
Yet will that cheer redound no less to me,
For where these greetings go, my heart shall be!

44. [To Edward L. Sechrist]

May Polynesian skies thy Yuletide bless,
And primal gods impart thee happiness;
Zimbabwe's wonders hint mysterious themes,
And ne'er a Dybbuk lurk to mar thy dreams!

45. [To John Russell]

To old Britannia's storied strand
    May Yuletide greetings glide,
As with a warm extended hand
    I brush the seas aside!

46. [To Jonathan E. Hoag, Samuel Loveman, and Eugene B. Kuntz]

Son of the Muse, may Yuletide bear
    A thousand joys to crown thy worth,
Whilst Fame supplies her curule chair
    To seat thee with the great of earth.

Sweet as the Musick of thy lyre   5
    Be all the coming year shall bring,
And with thine own Aonian fire
    May life to thee of beauty sing!

47. [To Rheinhart Kleiner]

A wreath to thee, whose double art
Can play the bard's and draughtsman's part,
And give to what thy visions trace
A setting worthy of their grace!
The monkish scribe, beat by thy hand,   5
Shares envy with the poet band;
Nor will th' impartial judge allow
That any do as well as thou.
Thus humbled, let us all draw near
To wish our victor Christmas cheer!   10

48. [To George Kirk]

Since Chelsea is old SANTA'S very home,
I trust he'll call before he starts to roam,
And find in KIRK a worthy youth to crown
With all the fame that MOORE of old laid down!

319

49. [To Arthur Leeds]

May Yuletide such beneficence evince
That thou mayst walk as gay as Pilsen's Prince;
Let wealth come fast, and sweet content still faster,
Till thou 'rt as placid as a Burgomaster!

50. [To Everett McNeil]

May Gallic shades thy Yuletide bless,
And all their pleasing lore express,
    Of wilderness and stream;
TONTY, successful, bids thee raise
For bold CHAMPLAIN thy potent praise,   5
    And revel in the theme!

51. [To Albert A. Sandusky]

Run out of slang, and far from fresh supplies,
I pen this feeble message to the wise:
Forgive the style, and grasp the good intent,
For ne'er was Christmas cheer more truly meant!

52. [To Edith Miniter]

From distant churchyards hear a Yuletide groan
As ghoulish Goodguile heaves his heaps of bone;
Each ancient slab the festive holly wears,
And all the worms disclaim their earthly cares:
Mayst thou, 'neath sprightlier skies, no less rejoice,   5
And hail the season with exulting voice!

53. [To Anne Tillery Renshaw and Wilfred B. Talman]

Each column by Potomac clear
    May Christmas wreaths entwine;
And may of all the season's cheer
    A goodly share be thine!

54. [To Edgar J. Davis]

May Santa bring to Harvard's brightest son
A Pickle for a Very Knowing One,
Whilst Father Charles and reed-crown'd Merrimack
Unite to swell with praise his gen'rous pack.

55. [To Alfred Galpin, Victor E. Bacon, and Wilfred B. Talman]

May good St. Nick, unaw'd by lights Parisian,
Bring thee rich blessings in his annual mission;
Long by thy chimney rest his pond'rous pack,
And leave with lessen'd weight upon his back.

56. [To Maurice W. Moe]

May Yuletide pow'rs thy worth reward,
And give thee happiness unmarr'd;
Attending angels guard thy path
And shield thee from celestial wrath.

57. [To Charles A. A. Parker]

Let Cliftondale to Yuletide croakings bark,
As the dull Raven greets the sprightly Lark!

58. [To James F. Morton]

Whilst cheaper souls extatick bark,
    And slop effusive o'er each page,
To milder purrs I bid thee hark,
    As feline Theobald greets a Sage.

When by the happy Yuletide fire   5
    There soars the Ave and Te Deum,
May Jersey's choicest cats conspire
    To fix their mews in thy Musaeum!

59. [To Rheinhart Kleiner]

The simple rustick here essays
To fan your urban Yuletide blaze,
And tincture with his clumsy bit
Sophistication's polish'd wit!

60. [To Frank Belknap Long]

As ev'ry year the Farmer's Almanack
Tells us that Christmas once again is back,
Our thoughts ancestral turn to former days,
And old dreams flicker o'er the fagot's blaze.
Take, then, this token, by a patriarch penn'd,   5
Who would to youth the antient lore commend,
Nor scorn that art which elder souls admire,
Flung whitely heav'nward in a Georgian spire!

61. [To Samuel Loveman, Victor E. Bacon, and Eugene B. Kuntz]

From Georgian byways, snowy, quaint, and steep,
To Hellas' temple, pois'd above the deep,
These Yuletide wishes fly, and bid you hold
Abundant revels, fill'd with joys of old.

62. [To George Kirk]

Where Chelsea's cluster'd steeples climb,
    And peaceful hearths at Christmas glow,
Let simple age direct a rhyme
    To sing the praise of long ago.

With wholesome boons may all be blest   5
    Who bide within thy happy door:
Charlie, small Oscar, and the rest—
    And thou, whose Art can highest soar!

63. [To Everett McNeil]

With happy heart let Theobald pitch in
To sing thy rescue from Hell's Kitchen;
So late himself from slums escap'd,
His joy with genuine warmth is shap'd!
Each with like words the season greets—   5
D—n 49th and Clinton Streets!

64. [To Wilfred B. Talman]

Colonial greetings!—tho' I sorrow much
That I can't send them fluently in Dutch.
Even the house this modest card commands
Savours but little of New-Netherlands!
But spite of that, believe the wishes good,   5
And that I'd curve the roof-line if I could;
Whilst genealogy assures you true
That old Saint Nick is Holland thro' and thro'!

65. [To Alfred Galpin]

Let simple Age melodick youth address,
And wish a Maestro Yuletide happiness.
From Georgian hills the cordial message flies,
To sing old days beneath the western skies.

66. [To Sonia H. Greene]

Once more the ancient feast returns,
And the bright hearth domestic burns
    With Yuletide's added blaze;
So, too, may all your joys increase
Midst floods of mem'ry, love, and peace,   5
    And dreams of Halcyon days.

67. [To Jonathan E. Hoag]

May Christmas gladness, nimble, warm, and witty,
Descend abundant on old Whipple City;
And bring a special blessing and reward
For Scriba, first as citizen and bard!

68. [To Lillian D. Clark]

Restor'd to ancient scenes where I belong,
Returning gladness fills my annual song;
And these fond wishes, bright with Yuletide's glow,
Take pleasure that they have not far to go!

69. [To Annie E. P. Gamwell]

As from the steeple, Georgian, white, and fair,
The bells of Christmas cheer the ancient air,
These greetings flow, wherein the past essays
With warm regard to fan your Yuletide blaze.

70. [To Albert A. Sandusky]

Here's the old stuff—without much pep
As measur'd by your zippy rep,
But warm and cordial-like clear thro',
And best a simple goof can do!

71. [To C. W. Smith]

Restor'd to ancient scenes where I belong,
Returning gladness fills my song;
And doubly glad I am when I address
Tryout, rejoicing in like happiness!

72. [To Edith Miniter]

Hark, from the nighted crypt a Georgian song
Of one restor'd to where he doth belong.

Encircling ghouls the daemon chorus swell,
And cordial ululations wish thee well!

73. [To Edward L. Sechrist]

From Georgian spires to Southern seas
    A wealth of blessings showers;
Abounding honey to thy bees,
    And peace to all thy hours!

74. [To W. Paul Cook]

May Athol as of yore be merry
With bright rejoicings Culinary,
And may no Christmas joy of old
Be Vagrant from the hearthside fold!

75. [To Rheinhart Kleiner]

St. John, whose art sublimely shines
In liquid odes and melting lines,
Let Theobald his regard express
In verse of lesser loveliness.
As now in regal state appear
The festive hours of Yuletide cheer,
My strongest wish is that you may
Feel ev'ry blessing of the day!

76. [To Alice M. Hamlet]

As gay Inzana with her light
Dispels the stars of Christmas night,
And happy gods intone an hymn
From blest Sardathrion to the Rim.

77. [To ?]

Accept, skill'd bard, a Yuletide line
From one whose gifts are less than thine.
If wanting in the words be aught,
Pray deem it present in the thought.

78. [To ?]

As you 'neath tropick skies enjoy
    The fav'ring sun's most genial rays,
And can your golden hours employ

In gentle summer's blissful ways,
Take the good wishes of an Arctick friend—   5
The only kind of warmth our clime can lend!

79. [To Felis (Frank Belknap Long's cat)]

Little Tiger, burning bright
With a subtle Blakeish light,
Tell what visions have their home
In those eyes of flame and chrome!
Children vex thee—thoughtless, gay—   5
Holding when thou wouldst away:
What dark lore is that which thou,
Spitting, mixest with thy meow?

80. [To Charles A. A. Parker]

May that fleet lark, whose late ambitious flight
Cheer'd my dull hours, and made my cottage bright,
Soar past such realms as these, and from the blue
Draw down, grave Clarence, some reward for you!

81. [To Edith Miniter]

Saturnalian cheer again at hand,
    With greens and holly on each door,
The tireless rhymer, smug and bland,
    Begins anew the annual bore.

Not his to vaunt a poet's bays,   5
    Whose bays may only reach the moon—
So trite and callous in my ways,
    I jazz once more the hackney'd tune.

82. [To Tat (Edith Miniter's cat)]

Tom Grey, 'tis no elegiack strain
    I sound in Yuletide gratulation,
For sure, I hope it still is plain
    Your state is one of animation.

As far from my Novanglian lea   5
    I meditate in many a boneyard,
The grey slabs turn my thoughts to thee,
    Yet purring gravely in thine own yard.

83. [To Albert A. Sandusky]

Well, Kid, I gotta leave it skip
Dat I have kinda lost my grip
In shootin' Mexpet since me gas
Got switched so fur from Cambridge, Mass.

But hell! les' hope that ol' Doc Time,   5
Touch'd by dis bevo'd fadeout rhyme,
Will some day patch the busted chain
An' tune de outfit up again!

84. [To Edward H. Cole]

CARBO, attend the Muses' pleasing flight
On this benignant Saturnalian night,
And let good will approach your holly'd gates
Deckt with those chaplets that the lyre creates:
But stay! by what ungentle thought impell'd,   5
You ask what poetry this card e'er held?

85. [To Edward L. Sechrist]

Minstrel of coral bow'rs whose limpid lay
Brings tropick visions ev'n on Christmas Day,
May golden seas stretch placid for thy proa,
And all for thee smile she of Hina-Moa!

86. [To Alice M. Hamlet]

May Christmas bring such pleasing boons
    As trolldom scarce can shew;
More potent than the Elf-King's runes
    Or Erl of long ago!
And sure, the least of Santa's spells   5
Dwarfs all of poor Ziroonderel's!

87. [To Sonia H. Greene]

Once more the greens and holly grow
Against the (figurative) snow
    To mark the Yuletide cheer;
Whilst as of old the aged quill
Moves in connubial fondness still,   5
    And quavers, "Yes, My Dear!"

May Santa, wheresoe'er he find
Thy roving footsteps now inclin'd,

His choicest boons impart;
Old Theobald, tho' his purse be bare,   10
Makes haste to proffer, as his share,
    Affection from the heart!

88. [To Lillian D. Clark]

Slight is the tour my lines essay,
But vast the fondness they convey:
And no less vast is all the throng
Of joys I'd like to send along!

89. [To Annie E. P. Gamwell]

No false address is this with which I start,
Since the lines come directly from my heart.
Would that the rest of me were hov'ring nigh
That spot where my soul rose, and where 'twill die.
But since geography has scatter'd round   5
That empty shell which still stalks on the ground,
To Brooklyn's shores I'll waft a firm command,
And lay a duty on the dull right hand:
"Hand," I will broadcast, as my soul's eyes look
O'er roofs of Maynard, Gowdy, Greene, and Cook,   10
Past Banigan's toward Seekonk's red-bridg'd brook,
"To daughter Anne a Yuletide greeting scrawl
Where'er her footsteps may have chanc'd to fall,
And bid her keep my blessing clear in view
In Providence, Daytona, or Peru!"   15

90. [To Rheinhart Kleiner]

For thee, Lothario, as the Yule
Revives the joy of Saturn's rule,
    Three boons I have in mind:
May Brooklyn thee her bard proclaim,
The world accord thee Elia's name,   5
    And all the fair be kind!

91. [To James F. Morton]

God rest thee, merry Gentleman, may naught
Intrude this Yuletide to dismay thy thought;
May woe in seven letters, clos'd with E,
Lie horizontal, and remote from thee,

Whilst thy sure fame, in vast museums stor'd,   5
Mounts vertical to join the heav'nly horde!

92. [To Everett McNeil]

On thee, skill'd scribe, whose magick touch distils
From all the past its choicest, keenest thrills,
May ev'ry age a Yuletide boon bestow,
Purg'd of each vestige of alloying woe:
May Sieur Du Lhut with noble rage inspire,   5
And Père Marquette call down his heav'nly fire!

93. [To Arthur Leeds]

May merry Yule—a festive, crisp, and bright one—
Beam o'er the hearth of Arthur Leeds—the right one;
And may the other—changeling red-flag Levy—
Reap Bolshevik confusion, hot and heavy!

94. [To Frank Belknap Long]

At thee, decadent Sir, this tome is hurl'd,
Appropriate to a purple-incense world;
O'er each strange leaf with Mediterranean zeal
The dodd'ring donor bids thy vision steal:
'Tis Greek to him—the simple country squire—   5
But youth is youth, and age respects its fire!

95. *To Mr. and Mrs. C. M. Eddy, Jr.*

Behold a pleasure and a guide
    To light the letter'd path you're treading;
Achievements with your own allied,
    But each the beams of polish shedding.

Here masters rove with easy pace,   5
    Open to all who care to spy them,
And if you copy well their grace,
    I vow, you'll catch up and go by them!

96. [To C. W. Smith and Harold Bateman Munroe]

Once more the festive day comes round,
    And all the air is filled with greeting;
A welcome, captivating sound,
    Tho' telling us that time is fleeing.
Well—let it fly on noiseless wings,   5

Whilst harmless joys make each day golden;
And hail the piny night that brings
    The breath of Yule, and mem'ries olden.

97. [To Edith Miniter]

The Shepherds' sign once more illumes the air,
And lights old Tremont's snowdrifts—if they're there.
The waits' sweet carols fill the maple wood,
And care is maul'd into a festive mood.
Holly and mistletoe flaunt gaudy banners,   5
Whilst Santa stocks all stockings with bananas.

98. [To Donald Wandrei?]

Health to the Tramp whose sturdy feet
    Along the vary'd highroads ramble;
May you with fav'ring fortune meet,
    Nor feel the stings of wayside bramble.
May plenty wait at ev'ry door,   5
    Exempt from bloodhounds' barb'rous teasing,
And may the junction 24
    Lead you to haystacks soft and pleasing!

99. *To an Author of Juvenile Fiction* [Everett McNeil?]

Behold a double blessing, sweet and mild,
This night of homage to the story'd child;
Thee, as thyself the angels once commend,
Then crown thee freshly as the children's friend!

100. [To Sonia H. Greene]

Sweets to the sweet, and beauties to beauty tend—
And sure, in PATER beauty knows no end!
What apter tribute for the fair design'd,
Than this assembled beauty of the mind?
The deft magician draws in golden page   5
Immortal glories from a shining age,
And keeps, a well of never-dying lore,
The titan raptures we can make no more.

101. [To ?]

Alas! what words can shew with fitting grace
Regard and blessings that the pen outrace!

Would that a monarch's pomp or conqueror's gold
Were mine to prove what else stands feebly told!

102. [To a cat]

With catnip deck the temple doors,
  And to the gods a fat mouse offer—
Tonight our annual praise outpours
  In pious purrs that mock the scoffer.
Let not a claw disturb the bliss,   5
  Let not a back in scorn be vaulted.
Lives there a cat with sceptick hiss
  Or meow for worship so exalted?

103. [To Lillian D. Clark]

Enclos'd you'll find, if nothing fly astray,
Cheer in profusion for your Christmas Day;
Yet will that cheer redound no less to me,
For where these greetings go, my heart shall be!

104. [To Annie E. P. Gamwell]

As when a pigeon, loos'd in realms remote,
Takes instant wing, and seeks his native cote,
So speed my blessings from a barb'rous clime
To thee and Providence at Christmas time!

105. [To Sonia H. Greene]

In Yuletide mood my pencil fain wou'd trace
The cheer I soon shall utter face to face,
And each crude line to warmth may well aspire,
Lit by Affection's bright enduring fire.

106. [To Frank Belknap Long]

Precocious Sir, who draw'st with wizardry
Charm from the sky, and horror from the sea;
Whose airy soul explores with lyrick art
All space and time where Beauty hath a part;
From fields of Fame one moment deign to gaze   5
On lower realms, whence rise inferior lays:
Mark antient Theobald—prosy, stiff, and drear,
Yet warm as any in his Christmas cheer!

107. [To Felis (Frank Belknap Long's cat)]

Haughty Sphinx, whose amber eyes
Hold the secrets of the skies,
As thou ripplest in thy grace,
Round the chairs and chimney-place,
Scorn on thy patrician face: 5
Hiss not harsh, nor use thy claws
On the hand that gives applause—
Good-will only doth abide
In these lines at Christmastide!

108. [To Frank Belknap Long]

A plain old soul, nor sharp nor analytical,
    Seeks here in all sincerity to please
A modern Child, sophisticate and critical,
    Who finds our world a wearisome disease.

Take then this volume, lofty and fastidious,   5
    Where Disillusion shakes its scornful head;
Ne'er will the donor frown with glance invidious,
    Tho' deep thou study what he hath not read!

109. [To Alfred Galpin]

A welcome home, Son! may you find
    The antient hearth a little pleasing,
And old-time folks a bit more kind
    Than city sirens with their teasing.
May flowing Fox without a sham   5
    Delight an eye with lakesides sated,
And may your ears prefer the dam
    To rumblings of the elevated!

May a fond parent's smile appeal
    A shade above collegiate smirking,   10
And birthplace leisure easier feel
    Than five-six-five-oh and hard working.
Include a look at A. H. S.,
    Where shades Mocratick lurk to cheer ye,
But shun that sneaking pythoness—   15
    That little flint-heart wretch O'Leary!

And as for me—why, Son, no change
    With aged Theobald seems to tamper;

You'll always find within your range
    The senile quaver of your Grampa.   20
And at this point that quaver grows
    To tones of festive benediction,
Whilst the Old Man sincerely throws
    Worlds of regards without one fiction!

110. [To Maurice W. Moe]

Hail, learned Mocrates, whose pious gaze
Reads CHRISTMAS in these genial holidays;
Accept my pagan blessings, tho' they be
A SATURNALIAN festival for me!

VI. Amateur Affairs

To the Members of the Pin-Feathers on the Merits of Their Organisation, and of Their New Publication, *The Pinfeather*

Hail! learned ladies, banded to protect
The lib'ral arts from undeserv'd neglect:
In whose skill'd numbers ev'ry grace appears;
Whose flowing prose is music to our ears.
How opportunely comes your gen'rous aid   5
To culture, crush'd by indolence and trade.
The modern scribbler doubly gives offence
From want of dignity and want of sense.
Content to pander to the half-taught mind,
He leaves the precepts of the Muse behind;   10
Forgets the purest phrases that he knows,
And makes vile verse, or scrawls in viler prose.
He tries his best all elegance to sink;
Meanly to write, and like a boor to think.
The stately words his sires so long have known   15
He casts aside as "formal" and "high-flown".
He lacks the patience all his gifts to waste
On careless readers, curs'd with peasants' taste.
How noble, cultur'd sisterhood, your task!
To spread true knowledge, and the false unmask.   20
How sadly does the shallow public need
Instruction how to think and what to read!
Your papers, writ with polish and with ease,
Shall serve at once to educate and please:
With truest art your topics shall be fix'd;   25
The grave and gay in just proportion mix'd.
Charm'd by the sound of each harmonious word,
Phoebus shall praise, and all the Nine applaud.
With youthful diffidence your pow'rs you rate
As being in the downy, new-fledg'd state;   30
Yet will the tender plumage amplify,
And clothe the wings that bear your fame on high.
What realms of learning can you then explore;
How far above Parnassus' hillside soar!
The richest fruits of all Aonia's soil   35
Will pay each scholar for her faithful toil.
May you upon your native Rocky Mount

335

Shew to the world a new Pierian fount,
And may old Greece her mind in you infuse,
Each member turning to a modern Muse.   40

To the Rev. James Pyke

On His Unpublished Verse

Accept, exalted Pyke, the honest praise
Of one who sits enraptur'd by your lays.
Scorn not applause from him you taught to know
The lyric strain, the true poetic glow.
Majestic bard! With what celestial skill   5
Your Muse can Nature in your verse instil!
Each sacred thought, each phase of joy or pain,
Flows forth in numbers from your fertile brain.
Vague, noble dreams, that slip the common grasp,
Your lofty lines in metric fetters clasp.   10
Singer sublime, your transcendental mind
Soars far above the realm of base mankind.
'Twas never meant you should so closely hide
The talents vast that in your soul reside.
To feel your pow'r is ev'ry human's due;   15
Hoard not the wealth the gods have lent to you.
With lib'ral pen revive the poet's art;
Exalt the spirit and arouse the heart.

To the Members of the United Amateur Press Association from the Providence Amateur Press Club

Before you all, in apprehension stand
The timid members of a new-form'd band.
With awkward pen, but eager of success,
Our sev'ral failings must we here confess;
Let critics treat us with a kindly sense,   5
And frown not on our inexperience.

As President above the others set,
Firm in his rule, see gifted Basinet.
By his bright genius all the club was made;
In ev'ry act his wisdom is display'd.   10
Of broadest sympathy, he seeks to lend
A pitying ear to all, and all befriend;

With fearless mien he scorns oppressive laws,
And stands a champion of the people's cause.
Next Dunn behold, whose active, well-stock'd mind   15
Is worth a hundred of the pompous kind.
Learned but modest, sure of what he knows,
His wit and sense in endless ways he shews.
Skilled in dispute, with none he fears to vie,
But picks up L———'s faults in history.   20
From his quick tongue the proofs abundant roll,
And Hugo's quoted 'gainst the mighty C———!
Turn now to Shehan; his pointed prose reveals
A man whose mind the censor's duty feels.
The flick'ring film, the moving picture stage,   25
Are lash'd in scorn by his discerning rage.
The bold reformer naught of vigour lacks,
And idle Pleasure shakes at his attacks.
Amidst the throng a shining light discern:
'Tis Kipling's own disciple, Mistress Kern.   30
Th' instructed fair, with ev'ry talent grac'd,
Decides the mode in literary taste.
Prepare ye now to shed unwonted tears,
As Mistress Miller with her pen appears:
The Queen of Fiction; with pathetic art   35
She melts the coldest and the hardest heart.
The reader tries to leave such scenes of pain,
Yet, charm'd against his will, he reads again.
Observe skill'd Reilly, erudite and wise,
Who all his art to stately prose applies.   40
Of matchless culture, and refinement rare,
His polish'd page reflects the author's care.
Next of the band, the quiet Byland see,
Whose gifts are mix'd with gentle dignity.
With forceful logic does the scholar think;   45
With pleasing style his thoughts are trac'd in ink.
Gaze last on H.P.L., whose bookish speech
But bores the auditors he tries to teach;
Whose stiff heroics ev'ry ear annoy;
Whose polysyllables our peace destroy.   50
The stilted pedant now can do no worse,
For he it is that writ this wretched verse!

Thus stand the club, to ev'ry eye reveal'd,
And not a fault or virtue left conceal'd.

If in your cultur'd ranks a place there be   55
For letter'd novices as crude as we,
That happy place we quickly would procure,
And each become a finish'd amateur.

The Bay-Stater's Policy

No kind fraternal love fills Thomson's heart,
Nor does he teach epistolary art.
In amateurs one thought he seeks to rub,
And shew them they're no correspondence club.
He calls on his associates to give   5
More samples of the "art preservative";
Yet should he cease to fret th' excited nerve,
But wait for something worthy to preserve.

To "The Scribblers"

> "Sumite materiam vestris, qui scribitis, aequam
> Viribus, et versate diu quid ferre recusent,
> Quid valeant humeri. Cui lecta potenter erit res,
> Nec facundia deseret hunc, nec lucidus ordo."
> —Horace.

United *Scribblers!* (Tho' your name belies
The earnest purpose of your enterprize)
Pray take this greeting from a friendly quill
That moves in praise, and sings your rising skill.
Whilst hireling verse and mercenary prose   5
Invade the art, as weed in garden grows;
When choicest words before Corruption flee,
And Worth becomes a curiosity,
With admiration we in you behold
A faithful few that cling to Culture's fold.   10
What keen respect for your attempts must claim us,
Since 'tis their grace that made Milwaukee famous!
But this with native excellence endow'd,
Be not content, nor rest supinely proud;
Tho' now with art and glorious talent fill'd,   15
Let not the fertile soil remain untill'd.
Whate'er of polish you possess will rise;
Seek no mere summits, but the arching skies!
If to your lot may fall the happy gift

338

To sound the lyre, and human thought uplift,   20
Think not that Nature will your rhymes excuse
When, tho' inspir'd, they scorn the polish'd Muse.
The loftiest line, obscur'd by garb uncouth,
Repels the mind, howe'er profound its truth.
Beware the dire effects of early praise,   25
That sates the soul, and checks continued lays.
Rest on no laurels, nor perfection claim;
Whate'er your heights, assume a higher aim.
Or if to prose your growing skill inclines,
Adopt each ancient precept that refines.   30
In cold contempt from modern counsels turn,
Nor fear that grace of classic style to learn.
Forbear to think your nascent work complete
Till you, unfearing, can the critic meet.
In this loose age, 'tis scarce enough to gain   35
The rules that make you fluent, terse, or plain;
We must needs grasp, since taste hath sunk so low,
Not only Knowledge, but *what not to know!*
Shun, as the serpent, him who would destroy
The laws that make the poet's art a joy;   40
The raving Vandal with reformer's gown,
Who seeks to tear our rhyme and metre down.
Then, too, the sneering cynics who despise
The dignity wherefrom our classics rise;
The careless crew that found their style upon   45
The bar-room's slang, and shun the lexicon.
Ye lab'ring learners, may the Muse attend
The cause to which your sev'ral efforts bend.
Tho' ill your task th' indifferent world repays,
For you await the scholar's loftier bays.   50
Let links fraternal all your band unite
And art, not fame, determine what you write.

R. Kleiner, Laureatus, in Heliconem

Blest by Apollo and th' admiring Nine,
On Helicon see tuneful KLEINER shine.
Euterpe close his piping lay attends,
And with his notes her own in concord blends.
Fleet Pegasus th' enchanting music hears,   5
And beats his pinions, and pricks up his ears;
Whilst the skill'd Erato, with sacred lyre,

Joins in the strain, and feels the noble fire.
Melpomene forgets her dark alarms,
And Polyhymnia lays aside her psalms: 10
The fair Thalia smiles with brighter grace,
And gay Terpsichore suspends her pace:
Calliope and Clio rest their quills,
As wise Urania at the chorus thrills.
The mighty Phoebus trembles on his throne,   15
For KLEINER'S chords are sweeter than his own!

Providence Amateur Press Club (Deceased) to the Athenaeum Club of Journalism

Hail! letter'd Bards, whose "voice from out the tomb"
Proclaims your progress and your coming bloom;
Whose solemn conclave speaks your good intent,
And shews your hours of leisure wisely spent:
Your card fraternal we with joy peruse,   5
Nor hide our pleasure at your cheering news.
'Tis yours, skill'd literati, to excite
The modest Muse, and scale th' Aonian height;
With art the Heliconian steed to tame,
And thrill Parnassus with your rising fame;   10
The bounding line and soaring verse to trace,
Till all the Nine confess an humbler pace.
In prose, in rhyme, in fiction, and in fact,
You teach our scribblers how to write and act!
What can we say, who on Rhode Island's shore   15
Were once a club, but are a club no more;
Whose puny petals ne'er to bloom unclos'd,
Nor on Pierus' sacred slopes repos'd:
Who stand apart, disorganis'd and weak,
With naught save one *Conservative* to speak?   20
Rent by the scythe of all-destroying Time,
We hide our sorrow and chagrin in rhyme!
To ye, industrious train, we fain would preach
The potent press, and circulated speech;
Save not your grace for mutual sight alone,   25
But make your products to your fellows known:
Of thought be gen'rous, and of words be free,
And let your flow'rs adorn a larger tree.
Rest not while only *Harvey* is delighted,

But blossom gaily o'er the whole *United!*   30
Arise, sweet Dempesy, whose trochaic line
No flaws obstruct, nor faulty rhymes confine;
Who rivals Romeo with his Song of Love,
And carols, flute-like, thro' the Paphian grove:
Enlarge thy audience, and diffuse thy lays;   35
With wider field, enjoy a wider praise!
Thou too, apt Thompson, whose dactylic flow
Recites a poet's and a Flivver's woe:
To ampler spheres thy well-turn'd stanzas fit,
And grow a very Hudibras in wit!   40
How fares skill'd Bradley, lately lab'ring hard
At once to be an editor and bard?
In Rudyard's style thy virile thoughts repeat,
And close by Hippocrene take thy seat!
Nor is the Muse reluctant to declare   45
The myriad talents of the letter'd fair;
Let authorship and editorial fame
In lib'ral measure grace a Wilbur's name.
Let Mistress Fairfield's head sustain the crown
Of polish'd prose, and narrative renown;   50
Let each the promptings of the Nine attend,
And ev'ry damsel prove the Muses' friend.
Now the learn'd chief, to all the crystal spring
Of prose and numbers, Heav'nly Goddess, sing!
Sing the keen mind that shap'd the course of youth,   55
And warm'd their love for beauty and for truth;
From buds to blossoms rear'd the aspiring band,
And rul'd the rising train with gentle hand;
School'd the young author in his careful art,
And taught the poet how to reach the heart;   60
Kind source of Knowledge—naught can stay or balk her—
Sing, Heav'nly Muse, the praise of Mistress Stalker!

Thus ends the bard (if bard indeed be he
Who writes mere rhyme, and fails at poesy).
His task is onerous, for here's the rub—   65
One pen must represent a vanish'd club!
Your kind indulgence for his faults he pleads,
And begs you judge his spirit, not his deeds!

To Mr. Lockhart, on His Poetry

Whilst the town poet, dodd'ring in decay,
With hopeless drivel drives the Muse away,
Pleas'd with the clatt'ring of some formless line
That only he can fathom or divine;
While sense and rhyme are banish'd as too hard   5
Till ev'ry chimney-sweep can turn a bard;
How great our joy to leave the free-verse throng,
And ease our ears with LOCKHART'S moving song!
Melodious LOCKHART! whose Aonian art
Transmits the pulsing of the simple heart;   10
Whose homely pen no languid soul dissects,
Whose polish'd lines no cultur'd fog reflects:
From Grecian stores he bears no tinsel pelf,
Content to be a classic in himself!
Let feebler wits their cumbrous couplets weight   15
With dry allusion—dulness' specious freight,
Or deck with sounding words the empty length
Of stilted odes, to hide their want of strength;
Our Milbank bard such formal trash disdains,
And fresh from Nature draws his rural strains.   20
'Tis not for him in solitude to scan
The pedant's page, and shun the haunts of man;
'Tis not for him in books alone to trace
The moods and passions of our mortal race:
Close to mankind, his deft, experienc'd quill   25
Portrays his fellows with familiar skill.
No borrow'd sentiment or mimic rage
Stalks coldly thro' our poet's glowing page;
Fancy's true visions ev'ry line inspire,
And fill each melody with genuine fire: 30
Charm'd by the sound, the cynic stops to hear,
And sheds against his will the human tear.
What rising fame will future ages bring
To LOCKHART, master of the lyric string?
With what fond honours will the minstrel move   35
Amongst the Muses of the sacred grove?
Skill'd in sweet harmonies, supremely blest
With all the genius of his native West,
His lofty brow deserves the laurel crown
That none hath worn, since RILEY laid it down!   40

To Jonathan E. Hoag, Esq.

On His Eighty-seventh Birthday, February 10, 1918

As wise Minerva with Olympian rage
Perceives the follies of a careless age;
Mourns the dull nonsense of Boeotian rhyme,
And trembles at the Vandal march of time;
As lab'ring Art, resentful of the wrong,   5
Deserts the precincts of unnatural song;
The languid Nine an heav'nly succour feel,
And daring magic stirs their sluggish zeal:
The blue-eyed maid, whose mercy never sleeps,
From the bright past a living minstrel keeps!   10

Hail, honour'd HOAG! whose Heliconian lay
Grows sweeter as thy laurell'd locks grow grey;
To whom the years but added graces bring,
As wintry stars outshine the skies of spring:
At birth baptis'd in Art's Pierian fount,   15
Four score and sev'n thy sunlit summers count;
Yet that kind Muse, by whom thy lyre was strung,
Pleas'd with her work, hath kept thee ever young!
Thine Attic garland, gay with many a flow'r,
Gains a fresh bloom with ev'ry song-blest hour: 20
In the fair dawn the tender buds unclose;
The noontide sees the richer full-blown rose;
Maturer blossoms deck the vesper scene,
And blend sedately with th' unfading green;
But rarest flow'r of all in mortal sight   25
Is the proud cereus of queenly night:
All those, Aonian bard, thou canst combine,
As the glad hours with endless radiance shine.
How fine thy fancy, whose swift glance can spy
The subtlest beauties that in Nature lie;   30
Whose dulcet lute can sing with moving skill
The ancient lays of stream and grove and hill:
Trace from primeval dust the verdant earth,
And sound once more the chant of Nature's birth.
To thee each rock an awesome tale imparts,   35
While foaming torrents bare their mighty hearts;
Forgotten glaciers, melted on the plain,
For thee their frigid journeys live again:

343

From ocean cave to snow-clad mountain spire,
The world is thine to praise with lyric fire!   40
Nor with less art canst thou in numbers tell
Of those who on its varied surface dwell:
Beneath thy brush the living Indian forms,
And wand'ring tribes defy the northern storms;
The rural home, the long-concluded fray,   45
The honest customs of another day,
The innocence of youth, the thoughts of age,
The visions of the singer and the sage,
The mourner's teardrop and the jester's smile,
The lore of far Hibernia's story'd isle;   50
These all are thine, yet thro' thy wizard pow'rs
They are not thine alone, but thine and ours!
But whilst the Muse, with fond maternal claim,
Seeks to enrobe thee in poetic flame,
The gods of prose a rival action press,   55
And bid thee wear a philosophic dress.
Thy facile pen the realm of thought explores,
And leads us on to unfamiliar shores;
Displays the mighty West's alluring zone,
And those grim heights that feet have never known;   60
Cleaves the clear ether, and expounds the blue
Where countless stars distract the questing view;
Nor deigns to pause till pois'd on that vast brink
Beyond whose depths no man may know or think.
Poet and Sage! But lest a point be miss'd,   65
Let none forget the valiant Moralist!
All praise to thee, whose potent pen and purse
Have served the right, and fought the Bacchic curse;
Silenus, newly sober, finds in thee
The staunchest friend of his morality,   70
And old Anacreon his red brow untwines,
Asham'd to flaunt his ancient wreath of vines.
How kind is Fate, whose mild decrees prolong
The work of virtue and the boon of song;
Who lends our day, of finer sense devoid,   75
The stately singer earlier days enjoy'd!
Elysium, rich in poets of the past,
Can well afford to leave on earth the last;
So thou, lov'd HOAG, whom generations crown
With choicest laurels of deserv'd renown,   80

Must long from thy calm Vista Buena shine,
And teach us all a sweetness like to thine:
Mayst thou, who bless'd the num'rous years before,
Delight our souls for eighty-seven more!

To Arthur Goodenough, Esq.

When fading faith with mangled morals vies
To drive Astraea to the shelt'ring skies;
When brazen times the silver age succeed,
And genius smothers in the folds of greed;
Amidst the wreck one ling'ring lamp behold,   5
Bright with the lustre of the age of gold;
Whilst virtue flickers, threat'ning to expire,
Brave *Goodenough* preserves the sacred fire!
Immortal bard, whose limpid lines sustain
Aonia's pow'r, and Saturn's blissful reign;   10
Whose skill Amphion vainly might contest;
Whose pious pen the fav'ring Gods have bless'd:
'Tis thine with art to cleanse our dismal day,
Lift up the soul, and smooth each sin away!
Happy the hour when first thy Doric reed   15
Thrill'd verdant mounts, and charm'd the flow'ring mead;
Pan with his pipes a softer strain rehears'd,
Content to copy where he once was first:
And since that time thy carols ne'er have ceas'd;
In number, as in melody, increas'd.   20
Whate'er thy manner, and whate'er thy theme,
Pierian ripples deck the copious stream,
Strength without bombast, virtue without cant;
The Nine to thee an endless genius grant:
Unstudy'd ease thy fecund pow'rs supply;   25
Full flows the fountain, never running dry.
We view thy songs, the fruit of many a year,
And as we gaze, fresh witcheries appear;
In vain we seek the loftiest to select,
For all excel, where lingers no defect: 30
Helpless to know what verses most to praise,
We laud the whole, and grant abounding bays.
How throb the pulses as we scan the page
Where low'r the portents of celestial rage,
Or as with sharp expectancy we turn   35
To read of Eric and his golden urn.

345

France's dead Queen thy bitt'rest scorn forgives,
So much of genius in thy censure lives;
Nor can we murmur when thy Roundhead pride
Contemns poor Charles, and sings the Regicide.   40
Great *Milton* thus thro' his Parnassian song
Made ev'n rebellion savour less of wrong.
What pleasures rise when in thy Attic strain
We hear the glories of our native plain:
There sachems stalk, and soldiers play their part,   45
And shades ancestral stir the Saxon heart;
The past in thee to second life is grown,
And old New-England claims thee as her own.
How swells the mind that knows thy sacred store,
And eager counts thy living lyrics o'er;   50
Verse upon verse diffuse a new delight,
Till each succeeding stanza seems more bright:
Tmolus the wise his classic judgment mends,
For Phoebus fails when *Goodenough* contends.

To the A.H.S.P.C., on Receipt of the Christmas *Pippin*

Like some astronomer, whose dazzled gaze
Looks for a star, but finds the moon's bright rays,
The carping critick trembles with surprise
As the new *Pippin* greets his awestruck eyes!
Precocious train, whose infant genius glows   5
In faultless verse and Addisonian prose;
Whose countless talents scintillate and shine
Thro' polish'd paragraph and lustrous line;
What ag'd assemblage can compare with you?—
Your gifts so many, yet your years so few!   10
High o'er the band euphonious HARPER tow'rs,
Blest with a poet's and a cynic's pow'rs;
Who can with equal skill and vigour shew
A press club's virtues, and November's snow,
And hold with majesty the office of a MOE.   15
Not less in altitude, nor less in wit,
See mighty GALPIN on his daïs sit;
Swiftest of bards, whose hasting pen can trace
Impromptu numbers—foremost in the race!
From him we turn to THAYER—refulgent star—   20
(Tho' *inter nos* methinks we turn not far:)
Experience gleams thro' each pathetic verse—

346

O leer ye not—some day you'll suffer worse!
But see!—above the present's tawdry theme
Soars a fleet WING, with high auspicious dream; 25
Prophetic singer! ere thy lines are done,
Rejoicing Freedom views the vanquish'd Hun!
All hail, FRANCISCO, who canst rhyme so well
Of the once-potent autocrat of h***:
Proud Lucifer a rival King must own, 30
Who keeps his evil, tho' he lose his throne!
Now comes the prose, but sure, the change is slight
When we behold YE ED'S ethereal flight:
With airy grace she sails celestial deeps,
And finds the wealth that pleasing Fancy keeps. 35
More fancy shines as we admiring look
At Santa's tale—Pieria's undammed brook;
With tranquil tide the stream melodious flows,
And poesy beams thro' the faultless prose.
The page now blazes with collegiate fire, 40
As M. PATRICIA smites the sounding lyre;
In classic halls a virtuous phantom see,
To mould the lives of heroes soon to be!
Christmas again! This time a RYAN'S quill
Describes the w. k. season of good will; 45
Each reader praises, as his eyes behold
A noble theme, and classic style, unroll'd.
Such are the parts—what language can we find
To sing the merits of the whole combin'd?
Superlatives in vain the critick tries 50
In praise of aught so witty and so wise.
Old age, with friendly grandpaternal glance,
Surveys each prodigy in swift advance:
If in the youthful mind such art appears,
What heights of glory wait your riper years? 55

Greetings

To Arthur Goodenough, Esq.

Son of the Muse, whose strains awake
The Dryads of the rural ways,
A lesser bard would bid thee take
His humble lines that chant thy praise.

*   *   *

May Yuletide find thee as of yore,   5
Content in virtue and in song,
Enrich'd in spirit more and more,
And arm'd to battle ev'ry wrong.

To W. Paul Cook, Esq.

I'd pray Saint Nick to send to thee
His choicest boons—the genial elf—
Did not thy generosity
Reveal thee as the Saint himself.

To E. Sherman Cole

(Born February 1918)

For reasons quite plain,
    'Twould lack polish and tone
To wish you the happiest
    Christmas you've known,
So I'll suit the conditions,   5
    And hope that your cheer
May this season be great,
    And be greater each year!

To the Silver Clarion

Clear thro' the land in Christmas fervour floats
The music of the Silver Clarion's notes;
Long may it ring, and with unfailing grace
Exalt our spirits and improve our race.

To Jonathan Hoag, Esq.

On His 88th Birthday, February 10, 1919

Once more auspicious Time, in annual round,
Shews a skill'd bard, with added laurels crown'd;
Whilst eager throngs, well pleas'd with lenient Fate,
Acclaim harmonious HOAG, turn'd eighty-eight!
What may we say, as we with joy behold   5
One who can flourish, never growing old;

Whose moving strains our list'ning grandsires knew,
Yet who can charm ourselves with art as true?
What may we write of his Parnassian lays—
Beyond our censure, and above our praise?   10
Life is a mountain, reaching to the sky,
With peak for ever hid, supremely high;
Its slipp'ry slopes each mortal seeks to scale—
Seeks but to pause, to falter, and to fail.
Who can predict the fame of him whose feet   15
Mount ever up, nor waver in retreat?
Thus climbs our Greenwich singer o'er the rest,
Attains the purer air, draws nigh the crest;
How wide and beauteous must his vision find
Life's spreading landscape, when he looks behind!   20
Well may his quill, in that exalted place,
At once the world's and Heaven's beauties trace;
In retrospection tell of stream and grove,
Yet with like art describe the scenes above.
So sounds the lyre that sweeter grows with age;   25
So gleam the lines on HOAG'S Pierian page;
Life, Death, and Immortality he sings,
Yet glads our fancy with terrestrial things.
How bright his picture of the simple school
Where rustic masters held benignant rule,   30
Or of the snow-clad slope, where light and free
The red-cheek'd coasters glide in youthful glee!
With magic notes his songs enchant our ears,
Revive the happy past, and melt the years.
May lesser bards compete with one whose Muse   35
Each year superior splendour can diffuse?
Who is so bold, that he can hope to gain
An equal skill, or chant an equal strain?
High on the mount our SCRIBA stands alone,
And blends a former aera with our own.   40
SCRIBA, for thee I wish a future bright
With ev'ry known, and yet unknown delight;
May the fond Fates that bless'd thy days of yore
On riper years repeated favours pour;
May Phoebus smile on thine increasing skill,   45
And Aesculapius shield thy form from ill;
May Nymphs and Dryads of the founts and woods
Preserve thy joy in sylvan solitudes;
May Jocus guide thy never-failing wit,

And sprightly Comus at thy banquets sit;   50
And best of all—mayst thou for ever live
Midst bliss as keen as that thy verses give!

In Memoriam: J. E. T. D.

The vales are silent for a little while,
    A mute, unwonted sadness brooding o'er;
For one whose harp so lately could beguile
    The peopled shades, will strike the strings no more.

Not with the hollow tones of borrow'd song   5
    Wak'd she the groves, or rous'd the echoing plain;
Life, rich and thoughtful, gentle, good, and long,
    Inspir'd each air, and throbb'd thro' ev'ry strain.

So deep a soul; so delicate an art
    Too seldom blend to make the world more fair;   10
Unfeign'd the grief with which the gen'ral heart
    Weeps for a singer whom it ill can spare.

To the A.H.S.P.C., on Receipt of the May *Pippin*

Dispense, ye shades of dulness and of gloom,
As welcome rays the letter'd realm illume;
Bright thro' the vapour of Boeotian reams
The fulgent lamp of youthful talent gleams:
Transported throngs acclaim th' increasing light,   5
And the blest *Pippin* greets our ravish'd sight!
Say, blameless babes grown wise beyond your years,
In whose rare pages ev'ry charm appears—
How is 't that you, with such perfection past,
Can make each issue loftier than the last?   10
First in the book, in witty rhymes unroll'd,
The honour'd members of the club behold;
Here wit and genius, art and learning shine,
And sacred Wisdom sheds her beams benign:
To verse and stanza pictures add their grace;   15
Each child displays a shining morning face;
Whilst high above (in inches and in brain),
Immortal GALPIN rules the infant train.
All-knowing youth, in whose capacious mind
The lore of all the ages is confin'd!   20
Next on the list, resplendent thro' the sky,

350

See flocks of wing'd heroicks gaily fly;
The critick murmurs with unwonted pleasure,
Glad to encounter his own fav'rite measure;
Pope was in luck so long ago to sing,   25
For we should else declare he copy'd WING!
Now for skill'd fiction must the gaze prepare,
As we observe bright CARY'S "First Affair";
With art and sympathy our author glows,
And charms the fancy with his vivid prose: 30
Struck with the lustre of the new-found star,
We swear in chorus—CARY will go far!
The Muse once more enchants our watching eyes
As PATTERSON'S and BRADFORD'S lines arise;
Pleas'd with the images so nobly wrought,   35
We laud the numbers, and commend the thought.
To this poetic pair we fain would add
The modest STEVENS, at his crudeness sad;
Henry, take heart! The peak is not so high
That thou needst miss it, if thou wilt but try!   40
(And as for roughnesses of taste and grammar—
Hast ever heard about a certain *Stammer?*
Compar'd to him, thou art already great—
The heir of genius, and the pet of Fate!)
And now, to quit a while the Yahoo kind,   45
In MORSE'S prose bright canine thoughts we find;
How pleas'd the heart, at human baseness pain'd,
To view the faithful dog, in soul unstain'd!
Such are the gems, from infant genius born,
That this gay crown of letter'd fame adorn;   50
Sing now the hand that with surpassing art
Chose and arrang'd each bright particular part:
All Hail, Learn'd ABRAHAM! whose magick skill
Hath mark'd thee out, great GALPIN'S place to fill;
Thy studious mind, each day more lofty grown,   55
Was sure design'd the nearest to his own:
Stars in their courses cast thy kindred fate,
For thou wert also born November 8!
Dazzled with art, the rhymester fain would know
How minds so young to such vast heights can go;   60
Abash'd, he pauses, conscious of a grace
His own dull pencil fruitless strives to trace.
Vain were the bard who still could court the ear,
When contrast shews him so much in the rear!

Helene Hoffman Cole: 1893–1919

The Club's Tribute

As when a storm-cloud, sudden form'd on high,
With instant gloom o'erspreads the morning sky;
Dims ev'ry scene so late with sunbeams gay,
And chills the vivid ardour of the day;
So sank the gen'ral heart from shore to shore,   5
When fell the word—HELENA is no more!
The mind, oppress'd by what it scarce can own,
Not soon in facile phrase or rhyme is shewn;
Yet tho' each mourner's dirge be crude and brief,
How vast the number, and how deep the grief!   10
Must we not rage at Fate's unfeeling might
When art, wit, virtue, thus are swept from sight?
All these in one auspiciously drew breath—
Yet for so short a time, when seiz'd by death!
Too few, alas, in these decadent days,   15
Deserve or earn an equal wealth of praise:
In paths of right her infant steps were led,
And in like goodness was the maiden bred;
A tender wife, in whose devoted mind
Alcestis and Andromache were join'd;   20
And last of all, that noblest work of heav'n—
A mother—proud of what the gods had giv'n!
But tho' from virtue she might justly claim
A saintly splendour, and a lasting fame,
Not that alone compos'd the glowing whole,   25
For height of mind was mixt with height of soul.
Choice were those gifts of Nature and of art
That cast their holder in a scholar's part;
Maternal care the budding talents train'd;
Each day some fresh accomplishment was gain'd;   30
Warm letter'd friendships lent their mellowing tone,
And she wed genius suited to her own.
Tho' few her years, those few with deeds were rife,
And in their span she liv'd a copious life;
Can many, dying at a greater age,   35
Leave in time's rolls a more inspiring page?
Ours, not hers, is all the present pain;
For bliss and honours form'd her happy train.
In grateful peace her blameless life was spent,

352

And calm she died, unwitting that she went.   40
Who can declare, that in eternity
She knows not far sublimer joys than we?

On Collaboration

1. *On Collaboration*

When two bright bards in friendly conf'rence sit,
To pool their genius and to join their wit,
Well may the world expect them to indite
A nobler lay than each alone could write;
Yet in their lines th' impartial mind must trace   5
A double labour, and but half the grace!

2.

In solemn truce behold the twain
    Who seek to draw three diff'rent ways;
Tho' serving sep'rate clubs, 'tis plain,
    We're both *UNITED* in thy praise!

3.

'Tis fitting that when poets meet,
    Their talents they should try;
In friendly odes and songs compete,
    And make the pencil fly.
But now, in spite of all our art,   5
    No lustrous lines appear;
For, tho' we play the poets' part,
    The Muses are not here!

4.

Two aged bards conferr'd one night,
    To test their letter'd skill;
Each vaunted his Aonian might,
    And felt a poet's thrill.

But when they sought to prove their pow'r,   5
    Their might they seem'd to miss;
And tho' they labour'd for an hour,
    They fashion'd only—THIS.

5.

Within these walls my fathers pray'd,
    With warm pragmatick zeal,
Tho' I, of coarser fabrick made,
    A lesser flame must feel.

But whilst I scorn a childish creed,   5
    A true respect I know,
When pond'ring o'er each Christian screed
    Of Kleiner, Cole, and Moe.

6.

The classic East in vain must seek
    (Tho' two exponents join their wits)
In purest melody to speak,
    When KUNTZ in loftiest ether flits.

7.

Whilst thou, McDONALD, with hot modern rage
Contemnst the ling'rers from a Georgian age;
Two tott'ring relics of the ancient time
Forgive thy scorn, and wish thee well in rhyme.

8.

In praise of a superior bard
    Two lowly pens industrious join;
Yet tho' we labour long and hard
    We cannot rise to verse like thine!

9.

If unaffected warmth atones
    For want of genius and of art,
Pray take our greetings, blest PINE CONES,
    Penn'd, tho' unskilful, from the heart!

10.

Thrice rev'rend sir, behold in each dull line
The wicked atheist with the Christian join;
KLEI hails thy soul in sanctify'd address,
Whilst pagan THEOBALD greets with warmth no less.

11. *To the Editor of the United Amateur*

As when two sober statesmen meet
    To mould a mighty nation,
See KLEINER and TIBALDUS sit
    In solemn convocation.

Here presidential minds unbend
    To light poetic passion,
And warm congratulations send
    In our poor halting fashion.

12.

Two scribblers of the presidential line
Their humble names in admiration sign,
And hail a brother, chieftain in his day,
Whose wits proclaim him greater far than they!

13.

Behold two bards of lesser fame
    Their bright superior jointly greet,
And in admiring tones proclaim
    The graces of a Muse complete.

14.

Leader, on whom unnumber'd hopes depend,
    Mayst thou the foe with wonted valour quell;
Let ev'ry force the hostile cohorts bend,
    Till we may write at last, here *lies Dowdell.*

15.

SCRIBA, accept the wishes kind
Of scribblers who with eager mind
Are here assembled, to behold
DUNSANY, Lord of Lands Untold!

16.

O wondrous stripling, to rehearse thy praise
Two timid bards their trembling voices raise;
But tho' ev'n Boston lend its Brahmin tone,
Our work must sink inferior to thine own!

17.

Bright bard, accept a hasty line
From two whose gifts are less than thine;
If wanting in the words be aught,
Pray deem it present in the thought.

18.

Madam, behold with startled eyes
A source of wonder and surprise;
Your humble serfs are two of many
Who will this night hear Lᵈ DUNSANY!

19.

Accept, inspir'd and tender bard,
Two dull Dunsanians' joint regard;
Nor scorn the spirit, tho' each line
Fall far below the worst of thine!

20.

Grave Sir, accept in weak uncertain lays
The atheist's and the pious Christian's praise;
Nor think the first, for all his wickedness,
Indiff'rent writes, or venerates thee less!

21.

Behold two bards with eager ear
When great DUNSANY lectures here.
Such art as his no peer can own
Save thine and GALPIN'S art alone!

22.

Great Sage of Athol, lend an ear
To wise DUNSANIANS gather'd here;
Soon shall we list to one whose grace
To CROSSMAN'S only must give place!

23.

Dear Madam, here in thine own cultur'd city
Behold the sessions of a grave committee;
This eve we hear with wondrous delectation
DUNSANY, Monarch of Imagination;

But tho' for prose he wear the laurel wreath,   5
JORDAN, with matchless *verse*, falls not beneath!

24.

Out of the vortices of cosmic space,
See KLEI appear with Heliconian grace;
A little while his roving soul remains
To join with THEOBALD in Parnassian strains.
Intent they strive, yet naught can they indite   5
Meet for AL FRIHDO, Peerless Prince of Light.

25.

The struggling bards, in rhythmic toil combin'd,
Strive to salute thee with composite mind;
Yet their lean verse, tho' from two sources grown,
Shines not so far as that thou mak'st alone!

[Poems written by Lovecraft in collaboration with
Rheinhart Kleiner; unbracketed lines are Lovecraft's.]

1.

Two heads, they say, a paltry one excel;
Hence these smooth couplets should be written well;
[And yet; in vain, one giddy poet strives
To reach the goal at which the first arrives.]

2.

[Hail Poet! From the city by the sea,
    Two fellow-bards by sportive fancy mov'd,]
In friendship send these halting lines to thee,
    Content with dulness, if by thee approv'd.

3.

From Eastern shores their joint esteem
    Two lab'ring rhymesters strive to send;
[And may you relish if the theme
    Sustain you to the bitter end.]

Ad Scribam

To Jonathan Hoag, Esq., Aetat LXXXIX. February 10, 1920

A health to thee, upon whose silver'd head
The mingled glow of Time and Art is shed;
Whose growing years, now full four score and nine,
In one vast beam of waxing glory shine!
Blessed is he, whose ev'ry hour can shew   5
Some virtuous effort or Aonian glow;
To such each added day fresh fame imparts,
Whilst mounting age endears him to our hearts:
SCRIBA, for thee a life of deeds well done
A lasting coronet of love hath won!   10
But tho' in gratitude we pause to scan
The welcome favour of thy lengthen'd span,
Counting alone reveals Time's number'd truth,
Since all thy works proclaim eternal youth!
In thy warm heart, with kindly genius sweet,   15
Life's golden morn and ripen'd evening meet;
No cynic hardness here hath found a place,
Where bloom perennial ardour, hope, and grace.
In thee the fragrance of forgotten Mays
Revives to bless our colder, drearier days;   20
Thy busy quill a story'd past recalls,
And with rare magic teaches and enthralls;
Legend and tale of regions far and near
On thy bright page in pleasing pomp appear,
While Nature, by thy hand sublimely drawn,   25
Yields copious lore of ages here and gone.
Happy the man who thus forever dwells
Close to the secrets that the brooklet tells;
Whose eager ear culls learning from the rose,
And gleans the truths Dionondawa knows;   30
Hears ev'ry message that the mountain breeze
Brings the high crags or whispers to the trees;
And thro' whose art, supreme and unimpair'd,
These living wonders with the world are shar'd!
Can hoary Time, whose stern, unyielding rod   35
Impartial rules the mortal and the god,
Whose deathless might Sardathrion's tow'rs o'erthrew,
And Babylonia's matchless splendour slew,

Tell by what art our poet tunes his lays
With nobler beauty thro' increasing days?   40
Can we not fancy that the stainless heart
Throbs with the rhythm of Nature's ev'ry part;
Each light-flown year in closer bonds ally'd,
Till the blest spirit joins the cosmic tide?
Thus the sweet song superior timbre gains,   45
And with long years achieves sublimer strains;
Blends with the chant of worlds beyond our sight,
And rides the aether in perpetual light:
The singer, one with harmonies of heav'n,
Not age, but youth, by grateful Time is giv'n!   50
So, SCRIBA, may unnumber'd honours crown
Thy golden years, and swell thy glad renown;
May a kind world spontaneous homage pay,
And ev'ry hearer praise thy potent lay.
Eighty and nine the years that lightly rest   55
Upon thy brow, by smiling Muses blest;
Yet may we hope that all thy joys before
Are less than what the future holds in store!

Ex-Poet's Reply

What Pangs of Envy animate my Breast
When hearing of the Pleasures of the Rest;
Joys I have miss'd, Pastimes that might have been
Had I but longer grac'd the festive Scene!
I glimpse in Fancy, the hot Sands upon,   5
The grave St. Julian and the wise St. John,
Whilst round the Twain the letter'd Nymphs are drap'd,
From urban Cares and musty Tomes escap'd.
Would I were there, that I might fondly gaze
O'er Massachusetts, fairest of the Bays!   10

To Two Epgephi

As by the shore you hear the breakers' song,
Why pause to wish there were a larger throng?
Sea, wind, and pines sufficient *noise* can brew,
While a throng's *wit* abides in just you two!

Theobaldian Aestivation

Chronicled under Compulsion for an Assemblage of the Hub Club
of the Massachusetts-Bay Colony, November 11, 1720.

I sing of summer—not because I choose,
    But in response to orders firm tho' kind,
For being ask'd, 'twere boorish to refuse
    This little off'ring at a feast of mind,
And yet, when all have heard my halting song   5
They'll wish my conscience had not been so strong!

The regal Phoebus up the zodiac soar'd,
    Turn'd in his course, and slowly started down;
'Twas July third, and aqueous torrents pour'd
    From leaden skies that held a threat'ning frown: 10
But sudden all was light—for thro' the rain
Beam'd godlike ST. JOHN, and divine HOUTAIN!

So vast a radiance ne'er before had glow'd
    Within the musty pedant's book-lin'd walls,
Th' Aonian bard his wingèd courser rode,   15
    And the roof shook with laughter that enthralls;
Homeric peals, with many a Zeus-like note,
Deep from the caverns of a GEORGIAN throat.

But all too soon the conclave must disperse,
    Since Boston calls the jovial knight away.   20
ST. JOHN and THEOBALD weep in dactyl verse,
    And for the storm-vex'd wand'rer's safety pray—
Tho' when he says he kiss'd the bards good-bye,
ST. JULIAN tells a metaphor—or . . . something analogous.

How tranquil breaks the blessed Sabbath morn;   25
    July the fourth, in local legend fam'd!
The gloomy rhymesters soon the scene adorn,
    And weight the air with epics loud declaim'd;
Then, having chosen backgrounds fair to see,
With kodaks gratify their vanity.   30

Thro' lane and garden, mead and shady grove,
    The sad-fac'd twain in meditation stroll;
In fancy spy the hoary shades that move
    Among the ancient scenes as years unroll:

To make it brief, they gawk and moon about 35
And prove themselves true bards beyond a doubt.

Night once more comes, and wondrous to relate
    Gives place in time to still another day!
July the fifth, whereon convene in state
    Some members of the proud U.A.P.A. 40
(I'll add, tho' merely in parenthesis,
That sev'ral National members share the bliss.)

Columbia's ATHOL—no, its ATHENS! is
    The shining goal of ev'ry member's tread,
So hither in the train our poets whizz, 45
    With rhymes to paint the dear old village red.
(Of course this is but figure—you must know
That both the bards are sad, sedate, and slow!)

Boston at last! And as grim poets should,
    ST. JOHN and THEOBALD seek th' Avernian cave. 50
Facile their swift descent, and in deep mood
    The wheels of Stygian chariots oft they brave:
Till as the Greek and Trojan did before,
They wend their way into the light once more!

Borne on the wings of Jove-descended pow'r, 55
    Along the green ALLSTONIAN plain they fly;
Till UNION-SQUARE'S bright domes before them tow'r,
    And they grow conscious that the goal is nigh:
A pleasant walk—then friendly voices greet
The pious pair at 20 WEBSTER STREET. 60

Who shall describe the pantheon there display'd;
    The gods and goddesses of letter'd fame?
Splendid they glitter'd thro' th' EPGEPHIAN shade,
    Each laurell'd deity of deathless name:
Rever'd Olympians, who a world can fill 65
With wit and wisdom in the *Hub Club Quill.*

High on his throne the great ALCALDE sat,
    Monadnock's thunders in his mighty hands,
While round his feet there strode the grey house-cat,
    As sacred here as in Nilotic lands. 70
And here, majestic in his cap and bells,
The lithe CONSERVER merry stories tells.

PLANCHETTE and OUIJA, Sibylline and wise,
    Thro' the vast crowd an astral force diffuse,
While shining golden from Pierian skies   75
    Is BERKELEY, favour'd daughter of the Muse.
And over all in dulcet numbers floats
The sunny sweetness of a LINNET'S notes!

And MICHAEL OSCAR, White, tho' almost Wilde
    When his black brothers bear the bard's disdain,   80
Or when he hears some word that is not mild
    Regarding the green, innocent Sinn Fein:
And who, when mov'd in quatrains to compete,
Can both old Omar and Fitzgerald beat!

Then J. BERNARD, supreme on ev'ry ground;   85
    Music and verse, biography and fiction,
Whose countless gifts my feeble pen confound,
    And drive me to quotation's mirror'd diction:
"A man so various, that he seem'd to be
Not one, but all mankind's epitome!"   90

MADAME LA MERE, for toothsome pastry fam'd;
    The PARKERS, genial enemies of gloom;
VIRTUE ALCALDE, soon to be proclaim'd
    The National's President and Dowdell's doom.
And Mistress FAIRBANKS, with a pleasing store   95
Of reminiscence and Colonial lore.

An HAMLET—tho' not he who rav'd and wept
    Round Elsinore for sundry tragic reasons,
Companion'd by a soul in art adept;
    A THOMPSON—tho' not he who writ "The Seasons".   100
Dorcastrian genius, here to add their light
To that of fulgent, black-befriending WHITE.

With such a company, 'tis scarcely queer
    That melancholy soon was sent away,
Yet vacant seats prompt many a furtive tear   105
    For those who share not in the festive day:
MORTONS are miss'd, a DENNIS does not dawn,
And EXAQUARIAE are to Cleveland drawn.

WAGNER is wanting, CUMMINGS, ELLIS—but
    Let me forbear to make a catalogue; 110
'Twere ill the thrice-bor'd list'ner's ear to glut
    With names, instead of vague poetic fog:
For poets should their province only touch—
A wealth of words, which mean not very much.

The banquet! Here the poet gains a theme 115
    Worthy of all his Heliconian pow'rs;
With what gay wit the genial diners gleam!
    With what keen zest HOUTAIN his bit devours!
And sure, each earns his sacred right to eat,
Since by rhym'd riddles he must find his seat! 120

But now to conquest must my epic turn,
    And tell how various victims quick were plighted,
Ere they could well their glorious fate discern,
    To the superior, Heav'n-ally'd UNITED!
Let me reflect . . . to what did they belong 125
Before they join'd the true Parnassian throng?

Wit, words, and writing close th' eventful eve,
    Each sage to fill th' EPGEPHIAN archives bid;
Pens fly or falter—none can gain reprieve,
    Or from Conserving eyes lie safely hid; 130
But some their Chief a vengeful snare lead into
By writing reams—and paying not the printer!

Thus night drew on apace, and each gay head
    Inclin'd—as yours must now—to gentle sleep;
While one by one the revellers sought bed, 135
    Their tryst with shadowy gods of dream to keep.
Nor will I here their blessed slumbers break—
'Twere well I stop, whilst you are still awake!

The Prophecy of Capys Secundus

(Apologies to T. Babington Macaulay)

> Nunc age, Dardaniam prolem quae deinde sequatur
> Gloria . . . Expediam dictis, et te tua fata docebo.
> —Virgil, *Aen.* vi, 756–9.

The Prologue

Tonight is solemn feasting, as by Epgephia's shrine
The priests and augurs gather, the future to divine.
Tonight the idle rhymester sits passive, aw'd, and dumb,
For ev'ry eye is strain'd to glimpse the mighty days to come.
In state broods ancient Capys, Capys the moody seer,   5
Who grinds out reams of dulness each empty, futile year.
And as the scene awakes him, he sees a wondrous gleam
That turns his mind from Georgian verse to high prophetic dream.
Before him yawns a vista of piercing crystal light,
The Hub Club's coming splendour, irradiate and bright.   10
So while the feasters tremble at tedium held in store,
The poor old fossil opes his lips and settles down to bore.

The Prophecy

Hail! band of matchless talents, of literate renown,
Whose fame for thirty twelvemonths hath brighten'd Boston town;
Hail! children of the Muses, resplendent in the glow   15
Of wisdom that the Delian god sent down from long ago.
For you no tawdry pleasures, no tinsel honours wait,
But all the gifts that genius demands from rigid Fate;
Let others count their silver, whilst you immortal shine
Beside the god whose gorgeous fane adorns the Palatine.   20
I look adown the ages, and spy with curious stare
A novel shrine of marble rear'd high on Copley Square;
Within is many a volume replete with art and wit,
Each one a deathless classic by Hubly author writ.
And on the hills of Allston in majesty there stands   25
A silent vast rotunda, the work of rev'rent hands;
Beneath the dome of crystal, around the curved wall,
There sit a marble circle presiding o'er the hall;
Each statue bears a tablet whereon the eye may trace
The glory that of old belong'd to one of Hubdom's race.   30

364

Behold in carven grandeur a proud patrician head
That stirr'd the world with melody in ages past and dead,
Whose numbers wak'd the echoes of many a distant clime,
And brought the fairies back to earth in captivating rhyme;
Each day before the statue young poets place a wreath,   35
While for a thousand marching years the bard hath slept beneath.
Close by there gleams another, that once could charm mankind
With tales whose searching verity explor'd the human mind;
The East and West united to sing their lofty praise,
And daily now the marble bears freshly gather'd bays.   40
Ten centuries of silence have lessen'd not the fame
Of one belov'd by all the Nine, and heir to Phoebus' flame.
Next shines a Roman visage where dignity and mirth
Are blent in just proportion to cheer a pensive earth;
And those who gaze upon it of grateful mem'ries quaff,   45
Recalling that a Dooley's wit first taught the land to laugh.
Upon a pedestal of bronze, engrav'd with moons and stars,
See now a stately image, wreath'd with white nenuphars;
A prophet of the seven spheres, whom modern sages know
As one who wrested from the sky its secrets long ago.   50
And here an ivory dais attracts the roving glance,
Whereon there rests a sculptur'd form adorn'd with flow'rs from France.
Unnumber'd tongues have chanted the blest musician's skill,
And oft at eve admiring choirs the temple shadows thrill.
Impressive in the twilight there looms a scholar's face,   55
At once the scion and the sire of an illustrious race;
From Persia's Gulf to Puget Sound that mighty name is known,
Nor thro' ten hundred weary years hath it less famous grown.
Bedeck'd with vivid verdure, and pleasing to the sight,
The Celtic form of fiction's king glows in the temple's light;   60
The ages sing his glory, the aeons praise his art;
For it is his informal law that moves the throbbing heart.
Made striking by the shadows cast back beneath its head
There stands a serious statue with aspect stern and dread;
The Congo chants his splendour in sempiternal song,   65
Who from their age-long bondage once rais'd the sooty throng.
But what is this I gaze on, set somewhat o'er the rest,
Is it Egyptian Pasht transferr'd to regions of the West?
In classic stone supreme there tow'rs, contented, calm, and fat,
The godlike, sleek, and well-fed form of an Egyptian Tat!   70
'Tis he! 'tis he, whose onyx shrine a million souls have deck'd,
God of the latest Asian fad—the holy Khâtist sect!

Beyond I spy—but dash it all! where have those feasters gone?
I've only made eight prophecies—the most are still undrawn!
Confound the wretches! How is this for base ingratitude?   75
They've left, whilst yet I'm going strong in prophesying mood!
How things have chang'd since Roman times, when I could keep a crowd
Agape with any nonsense, if I but mutter'd loud.
'Tis hard for any haruspice to meet these modern days
When people will be ennui'd howe'er I puff and praise!   80
I will not waste mine ancient bunk—I'll cease to be a prophet,
Or else I'll teach each cynic soul he's headed straight for Tophet!

(Wet) Dream Song

Homer had the pox,
Sappho had the itch,
But I'm just a vox-
Popular sonofabitch.

Mustard without cress,   5
Cakes without ale,
Satisfy me less
Than a cat without a tail.

I who loved the light
Of extinguished moons,   10
Chanted all night
My cacophonous tunes.

For hours and hours
On the arid Atlantic,
The clamour of flowers   15
Drove me quite frantic.

What should one do
When one's on the blink?
Have an oyster stew,—
Or another drink?   20

To Mr. Hoag

On His Ninetieth Birthday, February 10, 1921

As on the flow'ry Latmian crest
    Endymion ever young reposes,
With crystal dreams by Phoebe bless'd,
    And wreath'd in never-dying roses;
So, SCRIBA, thou, whose poet-eyes   5
    Have dwelt aloft in raptures rarest,
And won like favours from the skies,
    At ninety still youth's garland wearest!

Methinks I see thee where the moon
    On faery slopes sends down her splendour;   10
That realm of sempiternal June,
    Peopled by fauns and oreads tender,
Which sleeps unalter'd and unvex'd,
    Tho' with vast ills and changes direst
The world of waking be perplex'd—   15
    That fancy-heaven of the lyrist!

In such an aether dost thou dream
    Irradiate traceries to bear hither,
Rewarded by the boon supreme—
    A spirit that may never wither;   20
The years float by caressingly,
    Bestowing gifts but never robbing;
And now the ninetieth leaves thee free,
    Thy heart with youthful ardour throbbing.

Thus will it be in future time,   25
    Thy presence ever luminous beaming,
The while thou tell'st in beryl rhyme
    The winsome wonders of thy dreaming;
The queen of night thy path will strow
    With blossoms from the bow'rs Elysian,   30
And thou wilt sing amidst the dew,
    Rose-crown'd and young, a fadeless vision!

On a Poet's Ninety-first Birthday

(To Jonathan Hoag, Esq., February 10, 1922)

Blessings on thy natal day,
Lighter of the lengthen'd way!
Gorgeous be thy brother sun,
As thou turnest ninety-one!

Kindled in a happier time,   5
Burneth still thy torch sublime,
Destin'd for our joys to save
All that former ages gave.

Pure as crystal is the light;
Restful to the weary sight;   10
Would that all the world might shine,
SCRIBA, with such rays as thine!

Long hath been thy fulgent course,
Leading beauty from the source;
Grateful bow'rs their praise declare,   15
Sweeter for thy passing there.

And as now the years increase,
May thy beaming never cease;
Let the gold of evening glow
Like the morn of long ago.   20

Happy he whose eye may scan
Such a full, benignant span;
Years of song thou strow'st behind,
Like gay blossoms in the wind.

Youth and grace attend thy tread,   25
Fresh bays deck thy silver'd head;
Nor can springtime's note depart
From the tune within thy heart.

So as stars of evening hold
All the deep'ning sunset's gold;   30
Thou thy path mayst e'er prolong,
Vital in thy shining song!

To Saml: Loveman, Gent.,

With a fellow-martyr's heartfelt sympathy

From H: LOVECRAFT, CRITICK

See one by one the hapless criticks fall
Into the braggart bard's inglorious thrall.
First *Theobald* slips, and turns a witless slave;
Next *Morton* lays contentment in the grave.
And now, from heights still greater, crashes down   5
LOVEMAN, a god apprentic'd to be a clown!

To Mr. Hoag

Upon His Ninety-second Birthday, February 10, 1923

On the cold air with brighter ray
Dionondawa gleams today,
    To give a bard his due;
For SCRIBA, last of all the line
In whom our ancient glories shine,   5
    Is turning ninety-two!

As o'er the hills strange echoes rise
From bards who gaze with alien eyes
    Upon a changing land,
You, SCRIBA, who have known the past,   10
Will keep it living till the last,
    For those who understand.

'Tis yours a happier day to sing,
That spread too soon its golden wing;
    A day of hope and worth,   15
When young Columbia, proud and free,
Exulted in simplicity,
    And bless'd her recent birth.

For you the scene so few recall:
The village by the waterfall   20
    Where freemen dwelt unspoil'd;
Where the trim cottage lay embower'd,
Whilst o'er the trees the steeple tower'd,
    And swains contented toil'd.

The old farm home you knew so well,   25
Where homely virtue us'd to dwell,
    And strength in boundless store;
These but for you were dim in truth,
Yet in your lines gain second youth,
    And vivid rise once more.   30

Prais'd be the pow'r that keeps the fire
And living murmur of your lyre,
    And bids you linger here;
For thro' your eyes our hearts have learn'd
What thoughts within our fathers burn'd;   35
    What scenes to them were dear.

May all your days that radiance know
Which made them glad so long ago,
    By Hoosick's leaping tide;
When, charm'd by Nature's varying face,   40
You sang in lines of Doric grace
    Her ev'ry mood and side.

And may those fruitful days be long,
And garnish'd with unbroken song,
    That we may share delight;   45
May each calm year with tender care
Weave chaplets for your silver hair,
    And make the evening bright!

The Feast

(Hub Journalist Club, March 10, 1923)

"O vos qui stomacho laboratis, accurrite, et ego vos restaurabo."
    —From the Sign of the First Eating-House in Paris, 1774.

"Forsan et haec olim meminisse juvabit."
    —Virgil.

To WISECRACK SANDUSKY, Esq., B.I., M.B.O.
(Bachelor of Intelligence, Massachusetts Brotherhood of Owls)
Sir:—

    In dedicating to you this ponderous epick, I am but repaying the evil you have committed in soliciting a contribution from so obsolete an old country-gentleman as myself. It additionally delights me, however, to render a tribute to one who hath so considerably enrich'd the lighter part of our tongue; a task neglected since Dean Swift's essay on Genteel and Ingenious Conversation (1738), and by you perform'd with a zealous aptness which should be the model of every philologist and lexicographer.

I, Sir, am an old-fashion'd man still partial to the language of Dr. Johnson's aera; you are a creator of that lively speech which will be classical a century hence. Such a common aversion to the tame diction of this age, ought to establish betwixt us a bond of scholarship supplementing that bond of friendship already so firm; and in this hope I inscribe to you these immortal lines.

            Believe me, Sir, to be ever

                  Your most humble, most obedient Servant,

                                      H.P.L.

Providence, March 1923.

Lud, Sir! What's this you ask me to relate?
The Boston feast, and all I heard and ate?
Sure, that were hard, since Comus was so free
That sheer profusion clogs my memory!
Dazzled with art, and drugg'd with splendid fare,   5
My rustick pencil falters in despair,
And scarce commands the talent to set down
Such modish revels of a learned town!
Dark was the sky, when with expectant mind
I left my native rural shades behind;   10
A niveous mist oppress'd the leaden day,
As the fleet coach roll'd o'er the devious way,
Till close ahead in ancient pomp there rose
The spires and roofs that mark'd my journey's close.
But now behold! where once the scene was dark,   15
A radiant Cole supplies th' enlightening spark:
Dusk yields to light, and shades affrighted flit
Before the beams of Cantabridgian wit!
Now to the rout, where mirth and musick reign,
And Gaster vies with Jocus' pleasing strain.   20
Sink me! What splendour strikes my aged sight,
Where ev'ry face, and ev'ry word, is bright!
Thro' tavern halls the laugh decorous floats,
To join the lute's and viol's melting notes:
Swift flies the jest, whilst Priscian's shade grows pale   25
As novel terms, and new-coin'd quips, prevail.
'Zounds, what high syntax! what exalted speech!

Words that no Johnson's soaring skill could reach!
Sanduskian genius hurls the rules in limbo,
And sings the "gink", the "oil can", and the "bimbo";   30
"Lay off, old egg!" he cries, "your tank is leaking!"
(Piquant in metaphor, acute in speaking!)
"Nobody home there, bo—no use to knock on ye!
But bozo, can that line of low-grade Socony!"
Thus the glib tongue and nimble brain prolong   35
The gen'ral mirth, and season ev'ry song;
Lift the light step as all the crowd convene
Around the board, whilst cameras paint the scene.
Here eminence appears, austere and great,
The deathless Muses, and the Fourth Estate;   40
Here wit shines free from poverty's rude pinch,
And weaves a halo round imperial Lynch!
Fare in abundance (scan the luscious list!),
With melody ne'er eager to desist;
The song, the dance, the rebeck's golden chord;   45
The sprightly whisper pass'd along the board;
Then the grave pause, and as the meal is o'er,
The speakers reign—myself the only bore.
Demosthenes now lays aside The Crown,
And Cicero goes way back and sits down;   50
For Boston eloquence no peer hath known
Since the first founders kiss'd the Blarney Stone.
What wealths of wisdom win an exposition
From poet, pamphleteer, and politician!
Statesman and journalist with sense descant,   55
And the grave bard contests the wild gallant;
With senile voice my village jests I tell,
Whilst genius whelms me o'er with Machiavel:
Across our sight a thousand visions sail—
Florence and Fleet-Street, Helicon and gaol!   60
But hark! 'Fore Heaven! how agile Time hath pass'd,
Tho' each bright speech seems shorter than the last;
For peaks of thought, however high they tow'r,
Can't overawe the clock or stay the hour.
Gad's death!—'tis twelve, when honest toil reposes,   65
And in a brief half-hour the subway closes!
So on the scene the curtain's folds descend,
And the gay feast draws pensive to its end;
Join'd to the ages, planted in the sky

372

To wake the songs of better bards than I.   70
Pozz—now I'm done! And you, Sir, I entreat
To hide my couplets well within your sheet;
That the kind folk who heard my speaking thro'
May have less cause to curse my name anew!

Lines for Poets' Night at the Scribblers' Club

Cleveland, Octr. 13, 1923

A night for poets! send us, pow'rs above,
A proper moon to light Aonia's grove!
What's that—you tell me by the almanack
It sets at eight? I'll take my pleading back!
Sure, there's no need for sun or moon to shine   5
Where wit and genius here in numbers join!
Pox on 't, what luck! must I be helpless bound
To languish distant from the genial sound;
Chain'd to my hearth, whilst Erie's templed shore
Throbs to the tones that burning lutes outpour?   10
Such was the Fates' decree—but Gad! I'll beat 'em,
And send my spirit in your midst to cheat 'em!

Friends, Scribblers, Bards! excuse my Doric strains,
And rustic couplets coarse as clanking chains:
Awkward, unpolish'd, left from former times,   15
I come to praise, not emulate, your rhymes!
Unstudy'd zeal my ancient bosom fires,
And all my fancy kindles at your lyres.
How shall I name ye, whose commingled art
Tonight as one vast chorus charms the heart?   20
Some are old friends, yet in your waxing band
I spy new faces, bright on ev'ry hand:
'Zounds! but the Muse engulfs us ere we know it,
And all the town but me is grown a poet!

Yet one there is, whose radiant visage beams   25
With the rapt glow of more than common dreams;
Whose eyes are mellow with a prophet's light,
And wide and wise from many a cryptic sight;
Whose voice the gods a crystal song have made,
Whose thoughts are fauns from Tempe's arbours stray'd: 30

Hail to thee, LOVEMAN, ev'ry Scribbler's pride,
And soon to conquer all the world outside!

LOVEMAN, what throat but sings thee without end?—
The Delian minstrel and the loyal friend;
Adorn'd with gifts that might a monarch thrill   35
With vaulting pride, yet kind and modest still!
Set to thy praise, Invention hangs her head,
And warm Sincerity descants instead!
To thee, blest bard, the greenest bays belong—
Scanty enough for thy Saturnian song!   40
Thy soul it is, that down the ages leads
Untarnish'd hymns from Atlantean meads.
Thou, thou alone hast heard the piteous cry
Of bury'd gods that 'neath the mountains lie;
Deserted gods that in far caverns weep,   45
Or haunt their sunken temples in the deep:
'Tis thine to know, and knowing keep ablaze
Their exil'd altars thro' ungrateful days:
Thine to aspire—till Pan, once more releas'd,
Shall bless his fellow and exalt his priest!   50
Bright as the noons that o'er th' Aegean wave
To inland fanes a godlike splendour gave,
Thy chords ecstatic light the years behind,
And bring those fanes and noondays back to mind!
For thee no broken columns strow the plain,   55
Whose wizard song restores them fresh again:
Palace and temple, plinth and colonnade;
Ewer of gold, goblet of carven jade;
Wing'd brazen lion, sphinx of diorite,
And marble faun, an ode of living light;   60
Ionian moonbeams, bow'rs of Naxian vines,
Weird trains of Maenads, drunk with Thasian wines,
Rites that the gods themselves half fear'd to see,
And fever'd pomps of Phrygian sorcery;
Vistas of cities in the sunset clouds,   65
Black halls of Pharaohs in their nighted shrouds;
All that had pow'r to lift the mortal soul,
Maim'd on the rack of Time, thou giv'st us whole!

I pause abrupt, bewilder'd by the beam
Of lucent loveliness from such a theme.   70
Forgive, ye throng, the doting partial eye

That plucks your chief, and seems to pass ye by—
All I include, and split me! who can pray
A loftier symbol than our LOVEMAN'S lay?
A poets' night! egad, with so much splendour   75
I vow the title is a rank pretender!
Rather a poets' cresset, where as one,
Your joint aurora shames the midnight sun!

To Mr. Hoag

Upon His 93rd Birthday, February 10, 1924

Warm eastern winds, with Grecian perfumes fragrant,
    Play soft about thee tho' the plain be cold,
And music trembles from each airy vagrant
    That hails thee: "Ninety-three, but never old!"

Breezes from green Cithaeron call thee brother,   5
    Bearing the glow of many an ancient sun;
Arcadian airs to thee and one another
    Whisper the lore that makes ye all as one.

From Naxian shores a purple breath diurnal
    Brings dreams of vineyards basking sweet at noon,   10
Whilst Latmos sends a gift of youth supernal,
    Filch'd from the dow'r of an enamour'd moon.

And ev'ry gentle wanderer aërial
    Is vocal with the chant of elder choirs;
With songs of love divine and immaterial,   15
    Bright with the fervour of forgotten fires.

The Delian string for thee again is sounded,
    And Faunus wakes once more the oaten reed;
Old haunting tunes, of faery spells compounded,
    Distil thee flow'rs from a nymphaean mead.   20

Crystal and roseal, azure, gold, and argent,
    Flow'rs of a ripen'd wizardry of sight;
Flow'rs that adorn the visionary margent
    Of some celestial stream, or lake of light.

These dost thou ever, dreamer Apollonian,   25
    Weave in gay wreaths to deck our drear abode;

375

As on thy brow the nobler crown Aonian
    Sits to reward thee for each joy bestow'd.

Year upon year comes laden to thy portal,
    Swelling thy store with riches rare and pure;   30
Riches of mem'ry and of grace immortal,
    Hoarded for thee in antique vaults obscure.

So now as three and ninety years exalt thee
    To heights that winds ethereal touch and charm,
No pow'r of grosser earth may chain or halt thee,   35
    Or any fate thy singing spirit harm.

Kin of the aeons, rapt with visions olden,
    Flaming with sight of loveliness sublime,
'Tis thine to make all things about thee golden—
    Inspir'd, unfading, and unbow'd with time!   40

To Mr. Hoag

Upon His Ninety-fourth Birthday, February 10, 1925

Deep in the purple heaven,
    High by the clouds o'erfleec'd,
Carol the gods at even,
    Praising their elder priest.
Joyous above their altars,   5
    Chanting in tones of yore,
Writing in crystal psalters,
    "SCRIBA is ninety-four!"

Sprites of the lofty mountain,
    Gnomes of the nether caves,   10
Nymphs of the limpid fountain
    Where the green alder waves;
Tritons from antique oceans,
    Elves from the torrent steep,
Join in the glad devotions,   15
    Eager your day to keep!

True is the love they shew you,
    Grateful the hearts they bear,
Conscious of what they owe you—
    You, who have drawn them fair!   20

Never their debt ignoring,
    Look they for boons anew,
Knowing their loftiest soaring
    Rests with your lyre, and you!

So they have gladly granted   25
    All that they have to give;
Orpheus' sweet art transplanted,
    Sibyl's long days to live;
Voice that is always golden,
    Born of a soul sublime,   30
Gentle, serene, and olden,
    Safe from the rust of time.

Long may their kindness leave you
    Here in your native bow'rs,
Here where fond eyes perceive you,   35
    Here where your songs are ours!
Long may your lips enlighten,
    Genial and happy still,
Scribe whom the years but brighten,
    Scribe of the shining quill!   40

To Jonathan Hoag

(Upon His 95th Birthday)

Mellow burn the evening candles,
    O'er the snow the star-beams shine;
Down the sky in silver sandals
    Troop the laurel-bearing Nine.
Laden comes each tribute-bringer,   5
    Pleas'd with songs sublimely sung,
Crowning now the gentle singer—
    Ninety-five, and ever young!

Sparkling o'er the rugged granite,
    Dancing in a robe of spray,   10
First-born daughter of our planet,
    See Dionondawa play!
Measures stately and caressing
    Thro' the tranquil starlight float,
Wafting him a birthday blessing   15
    Who alone excels their note.

Neighb'ring fields attest his magic,
    Grateful that his golden lyre
Tells their stories, gay or tragic,
    In a voice of living fire;   20
Ancient roofs and spires that cluster
    Round his calm, sequester'd seat
All their mingled mem'ries muster,
    Quick their chosen bard to greet.

Farm and forest chant his praises,   25
    Song and legend own his pow'r,
Who with crystal pencil raises
    Visions of each vanish'd hour;
Time and space proclaim his talent—
    Master of their subtle spheres—   30
And in kinship proud and gallant,
    Grant him wisdom and long years.

Five and ninety! May he ever
    Sound the strings we love so well;
Peaceful, kindly, falt'ring never,   35
    Brother of bright Philomel;
SCRIBA, may the Muses bear you
    Gifts that art and worth repay,
And the years benignant spare you,
    That your lamp may light our way!   40

To Jonathan E. Hoag, Esq.

Upon His Ninety-sixth Birthday, February 10, 1927

There is magic today
    O'er the snow-mantled ground,
And the chant of a fay
    In the cataract's sound;
For the voice, clear and strong,   5
    That these marvels can fix
In the beauty of song,
    Has just turn'd ninety-six!

He has come down the years
    From a bright morning place,   10
With a message that cheers,
    And a vision of grace;

378

And of all that we prize
    He can make us a part,
As it lives in his eyes   15
    And resounds in his art.

From the white cottage home
    And the schoolhouse of red,
From the mountain's vast dome
    And the canyon's deep bed,   20
From the ocean that rolls,
    And the sunset that gleams,
He brings wealth to our souls
    And delight to our dreams.

He has tasted the past,   25
    And has brought to our door
All the wisdom amass'd
    In the calm days before;
In his heart there still bides
    What our age cannot reach,   30
Yet he dwells by our sides,
    The old lesson to teach!

He has quaff'd the rare glow
    Of a youth never gone
From the fountains that flow   35
    In the gardens of dawn;
And the spell of his tongue
    Weaves anew the far time
When the world was as young
    And the soul as sublime.   40

So as down the long lane
    The blest troubadour sings,
We must wish him again
    Happy summers and springs;
For his song claims a seat   45
    With the deathless and bright,
And immortal and sweet
    It will throb thro' the night!

The Absent Leader

In Memory of Mrs. Hazel Pratt Adams, of the Blue Pencil Club

Long miles away the bright familiar band
    Still gather, doubtless, by the autumn fire,
Or roam the Jersey woods or Brooklyn strand,
    Or where New-York lifts pinnacles and spire.

Again, perhaps, they walk where sunset fades   5
    Behind the mystic flatlands and the bay,
Or where the rim of rugged Palisades
    Throws a dim awe upon the short'ning day.

Still may it be they thread the lamplit street
    Or climb quaint stairways often climb'd before,   10
To some snug haven, hospitably meet
    For friendly pleasures and light letter'd lore.

But tho' these joys course unimpeded on,
    I cannot think their zest is quite so keen;
For since their founder and their guide has gone,   15
    There must be odd, new shadows in the scene.

Strange mists of absence that at evening rise,
    When from some home-bound trail or ferry slip
The city's lights are glimps'd against the skies,
    And the old times revive on pensive lip.   20

One cannot yet in inmost fancy own
    The kindly presence gone forever hence;
Ev'n now one half awaits her cheerful tone,
    Or leans upon her quiet competence.

In memory eternal life can bring   25
    To well-lov'd souls whose forms must elsewhere dwell;
Close may we feel the spirit hovering,
    As to the vanish'd voice we cry, farewell!

Ave atque Vale

To Jonathan E. Hoag, Esq.,

February 10, 1831–October 17, 1927

Wild on the autumn wind there comes a crying
    As from some mountain spirit griev'd and lone,
And thro' the woods resounds a deeper sighing
    Than throbb'd last night for summer overthrown.

Vapours of grief the waning moonbeams deaden   5
    That glint upon Dionondawa's spray,
And in the steeple all the chimes are leaden
    That toll o'er village square and hillside way.

The old farm home and rustic school seem blended
    With phantoms strange and wistful, wave on wave,   10
While on a spectral peak there fades untended
    The last weird campfire of the fabled brave.

Legend and song, and mem'ry's ancient treasures
    Slip half away, and glimmer more remote,
Robb'd of the life that SCRIBA'S magic measures   15
    Breath'd in their soul, and echoed in each note.

For he has paus'd amidst his crystal singing,
    Melting into the sunset's mystic gold;
He, who with Doric accents sweetly ringing,
    So long had charm'd us with his tales of old.   20

Poet whose annals were themselves a poem;
    Legate to us from brighter years than ours;
Beacon to all who had the boon to know him;
    Silver of head, but wreath'd in springtime's flow'rs.

Gentle and kindly, blest with upright vision,   25
    Valiant for truth and loveliness and right;
Learned and wise with active mind's precision,
    And radiant with the artist's lyric light.

Lib'ral, yet stern when sternness was a duty;
    Mellow with humour's quaint enliv'ning glow;   30

Eager and tender with the love of beauty,
    And courtly with the grace of long ago.

Honour's own self, whom many an honour garnish'd;
    Scion of proud Columbia's staunchest line;
Thrill'd with the wonder of a youth untarnish'd;   35
    Aw'd by the works of Nature's vast design.

Minstrel of cottage hearth and cloud-capt mountain;
    Fond, sprightly laureate of days long gone;
Teller of secrets of the woodland fountain,
    And hopeful prophet of a future dawn.   40

Ninety and six the years he bore so lightly,
    Close to the cherish'd fields that gave him birth;
Think him not old, whose spirit burn'd so brightly,
    One with the ageless things of heav'n and earth.

Think him not old, nor think him even vanish'd,   45
    Tho' now his well-lov'd form be laid to rest;
Can deathless song by Azraël's hand be banish'd,
    Or lifelong vision cease its starward quest?

Then let the mountain wind bewail no longer,
    Nor lasting gloom shroud any scene he knew;   50
He is still here, his olden song but stronger,
    Fix'd in the fulgent world his fancy drew!

VII. POLITICS AND SOCIETY

New-England Fallen

> Hic, ubi nocturnae Numa constituebat amicae,
> Nunc sacri fontis nemus et delubra locantur
> Judaeis, quorum cophinus faenunique supellex;
> Omnis enim populo mercedem pendere jussa est
> Arbor, et ejectis mendicat silva Camenis.
> —Juvenal, iii, 12–16.

When, long ago, America was young,
And held by yeomen from Britannia sprung,
New-England was with hardy rustics fill'd;
Green were her fields, and diligently till'd.
My grandsire John, beside a rocky hill,   5
'Mid pastures water'd by a sparkling rill,
Erected firm his unpretentious cot;
Sunk deep his well, laid out his garden-plot;
Built sheds for poultry, hives for honey-bees;
Barns for his cattle; clear'd the land of trees.   10
The meadows wide with walls he fenc'd around,
Builded of stones digg'd from the rocky ground.
From dawn to darkness reach'd his daily toil;
Each spring with seed he sow'd the fertile soil:
And in the heat of each midsummer day,   15
With sharpen'd scythe he mow'd the leaning hay.
'Neath harvest moon he reap'd the rip'ning crop;
In winter's blast his axe was heard to chop
The wind-sway'd oaks and maples of the wood
That on his hillside slopes majestic stood.   20
In grassy pastures, teeming with rich loam,
His brawny kine were wont to feed and roam;
Thus did he live, and call'd his humble acres "HOME".

The wooden farmhouse, painted snowy white,
Had in it more of broadness than of height.   25
A sloping roof its safe protection lent;
In vain the storms outside their fury spent.
Above the roof, the stone-built chimney tower'd,
Thro' which the smoke in inky torrents pour'd.
Around the door, the clinging ivy twin'd;   30
The sunny garden brilliant flow'rs confin'd.
The rooms within were scrubb'd until they shone

By the good wife of honest Farmer John.
Beside the fire at night the rustic sat,
And listen'd to the singing of his cat,   35
Or read the Scriptures to his wife and son,
Or thro' the window watch'd the rising moon.
His child by maxims wise and good was rear'd,
Virtue he lov'd, Immortal God he fear'd.
The vice and folly of the world he spurn'd,   40
But at the district-school true wisdom learn'd
From his kind master, who with precepts sage
Refin'd and shap'd the growth of tender age.
With no low trade his pliant mind was fill'd,
Nor was his wit by friv'lous notions kill'd.   45
Few were his studies, but with zeal pursu'd;
With solid learning was the youth imbu'd.
His hours of leisure were discreetly spent;
In harmless joys and sports he liv'd content.
Sturdy he grew, by Nature's certain law;   50
No towns he knew, nor crowded streets he saw.

Each Sunday in his stout capacious chaise,
John drove to meeting, God on high to praise.
New-shav'd, and in the finest of his coats,
The psalms he sang, with cheerful ringing notes.   55
With mind devout, his soul he sought to save,
Whilst lib'ral off'rings to the church he gave.
With ear attentive he the sermon heard;
The parson's counsels, and the holy word.
Blest was that parson, noblest of mankind;   60
True his belief, exalted was his mind.
Sinners he sav'd, and all creation lov'd;
By simple words, his flock to tears he mov'd;
Inspir'd he preach'd, and seraphim above approv'd.

The farmer's needs were few, and well supply'd   65
By laden ships that roll'd upon the tide,
From distant strands by fav'ring Zephyrs blown
Up to the wharves that grac'd each seaport town.
On wind-swept docks the Yankees, wond'ring, view'd
The swarthy sailors, freaks of alien blood.   70
They little fear'd, as they enjoy'd the breeze,
Their realm would soon be fill'd by such as these;
Unwarn'd they were; their ignorance was bliss;

They knew not how their land should go amiss.
Would that I might possess such nescience as this!   75

Oft to the village drove good Farmer John,
To stock his larder, and supply his barn.
'Mid shady streets he sought the village store,
And hail'd the rustics clutter'd 'round the door.
He bought with wisdom, and with honest heart   80
He'd trade in horses at the rural mart.
Then when night came, toward home John's wain inclin'd,
His new-bought nag a-trotting on behind.
And as he rode, with patriotic pride,
In sunset's glow he view'd the countryside.   85
The planted fields spread out before his gaze;
The steeple pierc'd the gath'ring evening haze,
Whilst here and there a tidy farmhouse shew'd
Its white expanse beside the dark'ning road.
Betwixt the trees, a wand'ring lane he saw;   90
Stone were its walls, and mossy was its floor.
The neighbours' boys addrest him thro' the gloam
As with their dogs they drove the cattle home.
Beside the brooklet stood the water-mill;
The day's work done, its pond'rous wheel was still.   95
Peace hover'd o'er each vale and gently rolling hill.

Agrestic bliss! Why canst thou not remain?
Why must the years bring evil in their train?
Why have the rustics' sons forsaken home,
In dismal towns and distant lands to roam?   100
Why have they left the meadows of their birth;
Quit rural ease for urban want and dearth?
Why are base foreign boors allow'd to dwell
Amongst the hills where Saxon greatness fell;
Live their low lives, themselves in filth degrade   105
As monkeys haunt a palace long decay'd?

Less fresh and green seem now New-England's hills,
The air is tainted by the smoke of mills;
The tott'ring houses, scarcely held erect,
Shake in the wind, and crumble from neglect,   110
Tho' in a few some wretched aliens dwell
'Midst hideous squalor, and repulsive smell.
The empty church with mould'ring rot decays;

387

The lofty steeple on its fast'ning sways:
Within its grass-grown yard, in peaceful sleep,   115
The parson lies, but none remain to weep.
The village rings with ribald foreign cries;
Around the wine-shops loaf with bleary eyes
A vicious crew, that mock the name of "man",
Yet dare to call themselves "American".   120
New-England's ships no longer ride the sea;
Once prosp'rous ports are sunk in poverty.
The rotting wharves as ruins tell the tale
Of days when Yankees mann'd the swelling sail.
The Indies yield no more their cargoes rare;   125
The sooty mill's New-England's present care:
The noisy mill, by foreign peasants run,
Supplants the glorious shipping that hath gone.
In arid fields, the kine no longer low;
The soil knows not the furrow of the plough;   130
The rolling meadows all neglected lie,
Fleck'd here and there by some foul alien's sty.
The school no more contains the busy class;
The walls are down, the ruins chok'd with grass.
Within the gate-post swallows build their nests;   135
Upon the hill, the gentle master rests.
The mossy lane with briers is o'ergrown;
The bound'ry walls are shapeless heaps of stone,
And thro' the mourning trees the winds in sorrow moan.

Whence comes this devastation of the land,   140
This awful blow of the Almighty's hand?
Where is New-England, that our fathers knew,
Where pious men in rugged virtue grew?
Where law and order rul'd the rustic realm,
And honour stood unconquer'd at the helm?   145
Gone! with the noble race that gave it life,
And given o'er to foreign crime and strife.
The Saxon yeoman made New-England great,
And when he leaves, he leaves it to foul fate.
No baser tribe can take his honour'd place,   150
And with like virtues old New-England grace.
This pow'r lies lock'd within the noble BRITISH race!

388

On the Creation of Niggers

When, long ago, the Gods created Earth,
In Jove's fair image Man was shap'd at birth.
The beasts for lesser parts were next design'd;
Yet were they too remote from humankind.
To fill this gap, and join the rest to man,   5
Th' Olympian host conceiv'd a clever plan.
A beast they wrought, in semi-human figure,
Fill'd it with vice, and call'd the thing a NIGGER.

On a New-England Village Seen by Moonlight

(The peaceful old villages of New England are fast losing their
original Yankee inhabitants and their agricultural atmosphere, being
now the seats of manufacturing industries peopled by Southern
European and Western Asiatic immigrants of low grade.)

The squalid, noisome village lies asleep;
The dusk and quiet hide the monstrous mill:
The bats their melancholy watches keep,
Whilst all the rabble's daytime cries are still.

A friendly wind, soft sweeping from the seas,   5
The tainted air for one brief moment clears;
A friendly moon, dim shining thro' the trees,
Conceals the ruin wrought by evil years.

The alien serfs escape our sorrowing view;
The tortur'd mind is lighten'd of its pain;   10
Our own ancestral spirits reign anew,
And old New-England seems to live again.

An idle moonbeam in the village square
Lights up the fountain and the empty green;
Plays o'er the ancient structures rotting there,   15
Yet veils the sad decadence of the scene.

Yon rustic cottage on the mountain's side
Seems still some pious farmer's simple home;
The sordid crew, that in it now abide,
Are sunk in sleep, and swath'd in grateful gloom.   20

A stealthy ray illumes the mounting spire
That crowns the temple where our fathers pray'd,

But, wisely kind, the light ascends no high'r,
And leaves the new-built Popish cross in shade.

Where dwells that race, beneath whose rule benign   25
The village rich in bliss and virtue grew,
The moonlight shews us, when its pencils shine
Amongst the mounds and tablets by the yew.

The hopeful cry, that from the woes which blend
In modern times, new blessings shall emerge;   30
But Contemplation mourns New-England's end,
And, drap'd in sack-cloth, chants her country's dirge.

To General Villa

AL INTREPIDO SEÑOR, General Francisco Villa, Comandante del Ejercito
de la Constitucion.

'Tis true, Don Francisco, you're only a thief;
A cut-throat, a bandit, a low rustling chief;
But in justice, old fellow, I really must own
That you know how to fight, if you are a ladron.

As a Spanish hidalgo, you cut little figure;   5
You're three-quarters Injun, and tainted with nigger;
You can't read a word; your own name you can't write,
But ¡Santa Maria! you know how to fight.

When we look for a treaty, or ponderous answer,
We turn to the dignified Señor Carranza;   10
But Mexico waits for another to free her
And places her hopes in the poor mongrel Villa.

So while crafty old Huerta, half drunk with bad brandy,
Still clings to his throne, 'cross the far Rio Grande,
'Tis to you our friend Bryan would lend his assistance: 15
Si, General Villa, you'll do—at a distance.

The Teuton's Battle-Song

"Omnis erat vulnus unda
Terra rubefacta calido
Frendebat gladius in loricas
Gladius fludebat clypeos—
Non retrocedat vir a viro

390

Hoc fuit viri fortis nobilitas diu—
Laetus cerevisiam cum Asis
In summa sede bibam
Vitae clapsae sunt horae
Ridens moriar."
        —REGNER LODBROG

The mighty Woden laughs upon his throne,
And once more claims his children for his own.
The voice of Thor resounds again on high,
While arm'd Valkyries ride from out the sky:
The Gods of Asgard all their pow'rs release   5
To rouse the dullard from his dream of peace.
Awake! ye hypocrites, and deign to scan
The actions of your "brotherhood of Man".
Could your shrill pipings in the race impair
The warlike impulse put by Nature there?   10
Where now the gentle maxims of the school,
The cant of preachers, and the Golden Rule?
What feeble word or doctrine now can stay
The tribe whose fathers own'd Valhalla's sway?
Too long restrain'd, the bloody tempest breaks,   15
And Midgard 'neath the tread of warriors shakes.
On to thy death, Berserker bold! and try
In acts of Godlike bravery to die!
Who cares to find the heaven of the priest,
When only warriors can with Woden feast?   20
The flesh of Schrimnir, and the cup of mead,
Are but for him who falls in martial deed:
Yon luckless boor, that passive meets his end,
May never in Valhalla's court contend.
Slay, brothers, slay! and bathe in crimson gore;   25
Let Thor, triumphant, view the sport once more!
All other thoughts are fading in the mist,
But to attack, or if attack'd, resist.
List, great Alfadur, to the clash of steel;
How like a man does each brave swordsman feel!   30
The cries of pain, the roars of rampant rage,
In one vast symphony our ears engage.
Strike! Strike him down! whoever bars the way;
Let each kill many ere he die today!
Ride o'er the weak; accomplish what ye can;   35

391

The Gods are kindest to the strongest man!
Why should we fear? What greater joy than this?
Asgard alone could give us sweeter bliss!
My strength is waning; dimly can I see
The helmeted Valkyries close to me.   40
Ten more I slay! How strange the thought of fear,
With Woden's mounted messengers so near!
The darkness comes; I feel my spirit rise;
A kind Valkyrie bears me to the skies.
With conscience clear, I quit the earth below,   45
The boundless joys of Woden's halls to know.
The grove of Glasir soon shall I behold,
And on Valhalla's tablets be enroll'd:
There to remain, till Heimdall's horn shall sound,
And Ragnarok enclose creation round;   50
And Bifrost break beneath bold Surtur's horde,
And Gods and men fall dead beneath the sword;
When sun shall die, and sea devour the land,
And stars descend, and naught but Chaos stand.
Then shall Alfadur make his realm anew,   55
And Gods and men with purer life indue.
In that blest country shall Abundance reign,
Nor shall one vice or woe of earth remain.
Then, not before, shall men their battles cease,
And live at last in universal peace.   60
Thro' cloudless heavens shall the eagle soar,
And happiness prevail for evermore.

1914

"Parcere subjectis, et debellare superbos."
—Virgil, *Aen.* lib. vi.

Arise, Britannia! at thy sisters' plea,
And crush the mighty foe of liberty.
Behold the hour for thee to prove thy place
As friend and guardian of the human race.
Th' insatiate Goth, with naked, murd'rous sword,   5
Defies thy edict, and ignores thy word;
E'en daring, as he plays the fuming brute,
To scorn thy greatness, and thy pow'r dispute.
Thou Queen of Nations! smite into the dust
The proud invader, savage and unjust,   10

Whose madden'd hordes, like ancient vandals, seek
To wrong the guiltless, and despoil the weak;
Who all his boasted culture misemploys,
In art creating less than he destroys.
Imperial Mother! cast thy pitying eyes   15
On that sad spot where shatter'd Louvain lies,
Or on yon crumbling wall and formless mound
Where Gallia's stately monarchs once were crown'd.
From north and east the bold barbarians pour
And dye the flowing Axona with gore.   20
The outrag'd Gauls, defeated and dismay'd,
Survive alone thro' England's potent aid.
Vainglorious Prussia, with a Teuton's pride,
By force of arms would thrust the weak aside;
Above the sphere of lesser tribes ascend,   25
And martial sway o'er all the earth extend.
But thou, Britannia, art by heav'n endow'd
To spare the humble, and subdue the proud:
Thy stalwart sons have Teuton blood as true
As e'er the banks of Rhenus' waters knew!   30
What race can boast a better, braver strain
Than noble Norman, Saxon, Jute, and Dane?
No native island can such pow'r confine:
The widespread world, O Englishman, is thine!
From Afric Cape and Island Continent,   35
Stout hearts of oak to face the Goth are sent;
The swarthy Rajah, skill'd in Indian wars,
Supplies his subjects to assist the cause,
And legions from Canadian shores have come
To drive the raging Prussian to his doom.   40
In vain the Goth his monstrous cannon loads;
In vain his mine beneath the wave explodes;
In vain his zeppelin patrols the sky,
In vain his ships upon the ocean lie;
For Gallia's fields, encrimson'd with the slain,   45
Shall never in the Prussian's hands remain!
Insensate German! blindly to oppose
A conqu'ring race that naught but vict'ry knows.
How couldst thou dream successfully to fight,
When English, Irish, Scotch, and Welsh unite?   50
E'en thy brave cohorts constantly prepar'd
To strike such mighty foes should not have dar'd.

393

For each success gain'd early in the fray,
How great a price will Prussia have to pay!
Ere long the nations once again shall learn 55
On whom fair Europe's fate must ever turn;
Before whose strength the fiercest foemen fall,
From ancient Crécy to Sebastopol;
Whose task it is, true justice to dispense,
And strike the braggart for his gross offence. 60

Thou right arm of Astraea! speed the hour
When peace and order shall reward thy pow'r;
When grateful lands, deliver'd from despair,
Shall bless Britannia for her kindly care;
When ev'ry king and country shall resort 65
To England's judgment as the final court,
And when the mighty Empire shall become
A world itself—the deathless heir of Rome!

The Crime of Crimes

Lusitania, 1915

"Virescit vulnere virtus."

Craz'd with the Belgian blood so lately shed,
The bestial Prussian seeks the ocean's bed;
In Neptune's realm the wretched coward lurks,
And on the world his wonted evil works.
Like slinking cur, he bites where none oppose; 5
Victorious over babes, his valour grows.

One fateful day (may such be never more)
A stately vessel left Columbia's shore;
Upon the wave in dauntless grandeur rode,
Nor fear'd to bear its blameless, helpless load. 10
No human risk the watchful captain ran,
Protected by the common laws of man.
The laws of man! What laws can curb or sway
The Prussian wolf, with manhood cast away?
His idle threat, too hideous for belief, 15
With its foul truth plung'd nations into grief.
The sun was bright, the sea by wind untoss'd,
As the proud ship lay off Hibernia's coast.

Secure in innocence, she plough'd the brine,
And scorn'd the dread of hostile craft or mine.   20
O matchless infamy! Could mortal brain
Conceive the foe that lurk'd along the main;
Who eyed with gory glee the watchful band
That pac'd the deck, and view'd the distant land?
Stay, weeping Muse! Dwell not upon the sight   25
That turn'd the shining day to hellish night;
Sing not the missile, sent with fiendish aim,
Its toll of unoffending lives to claim:
Such things as these to humans scarce belong,
Nor form a lawful theme for rhyme or song.   30
Struck by the dastard's dart, a fated mark,
Beneath the sea descends the hapless bark.
Her sister ships, by Prussian threats delay'd,
Tho' eager, yet are impotent to aid.
Thrice cursed Goth! Thy prey already down,   35
Yet thou must needs have helpless hundreds drown!
The crime accomplish'd, now the foe recedes,
And in his craven flight recounts his deeds.
Vengeance! From kindred nations comes the cry.
Shall mortals thus for no offences die?   40
Shall rabid wolves unpunish'd prowl the wave,
And strike at random when no man can save?
Laws of the world! have ye no force to blast
Th' infernal hordes that set the world aghast?
Shall man beneath the Prussian madness fall,   45
And black barbarity engulf us all?
Awake! ye torpid hemispheres, to strike
The serpent that defies us all alike!
The snake that spreads his writhing, pois'nous coils
O'er the fair land, and all he sees despoils.   50
Have ye not ever in your childhood heard
The mystic utt'rance of the Holy Word,
That he, the serpent who shall bruise our heel,
Must in his turn our stronger bruises feel?
The time is here, our heel hath felt his sting;   55
Let now our righteous wrath his downfall bring.
Let man, united, crush the hissing head
That all the world hath learn'd to hate and dread.
Choke the vile threat that opens but to lie,
And in his poison let the adder die.   60

To arms! ye nations, and acclaim the dawn
Wherein a second freedom shall be born!

An American to Mother England

England! My England! Can the surging sea
That lies between us tear my heart from thee?
Can distant birth and distant dwelling drain
Th' ancestral blood that warms the loyal vein?
Isle of my Fathers! hear the filial song   5
Of him whose sources but to thee belong!
World-conqu'ring Mother! by thy mighty hand
Was carv'd from savage wilds my native land:
Thy matchless sons the firm foundation laid;
Thy matchless arts the nascent nation made: 10
By thy just laws the young republic grew,
And thro' thy greatness, kindred greatness knew:
What man that springs from thy untainted line
But sees Columbia's virtues all as thine?
Whilst nameless multitudes upon our shore   15
From the dim corners of creation pour,
Whilst mongrel slaves crawl hither to partake
Of Saxon liberty they could not make,
From such an alien crew in grief I turn,
And for the mother's voice of Britain burn.   20
England! Can aught remove the cherish'd chain
That binds my spirit to thy blest domain?
Can Revolution's bitter precepts sway
The soul that must the ties of race obey?
Create a new Columbia if ye will;   25
The flesh that forms me is Britannic still!
Hail! oaken shades, and meads of dewy green,
So oft in sleep, yet ne'er in waking seen.
Peal out, ye ancient chimes, from vine-clad tow'r
Where pray'd my fathers in a vanish'd hour: 30
What countless years of rev'rence can ye claim
From bygone worshippers that bore my name!
Their forms are crumbling in the vaults around,
Whilst I, across the sea, but dream the sound.
Return, Sweet Vision! Let me glimpse again   35
The stone-built abbey, rising o'er the plain;
The neighb'ring village with its sun-show'r'd square,
The shaded mill-stream, and the forest fair,

396

The hedge-lin'd lane, that leads to rustic cot
Where sweet contentment is the peasant's lot;   40
The mystic grove, by Druid wraiths possess'd,
The flow'ring fields, with fairy circles blest;
And the old manor-house, sedate and dark,
Set in the shadows of the wooded park.
Can this be dreaming? Must my eyelids close   45
That I may catch the fragrance of the rose?
Is it in fancy that the midnight vale
Thrills with the warblings of the nightingale?
A golden moon bewitching radiance yields,
And England's fairies trip o'er England's fields.   50
England! Old England! in my love for thee
No dream is mine, but blessed memory;
Such haunting images and hidden fires
Course with the bounding blood of British sires:
From British bodies, minds, and souls I come,   55
And from them draw the vision of their home.
Awake, Columbia! scorn the vulgar age
That bids thee slight thy lordly heritage.
Let not the wide Atlantic's wildest wave
Burst the blest bonds that fav'ring Nature gave: 60
Connecting surges 'twixt the nations run,
Our Saxon souls dissolving into one!

Temperance Song

[Tune: "The Bonnie Blue Flag."]

1.   We are a band of brothers
       Who fight the demon Rum,
       With all our strength until at length
       A better time shall come.

(Chorus)
Hurrah! Hurrah! for Temperance, Hurrah!   5
'Tis sweet to think that deadly drink
Some day no more shall mar!

2.   We'll drive from off our table,
       We'll drive from out our gate
       The gross offence that clouds our sense,   10
       And leads to dismal Fate.

3.   We'll stop the bloated brewer,
We'll close the foul saloon,
We'll teach the land to understand
How mighty is our boon.   15

4.   If aught our progress hinder,
Or check our upward course,
We'll scorn the hand that threats our stand
And strive with double force.

5.   And when at last we triumph;   20
When whiskey fades from view;
The drunkard slave no more shall crave,
But join our legions, too!

The Rose of England

At morn the rosebud greets the sun
    And sheds the evening dew,
Expanding ere the day is done,
    In bloom of radiant hue;
And when the sun his rest hath found,   5
Rose-petals strow the garden round!

Thus that blest Isle that owns the Rose
    From mist and darkness came,
A million glories to disclose,
    And spread BRITANNIA'S name;   10
And ere Life's Sun shall leave the blue,
ENGLAND shall reign the whole world thro'!

Lines on Gen. Robert Edward Lee

Born Jan. 19, 1807

              "Si veris magna paratur
    Fama bonis, et si successu nuda remoto
    Inspicitur virtus, quicquid laudamus in ullo
    Majorum, fortuna fuit."
                —Lucan.

Whilst martial echoes o'er the wave resound,
And Europe's gore incarnadines the ground;
Today no foreign hero we bemoan,
But count the glowing virtues of our own!

Illustrious LEE! around whose honour'd name   5
Entwines a patriot's and a Christian's fame;
With whose just praise admiring nations ring,
And whom repenting foes contritely sing!
When first our land fraternal fury bore,
And Sumter's guns alarm'd the anxious shore;   10
When Faction's reign ancestral rights o'erthrew,
And sunder'd States a mutual hatred knew;
Then clash'd contending chiefs of kindred line,
In flesh to suffer and in fame to shine.
But o'er them all, majestic in his might,   15
Rose LEE, unrivall'd, to sublimest height:
With torturing choice defy'd opposing Fate,
And shunn'd Temptation for his native State!
Thus Washington his monarch's rule o'erturn'd
When young Columbia with rebellion burn'd.   20
And what in Washington the world reveres,
In LEE with equal magnitude appears.
Our nation's Father, crown'd with vict'ry's bays,
Enjoys a loving land's eternal praise:
Let, then, our hearts with equal rev'rence greet   25
His proud successor, rising o'er defeat!
Around his greatness pour disheartening woes,
But still he tow'rs above his conqu'ring foes.
Silence! ye jackal herd that vainly blame
Th' unspotted leader by a traitor's name: 30
If such was LEE, let blushing Justice mourn,
And trait'rous Liberty endure our scorn!
As Philopoemen once sublimely strove,
And earn'd declining Hellas' thankful love;
So follow'd LEE the purest patriot's part,   35
And wak'd the worship of the grateful heart:
The South her soul in body'd form discerns;
The North from LEE a nobler freedom learns!
Attend! ye sons of Albion's ancient race,
Whate'er your country, and whate'er your place: 40
LEE'S valiant deeds, tho' dear to Southern song,
To all our Saxon strain as well belong.
Courage like his the parent Island won,
And led an Empire past the setting sun;
To realms unknown our laws and language bore;   45
Rais'd England's banner on the desert shore;

Crush'd the proud rival, and subdu'd the sea
For ages past, and aeons yet to be!
From Scotia's hilly bounds the paean rolls,
And Afric's distant Cape great LEE extols; 50
The sainted soul and manly mien combine
To grace Britannia's and Virginia's line!
As dullards now in thoughtless fervour prate
Of shameful peace, and sing th' unmanly State;
As churls their piping reprobations shriek, 55
And damn the heroes that protect the weak;
Let LEE'S brave shade the timid throng accost,
And give them back the manhood they have lost!
What kindlier spirit, breathing from on high,
Can teach us how to live and how to die? 60

Britannia Victura

When Justice from the vaulted skies
    Beheld the fall of Roman might,
She bade a nobler realm arise
    To rule the world and guard the right:
She spake—and all the murm'ring main, 5
    Rejoicing, hail'd Britannia's reign!

The mind of Greece, the law of Rome,
    The strength of Northern climes remote,
On one fair Island made their home,
    And in one race their virtues wrote: 10
The blended glories of the past
    In England evermore shall last!

Untrodden wilds beyond the sea,
    And savage hordes in lands unknown,
At Albion's touch rose great and free, 15
    And bless'd the sway of England's throne:
Discordant tribes, with strife o'errun,
    Grew Britons, and join'd hands as one!

When Greed and Envy stand array'd,
    And Madness threats a peaceful earth, 20
Britannia's sons with sacred blade
    Defend the soil that gave them birth:
Nor is their cause to that confin'd—
    They fight for Justice and Mankind.

Tho' Fortune frown and trials press;   25
    Tho' pain and hardship weight the heart;
The dawn of vict'ry soon will bless
    Each Briton who sustains his part:
For Heav'n's own pow'r is close ally'd
    To Virtue's and Britannia's side!   30

Pacifist War Song—1917

We are the valiant Knights of Peace
    Who prattle for the Right:
Our banner is of snowy fleece,
    Inscribed: "TOO PROUD TO FIGHT!"

By sweet Chautauqua's flow'ry banks   5
    We love to sing and play,
But should we spy a foeman's ranks,
    We'd proudly run away!

When Prussian fury sweeps the main
    Our freedom to deny;   10
Of tyrant laws we ne'er complain,
    But gladsomely comply!

We do not fear the submarines
    That plough the troubled foam;
We scorn the ugly old machines—   15
    And safely stay at home!

They say our country's close to war,
    And soon must man the guns;
But we see naught to struggle for—
    We love the gentle Huns!   20

What tho' their hireling Greaser bands
    Invade our southern plains?
We well can spare those boist'rous lands,
    Content with what remains!

Our fathers were both rude and bold,   25
    And would not live like brothers;
But we are of a finer mould—
    We're much more like our mothers!

Iterum Conjunctae

Hail! mighty kindred, ever bound
    By ties of freedom, blood, and speech;
Whose mingled empires girdle round
    The teeming earth's expansive reach.

Our mother BRITAIN taught the brave   5
    Their sacred rights with zeal to hold;
To spread their glory o'er the wave,
    And liberty to all unfold.

From such a source COLUMBIA grew,
    And fill'd the West with freedom's light;   10
A second world uprear'd to view,
    And aw'd the nations with her might.

Let now th' aspiring Vandal quake,
    And shrink affrighted from the plain,
For ancient bonds at last awake,   15
    And SAXONS stand as one again!

The Peace Advocate

(Supposed to be a "pome", but cast in strictly modern metre.)

The vicar sat in the firelight's glow,
    A volume in his hand;
    And a tear he shed for the widespread woe,
    And the anguish brought by the vicious foe
        That overran the land.   5

But ne'er a hand for his King rais'd he,
    For he was a man of peace;
    And he car'd not a whit for the victory
    That must come to preserve his nation free,
        And the world from fear release.   10

His son had buckled on his sword,
    The first at the front was he;
    But the vicar his valiant child ignor'd,
    And his noble deeds in the field deplor'd,
        For he knew not bravery.   15

On his flock he strove to fix his will,
  And lead them to scorn the fray.
He told them that conquest brings but ill;
That meek submission would serve them still
  To keep the foe away.   20

In vain did he hear the bugle's sound
  That strove to avert the fall.
The land, quoth he, is all men's ground,
What matter if friend or foe be found
  As master of us all?   25

One day from the village green hard by
  The vicar heard the roar
Of cannon that rivall'd the anguish'd cry
Of the hundreds that liv'd, but wish'd to die
  As the enemy rode them o'er.   30

Now he sees his own cathedral shake
  At the foeman's wanton aim.
The ancient tow'rs with the bullets quake;
The steeples fall, the foundations break,
  And the whole is lost in flame.   35

Up the vicarage lane file the cavalcade,
  And the vicar, and daughter, and wife
Scream out in vain for the needed aid
That only a regiment might have made,
  Ere they lose what is more than life. 40

Then quick to his brain came manhood's thought,
  As he saw his erring course;
And the vicar his dusty rifle brought
That the foe might at least by one be fought,
  And force repaid with force.   45

One shot—the enemy's blasting fire
  A breach in the wall cuts thro',
But the vicar replies with his waken'd ire;
Fells one arm'd brute for each fallen spire,
  And in blood is born anew.   50

Two shots—the wife and daughter sink,
  Each with a mortal wound;
And the vicar, too madden'd by far to think,

Rushes boldly on to death's vague brink,
    With the manhood he has found.   55

Three shots—but shots of another kind
    The smoky regions rend;
And upon the foeman with rage gone blind,
Like a ceaseless, resistless, avenging wind,
    The rescuing troops descend.   60

The smoke-pall clears, and the vicar's son
    His father's life has sav'd;
And the vicar looks o'er the ruin done,
Ere the vict'ry by his child was won,
    His face with care engrav'd.   65

The vicar sat in the firelight's glow,
    The volume in his hand,
That brought to his hearth the bitter woe
Which only a husband and father can know,
    And truly understand.   70

With chasten'd mien he flung the book
    To the leaping flames before;
And a breath of sad relief he took
As the pages blacken'd beneath his look—
    The fool of Peace no more!   75

Epilogue

The rev'rend parson, wak'd to man's estate,
Laments his wife's and daughter's common fate.
His martial son in warm embrace enfolds,
And clings the tighter to the child he holds.
His peaceful notions, banish'd in an hour,   80
Will nevermore his wit or sense devour;
But steep'd in truth, 'tis now his nobler plan
To cure, yet recognise, the faults of man.

To Greece, 1917

Ye sons of Greece! by true descent ally'd
To Athens' glory, and to Sparta's pride;
Heirs to the spark that set the world ablaze
With new-born Freedom's first awak'ning rays;
Children of Hellas, from whose deathless heart   5

Sprang all we have of wisdom and of art:
Can ye, unblushing, bear upon your throne
A slave of gods and cultures not your own?
Heav'ns! would Pelides, foremost in the fray,
Bow thus to Thor's and Woden's frost-mad sway?   10
Would Agamemnon drop his glist'ning shield,
And passive to barbarian Wilhelm yield?
Shame on thee, Constantinos! Reign no more,
Thou second Hippias of the Attic shore!
Rise from your tombs, ye Marthonian slain!   15
Ye shades of Salamis, adorn the main!
Appear, ye martyrs of th' embattled free,
Whose sacred mem'ry guards Thermopylae!
With ancient valour teach your native Greece
To scorn the Goth, and spurn a coward's peace!   20
As once your hands, invincible and just,
Smote tyrant Xerxes prostrate in the dust;
Disarm'd th' oppressor, and preserv'd the brave;
Snatch'd infant Europe from a Persian grave;
So may ye now against the despot stand,   25
And stir the sleeping glories of your land!
Need any tongue before your ears rehearse
The monstrous menace of the Vandal curse?
Need bard or prophet sound the mourning lyre,
Or Delphic riddles rouse your smould'ring fire?   30
Behold the Teuton, threat'ning in his guilt
The laws and arts your matchless Athens built;
Your laws and arts, by Roman prowess spread
Thro' grateful Europe, and to Britain led;
By British pow'r sent o'er the ocean crest   35
Where young Columbia rules th' expansive West;
Gaze on the Hun, his bestial cohorts hurl'd
Against the freedom of a Grecian world!
See great Italia soar again to fame,
Till monarchs shudder at the Roman name;   40
See fiery Gaul achieve a nobler height,
And shew the neighb'ring nations how to fight;
And proud o'er all the rest, with ties renew'd,
See brother Saxons cow th' invading brood!
All these behold—these scions of your mind—   45
Shall Hellas, source of all, remain behind?
Say not, ye Greeks, that those bold men are gone

Who yesteryear your conqu'ring hosts led on;
Say not your plains of heroes are bereft,
Nor cry that Clisthenes no heir hath left; 50
False is the tongue that such a slander gives
To Grecian soil, while VENIZELOS lives!
With such a chieftain could your country know
The fame and liberty of long ago;
Once more would tyrants meet their well-earn'd fate, 55
And Grecian freedom bless the Grecian state:
A Cretan Pericles the helm would hold,
That Greece might sail to glory as of old!
Cloud-crown'd Olympus! may thy godlike train
Rule as of yore, and haunt the groves again; 60
May Zeus with thunders scourge the martial scene
Where Woden tramples o'er th' unhappy green;
May arm'd Athena with her aegis soar
Above the phalanx of encroaching Thor,
While gruff Poseidon's trident, pois'd with care, 65
Smites the dread serpent in its ocean lair!
Gods! Heroes! Men of Greece! at last come forth
Against the crawling Hydra of the North:
Achaia's pow'r eternally endures—
The past, the blood, the leader, all are yours! 70

Ode for July Fourth, 1917

As Columbia's brave scions, in anger array'd,
    Once defy'd a proud monarch and built a new nation;
'Gainst their brothers of Britain unsheath'd the sharp blade
    That hath ne'er met defeat nor endur'd desecration;
        So must we in this hour 5
        Shew our valour and pow'r,
And dispel the black perils that over us low'r:
    Whilst the sons of Britannia, no longer our foes,
    Will rejoice in our triumphs and strengthen our blows!

See the banners of Liberty float in the breeze 10
    That plays light o'er the regions our fathers defended;
Hear the voice of the million resound o'er the leas,
    As the deeds of the past are proclaim'd and commended;
        And in splendour on high
        Where our flags proudly fly, 15
See the folds we tore down flung again to the sky:

For the Emblem of England, in kinship unfurl'd,
Shall divide with Old Glory the praise of the world!

Bury'd now are the hatreds of subject and King,
    And the strife that once sunder'd an Empire hath vanish'd.   20
With the fame of the Saxon the heavens shall ring
    As the vultures of darkness are baffled and banish'd:
        And the broad British sea,
        Of her enemies free,
Shall in tribute bow gladly, Columbia, to thee: 25
    For the friends of the Right, in the field side by side,
    Form a fabric of Freedom no hand can divide!

An American to the British Flag

In zealous rage our fathers swore
To fly the ancient flag no more;
    To trail it in the dust:
They curs'd the holy cross of red,
For which th' embattled free had bled,   5
    And deem'd their hatred just.

Another flag in pomp they rais'd,
And whilst the world stood by amaz'd,
    A nation had its birth.
Forgetful of the blood that gave   10
Their pow'r to prosper, free and brave,
    They welcom'd all the earth.

The Land that English prowess made,
A horde of mongrel breed display'd;
    The scourings of mankind.   15
The pauper and the weakling swarm'd
O'er realms our English fathers form'd:
    O nation proudly blind!

Our dear ancestral glories wane
From teeming town, from grove and plain,   20
    And well-remember'd leas.
'Mid changing scenes we sadly plod
As strangers on our native sod,
    And live in memories.

O Flag of Old! At last we hail   25
Once more thy ripples in the gale,
    And watch thy wistful face.
Thy folds remain, tho' aliens rise
To taint each story'd scene we prize,
    Thou symbol of our race.   30

The Volunteer

(A Reply to the Lines of Sergt. Miller in *The National Enquirer*)

Tho' today all the bands are playing
    For the fellow who had to go;
For the man of faint heart, who needed a start,
    And was caught in the current's flow;
Never think that we're scorned or slighted,   5
    Or that ever we hold less dear
The hero we raise above all common praise—
    The valorous volunteer!

In the turmoil of black disaster,
    When the nations totter and reel,   10
When our soft, fat race started awake to face
    The mad monster of blood and steel;
Then our hearts are tried in the furnace,
    And our souls are sounded for fear,
And while pity must go to the weak and the slow,   15
    We worship the volunteer!

We honour the ranks of the conscripts,
    For we know they are average men—
The plumber and clerk snatched up from their work
    To be thrown in the dragon's den;   20
They are bearing their fate rather nobly,
    Who is perfect enough to sneer?
But the laurels of fame and the patriot's name
    Go first to the volunteer!

'Tis not easy to leave all we cherish,   25
    To lose half our hope of life;
To suffer more than we dreamed of before,
    And conquer our dread of strife;
So we grudge none the pomp and the music
    That are needed to hearten and cheer;   30

There's just one in the throng who can fight without song—
    The man who can volunteer!

For his heart is the heart of our fathers,
    Who knew how to conquer or die,
Who could offer their all at their country's call,   35
    And knew never a tremor or sigh;
He has given himself to the ages,
    He has soared to the godlike sphere;
What honour needs he, but to feel and to be
    A Liberty volunteer?   40

So when victory breaks thro' the war-clouds,
    And peace comes to bless us once more,
And each man on the roll searches deep in his soul
    For the thoughts of the conflict before,
Who can hold up his heart to the daylight   45
    With a conscience so joyous and clear
As the fellow who fought uncompelled and unsought—
    The chivalrous volunteer?

Ad Britannos—1918

Ye legions of England, supernal in glory,
    The sons of the mighty and lords of the main,
Awake to the lustre of ballad and story,
    And drench the torn earth with your enemies slain!

Too long have we falter'd in kindly illusion,   5
    Too long have we pleaded for justice and right,
Too dim have we seen thro' a combat's confusion
    The death of our dreams and the triumph of might.

Untouch'd by the centuries' softening finger,
    Untaught by the delicate precepts of time,   10
See the shade of Arminius defiantly linger,
    And mock the soft world with his wassail of crime.

Whilst we shrink in disgust at the carnage and clamour,
    And defend our lov'd ground in incredulous woe,
Hear the gay, ghastly swing of Thor's thundering hammer,   15
    As his children delight in each dastardly blow!

Not a steeple or dome knows the Hun's veneration;
    Not a relic or shrine can restrain his mad hand;

Not a scruple or law stems his wild profanation,
 As exultant he stalks thro' the sore-stricken land.   20

'Tis the blood of the past that is raging within him,
 The hot blood of pillagers ruthless and bold;
The murderous madness he summons to win him
 Such a realm as would glad his stern fathers of old.

Can we patiently stand in our honour and meekness,   25
 And hope to prevail against forces like these;
When mercy is folly and pity is weakness,
 And black-shrouded hate haunts the plains and the seas?

What strength can we draw from our modest position?
 What watchword have we to inflame the slow mind?   30
What passion of ours may reduce to submission
 The blond beast of the barracks, beserker and blind?

Shall our ardour be stirr'd but by doctrine and sermon,
 By high thoughts of liberty, abstract and grave?
Shall we frown on the War-Lord, but love each poor German   35
 Who bows to his sceptre, a glad willing slave?

Shall we cherish the monsters that slaughter and ravage?
 Forgive their red sins and condone their dark plan?
Shall we open their hearts to the fiend and the savage,
 And name him our brother, our dear fellow-man?   40

Shall we lecture and wail at the tyrant's oppression;
 With leaden hearts labour to stem the black tide;
Shall we prate of the law whilst he glows with possession,
 Nor avenge the mourn'd hosts that have suffer'd and died?

Come, rise, ye bold Britons, on Victory's pinion,   45
 Recall the proud blood that leaps warm in your veins;
Your country was fashion'd for pow'r and dominion,
 Your Muse was created for high martial strains!

Forget not your birthright of greatness and valour,
 Forget not the might that your fathers could wield;   50
Forget not the foemen who trembled in pallor
 When Saxons and Normans appeared on the field!

For our blood is the same the vandals are vaunting;
 We too are the stout sons of Woden and Thor;

Our past is their past—let no fervour be wanting 55
    To expand us with pride and exalt us in war!

When Hengist and Horsa our blessed isle gain'd us,
    Like feathers before us the poor Celts were blown:
What native resisted, what chieftain restrain'd us,
    As we swept from the land ev'ry race but our own? 60

Alfadur smil'd sweet on our fair-flashing sabre,
    And roar'd with delight as we smote the base foe;
He laugh'd as we vanquish'd each insolent neighbour,
    And drank deep to the health of the English long bow.

So spring up again at the challenge of madness, 65
    To the ages proclaim that the past is not dead;
Let the javeline be flung more in glee than in sadness,
    And a wild song of conquest lend wings to our lead.

As our battle-brave Beowulf, valiant and joyous,
    Slew monsters and dragons that threaten'd his realm, 70
So must we face the serpents that seek to destroy us,
    And with spirit as light, ev'ry fiend overwhelm!

Let us redden each stream with the blood of our foemen,
    And gorge the lean wolves with the wretches we slay;
Let the buzzards be hail'd as a glad welcome omen, 75
    As they circle above us, awaiting their prey!

What is Death to the hero of courage and spirit,
    Whose soul to his country full loyalty gives:
What Briton so base not to heed it or fear it,
    If he knew that Old England in triumph yet lives? 80

See the sons of Britannia surge forth in their splendour
    From the dear native isle and the far distant shore;
From the plains of Columbia behold the defender
    Rise proud by the side of the mother once more!

In the cloud-laden skies the Valkyries are soaring 85
    And calling the brave to their long blissful rest;
On the struggle-scarr'd field our stern legions are pouring,
    Each hot for the fray, and prepar'd for the test.

So onward, bold Saxons, who carry behind ye
    A valorous heritage none can excel; 90

May the shades of your world-winning fathers remind ye
    To rival their glories, and battle as well!

On a Battlefield in Picardy

      Here all is dead.
The charnel plain a spectral legion knows,
      That cannot find repose,
And blank, grey vistas endless stretch ahead,
        Mud-carpeted,   5
     And stain'd with red.
       Where Valour's sons for Freedom bled.
       And in the scorching sky
       The carrion ravens fly,
Scanning the treeless waste that rots around,   10
Where trenches yawn, and craters pit the ground.
And in the night the horn'd Astarte gleams,
       And sheds her evil beams.

Yet there so lately bloom'd the fragrant grove
       Where linnets chirp'd their love,   15
And dreaming pastures, pied with daffodils,
Where Satyrs sang by Naiad-peopled rills,
And where Endymion at the close of day
       Beneath the moonbeams lay.
Dread Desolation, ruling now the scene,   20
How little recks the beauties that have been!
Sear'd is the plain across whose face hath trod
       The twisted Scourge of God.
       But sometimes in the breeze
That stirs at dusk, come mystic prophecies   25
Of never-dying Pan and meadows green!

The Link

By distant shores two Empires lie,
    As one in language, race, and laws,
And like the Brethren of the Sky,
    Together join'd in Honour's cause.

One mighty source these giants knew;   5
    One mighty soul thro' time they share;
For the young oak that westward grew,
    Was nurs'd in English soil and air.

Hesperia! ere thy glowing glance
    Explores the sunset path of Fate,   10
Look backward o'er the wave's expanse,
    And bless the blood that made thee great!

To Alan Seeger

Author of "A Message to America", who fell in the Cause of Civilisation
at Belloy-en-Santerre, July, 1916.

SEEGER! whose soul, with animated lyre,
Wak'd the dull dreamer to a manlier fire;
Whose martial voice, by martial deeds sustain'd,
Denounc'd the age when shameful peace remain'd;
Let thy brave spirit yet among us dwell,   5
And linger where thy form in valour fell:
Proudly before th' invader's fury mass'd,
Behold thy country's cohorts, rous'd at last!
It was not for thy mortal eye to see
Columbia arm'd for Right and Liberty;   10
Thine was the finer heart, that could not stay
To wait for laggards in the vital fray,
And ere the millions felt thy sacred heat,
Thou hadst the gift to Freedom made complete.
But while thou sleepest in an honour'd grave   15
Beneath the Gallic sod thou bledst to save,
May thy soul's vision scan the ravag'd plain,
And tell thee that thou didst not fall in vain:
Here, as thou pray'dst, a million men advance
To prove Columbia one with flaming France,   20
And heeding now the long-forgotten debt,
Pay with their blood the gen'rous LAFAYETTE!
Thy ringing odes to prophecies are turn'd,
Whilst legions feel the blaze that in thee burn'd.
Not as a lonely stranger dost thou lie,   25
Thy form forsaken 'neath a foreign sky,
On Gallic tongues thy name forever lives;
First of the mighty host thy country gives:
All that thou dreamt'st in life shall come to be,
And proud Columbia find her voice in thee!   30

Germania—1918

For four long years on daemon malice bent,
To shake a world, and burn a continent,
See the mad Goth each impious boast recall,
And start in terror at his coming fall!
How late the day, when big with martial pride,   5
The rav'ning beast a peaceful earth defy'd;
Sure of his skill, contemptuous of his foe,
Inspir'd by counsel from the pit below,
By laws unhinder'd, and by rights uncheck'd,
With slaves to fight, and madmen to direct;   10
The savage, thirsty for accustom'd gore,
Burst from his lair as many a time before.
So swarm'd his Cimbrian fathers on the plain
Where Marius only could their force restrain;
So Ariovistus, merciless and bold,   15
Spread havoc till by Caesar's might controll'd;
So the curs'd Alaric a mournful fate
Brought on the weak declining Roman state:
So in each age the German wolf we find,
The spoiler, scourge, and terror of mankind.   20
In evil pomp dark Wilhelm's form discern,
Resolv'd the weak'ning nations to o'erturn;
Close by his side his chinless Princeling sits,
As rich in arrogance as poor in wits:
Around the two a herd obsequious throng,   25
Flatt'rers in folly, counsellors in wrong;
Agreed on crime, the knavish train essay
To wake the horrors of a former day.
O'er Belgian ground the noisome rabble spread,
Murder and arson in their hated tread;   30
Gallia's fair meads the bestial presence feel,
And helpless children know the wanton steel:
Steeples and tow'rs, mute suppliants to the sky,
For sport are levell'd as the fiends march by;
Heavens and sea unwonted evil bear,   35
And anguish'd earth bewails her thick'ning care;
Meanwhile the suff'rers, brave thro' all their woes,
In Saxon valour ev'ry hope repose:
A Roman pow'r in British blood perceive,
The strong to crush, the humble to relieve: 40
Britannia hears the call, and proudly wields

414

Her arms, victorious on a thousand fields;
New Marlboroughs rise, and o'er the troubled main
Pour the stout heirs of many a bright campaign.
Thus, as of old, we see our valiant line   45
A planet's saviour, and a force divine.
The Goth, incens'd, delivers blow for blow,
In Justice conscious of an ancient foe;
Preserves his boldness as his elders tell
How Varus perish'd, and how Cassius fell: 50
Plots and intrigues an evil aid afford,
And treachery upholds the German sword.
The fickle Russian, helpless, quits the fray;
Ausonia's frighten'd legions stand at bay;
Teutonic might on ev'ry tongue resounds,   55
Whilst red Germania swells beyond her bounds;
Thro' Dacian lands the empire is increas'd,
And stretches threat'ning to the mystic East;
Wild Scythian wastes endure the anarch flame,
And barb'rous regions ring with Wilhelm's name.   60
Thus Europe trembles till from Western shores
The crowning gift of English freedom pours;
Columbia, potent in her Saxon pride,
Beholds and seeks her lab'ring mother's side:
On ev'ry wave Columbian barques appear,   65
And Freedom watches with returning cheer.
The Goth, unheeding, plans continued wrong,
And ruthless drags his brutish horde along,
When swift and sudden in his wild advance
He meets and feels an unfamiliar lance.   70
Yet unbelieving, stolid to the last,
He scorns the foe, and strives to struggle past;
But as he strives, he finds his legions led
In paths strategic rather than ahead;
Unnumber'd vict'ries may his voice proclaim,   75
Yet each one takes him back from whence he came!
O Glorious Fortune! with triumphal notes
O'er Saint Mihiel the conquering German gloats;
Yet strange to say, he gains his just renown
For giving up, not capturing, the town!   80
And now o'er all th' ensanguin'd field of Mars
Floats the new banner with its stripes and stars.
Unending cohorts crowd the plains around,

And Gallia smiles for her recover'd ground.
The baffled savage, burning as he flees,   85
Turns pale, and shivers for his native leas;
Dreads the sure day when Saxon steel shall shine
Beyond the waters of his sacred Rhine:
He knows his doom—what Caesar did before,
Foch, Haig, and Pershing can effect once more!   90

How can I sing, without Ovidian skill,
The metamorphos'd Goth in time of ill?
That sov'reign, who for nations lately sigh'd,
Whines for his stricken land, and chokes his pride;
No more he flings his challenge to the air,   95
But begs th' indignant foe his race to spare;
The injur'd, peaceful monarch fain would know
Why the cold world dislikes his people so!
"Let us have Peace!" To Heav'n resounds the plea
From lips defil'd with all iniquity,   100
"Let us converse," (those chasten'd lips implore)
"And seek our weary'd countries to restore."
The gen'rous beast a blood-stain'd paw extends,
And as a peer, permits us to be friends!
Yet sad to say, our cynic thought adheres   105
To certain trifles of preceding years;
Belgium, despoil'd, a moment claims our mind,
And scraps of paper leave their doubts behind;
Mem'ry, if stretch'd, at times can ev'n include
Some ocean pastimes which at least were rude.   110
In short, we feel that sev'ral things prevent
A barter'd peace, and equal settlement!

Victorious Foch! in whose rare soul unite
Great Churchill's valour, and Eugenio's might;
Whose art with pride Napoleon's self could scan,   115
Well pleas'd to own thee of his Gallic clan:
'Tis thine the terms of lasting peace to draw
With shot and steel—Germania's chosen law.
'Tis thine with conqu'ring sword to fix the fate
Of guilty princes and an outlaw'd state!   120
In thy bold ranks the sons of ev'ry land
Soar to new glories at thy wise command;
Thou guid'st the mighty Briton, proud and free,
And vast Columbia owns a chief in thee;

The Nervian hero 'neath thy banner toils   125
To rob th' invader of his precious spoils,
Whilst Italy, that once the Gaul o'erthrew,
Strives, 'neath a Gaul, her lustre to renew!
The wolf is gaunt, his tatter'd ranks are thin,
And burden'd with a daemon load of sin;   130
On draws the hour when for each deed of shame
His land, accurst, must pay in death and flame.
Abroad Britannia checks him on the wave;
Approaching armies hollow out his grave;
Madden'd he sees his proud delusion o'er,   135
His ancient splendour to return no more.
What he shall be, his will can never guide,
For others now his future must decide:
Whipp'd, cow'd, degraded, he can only pray,
"Mercy! have mercy!—Freedom! I obey!"   140

The Conscript

I am a peaceful working man—
    I am not wise or strong—
But I can follow Nature's plan
    In labour, rest, and song.

One day the men that rule us all   5
    Decided we must die,
Else pride and freedom surely fall
    In the dim bye and bye.

They told me I must write my name
    Upon a scroll of death;   10
That some day I should rise to fame
    By giving up my breath.

I do not know what I have done
    That I should thus be bound
To wait for tortures one by one,   15
    And then an unmark'd mound.

I hate no man, and yet they say
    That I must fight and kill;
That I must suffer day by day
    To please a master's will.   20

I used to have a conscience free,
    But now they bid it rest;
They've made a number out of me,
    And I must ne'er protest.

They tell of trenches, long and deep,   25
    Fill'd with the mangled slain;
They talk till I can scarcely sleep,
    So reeling is my brain.

They tell of filth, and blood, and woe;
    Of things beyond belief;   30
Of things that make me tremble so
    With mingled fright and grief.

I do not know what I shall do—
    Is not the law unjust?
I can't do what they want me to,   35
    And yet they say I must!

Each day my doom doth nearer bring;
    Each day the State prepares;
Sometimes I feel a watching thing
    That stares, and stares, and stares.   40

I never seem to sleep—my head
    Whirls in the queerest way.
Why am I chosen to be dead
    Upon some fateful day?

Yet hark—some fibre is o'erwrought—   45
    A giddying wine I quaff—
Things seem so odd, I can do naught
    But laugh, and laugh, and laugh!

To Maj.-Gen. Omar Bundy, U.S.A.

"The American Flag has been compelled to retire. This is
unendurable, and none of our soldiers would be able to understand not
being asked to do whatever is necessary to reëstablish a situation which is
humiliating to us and unacceptable to our country's honor. We are going
to counter-attack." Major General Omar Bundy, U.S.A., author of the
above quotation, and commanding the Fifth United States Army Corps,
at Chateau-Thierry, on July 15th, 1918, commenced the offensive which
conquered Germany.

A wreath to him whose Saxon heart
    A nation's pride thro' stress upheld:
Who nobly play'd the hero's part,
    And peril's thick'ning cloud dispell'd.

When Gothic hordes with vile intent   5
    Spread fierce and mighty on the plain,
And Gallia mourn'd, her forces spent,
    'Twas thou who turn'dst the tide again.

Dark was the day when pour'd the foe
    Across the Marne's encrimson'd wave;   10
The star of Liberty burn'd low,
    And sadness fill'd the lab'ring brave.

In endless ranks the fiends attack,
    Till not a Gaul the charge can meet,
And tearful chieftains summon back   15
    Their cohorts to a new retreat.

But thou alone, of prouder race,
    Recall'st COLUMBIA'S ancient pow'r;
Thy spirit spurns the deep disgrace
    Of weakness at the crucial hour.   20

Thy legions, bred in Freedom's land,
    As victors only wage their fray;
Such men the conqueror's part demand,
    Unknowing how to turn away.

Such dost thou feel, when from thy tongue   25
    Straight fall those words of pride sublime;
Those words in glory to be sung
    Till Dis shall halt the march of Time.

"We grieve to scorn the mandate kind
    That bids us quit the anxious field,   30
But Yankees cannot glance behind,
    Or to a winning foeman yield.

"Our legions, valiant to the end,
    Their flag in triumph only fly;
No other course they comprehend—   35
    Today we subjugate or die!"

Quick gleams the bright unsully'd steel
    Of ev'ry hero on the plain;
Columbian ranks the impulse feel,
    And charge, unmindful of the slain.   40

In that great hour the past bequeaths
    A heritage of dauntless might;
Each Saxon shade his sword unsheaths,
    To aid his children in the fight.

A thousand mem'ries lend their sway   45
    From Eastern and from Western shore;
Quebec, Manila, Monterey,
    And Agincourt are liv'd once more.

Th' astonish'd Gaul in wonder sees
    Disaster turn'd to proud success;   50
The trembling Goth in terror flees,
    As on and on the victors press.

Thy valour, BUNDY, check'd the foe,
    That now his vanquish'd lot bewails;
Thy deathless words in state shall glow   55
    Whilst courage lives, and right prevails.

So ever shine COLUMBIA'S brave,
    First in the fray, unconquer'd still;
Whose glories echo o'er the wave,
    And ev'ry land triumphant fill!   60

Theodore Roosevelt

1858–1919

Last of the giants, in whose soul shone clear
    The sacred torch of greatness and of right,
A stricken world, that cannot boast thy peer,
    Mourns o'er thy grave amidst the new-born night.

Sage, seer, and statesman, wise in ev'ry art;   5
    First to behold, and first to preach, the truth;
Soldier and patriot, in whose mighty heart
    Throbb'd the high valour of eternal youth.

Foremost of citizens and best of chiefs,
    Within thy mind no weak inaction lay;   10
Leal to thy standards, firm in thy beliefs;
    As quick to do as others are to say.

Freeman and gentleman, whose spirit glow'd
    With kindness' and with goodness' warmest fire;
To prince and peasant thy broad friendship flow'd,   15
    Each proud to take, and eager to admire.

Within thy book of life each spotless page
    Lies open for a world's respecting view;
Thou stand'st the first and purest of our age,
    To private, as to public virtue true.   20

In thee did such transcendent greatness gleam,
    That none might grudge thee an Imperial place;
Yet such thy modesty, thou need'st must seem
    The leader, not the monarch, of thy race.

Courage and pow'r, to wit and learning join'd,   25
    With energy that sham'd the envious sun;
The ablest, bravest, noblest of mankind—
    A Caesar and Aurelius mixt in one.

At thy stern gaze Dishonour bow'd its head;
    Oppression slunk ingloriously away;   30
The virtuous follow'd where thy footsteps led,
    And Freedom bless'd thy uncorrupted sway.

When from the East invading Vandals pour'd,
    And selfish ignorance restrain'd our hand,
Thy voice was first to bid us draw the sword   35
    To guard our liberties and save our land.

Envy deny'd thee what thy spirit sought,
    And held thee from the battle-seething plain;
Yet thy proud blood in filial bodies fought,
    And poppies blossom o'er thy QUENTIN slain.   40

'Twas thine to see the triumph of thy cause;
    Thy grateful eyes beheld a world redeem'd;
Would that thy wisdom might have shap'd the laws
    Of the new age, and led to heights undream'd!

Yet art thou gone? Will not thy presence cling   45
    Like that of all the great who liv'd before?
Will not new wonders of thy fashioning
    Rise from thy words, as potent as of yore?

Absent in flesh, thou with a brighter flame
    Shin'st as the beacon of the brave and free;   50
Thou art our country's soul—our loftiest aim
    Is but to honour and to follow thee!

North and South Britons

Man is so much with prejudice imbu'd,
That love and hate arise from latitude;
What else can cause such petty strife to breed
Along the Cheviots and flowing Tweed?
No sober sense could disagreement bring   5
'Twixt Britons with one country and one King.
Beyond the seas, the Colonies are built
Alike by men of breeches and of kilt;
On fields of war, with blood of heroes dy'd,
Stand sturdy Scots and Saxons side by side: 10
In harmony the martial music comes
From Scottish bagpipes and from English drums;
Amid such scenes none stops to boast his birth
As being north or south of Solway Firth;
There Fife and Devon, Ayr and Dorset blend,   15
And all for one united land contend.
How strange that men, so brotherly abroad,
Cannot be brothers on their native sod!
Would that each Scot and Saxon might be free
From local feuds, and childish jealousy.   20
Who shall the one above the other place,
When both are mix'd in one imperial race?
Rule on, belov'd Britannia, rule the waves—
No Britons, North or South, shall e'er be slaves!

422

VIII. PERSONAL

[To His Mother on Thanksgiving]

Dear Mother:—
If, as you start toward Lillie's festive spread,
You find me snoring loudly in my bed,
Awake me not, for I would fain repose,
And thro' the day in quiet slumbers doze.
But lest I starve, for lack of food to eat,   5
Leave here a dish of Quaker Puffèd Wheat,
Or breakfast biscuit, which, it matters not,
To break my fast when out of bed I've got.
And if to supper you perchance should stay,
Thus to complete a glorious festive day,   10
Announce the fact to me by Telephone,
That whilst you eat, I may prepare my own.

An Elegy on Franklin Chase Clark, M.D.

(Died April 26, 1915)

Can learned Clark in truth have ceas'd to be,
    As Reason's bitter voice hath coldly said?
Can vibrant intellect, of earth so free,
    Like peasant clay be lost among the dead?

But yesterday the lustre of his mind   5
    Had force to pale obscurity away:
In its stern glare, the folly of mankind
    Shrunk, like the shadows at the noon of day.

A changing world of strife about him seeth'd;
    Ideals less'ning, and the pure disdain'd;   10
But in his soul untainted wisdom breath'd,
    And linger'd round him whilst his form remain'd.

A fleeting fame, or momentary praise,
    How little wish'd he, and how nobly scorn'd.
How oft were Learning's deeper, richer ways   15
    Sought out by him, and by his hand adorn'd.

Whilst empty multitudes in frenzy crave
    The glitt'ring gold, or honours of a lord,
In quiet he his best endeavour gave,
    Content to serve; unthinking of reward.   20

425

Let lesser men display the laurell'd brow,
　　And beg for homage to the world beneath.
In silence lies a greater master now,
　　E'en tho' his laurel be his fun'ral wreath.

Say not that in the void beyond Death's door   25
　　The mighty and the lowly are the same;
Can boorish dust, in life but little more,
　　Equality with mental essence claim?

His voice is still'd; his body run its course;
　　But have those waves of intellect decay'd?   30
Can subtle energy, eternal force,
　　As mortal flesh within the tomb be laid?

Have not these waves, sent forth by matchless mind,
　　An endless path in boundless space to run?
To flow unseen; alive, yet undefin'd,   35
　　But never, like the body, to be done?

Who can declare that such unbody'd thought,
　　Sent forth by sages of an earlier time,
Thro' other, living bodies hath not wrought
　　The good of ev'ry age and ev'ry clime?   40

So tell me not that he no more remains,
　　Whose silent form no word responsive gives:
His body sleeps, reliev'd of earthly pains,
　　But he, the guiding soul, immortal lives!

[The Solace of Georgian Poetry]

Benignant spirits bless th' adjacent mead,
And swains their flocks thro' fertile pastures lead;
The friendly Fauns the neighb'ring grove protect,
Whilst crystal founts a Naiad train reflect.
At eventide sweet Orpheus tunes his lay   5
To lull the hills, and speed the fading day;
Nor sings alone, for o'er th' expansive wold
Fair Philomela chants from throat of gold.
Such joys as these no others can excel;
In this sweet country ever would I dwell!   10
No sordid sight or tainted thought intrudes,
But all is shap'd to suit my changing moods:

All churls are honest, and all squires are kind,
And King and boor enjoy th' untarnish'd mind.
'Tis ever sunshine when I wish it so,   15
But at my will the gentle torrents flow.
The bard is here supreme in ev'ry joy,
No cares oppress, or cruel truths annoy:
When all the world my weary spirit pains,
May I not flee where Pan, idyllic, reigns?   20
Seize on my pencil, and in rhyme depart
For regions where fond mem'ry warms the heart?
Stay! vandal critick, ere thy ruthless line
Destroy the only solace that is mine!

[On Phillips Gamwell]

Whilst town astronomers, with straining eyes,
Search out the wonders of the distant skies;
With optic tube in feeble fashion trace
The cloud-film'd features of ethereal space;
While scribbling pedants paint with prosy line   5
The various orbs, and when and how they shine;
(Those orbs so faintly and so little known—
Realities in books and globes alone—)
On Zoar's proud height, of heav'n itself a part,
Gamwell sees all, without the need of art!   10

An Elegy on Phillips Gamwell, Esq.

April 23, 1898–December 31, 1916

If Fate can at her own unkindness grieve,
And vainly wish her edicts to retrieve,
Let her now bear the sting of bitterest ruth
For GAMWELL'S loss, in morn of blameless youth.
Who can but weep that one so pure must haste   5
From scenes his presence all too briefly grac'd?
Our falt'ring numbers take a feebler tone,
For poets into mourners now are grown.
What pen shall sing the glowing heart and mind
Where innocence and learning both were join'd;   10
The gentle speech, whose modesty deny'd
The copious wit and sense it could not hide;
The earnest face, in equal measure bright

With beauty's and with virtue's inward light;
And the fair mien, that pride-fill'd eyes would scan   15
To trace within the boy the coming man?
Such song should vie with Phoebus' sorrowing strain
For tender Hyacinthus, lately slain;
Or that soft lay which Cytheraea breath'd
When she with flow'rs the lost Adonis wreath'd;   20
And yet, the pen that would his praise bestow
Pauses for words, and halts from recent woe!
Can he, whose form so vividly appears;
Whose manly accent lingers on our ears;
Whose sturdy step, that still our fancy loves,   25
So lately trod th' accustom'd walks and groves;
Can he, whom all in proud affection bore,
Indeed be gone, to bless our sight no more?
This none can think! His soul must rather dwell
Among the blossoms of some forest dell   30
Where, shaded from the jealous western breeze,
Spring hyacinths and sweet anemones:
Symbolic petals strow th' embroider'd green,
And speak the Delian God and Paphian Queen;
Whilst added fragrance in the flow'r-fill'd air   35
Tells the fond oaks young GAMWELL lingers there.
Tho' well the clod that sails the mortal main
From birth to bier with unperfected brain,
May from poor dust to kindred dust return,
Could GAMWELL'S spirit own the fun'ral urn?   40
From ancient stem the comely shoot arose,
And knew the care that tender love bestows;
The budding twig, to Virtue's mould inclin'd
By guiding culture and informing mind,
Outstripp'd the promise of auspicious birth,   45
And to great learning join'd superior worth:
So rich a store of grace did Heav'n allow,
That the whole tree ador'd its youngest bough!
Such was the youth, whose stainless mind and heart
Combin'd the best of Nature and of Art;   50
Such was the life, which tho' untimely flown,
Shews rising ages how to lead their own:
A thing so rare, so precious, and so pure,
Must needs in spirit, if not flesh, endure!

Sonnet on Myself

A transient speck in wide infinity,
A needless incident of endless time,
An empty fool of measure and of rhyme,
One who is not but only seems to be
Alive to intellect and melody—   5
Whose struggling thoughts a puny soul confines
Till their small wit must hide in sounding lines,
Whose only wisdom is to know and see
That he is nothing, and to guard his pen
Against those flights of arrogant conceit   10
Which soar to mocking Heav'n from bards more bold;
From lords and peasants, great and little men,
Who deem their vain thoughts worthy to repeat,
I tell, for ease, what were as well untold!

Phaeton

Critic, whose soul a busy world hath slain,
    Whose taste is but the impress of the times,
Bid me no more my eager quill restrain,
    Or court the multitude in earthy rhymes.

Say not again that passion, bliss, and woe,   5
    The hackney'd feelings of the gen'ral heart,
Must fill my days, in all my visions glow,
    And throb triumphant thro' my labour'd art.

Let the stout swain, whom no reflections wake,
    Chant of his Phillis, and his hopes and fears;   10
Let earth-bound clods of such tame things partake,
    Dance with vain joys, and shed their trivial tears.

Why should I fret in microscopic bonds
    That chafe the spirit, and the mind repress,
When thro' the clouds gleam beckoning beyonds   15
    Whose shining vistas mock man's littleness?

Can seeing intellect contented lie
    Within the confines of our tiny race,
When overhead yawns wide the starry sky,
    Pregnant with secrets of unfathom'd space?   20

429

Monos: An Ode

    Mine be the boon to sleep
    On warm Hymettus' flow'r-sweet steep,
Lull'd by the lays that mountain torrents sing,
    And Lydian carolling
Of choirs celestial, heard by none but me,   5
    A faery minstrelsy
Of sound as subtle as the living light
    Which wings its flight
From immaterial spheres, remote and free.

    Let not intrude   10
    Into this sacred solitude
Aught of the Satyr-shades of mortal mind;
Grossness that galls, empiric thoughts that bind;
    But let my fancy soar
Above the clouds that veil our planet o'er,   15
Far from the seeming forms and dreams of earth,
    To deeps of Nature's birth
Where pure, unparticled, and splendid course
Th' ethereal founts of entity and force;

    And circling as begun,   20
    All cosmic being is as one,
And Time, Space, Change, and varied Nature blend
In cycles infinite and without end,
    Till Reason, beaming clear,
    Sees disappear   25
All that is complex, earthy, vile, or drear;
    And may at last behold
    Matter and life unfold
To Unity unbody'd and divine,
    Throughout whose fabric fine   30
Beauty and Purity unsully'd shine.

Oct. 17, 1919

The filial pen, unblest with poet's grace,
In rugged lines a birthday wish would trace;
And begs you take, in lieu of pleasing art,
The thought that springs uncolour'd from the heart:
Thus let me write, tho' feeble be my skill,   5

With keen sincerity to guide my quill:
And sing the hope, that future birthdays bright
May this excel, as noon excels the night!

To S. S. L.—October 17, 1920

In these confections would the bard essay
To send his greetings on your natal day;
For sure, such sweets can better bring his thought
Than creaking lines, by clumsy pencil wrought.
May ev'ry morsel, with symbolic pow'r,   5
Lend sugar'd pleasure to the passing hour;
And shew that life, howe'er its course unfold,
Amidst the gall some sweetness yet can hold.

S. S. L.: Christmas 1920

These trivial tokens of a festive day
How little of the giver's wish convey,
For in each sep'rate one he fain would send
Regards untold, and blessings without end.
Yet all, perhaps, in their slight way suggest   5
The annual spirit and the ancient zest;
Disclosing still amidst the wintry shade
A Christmas cheer which never quite may fade!

To Xanthippe, on Her Birthday—March 16, 1925

Again the whirling year brings round
Your natal day with festive sound,
As wak'ning earth with vernal glee
Salutes you in each budding tree.
And may each joy the moments hold   5
Be hours as brighter days unfold,
Till all the mountain springtime zest
Find lasting echoes in your breast!

Εἰς Σφίγγην

To Georgian meads in triumph now restor'd,
Hear antient Theobald croak the Yuletide word,
And shout, that all th' archaick world may know,
God save the King, and Providence, and MOE!

[On Cheating the Post Office]

The law, despite its show of awe, a soft thing to infract is,
And crime, mere theory in its time, too soon is put in practice!
My soul, now on its downward roll, in crafty scheming romps on,
And ne'er will rest till I can best a Bickford or a Thompson.

An Epistle to the Rt. Honble Maurice Winter Moe, Esq. of Zythopolis, in the Northwest Territory of HIS MAJESTY'S American Dominions

Thanks for the gift, nor blame me if I Teter
And slip into mine antient vice of metre,
For sure, your kindness piles Temptation on
With this new Handy Guide to Helicon!
Tho' brief, 'tis clear, with no false precepts strown,   5
Nor fashion'd for the pedant's mind alone;
Each turn of stile, and each mechanick art,
The cogent author can with skill impart:
Bright beyond rivals, peerless three or four ways—
A fitting pair of steps to reach your Doorways!   10

    Yet such a tome must take its proper place,
Nor vie with your own volume in the race!
Lud, Sir, but what new marvels daily come
Full-arm'd from the Mocratick cerebrum!
Tests, outlines, drills—and now your genius adds   15
New leaves of wonder in your sep'rate pads!
Macmillan sure would prove a brainless dolt
Did he not vie in eagerness with Holt—
But be their sense of judgment more or less,
You need not care—for you've the Kenyon Press,   20
Nurse of the arts—hail, Mater Gloriosa!
The press that carry'd fame to Wauwatosa!

    And now in meekness let my fancy glance
At these sly tests which prov'd my ignorance—
Those tricky snares which ev'n Mortonian mind   25
Could scarcely meet and scatheless leave behind!
The prose I view with less disorder'd pride,
And by my pristine verdicts still abide:
D may be Tark's—but still I vow it groans
With needless weight, and talks in cumbrous tones;   30

Labours for pow'r, forgetting to be neat,
And trades its birthright for a cheap conceit.
As for trite F, I censur'd not its stream
Of thought, nor held it faithless to its theme;
My wildest wish was for less verbal pelf, 35
And for more freshness from the scribe himself!
But E—oh priceless pearl! how quick mine eye
Caught the bright vision from an age gone by!
Past my pleas'd mind in long procession ran
The assembl'd genius of the a. j. clan: 40
Lynch, Haughton, Fritter, roving Hennessy;
Hasemann—don't choke!—and deathless David V.—
Lehmkuhl and Crowley, and—young imps of hell—
Porter and Moitoret and Kid Dowdell—
Woodbee and Warrenite the foreground take, 45
Whilst over all immortal soars Our Jake!

    Dropping to poesy—my head drops, too,
As my illit'rate score I dumbly view!
(So dumb, eheu, my mental equipage,
I think Iambus was a Grecian sage!) 50
What can I say when here I stand confest
I can't pick Shelley in a blindfold test?
How can I face the world—a crawling midge
Who puts a Wordsworth tag on Coleridge?
I say no more! May all the Muses chide me . . . 55
But, damn it, Morton's in the soup beside me!

    I now with pleasure hear, whilst you relate
Your recent deeds, and how you aestivate.
Pox on't, but how you crown the flying hours
With new-made proofs of your scholastic pow'rs! 60
Your leisure's like my toil—and when *you* labour,
You rise to heights that leave you not a neighbour!
I still await my cherisht chance to quaff
The nectar of your class-day MOE-KNOW-GRAPH.
Ah, me! can 't be that twenty years and more 65
Have pass'd since that blest Golden Age—'04?
A quarter century! And old and grey,
We see it still as if 'twere yesterday!
Old Nineteen-hundreds! What would we not give
Once more amid your artless hours to live? 70
Puff ties and cake-walks, cloak-and-sword romance,

433

And Teddy fighting back the trusts' advance;
Queer horseless carriages on cobbled streets,
And new-found radium in the science sheets:
Wireless—the latest—(never'll be much use!)   75
Japan—not yet a mark for our abuse—
"Bedelia" light on ev'ry whistler's lip,
And rearward seating still the smartest quip:
St. Louis' glory—crowds in fairward push
To rest beneath the broad Anheuser Busch.   80
Edwardus Rex on Britain's antient throne,
And "Hiawatha" on the graphophone:
Hope still triumphant, and the cold grey morn
Of Mencken, Krutch, and Einstein yet unborn:
Harper's chaste leaves with polisht mildness rife,   85
And prim McClure's a stranger still to life.
Gilder still gilding with decorous mien,
And Winter freezing o'er the painted scene;
Van Dyke and Aldrich saying in fresh rhymes
The borrow'd thoughts and saws of other times—   90
Vague pleasing dreams of futures ever young;
"The Simple Life" on ev'ry trusting tongue;
Graft and muckraking in their genial fights,
And prophets soon to set the world to rights;
Dowie, Lyme Abbott, Parkhurst, and the rest   95
With various plans to put us 'midst the blest;
Bryan and Hanna, nigger-minstrel shows,
Elb Hubbard posing o'er his Windsor bows,
Corbett, Fitzsimmons, Sharkey, and Old Jeff,
Pete Dailey, Weber-Fields, and Fritzi Scheff,   100
Young Buster nosing out the Yellow Kid,
And ev'ry newsboy in an "Old Coon" lid;
"Extry—Port Arthur Falls"—we stand aghast—
But "Russia's Czar has got a son at last"—
Santos-Dumont displays a fresh balloon,   105
And Langley vows his gliders will fly soon.
Bill Pick'ring vainly tells a sceptick nation
Of finding signs of lunar vegetation,
Nor can Park Lowell gather many pals
To hear about his precious Mars-canals!   110
Dear bygone days! Could modern genius hatch
A Mrs. Wiggs from any Cabbage Patch?

Could modern talent make us gape and marvel
At Zenda, Haddon Hall, or Richard Carvel?
'04 *produced* what modern throats but whine— 115
The Flower of My Heart—Sweet Adeline!
Then Pilsen's Prince in tuneful splendour reign'd,
And "Woodland" bloom'd, by jazz yet unprofan'd:
Boston was still a sep'rate realm from Cork,
Whilst English yet was spoken in New York! 120

Shades of the past! And have I liv'd to view
A scene so diff'rent, and a world so new?
Have five and twenty years in truth gone by,
While still the old days seem so clear and nigh?
'Zounds! 'Tis a dream—this is not I at all— 125
This greybeard in the mirror on the wall!
What nonsense—when but lately I dar'd don
A derby hat, and put long trousers on!
Of course 'tis dreaming—merely look about
And see how all reality's in rout! 130
Autos in droves, men flying o'er the mist,
And talk of things that simply can't exist! . . .
Shucks! There's the proof! Sure, we need fret no more,
Because it must be still our old '04!
We're merely dizzy—say, from overeating, 135
Or from some thought of Time's relentless fleeting:
Sing, boys, in chorus—put the nightmare down
With "Bluebell", "Creole Belles", or "Nancy Brown".
All—one—two—three—nor let your voices fail ye—
"Won't you come home"—here, mind the pitch!—"Bill Bailey?" 140
No—that won't do—try this: "O Karama,"
(Too high, I fancy) "be my guiding star!"
What's this? No rhyme? O damn such close precision!
I hold these Western rrrrrh's in deep derision!
Not on your life—I vow you're off your trolley 145
To think I'd listen to such upstart folly!
A fight! A fight! Here, knock his block off, Joe!
Eat him up, Jack; dump him at Buffalo!
Bust in his coc'nut! Lam him on the bean!
Go bite his head off! Puncture his canteen! 150
Bats in your belfry—you're another, Jack!
Bum—bughouse—looney—go sit on a tack! . . . . .

Thus down the years the virile echoes pour,
Fresh with the vigour of the days of yore:
While such survive, is it not still '04?   155

    Oh, yes, those magazines which presently
Will saunter westward to 2303:
In one vast packet safely I'll return all—
Mags, Doorways, and that pleasing *English Journal*.
The latter—thanks—sheds an informing blaze   160
On your young charges' editorial ways:
I see—I know—and with new zeal extend
Congrats on what each hopeful chick hath penn'd.
So gifted Franklin turns the other Cheek
In fistick fashion, vigilant to seek   165
Ways to knock guys to the middle of next week!
Attaboy, Frank! An' don'tcha let no bimbo
Knock ya down hill into de has-been's limbo!
Keep right and left glov'd, dauntless and on edge,
Till ev'ry knuckle grows to be a sledge: 170
Punch 'em to pulp, and let Manila's shoar
Grow vocal in one tributary roar;
But keep art's cunning in the mitt that slugs—
Pug among painters, painter among pugs!

    I thrill with joy if Rems devoid of sound   175
Will bring Mocratick lines more frequent round!
For my part, nothing like a damn'd machine
Will give my thought a free and fair demesne.
'Tis too unnatural for an old man still
A dweller in the realm of script and quill—   180
Words pause embarrassed, images depart
At sight of such an enemy to art:
When thoughts pile up, a pen must set 'em free—
My grandsire's ways are good enough for me!!

    Well, Sir, my days in wonted fashion run   185
Beneath Rhode Island's classick Georgian sun.
Last week a guest adorn'd the local strand—
Victor E. Bacon, of the a. j. band;
Fresh from convention, he declar'd his fellows
Had nurs'd the dying flame with frantick bellows: 190
An happier twelvemonth he discerns ahead,
The National still declining to be dead.

Six years had pass'd since I the youth had seen
In visual form, and I recall'd him lean;
Fancy my thoughts to find *him* deck'd today   195
In all the poundage *I* have cast away!
His stay was brief, yet fill'd with lib'ral cheer
And season'd with our Georgian atmosphere.
To Newport's antient shoar I bade him rove,
And old Pawtuxet, dreaming by its cove.   200
Of much we spoke, the past more than the present—
So that the passing hours to both were pleasant.

    And so it goes. But Lud! you must be yawning
At these misshapen lines my quill is spawning!
Pardon, Sir—pardon—yet pray don't omit   205
To mind that Teter set me doing it!
A brief recess—now back to art's dim last row,
To doctor that curst junk by old De Castro!
Hail and farewell—and may my trembling hand
Clasp yours some morning in a better land—   210
Some Delian isle or mild Ionian shoar
Where 'twill be ever summer—and '04!

[Anthem of the Kappa Alpha Tau]

Here we are,
The Kappa Alpha Tau boys;
We'll give a great meow, boys,
For Bast, and Sekhmet too.
Near and far,   5
We gather here as fellows,
And none may e'er excel
The Kappa Alpha Tau!

Here we shine,
The Kappa Alpha Tau boys;   10
Brave soldiers all allow, boys,
With many a victory.
Foes canine
In vain may seek to flout us,
For naught can ever rout   15
The Kappa Alpha Tau!

Edith Miniter

Born on Wilbraham Mountain, Massachusetts, May 19, 1869.
Died at North Wilbraham, Massachusetts, June 4, 1934.

Through her the hills their age-long memories told;
 Their centuried heritage unmixed she bore;
And now those rock-strown slopes at last enfold
 Her kindred dust—a child come home once more.

She knew the lore of distant, crowded ways;   5
 The sights and language of the market-place;
But deep within, there flowed through all her days
 The currents of New England's changeless race.

No lyric lay of golden dreams was hers;
 She held a mirror to the world she saw.   10
Vain hopes she left to fools and flatterers,
 Content with what a truthful pen could draw.

Others might sing of heroes, pomps, and powers—
 For her the quiet substance of the age.
She caught the faint, dull tones of common hours   15
 Till living figures thronged each vital page.

Mankind she studied with a searching sight;
 Folly she pictured with a smiling mind;
Whilst over all she felt the hovering light
 Of brooding years and what they leave behind.   20

Always she dwelt amidst the ancient things—
 The household relique, and the crumbling tome;
Her ears could catch the beat of hidden wings
 By moss-grown grave, and lonely hillside home.

Wit, learning, art, were hers in amplitude,   25
 And kindliness that helped the loyal friend,
And charm and skill that fostered and renewed
 Parnassian dreams in others without end.

Merged with the meadows where her fathers sleep,
 The wearied clay has come into its own;   30
The mind, too keen for any tomb to keep,
 Lives in the fruits and memories it has sown.

[Little Sam Perkins]

The ancient garden seems tonight
    A deeper gloom to bear,
As if some silent shadow's blight
    Were hov'ring in the air.

With hidden griefs the grasses sway,   5
    Unable quite to word them—
Remembering from yesterday
    The little paws that stirr'd them.

IX. ALFREDO; A TRAGEDY

Alfredo; a Tragedy

By Beaumont and Fletcher

Dramatis Personae

RINARTO, King of Castile and Aragon
ALFREDO, the Prince Regent
TEOBALDO, the Prime-Minister
MAURICIO, a Cardinal
OLERO
MARCELLO
GONZAGO
MARGARITA, daughter to OLERO
AMALIA ⎤
BEATRIZ ⎮
CARLOTA ⎬ Young Gentlewomen of the Court
DOROTEA ⎮
ELENA ⎦
HYPATIA, daughter to MARCELLO
HECATISSA, a noble Eastern lady

Ladies and Gentlemen of the Court

Scene—MADRID

Act I.
Sc. I. Throne Room of the Palace

The King discovered in Full Armour on the Throne, Attended by Soldiery.
Mauricio, Alfredo, and Teobaldo standing before throne.

RIN. Alfredo, since it suits our royal pleasure
To quit the Palace for the noisy camp,
Grasp shield and spear, and in the clash of war
Renew the glories of our ancient line,
Do thou with law and grace administer   5
The fortunes of our realm. I charge thee tend
With constant vigilance the gen'ral weal,
Nor give our people cause for just complaint.
Be firm, yet kind, nor falter in thy course;
Virtue alone thy guide. And, Teobaldo,   10
To thee I leave an equal care, to guide
The young prince in the mysteries of rule,

Mould the quick mind, and check the ardent heart
That beats too strongly for the soft and fair.
Mauricio, Rev'rend Father, thee I beg   15
T' invoke upon our arms thy Pope's good will;
With Holy Water sprinkle o'er our swords,
And strengthen us against the turban'd Moor.

(Rises. Mauricio advances with silver basin and besprinkles with
Holy Water the lances of the soldiery.)

MAU. In name of Father, Son, and Holy Ghost,
Your mission I do bless, and may the Cross   20
Of righteousness e'er triumph on the field.

(Fanfare of trumpets. Soldiery form in marching order.)

ALF. Dear Sire, fear nothing for the Kingdom's fate.
I am not old, but as thou know'st, have drunk
Deep of the learning of the age and clime.
Cordova's volumes are not strange to me,   25
And tho' my fiery passions rouse thy doubt,
I vow them but reflections of thine own,
Temper'd with thoughts of high infinity.
Thy deeds in me a ready glow shall wake,
As couriers tell the wonders thou shalt do: 30
My deepest woe is, that by Fate deny'd,
I may not march and battle by thy side!

(Exeunt omnes, in military order.)

Sc. II. An Antechamber in the Palace

Enter Alfredo, preceded by Margarita.

MARG. Stay, good my lord, why should I speak with thee,
When that thy words are alien to mine ears?
I fain would seek the maidens of the court,   35
Who, in the garden gather'd, pass the time
With carols innocent and bright withal.

ALF. Aye, gentle maid, but list unto their import.
Tells not each one of sempiternal spring,
Woods, bow'rs, and pansied pastures lightly trod   40
By the warm swains and yielding nymphs of old,
Whose storied pleasures need not pass our own?

444

(Song from without the window)

> Hither come, with vernal zest,
> Thou with roseate blossoms drest,
>   Seek these lilied bow'rs: 45
> Pan with gracious pow'r presides,
> Cyprian musick gently glides
>   Thro' the golden hours.

MARG. The tune is pretty, tho' the words escape.
Delay me not, for in thy eager voice   50
Is that which irks me. I would to the green,
And add my carols to the virgin choir.

ALF. Thou know'st my heart, a royal heart, 'tis true,
Yet which can find a place for such as thou.
Wilt thou not hear?

MARG.   Of suppliance I am sick.   55
Thou art too grave to suit my airy will.
Get thee unto thy chamber, there to lose
Thyself in tomes of antiquated lore,
Or stroll upon the porticoes at eve
With grave Mauricio, or discourse at length   60
With gloomy Teobaldo, whose cold heart
Fills thee with coldness like its own, or go
Unto the throne-room where in glitt'ring pomp
Repose the symbols of thy rank and state.
Content thyself with sovereignty and art,   65
And leave to sprightlier swains the female heart!

(Exit Margarita.)

ALF. (Solus) How burns my soul for heavens unattain'd!
What paradise in her fair face doth dwell!
So fair and yet so cold! Claim me, kind Death,
If Margarita smile not on my suit.   70
But who comes here?

(Enter Hecatissa)

HEC.   'Tis I, my noble Prince,
Admirer of thy learning and thy grace,
Nay, flee me not, what horror may reside
In my poor glance, that thou should'st shun me so?

Did I not come from a far Eastern shore; 75
Is my proud lineage not as great as thine?

    (Exit Alfredo unobserved)

Alas, grim Fate, that the young Prince shou'd be
So warm to other maids, yet cold to me!

(Curtain)

Act II.
Sc. I. A Hall in the Palace

    (Alfredo and Hypatia discovered seated at a table, a large volume
betwixt them.)

    HYP. See, prince, the poet falters in this line,
It likes me not that he should break the flow 80
Of his impassion'd numbers. Think not thou
He might have smoother writ his glowing thoughts?

    ALF. 'Tis even as thou say'st. I find my taste
Ever and ever moulded close to thine,
As tho' some strange bewitchment seiz'd my soul 85
When I with thee con o'er this letter'd lore;
Yet I do know myself to be devoid
Of all that passion which beclouds the mind,
And burns not for the thoughtful and the wise.

    HYP. Yet thou didst call me beauteous on that day 90
When in the garden we convers'd at eve.
But hark! Methinks I hear an heavy step
As of that ancient prattler Teobaldo,
Whose very face casts gloom on youthful bliss.
I will begone.

    (Exit Hypatia. Enter Teobaldo)

    TEO.   How now, my studious youth? 95
Art deep as ever in the mystic page
Of Aristotle or the Abderan?
Methinks I note of late upon thy brow
A darkling cloud, as of some secret sorrow.
Come, tell me all, for age can e'er advise! 100

    ALF. It is the lady Margarita, Sir,

Who shuns my steps, and never will be kind,
But smiles, and seeks her fellow-nymphs without.
Her must I have, else I in flames shall die,
For sure, there is no other hath my heart. 105
Tell if thou canst, thyself unmov'd by love,
What refuge from despair I may attain?

TEO. Alfredo, tho' my long-encrusted heart,
Cold as the virgin snows of Rhodope,
Disdains a melting flame, I yet have read 110
Much of thy pleasing phrensy in the lore
That the warm poets sing for future time.
I pity thee, and by our Jhesu's blood
I swear to help thee in thy sad amour.
This much I know of nymphs, that poets say 115
They shun the ardent swain, but follow him
Whose fancy they have cause to think engag'd
Upon another nymph. Therefore seek out
Some kinder fair, who to thyself inclin'd,
Will bear thee company in publick spots 120
Where Margarita cannot fail to see.
But t'other day I mark'd a pensive maid
Attentive on thy footsteps. One whose face
Is by her rank surpass'd, yet who could serve
A little while t' excite a jealous pang. 125
Court then the lady Hecatissa——

ALF.   'Zounds!
Old man, thou dost presume upon our friendship!
Think'st thou I could so ill a nymph endure
Ev'n for a moment's casual discourse?
She that might move my fair to kinder thought 130
Would my companions rouse to galling jest.
But yesternight the young Gonzago smil'd
As Hecatissa dogg'd me like a shadow.
Nay, ancient man, back to thy learned lore;
I go to find Hypatia.

TEO.   Stay, young Sir. 135
The name excites my thought. Is it not she,
The Duke Marcello's daughter, fair of face,
Yet fairer still in godlike mind and soul?

ALF. The same, with whom in purest friendship link'd

I share my studious hours. A wondrous nymph   140
That to Minerva's mind joins Venus' grace.

    TEO. Unseeing youth! O stripling more than blind!
Here were a maid well suited to thy life;
A wise companion and discerning friend,
Who like to thee enjoys the bookish moments   145
When Margarita, being thy wife, would yawn,
Or fret thee with those naggings known to wives,
Which make celibacy an heav'nly boon.
Know then, that all young nymphs are so alike,
Save as their mind gives them a varying bent,   150
That it were madness to permit thy rage
And amorous phrensy to direct thy choice.
Banish all thoughts of thy unyielding fair,
That cruel nymph whose poor inferior birth
Unfits her for the throne thy bride must know,   155
And get thee to Hypatia, she whose rank
Is like her mind, congenial to thine own.
An circumstance refuse an early love,
Dote on her friendship, till from constant sight
You both insensibly to love incline.   160
I go, and mayest thou soon to sense return;
The wench forget, and for Hypatia burn.

(Exeunt)

Sc. II. The Garden

    (Margarita, Hypatia, Amalia, Beatriz, Carlota, Dorotea, Elena, and
Hecatissa discovered at games)

    AMAL. What now, dull Margarita, wilt thou quit
These our diversions ere the game's half play'd?
Marry! for days I have observ'd thee thus,   165
With downcast eye and a funereal look
As tho' thy father or thy pet cat ail'd;
Where now the smile that us'd to deck thy brows?

    MARG. Plague on thee! get thou gone! must I endure
The prattling of thy light unthinking train?   170
My thoughts are mine. Say that I mourn the absence
Of our good King, or grieve upon the fate
Of the young maiden in yon French romance.

BEAT. A song! fie on the maid who could today
In melancholy waste the sweets of morn. 175
See how the sun shines! Come, Carlota, sing
That chanson taught thee by the troubadour,
Whilst Dorotea makes the sportive lute!

(Carlota sings, accompanied by Dorotea)

> The lilies lay white on the mead,
>> When Colin his Lycë address'd; 180
> In vain did the young shepherd plead,
>> For coyness had frozen her breast.

> But Phoebus shone hot from above,
>> And Cupid fill'd all the warm air,
> So Colin, exchanging his love, 185
>> Found Doris more pleasing and fair!

MARG. Cease your rude noise! The lute is out of tune.

DOR. No more than are thy thoughts, ungrateful nymph!

CAR. I swear, the music well did fit my song!

MARG. Because thy croaking, likewise, was awry! 190

HYP. Ladies, for shame! what discord can be yours?

MARG. Behold the poetess—who'd bore us worse
With wretched pilfer'd sonnets of her own!
Say, learned maid, how many frigid reams
Of dulness hast thou plagiaris'd today? 195

HEC. I saw her lately at a mighty book;
Were we to look well we should find therein
Much of her late-sung songs, I doubt me not!

HYP. (in tears) Wherefore these taunts, ungentle and untrue?
Have I by some mischance conferr'd offence 200
On any damsel here? If so my heart
Grants that repentance that my tongue would tell
Did it but know wherein th' offence might lie.

ELE. Nay, sweet Hypatia, if offence there be,
Thine is the last tongue that could bear the blame. 205
But stay, the Prince Alfredo comes!

(Enter Alfredo with book; the maidens flock about him)

ALF.   Fair nymphs,
I greet you all! No lovelier train e'er danc'd
O'er velvet turf, and 'mid the vernal flow'rs,
Since Cytheraea, fresh from Paphos, led
Her melting followers o'er Arcadian meads!   210

MARG. Good morrow, Prince, how does my lord today?

AMAL. (aside) Our Margarita learns a brighter tone!

ALF. (to Marg.) Well, well, good nymph. (To Hyp.) And art thou
    yet prepar'd
To scan our daily lesson o'er, and read
The lines thou said'st were nearly writ? Methinks   215
Yon verdurous bow'r well suits the student mind;
Let's to its shade, by no bleak walls confin'd!

(Exeunt Alfredo and Hypatia, attended by all save Margarita and
Hecatissa.)

HEC. Sister, our Prince seems humoursome today.
Hypatia likes him well, or else his books
Have much subdu'd the raging of his heart.   220

MARG. Have none of this! Some evil influence works
In all my veins, and dark imaginings
Fill my long sleepless nights.

HEC.   'Tis so with me,
For young Alfredo's scorn I illy bear.
There is a custom in the fervid East,   225
From whence I come, whereby an injur'd maid
Sometimes doth ease her pride with odd revenge.
I'd speak with thee alone, good Margarita,
Sister in suff'ring, join'd to me in hate.
Haply the swain my own Hypatia's pow'r,   230
But many a day precedes the nuptial hour!

Act III.
Sc. I. An Antechamber

(Enter Alfredo, Hypatia, Teobaldo, Marcello, Olero, Mauricio,
Margarita, and Hecatissa.)

MAU. Are now the rites prepar'd? This day I own
The greatest joy of an eventful life;
To join in holiest wedlock of the Church
My prince Alfredo and the fair Hypatia!   235
Is 't true your royal parent quits the fray
For a brief space to witness these rejoicings?

    ALF. He hath advis'd me so, your Eminence,
In letters sent by Duke Marcello, here,
Who being father to the maid I wed,   240
Was chosen to precede him, and to plan
The masque we do enact to glad the day.

    MAU. What of the masque? I know that Teobaldo,
Delving in antique lore, hath writ a play
Of heathen gods and naiads, but no more   245
He told me, since he gave the acting o'er
To younger hands, his own share being done.

    TEO. Dost not remember, reverend Mauricio,
It was a pastoral fancy, a light thing
About young Glaucus and the nymphs, wherein   250
Alfredo hath a leading part to play,
Whilst round him several fair maids do act,
Chief among these Hypatia, drest as Scylla.
The purport of the myth I have improv'd
Just far enough to make a happy end,   255
So that the pair, given a proper potion,
Take mortal form again and dwell on earth.
At this part of the pageant must your Eminence,
Ready with book and ring, the masque conclude
By joining the young twain in genuine bonds.   260

    MAU. A pretty notion, one that likes me well,
And fear not but that I shall play my part.

    OLERO. Look you upon my daughter, mark how fair
She is bedight as Circe. I shall act
The green Oceanus.

    MARCEL.   Look on my child,   265
The image of my sainted Ynes, when
Upon mine arm to similar rites she went.
Would that she might have liv'd to see this hour!

451

OLERO. The hour, my Duke, is not yet o'er.

MAU.   How now,
Dost fear some trifle like to go amiss?   270

OLERO. Nay, Eminence, I think all will go well—
Most well.

MARCEL.   Come, now, the time is growing short.
Hast thou prepar'd the goblet, Hecatissa,
Ready to use when that the play demands?

HEC. My lord, I have, even as I agreed.   275
My face, unequal to the masque, hath not
Withheld me from a lesser, useful part.
The wine is of old vintage, old and rare;
No man or woman here hath drunk such wine.
'Tis from the East, whence, as you know, I come.   280

(Hautboys play without the door.)

ALF. It is the King, my noble sire, Rinarto,
Let's to the hall and greet him as he comes!

MARG. (aside) Welcome, great King! Watch close the moving play,
For great events are like to hap this day!

(Exeunt)

Sc. II. The Great Hall

(Curtains drawn before a stage. Rinarto, Teobaldo, Ladies,
Gentlemen, and Soldiers seated as spectators.)

RIN. How goes it now, most learned Teobaldo;   285
Will the last act suffice to break the spell?

TEO. So have I written it, my lord. As now
Thou'st seen the ill of Circe's wrath, thou shalt
Hereafter view the sweet Endymion—play'd
By young Gonzago, noble Castro's son—   290
Bring from the moon a draught of magic nectar,
Which drunk, restores th' enchanted pair to earth.

RIN. It likes me well, I thank thee for the pains
Thou hast extended on the revelry.
Alfredo bears him well—

TEO.   But lo, my lord,   295
The curtains part again—attend the scene!

(Curtains reveal a scene representing rocks and seashore. Enter
Gonzago drest as Endymion, bearing a goblet. He blows on a conch shell.)

GONZ. Spirits from your oozy deeps
Where the sea-god lightly sleeps,
Wat'ry nymphs that ride the waves,
Naiads from your ocean caves,   300
Rise above your native foam,
Where the docile dolphins roam.
Rise, ye lovely mermaid throngs,
Pensive with fair Scylla's wrongs,
Kind Leucothea, friend of man,   305
Come, the joyful rites to scan.

(Enter many young maids drest as sea-goddesses, together with
Margarita, drest as Circe.)

MARG. Begone, intruder from the skies
And from fair Latmos' flow'ring meads;
For you no potent sea-gods rise,
    Not yours to meddle with my deeds.   310

GONZ. Circe, thy foul debasing pow'r hath fled,
As Dian, shining o'er thy sinful head,
    Exerts superior sway.
Within my hand a magic draught I bear,
Thy noxious ills forever to repair,   315
    And wash thy charms away.
Glaucus and Scylla, from your depths appear,
Endymion calls—deliverance is here—
    By Cynthia's mercy wrought.

(Enter Alfredo and Hypatia as Glaucus and Scylla. Gonzago as
Endymion extends them goblet.)

Drink deep of this the golden moon hath sent,   320
And know at last an unalloy'd content,
    To human likeness brought.

(Gives cup to Alfredo, who permits Hypatia to drink, then drinks
himself.)

ALF. As light as the billows that bound on the foam
Beats my heart as I turn to my own native home.
Fair Scylla my bride ere the nightfall shall be,   325
And we'll linger no more by the rocks and the sea.

(Reels a trifle, but steadies himself)

HYP. (tremulously) Cynthia, unspotted maid,
That send'st thy blessed aid,
Thy altars, rich . . .

(Falls in Alfredo's arms)

I faint, Alfredo! What is this strange fire   330
That courses madly thro' each aching vein?

ALF. Hypatia! Love! what have the Furies wrought?
A venom'd anguish burns my very soul—
Father, my Royal Sire, thou, Teobaldo,
Attend us in this sudden new distress!   335

(Alfredo and Hypatia sink to floor; Rinarto and Teobaldo
approach them. Rinarto takes Alfredo in his arms. Enter Hecatissa and
Olero from behind the scenes.)

RIN. My son, Alfredo! speak to me, my child!

HEC. How now, is Eastern wine a shade too strong
For obdurate princes and designing maids?

(Gonzago draws his sword)

GONZ. Exotick fiend! Thine was the guilty hand,
But 'twill no second act of mischief do!   340

(Kills her)

(Olero draws sword from beneath his masque costume and gives
battle to Gonzago)

OLERO. This for my daughter, slighted by the Prince
Thou serv'st with such unreasoning devotion!

(Inflicts a mortal wound)

GONZ. I die, most noble King! (Dies)

(Teobaldo draws and engageth Olero)

454

TEO.   Thou damn'd churl,
Accept the fate that is too good for thee,
Being worthy only of the hangman's noose!   345

    (Mortally wounds Olero. Margarita steals up behind Teobaldo)

    OLERO. Daughter, avenge me! (Dies)

    (Margarita stabs Teobaldo in the back)

MARG.   Ancient wretch, take this
For my poor father and for me, whose woes
Came from thy knavish counsel to Alfredo!

    (Alfredo, dying, crawls from out his father's arms, grasps sword
of the dead Gonzago, and approaches Margarita from behind.)

    TEO. Pox on the wench! Rinarto, my time's here,
Yet would I have thee know I die right gladly   350
In service of my King.

    (Alfredo stabs Margarita)

ALF.   This, cursed nymph,
For Teobaldo, and for all the grief
That thy caprice and vanity have wrought!
Foul Murderess—

MARG.   I perish by thy hand,
Belov'd Alfredo, loving thee the more.   355
'Tis a sweet death—I should have kill'd myself
Hereafter, being loath to live without thee,
But I could not permit thee wed Hypatia!

    (Dies)

    TEO. (to Alf.) Kind youth, I am aveng'd! We go together
To regions of infinity and light.   360

    (Alfredo and Teobaldo die. Enter Marcello from behind the scenes
of masque.)

    MARCEL. What means this sight of horror! Child! Hypatia!
They say that thou art poison'd—tell me, child!

    (Goes to his daughter)

HYP. Father, I die, but die not unaveng'd,
For those that plotted this fell thing are slain.
It is as well, for I have ever thought 365
That death itself is but a kind of marriage,
And that I shall in realms of ether rove
With my Alfredo, tasting loftier joys
Than we on earth might ever have possess'd.
See yon gold goblet, wherefrom we did drink 370
The fatal draught which us in death does link!

(Dies)

RIN. Our belov'd children both are slain, Marcello.
I have my Kingdom, but of what avail
Were twenty Kingdoms to a soul bereav'd!

(Marcello picks up the goblet and drinks therefrom)

MARCEL. My liege, I go! I am too old to live 375
An empty frame whereof the heart is dead.

RIN. Marcello! who shall say a father's grief
Is greater in a Duke than in a King?
Give me the goblet!

MARCEL. (weakly) Nay, my lord Rinarto!
The State requires the guidance of thy hand. 380
'Tis thine to live—

RIN. No more! Give me the vessel—
It is thy King that bids! Mauricio here,
An honour'd Cardinal of the Holy Church,
Will rule by the Pope's edict till my brother
Comes back from Sicily to take the throne. 385

(Takes goblet and drinks)

'Tis done! I took an heavier draught than thine
That I might die the sooner, and with thee.
We have been friends, Marcello, in the midst
Of roaring battle and unmeasur'd pow'r.
Here, take my hand—

MARCEL. I think it is the end. 390

RIN. It is indeed the end. (To Mau.) Godly Mauricio,
Say o'er our sev'ral bodies those grave rites,
Couch'd in Latin, which thy Church prescribes
For them that die. And to succeeding times
Impart a knowledge of these dire events,   395
Drawing such morals as thy cloth deviseth.
I come, Alfredo, nearest to my heart,
Whom death from me could but a moment part.

(Rinarto and Marcello die)

MAU. See to what ills doth female malice tend!
Our King Rinarto, his proud son, the fair   400
Hypatia, and the learned Teobaldo,
Marcello, noble Duke, the young Gonzago,
All slain, tho' to avenge them lifeless lie
The damn'd Margarita, and her sire
Treacherous Olero, and the Eastern dame   405
Whose crimes in hideousness outrank her aspect.
Ye grave assembled guests, I pray you all
For a brief time depart, till fun'ral rites
Be substituted for yon nuptial settings.
My heart cries out 'gainst these o'erwhelming deeds—   410
I'll to the chapel and count o'er my beads!

END OF THE TRAGEDY.

X. FRAGMENTS

1.

Armed against an arrogant attack,
Bold BELGIUM beats barbaric braggarts back.

2.

But (past belief) a dolphin's arched back
Preserv'd Arion from his destin'd wrack;
Secure he sits, and with harmonious strains
Requites his bearer for his friendly pains.

3.

The winged steed above th' horizon flies,
And lends his lustre to the vaulted skies;
But whilst we view him in the distant space,
Kleiner leaps on, and guides his flight with grace!

4.

With rotting rib and salt-encrusted spar,
See yonder hulk upon the Ipswich bar;
Thro' shatter'd side the surging ocean streams,
While sea-gulls nest amid the ancient beams.
The keel sinks idly in a sandy bed,   5
And seaweeds hide the grinning figurehead.
Upon the drooping deck at noon of day
The fishers' children come, to dream and play;
In infant fancy man the swelling sail,
And in their dauntless barque defy the gale: 10
With pleasing sport they roam the wreckage o'er,
And act the parts their grandsires liv'd before.
So rests the vessel, in decrepit ease,
That once in grandeur rode the billowy seas:
Her ruin'd timbers o'er the beach bestrown;   15
Her name and fortune to the world unknown.
Yet not unknown—for he whose form you spy
In trembling tread upon the sand close by,
Whose matted locks a chalky whiteness bear
Who sweeps the ruin with a senile stare—   20
He can repeat a wondrous tale and wild;
Told by old men, whilst he was yet a child.

5.
As London wits at Will's or Button's knew
The letter'd leisure of a favour'd few;
So our small band, more scatter'd and less able,
May meet in mind, if not about the table!
                    LUDOVICUS THEOBALDUS, JUN.

6.
The cluster'd spires and roofs that gaily gleam
Across the verdant plain and glist'ning stream.
[. . .]
The bending corn that in profusion grows
Where rural virtue earns its calm repose.
[. . .]
The twining thicket and the shady grove   5
Where supple Fauns in artless pleasure move.

7.
Slumber, watcher, till the spheres
Six and twenty thousand years
Have revolv'd, and I return
To the spot where now I burn.
Other stars anon shall rise   5
To the axis of the skies;
Stars that soothe and stars that bless
With a sweet forgetfulness:
Only when my round is o'er
Shall the past disturb thy door.   10

8.
Whilst you, Menalcas, feed your tender goats,
And calm your restless herds with Dorick notes,
In pensive strains amongst the mountain rocks,
I tell the Oreads of my absent flocks [. . .]

9.
All Hail, exponent of aesthetic pow'r—
Whose lucent lines display the present hour;
List to the strains of those whose ancient mind
Reflects the ages that have gone behind.

10.
That is not dead which can eternal lie,
And with strange aeons even death may die.

462

11.
The wise to care a comic strain apply,
And shake with laughter, that they may not cry.

12.
There is a quaint fellow call'd Fritter,
An amiable sort of a critter.
    But when he slung lead
    At Old Theobald's head
The votes shew'd him up as a bum hitter!   5

13.
Intent to prove esteem by lines of worth,
I scann'd my songs, and shudder'd at the dearth,
When the clear way by HOAG was nobly shewn,
And I found voice in couplets not my own!

14.
Bright are the blooms I gaily pick on
The piny steeps of Wissahickon!

15.
What leap so vast, what flame so quick to start,
As that great elder dawn of soul and art?
Chain'd in the darkness of an hour accurst,
Prometheus stretch'd—and truth phlogistick burst.
Fast spread the blaze, and where confusion lay,   5
There leap'd forthwith the beams of order'd day:
Monk turn'd to sculptor, priest a sage became,
And beauty seiz'd what creed no more cou'd claim.
'Tis then, ITALIA, thou could'st raise anew
The mighty splendours Virgil's pencil drew: 10
With pagan glow the vital figure mould,
And lift afresh the glitt'ring dome of gold;
The heart disburthen of its weight of rust,
The fancy beckon from somnifick dust;
Reach to the light beyond the years of gloom,   15
Revive old Greece, and Roman pomp resume!
And now this beauty, limn'd with beauteous skill
By Pater's pen, a beauteous mind wou'd fill.
Short is the search, when swift the postboy rides
To that green vale where sweet Xanthippe bides!   20
There, in a Grecian steeple's mellow shade,
Let the bright fair this added light invade—

463

Nor blame the donor if herself outshine,
In grace celestial, any mortal line!

16.
Madam, what thankful Raptures rouse my breast,
Cut from the native Shades I love the best;
I pine for Greens and Groves I cannot see,
And lo! Novanglia's Woodlands come to me!

17.
The hour is TEN, as to my couch I creep,
In quest of slumbers visionless and deep;
The drowsy god his subtlest spell prepares,
And with oblivion scatters all my cares.

18.
Never say I chose this metre just to skimp on things like rhyme;
What indeed could e'er be neater, or more fitted to the time?

19.
No modern menace here our joy may blast;
Who sees *Old Newport* sees the beauteous past!

20.
To Bossy's Brawn the lofty Lid we doff:
He tells the cock-ey'd World where it gets off!

21.
Nor can decadent change unchalleng'd thrive
While Foster and Old Theobald both survive!

22.

Observe dull { ———, whose sluggish mind (if name is trisyllabick)
——— , whose unfinisht mind (if name is disyllable)
——— , whose microscopick Mind (if name is monosyllable)
Rejects the precepts known to all mankind:
Scorns ev'ry fact, & scours the world to reach
Some height of folly new to human speech:
Begot by b———s, in a bedlam born,   5
Well-shap'd a gaol or madhouse to adorn;
Void of all things that Art and Virtue praise,
But fashion'd fit for these degen'rate days:
Pattern of all that wakes our honest spleen,
And brother to his own belov'd machine!   10

23.
Black and unform'd, as pestilent a Clod
As dread Sadoqua, Averonia's God.

24.
'Tis a sprig of green shamrock grown fresh with the dew
    Of the far-distant isle that I love,
And in ev'ry trim petal there rise into view
    The dear scenes where I'm longing to rove.

Sure the leaves as they sway seem to sing with the wind   5
    That plays round the blest cot of my birth,
Till among the strange faces about me I find
    The lost dream of my own native earth.

And when death comes at last my long exile to break,
    And my ashes in foreign soil rest,   10
Plant the sprig o'er my grave that my soul may awake
    Midst the kindred it cherishes best!

APPENDIX 1: LOVECRAFT'S REVISIONS OF POETRY

A Prayer for Universal Peace

Robert L. Selle, D.D.

"They shall beat their swords into ploughshares, and their spears into pruning-hooks: nation shall not lift up sword against nation, neither shall they learn war any more." Isa. 2:4.

How long, O Lord, must suffering Man withstand
The martial throes that shake th' extended land?
Supreme Jehovah! hear the anguish'd plea
Of Thy sad children, wreck'd with misery.
How long must brothers thus in hatred meet   5
On fields of War, and with Destruction greet;
Whilst cannon's echoes stir the trembling ground,
And seas of blood grow deeper at the sound:
When men, like cattle, feel the slaught'rous blow
That fells in rage, nor spares the noblest foe?   10
Father, may Thy unbounded mercy save
The men who stop the breath Thy judgment gave!
How long, O Lord, must monarchs call to arms
Their bravest subjects, roused by War's alarms;
In weeping majesty their legions send   15
To face without retreat a fruitless end:
Where steel meets steel, and in th' increasing fray
Not courage, but mad fury gains the day?
How long, Lord! ere man can be so free
That he will bow to Reason, and to Thee?   20

The scenes of War! what tongue would dare relate
The fiendish work of universal hate?
For food the child and widow cry in vain,
Since he who earned it ne'er can earn again.
Bereft of strength, deprived of filial care,   25
The aged mother totters in despair.
Another mother, with her infant load,
Laments the fate that War's disasters bode:

467

Will her blest burden, to full manhood grown,
Fall on the field, while she must sigh alone? 30
Behold the wife, whose Heav'nly love enfolds
The man whose heart a like affection holds;
Must that brave man, to whom she gave her all,
Take last farewell, and in the battle fall?
Alas! what useless toll the conflict claims, 35
With its foul chaos, and uncertain aims!
The loving husband, and the cherish'd son,
Would fain enjoy the peace their fathers won,
But War, the tyrant, scorns domestic joys;
Surveys the nations, and the world destroys. 40

O Prince of Peace! at whose unspotted birth
The star of brotherhood beamed o'er the earth,
And choirs angelic, in melodious glee,
Proclaimed the age of love and charity;
O Prince of Peace, whose holy life was spent 45
That War might end, and harden'd hearts relent;
Behold the crimes of those who falsely pray,
And from Thy Heavenly precepts turn away!
Saviour Divine! through what unholy greed
Hath Man forborne Thy righteous word to heed? 50
Thrice-wicked Man, who in his worldly pride,
Leads on to death, and wakes the fratricide!
O Prince of Peace! whose undisputed reign
Can give security to earth's domain;
Whose blessed power can heal the wounded land, 55
And banish bloodshed at divine command:
Thou, Thou alone, appear'st in holy state,
To raise the soul, and brutish strife abate.

Come, blest Redeemer, with Thy sweet relief,
And purge our hearts of hatred and of grief! 60
Give Thou to us, O mighty Lord of Lords,
The boons that Peace, not bloody War, affords;
Let teeming fields of golden grain arise,
Whilst Education clears our blinded eyes;
Let Rum, the noxious demon, be no more, 65
And Christian Majesty above us soar.
May weary soldiers, freed from battle's rage,
'Mid scenes domestic all their lives engage.
May battle-steel, its deadly function spent,

In peaceful ploughshares by our sons be bent,   70
By that which hath th' encrimson'd world distress'd,
May Earth, forgiving, in the end be blest!
Lend, O Creator, Thy all-pitying aid,
To those who bear the ills that War hath made;
Lift up the weeping, and Thy bounty pour   75
On sadden'd throngs whose lov'd ones speak no more.

Revive, Almighty Lord, throughout the lands,
The laws wherein domestic virtue stands;
Teach every man to hold his peaceful place,
And shower Thy Heav'nly blessings on his race.   80
Before Thy sacred altars, Lord, we pray,
That Thou may'st grant us a sublimer day,
When erring Man of hatred shall be free,
And dwell at peace in pious harmony.
The clouds of War fill now the seething sky,   85
And bank'd the blackness, grieve the godly eye:
What dire events behind the blood-mist low'r?
Curs'd is the time; portentous is the hour!
Lord, may we who scan the darkened space
Behold a rift to mark Thy boundless grace;   90
A rift whose breadth in mercy may increase
Till all the heav'ns are clear with final peace.
Mankind, awake! Hath not experience
Preach'd lasting Peace to your half-slumb'ring sense?
Look on the blood in needless battle shed: 95
What victory can replace the honor'd dead?
Almighty Lord! to Thee ascends our pray'r;
Wilt not through Jesus for our nations care?
Spread Peace and Love throughout Thy boundless ken,
Whilst we, in humble suppliance, cry AMEN!   100

[On the Duke of Leeds]

Unknown

When Gallant LEEDS auspiciously shall wed
The virtuous Fair, of antient Lineage bred,
How must the Maid rejoice with conscious Pride
To win so great an Husband to her Side!

Mors Omnibus Communis

(Written in a Hospital)

Sonia H. Greene

On ev'ry hand the shrieks of woe,
　　The moans of human pain;
The wailing as from pits below
　　Where souls are lash'd and slain.

On eye and ear and heart and soul　　　　　　　　　5
　　Thro' night's abyss they pour,
As if each suff'rer glimps'd a goal
　　Of hell for evermore.

Down aisles of grief, with silent tread
　　Stalk spectres curs'd and drear;　　　　　　　　10
The shadows of the coming dead,
　　Whose touch is chill with fear.

And as the dying groan and scream
　　Beneath the futile knife,
They pray their gods to end the dream;　　　　　　15
　　The noxious dream call'd life.

They mutter at the vacant sky,
　　And plead with empty air;
They whine to myths of days gone by
　　In unavailing prayer.　　　　　　　　　　　　20

But still the monster Death assails
　　With all-encroaching claw;
And slave and king with kindred wails
　　Are crush'd within his maw.

The thief and saint, the old and young,　　　　　　25
　　Impartial torments feel,
Till each in that mute gulf is flung,
　　Whose horrors none reveal.

Alone

Jonathan E. Hoag

Oft have I wander'd, mute and lone,
    Where Autumn turns the green to gold,
And frosted Leaves are downward blown
    To feed the coming Springtime's Mould.

Oft have I trod those Realms of Mind   5
    Where Silence breathes with voiceless Breath,
And Footsteps scarce an Echo find
    In Solitudes of Dream and Death.

Oft have I viewed from Lands apart
    The Myriad Scenes long gone before,   10
The Childhood Days of happy Heart,
    And all the Light and Life of yore.

So seek I still dim Vales where far
    The Thrush and Waterfall are heard;
Where worldly Cares may never mar,   25
    Nor Folly sound o'er Wisdom's Word.

Unity

Unknown

My soul has the arms of an octopus
    To cuddle the whole world in;
O'er the cosmick sea, with emotion plus
    I float on a fluttery fin.

For Buddha has bidden my bosom burst   5
    The collar that cramps us so—
And I sprinkle all space with the love that erst
    Was lavish'd on Lima, O.

The Dweller

William Lumley

Dread and potent broods a Dweller
    In an evil twilight space,
Formless as a daemon's shadow,

Void of members and of face.

Heeding not the shaped or human,   5
    Past the reach of time or law—
Never may our minds conceive It
    Save as clouds of fright and awe.

When It crawls malignly on us,
    Lethal mists of leaden grey,   10
Rising vaguely in the distance,
    Veil its hideous bulk away.

And Its mutterings of horror,
    Foul with lore of charnel ground,
Lose themselves in troubled thunders   15
    That from far horizons sound.

Dreams of Yith

Duane W. Rimel

I

In distant Yith past crested, ragged peaks;
    On far-flung islands lost to worldly eyes,
A shadow from the ancient star-void seeks
    Some being which in caverns shrilly cries
A challenge; and the hairy dweller speaks   5
    From that deep hole where slimy Sotho lies.
But when those night-winds crept about the place,
They fled—for Sotho had no human face!

II

Beyond the valleys of the sun which lie
    In misty chaos past the reach of time;
And brood beneath the ice as aeons fly,
    Long waiting for some brighter, warmer clime;
There is a vision, as I vainly try   5
    To glimpse the madness that must some day climb
From age-old tombs in dim dimensions hid,
And push all angles back—unseal the lid!

472

III

Beside the city that once lived there wound
  A stream of putrefaction writhing black;
Reflecting crumbling spires stuck in the ground
  That glow through hov'ring mist whence no stray track
Can lead to those dead gates, where once was found   5
  The secret that would bring the dwellers back.
And still that pitch-black current eddies by
Those silver gates of Yith to sea-beds dry.

IV

On rounded turrets rising through the visne
  Of cloud-veiled aeons that the Old Ones knew;
On tables deeply worn and fingered clean
  By tentacles that dreamers seldom view;
In space-hung Yith, on clammy walls obscene   5
  That writhe and crumble and are built anew;
There is a figure carved; but God! those eyes,
That sway on fungoid stems at leaden skies!

V

Around the place of ancient, waiting blight;
  On walls of sheerest opal rearing high,
That move as planets beckon in the night
  To faded realms where nothing sane can lie;
A deathless guard tramps by in feeble light,   5
  Emitting to the stars a sobbing cry.
But on that path where footsteps should have led
There rolled an eyeless, huge and bloated head.

VI

Amid dim hills that poison mosses blast,
  Far from the lands and seas of our clean earth,
Dread nightmare shadows dance—obscenely cast
  By twisted talons of archaean birth
On rows of slimy pillars stretching past   5
  A daemon-fane that echoes with mad mirth.
And in that realm sane eyes may never see—
For black light streams from skies of ebony.

VII

On those queer mountains which hold back the horde
    That lie in waiting in their mouldy graves,
Who groan and mumble to a hidden lord
    Still waiting for the time-worn key that saves;
There dwells a watcher who can ill afford   5
    To let invaders by those hoary caves.
But some day then may dreamers find the way
That leads down elfin-painted paths of gray.

VIII

And past those unclean spires that ever lean
    Above the windings of unpeopled streets;
And far beyond the walls and silver screen
    That veils the secrets of those dim retreats,
A scarlet pathway leads that some have seen   5
    In wildest visions that no mortal greets.
And down that dimming path in fearful flight
Queer beings squirm and hasten in the night.

IX

High in the ebon skies on scaly wings
    Dread batlike beasts soar past those towers gray
To peer in greedy longing at the things
    Which sprawl in every twisted passageway.
And when their gruesome flight a shadow brings   5
    The dwellers lift dim eyes above the clay.
But lidded bulbs close heavily once more;
They wait—for Sotho to unlatch the door!

X
Now, through the veil of troubled visions deep
    Is draped to blind me to the secret ways
Leading through blackness to the realm of sleep
    That haunts me all my jumbled nights and days,
I feel the dim path that will let me keep   5
    That rendezvous in Yith where Sotho plays.
At last I see a glowing turret shine,
And I am coming, for the key is mine!

[On John Donne]

Lee McBride White

Not sweet, this man: more he implacable:
Unreconciled to sugar of Shakspere,
Or music of the mighty-lined Marlowe
Combined of rare components, he remained
Supple, infrangible, with prism-perception   5
Of a vast world and of himself in it.
Below, above, beyond, this man; his view
Wide, metasensual; his rugged words
Dimensioned by mind, soul, body—bound
By four stern walls of closely coffined space.   10
All shining metal, this man's leaping verse—
The mercury of fluid lyric love
Silver of resonant God-pointing hymn,
Rough ore of youthful satire, grating harsh. . . .
Nor ever sags the bold arc of his flight: 15
A force centrifugal keeps tautly strung
The thin cool wires of subtle intellect.
Of bright and sudden tangent-thought composed—
This man, light-winged, eccentric of good things:
Body of woman, mind of man, God's soul—   20
Long time before his fire shall flicker out,
Yet molder now the canons he defy'd.

The Wanderer's Return

Wilson Shepherd

Far out past the dim horizon,
    In the depths of star-filled space,
To a million alien planets
    I went with a smiling face.

But when after years of roving   5
    My ship took the homeward track,
There was no smile on my haggard face,
    And the look in my eyes was black.

The great of the earth flocked round me,
    And gaped at my space-wide flight,   10

Yet looked askance when I hinted
    Of things in the gulf of night.

They tapped their heads when I told them
    Of the million lightless suns
That reel in the outer darkness   15
    Where the stream of dead dust runs.

And none of them cared to listen
    When I spoke of the nightmare deeps
Where evil leers in a trillion shapes,
    And the god of chaos sleeps.   20

They stopped their ears when my story
    Made light of their creeds and laws,
And proved that their vaunted science
    Was a tissue of worn-out saws.

They balked at the task of facing   25
    The truths that my quest unrolled,
Reluctant to learn a lesson
    From the horrors I glimpsed and told.

And now they have seized and chained me
    In a madman's hopeless thrall,   30
The while there is closer creeping
    A doom to engulf them all.

They eye me with lofty pity,
    And laugh at my words of fear—
But how will they meet the Outer Shapes   35
    When the ships from the Void draw near?

Appendix 2: Poems by Others

Metamorphoses 1.1–88

Ovid (P. Ovidius Naso)

In nova fert animus mutatas dicere formas
corpora; di, coeptis (nam vos mutastis et illas)
adspirate meis primaque ab origine mundi
ad mea perpetuum deducite tempora carmen!
Ante mare et terras et quod tegit omnia caelum   5
unus erat toto naturae vultus in orbe,
quem dixere chaos: rudis indigestaque moles
nec quicquam nisi pondus iners congestaque eodem
non bene iunctarum discordia semina rerum.
Nullus adhuc mundo praebebat lumina Titan,   10
nec nova crescendo reparabat cornua Phoebe,
nec circumfuso pendebat in aere tellus
ponderibus librata suis, nec bracchia longo
margine terrarum porrexerat Amphitrite;
utque erat et tellus illic et pontus et aer,   15
sic erat instabilis tellus, innabilis unda,
lucis egens aer; nulli sua forma manebat,
obstabatque aliis aliud, quia corpore in uno
frigida pugnabant calidis, umentia siccis,
mollia cum duris, sine pondere, habentia pondus.   20
Hanc deus et melior litem natura diremit.
nam caelo terras et terris abscidit undas
et liquidum spisso secrevit ab aere caelum.
Quae postquam evolvit caecoque exemit acervo,
dissociata locis concordi pace ligavit: 25
ignea convexi vis et sine pondere caeli
emicuit summaque locum sibi fecit in arce;
proximus est aer illi levitate locoque;
densior his tellus elementaque grandia traxit
et pressa est gravitate sua; circumfluus umor   30
ultima possedit solidumque coercuit orbem.
Sic ubi dispositam quisquis fuit ille deorum
congeriem secuit sectamque in membra coegit,
principio terram, ne non aequalis ab omni
parte foret, magni speciem glomeravit in orbis.   35

Tum freta diffundi rapidisque tumescere ventis
iussit et ambitae circumdare litora terrae;
addidit et fontes et stagna inmensa lacusque
fluminaque obliquis cinxit declivia ripis,
quae, diversa locis, partim sorbentur ab ipsa,   40
in mare perveniunt partim campoque recepta
liberioris aquae pro ripis litora pulsant.
Iussit et extendi campos, subsidere valles,
fronde tegi silvas, lapidosos surgere montes,
utque duae dextra caelum totidemque sinistra   45
parte secant zonae, quinta est ardentior illis,
sic onus inclusum numero distinxit eodem
cura dei, totidemque plagae tellure premuntur.
Quarum quae media est, non est habitabilis aestu;
nix tegit alta duas; totidem inter utramque locavit   60
temperiemque dedit mixta cum frigore flamma.
Inminet his aer, qui, quanto est pondere terrae
pondus aquae levius, tanto est onerosior igni.
Illic et nebulas, illic consistere nubes
iussit et humanas motura tonitrua mentes   55
et cum fulminibus facientes fulgura ventos.
His quoque non passim mundi fabricator habendum
aera permisit; vix nunc obsistitur illis,
cum sua quisque regat diverso flamina tractu,
quin lanient mundum; tanta est discordia fratrum.   60
Eurus ad Auroram Nabataeaque regna recessit
Persidaque et radiis iuga subdita matutinis;
vesper et occiduo quae litora sole tepescunt,
proxima sunt Zephyro; Scythiam septemque triones
horrifer invasit Boreas; contraria tellus   65
nubibus adsiduis pluviaque madescit ab Austro.
Haec super inposuit liquidum et gravitate carentem
aethera nec quicquam terrenae faecis habentem.
Vix ita limitibus dissaepserat omnia certis,
cum, quae pressa diu fuerant caligine caeca,   70
sidera coeperunt toto effervescere caelo;
neu regio foret ulla suis animalibus orba,
astra tenent caeleste solum formaeque deorum,
cesserunt nitidis habitandae piscibus undae,
terra feras cepit, volucres agitabilis aer.   75
Sanctius his animal mentisque capacius altae
deerat adhuc et quod dominari in cetera posset:

478

natus homo est, sive hunc divino semine fecit
ille opifex rerum, mundi melioris origo,
sive recens tellus seductaque nuper ab alto   80
aethere cognati retinebat semina caeli.
Quam satus Iapeto, mixtam pluvialibus undis,
finxit in effigiem moderantum cuncta deorum,
pronaque cum spectent animalia cetera terram,
os homini sublime dedit caelumque videre   85
iussit et erectos ad sidera tollere vultus:
sic, modo quae fuerat rudis et sine imagine, tellus
induit ignotas hominum conversa figuras.

Our Apology to E. M. W.

John Russell

'Tis the voice of the knocker,
Just hear him complain:
"Here's Lovecraft and Russell,
With verses again.
I really do think   5
It is a disgrace
The way they use up
Your valuable space.
The Log-Book is just
For critical use,   10
And not, as they think,
For sarcastic abuse.
So please, Mr. Editor,
Tell them to quit,
Or they will both finish   15
By thinking they're IT."

Don't vex yourself more,
My dear E. M. W.,
For we'll never again
With our verses trouble you.   20

Florida

John Russell

When the wild and wily moccasin glides gently round your tent,
And when the rattler crawls around, on evil purpose bent,
Or when the giddy 'gator roams around your only well,
If then you're asked about your land, you'll answer: "Sure, it's HELL."

Then when the gay mosquito starts, it keeps you on the run,   5
And the lovely little chigger starts in to help the fun;
Then if a colony of ants begin to bite as well,
If then you're asked about your land, you'll answer: "Sure, 'tis HELL."

And when the rainy season comes, the rain in torrents pours;
You see the lightning's vivid flash and hear the thunder roars;   10
You see your land beneath the flood, your tent is soaked as well,
Then if you're asked about your land, you'll answer: "It's sure HELL."

But when the late September comes, the climate seems to change;
Then peace and comfort once again come stealing o'er the range;
Your hogs begin to fatten, and the sweet potatoes swell,   15
Then if you're asked about your land, you'll say: "SURE, THIS BEATS HELL!"

Regner Lodbrog's Epicedium

Olaus Wormius

1.

Pugnavimus ensibus
Haud post longum tempus
Cum in Gotlandia accessimus
Ad serpentis immensi necem
Tunc impetravimus Thoram   5
Ex hoc vocarunt me virum
Quod serpentem transfodi
Hirsutam braccam ob illam ceem
Cuspide ictum intuli in colubrum
Fero lucidorum stupendiorum.   10

2

Multum juvenis fui quando acquisivimus
Orientem versus in Oreonico freto

Vulnerum amnes avidae serae
Et flavipedi avi
Accepimus ibidem sonuerunt   15
Ad sublimes galeas
Dura ferra magnam escam
Omnis erat oceanus vulnus
Vadavit corvus in sanguine Caesorum.

3.

Alte tulimus tunc lanceas   20
Quando viginti annos numeravimus
Et celebrem laudem comparavimus passim
Vicimus octo barones
In oriente ante Dimini portum
Aquilae impetravimus tunc sufficientem   25
Hospitii sumptum in illa strage
Sudor decidit in vulnerum
Oceano perdidit exercitus aetatem.

4.

Pugnae facta copia
Cum Helsingianos postulavimus   30
Ad aulum Odini
Naves direximus in ostium Vistulae
Mucro potuit tum mordere
Omnis erat vulnus unda
Terra rubefacta Calido   35
Frendebat gladius in loricas
Gladius findebat Clypeos.

5.

Memini neminem tunc fugisse
Priusquam in navibus
Heraudus in bello caderet   40
Non findit navibus
Alius baro praestantior
Mare ad portum
In navibus longis post illum
Sic attulit princeps passim   45
Alacre in bellum cor.

6.

Exercitus abjecit clypeos
Cum hasta volavit
Ardua ad virorum pectora
Momordit Scarforum cautes   50
Gladius in pugna
Sanguineus erat Clypeus
Antequam Rafno rex caderet
Fluxit ex virorum capitibus
Calidus in loricas sudor.   55

7.

Habere potuerunt tum corvi
Ante Indirorum insulas
Sufficientem praedam dilaniandam
Acquisivimus feris carnivoris
Plenum prandium unico actu   60
Difficile erat unius facere mentionem
Oriente sole
Spicula vidi pungere
Propulerunt arcus ex se ferra.

Hugh Blair:

We have fought with our swords. I was young, when, towards the east, in the bay of Oreon, we made torrents of blood flow, to gorge the ravenous beast of prey, and the yellow-footed bird. There resounded the hard steel upon the lofty helmets of men. The whole ocean was one wound. The crow waded in the blood of the slain.

When we had numbered twenty years, we lifted our spears on high, and every where spread our renown. Eight barons we overcame in the east, before the port of Diminum; and plentifully we feasted the eagle in that slaughter. The warm stream of wounds ran into the ocean. The army fell before us.

When we steered our ships into the mouth of the Vistula, we sent the Helsingians to the Hall of Odin. Then did the sword bite. The waters were all one wound. The earth was dyed red with the warm stream. The sword rung upon the coats of mail, and clove the bucklers in twain.

None fled on that day, till among his ships Heraudus fell. Than him no braver baron cleaves the sea with ships; a cheerful heart did he ever bring to the combat.

Then the host threw away their shields, when the uplifted spear flew at the breasts of heroes. The sword bit the Scarfian rocks; bloody was the shield in battle, until Rafno the king was slain. From the heads of warriors the warm sweat streamed down their armour.

The crows around the Indirian islands had an ample prey. It were difficult to single out one among so many deaths. At the rising of the sun I beheld the spears piercing the bodies of foes, and the bows throwing forth their steel-pointed arrows. Loud roared the swords in the plains of Lano.—The virgins long bewailed the slaughter of that morning.

A Prayer for Universal Peace

Robert L. Selle, D.D.

Give Thou to us O Lord give us,
Instead of war revivals four—
Agriculture, Education,
Temperance and Christian religion.
[. . .]
Revive, Revive, O Lord, revive,   5
For every man throughout the land
The things that'll make for home and state
Conditions right for man's best plight.

To Mary of the Movies

Rheinhart Kleiner

You palpitate upon the screen,
    A shadowy delusion,
And live your crowded hour between
    Beginning and conclusion.
But sometimes I forget that you   5
    Are just a passing flicker,
And wonder if your eyes are blue
    That make my heart beat quicker!

I've seen you as a haughty dame,
    Aloof, aristocratic;   10
Or one who turned, when evening came,
    From factory to attic.
I've found that you are just as sweet
    A princess as a peasant—
Whatever ways your little feet   15
    Traversed to me were pleasant!

Shy maid, may all the winsome grace,
    As pictured on the screen there,
Forever shine upon your face,
    And never frown be seen there!   20
May every ill that mars the day
    Or care that looms above you,
Prove fleeting as a phantom play
    At thought of all who love you!

And tho' we'll never meet, I know,   25
    Yet when you're most beguiling
I wish 'twere you that thrill me so,
    Not just your shadow, smiling.
And still for each remembered time
    Your art had power to cheer me,   30
I sing to you this little rhyme,
    Tho' you may never hear me!

A Prayer for Peace and Justice

Henry F. Thomas

Great God, our Father—Source of Peace,
When shall earth's bloody warfare cease?
We pray and plead on bended knee
And fain to love—and worship Thee.
While to our shame—we cry: "Prepare"   5
For strife and conflict ev'rywhere.
We waste our force on armed defence
Where arbitration were more sense.

Aid us O Lord to mend our way,
To be consistent when we pray: 10
"Thy Kingdom come, Thy will be done
On earth, as it in Heav'n is done."
Let us not live on daily bread
That has been earned by other's sweat.
But let us build—not to destroy,   15
And thus create world-lasting joy.

Real songs of praise would fill the air
If ev'ry soul reaped its full share
Of blessings from their source of toil.
No blood for greed would stain God's soil,   20

484

When all the world co-operates
And well conserves what it creates.
Success and blessings cannot fail—
For Peace and Justice will prevail.

The Modern Business Man to His Love

(With Apologies to Kit Marlowe)

Olive G. Owen

Come live with me and be my love.
    I swear by all the pow'rs above
That none in all this fair, wide land
    Shall be more worthy of thy hand!

We'll go upon our honeymoon   5
    Where falling waters sweetly croon:
To Glacier or to Yellowstone;
    To Palm Beach, or to foreign zone.

If thou of autos lik'st the whir,
    Behold—a seven passenger!   10
Or if the waves thou lik'st to churn,
    My yacht, pure white, from stern to stern.

I'll buy the silks of shimm'ring sheen,
    The finest that the world has seen;
And diamonds, pearls, and sapphires, too,   15
    Deep as the ocean's deepest blue.

A summer house—a winter home—
    And much in foreign lands we'll roam.
And then a nifty bungalow,
    Where sweet birds sing and flowers grow!   20

All sanitary shall there be,
    Where not a germ shall laugh in glee;
Nor any fly—of all the worst,
    For I believe in "safety first."

If thou an air-ship should'st admire,   25
    We will forsake our rubber tire;
And if a moment thou wilt wait
    Behold! I'll have one at the gate.

O Grace, dear Grace, if all these things
 Should prove to thee as leading strings,   30
I pray (O hear, ye pow'rs above!)
 Thou'lt come with me and be my love!

His Frank Self-Expression

Paul Shivell

Obscure and down and out as the world goes,
 I know I am a seer in plain disguise,
 Living above ambition, for a prize
 Which angels see, but no man living knows,
And few have ever cared for. I compose   5
 Out of my unapplauded sacrifice
 An immortality which proves me wise,
 And makes my life acceptable with those
Who shall hereafter understand its aim.
 For I who seem to muse of self am singing   10
 The sacred song given me to impart,
The song that was born in me. I disclaim
 Fictitious verse, and am through sorrow bringing
 Unto my people all I have, my heart.

To a Movie Star

Rheinhart Kleiner

We see you as you love or hate;
 And dry our tears or hush our laughter,
While trembling at relentless Fate
 That where you go must follow after!

Yet joy and pain seem strangely sweet   5
 When shown by charm so captivating;
And twenty reels were all too fleet
 In which you moved, our hearts elating!

Now please take care—from yonder cliff
 The "heavy's" very apt to throw you;   10
We shudder when we wonder if—
 But, ah, the hero's there below you!

And though, perhaps, you love in vain
 Today, and sicken with your sorrow;
We'll dry our eyes; forget our pain;   15
 And hope for better luck tomorrow!

[On the Duke of Leeds]

Unknown

When the Duke of *Leeds* shall marry'd be
To a fine young Lady of high Quality
How happy will that Gentlewoman be
In his Grace of *Leeds'* good Company.

Ruth

Rheinhart Kleiner

Oh, it was you, whom I had always held
So cold and weary and so passionless,
Long disillusioned, with all hopes dispelled
That once might please or trouble or distress.

Sweet, very sweet that moment of surprise   5
With which I glimpsed your spirit's hidden deep,
And came to know that you were not too wise
Nor yet too weary or too worn to weep.

Only a Volunteer

Sergt. Hayes P. Miller, 17th Aero-Squadron, U.S.A.

Why didn't I wait to be drafted,
 And be led to the train by a band,
Or put in a claim for exemption,
 Oh, why did I hold out my hand?
Why didn't I wait for the banquets,   5
 Why didn't I wait to be cheered,
For the drafted man gets credit,
 While I only volunteered!

For no one gave me a banquet,
 No one said just one kind word;   10
A puff of the engine, a grind of the wheels,

Were all the goodbye that I heard.
Then off to a camp I was hustled,
    To be trained for the next half year,
In the shuffle I was forgotten—   15
    I was only a volunteer!

I have builded the others their barracks,
    While roasting alive in a tent;
I have cleaned off a dozen parade grounds
    For the fellows that "only were sent."   20
And to me it was made very clear
    That the honor goes to the drafted man,
And the work to the volunteer!

I have waded the mud in Texas,
    I have frozen in Canada cold,   25
I've walked my posts in the moonlight
    Till this army is getting old;
But I'm not on their roll of honor,
    And though someone may shed a tear,
By all the rest I'm forgotten,   30
    For I'm only a volunteer.

And I dreamed that in far-off Flanders,
    On that bloody field of hate,
I went over the top—by a bullet was stopped,
    Then I knocked at the pearly gate.   35
And I heard Saint Peter saying,
    "We've no room for your kind here,
We're reserved for the National Army,
    Hell was made for the volunteer."

And perhaps some day in the future,   40
    When my little boy sits on my knee,
And asks what I did in the great war
    As he looks up at me,
I will have to look into those eyes
    That at me so trustingly peer,   45
And tell him I was not drafted—
    I was only a volunteer!

John Oldham: 1653–1683

Rheinhart Kleiner

Written after a perusal of his poems, the same having been presented to the writer by a friend.

Neglected Oldham! Who will heed
The rhymes that Dorset lov'd to read?
Moderns, I fear, would call him dunce,
Tho' he was prais'd by Dryden once!
His long-admir'd satiric vein   5
Seems strangely stupid and inane;
His wit has pall'd; his rhymes are flat;
No two opinions as to that!
But if we seek a fitting cause
For some slight measure of applause,   10
Be it in this: he made it pay,
In that old Restoration day!

To Miriam

Rheinhart Kleiner

Oh, Miriam, if I had only spent
One half the pains which I was wont to do,
On rhymes and verse of sweetest sentiment,
That celebrated Love and Youth and You;
If I had brought as much of tender care   5
To these accounts and figures in my books,
As to the lines which said that you were fair
As any movie actress in your looks;
Had I but counted, with as sharp an eye,
Discounts and rebates; credits gone to waste   10
Instead of beats and pauses—arts that lie
In verse—so all I wrote might please your taste;
My fame and fortune were less far to seek,
And I'd be earning more than twelve a week!

Ethel: Cashier in a Broad Street Buffet

Rheinhart Kleiner

Beautiful and calm and proud,
Only Ethel's soul seems bowed;
Throngs may pass her, kind or curt,
They can neither heal nor hurt;
There she sits with manner strange,   5
Taking checks and making change!

Eyes are dark, but something fled
Leaves them heavy as the dead;
Brow is white, but something there
Lingers like an old despair;   10
Lips are sweet, but coldly curled—
Oh, so weary of the world!

Ethel's always dressed in black;
Parting thus may leave its track.
Ethel's always wan and pale;   15
Pining is not known to fail.
Though a life or love you rue,
Ethel, how I pity you!

Pastorale

Hart Crane

No more violets,
and the year
broken into smoky panels.
What woods remember now
her calls, her enthusiasms.   5

That ritual of sap and leaves
the sun drew out,
ends in this latter muffled
bronze and brass. The wind
takes rein.   10

If, dusty, I bear
an image beyond this
already fallen harvest,

490

I can only query, "Fool—
have you remembered too long;   15

or was there too little said
for ease or resolution—
summer scarcely begun
and violets,
a few picked, the rest dead?"   20

Odes 3.9

Horace (Q. Horatius Flaccus)

    Donec gratus eram tibi
nec quisquam potior bracchia candidae
    Cervici iuvenis dabat,
Persarum vigui rege beatior.
    "donec non alia magis   5
arsisti neque erat Lydia post Chloen,
    multi Lydia nominis
Romana vigui clarior Ilia."
    me nunc Thraessa Chloe regit,
dulcis docta modos et citharae sciens,   10
    pro qua non metuam mori,
si parcent animae fata superstiti.
    "me torret face mutua
Thurini Calais filius Ornyti,
    pro quo bis patiar mori,   15
si parcent puero fata superstiti."
    quid si prisca redit Venus
diductosque iugo cogit aeneo,
    si flava excutitur Chloe
reiectaeque patet ianua Lydiae?   20
    "quamquam sidere pulchrior
ille est, tu levior cortice et improbo
    iracundior Hadria,
tecum vivere amem, tecum obeam libens."

[On John Donne]

Lee McBride White

Not sweet, this man: more he implacable:
Non-reconciled to sugar of Shakspere
Music of Mighty-lined Marlowe
Combined of rare component,
Supple, infrangible, prism-perception   5
Of a vast world and of himself in it.
Infra-ultra, this man metasensual;
Dimensioned by mind, soul, body
Bound by four walls of coffins.
All metal, verse of this man   10
Mercury of fluid love lyric
Silver of God-pointing hymn,
Rough ore of youthful satire.
Never sagged the arc of his flight:
The centrifugal force keeps taut   15
The thin cool wires of intellect.
Of bright sudden tangent-thought this man
Eccentric of good things:
Body of woman, mind of man, soul of God:
Long time before flash of his fire shall be dying   20
Yet molders the canon of his defying.

Irony

Wilson Shepherd

Far out o'er the dim horizon
In the depths of star-filled space
To a thousand foreign worlds
I went with a grin on my face.

And I returned o'er the dim horizon   5
From the depths of star-filled space.
My eyes were as grim as Fate itself—
And the grin was wiped from my face.

Mighty was the ovation they gave me
They wined me and dined me until dawn,   10
But none of them cared to ask me
What those far away planets had spawned.

Yes, none of them cared to ask me—
Of the thousand nightmare wrongs—
The terrible things—the horrible things   15
That I saw in the star-sprinkled dawns!

And none of them wanted to listen
When I tried to set them to right
Of the foolish scientific ideas
That eats on their brains like a blight.   20

I would have told them many things,
And disproved their theorys and laws, so bright!
And showed them how foolish they really were—
In the midst of this Cosmic Might.

But none of them cared to listen   25
And they began to look askant,
And I saw that perhaps I was crazy,
When I suggested that they try to think!

And now they have stuck me in a "home"
To recuperate—so they say   30
Well, let them go their inane ways,
And I will only say:—

That God helps those that help themselves,
And fools—well God made them so. . . .

NOTES

Abbreviations used in the notes:

AG	*Letters to Alfred Galpin* (Hippocampus Press, 2003)
AHT	Arkham House transcripts of HPL's letters
AMS	autograph manuscript
CB	*Commonplace Book*, ed. David E. Schultz (Necronomicon Press, 1987)
CE	*Collected Essays* (Hippocampus Press, 2004–06; 5 vols.)
CoC	*Crypt of Cthulhu*
CP	*Collected Poems* (Arkham House, 1963)
D	*Dagon and Other Macabre Tales* (Arkham House, 1986)
DH	*The Dunwich Horror and Others* (Arkham House, 1984)
DPC	"Department of Public Criticism" (*United Amateur*)
ES	*Essential Solitude: The Letters of H. P. Lovecraft and August Derleth* (Hippocampus Press, 2008)
FDOC	*H. P. Lovecraft: Four Decades of Criticism*, ed. S. T. Joshi (Ohio University Press, 1980)
FP	first publication
HM	*The Horror in the Museum and Other Revisions* (Arkham House, 1989)
IAP	S. T. Joshi, *I Am Providence: The Life and Times of H. P. Lovecraft* (Hippocampus Press, 2010)
J	*Juvenilia: 1897–1905* (Necronomicon Press, 1984)
JFM	*Letters to James F. Morton* (Hippocampus Press, 2011)
JHL	John Hay Library, Brown University (Providence, RI)
LL	S. T. Joshi, *Lovecraft's Library* (3rd rev. ed. Hippocampus Press, 2012)
LNY	*Letters from New York* (Night Shade, 2005)
LS	*Lovecraft Studies*
M	*Medusa and Other Poems* (Cryptic Publications, 1986)
MM	*At the Mountains of Madness and Other Novels* (Arkham House, 1985)
MTS	*Mysteries of Time and Spirit: The Letters of H. P. Lovecraft and Donald Wandrei* (Night Shade, 2002)
MW	*Miscellaneous Writings* (Arkham House, 1995)
NAPA	National Amateur Press Association
OFF	*O Fortunate Floridian: H. P. Lovecraft's Letters to R. H. Barlow* (University of Tampa Press, 2007)
RK	*Letters to Rheinhart Kleiner* (Hippocampus Press, 2005)
S	*Saturnalia and Other Poems* (Cryptic Publications, 1984)
SL	*Selected Letters* (Arkham House, 1965–76; 5 vols.)
TMS	typed manuscript
UAPA	United Amateur Press Association
WW	*A Winter Wish* (Whispers Press, 1977)

The Absent Leader: AMS, TMS (JHL), dated 12 October 1927; FP: *In Memoriam: Hazel Pratt Adams*, ed. anon. ([Brooklyn, NY?: Blue Pencil Club?], 1927), 11–12. Hazel Pratt Adams was one of the founders of the Blue Pencil Club (originally the Brooklyn Amateur Journalists Club). HPL met her on a few occasions during his New York stay of 1924–26.

Ad Balneum: Text derived from a letter to the Kleicomolo, October 1916 (AHT; *RK* 45–46). It is a satiric "ode" to a bathtub, meant to parody the "low" or inapposite subjects chosen by some modern poets of HPL's day. The references in ll. 11–13 are to Odysseus (rendered in Latin as Ulysses), hero of Homer's *Odyssey;* Horatio Nelson, 1st Viscount Nelson (1758–1805), commander of the British Royal Navy who defeated Napoleon at the Battle of Trafalgar (1805), during which he died; and Cn. Pompeius Magnus (106–48 B.C.E.; called "Pompey" in English), Roman military leader who waged a largely successful campaign against piracy in the Mediterranean in the 60s.

Ad Britannos—1918: FP: *Tryout* 4, No. 4 (April 1918): [3–6]; rpt. *National Enquirer* 6, No. 4 (25 April 1918): 10. In l. 11 HPL refers to Arminius (18? B.C.E.–21 C.E.), a Germanic chieftain who dealt a crushing defeat to the Roman army in the battle of the Teutoburgian Forest in 9 C.E., where three entire Roman legions were largely annihilated.

Ad Criticos: AMS (JHL); FP: *Argosy* 74, No. 2 (January 1914): 479–80 (Liber Primus; as "Lovecraft Comes Back: Ad Criticos"); 74, No. 3 (February 1914): 715–16 (Liber Secundus; as "Ad Criticos: Liber Secundus"); *M* (Liber Tertius and Liber Quartus). HPL's celebrated verse satires on the romance writer Fred Jackson and his defenders in the *Argosy* and *All-Story.* The title is Latin for "To [my] critics." Curiously, Liber Tertius and Liber Quartus were never published in the *Argosy,* even though the editor expressed his openness to publishing HPL's comments. Liber Quartus is largely a response to a very cutting verse letter by Russell in the May 1914 issue. The entire controversy has been reprinted in *H. P. Lovecraft in the Argosy* (Necronomicon Press, 1994).

In Liber Primus, l. 11, the *Argosy* printed "shew" as "show," on the mistaken assumption that the former was pronounced "shoo." HPL wrote a prose letter about this error, published as "Correction for Lovecraft," *Argosy* 74, No. 4 (March 1914): 956. "Russell" (l. 7) is John Russell, the Scotsman from Tampa, Florida, who began the practice of writing verse letters, beginning in the November 1913 issue. "Crean" (l. 20) is T. P. Crean of Syracuse, NY, who stated in the November 1913 issue that "I am personally of the opinion that the letter [by HPL] was merely to display to THE ARGOSY world his vocabulary; or he may be a less successful author." "Fonetik Bennett" (l. 32) is F. V. Bennett of Hanover, IL, who in the November 1913 issue wrote an illiterate letter containing such spellings as "jiant" and "sutch." (Bennett had actually initiated the controversy by writing a letter in the July 1913 issue criticising Jackson.)

In Liber Secundus, "Saunders" (l. 7) is F. W. Saunders of Coalgate, OK, who in the December 1913 issue wrote a long letter titled "Bomb for Lovecraft." In it, he criticised HPL for fashioning (in his prose letter published in the September 1913 issue) such words as "Jacksonian," "Jacksonine," and "Hanoverian"; the last, he claimed, was not in his dictionary ("in looking for 'Hanoverian' I find a skip from 'hanker' to 'hansom'"). Saunders concluded: "However, I am a kangaroo when it comes to jumping, so I made the leap in perfect safety." "Laconic Bonner" (l. 21) is G. E. Bonner of Springfield, OH, who wrote: "I read Mr. Lovecraft's condemnation of Fred Jackson's stories, so I thought I would write another Josh Billings-gate classic." "Madam Loop" (l. 25) is Elizabeth E. Loop of Elmira, NY, who stated: "If he would use a few less adjectives and more words which the general public are more familiar with than labyrinthine, laureled, luminary, lucubrations, and many others." "Mistress Blankenship" (l. 36) is Miss E. E. Blankenship of Richmond, VA, who wrote of HPL: "Your words 'erratic fiction' I fail to acknowledge. Instead I find pages filled with innocence, sweetness, loveliness, and fascination."

In Liber Tertius, "Butler" (l. 5) refers to Samuel Butler (1612–1680), author of the satirical poem *Hudibras* (1663–78), in which a pompous and ignorant character named Sir Hudibras is featured. In l. 14, the references are to Charles Dickens (1812–1870), whose early works were published under the pseudonym "Boz"; James Fenimore Cooper (1789–1851); William Shakespeare (1564–1616), whose hometown, Stratford-upon-Avon, is on the banks of the Avon river; and Sir Walter Scott (1771–1832). (Russell had referred to these writers in a verse letter published in the April 1914 issue.) "Saunders" (l. 20) is F. W. Saunders, who wrote a verse letter entitled "Ruat Caelum" [may the heavens shake] in the April 1914 issue. "Isenhour" (l. 32) is D. W. Isenhour, who wrote a letter supporting HPL in the January 1914 issue. "Rahs" (l. 36) is E. P. Rahs of Berkely, CA, who objected to the "unmerciful and unnecessary 'criticism' of Fred Jackson" (April 1914). "Forrest" (l. 41) is Ira B. Forrest of Messick, VA, who claimed that HPL was "a grouchy old bachelor and dislikes sentiment in any form" (April 1914).

In Liber Quartus, l. 1 refers to a verse letter by John Russell in the May 1914 issue making fun of HPL's letter "Correction for Lovecraft." "Cummings" (l. 9) is J. C. Cummings of Chicago, who wrote a combined prose-verse letter in the May 1914 issue who made a pun on HPL's name ("I think, indeed, he has no sense / When he has no *love* for Jackson, / For, unlike the bard of Providence, / His *craft* brings satisfaction"). "Forster" (l. 16) is Richard Forster of Rothwell, WY, who also wrote a prose-verse letter in the May 1914 issue.

Ad Scribam: FP: *Tryout* 6, No. 2 (February 1920): [9–10]; rpt. *The Poetical Works of Jonathan E. Hoag*, ed. H. P Lovecraft (New York: [Privately printed,] 1923), 64–65. "Scriba" (Latin for "scribe" or, more generally, "writer") was Hoag's nickname, derived from a signature that Hoag used when he sent letters to newspapers. "Dionondawa" (l. 30) refers to Dionondawa (more properly Dionondehowa) Falls, a waterfall near Hoag's home in Greenwich, NY. For "Sardathrion" (l. 37), see note on "[Christmas Greetings]" (no. 77).

Alfredo; a Tragedy: AMS (JHL), dated 14 September 1918; FP: *The Dark Brotherhood and Other Pieces* (1966). The only verse play HPL is known to have written. Beaumont and Fletcher are, of course, the celebrated and prolific Elizabethan dramatists Francis Beaumont (1584–1616) and John Fletcher (1579–1625), who collaborated on many plays. The play's characters are all derived from HPL's amateur associates: "Rinarto" (Rheinhart Kleiner); "Alfredo" (Alfred Galpin); "Teobaldo" (HPL); "Mauricio" (Maurice W. Moe); "Margarita" (perhaps Margaret Abraham). Like the "Damon and Delia" poems, the play deals with Galpin's high-school love affairs. Rinarto is King and Alfredo the Prince Regent because Kleiner was President and Galpin First Vice-President of the UAPA at the date of writing. "Cordova's volumes" (l. 25) refers to the fact that, during the mediaeval era, the city of Cordoba, in south-central Spain, had one of the greatest libraries in the world. "The Abderan" (l. 97) refers to Democritus (460?–370 B.C.E.), the Greek Presocratic philosopher (cofounder, with Leucippus, of the atomic theory) who was born in Abdera, in Thrace. In l. 158, "An" is an archaic term meaning "if."

Ambition: FP: *United Co-operative* 1, No. 1 (December 1918): 5 (as by "Ward Phillips"). In DPC (January 1919) HPL makes mention of "Ward Phillips, whose heavy lines on 'Ambition' reveal his usual attitude concerning the insignificance of man and the futility of things in general" (*CE* 1.221).

An American to Mother England: TMS (included in a letter to John T. Dunn, 10 June 1916 [JHL]); FP: *Poesy* 1, No. 7 (January 1916): 62; rpt. *Dowdell's Bearcat* No. 16 (November 1916): [12–14]. The poem is mentioned as having appeared "last January" in a letter to Arthur Harris dated 1 July 1915, but the letter is clearly misdated and was written on 1 July 1916.

An American to the British Flag: FP: *Little Budget of Knowledge and Nonsense* 1, No. 9 (November 1917): 110.

Amissa Minerva: FP: *Toledo Amateur* (May 1919): 11–14; rpt. *National Enquirer* 8, No. 5 (1 May 1919): 3. A remarkably compact survey of English poetry and a condemnation of what HPL felt to be the freakish innovations of his contemporaries. The citation from Horace's *Ars Poetica* is from ll. 1–5: "Suppose a painter should at fancy's beck / Join to a human head a horse's neck, / And, bringing limbs of every beast together, / Stick on them plumes of parti-coloured feather, / So that a woman beautiful and nesh / Should tail off to a shocking ugly fish, / Could you, my friends, admitted to the sight, / Refrain from laughing at the thing outright?" (tr. Alexander Murison). For "Maro" (l. 6), see note on "The Bookstall." In l. 66, HPL refers to the practitioners of *vers libre*, or free verse (see his essay "The Vers Libre Epidemic" [1917]; *CE* 2.19–21);

498

Cubism, chiefly an artistic movement but associated with the literary work of Gertrude Stein and others; and Spectrism, a movement spawned by the book *Spectra: A Book of Poetic Experiments* (1916), edited by Witter Bynner and Arthur Davidson Ficke (the editors compiled the book as a joke, maintaining that the material in it was intended to reflect the kaleidoscopic fragmentation of thoughts and images in the brain, but Spectrism became an actual if short-lived literary movement). For "odes to bathtubs" (l. 60), see "Ad Balneum." "Lowell" (l. 63) refers to Amy Lowell (1874–1925), leader of the Imagist school of poetry, condemned by HPL in "The Vers Libre Epidemic." "Masters" (l. 64) refers to Edgar Lee Masters (1868–1950), author of *Spoon River Anthology* (1915). "Gould" (l. 65) presumably refers to John Gould Fletcher (1886–1950), American Imagist poet. "Sandburg" (l. 66) refers to Carl Sandburg (1878–1967), American poet who gained celebrity with his *Chicago Poems* (1916). For an exhaustive commentary on the poem see Steven J. Mariconda, "On Lovecraft's 'Amissa Minerva,'" *Etchings and Odysseys* No. 9 [1986]: 97–103; rpt. *H. P. Lovecraft: Art, Artifact, and Reality* (New York: Hippocampus Press, 2013).

The Ancient Track: AMS, TMS (JHL), dated 26 November 1929; FP: *Weird Tales* 15, No. 3 (March 1930): 300. The poem contains the only other mention of Dunwich (see l. 22) in HPL's corpus aside from "The Dunwich Horror" (1928). "Zaman's Hill" (l. 11) was later used in a sonnet of the title in *Fungi from Yuggoth*.

[Anthem of the Kappa Alpha Tau]: Text derived from a letter to E. Hoffmann Price, 7 August 1934 (AMS, JHL). The Kappa Alpha Tau was HPL's name (in imitation of a fraternity, since he lived on Brown University's fraternity row) for a group of cats who sunned themselves on the roof of a shed across the back garden from his residence at 66 College Street. In l. 4, HPL refers to Bast, a goddess in the shape of a cat worshipped an ancient Egypt, and Sekhmet, another Egyptian goddess with the face of a lion.

April: FP: [Providence] *Evening News* 50, No. 121 (24 April 1917): 6; rpt. *Tryout* 4, No. 3 (March 1918): [3–5]. Included in a letter to the Kleicomolo (April 1917 [AHT]; *RK* 85–86; as "Spring").

April Dawn: FP: *National Enquirer* 8, No. 2 (10 April 1919): 3; rpt. *Silver Clarion* 4, No. 1 (April 1920): 1.

Arcadia: AMS, TMS (JHL); FP: *WW*. See "Dead Passion's Flame." In ll. 4 and 11 HPL refers to well-known locales in Greenwich Village, New York City.

Astrophobos: FP: *United Amateur* 17, No. 3 (January 1918): 38 (as by "Ward Phillips"). Written in mid-November 1917, as HPL notes in a letter to Rheinhart Kleiner (17 November 1917; *RK* 121) that it had been written a day or two earlier. The title means "[One who is] afraid of stars." In DPC (May 1918) HPL, writing pseudonymously, comments: "'Astrophobos', by Ward Phillips, is another recipe poem; although his recipe is so much more intricate [than a poem previously mentioned] that it is not to be recommended for the Freshman. The critic would denominate a poem composed according to this recipe a ulalumish poem, as it has so many earmarks of Poe. True to type, it is ulaluminated with gorgeous reds and crimsons, vistas of stupendous distances, coined phrases, unusual words, and general thoughts of either mysticism or purposeless obscurity. Such a poem is a feast for epicures who delight in intellectual caviar, but it is not half so satisfying to the average poetic taste as Mr. Kleiner's 'Ruth'" (*CE* 1.196–97). For HPL's response to Kleiner's "Ruth," see "Grace" (1918).

August: FP: *Tryout* 4, No. 8 (August 1918): [3]; rpt. *National Enquirer* 6, No. 21 (22 August 1918): 10; *Californian* 5, No. 1 (Summer 1937): 25.

Autumn: FP: *Tryout* 3, No. 12 (November 1917): [3–5]; rpt. [Providence] *Evening News* 51, No. 125 (5 November 1917): 3; *National Enquirer* 9, No. 4 (23 October 1919): 7.

Ave atque Vale: TMS (JHL), dated 18 October 1927; FP: *Tryout* 11, No. 10 (December 1927): [3–4]. The title is Latin for "hail and farewell." For "Dionondawa" (l. 6) and "Scriba" (l. 15), see note on "Ad Scribam."

Ye Ballade of Patrick von Flynn: FP: *Conservative* 2, No. 1 (April 1916): 3–4 (as by "Lewis Theobald, Jun."). Written no later than 23 August 1915, for on that date HPL discusses the poem in a letter to Arthur Harris: "I am rather anxious for you to read my comic satirical verse entitled 'The Ballade of Patrick von Flynn.' This ridicules the miserable anti-English Irishmen residing in the States, who are just now violently espousing the German cause. . . . The character of Patrick von Flynn is drawn from life, and represents a certain Irish-American member of the United" (AMS, JHL; quoted in *Books at Brown* 38–39 [1991–92]: 181n7). The person referred to is apparently John T. Dunn, a member of the Providence Amateur Press Club. The epigraph is HPL's Latin coinage ("more German than the Germans themselves"). Oddly, the poem was written months before, but published just at the time of, the Easter Rebellion of April 1916, when a plot by Irish radicals collaborating with the Germans to overthrow British rule in Ireland was discovered in Dublin and ruthlessly suppressed. In DPC (September 1916) HPL comments: "'Ye Ballade of Patrick von Flynn' is a comic delineation of the cheap pseudo-Irish, England-hating agitators who have been so offensively noisy on this side of the Atlantic ever since the European war began, and particularly since the late riots in Dublin" (*CE* 1.130). "shebeens" (l. 8) are unauthorised pubs or bars where alcoholic beverages are served without a licence. In l. 42, HPL refers to "Die Wacht am Rhein" (1854), a German patriotic hymn, and "The Wearing of the Green" (1798), an Irish street ballad.

The Bay-Stater's Policy: FP: *Bay-Stater* 4, No. 3 (June 1915): [3]. A poem about the amateur journal, the *Bay-Stater*, edited by George A. Thomson of West Medford, MA.

The Beauties of Peace: TMS (included in a letter to John T. Dunn, 28 June 1916 [JHL]); FP: [Providence] *Evening News* 49, No. 123 (27 June 1916): 6. The epigraph is HPL's Latin coinage ("I prefer the most unjust peace to the most just war"). For Thomas's poem see Appendix 2. "Villa" (l. 15) and "Carranza" (l. 16) refer to Pancho Villa (1878–1923) and Venustiano Carranza (1859–1920), leading participants in the Mexican Civil War. In late 1915, the United States had recognised Carranza as president of Mexico. Villa, enraged, killed several Americans in Mexico in early 1916 and invaded New Mexico and Texas in March and May; in response, President Wilson sent 10,000 troops commanded by General John Pershing to capture Villa. "Obregon" (l. 40) is Álvaro Obregón Salido (1880–1928), Carranza's minister of war (1915–17) and later president of Mexico (1920–24). He had lost his arm in a battle with Villa in 1915. In l. 58, HPL refers to Henry Ford (1863–1947) and William Jennings Bryan (1860–1925), who both opposed US entry into World War I. Bryan had been secretary of state in 1913–15.

Bells: FP: *Tryout* 5, No. 12 (December 1919): [9–10] (as by "Ward Phillips"). One manuscript (AHT) dates the poem to 11 December 1919. (The *Tryout* often appeared later than its issue date.) Cf. HPL's later poem "The Bells" (in *Fungi from Yuggoth*). Neither of the poems seems to bear much resemblance to Poe's remarkable exercise in onomatopoeia, "The Bells" (1848).

Birthday Lines to Margfred Galbraham: AMS (JHL), written on an envelope postmarked 3 November 1919; FP: *S*. Another poem on the joint birthday of Alfred Galpin and Margaret Abraham; see "To the Eighth of November."

The Bookstall: FP: *United Official Quarterly* 2, No. 2 (January 1916): [9–11]. The poem alludes to several of the choicest books in HPL's own library, including, in l. 23, Robert Wittie's *Ouranoskopia* (1681; *LL* #967); in l. 25, Cotton Mather's *Magnalia Christi Americana* (1702; *LL* #598); and, in l. 50, Samuel Garth's *The Dispensary* (1699; *LL* #343). Other books and authors referred to include: in l. 24, Samuel Johnson (1709–1784), noted man of letters who, in 1762, was part of a commission to investigate claims that a ghost was haunting a house in Cock Lane, London (the commission concluded that the ghost was a fraud); in l. 26, John Hawkesworth (1715?–1773), British author who edited the travel accounts of Captain James Cook; in l. 29, the celebrated Latin author P. Vergilius Maro (70–19 B.C.E.), or Virgil, author of the *Aeneid* who was born near Mantua (l. 33); in l. 45, Latin author M. Annaeus Lucanus (39–65 C.E.), or Lucan, author of the *Pharsalia* or *Civil War* (it was translated into English in 1718 by Nicholas Rowe [l. 46]); in l. 48, Sir Charles Abraham Elton (1778–1853), British translator; in l. 52, James Knapton (d. 1738), British publisher; in l. 57, Philip Dormer Stanhope, 4th Earl of Chesterfield (1694–1773), British statesman and man of letters; and, in l. 59, John Wilmot, 2nd Earl of Rochester (1647–1680), British poet. In DPC (April 1916) HPL refers to the poem as a "metrical monstrosity" (*CE* 1.108).

Bouts Rimés: TMS (JHL), dated 23 May 1934. The poems were written in collaboration with R. H. Barlow, who devised the end-rhymes; HPL then wrote the rest of the lines to fit. The title literally means "end-rhymes." For Zimbabwe see "The Outpost" (1929).

Britannia Victura: FP: *Inspiration,* Tribute number (April 1917): 3–4; rpt. *Little Budget of Knowledge and Nonsense* 1, No. 2 (May 1917): 27–28; *National Enquirer* 6, No. 8 (23 May 1918): 10. The title translates to "Britain About to Be Victorious." In a letter to Arthur Harris (29 April 1917; ms., JHL), HPL indicates that the poem was written in January 1917.

Brotherhood: TMS (JHL); FP: *Tryout* 3, No. 1 (December 1916): [7] (as by "Lewis Theobald, Jun."); rpt. *National Magazine* 45, No. 3 (December 1916): 415.

Brumalia: FP: *Tryout* 3, No. 1 (December 1916): [1]; rpt. [Providence] *Evening News* 51, No. 152 (7 December 1917): Sec. 2, p. 2. In the *Tryout* (p. [22]) HPL has added a note entitled "Brumalia":

Brumalia commemorates the prehistoric winter festival held by all primitive races to celebrate the northward turning of the sun at the Winter Solstice. On December 21st the days are at their shortest, and the weather is drawing toward its coldest; but the act of the sun in commencing its return to the north is a prophecy of Spring, to be hailed with rejoicing, and typified by evergreen wreaths symbolic of the survival of Nature. The Yule Log, with its blazing glow, is representative of warmth presaged by the return of the sun to its northward track.

This type of festival was amongst the early Latin <races> called "Brumalia", from the word "bruma", which signifies winter, or the winter solstice. In later days, when Rome became the seat of learning and government, Brumalia became the Saturnalia, or festival of Saturn, though it was some time before the primitive significance was really lost. Late in the Imperial age, after the adoption of Christianity, the 25th of December, heretofore the date of the Saturnalia, was selected as the proper time to observe Christmas: a festival previously held on Epiphany, or January 6th, since the day and month of Our Saviour's birth are unknown. Thus the immensely ancient Brumalia may be considered, in a sense, as the primitive pagan ancestor of our Christmas celebration.

C.S.A.: 1861–1865: Text derived from a letter to Rheinhart Kleiner (16 November 1916; *RK* 72), in which HPL dates the poem to 1902. He remarks that he impishly placed it on the desk of Abbie A. Hathaway (principal of the Slater Avenue School), whose father was a soldier on the Union (Federal) side in the Civil War. C.S.A., of course, stands for Confederate States of America. HPL, although a Yankee, exhibited lifelong support for the Confederate cause; cf. "De Triumpho Naturae."

The Cats: AMS (JHL), dated 15 February 1925; FP: *WW.* HPL curiously made no apparent attempt to publish this fine poem, even in the amateur press.

Chloris and Damon: TMS (JHL), dated "Jan. 1723" [i.e., 1923]; FP: *Tryout* 8, No. 8 (June 1923): [12–13] (as by "Edward Softly"). Another poem to Galpin.

Christmas: FP: *Tryout* 6, No. 11 (November 1920): [16] (as by "Edward Softly"). A variant, substituting "sing" for "shake" (l. 7), can be found written on the same page as "[Christmas Greetings]" nos. 14–18, under the heading "Christmas—1919" (see note on "[Christmas Greetings]").]

[Christmas Greetings]: AMS (JHL), with dates ranging from 1919 to 1926. HPL has usually scribbled the recipients (sometimes merely by initial) in the margins of the poems. Nos. 14–18 are found on a page labelled "Christmas—1919." No. 28 is dated 1920, so perhaps the others on this ms. page (Nos. 27–31) are of this date. Nos. 32–33 are dated 1921. Nos. 36–40 are on a page dated "Chr[istmas] 1921." Nos. 58–63 are on a page dated 1926. No. 7 ("A Brumalian Wish") is a parody of HPL's own "Nemesis." Nos. 41–42, 44–52, and 54 are also found in a letter to Lillian D. Clark, 22–23 December 1925 (AMS, JHL); Nos. 106–8 are found only there. No. 104 is also found on a postcard to Lillian D. Clark (postmarked 23 December 1925; AMS, JHL). No. 35 was published in *Tryout* 7, No. 9 (December 1921): [35]. It is not entirely clear whether Nos. 100 and 109 are Christmas poems; No. 100 was meant to accompany a gift of a volume of Walter Pater to Sonia H. Greene, while No. 109 greeted Alfred Galpin's return to Appleton, WI, possibly from a trip overseas.

No. 7 is a parody of HPL's own "Nemesis." "Weir" (l. 2) is derived from Poe's "Ulalume" (1847). "Galba" (l. 11)—the Roman emperor Servius Sulpicius Galba Augustus (r. 68–69)—was HPL's nickname for Alfred Galpin. The signature alludes to Edward John Moreton Drax Plunkett, 18th baron Dunsany and Ambrose Bierce. No. 10 and other poems to Albert A. Sandusky are written in the slang for which Sandusky was well known in amateurdom (see "The Feast"). In no. 13, "Eliot" (l. 6) refers to T. S. Eliot. In no. 21, Mary Faye Durr was the president of the UAPA in 1919–20, and the Official Printer was E. E. Ericson of Elroy, WI (see l. 4). In no. 23, HPL writes a poem to John Milton Samples, editor of the *Silver Clarion*, published in Macon, GA (see l. 4). In no. 24, for Tityrus (l. 1), see note on "To Delia, Avoiding Damon." In no. 26, for "Scriba" (l. 4), see note on "Ad Scribam."

In no. 41, "thy bright *Recluse*" (l. 6) refers to the *Recluse* (1927), a one-shot periodical that W. Paul Cook issued, containing HPL's "Supernatural Horror in Literature." In no. 42, HPL refers to James F. Morton's position as curator of the Paterson (NJ) Museum, which featured displays of minerals. For the references in no. 44, see note on "The Outpost." In no. 48, for "Moore" (l. 4), see note on "To George Willard Kirk . . ." In no. 50, HPL refers to *Tonty of the Iron Hand* (1925) by Everett McNeil (1862–1929), a member of the Kalem Club. The historical novel dealt with Samuel de Champlain (1567?–1635), one of the first colonisers of French Canada. In no. 52, "Goodguile" (l. 2) refers to Edith Miniter's parody of HPL's weird tales, "Falco Ossifracus: By Mr. Goodguile"

(*Muffin Man,* April 1921). In no. 54, HPL refers to "Lord" Timothy Dexter (1748–1806), author of an eccentric autobiographical work entitled *A Pickle for the Knowing Ones* (1798). The references in l. 3 are to the Charles River, which runs through Cambridge, MA (where Edgar J. Davis was attending college at Harvard) and the Merrimack River, which runs through Newburyport, MA, where Dexter lived and which HPL visited with Davis in 1923.

In no. 57, "Cliftondale" (l. 1) refers to a town in Massachusetts (now included in the town of Saugus); possibly Charles A. A. Parker was living there at the time. "Lark" (l. 2) refers to his amateur journal *L'Alouette* (French for "lark"). In no. 62, "Charlie [and] small Oscar" (l. 7) presumably refer to cats (see "In Memoriam: Oscar Incoul Verelst of Manhattan"). In no. 63, "Hell's Kitchen" (l. 2) refers to a rough neighbourhood on the West Side of Manhattan where Everett McNeil used to live. Around 1929 McNeil moved to Tacoma, WA. In no. 73, l. 3 refers to the fact that Sechrist was a beekeeper. In no. 74, l. 4 refers to Cook's amateur journal, the *Vagrant.* In no. 76, HPL alludes to the fact that Alice M. Hamlet introduced him to the work of Lord Dunsany. "Inzana" (l. 1) is a character in the story "A Legend of the Dawn"; "Sardathrion" (l. 4) is a city cited in "Time and the Gods" (both in *Time and the Gods,* 1906). In no. 79, HPL parodies William Blake's famous poem "The Tyger" (1794). In no. 80, "lark" (l. 1) again refers to Parker's amateur journal *L'Alouette.*

In no. 83, "Mexpet" (l. 3) refers to Mexican Petroleum. In no. 84, "Carbo" (Latin for "coal") is a pun on Edward H. Cole's name. In no. 86 there are more allusions to the work of Lord Dunsany: "Elf-King's runes" (l. 3), "Erl" (l. 4) [a place-name], and "Ziroonderel" (l. 6) [a witch] all allude to the novel *The King of Elfland's Daughter* (1924). In no. 90, "Elia" (l. 5) refers to the British essayist Charles Lamb (1775–1834), author of *Essays of Elia* (1823). In No. 91, ll. 3–4 refer to Morton's fascination with crossword puzzles. In no. 92, ll. 5–6 allude to McNeil's historical novel *Daniel Du Luth; or, Adventuring on the Great Lakes* (1926). No. 98, if it is indeed addressed to Donald Wandrei, may refer to his hitchhiking from St. Paul, MN, to Providence and back in 1927. In no. 109, "A. H. S." (l. 13) refers to Appleton High School (Appleton, WI), where Galpin went to school.

Cindy: Scrub-Lady in a State Street Skyscraper: FP: *Tryout* 6, No. 6 (June 1920): [19–20] (as by "L. Theobald, Jun."). The poem was written in response to Rheinhart Kleiner's "Ethel: Cashier in a Broad Street Buffet," published just prior to HPL's in the same issue of the *Tryout* (p. [19]). (For the text, see Appendix 2.) State Street is presumably the street in Boston. If the poems relate actual incidents or refer to actual individuals, HPL and Kleiner may have derived the inspiration for their works on their trip to Boston in October 1919, when HPL heard Lord Dunsany lecture.

The City: FP: *Vagrant* No. 10 (October 1919): 6–7 (as by "Ward Phillips"); rpt. *Weird Tales* 42, No. 5 (July 1950): 48–49. See Dirk W. Mosig, "Poet of the

Unconscious," *Platte Valley Review* 6, No. 1 (April 1978): 60–66; rpt. *CoC* No. 20 (Eastertide 1984): 22–24 (as "Poet of the Unknown").

The Conscript: AMS (JHL); FP: *WW*. Presumably dates to 1918. A strange poem for HPL to have written, unless it is somehow meant parodically. Its message seems antipodal to that found in "The Volunteer."

Content: FP: *United Amateur* 15, No. 11 (June 1916): 150. The epigraph from Horace is from *Epodes* 2.1–3: "Happy the man who, far away from business cares, like the pristine race of mortals, works his ancestral acres with his steers" (tr. C. E. Bennett). Morven (l. 18) is a mythical kingdom cited in Ossian's poem *Fingal* (1762). Ll. 65–66 are copied from HPL's juvenile poem "On the Vanity of Human Ambition." The final couplet is an adaptation of the last two lines of that poem. Kleiner's "Another Endless Day" appeared in HPL's own *Conservative* (April 1916).

The Crime of Crimes: FP: *Interesting Items* No. 459 (July 1915): 8–10; rpt. Llandudno, Wales: A[rthur] Harris, [1915]. The pamphlet is the first separate appearance of a work by HPL. The epigraph ("Courage flourishes from injury") is from the obscure Latin poet A. Furius Antias (fl. 100 B.C.E.) as cited in Aulus Gellius' *Noctes Atticae* 18.11. The *Lusitania*, a British passenger ship, was sunk by a German submarine on 7 May 1915 about 100 miles off the coast of Ireland (see l. 18). Among the 1200 killed were 128 Americans, but the incident still did not persuade either the American people or the government to enter the war on the side of the Allies, as HPL would have wished. In a letter to Arthur Harris (20 June 1915; ms., JHL), HPL elucidates the genesis of the poem: "Your letter was in a way an inspiration. I had wished to express in verse my horror at the Lusitania murders, yet had viewed the subject with so much awe that I scarce dared attempt to treat of it. But the sight of my printed piece [i.e., "1914"], and the suggestion in your letter, gave me the necessary impetus, and the enclosed lines, entitled 'The Crime of Crimes' were written by me last evening within the space of two hours."

A Cycle of Verse: FP: *National Enquirer* 7, No. 25 (20 March 1919): 3 ("Oceanus" and "Clouds"); 7, No. 26 (27 March 1919): 3 ("Mother Earth"); rpt. as "A Cycle of Verse" in *Tryout* 5, No. 7 (July 1919): [19–22] (as by "Ward Phillips"). The poems have subsequently appeared separately on many occasions. "Oceanus" and "Clouds" appear in a letter to Rheinhart Klemer, 25 November 1918 (*RK* 150); "Mother Earth" appears in a letter to Kleiner, 4 December 1918 (*RK* 150–51).

Damon: A Monody: FP: *United Amateur* 18, No. 5 (May 1919): 106 (as by "Theobaldus Senectissimus, Esq."). On Galpin's love affairs. "Mocrates" (l. 15) is HPL's affectionate name for Maurice W. Moe.

Damon and Delia, a Pastoral: FP: *Tryout* 4, No. 8 (August 1918): [23–26] (as by "Edward Softly"). Another poem on Galpin's love affairs. "Consul Hasting" is Galpin's pseudonym. It is possible that "Delia" is Margaret Abraham, a girl exactly one year younger than Galpin; both were in the Appleton High School Press Club. See also *Alfredo* (1918).

Damon and Lycë: AMS (JHL), dated 13 December 1723 [i.e., 1923], as by "L. Theobald Jun."; FP: *S.* Another poem to Galpin. Lyce is a woman cited in Horace's *Odes* 4.13.1. The name Nea (l. 58) does not appear in any Latin or Greek text. Glaber (l. 70) is a young slave cited in Catullus 61.142. The word *glaber* means "bald" in Latin. "Sapphic death" (l. 106) refers to the legend that Sappho killed herself by jumping off the Leucadian cliffs out of love for a ferryman named Phaon.

De Scriptore Mulieroso: AMS (JHL); FP: *H. P. Lovecraft in the Argosy* (1994). The title is Latin for "On an effeminate writer." The poem is in response to the verse letter by John Russell in the *Argosy* (June 1914) claiming that HPL's distaste for love stories is a product of his own disappointment in a love affair.

De Triumpho Naturae: AMS (JHL), dated July 1905; FP: *J.* William Benjamin Smith's *The Color Line: A Brief in Behalf of the Unborn* (New York: McClure, Phillips & Co., 1905) is a viciously racist work by a Southerner distressed by the political and social emergence of African Americans. Extracts are quoted in S. T. Joshi's *H. P. Lovecraft: The Decline of the West* (Mercer Island, WA: Starmont House, 1990), 75–78. The argument of the book (and hence the poem, although it is not clear in the latter) is that blacks, now that they are freed, will descend into "vice" and disease and thereby die off, whereas they could have remained contented under slavery.

The Dead Bookworm: TMS (JHL), signed "Lewis Theobald, Junr."; FP: *United Amateur* 19, No. 1 (September 1919): 1 (as by "John J. Jones"). The poem was included in a letter to Maurice W. Moe (29 August 1916; AHT). An exquisite self-parody; see also "On the Death of a Rhyming Critic" (1917).

Dead Passion's Flame: AMS, TMS (JHL); FP: *WW.* This and the two following poems may have been written jointly with R. H. Barlow, apparently in the summer of 1935; in the TMS (prepared by Barlow) they form part of a purported magazine (presumably a parody of the amateur journal *Hodge Podge*) entitled *Tosh Bosh: An Hourly Devoted to the Mutual Puffing of the Tosh Bosh Clique*, Vol. 365, No. 5280 (no date). There are a few prose pieces on the AMS and TMS as well.

The Decline and Fall of a Man of the World: AMS (JHL). The handwriting dates the poem to c. 1919. For HPL and temperance see "[On Prohibition]." "Damon" is presumably not a reference to Alfred Galpin. In l. 4 HPL provides the chemical formula for ethyl alcohol; in l. 9, the chemical formula for nicotine; in ll. 13–14, the chemical formula for morphine. In l. 16 HPL refers to British author Thomas De Quincey (1785–1859), celebrated for his use of opium.

"KCN solution" (l. 20) is potassium cyanide. L. 21, in the form of an epitaph, is Latin for: "Here lies unhappy Damon."

Despair: TMS (JHL); FP: *Pine Cones* 1, No. 4 (June 1919): 13 (as by "Ward Phillips"). HPL notes (*SL* 1.79 [19 Feb. 1919]) that the poem was written in response to the illness of his mother (by March Mrs. Lovecraft would enter Butler Hospital, dying two years later). Although the poem is clearly heartfelt, it appears to owe much of its imagery and language to Poe's late poem "For Annie" (1849).

Dirge of the Doomed: FP: Wilfred B. Talman, "The Normal Lovecraft," *The Normal Lovecraft* (Saddle River, NJ: Gerry de la Ree, 1973), 9. Apparently enclosed in an unspecified letter to Talman. It recounts the destruction of Talman's former residence at 256 Benefit Street to make way for the new courthouse (built 1928–33); hence it probably dates to 1927–28. The epigraph ("Dulce et decorum . . .": "It is sweet and honorable to die for [one's] church") is a parody of Horace's celebrated line *Dulce et decorum est pro patria mori* (*Odes* 3.2.13): "It is sweet and honorable to die for one's country." "Jacques" (l. 28) refers to a restaurant in a working-class area in Providence that HPL, Talman, and others liked to frequent. It closed in 1935 (see *JFM* 368).

The Dream: FP: *Tryout* 6, No. 9 (September 1920): [15–16] (as by "Edward Softly"). Another poem on Galpin.

Earth and Sky: FP: *Little Budget of Knowledge and Nonsense* 1, No. 4 (July 1917): 43; rpt. *Pine Cones* 1, No. 1 (December 1918): 1. The poem testifies to the philosophical ramifications of HPL's study of astronomy; see further *SL* 1.301–2. In DPC (January 1919) HPL comments that the poem is "a piece of verse in *ottava rima* . . . In metre and general form this production seems tolerable, though its intellectual rather than emotional appeal would in the opinion of many critics debar it from classification as poetry" (*CE* 1.217).

The East India Brick Row: FP: *Providence Journal* 102, No. 7 (8 January 1930): 13. The poem was written in early to mid-December 1929 (the date of 7 December given in *CP* is unverified) in a vain attempt to save some early 19th-century warehouses on South Water Street in Providence from destruction. HPL notes that it received such a favourable response from readers in the newspaper that the editor wrote HPL a cordial letter (HPL to August Derleth, [mid-January 1930]; *ES* 1.244).

Edith Miniter: AMS, TMS (JHL), dated 10 September 1934; FP: *Tryout* 16, No. 8 (August 1934): [5–6]. The TMS has a blank where the day of Miniter's birth should be; the *Tryout* appearance (the issue was clearly much delayed) supplies "May 5"; the AMS supplies the correct date. Miniter was one of HPL's closest amateur colleagues; see the memoir "Mrs. Miniter—Estimates and Recollections" (1934; *CE* 1.378–86). After her death HPL spent considerable effort gathering material for a memorial volume on Miniter to be published by W. Paul Cook, but the project never materialised.

The Eidolon: FP: *Tryout* 4, No. 10 (October 1918): [3–6] (as by "Ward Phillips"). This poem, as well as "The Nightmare Lake" and several others, utilises the iambic trimeter metre found in many of Poe's horrific poems. In "Dream-Land" (1844) the expression "an Eidolon, named Night" is found (l. 3). "Aidenn" (l. 77) is a variant spelling of "Eden" used frequently by Poe (e.g., "The Raven," l. 93).

Εἰς Σφίγγην: Text derived from a facsimile of the AMS printed on p. [14] of *An Epistle to . . . Maurice Winter Moe, Esq.* The title translates to "To the Sphinx." Under the poem is written: "House of Theobaldus / 10 Barnes St., / PROVIDENCE, / RHODE-ISLAND / 1926." The context establishes that it was written around Christmas 1926, commemorating HPL's return (in April 1926) to Providence from New York.

An Elegy on Franklin Chase Clark, M.D.: FP: [Providence] *Evening News* 46, No. 137 (29 April 1915): 6. Clark (1847–1915), the husband of HPL's aunt Lillian, was a significant influence on HPL's intellectual maturation. He is the source of the character Elihu Whipple in "The Shunned House" (1924).

An Elegy on Phillips Gamwell, Esq.: FP: *Cambridge Chronicle*, 6 January 1917, p.5; [Providence] *Evening News* 50, No. 129 (5 January 1917): 8; rpt. *Cambridge Tribune*, 13 January 1917, p.5. Phillips Gamwell, the son of HPL's aunt Annie E. Phillips Gamwell, was the only close family member of HPL's own generation. In the printed text l. 49 was dropped, but HPL has supplied it in a clipping (JHL).

The End of the Jackson War: FP: *Argosy* 77, No. 3 (October 1914): 718. Written at the request of T. N. Metcalf, an editor at the *Argosy*, who wished the letter/poetry controversy regarding Fred Jackson to end. The poem was published under the collective heading "The Critics' Farewell"; John Russell's poem "Our Apology to E. M. W." (see Appendix 2) followed HPL's. L. Sprague de Camp believed the latter to be HPL's, but surely "The End of the Jackson War," written in HPL's usual heroic couplets, is more typical of his work than the iambic trimeter of "Our Apology . . .," a metre used frequently by Russell. The two poems are jointly signed by HPL and Russell at the bottom, so that it is not immediately clear which poem was written by whom. HPL definitively notes his authorship of "The End of the Jackson War" in a letter to Rheinhart Kleiner (16 November 1916; *RK* 77), where the poem is quoted in its entirety.

[Epigrams]: AMS (JHL); FP: *S*. The various poems appear to deal with various amateur writers; they date perhaps to around 1920. In "On a Poem for Children, Writ by J. M. W.," "Widdows" is J. Morris Widdows, to whom HPL refers in DPC (May 1917) as a "Hoosier exponent of rural simplicity. Mr. Widdows has enjoyed considerable success in the professional world as a poet, song-writer, and musical composer; hence it is no untried or faltering quill which he brings within our midst" (*CE* 1.154–55). In "On ——'s Gaining in Weight," Mrs. M—— is the diminutive Verna McGeoch (pronounced Ma-GOO), while Mrs. H——n is the bulky Ida C. Haughton (see "Medusa: A Portrait"). In "On a Pathetick Poem, by J. M. W.," "Tears, idle Tears" (l. 1) is a quotation from the first line of a poem by that title (1847) by Alfred, Lord Tennyson. In "Idle Lines on a Poetick Dunce," "Selle" (l. 5) is the Rev. Robert L. Selle; "Bush" (l. 5) is HPL's pestiferous revision client David Van Bush.

An Epistle to . . . Maurice Winter Moe . . .: TMS (private collection); FP: *An Epistle to the Rt. Honble Maurice Winter Moe, Esq.*, ed. R. Alain Everts (Madison, WI: Strange Co., [1987]). HPL notes in a letter to James F. Morton (30 July 1929): "By the way—some recent heroicks of mine, on the departed glories of 1904, are about to be seen by every member of the U. of Wis. class of '04! How come? This way. Moe told me he was going to prepare a festive booklet to give each member of the class—commemorating the twenty-fifth anniversary—and the idea of '04 memories mov'd me to write him a reminiscent letter about old days and ways. It happened to be composed entirely in heroicks, and Moe liked it—so he took all the impersonal couplets and put 'em in his booklet!" (*JFM* 175). This booklet, if it actually appeared, has not been located. The poem begins as a rumination on 1904, then becomes a verse response to Moe's previous letter to HPL. "Zythopolis" is HPL's Greek coinage (meaning "beer-city," from the Greek *zythos,* an Egyptian beer brewed from barley) for Milwaukee, where Moe resided.

"Teter" (l. 1) refers to George E. Teter, *An Introduction to Some Elements of Poetry* (Wautatosa, WI: Kenyon Press, 1927; *LL* #868). It is possible that Moe or HPL had something to do with the preparation of this 46-page booklet. "Doorways" (l. 10) refers to *Doorways to Poetry,* a book of poetic appreciation that Moe was working on, with HPL's help; it appears to have been under consideration by the publishers Macmillan (l. 17) and Henry Holt (l. 18). Kenyon Press (l. 20), based in Wauwatosa, WI (l. 22), was apparently a press with which Moe was involved. "Tark" (l. 29) may be an allusion to American novelist Booth Tarkington (1869–1946). In l. 41–45 HPL refers to the amateur journalists Joseph Bernard Lynch, Ida C. Haughton, Leo Fritter, James J. Hennessey (not Hennessy), John H. Hasemann, Harry M. Lehmkuhl, James Laurence Crowley, Wilson H. Porter, Anthony F. Moitoret, and William J. Dowdell. "David V." (l. 42) refers to HPL's pestiferous revision client David Van Bush. In l. 45 HPL refers to the amateur journalist groups the Woodbees (see "Medusa: A Portrait") and those in the town of Warren, OH. "Our Jake" (l. 46) is possibly an allusion to the restaurant Jacques' (see note on "Dirge of the Doomed").

In l. 72 HPL refers to Theodore Roosevelt's battles against the "trusts" (monopolies), leading to the breakup of the Standard Oil Company and other antitrust measures. "Bedelia" (l. 77) is the title of a popular 1903 song written by Billy Jerome and Jean Schwartz. HPL supplies the lyrics at *SL* 4.365. In l. 79

HPL refers to the World's Fair (Louisiana Purchase Exposition) in St. Louis in 1904. "Edwardus Rex" (l. 81) refers to King Edward VII (r. 1901–1910) of England. In l. 82 HPL apparently refers to the song "Hiawatha" (1903), by Neil Moret and James O'Dea. The graphophone was an improved version of the phonograph manufactured by the Volta Company. In l. 84 HPL refers to H. L. Mencken (1880–1956), Joseph Wood Krutch (1893–1970), and Albert Einstein (1879–1955), none of whom were famous in 1904 (Einstein's theory of relativity was first propounded in a paper published in 1905). In ll. 85–86 HPL refers to the magazines *Harper's Monthly* and *McClure's*. In ll. 87–89 he refers to the literary figures Richard Watson Gilder (1844–1909), poet and longtime editor of the *Century Magazine;* William Winter (1836–1917), drama critic; Henry Van Dyke (1852–1933), clergyman and author; and Thomas Bailey Aldrich (1836–1907), poet and novelist. In l. 92 HPL refers to *The Simple Life* (1904), a translation of a French inspirational work (*La Vie Simple,* 1905) by Charles Wagner (1852–1918).

In l. 95 HPL refers to John Alexander Dowie (1847–1907), a Scottish evangelist who had been preaching in the United States since 1888; Lyman Abbott (1835–1922), American Congregationalist theologian; and Charles Henry Parkhurst (1842–1933), American clergyman and reformer. In l. 97 HPL refers to William Jennings Bryan (1860–1925), the Democratic candidate for president in 1896, 1900, and 1908; and Mark Hanna (1837–1904), U.S. senator from Ohio (1897–1904) and chairman of the Republican National Committee. In l. 98 HPL refers to Elbert Hubbard (1856–1915), American author and publisher who was considered something of a dandy. In l. 99 HPL refers to the boxers James J. Corbett (1866–1933), Bob Fitzsimmons (1863–1917), Tom Sharkey (1873–1953), and James J. Jeffries (1875–1953). In l. 100 HPL refers to Peter F. Dailey (1868–1923), American burlesque performer and comedian; Weber and Fields, the comedy duo of Joe Weber (1867–1942) and Lew Fields (1867–1941); and Fritzi Scheff (1879–1954), American actress and opera singer.

In l. 101 HPL refers to two comic strip characters created by Richard Felton Outcault, Buster Brown (1902f.) and the Yellow Kid (in *Hogan's Alley,* 1894f.). In ll. 103–4 HPL refers to the Battle of Port Arthur (8–9 February 1904), in which the Japanese army defeated the Russian army at Port Arthur, Manchuria, thereby initiating the Russo-Japanese War (1904–05); and to the birth of Nicholas II of Russia's first and only son, Alexei Nikolaevich (b. 12 August 1904). In ll. 105–6 HPL refers to two early aviators, the Brazilian Alberto Santos-Dumont (1873–1932) and the American Samuel Pierpont Langley (1834–1906). In ll. 107–10 HPL refers to the astronomers William H. Pickering (1858–1938) and Percival Lowell (see note on "Percival Lowell"). In l. 112 HPL refers to *Mrs. Wiggs from the Cabbage Patch* (1901), a sentimental novel by Alice Hegan Rice that was turned into a play in 1903. In l. 114 HPL refers to other popular novels: *The Prisoner of Zenda* (1894) by Anthony Hope; *Dorothy Vernon of Haddon Hall* (1902) by Charles Major (turned into a play in 1903); and *Richard Carvel* (1899) by the American novelist Winston Churchill (turned into a play in 1900).

In ll. 116–18 HPL refers to the song "You're the Flower of My Heart, Sweet Adeline" (1903) by Richard H. Gerard and Harry Armstrong; and two operas by Gustav Luders and Frank Pixley, *The Prince of Pilsen* (1902) (HPL's ms. erroneously reads "Pilen's") and *Woodland: A Forest Fantasy* (1904). In l. 138 HPL refers to the songs "Blue Bell" (1904) by Edward Madden, Dolly Morse, and Theodore F. Morse; "Creole Belles" (1904) by Bodewalt Lampe; and "Nancy Brown" (1902) by Marie Cahill. For the song "Won't You Come Home, Bill Bailey?" see note on "Waste Paper" (l. 17). The song alluded to in ll. 141–42 is "Karama: A Japanese Romance" (1904) by Vivian Grey. "Rems devoid of sound" (l. 175) refers to a Remington Noiseless typewriter, introduced around 1928. Victor E. Bacon (l. 188) was an amateur journalist and editor of *Bacon's Essays*. In l. 208 HPL refers to revision work for Adolphe de Castro (1859–1959), possibly "The Electric Executioner."

Epitaph on yᵉ Letterr Rrr........: Text derived from a letter to Maurice W. Moe (29 August 1916; AHT). The poem was written as part of a dispute with Moe regarding the propriety of dropping the letter *r* in such words as "far" or "father" (Moe had objected to HPL's rhyming "born" and "dawn" in a poem). The poem is signed "Lvdovicvs Theobaldvs Ivnior" (Latinisation of "Lewis Theobald, Junior").

Ex-Poet's Reply: FP: *Epgephi* (September 1920): 14 (as by "L. Theobald, Jr."). The poem commemorates a convention in Allston (a suburb of Boston) in early July 1920; HPL had stayed on July 4–5, but the convention went on for at least a day or two more. In l. 5, "St. Julian" is George Julian Houtain, "St. John" is Rheinhart Kleiner.

Fact and Fancy: FP: *Tryout* 3, No. 3 (February 1917): [7]; rpt. *National Magazine* 46, No. 11 (August 19171): 718. In l. 5, Zeno of Citium (334?–262? B.C.E.) was the founder of the Stoic school of philosophy.

The Feast: FP: *Hub Club Quill* 15, No. 2 (May 1923): [13–15]. The first epigraph ("O you whose stomachs are in distress, come running, and I will restore you") is an adaptation of the line *Venite ad me omnes qui stomacho laboratis, et ego vos restaurabo*, a parody of Mark 11:28, affixed on a sign in a Paris restaurant in 1765 (not 1774). The second epigraph is a celebrated phrase from Virgil's *Aeneid* (1.203) when Aeneas tells his compatriots after they have fled Troy and are on their way to found Rome: "Perhaps it will one day be pleasant to remember even these things." The poem commemorates a gathering of the Hub Club in Boston on March 10–11, in which HPL participated. Albert A. Sandusky was a longtime associate of HPL's who was much given to the use of slang. The pun in l. 16 is a nod to HPL's host, Edward H. Cole. In l. 20, "Gaster" and "Jocus" are Latin for "stomach" and "jest," respectively. "Priscian" (l. 25) is a personification of *priscus* ("ancient"). "Lynch" (l. 42) refers to Joseph Bernard Lynch. In l. 49, HPL refers to the celebrated Greek orator Demosthenes (384–322 B.C.E.), whose most famous oration was *On the Crown* (330 B.C.E.).

Festival: AMS (JHL); FP: *Weird Tales* 8, No. 6 (December 1926): 846 (without final stanza; as "Yule Horror"). The poem was designed as a Christmas greeting in 1925 for *Weird Tales* editor Farnsworth Wright, who liked it so much that he published it, omitting the last stanza and its reference to himself.

Fragment on Whitman: Text derived from "In a Major Key," *Conservative* 1, No. 2 (July 1915): 9–11, where it is mentioned as "written several years ago as part of an essay on the modern poets"; title supplied by HPL at *SL* 1.57. HPL cites it in his essay in attempted refutation of the remarks of Charles D. Isaacson in his amateur journal *In a Minor Key* in regard to the poetic greatness of Walt Whitman. HPL owned a volume of Whitman, but it dates to 1927 (*Selections from Whitman* [New York: Macmillan]; *LL* #952), so it is not clear how much of Whitman HPL had read. The poem probably dates to c. 1912. The reference to Ovid (l. 4) is to Ovid's poems *Ars Amatoria* (The Art of Love) and *Remedia Amoris* (The Remedy of Love), which frankly discuss sexual activity. Cf. HPL's letter to Helen Sully, 17 October 1933, criticising the dissipated "young modern": "He gets on finely with Ovid's *Ars Amatoria*, but doesn't understand what the tale of Baucis & Philemon in the same author's *Metamorphoses* is about" (*SL* 4.285).

Frustra Praemunitus: AMS (JHL); FP: *M*. The title is Latin for "Forearmed in vain." The poem is in response to a verse letter by John Russell in the *Argosy* (June 1914) expressing wonder at what HPL would think of Fred Jackson's newest story, "Winged Feet" (*Argosy*, February 1914). "Calamity" (l. 22) refers to Russell's lines: "For sure he's bound to make a fuss / And give us liber tertius. / If this calamity befall us / We'll swallow it 'cum grano salis.'"

Fungi from Yuggoth: AMS, TMS (JHL), dated 27 December 1929–4 January 1930. The sonnet cycle as a whole was not published in its entirety until *Beyond the Wall of Sleep* (Arkham House, 1943); the separate appearance *Fungi from Yuggoth* ([Washington, DC:] Bill Evans, June 1943) lacks the final three sonnets. R. H. Barlow was planning an edition of the cycle around 1935 and typeset several sonnets, but never completed the job; it was, however, only at this time that the cycle achieved its present form (see below on "Recapture" [XXXIV]). HPL had no compunction allowing the sonnets to appear separately and in fact aggressively sold many to professional markets in 1930, including *Weird Tales* and the *Providence Journal*. Others he gave to amateur or fan publications.

The name Yuggoth, first cited in the title of the cycle, was later mentioned in a letter in which HPL noted the discovery of Pluto: "Whatcha thinka the NEW PLANET? HOT STUFF!!! It is probably Yuggoth" (HPL to James F. Morton, [15 March 1930]; *JFM* 225). This statement was written when HPL was writing "The Whisperer in Darkness," where Yuggoth is identified with Pluto.

For various discussions of the sonnet cycle, see R. Boerem, "The Continuity of the *Fungi from Yuggoth*," in *FDOC;* David E. Schultz, "H. P. Lovecraft's *Fungi from Yuggoth*," *CoC* No. 20 (Eastertide 1984): 3–7; Ralph E. Vaughan, "The Story in *Fungi from Yuggoth*," *CoC* No. 20 (Eastertide 1984): 9–11; David E. Schultz, "The Lack of Continuity in *Fungi from Yuggoth*," *CoC* No. 20 (Eastertide 1984): 12–16; Robert M. Price, "Second Thoughts on the *Fungi from Yuggoth*," *CoC* No. 78 (St. John's Eve 1991): 3–8; Robert H. Waugh, "The Structural and Thematic Unity of *Fungi from Yuggoth*," *LS* No. 26 (Spring 1992): 2–14; Dan Clore, "Metonyms of Alterity: A Semiotic Interpretation of *Fungi from Yuggoth*," *LS* No. 30 (Spring 1994): 21–32; David A. Oakes, "This Is the Way the World Ends: Modernism in 'The Hollow Men' and *Fungi from Yuggoth*," *LS* No. 40 (Fall 1998): 33–36, 28.

I. The Book: FP: *Fantasy Fan* 2, No. 2 (October 1934): 24; rpt. *Driftwind* 11, No. 9 (April 1937): 342. Possibly based on *CB* entry 144: "Hideous book glimpsed in ancient shop—never seen again"; also perhaps entry 78: "Wandering thro' labyrinth of narrow slum streets—come on distant light—unheard-of rites of swarming beggars—like Court of Miracles in Notre Dame de Paris." It appears as if HPL rewrote the first three sonnets—which form a continuous narrative, as the rest of the cycle does not—into prose in the fragment "The Book" (1933?); see my article, "On 'The Book,'" *Nyctalops* 3, No. 4 (April 1983): 9–13; rpt. *CoC* No. 53 (Candlemas 1988): 3–7, and in my *Primal Sources: Essays on H. P. Lovecraft* (New York: Hippocampus Press, 2003), 190–94.

II. Pursuit: FP: *Fantasy Fan* 2, No. 2 (October 1934): 24. Possibly based on *CB* entry 55: "Man pursued by invisible thing."

III. The Key: FP: *Fantasy Fan* 2, No. 5 (January 1935): 72.

IV. Recognition: FP: *Driftwind* 11, No. 5 (December 1936): 180.

V. Homecoming: FP: *Fantasy Fan* 2, No. 5 (January 1935): 72; rpt. *Science-Fantasy Correspondent* 1, No. 1 (November–December 1936): 24; rpt. *HPL* (Bellville, NJ: Corwin F. Stickney 1937); *Weird Tales* 37, No. 5 (May 1944): 52–53.

VI. The Lamp: FP: *Driftwind* 5, No. 5 (March 1931): 16; rpt. *Weird Tales* 33, No. 2 (February 1939): 151. Based on *CB* entry 146: "Ancient lamp found in tomb—when filled & used, its light reveals strange world."

VII. Zaman's Hill: FP: *Driftwind* 9, No. 4 (October 1934): 125; rpt. *Weird Tales* 33, No. 2 (February 1939): 151. "Zaman's Hill" is first cited in "The Ancient Track." Aylesbury (l. 11) is a minor town in HPL's imaginary New England topography, first cited in "The Dunwich Horror" (1928).

VIII. The Port: FP: *Driftwind* 5, No. 3 (November 1930): 36; rpt. *Weird Tales* 39, No. 7 (September 1946): 65. Based on *CB* entry 155: "Steepled town seen from afar at sunset—*does not light up at night.* Sail has been seen putting out to sea."

Innsmouth is cited here for the first time since its use in "Celephaïs" (1920), where it was located in England; here it appears to be in New England (as in the later "The Shadow over Innsmouth" [1931]). Boynton Beach (fictitious) is never cited again.

IX. The Courtyard: FP: *Weird Tales* 16, No. 3 (September 1930): 322. Based on *CB* entry 149: "Evil alley or enclosed court in ancient city—Union or Milligan Pl." (Union Place is in Brooklyn, Milligan Place in Greenwich Village in Manhattan.) The poem appears to be a retelling of "He" (1925), where the "courtyard" mentioned in the story is located at 93 Perry Street in Manhattan.

X. The Pigeon-Flyers: FP: *Fungi from Yuggoth* (1943); rpt. *Weird Tales* 39, No. 9 (January 1947): 96. HPL remarks that the "appreciation [of the poem] depends upon a familiarity with the actual customs of the 'Hell's Kitchen' slum in New York, where bonfire-building & pigeon-flying are the two leading recreations of youth" (HPL to August Derleth, [early January 1930]; *ES* 1.242). "Thog" (l. 12) is cited only here, but cf. "Thok" in "To a Dreamer" and other poems.

XI. The Well: FP: *Providence Journal* 102, No. 116 (14 May 1930): 15; rpt. *Phantagraph* 6, No. 3 (July 1937): 1; *Weird Tales* 37, No. 5 (May 1944): 53. Two discarded drafts of the poem were published in *CoC* No. 20 (Eastertide 1984): 8. Based on *CB* entry 143: "Strange well in Arkham country—water gives out (or was never struck—hole kept tightly covered by a stone ever since dug)—no bottom—shunned & feared—what lay beneath (either unholy temple or other very ancient thing, or great cave-world)." A Professor Atwood is mentioned in *At the Mountains of Madness* (1931), and a Rev. Silas Atwood in "The Horror in the Burying-Ground" (1933).

XII. The Howler: FP: *Driftwind* 7, No. 3 (November 1932): 100; rpt. *Weird Tales* 34, No. 1 (June–July 1939): 66. Zoar is a real town in northwestern Massachusetts near the Vermont border (see *SL* 2.347). In the Bible, it is a city in Egypt where Lot took refuge from the destruction of Sodom (Genesis 13:10).

XIII. Hesperia: FP: *Weird Tales* 16, No. 4 (October 1930): 464. "Hesperia" is Greek for "land of the West," generally referring to a conjectured realm beyond the Straits of Gibraltar.

XIV. Star-Winds: FP: *Weird Tales* 16, No. 3 (September 1930): 322. The planet Nithon is cited only here.

XV. Antarktos: FP: *Weird Tales* 16, No, 5 (November 1930): 692. "Antarktos" is HPL's Greek coinage referring to the Antarctic regions.

XVI. The Window: FP: *Driftwind* 5 (April 1931 [Special issue]): 15; rpt. *Weird Tales* 37, No. 5 (May 1944): 53.

XVII. A Memory: FP: *Fungi from Yuggoth* (1943); rpt. *Weird Tales* 39, No, 10 (March 1947): 69.

XVIII. The Gardens of Yin: FP: *Driftwind* 6, No. 5 (March 1932): 34; rpt. *Weird Tales* 34, No. 2 (August 1939): 151. The name Yin (as well as the general imagery) may be derived from Robert W. Chambers's "Yian," a fictitious Chinese city described in the novelette "The Maker of Moons" (in *The Maker of Moons* [1896]); HPL certainly borrowed the latter for Yian-Ho in "Through the Gates of the Silver Key" (1932–33) and "The Diary of Alonzo Typer" (1935). In the summer of 1930 HPL felt that Maymont Park in Richmond, VA, was the Gardens of Yin come to life (*SL* 3.150).

XIX. The Bells: FP: *Weird Tales* 16, No. 6 (December 1930): 798. Cf. HPL's earlier poem "Bells" (1919). See also Donald R. Burleson, "Notes on Lovecraft's 'The Bells': A Carillon," *LS* No. 17 (Fall 1988): 34–35.

XX. Night-Gaunts: FP: *Providence Journal* 102, No. 73 (26 March 1930): 15; rpt. *Phantagraph* 4, No. 3 ([June] 1936): 8; *HPL* (Bellville, NJ: Corwin F. Stickney, 1937); *Weird Tales* 34, No. 6 (December 1939): 59. The night-gaunts were strange creatures that HPL had been dreaming about since the age of five (see *SL* 1.35), brought on apparently by the funereal atmosphere of his home following the death of his maternal grandmother. They were utilised first in *The Dream-Quest of Unknown Kadath* (1926–27). Thok was invented in "To a Dreamer" (1920). The "shoggoths" are first cited here, although their most memorable appearance is of course in *At the Mountains of Madness* (1931).

XXI. Nyarlathotep: FP: *Weird Tales* 17, No. 1 (January 1931): 12. The history of HPL's use of Nyarlathotep is too involved for discussion here. HPL dreamed the name in late 1920 (*SL* 1.161 [letter misdated 14 December 1921]) and wrote the beginning of the prose-poem "Nyarlathotep" (1920) while not fully awake. Nyarlathotep makes frequent appearances in HPL's fiction, notably *The Dream-Quest of Unknown Kadath* and "The Haunter of the Dark" (1935). For the plausible conjecture that the entity was based in part on the eccentric scientist Nikola Tesla, see Will Murray, "Behind the Mask of Nyarlathotep," *LS* No. 25 (Fall 1991): 25–29. Robert Bloch quoted much of the poem in "The Shadow from the Steeple" (*Weird Tales*, September 1950), his "sequel" to "The Haunter of the Dark." The term "fellas" (1. 2) refers to *fellaheen* (singular *fellah*), the Arabic term for a peasant or manual laborer.

XXII. Azathoth: FP: *Weird Tales* 17, No. 1 (January 1931): 12. Azathoth was first cited in the title of HPL's unfinished "novel," "Azathoth" (1922), although the name is not mentioned in the 500 words of the extant text; thereafter, Azathoth became the chief deity in HPL's pantheon of imagined gods. The image of daemon flute-players recurs frequently in HPL's fiction; it is first cited in "The Festival" (1923). The phrase "I am his Messenger" (1. 12) has been taken to be an allusion to Nyarlathotep; cf. "The Whisperer in Darkness": "To Nyarlathotep, Mighty Messenger, must all things be told" (*DH* 226).

XXIII. Mirage: FP: *Weird Tales* 17, No. 2 (February–March 1931): 175. The composer Harold S. Farnese (1885–1945) set this sonnet and "The Elder Pharos" to music in 1931. See Donald R. Burleson, "Scansion Problems in Lovecraft's 'Mirage,'" *Lovecraft Studies* No. 24 (Spring 1991): 18–19, 21.

XXIV. The Canal: FP: *Driftwind* 6, No. 5 (March 1932): 34; rpt. *Harvest: A Sheaf of Poems from* Driftwind, ed. Walter J. Coates (North Montpelier, VT: Driftwind Press, May 1933), 33; *Weird Tales* 31, No. 1 (January 1938): 20. Based on *CB* entry 15: "Bridge & slimy black waters."

XXV. St. Toad's: FP: *Fungi from Yuggoth* (1943); rpt. *Weird Tales* 37, No. 5 (May 1944): 52. The name St. Toad's may have been inspired by St. Michael's Episcopal Church in Frog Lane in Marblehead, MA. See Robert M. Price, "St. Toad's Church," in Price's *H. P. Lovecraft and the Cthulhu Mythos* (Mercer Island, WA: Starmont House, 1990), 71–73.

XXVI. The Familiars: FP: *Driftwind* 5, No. 1 (July 1930): 35; rpt. *Weird Tales* 39, No. 9 (January 1947): 96. The name Whateley clearly derives from "The Dunwich Horror" (1928). For Aylesbury (l. 11), see note on "Zaman's Hill" (VII).

XXVII. The Elder Pharos: FP: *Weird Tales* 17, No. 2 (February–March 1931): 175. The word pharos is Greek for lighthouse; the most celebrated lighthouse in antiquity was in the harbour of Alexandria in Egypt. The name Leng was first cited in "The Hound" (1922) and used frequently by HPL thereafter. The imagery of the sestet seems taken from a passage in *The Dream-Quest of Unknown Kadath* and is perhaps based ultimately on *CB* entry 69: "Man with unnatural face—oddity of speaking—found to be a *mask*—Revelation." Harold S. Farnese set this sonnet to music in 1931. See Will Murray, "Illuminating 'The Elder Pharos,'" *CoC* No. 20 (Eastertide 1984): 17–19.

XXVIII. Expectancy: FP: *Fungi from Yuggoth* (1943).

XXIX. Nostalgia: FP: *Providence Journal* 102, No. 61 (12 March 1930): 15; rpt. *Phantagraph* 4, No. 4 (July 1936): 1; *HPL* (Bellville, NJ: Corwin F. Stickney, 1937).

XXX. Background: FP: *Providence Journal* 102, No. 91 (16 April 1930): 13; rpt. *Galleon* 1, No. 4 (May–June 1935): 8; *Lovecrafter* 47, No. 1 (20 August 1936): [1] (as "A Sonnet"). The octet now appears on the H. P. Lovecraft Memorial Plaque in the garden of the John Hay Library of Brown University, Providence, RI.

XXXI. The Dweller: FP: *Providence Journal* 102, No. 110 (7 May 1930): 15; rpt. *Phantagraph* 4, No. 2 (November–December 1935): [3]; HPL (Bellville, NJ: Corwin F. Stickney, 1937); *Weird Tales* 35, No. 2 (March 1940): 20.

XXXII. Alienation: FP: *Weird Tales* 17, No. 3 (April–May 1931): 374. The poem seems to be an adaptation of "The Strange High House in the Mist" (1926).

Yaddith and the Ghooric Zone are first cited here; the former would later be used in "Through the Gates of the Silver Key" (1932–33).

XXXIII. Harbour Whistles: FP: *Silver Fern* 1, No. 5 (May 1930): [1]; rpt. *L'Alouette* 3, No. 6 (September–October 1930): 161; *Phantagraph* 5, No. 2 (November 1936): 1; *HPL* (Bellville, NJ: Corwin F. Stickney, 1937); *Weird Tales* 33, No. 5 (May 1939): 134. See Donald R. Burleson, "On Lovecraft's 'Harbour Whistles,'" *CoC* No. 74 (Lammas 1990): 12–13.

XXXIV. Recapture: AMS (JHL); FP: *Weird Tales* 15, No. 5 (May 1930): 693; rpt. *Weird Tales* 39, No. 3 (January 1946): 37. The poem was written in mid-November 1929 (see HPL to Clark Ashton Smith, [19 November 1929]; *Dreams and Fancies* [1962], 26), well prior to the other sonnets in the cycle; it was only incorporated into the cycle in 1936 on the suggestion of R. H. Barlow. Barlow had placed it last, but HPL felt that its placement here would allow the cycle to conclude more satisfactorily: "I think 'Recapture' had better be *#34*—with 'Evening Star' as *35* & 'Continuity' as *36*. 'Recapture' seems somehow more *specific* & *localised* in spirit than either of the others named, hence would go better before them—allowing the Fungi to come to a close with more diffusive ideas" (*OFF* 341–42).

XXXV. Evening Star: FP: *Pioneer* 2, No. 4 (Autumn 1932): 16; rpt. *Weird Tales* 37, No. 5 (May 1944): 52.

XXXVI. Continuity: FP: *Pioneer* 2, No. 2 [i.e. 3] (Summer 1932): 6; rpt. *Causerie* (February 1936): 1.

Futurist Art: FP: *Conservative* 2, No. 4 (January 1917): [2]. Futurism was a very short-lived aesthetic movement founded by the Italian poet Filippo Marinetti (1876–1944) in 1909 and purporting to address directly the phenomena of the modern world by attempting to depict movement rather than static still-life. Cf. HPL's comment in *At the Mountains of Madness* (1931) in reference to the bas-reliefs of the Old Ones: "Those who see our photographs will probably find its closest analogue in certain grotesque conceptions of the most daring futurists" (*MM* 57).

A Garden: AMS (signed "L. Theobald, Junr."), TMS (JHL); FP: *Vagrant* [Spring 1927]: 60. Included in a letter to the Kleicomolo (April 1917 [AHT]; *RK* 91); HPL erroneously dates the poem to 1918 at *SL* 1.59. The issue of the *Vagrant* was long delayed and should have emerged as early as 1923.

Gaudeamus: AMS (JHL), where it is included in a fragment of an undated letter to an unknown correspondent. The poem was evidently written in response to another drinking-song of the same type by another writer. HPL writes: "As for 'Gaudeamus', the best I can say is, that its rather too Epicurean subject is as ancient as literature itself, and its treatment mediocre. I believe, without any egotism, that I could do better myself—witness the following . . ." The poem was used in "The Tomb" (1917; FP: *Vagrant*, March 1922) and has been published separately as "Drinking Song from 'The Tomb.'" It probably predates the story, perhaps by several years; it could date to as early as 1914. It may have been influenced by a similar song included in Richard Brinsley Sheridan's play *The School for Scandal* (1777), a more likely source than Thomas Morton's *New English Canaan or New Canaan* (1637) as suggested by Will Murray, "A Probable Source for the Drinking Song from 'The Tomb,'" *LS* No. 15 (Fall 1987): 77–80.

Gems from *In a Minor Key*: FP: *Conservative* 1, No. 3 (October 1915): 8 (unsigned). The poems are all based upon quotations from *In a Minor Key* No. 2 [1915]. George Sylvester Viereck [not Vierick] (1884–1962) was a German-American poet and propagandist who supported the Germans in World War I. "Horatius at the bridge" (l. 9) refers to the poem by Thomas Babington Macaulay (1800–1859), "Horatius," in *Lays of Ancient Rome* (1842), retelling the celebrated legend from early Roman history of Horatius Cocles and two others who guarded a bridge leading into Rome against an onslaught by the Etruscan army. HPL owned a copy of *Lays of Ancient Rome* (LL #560).

Germania—1918: FP: *Tryout* 4, No. 11 (November 1918): [3–7]. In ll. 13f. HPL refers to various battles between the ancient Germanic tribes and the Romans. The Roman general C. Marius (147–86 B.C.E.) battled the Cimbri and the Teutones in 104–101 B.C.E., ultimately defeating them. Ariovistus was a Germanic leader who conquered several Gallic tribes before being defeated by Julius Caesar in 58 B.C.E. Alaric I (370–410) was king of the Visigoths and sacked Rome in 410. In ll. 21–24 HPL refers to Kaiser Wilhelm II (1859–1941; r. 1888–1918) and his eldest son, Crown Prince Wilhelm (1882–1951). Both of them fled Germany after the end of the war. In l. 40 HPL presents another version of the Virgilian line *Parcere subiectis et debellare superbos* (see epigraph to "1914"). "Marlboroughs" (l. 43) refers to John Churchill, 1st Duke of Marlborough (1650–1722), a noted British general who fought in the War of the Spanish Succession and other conflicts. In l. 50, HPL refers to P. Quinctilius Varus (46 B.C.E.–9 C.E.), the Roman general who lost the battle of the Teutoburgian Forest to Arminius (see note on "Ad Britannos—1918"), and to L. Cassius Longinus (consul 107 B.C.E.), who was killed in a battle with the Cimbri. Ausonia (l. 54) is the Roman name for a region in southern Italy. "Dacian lands" (l. 57) refers to the Roman province of Dacia, approximately equivalent to the modern countries Romania and Moldavia. "Scythian wastes" (l. 59) refers to Scythia, the Graeco-Roman name for a large area east of Dacia extending into modern-day Russia. In ll. 77–80 HPL refers to the Battle of Saint-Mihiel (12–15 September 1918), in northeastern France, in which the American and French army fought the Germans. In l. 90 HPL refers to Ferdinand Foch (1851–1929), French general who in early 1918 was named Supreme Commander of the Allied Armies; Douglas Haig (1861–1928), British field marshal who commanded the British Expeditionary Force (1915–18); and John J. Pershing (1860–1948), American general who led the American Expeditionary Force (1917–18). In l. 114 HPL apparently refers to the Duke of Marlborough (see above on l. 43); "Eugenio" is unidentified.

Grace: FP: *Conservative* 4, No. 1 (July 1918): 7 (as by "Ward Phillips"). For Rheinhart Kleiner's "Ruth" see Appendix 2. The poem was quoted in full (under the title "Grayce") in a letter to Alfred Galpin, 27 May 1918 (*AG* 22). As published, the poem was part of an article entitled "Ward Phillips Replies" and was prefaced by the following note:

> The *Conservative* acknowledges a communication from Ward Phillips, Esq., whose recent ulalumish poem entitled "Astrophobos" was so unfavourably contrasted with Mr. Kleiner's "Ruth" by a reviewer in the May *United Amateur.* Mr. Phillips would make it plain, that if he so desired he could work with perfect ease in a simpler, tenderer, and more popular medium; and as an answer to his critics he has graciously favoured this office with the following effusion, in the metre and manner of his distinguished contemporary: . . .

The writer in the May 1918 *United Amateur* to whom HPL refers was HPL himself (see note on "Astrophobos").

The Greatest Law: Text derived from AHT, where it is undated. "C. Raymond" is presumably Clifford Raymond, the reporter for the *Chicago Tribune* whose work HPL paraphrased for the poem "Spring" (1917). The first part of the poem is a variant of "Spring." The rest of the poem is about Galpin (Damon), perhaps dating to 1920–21.

Greetings: FP: *Silver Clarion* 2, No. 10 (January 1919): 3. For Goodenough see note on "To Arthur Goodenough, Esq." W. Paul Cook was a longtime associate of HPL's, especially instrumental in HPL's resumption of fiction writing in 1917. E. Sherman Cole was the infant son of Edward H. and Helene Hoffman Cole. The *Silver Clarion* was edited by John Milton Samples.

Gryphus in Asinum Mutatus: AMS (JHL); FP: *S.* The poem is undated, but presumably dates to sometime after "On a Modern Lothario," as it is a more exhaustive satire on W. E. Griffin's views on flirting than that poem. In the prefatory note, HPL quotes from Sir William Smith (1813–1893), *A Smaller Classical Dictionary of Biography, Mythology, and Geography* (New York: American Book Co., [1852?]; *LL* #823). The quotation from Milton's *Paradise Lost* occurs at 2.943–47.

H. Lovecraft's Attempted Journey . . .: AMS (JHL); FP: *J.* Like *The Poem of Ulysses,* the poem is prepared like a booklet and is dated 1901. The present title is derived from the cover; on the title page there is a variant title: *An Account in Verse of the Marvellous Adventures of H. Lovecraft, Esq. Whilst Travelling on the W. & B. Branch N.Y.N.H.&H.R.R. in Jany. 1901 in One of Those Most Modern of Devices, to Wit: An Electric Train.* The trolley line in question is the New York, New Haven, and Hartford Railroad, the leading company of its kind in New England at the time. Osgood Bradley (1800–1884) founded the Osgood Bradley Car Company in 1820 or 1822.

Hallowe'en in a Suburb: FP: *National Amateur* 48, No. 4 (March 1926): 33 (as "In a Suburb"); rpt. *Phantagraph* 6, No. 2 (June 1937): 3–4; *Weird Tales* 44, No. 6 (September 1952): 9.

Hedone: AMS (JHL), dated 3 January 1927; FP: *S.* "Hedone" is Greek for "pleasure": the poem contrasts two kinds of pleasure, physical and mental, typified by the two Roman poets Catullus and Virgil.

Helene Hoffman Cole: 1893–1919: FP: *Bonnet* 1, No. 1 (June 1919): 8–9 (unsigned). The poem has been attributed to HPL on internal evidence. The *Bonnet* was the organ of the United Women's Press Club of Massachusetts (Anne Tillery Renshaw, Official Editor). Cole—the wife of HPL's close associate Edward H. Cole—died on 25 March 1919. See also HPL's essay "Helene Hoffman Cole—Litterateur" (*United Amateur*, May 1919; *CE* 1.229–30).

Hellas: FP: *United Amateur* 18, No. 1 (September 1918): 3. In DPC (November 1918) HPL writes: "'Hellas', a piece of rather obvious hack-writing by H. P. Lovecraft, is even in metre and correct in grammar, but falls flatly beneath the level of inspiration its subject causes us to expect" (*CE* 1.213).

The House: FP: *National Enquirer* 9, No. 11 (11 December 1919): 3; rpt. *Philosopher* 1, No. 1 (December 1920): 6 (as by "Ward Phillips"). The poem is quoted in a letter to Rheinhart Kleiner, 16 July 1919 (*RK* 161–62). HPL later noted (*SL* 1.357) that it was inspired by the house at 135 Benefit St. that later served as the inspiration for "The Shunned House" (1924).

Hylas and Myrrha: A Tale: TMS (JHL); FP: *Tryout* 5, No. 5 (May 1919): [6–11] (as by "Lawrence Appleton"). Another poem on Galpin, who was about to enter Lawrence College in Appleton, Wisconsin (hence HPL's pseudonym). In l. 51, Praxiteles (4th century B.C.E.) was one of the most famous sculptors in ancient Greece.

In a Sequester'd Providence Churchyard . . .: AMS (JHL); FP: *Four Acrostic Sonnets on Edgar Allan Poe* ([Milwaukee, WI: Maurice W. Moe, 1936]); rpt. *Science-Fantasy Correspondent* 1, No. 3 (March–April 1937): 16–17 (as "In a Sequestered Churchyard Where Once Poe Walked"); *HPL* (Bellville, NJ: Corwin F. Stickney, 1937); *Weird Tales* 31, No. 5 (May 1938): 578 (as "Where Poe Once Walked"). The poem was written on 8 August 1936 in St. John's Churchyard in Providence, where HPL, R. H. Barlow, and Adolphe de Castro wrote acrostic "sonnets" (hardly the right word, as the poems lack one line for a true sonnet) to Poe, who used to haunt the churchyard when he was courting Providence poet Sarah Helen Whitman in 1848–49. De Castro had the presence of mind to send his poem to *Weird Tales*, where it was quickly accepted, appearing in the May 1937 issue; HPL's and Barlow's were rejected, as Farnsworth Wright wished only one such poem. Maurice W. Moe hectographed the three poems, along with one of his own; later Henry Kuttner wrote one. See David E. Schultz, "In a Sequester'd Graveyard," *CoC* No. 57 (St John's Eve 1988): 26–29; Donald R. Burleson, "Lines of Verse Evoking Close Reading: Acrostic-Formulated Text," *CoC* No. 85 (Hallowmas 1993): 9–12.

In Memoriam: J. E. T. D.: FP: *Tryout* 5, No. 3 (March 1919): [6] (as by "Ward Phillips"); rpt. *In Memoriam: Jennie E. T. Dowe*, ed. Michael White (Dorchester, MA: [W Paul Cook,] Sept. 1921), 56. Dowe was the mother of Edith Miniter. In 1934 HPL went to central Massachusetts to scatter Dowe's ashes in her native region in accordance with her final wishes. In the booklet the following note, entitled "A Singer of Ethereal Moods and Fancies," prefaces the poem:

> The accompanying lines were prepared in 1919 at the request of C. W. Smith for a booklet to be dedicated to Mrs. Dowe's memory. Since the writer was not personally acquainted with the poet and had seen but a limited amount of her work at the time, the piece was offered under a pseudonym; thus appearing in *The Tryout* after the plan for a booklet was abandoned.
>
> It is with gratification that the stanzas are now presented for reprinting; for while the writer is conscious of his total want of merit as a bard, he is glad of the opportunity to express, under his own signature, his appreciation of a rare poet. Mrs. Dowe was a poet in the highest sense—a singer of ethereal moods and fancies, who never confused her art with lesser arts, or allowed it to break up into abnormal fragments in the modern manner. Hers was the delicate fancy from which real images are born, and in her death literature lost an exponent who can never be replaced.

In Memoriam: Oscar Incoul Verelst of Manhattan: Text and title derived from a postcard to George Kirk postmarked 2 August 1926 (AMS, private collection), although the poem (without title or with variant titles) was copied in various other letters of the period; the earliest is a letter to James F. Morton, 28 June 1926 (*JFM* 111). FP: *SL* 2.60; cf. also *LS* No. 28 (Spring 1993): 15. Oscar was a cat owned by a neighbour of Kirk's that was killed by an automobile. HPL had by this time returned to Providence, so he only heard of the incident from members of the Kalem Club in New York. "Oscarus fuit" is Latin for "Oscar was" (i.e., is no more).

Inspiration: TMS (JHL); FP: *Conservative* 2, No. 3 (October 1916): [2] (as by "Lewis Theobald, Jun."); rpt. *National Magazine* 45, No. 2 (November 1916): 287. In DPC (March 1917) HPL writes: "The form and rhythm of this piece are quite satisfactory, but the insipidity of the sentiment leaves much to be desired. The whole poem savours too much of the current magazine style" (*CE* 1.140).

The Introduction: FP: *O-Wash-Ta-Nong* 2, No. 3 (December 1937): [10] (as by "Humphry Litttewit, Esq., of Grubstreet Manor"). Presumably written around 1917, when three other poems ("Unda; or, The Bride of the Sea," "The Peace Advocate," "A Summer Sunset and Evening") were apparently written and/or gathered as "Perverted Poesie or Modern Metre." "The Introduction" was apparently written last, as a summary of HPL's attempts to break out of the 18th-century heroic couplet. Cf., however, a comment in late 1914: "Once I privately tried imitations of modern poets, but turned away in distaste" (*SL* 1.4). But a reference to "Perverted Poesie" seems unlikely; certainly "A Summer Sunset and Evening," an imitation/parody of the Elizabethan Thomas Drayton, is certainly not an imitation of a "modern" poet. "Charles' Return" (l. 31) refers to the restoration of King Charles II to the English throne in 1660.

The Isaacsonio-Mortoniad: AMS (JHL); FP: *S*. Written no later than 14 September 1915, for that is the date on which HPL copied the poem in a letter to Rheinhart Kleiner (*RK* 20). The poem attacks various utterances by Charles D. Isaacson and James F. Morton in Isaacson's amateur journal *In a Minor Key* No. 2 [1915], which themselves were a response to HPL's "In a Major Key" (*Conservative*, July 1915). The epigraph ("Of arms and men I sing") is a parody of the opening words of Virgil's *Aeneid* ("Arma virumque cano" = "Of arms and the man [i.e., Aeneas] I sing"). Morton was at this time not personally acquainted with HPL, but would become one of his closest friends from 1922 onward. HPL wisely did not allow this poem to be published in his lifetime. In ll. 15f., the references are to Geoffrey Chaucer (1343?–1400), Queen Elizabeth I of England (1533–1603; r. 1558–1603), Sir Walter Ralegh [this spelling preferred to "Raleigh"] (1554?–1618), George Frideric Handel (1685–1759), Richard Lovelace (1618–1657) (who was imprisoned in 1641 and 1648–49 for various religious offences), Robert Herrick (1591–1674), and Alexander Pope (1688–1744). Contrary to HPL's implication, Isaacson did not suggest that these figures were contemporaries. "Honi soit qui mal y pense" ("Shame on him who thinks evil of it") is in fact the motto of the English Order of the Garter; Isaacon claimed it was "a saying of the French court." In l. 54, HPL refers to the *Jeffersonian* (1907–65), a weekly newspaper published in Jeffersontown, KY. Isaacson had stated: "Anything which incites to prejudice of any sort should be restrained." "Goodwin" (l. 62) is presumably a reference to W. H. Goodwin, another contributor to *In a Minor Key* (see "Gems from *In a Minor Key*"). "Vanbrugh" (l. 79) refers to Sir John Vanbrugh (1664–1726), British architect and the author of several sexually suggestive plays. The reference to Billy Sunday (l. 136) is prescient, as Morton in fact contributed to a tract—*The Case of Billy Sunday* (1915)—about the flamboyant evangelical preacher.

Iterum Conjunctae: FP: *Tryout* 3, No. 6 (May 1917): [3]; rpt. [Providence] *Evening News* 51, No. 8 (12 June 1917): 6; *Little Budget of Knowledge and Nonsense* 1, Nos. 5–6 (August–September 1917): 77; *National Enquirer* 6, No. 5 (2 May 1918): 10

(with subtitle: "America and England, 1918"); *Tryout* 19, No. 3 (May 1938): [16] (as "Intrum Donjunctae"). The poem (whose title translates to "Conjoined Again") commemorates the renewed association of England and the United States upon the latter's entry into World War I in April 1917.

January: FP: *Silver Clarion* 3, No. 10 (January 1920): 1 (as by "H. Paget-Lowe").

John Oldham: A Defence: FP: *United Co-operative* 1, No. 2 (June 1919): 7. The poem was written in response to Rheinhart Kleiner's "John Oldham: 1653–1683," published on the same page as HPL's poem (see Appendix 2). Oldham was a British satirist and translator.

A June Afternoon: FP: *Tryout* 4, No. 6 (June 1918): [1]; rpt. *National Enquirer* 6, No. 12 (20 June 1918): 10; *Vanity Fair* No. 13 (September 1919): 8.

Laeta; a Lament: FP: *Tryout* 4, No. 2 (February 1918): [15–16] (as by "Ames Dorrance Rowley"). The pseudonym is a parody on the name of the amateur poet James Laurence Crowley, whose saccharine verses HPL repeatedly criticised in DPC. The poem may also be a parody of Crowley's verse. Consider this remark from DPC (April 1916): "'My Dear, Sweet Southern Blossom' . . . is a saccharine and sentimental piece of verse reminiscent of the popular ballads which flourished ten or more years ago. Triteness is the cardinal defect, for each gentle image is what our discerning private critic Mr. Moe would call a 'rubber-stamp' phrase" (*CE* 1.105).

Life's Mystery: AMS (JHL); FP: *WW*. An obvious parody of modernistic verse. The handwriting dates it to around 1915.

Lines for Poets' Night 1t the Scribblers' Club: TMS (JHL); FP: *National Amateur* 46, No. 3 (January 1924): 25; rpt. *Pegasus* No. [2] (February 1924): 31–33. The Scribblers' Club is probably not the same group for which HPL had written the poem "To 'The Scribblers.'" The poem ends up being largely a paean to Samuel Loveman. In 1922–23 HPL had been embroiled in an amateur controversy over the merits of Loveman's verse; see *LAP* 1.475–77.

Lines on Gen. Robert Edward Lee: FP: *Coyote* 3, No. 1 (January 1917): 1–2. The epigraph from Lucan's *Bellum Civile* (or *Pharsalia*) is from 9.593–96: "If great renown is won by real merit, if excellence is examined naked with success removed, whatever in any of our great ancestors we praise—was luck" (tr. S. H. Braund). For HPL's Confederate sympathies see note on "C.S.A.: 1861–1865" (1902). "Sumter" (l. 10) refers to Fort Sumter, in the harbour of Charleston, S.C., where, on 12 April 1861, the first shots of the Civil War were fired. In l. 33, Philopoemen (253–183 B.C.E.) was a Greek general who waged a number of successful battles against the Spartans from the 220s to the 180s.

Lines on Graduation . . .: TMS (included in a letter to John T. Dunn, 13 January 1917 [JHL]); FP: *Tryout* 3, No. 3 (February 1917): [15–17] (attributed to John T.

Dunn). The poem was written for Dunn, an Irish-American associate of HPL's in Providence (a co-member of the Providence Amateur Press Club), to be read by Dunn's sister. In his letter to Dunn HPL remarks: "You suggested something of from 6 to 12 lines, but the nature of the subject prohibited anything so short. Class poems are a definite type in literature, requiring substantial length, and a certain classic atmosphere and versification. I am sure that the length of time required to recite it will not be excessive; in fact, it is only half or a third the length of many class poems. I think I have included the various points you mentioned, and have also thought it appropriate to pay a tribute to the noble character of the nurses' profession, a nobility which makes it a very suitable and inspiring subject for treatment in verse" (*Books at Brown* 38–39 [1991–92]: 211). See also HPL's poem "To the Nurses of the Red Cross" (1917).

Lines on the 25th. Anniversary . . .: FP: *Tryout* 4, No. 1 (December 1917): [3–5]; rpt. [Providence] *Evening News* 51, No. 154 (10 December 1917): 7 (as "Our 25th Anniversary, 1892–1917"). HPL was a columnist for the *Evening News* at this time, writing monthly astronomy columns. "Heaton" (l. 38) evidently refers to Heaton, Langtry & Co., the original publisher of the paper. "Brown" (l. 46) refers to D. Russell Brown, who took over the publication of the paper in 1913.

Lines upon the Magnates of the Pulp: FP: *Leaves* No. 1 (Summer 1937): 60–61 (in R. H. Barlow's column "Obiter Scriptum"). Text derived from the AMS (JHL), titled (apparently by R. H. Barlow) "On the Achievements of a Popular Writer," written on an envelope postmarked 1 November 1929; title derived from a letter to Maurice W. Moe (c. 1929; AHT). In the AMS, HPL has provided some variant lines: for ll. 25–26, "Our newer band opposing ways pursue, / And lose the freeman in the griping Jew"; for ll. 29–30: "To drown their yearnings and their freeman's right / In swamps o'ergrown with thorn and aconite." HPL's hostility to pulp writing needs no documentation.

The Link: FP: *Tryout* 4, No. 7 (July 1918): [7]; rpt. *National Enquirer* 6, No. 21 (22 August 1918): 10. On the same basic subject as "Iterum Conjunctae" (1917).

[Little Sam Perkins]: Text derived from a letter to James F. Morton (24 September 1934) as published in *Olympian* No. 35 (Autumn 1940): 36; the poem is also included in AMS letters to Edward H. Cole (17 September 1934), R. H. Barlow (25 September 1934), Elizabeth Toldridge (6 October 1934), and Duane W. Rimel (8 October 1934) (all JHL). In all these instances the poem is printed without title; oddly enough, the first appearance of the poem with a title is in *Cats in Prose and Verse*, ed. Nelson Antrim Crawford (New York: Coward-McCann, 1947), 76 (presumably the text was supplied to Crawford by August Derleth). Sam Perkins was a small black cat who died of unknown causes at the age of four months. See Donald R. Burleson, "Lovecraft's Cheshire Cat," *CoC* No. 76 (Hallowmas 1990): 19–22.

Lullaby for the Dionne Quintuplets: AMS, TMS (JHL); FP: *WW*. See "Dead Passion's Flame."

The Magazine Poet: FP: *United Amateur* 15, No. 3 (October 1915): 51.

March: FP: *United Amateur* 14, No. 4 (March 1915): 68; rpt. [Providence] *Evening News* 52, No. 66 (1 March 1918): 7. In DPC (September 1915) HPL states: "'March', by ourselves, is a gem of exquisite poesy, etc., etc., which we have here praised because no one else could ever conscientiously do so" (*CE* 1.70).

Medusa: A Portrait: TMS (JHL); FP: *Tryout* 7, No. 9 (December 1921): [32–34] (as by "Jeremy Bishop"). One of the TMSs and the published appearance lack the introductory letter to Haughton. The other TMS (which is dated 29 November 1921) is presented as a letter to the Gallomo (the round-robin correspondence between HPL, Alfred Galpin, and Maurice W. Moe); see *AG* 116–18. Ida C. Haughton was President of the UAPA for 1921–22, when HPL was serving as Official Editor. HPL in letters claims that Haughton "ran the very gamut of abuse & positive insult—culminating even in an aspersion on my stewardship of the United funds!" (HPL to Maurice W. Moe, 15 June 1925; AMS, JHL). Hence the poem, the most vicious satire HPL ever wrote. "Woodby" is a play on the *Woodbee*, an amateur journal edited by Haughton and her associates in Cleveland, who had formed a press club called the Woodbees. Haughton was apparently a woman of considerable bulk; HPL satirises her girth here as well as in the undated epigram, "On ——'s Gaining in Weight." HPL's signature at the end of the letter translates to: "The Most Elderly Theobald, Esquire."

The Members of the Men's Club . . .: AMS (JHL); FP: *S*. Undated, but probably dates to 1908–12. The First Universalist Church was at this time located at the corner of Westminster and Greene Streets in downtown Providence. One suspects that HPL's mother urged HPL to join this club, possibly as a way of getting him out of the house during his "recluse" period of 1908–13. There is no indication of who the president of the club was.

The Messenger: AMS (JHL), dated 30 November 1929, 3:07 a.m.; FP: *Weird Tales* 32, No. 1 (July 1938): 52. The poem was quoted in its entirety in B. K. Hart's column, "The Sideshow," *Providence Journal* (3 December 1929): 14. Hart had encountered HPL's "The Call of Cthulhu" in T. Everett Harré's anthology *Beware After Dark!* (1929) and was startled to discover that the dwelling of the artist Wilcox (7 Thomas Street) was a place Hart himself had occupied. Hart professed mock umbrage: ". . . I shall not be happy until, joining league with wraiths and ghouls, I have plumped down at least one large and abiding ghost by way of reprisal upon his own doorstep at Barnes street. . . . I think I shall teach it to moan in a minor dissonance every morning at 3 o'clock sharp, with a clinking of chains" (*Providence Journal* [30 November 1929]: 10). Winfield Townley Scott (in *FDOC*) called the sonnet "perhaps as wholly satisfactory as any poem [HPL] ever wrote."

[Metrical Example]: Text derived from a letter to Elizabeth Toldridge, 27 February [1935] (AMS, JHL). In the letter HPL has marked the long and short syllables to indicate the proper use of triple rhymes (*cheerily-drearily*).

A Mississippi Autumn: FP: *Ole Miss'* No. 2 (December 1915): 5–6 (as by "Howard Phillips Lovecraft, Metrical Mechanic"). "Mrs. Renshaw" is Anne Tillery Renshaw, editor of *Ole Miss'*. In DPC (April 1916) HPL remarks: "'A Mississippi Autumn' was written as prose by Mrs. Renshaw, and set in heroic verse without change of ideas by the present critic. The metaphor is uniformly lofty and delicate, whilst the development of the sentiment is facile and pleasing. It is to be hoped that the original thoughts of the author are not impaired or obscured by the technical turns of the less inspired versifier" (*CE* 1.105).

Monody on the Late King Alcohol: *Tryout* 5, No. 8 (August 1919): [15–16] (as by "Lewis Theobald, Jun.").

Monos: An Ode: FP: *Silver Clarion* 2, No. 7 (October 1918): 3–4. In DPC (November 1918) HPL writes: "'Monos; An Ode' is a pleasantly meaningless philosophical Pindaric by an author more accustomed to iambic pentameter" (*CE* 1.212).

My Favourite Character: AMS (JHL), dated 31 January 1925; FP: *Brooklynite* 16, No. 1 (January 1926): 1 (as "My Favorite Character"). Written for a gathering on 31 January of the Blue Pencil Club, a Brooklyn amateur press club; members were asked to prepare literary contributions on a given topic. The references in ll. 17–18 are to James Branch Cabell's novel *Jurgen* (1919); Clerk Nicholas, a character in "The Miller's Tale," in Chaucer's *Canterbury Tales;* and Giovanni Boccaccio's *Decameron* (14th c.). In l. 24 HPL cites the protagonists of several series of dime novels: Frank Merriwell, an athlete featured in novels and tales written by Burt L. Standish (pseudonym of Gilbert Patten, 1866–1945), beginning in 1896; Nick Carter, a detective originally created by John R. Coryell in the dime novel *The Old Detective's Pupil* (1886) and who subsequently appeared in the long-running *Nick Carter Weekly* (1897–1912); and Fred Fearnot, a character created by Hal Standish (pseudonym of Harvey King Shackelford, 1841–1906) in hundreds of novels written between 1899 and 1906. HPL read dime novels extensively in his youth. In l. 30, HPL alludes to Anglo-American poet T. S. Eliot, author of *The Waste Land* (1922), which originally appeared in the US in the November 1922 issue of the *Dial*, a long-running periodical (1840–1929) that in 1920 became an avant-garde literary journal.

My Lost Love: TMS (JHL), signed "J. Lewis Theobald"; FP: *S*. Written no later than 10 June 1916, for on that date it was included in a letter to John T. Dunn. The poem is a parody of the saccharine verse of amateur poet James Laurence Crowley. HPL comments in the letter: "I recently composed a 'take off' on James L. Crowley's silly songs and 'poems' . . ." (*Books at Brown* 38–39 [1991–

92]: 179). The poem is presumably also an imitation of the barbershop tunes HPL and his friends used to sing as teenagers (see *SL* 4.365–66).

Myrrha and Strephon: FP: *Tryout* 5, No. 7 (July 1919): [9–10] (as by "Lawrence Appleton"). Another poem on Galpin.

Nathicana: AMS (JHL); FP: *Vagrant* [Spring 1927]: 61–64 (as by "Albert Frederick Willie"). The poem was written, probably no later than 1920, in conjunction with Alfred Galpin (hence the pseudonym, Al[bert] Fred[erick] Willie—Willy being Galpin's mother's maiden name). The *Vagrant* issue in which it appeared was long delayed, having been scheduled to appear in 1923 or earlier. HPL meant it as "a parody on those stylistic excesses which really have no basic meaning" (HPL to Donald Wandrei, [2 August 1927]; *MTS* 138); the focal point of the parody being Poe with his sonorous repetition, especially in such a poem as "Ulalume" (1848). Donald Wandrei, however, when reading the poem, commented: "It is a rare and curious kind of literary freak, a satire too good, so that, instead of parodying, it possesses, the original" (Donald Wandrei to HPL, 12 August 1927; *MTS* 149). All the proper names in the poem are imaginary and cited only here; also imaginary are the terms nephalotë (l. 3) and astalthon (l. 35), evidently the names of flowers.

Nemesis: FP: *Vagrant* No. 7 (June 1918): 41–43; rpt. *Weird Tales* 3, No. 4 (April 1924): 78. Written the night after Hallowe'en 1917 (*SL* 1.51). HPL goes on to say: "It presents the conception, tenable to the orthodox mind, that nightmares are the punishment meted out to the soul for sins committed in previous incarnations—perhaps millions of years ago!" HPL quotes ll. 8–10 as the epigraph to "The Haunter of the Dark" (1935). Cf. HPL's parody of the poem in "A Brumalian Wish" in the Christmas greetings. The metre of this and other similar poems is a fusion of Poe's "Ulalume" and Swinburne's *Hertha*. Alfred Galpin's poem "Selenaio-Phantasma" (*Conservative*, July 1918) is "Dedicated to the Author of 'Nemesis'"; the poem itself is a combined pastiche and parody of HPL's poem. (For the text, see *AG* 235.) See Donald R. Burleson, "On Lovecraft's 'Nemesis,'" *LS* No. 21 (Spring 1990): 40–42.

New England: FP: [Providence] *Evening News* 46, No. 26 (18 December 1914): 11. The poem appeared on the same page as John Russell's "Florida" (reprinted from the *Tampa Times*) under the general heading "Heat and Cold." It shows that HPL kept in touch with Russell even after the end of the *Argosy* controversy.

New-England Fallen: AMS (JHL), dated April 1912; FP: *Beyond the Wall of Sleep* (1943). The epigraph from Juvenal's third satire translates to: "Here Numa erst his nightly visits paid / And held sweet converse with the Egerian maid. / Now the once-hallowed fountain, grove, and fane / Are let to Jews, a wretched wandering train / Whose furniture's a basket and some hay, / Since every tree is forced a tax to pay, / And the Camenae far in exile rove, / A-begging stands the consecrated grove" (tr. William Gifford).

The Nightmare Lake: FP: *Vagrant* No. 12 (December 1919): 13–14; rpt. *Scienti-Snaps* 3, No. 3 (Summer 1940): 13–14. Zan (l. 1) is imaginary, but cf. a similar imaginary realm, Zin, cited in "To a Dreamer."

1914: TMS (JHL); FP: *Interesting Items* No. 457 (March 1915): 3–5. The epigraph from Virgil's *Aeneid* (6.853) is the celebrated phrase in Anchises' prophecy to Aeneas: "To spare the conquered, and to subdue the proud." (See l. 28 for HPL's rendition.) "Louvain" (l. 16) is the French name for the Flemish city of Leuven, which was overrun by the Germans on 25 August 1914. "Axona" (l. 20) is the Latin name for the Aisne river in northeastern France. The First Battle of the Aisne (13–15 September 1914) resulted in a stalemate that led to the initiation of trench warfare. "Rhenus" (l. 30) is the Latin name for the Rhine river. In l. 58 HPL refers to British victories at Crécy, in northern France, in 1346, during the Hundred Years' War, and at Sebastopol (more properly Sevastopol), in the Crimea, 1854–55, during the Crimean War.

North and South Britons: FP: *Tryout* 5, No. 5 (May 1919): [13] (as by "Alexander Ferguson Blair"). The attribution of this poem to HPL was first made by Tom Collins in *WW*. In l. 4 HPL refers to the Cheviot Hills, just south of the Scottish border in England, and the River Tweed, just north of the border. In ll. 14–15 HPL refers to Solway Firth, which forms part of the western border between England and Scotland; Fife, a county in central Scotland; Devon, a county in southwestern England (where HPL's paternal relations originated); Ayr, a city in southwestern Scotland situated on the Firth of Clyde (although HPL may be using the name as a synecdoche for the county of Ayrshire); and Dorset, a county in southwestern England. The last line alludes to the celebrated line "Britons never will be slaves!" from the patriotic song "Rule, Britannia!" (1740; words by James Thomson, music by Thomas Augustine Arne).

The Nymph's Reply to the Modern Business Man: FP: *Tryout* 3, No, 3 (February 1917): [2] (as by "Lewis Theobald, Jr."). A reply to Olive G. Owen's poem, "The Modern Business Man to His Love" (see Appendix 2). The "apologies" to Walter Raleigh are offered because Owen offered apologies to "Kit Marlow [*sic*]" (i.e., Christopher Marlowe).

Oct. 17, 1919: AMS (JHL); FP: *WW*. A poem on the birthday of HPL's mother, Sarah Susan Lovecraft (1857–1921), who was at this time confined in Butler Hospital for nervous ailments.

October [I]: FP: *Tryout* 6, No. 10 (October 1920): [17] (as by "Henry Paget-Lowe").

October [II]: TMS (JHL), dated 30 October 1925; FP: *Tryout* 10, No. 7 (January 1926): [3–5].

Ode for July Fourth, 1917: FP: *United Amateur* 16, No. 9 (July 1917): 121; rpt. *National Magazine* 45, No. 10 (July 1917): 616 (as "Ode to July 4th: 1917"); [Providence] *Evening News* 51, No. 26 (3 July 1917): 3.

The Odes of Horace: AMS, TMS (JHL), dated 22 January 1736 [i.e., 1936]; FP: *Sappho* 1, No. 4 [1940s]: 11 (as "Horace: Book III Ode IX: Theobald's Translation"). The first translation from a classical work by HPL since his translation of Ovid's *Metamorphoses* as a boy.

Old Christmas: TMS (JHL) [fragment—p. 1 only]; FP: *Tryout* 4, No. 12 (December 1918): [1–11]; rpt. *National Enquirer* 9, No. 13 (25 December 1919): 3. Written in late 1917 (see HPL to Rheinhart Kleiner, 5 June [1918]; *RK* 143). The longest single poem HPL ever wrote. The epigraph is the refrain from the "Boar's Head Carol" (1521); it translates to: "I carry the head of the boar, / Conveying praises to [my] lord." When HPL sent the poem through the Transatlantic Circulator (an Anglo-American correspondence group), the Canadian amateur John Ravenor Bullen remarked: "His devotion to Queen Anne style may make his compositions seem artificial, rhetorical descriptions to contemporary critics, but the ever-growing charm of eloquence (to which assonance, alliteration, onomatopoeic sound and rhythm, and tone colour contribute their entrancing effect) displayed in the poem under analysis, proclaims Mr Lovecraft a genuine poet, and 'Old Christmas' an example of poetical architecture well-equipped to stand the test of time." For Bullen's entire quotation see *IAP* 1.195–96. HPL himself commented: "'Old Christmas' is a rhymed essay—light verse, verging on the whimsical" ("The Defence Reopens!"; *CE* 5.49). "ANNA'S virtuous reign" (l. 10) refers to the reign of Queen Anne (Queen of England, 1702–14), when such writers as Jonathan Swift and Joseph Addison were in their prime. "Apicius" (l. 51) refers to M. Gavius Apicius (1st century C.E.), a Roman gourmet who was falsely thought to be the author of a cookbook dating to the 4th or 5th century C.E. HPL owned a volume, *Apician Morsels; or, Tales of the Table, Kitchen, and Larder* (1829) by Dick Humelbergius Secundus (*LL* #451). For Lucullus (l. 53), see note on "The Poe-et's Nightmare."

On a Battlefield in Picardy: FP: *National Enquirer* 6, No. 9 (30 May 1918): 10; rpt. *Voice from the Mountains* (July 1918): 11 (as "On a Battlefield in France"). A fine ode, showing what HPL could do when not self-constrained within the narrow limits of the heroic couplet and of political prejudice. In DPC (September 1918) HPL writes that the poem is "a Pindaric ode containing one or two vivid pictures despite its now hackneyed theme. We are of the opinion that the author might have conveyed his thought more effectively in a different metre" (*CE* 1.208). Picardy is a province in the north of France; its capital is Amiens. The Battle of the Somme (July–November 1916) took place there.

On a Grecian Colonnade in a Park: TMS (JHL), dated 20 August 1920 (HPL's thirtieth birthday); FP: *Tryout* 6, No. 9 (September 1920): [11–12] (as by "Henry

Paget-Lowe"). The poem does not bear any appreciable resemblance to Keats's celebrated "Ode on a Grecian Urn."

On a Modern Lothario: FP: *Blarney Stone* 2, No. 4 (July–August 1914): 7–8. The poem was written in response to an article by W. E. Griffin, "My Favorite Pastime—Flirting," *Blarney Stone* 2, No. 3 (May–June 1914): 1–2. See also "Gryphus in Asinum Mutatus." In DPC (January 1915) HPL comments on an article that defended Griffin: "The Modern Lothario is fortunate in having so competent and experienced a champion. However, we cannot wholly endorse the sentiments of these excellent writers. The statement that 'all amateur journalists are flirts, more or less', is a base and unwarranted libel which we are prepared completely to refute" (*CE* 1.21). The two blanks at the end of the poem are meant to be filled in by the words "Blarney Stone."

On a New-England Village Seen by Moonlight: AMS (JHL), dated 7 September 1913; FP: *Trail* No. 2 (Summer 1915): 8–9. Lines 25–28 were quoted in a letter to Lillian D. Clark, 29–30 September 1924 (AMS, JHL; *LNY* 72–73) as a description of a cemetery in the Bowery, in lower Manhattan.

On a Poet's Ninety-first Birthday: FP: *Troy* [NY] *Times* (10 February 1922); rpt. *Tryout* 7, No. 11 (March 1922): [15–16] (as by "Lewis Theobald, Jun."); in *The Poetical Works of Jonathan E. Hoag*, ed. H. P. Lovecraft (New York: [Privately printed,] 1923), 66.

[On a Politician]: Text derived from a letter to Lillian D. Clark, 24–27 October 1925 (AMS, JHL). It was inspired by a street-corner political rally HPL stumbled upon in Brooklyn. The politician in question was Algernon Nova, who was in fact elected Kings County Judge (HPL makes reference in the poem to the fact that a card he was handed printed Nova's first name incorrectly). "Grover" (l. 2) refers to President Grover Cleveland. Under the word "early" (l. 14) HPL has supplied the annotation "= oily" (indicating the local pronunciation of the word).

[On a Room for Rent]: Text derived from a letter to Lillian D. Clark, 24–27 October 1925 (AMS, JHL). It was inspired by an advertisement in a subway car: "Rooms for rent, / Prices right; / Dandy rooms— / Large & light!" HPL's comment about heat refers to his constant complaints about the lack of heat supplied at 169 Clinton Street by his landlady, Mrs. Burns (although there was a coal strike in New York at this time), forcing HPL to purchase an oil heater for his apartment.

[On a Scene in Rural Rhode Island]: Text derived from a letter to Frank Belknap Long, 8 November 1923 [AHT]; FP: *SL* 1.266. The poem was inspired by a visit to the village of Chepachet and the surrounding vicinity, as HPL and C. M. Eddy attempted (and failed) to find the mysterious Dark Swamp. The poem specifically reflects a scene witnessed by HPL from the farmhouse of Ernest Law.

[On Ambrose Bierce]: Text derived from an undated letter (c. June 1927) to Frank Belknap Long (AHT). The poem emerged from a dispute between HPL, Long, and Samuel Loveman over the precise colours conjured up by Bierce's "verdant atmospheric effects": Loveman claimed to see blue, whereas Long saw green.

On an Accomplished Young Linguist: AMS (JHL); FP: *S*. The handwriting dates the poem to c. 1915. There is no clue as to the identity of "Paul," assuming this is a reference to a real individual.

On an Unspoil'd Rural Prospect: AMS (JHL), dated 30 August 1931; FP: *S*. In a letter to Maurice W. Moe (30 August 1931; AHT) HPL copies the poem with a variant title: "On an Unchang'd Rural Prospect." The epigraph from Ovid's *Metamorphoses* translates to: "Warm drops fall upon the earth, / The ground is verdant, flowers and soft fodder arise." The poem was written when HPL was "sitting on the ancient riverbank & looking into a splendid ravine" (HPL to August Derleth, 2 September 1931; *ES* 1.373)—i.e., the bank of the Seekonk River, several miles east of HPL's residence at 10 Barnes Street in Providence.

[On Cheating the Post Office]: Text derived from a postcard to Maurice W. Moe (c. 14 August 1927), reproduced in facsimile in *Marginalia* (1944), facing p. 278. HPL had wagered that two letters could be sent for the price of one. He received a letter from Alfred A. Knopf, steamed it open, inserted the postcard with the verses on it, resealed the envelope, crossed out his address, and "forwarded" the letter to Moe.

On Collaboration: AMS (JHL); FP: *S*. Poems written in Boston just prior to seeing Lord Dunsany lecture at the Copley Plaza on 20 October 1919. No. 6 is written to Eugene B. Kuntz, an amateur poet; No. 7 to Prof. Philip B. McDonald (for whom see "The Case for Classicism," *United Co-operative*, June 1919; *CE* 2.36–38); No. 9 to John Clinton Pryor, editor of *Pine Cones;* No. 11 to Anne Tillery Renshaw; No. 14 to William J. Dowdell; No. 15 to Jonathan E. Hoag; No. 16 to "Galba" (Alfred Galpin); No. 18 to Verna McGeoch; No. 19 to Rheinhart Kleiner; No. 20 to Maurice W. Moe; No. 21 to Muriel P. Kelly; No. 22 to W. Paul Cook (l. 4 refers to Cook's pseudonym, Willis Tete Crossman); No. 23 to Winifred Virginia Jordan; No. 24 to Alfred Galpin.

[On J. F. Roy Erford]: Text derived from a letter to James F. Morton, 18 June [1927] (AMS, JHL; *JFM* 141). Erford was the head of the United Amateur Press Association of America, a faction of the UAPA that had split over a contested election in 1912. HPL's "A Matter of Uniteds" (*Bacon's Essays*, Summer 1927; *CE* 1.358–60) is a summary of the controversy, written because Erford had recently made what HPL believed to be inaccurate and uncharitable remarks about the other faction of the UAPA (which HPL had joined in 1914). The poem was written in the expectation (not, apparently, realised) that Erford might write a response to HPL's article. HPL notes that the poem is consciously written in the manner of "The Isaacsonio-Mortoniad" (1915).

[On Kelso the Poet]: AMS (JHL). The "Kelso" in question appears to be Guy H. Kelso, a member of the Providence Amateur Press Club. In a letter to John T. Dunn, 14 October 1916 (*Books at Brown* 38–39 [1991–92]: 199) HPL refers to "the rather hopeless nature of his verse." HPL's poem presumably dates to this approximate period.

[On Marblehead]: Text derived from a letter to Maurice W. Moe, 10 July 1923 (AHT). The poem is part of a description of a trip to Marblehead, MA, that HPL had taken in July 1923. Specifically, the poem describes the scenery behind the Old Burying Hill. HPL's first visit to Marblehead in 1922 was, as he confessed in 1930, "the most powerful single emotional climax experienced during my nearly forty years of existence" (*SL* 3.126). The town became identified with the fictitious city of Kingsport in "The Festival" (1923) and later stories.

On Mr. L. Phillips Howard's . . .: AMS (JHL), written on the same page as "Life's Mystery"; FP: *WW*.

[On Newport, Rhode Island]: Text derived from a letter to Annie E. Phillips Gamwell, 17 September 1927 (AMS, JHL); FP: *SL* 2.169 (where the recipient is mistakenly given as Frank Belknap Long). The poem concludes a lengthy travelogue of Newport (written, apparently, from memory) for Mrs. Gamwell, who was about to visit the town. "Berkeley" is Bishop George Berkeley (1685–1753), the British philosopher who wrote the first version of *Alciphron; or, The Minute Philosopher* (1732) during his several-year stay in Newport.

[On *Old Grimes* by Albert Gorton Greene]: AMS (JHL); also included in a letter to Marion F. Bonner, 9 April 1936 (AMS, JHL). The poem is about a poem, *Old Grimes* (Providence: S. S. Rider & Brother, 1867; *LL* #374), by the Rhode Island writer Albert Gorton Greene (1802–1868), with illustrations by Rhode Island book illustrator Augustus Hoppin (1828–1896). It was given to HPL by his aunt Lillian D. Clark in late December 1925 (see HPL to Lillian D. Clark, 22–23 December 1925 [AMS, JHL]), in a copy that had been rebound by a Providence bookseller. HPL notes in the letter to Bonner that his poem was written upon receipt of the volume.

[On Phillips Gamwell]: Text derived from the essay "September Skies," [Providence] *Evening News* 49, No. 79 (1 September 1916): 6 (*CE* 3.197). Phillips Gamwell (1898–1916) was HPL's cousin, the son of HPL's aunt Annie E. P. Gamwell. He died at the very end of 1916. For Zoar see "The Howler" (*Fungi from Yuggoth* XII).

[On Prohibition]: AMS (JHL), dated June 30–Midnight [i.e., 1919]. Prohibition went into effect on either 1 July or 4 July 1919, depending upon the state, and this poem was presumably written the night before Prohibition was to commence in Rhode Island. HPL had long been a temperance advocate; see

"The Decline and Fall of a Man of the World," "The Road to Ruin," "Temperance Song," and "Monody on the Late King Alcohol."

On Reading Lord Dunsany's *Book of Wonder:* FP: *Silver Clarion* 3, No. 12 (March 1920): 4. *The Book of Wonder* was first published in 1912. HPL owned the Modern Library edition of 1918, in which that volume was combined with *Time and the Gods* (1906).

On Receiving a Picture of Swans: FP: *Conservative* 1, No. 4 (January 1916): 2–3. The poem is quoted in a letter to Rheinhart Kleiner, 14 September 1915 (*SL* 1.12–13), in which HPL says he wrote it in about ten minutes. It was based upon a postcard he had received bearing a picture of swans on a placid stream. It is quoted in its entirety in "August Skies," [Providence] *Evening News* 49, No. 52 (1 August 1916): 6 (*CE* 1.193).

On Receiving a Picture of the Marshes at Ipswich: TMS (JHL); FP: *National Magazine* 45, No. 4 (January 1917): 588; rpt. *Merry Minutes* 3, No. 12 (March 1917): 3. The poem may be the first work by HPL to have been initially published in a professional magazine. HPL had probably not visited Ipswich, MA, at this time. It is frequently mentioned in "The Shadow over Innsmouth" (1931).

On Receiving a Picture of yᵉ Towne of Templeton . . .: Text derived from facsimile of AMS in *Arkham House Catalogue* (1949): 18[c]; FP: *Vagrant* No. 5 (June 1917): 5 (as "To Templeton and Mount Monadnock"). Templeton is in north-central Massachusetts, midway between Athol (where W. Paul Cook resided) and Gardner. Mt. Monadnock is just over the Massachusetts border in New Hampshire, about 15 miles from Templeton.

On Receiving a Portraiture . . .: AMS (JHL), dated 25 December 1920; as by "L. Theobald Junr"; FP: *S.* "Elizabeth Neville Berkeley" is the pseudonym of Winifred Virginia Jordan, who by this time was divorced and had resumed her maiden name Jackson. The fact that she sent HPL a photograph of herself as a Christmas present may augment the supposition of a romance between the two.

On Religion: TMS (JHL); FP: *Tryout* 6, No. 8 (August 1920): [18] (as by "Henry Paget-Lowe"). HPL's hostility to organised religion is well documented. See now the compilation *Against Religion: The Atheist Writings of H. P. Lovecraft,* ed. S. T. Joshi ([New York]: Sporting Gentlemen, 2010).

[On Rheinhart Kleiner Being Hit by an Automobile]: Text derived from a letter to Lillian D. Clark, 1 August 1924 (ms., JHL).

[On Robert Browning]: Text derived from a letter by HPL to Rheinhart Kleiner, 28 March 1915 (*RK* 16), where HPL remarks that it was "one of my old attempts." It may be part of the "essay" on modern poets that HPL discusses in regard to "Fragment on Whitman."

[On Slang]: FP: *Conservative* 1, No. 1 (April 1915): [6]. HPL prefaces the poem with the remark: "Rheinhart Kleiner, in the concluding paragraph of *The Piper*, refers very wittily to the prevalence of slang in amateur journalism. His epigram on this subject deserves versified form." The reference is to a comment (not seen) by Kleiner in the *Piper* No. 1, dating to early 1915.

On the Cowboys of the West: FP: *Plainsman* 1, No. 4 (December 1915): 1–2. For Cole, see note on "To the Recipient of This Volume." Cole appended a note to the poem (pp. 2–3) praising it: "I can think of no better comparison, no more appropriate name than the poet has given them [cowboys]. 'Children'—yes, they were children; they were young gods, they were heroes. . . . I feel it a great honor that words of mine should inspire so worthy a poet as Howard P. Lovecraft to the writing of lines like the above." No doubt Cole spoke extensively of cowboys in his letters to HPL.

On the Creation of Niggers: TMS (hectographed copy), JHL, dated 1912 (whether in HPL's hand or not is unclear); FP: *S* (but quoted in its entirety in L. Sprague de Camp's *Lovecraft: A Biography* [1975]). The fact that HPL hectographed this poem must mean that he distributed it at least to friends and family.

On the Death of a Rhyming Critic: FP: *Toledo Amateur* (July 1917): 11–12. Another exquisite self-parody. For "Macer" (l. 2), see note on "To Rheinhart Kleiner, Esq." The final lines make reference to HPL's extensive revision of others' poetry.

[On the Double-R Coffee House]: Text derived from a letter to Annie E. P. Gamwell, 10 February 1925 (AMS, JHL). The poem was written on 1 February at a meeting of the Kalem Club at the coffee house (on 44th Street in Manhattan), one of the gang's favourite gathering-places.

[On the Pyramids]: Text derived from an undated letter (c. late February 1924) to Frank Belknap Long (AHT). The verses were written as HPL was finishing the writing of "Under the Pyramids," the tale ghostwritten for Houdini.

On the Return of Maurice Winter Moe . . .: FP: *Wolverine* No. 10 (June 1921): 15–16 (as by "Lewis Theobald, Jun."). HPL wrote in "News Notes" (*United Amateur*, November 1920): "Maurice Winter Moe is receiving felicitations on his return to the teaching profession, for which he is so conspicuously well fitted. He now fills a post at the West Division High School, Milwaukee, Wis., where his success is already notable, and in addition conducts much valuable work in connexion with boys' clubs and the Y. M. C. A." (*CE* 1.264).

[On *The Thing in the Woods* by Harper Williams]: Text derived from a letter to Lillian D. Clark, 29 November 1924 (AMS, JHL), in which HPL announces that he had written it into a copy of *The Thing in the Woods* (New York: Robert M. McBride & Co., 1924), presented to Frank Belknap Long for his assistance in finding books for HPL at the Scribner Book Shop on 9 October 1924 (see

SL 1.355–56). The novel may well have influenced HPL's own "The Dunwich Horror." The author has now been identified as British-born novelist Margery Williams Belasco (1881–1944). *The Thing in the Woods* was first published in the UK in 1913. For the text, see *Tales out of Dunwich*, ed. Robert M. Price (New York: Hippocampus Press, 2005), 13–137.

[On "Unda; or, The Bride of the Sea"]: Text derived from a letter to Rheinhart Kleiner, 30 September 1915 (*RK* 24), where the poem is appended to "Unda." The quatrain is addressed to Maurice W. Moe, who was repeatedly urging HPL to abandon the heroic couplet for other, more modern verse forms (see *SL* 1.4).

The Outpost: AMS, TMS (JHL), dated 26 November 1929; FP: *Bacon's Essays* 3, No. 1 (Spring 1930): 7; rpt. *Fantasy Magazine* 3, No. 3 (May 1934): 24–25; *O-Wash-Ta-Nong* 3, No. 1 (January 1938): 1. The poem was rejected by *Weird Tales* for excessive length. Some of the plot and imagery appears to derive from stories about Zimbabwe told to HPL by his amateur colleague Edward Lloyd Sechrist, who had actually visited the ruins of Zimbabwe in Africa (HPL to Lillian D. Clark, [6 May 1929]; ms., JHL). The phrase "Fishers from Outside" (l. 33) was later used in HPL's revision of Hazel Heald's "Winged Death" (1933), in reference to ruins found in Uganda: "They say these megaliths are older than man, and that they used to be a haunt or outpost of 'The Fishers from Outside'—whatever that means—and of the evil gods Tsadogwa and Clulu" (*HM* 247). See Will Murray, "The First Cthulhu Mythos Poem," *CoC* No. 20 (Eastertide 1984): 27–29.

Ovid's Metamorphoses: AMS (JHL); FP: *J*. The poem is a fairly literal translation of the first 88 lines of Ovid's *Metamorphoses* (for the Latin text, see Appendix 2). It is undated; but in a "Catalogue of the Prov. Press Co." at the rear of *The Poem of Ulysses* the work is listed as "Soon to be Published"; in another catalogue at the rear of *Poemata Minora, Volume II* (1902) the work is listed for sale, hence presumably completed. It may be a fragment, as the text proceeds to the very bottom of the last ms. page. It bears little resemblance to Dryden's translation of Book I of Ovid (included in "Garth's Ovid" [1717], which HPL had read by 1898 [*SL* 1.7]). The Latin original of the phrase "a raw unfinish'd mass" (l. 3), *rudis indigestaque moles*, was used as the title of HPL's attack on T. S. Eliot's *The Waste Land* (*Conservative*, March 1923; *CE* 2.63–65). "Nabathaea" (l. 74) refers to the ancient kingdom of Nabataea, located between the Sinai Peninsula and the Arabian Peninsula. It was annexed by the Romans in 106 C.E. In l. 100 HPL probably meant to write "creature" (= Ovid's *animale*) for "king," as the line does not scan otherwise.

Pacifist War Song—1917: FP: *Tryout* 3, No. 4 (March 1917): [10] (as by "Lewis Theobald, Jun."). The expression "Too proud to fight" (l. 4) was coined by Woodrow Wilson as part of his successful campaign for re-election as president in 1916, since Wilson correctly gauged that the American people wished to remain uninvolved in World War I. The reference to "hireling Greaser bands" (l. 21) is to suspicions that the Germans were inciting Mexico to invade the United States to distract the nation so that it would not enter World War I on the side of the Allies. The plan (recorded in the so-called Zimmerman Telegram) was discovered and ironically led to US entry into the war.

A Pastoral Tragedy of Appleton, Wisconsin: Text derived from a letter to Alfred Galpin, 27 May [1918] (AMS, JHL; *AG* 16–17), signed "Kleinhart Reiner, Esq." (an obvious parody on Rheinhart Kleiner). The first of many poems on the high-school romances of Alfred Galpin (1901–1983) at Appleton High School (which include all the "Damon and Delia" poems). The situation described in the poem—in which Strephon (Galpin) is pursued by Hecatissa but longs instead for Chloë, who scorns him—was an actual one being faced by Galpin.

The Pathetick History of Sir Wilful Wildrake: Text derived from a letter to Frank Belknap Long, 7 February 1924 (*SL* 1.306–9), where HPL says he wrote the poem three years before. A letter to Kleiner (who had not hidden his tender sentiments toward women) addressed to "Sir Wilful Wildrake, Bt." and dated 13 May 1921 (*SL* 1.131) suggests that the poem had been written by this time. "Charles" (l. 3) refers to Charles II (King of England, 1660–85), whose reign was thought to have been characterised by licentiousness in both life and literature. *"Jus Trium Librorum"* (l. 18), more properly *ius trium liberorum*, is Latin for "the right of three children," referring to certain privileges bestowed upon Roman citizens if they bore three children.

The Peace Advocate: FP: *Tryout* 3, No. 6 (May 1917): [12–14] (attributed to "Elizabeth Berkeley"); rpt. *O-Wash-Ta-Nong* 2, No. 3 (December 1937): [11–12] (as part of "Perverted Poesie or Modern Metre"). For the attribution in the *Tryout* see note on "The Unknown" (1916). The subtitle and epilogue appear only in the second appearance.

The Pensive Swain: FP: *Tryout* 5, No. 10 (October 1919): [20] (as by "Archibald Maynwaring"). For the pseudonym see note on "Wisdom." "P. M." has not been identified; it may possibly be Philip B. McDonald, a professor whom HPL criticised in the essay "The Case for Classicism" (1919).

Percival Lowell: FP: *Excelsior* 1, No. 1 (March 1917): 3. Lowell, the celebrated astronomer, died on 12 November 1916. In DPC (May 1917) HPL refers to the poem as "an abominably dull elegiac piece of heavy verse" (*CE* 1.149). For HPL's youthful encounter with Lowell in 1907, see *SL* 1.21–22. Lowell is frequently mentioned in HPL's astronomy columns of 1906–18, especially in regard to his hypotheses on the Martian canals.

Phaeton: FP: *Silver Clarion* 2, No. 5 (August 1918): 3; rpt. *Californian* 5, No. 1 (Summer 1937): 24; *Golden Atom* 1, No. 10 (Winter 1943): 22–23. Phaeton (more properly Phaethon) was a son of Apollo who, reluctantly receiving permission to steer the chariot of the sun, was unable to control the impetuous horses and was killed by Zeus. The story is told in Ovid's *Metamorphoses* 1.755f. Here the myth seems to be used metaphorically to indicate HPL's cosmic yearnings. In DPC (November 1918) HPL writes: "'Phaeton' is the author's metrical protest against those pragmatical critics who have termed his verse too ethereal in subject and deficient in human interest. The rhymes are correct and the prosody smooth, though as a purist we must protest against the rhetorical enallage whereby the adverb or preposition *beyond* is made to serve as a noun" (*CE* 1.211). The reference is to line 15.

Plaster-All: TMS (private collection); FP: *LS* No, 27 (Fall 1992): 30–31. A loose parody of Hart Crane's "Pastorale" (see Appendix 2). The poem reflects HPL's visit to Cleveland in August 1922, where he met Crane, Samuel Loveman, Alfred Galpin, and other members of Crane's circle. In form the poem naturally bears affinities to "Waste Paper." Steven J. Mariconda has plausibly conjectured that the first-person narrator is meant to be Crane. "Bill Sommer" (l. 6) is William Sommer (1867–1949), Modernist painter. "Willy Lescaze" (l. 12) is William Lescaze (1896–1969), later to become an internationally known architect. *"Spittle Review"* (l. 26) is a parody of *Little Review* (1914–29), an avant-garde journal edited by Margaret Anderson (see l. 60), where Crane published some of his poetry. The references in ll. 29–30 refer to an actual brand of chocolates, Crane's Mary Garden Chocolates (apparently sponsored by the soprano Mary Garden, 1874–1967), an ad for which appeared in the *Little Review*. "Hatfield" (l. 39) is Gordon Hatfield, a minor composer who was gay; HPL wrote of him: "I didn't know whether to kiss it or kill it!" (*SL* 1.280). "Guenther" (l. 39) and "Dave Gordon" (l. 68) are unidentified. In l. 75, HPL refers to Jules Laforgue (1860–1887), French Symbolist poet who was a major influence on T. S. Eliot's early poetry.

The Poe-et's Nightmare: FP: *Vagrant* No. 8 (July 1918): [13–23]; rpt. *Weird Tales* 44, No. 5 (July 1952): 43–46 ("Aletheia Phrikodes" section only). Dated to 1916 by HPL (*SL* 1.59). The epigraph (presumably of HPL's own devising) translates to: "Disturbance is always caused by excess." As R. Boerem ("A Lovecraftian Nightmare" in *FDOC*) has pointed out, the name Lucullus Languish derives from the Roman general L. Licinius Lucullus (a noted gourmand) and Lydia Languish, a character in Sheridan's *The Rivals*. Late in life, when R. H. Barlow contemplated an edition of HPL's collected poems, HPL stated that he wished to retain only the central section (in blank verse) of the poem, thinking that the comic beginning and ending subverted the message of the cosmic central portion (see *OFF* 342). "Aletheia Phrikodes," the title of the central section, is Greek for "the frightful truth." The Latin epigraph to this section (of HPL's devising) translates to: "All is laughter, all is dust, all is nothing." HPL translated the phrase into Greek as the epigraph to "Waste Paper." In ll. 23–24, Auber and Yaanek refer to imaginary realms invented in Poe's poem "Ulalume" (1847); the latter term was also cited in HPL's *At the Mountains of Madness* (1931), as HPL claimed that Poe was identifying Yaanek with Mt. Erebus in Antarctica (*MM* 8). "Homer's well-known catalogue of ships" (l. 48) occurs in Book 2 of the *Iliad*. "On those who dine not wisely, but too well" (l. 58) is a parody of Shakespeare's "Of one that loved not wisely but too well" (*Othello* 5.2.343). The reference in l. 60 is to Oliver Wendell Holmes's poem "Rip Van Winkle, M.D.," in *Songs of Many Seasons* (1875), in which it is suggested that the physician takes a drug called "Elixir Pro" that is largely constituted of alcohol. Ll. 142–46, 150–55, and 159–60 were, with slight revisions, quoted in "May Skies" ([Providence] *Evening News*, 1 May 1917; *CE* 3.222). In DPC (September 1918) Alfred Galpin writes at length on the poem.

The Poem of Ulysses: AMS (JHL); FP: *The Young Folks' Ulysses* (Toronto: Soft Books, 1982); also in *J*. In the AMS the poem is prepared like a booklet and bears the imprint of the "Providence Press Co."; it is labelled a "Second Edition" and dated 8 November 1897. The title I have used appears on the cover; throughout the book there are other titles: "The Poem of Ulysses: Written for Young People"; "The Young Folks' *Ulysses;* or the *Odyssey* in plain Old *English* Verse: An Epick Poem"; "The New Odyssey or Ulyssiad for the Young." The poem is, of course, a highly condensed retelling of Homer's *Odyssey*. In an acknowledgment HPL gives thanks to Pope's *Odyssey* (1725–26), Bulfinch's *Mythology* (1855), and a volume that he calls "Harpers Half Hour series." Harper's Half-Hour Series was a series of small books of essays, poetry, plays, and other short works selling for a quarter. There does not seem to have been any edition (even an abridged one) of Homer or of the *Odyssey*, and I suspect the work in question was Eugene Lawrence's *A Primer of Greek Literature* (1879), which may have had a summary of the *Odyssey*. In "A Confession of Unfaith" (*CE* 5.145) HPL describes the volume as a "tiny book in the private library of my elder aunt" (i.e., Lillian D. Phillips).

Poemata Minora, Volume II: AMS (JHL). First published in complete form in *J*. In the AMS it is prepared like a booklet, with the imprint of "The Providence Press" and dated 1902 (preface dated September 1902). There is a dedication: "To the Gods, Heroes, & Ideals of the Ancients This Volume Is Affectionately Dedicated by a Great Admirer." Volume I (non-extant) apparently dates to 1901 (see HPL to Maurice W. Moe, 27–29 July 1929; AHT).

Ode to Selene or Diana: FP: *Tryout* 5, No. 4 (April 1919): [8] (as "To Selene"; as by "Edward Softly"). HPL quotes the final stanza in a letter to Edwin Baird, 3 February 1924 (*SL* 1.301), as emblematic of his devotion to the past. **To the Old Pagan Religion:** FP: *Tryout* 5, No. 4 (April 1919): [17] (as "The Last Pagan Speaks"; as by "Ames Dorrance Rowley"). The third stanza appears to refer to HPL's claim (made in "A Confession of Unfaith" [1922]) that, at the age of seven, "I have in literal truth built altars to Pan, Apollo, Diana, and Apollo, and

I have watched for dryads and satyrs in the woods and fields at dusk. Once I firmly thought I beheld some of these sylvan creatures dancing under autumnal oaks" (*CE* 5.146). **On the Ruin of Rome:** FP: *J.* **To Pan:** FP: *Tryout* 5, No. 4 (April 1919): [16] (as "Pan"; as by "Michael Ormonde O'Reilly"); rpt. *Tryout* 13, No. 2 (September 1929): [15] (as "Pan"; as by "M. O. O."). **On the Vanity of Human Ambition:** FP: *J.* An adaptation of the sentiments expressed in Samuel Johnson's *The Vanity of Human Wishes* (1749), itself a paraphrase of Juvenal's tenth satire. The final line much more closely echoes Juvenal's *mens sana in corpore sano* (10.356; "a sound mind in a sound body") than Johnson's "healthful Mind, / Obedient Passions, and a Will resign'd" (ll. 359–60).

The Poet of Passion: FP: *Tryout* 3, No. 7 (June 1917): [25] (as by "Louis [*sic*] Theobald, Jun.").

The Poet's Rash Excuse: FP: *Tryout* 6, No. 7 (July 1920): [13] (as by "L. Theobald, Jun."). For "Waller" (l. 6), see note on "To the Late John H. Fowler, Esq."

"The Poetical Punch" . . .: AMS (JHL); FP: *S.* The handwriting dates the poem to around 1913. It may be an offshoot of the *Argosy*/*All-Story* controversy: l. 4 seems to refer to De Lysle Ferrée Cass, a writer whom HPL castigated for his sexual explicitness in a letter to the *All-Story* for 7 March 1914 (see *H. P. Lovecraft in the Argosy*, 35). The hypothesis that Cass's short novel *As It Is Written* is a pseudonymous work by Clark Ashton Smith has now been proven to be false.

The Power of Wine: A Satire: FP: [Providence] *Evening News* 46, No. 46 (13 January 1915): 5; rpt. *Tryout* 2, No. 5 (April 1916): [5–7]; *National Enquirer* 5, No. 26 (28 March 1918): 3. The poem was included with HPL's letter to Maurice W. Moe (8 December 1914; AHT). It is not surprising that it was reprinted in the *National Enquirer*, as that Indianapolis magazine was a temperance journal. HPL published many poems on a variety of subjects in it. The epigraph from Horace is from *Odes* 4.12.19–20: "[Such a drink] expands hopes in the heart and works wonders washing our cares away" (tr. Charles E. Passage).

Primavera: FP: *Brooklynite* 15, No. 2 (April 1925): 1.

Prologue to "Fragments from an Hour of Inspiration": FP: *Tryout* 3, No. 8 (July 1917): [17]; rpt. *The Poetical Works of Jonathan E. Hoag*, ed. H. P. Lovecraft (New York: [Privately printed,] 1923), 41 (as "Prologue" to "Amid Inspiring Scenes"). Hoag (1831–1927) was an aged amateur poet living in Greenwich, NY. HPL later wrote many birthday odes to him, as well as editing his *Poetical Works*. "Dillon's pleasing heights" (l. 4) is unidentified; presumably it is a locale near Hoag's home. "Burgoyne" (l. 16) refers to General John Burgoyne (1722–1792), British army officer who, during the American Revolution, suffered a humiliating defeat at Saratoga, NY, on 17 October 1777.

The Prophecy of Capys Secundus: TMS (JHL), dated 11 January 1921 (as by "Lewis Theobald, Jun."); FP: *WW*. The title is a takeoff of Thomas Babington Macaulay's poem "The Prophecy of Capys," in *Lays of Ancient Rome* (1842). (See note on "Gems from *In a Minor Key*.") The poem commemorates various Hub Club members. In the TMS HPL has indicated in pencil the persons alluded to in the poem: ll. 31–36, Winifred Virginia Jordan; ll. 37–42, Edith Miniter; ll. 43–46, Laurie A. Sawyer; ll. 47–50, K. Leyson Brown; ll. 51–54, S. Lilian McMullen ("Lilian Middleton"); ll. 55–58, Nelson Marden; ll. 59–62, Joseph Bernard Lynch; ll. 63–66, Michael Oscar White; ll. 67–72, Tat (a cat). The epigraph from Virgil's *Aeneid* translates to: "Come now, relate in words the glory which thereupon followed the Dardanian offspring, and I will teach you your own fate." "Dooley's wit" (l. 46) refers to Mr. Dooley, a garrulous Irishman created in sketches written by Finley Peter Dunne (1867–1936) and published in various Chicago newspapers, and also in book form, beginning in the 1890s.

Providence: FP: *Brooklynite* 14, No. 4 (November 1924): 2–3; rpt. *Brooklynite* 17, No. 2 (May 1927): 1; *Californian* 5, No. 1 (Summer 1937): 26–27. (A TMS at JHL is a transcript of the second *Brooklynite* appearance.) HPL wrote the poem on 26 September 1924 for a meeting of the Blue Pencil Club on the topic "The Old Home Town"; he polished it the next day (HPL to Lillian D. Clark, 29–30 September 1924; AMS, JHL). It was also published in the *Providence Evening Bulletin* in early to mid-November 1924 (HPL to Lillian D. Clark, 17–18 November 1924; AMS, JHL), but this appearance has not been located. "A hidden churchyard's crumbling proofs" (l. 21) refers to St. John's Churchyard, the burial ground of St. John's Episcopal Church (1810) on North Main Street.

Providence Amateur Press Club . . .: AMS (JHL), dated 24 November 1916; FP: *S*. The poem, if nothing else, indicates that the Providence Amateur Press Club had folded by this time. It had published issues dated June 1915 and February 1916. The Athenaeum Club of Journalism was based in Harvey, IL, and published the amateur journal *Literary Buds*. The members cited by HPL are unidentified. For "Hudibras" (l. 40), see note on "Ad Criticos."

Providence in 2000 A.D.: FP: [Providence] *Evening Bulletin* 50, No. 55 (4 March 1912): Sec. 2, p. 6. HPL's first published poem.

Psychopompos: TMS (JHL); FP: *Vagrant* No. 10 (October 1919): 13–22; rpt. *Weird Tales* 30, No. 3 (September 1937): 341–48. HPL remarks that the poem was begun in late 1917, but was put aside and was not finished until the summer of 1918 (HPL to the Gallomo, [April 1920]; *AG* 82). The title means "Conveyer of souls [i.e., to Hades]," usually an attribute of Hermes; but the poem is about werewolves, not psychopomps. For the latter see "The Dunwich Horror" (1928) The name Blois can be found on some headstones in St. John's Churchyard in Providence. The opening quatrains are very similar to portions of Winifred Virginia Jackson's poem "Insomnia," *Conservative* 2, No. 3 (October

1916): [2–3]. The final two lines in the *Vagrant* read: "For Sieur de Blois (the old wife's tale is through) / Was lost eternally to mortal view." A member of the Transatlantic Circulator correspondence cycle, John Ravenor Bullen, objected to the use of "through," finding it colloquial (see *CE* 5.53). HPL made a similar change to the poem in "Polaris."

Quinsnicket Park: FP: *Badger* No. 2 (June 1915): 7–10; rpt. [Providence] *Evening News* (8 February 1916): 8. In "The Defence Remains Open!" (*CE* 5.54) HPL dates the poem to 1913. The park (now called Lincoln Woods Park) was one of HPL's favourite sylvan retreats. The epigraph from Virgil is from *Georgics* 2.468–71: "The Country King his peaceful Realm enjoys: / Cool Grots, and living Lakes, the Flow'ry Pride / Of Meads, and Streams that thro' the Valley glide; / And shady Groves that easie Sleep invite, / And after toilsome Days, a soft repose at Night" (tr. John Dryden). In all appearances the following "Note" appears after the epigraph and before the poem proper:

> Quinsnicket Park, the most attractive spot in the state of Rhode Island, lies in the town of Lincoln, about four miles north of Providence. It is a bit of old New-England, containing a considerable extent of primeval forest with beautiful takes, hills, and glens, and much farming land, on which remain unchanged the old houses of two centuries or more ago.
>
> A visit to this rustic tract is far more instructive than any amount of study in books on New-England history and antiquities. The name "Quinsnicket" is the Indian equivalent for "stone huts", and refers to the old practice of the savages in making their winter homes in the clefts of the great split rocks which abound in this rugged district. Quinsnicket Park is a state reservation, so that its ancient condition will be preserved permanently.

In DPC (September 1915) HPL comments: "Our own poetical attempt . . . contains 112 lines, and spoils three and a half otherwise excellent pages. It is probable that but few have had the fortitude to read it through, or even to begin it, hence we will pass over its defects in merciful silence" (*CE* 1.62).

R. Kleiner, Laureatus, in Heliconem: FP: *Conservative* 2, No. 1 (April 1916): 2. The title translates to: "Rheinhart Kleiner, the Laureate, in Helicon" (a mountain in Boeotia sacred to Apollo and the Muses). The reference is to Kleiner's winning the Poetry Laureateship in the UAPA for 1915–16.

Regner Lodbrog's Epicedium: AMS (JHL): FP: *Acolyte* 2, No. 3 (Summer 1944): 11–15 (as "Regnar Lodbrug's Epicedium"). The poem was written in late 1914 (see HPL to Maurice W. Moe, 17 December 1914 [AHT]) and is a translation of a Latin translation by Magnús Ólafsson of Laufás published by Olaus Wormius (Ole Wurm, 1588–1654) of a Runic poem, quoted in Hugh Blair's *A Critical Dissertation on the Poems of Ossian* (1763). The original poem, *Krákumál*, was probably composed in the 12th century; Regner Lodbrog—insofar as he is based on an historical person—lived in the 9th century (a Viking chief named Ragnar, who has been identified as one of the inspirations for Lodbrog, sacked Paris in 845). HPL was assisted in his translation by Blair's English prose translation of all but the first stanza (which is perhaps why HPL's first stanza has more gaps than the others). (For Wormius's Latin text and Blair's English paraphrase, see Appendix 2.) HPL quotes some lines from the Latin version as the epigraph to "The Teuton's Battle-Song" (1916). It was HPL's misconstrual of Blair's comments on Wormius that led him to believe that Wormius lived in the 13th century; he was later deemed the Latin translator of the *Necronomicon*. On the whole matter see S. T. Joshi, "Lovecraft, Regner Lodbrog, and Olaus Wormius," *CoC* No. 89 (Eastertide 1995): 3–7; rpt. *Primal Sources: Essays on H. P. Lovecraft* (New York: Hippocampus Press, 2003), 145–53. An epicedium is a funeral ode. Regner Lodbrog was a legendary king of Denmark. "Gothland" (l. 2) or Götaland is the southernmost of the three old lands of Sweden (not to be confused with the island of Gotland). "Thor" (l. 5) is a misunderstanding; the Old Norse original refers to Thora, Regner's first wife, the daughter of Herröd ("Heraudus" of l. 46). The "channel of Oreon" (l. 14) is the straits of Öresund between the Danish island Zealand and the Swedish province Scania (it is cited as the "bay of Oreon" by Blair). Vistula (l. 35) is a long river in Poland; its identification with the Íva of the Old Norse original is dubious. "Helsingian" (l. 38) is the adjectival form of Helsingia, the English name for the province of Hälsingland, in central Sweden. "Scarfian rocks" (l. 54) and "Indirian islands" (l. 61) are unidentified; the phrases are copied directly from Blair. "Lano's plain" (l. 67) is Ulleråker near Uppsala in Sweden; HPL's translation—copied from Blair—is a mistranslation of Latin "Laneo campo" (field of wool), which in turn is a mistranslation of Old Norse "Ullarakri," arising from a confusion between the word for "wool" ("ull") and the name of the Norse God Ullr. See Martin Andersson, "Of Regner Lodbrog, Hugh Blair, and Mistranslations," *Lovecraft Annual* No. 6 (2012): 36–42.

Respite: FP: *Conservative* 2, No. 3 (October 1916): [6–7]; rpt. *National Magazine* 45, No. 6 (March 1917): 826. In DPC (March 1917) HPL writes: "'Respite' is a lachrymose lament in five stanzas by the present critic. The metre is regular, which is perhaps some excuse for its creation and publication" (*CE* 1.140).

The Return: TMS (JHL); FP: *Tryout* 11, No. 1 (December 1926): [7–8]. On Charles W. Smith, editor of the *Tryout*.

Revelation: FP: *Tryout* 5, No. 3 (March 1919): [34]; rpt. *National Enquirer* 8, No. 4 (24 April 1919): 3. For "Aidenn" (l. 5), see note on "The Eidolon."

The Road to Ruin: AMS (JHL), found on the verso of "The Decline and Fall of a Man of the World." For the chemical formula in l. 8, see note on that poem.

The Rose of England: FP: *Scot* No. 14 (October 1916): 7.

A Rural Summer Eve: FP: *Trail* 1, No. 2 (January 1916): 12–13.

The Rutted Road: FP: *Tryout* 3, No. 2 (January 1917): [17] (as by "Lewis Theobald, Jun."); rpt. *Tryout* 10, No. 8 (March 1926): [17].

S. S. L.: Christmas 1920: AMS (JHL); FP: *S.* A Christmas poem to HPL's mother.

Saturnalia: AMS (JHL). The handwriting dates the poem to the mid-1920s. For "Morven's Mead" (l. 1) see note on "Content."

The Simple Speller's Tale: FP: *Conservative* 1, No. 1 (April 1915): [1]. One of HPL's many attacks on simple spelling; see the later essay "The Simple Spelling Mania" (1919; *CE* 2.34–35). The couplet at the end refers to Brander Matthews (1852–1929), an American literary critic who was a vigorous proponent of simplified spelling.

Simplicity: A Poem: Text derived from a letter to Maurice W. Moe, 18 May 1922 (AHT). In l. 55 (and footnote), HPL refers to *Main Street* (1920) by Sinclair Lewis (1885–1951). In l. 56 (and footnote), he refers to Sherwood Anderson (1876–1941), whose story collection *Winesburg, Ohio* (1919) was a landmark in social realism (HPL later admitted it was a partial influence on "Facts concerning the Late Arthur Jermyn and His Family" [1920]; see *MW* 508). The third footnote, about German philosopher Arthur Schopenhauer (1788–1860), refers to a passage in the essay "The Vanity of Existence": "The scenes of our life are like pictures done in rough mosaic. Looked at close, they produce no effect. There is nothing beautiful to be found in them, unless you stand some distance off." *Studies in Pessimism,* tr. T. Bailey Saunders (London: Swan Sonnenschein, 1893), 36. In a letter to Anne Tillery Renshaw, 14 June 1922 (AHT), HPL quotes ll. 9–10 and 17–18, but precedes them with four original lines: "Wide rolling pastures, till'd by many a swain, / And teeming orchards scatter'd o'er the plain; / Unbounded prospects o'er the vales and hills, / With fat kine quaffing at the crystal rills."

Sir Thomas Tryout: TMS (JHL); FP: *Tryout* 7, No. 9 (December 1921): [31–32] (as by "Ward Phillips"); rpt. *Tryout* 21, No. 1 (March 1941): [3–4]. On Charles W. Smith's cat.

The Smile: FP: *Symphony* No. 12 (July 1916): [3–4]; rpt. *Little Budget of Knowledge and Nonsense* 1, Nos. 5–6 (August–September 1917): 68. The epigraph ("Laugh, if you are wise") is from Martial (*Epigrams* 2.41.1); it is quoted as the epigraph to the *Spectator* No. 47 (24 April 1711). "Maestus" (l. 8) and "Laetus" (l. 49) are, respectively, Latin for "sad" and "happy." Cf. HPL's essay "The Symphonic Ideal" (*Conservative,* October 1916; *CE* 5.25–26), which elaborates upon the ideas expressed in this poem.

[The Solace of Georgian Poetry]: Text derived from a letter to Maurice W. Moe,

18 May 1916 (AHT), where HPL declares that it is an "impromptu" verse designed to testify to the psychological effects that writing Georgian poetry has on his temperament: "what a quaintly idyllic little world those artificial writers [of the Georgian age] made for themselves and their publick! I would fain dwell therein forever—blest with sights that have never been seen, and happiness that has never existed!"

Solstice: AMS (JHL), dated Christmas 1924; FP: *Tryout* 9, No. 11 (January 1925): [8].

Sonnet on Myself: FP: *Tryout* 4, No. 7 (July 1918): [2] (as by "Lewis Theobald, Jun."). Included in a letter to the Kleicomolo (April 1917; *RK* 100) under the title "Lewis Theobald, Jun., on Himself." HPL here declares that the poem is his first sonnet and goes on to state that the poem was written in response to a poem by Paul Shivell, "His Frank Self-Expression" (see Appendix 2). (HPL renders the title as "My Frank Self-Expression.")

[Sonnet Study]: TMS (JHL); FP: *WW*. The text exists on a mimeographed sheet (with the title "Sonnet Study," presumably supplied by Maurice W. Moe) with accompanying "analysis" (also presumably by Moe). The first poem is in the Italian sonnet form, the second in the Elizabethan or Shakespearean sonnet form. (A third sonnet, by Richard Watson Gilder, is also on the mimeographed sheet.) The poems were presumably written either for Moe's high school classes or for use in Moe's abortive book on poetry appreciation, *Doorways to Poetry*, on which HPL was supplying considerable assistance in the late 1920s. If these poems were written prior to *Fungi from Yuggoth*, they may have helped to direct HPL's attention to the aesthetic potential of the sonnet, as HPL had written few sonnets heretofore.

Sors Poetae: AMS (JHL); FP: *S*. The handwriting dates the poem to around 1915. The title is Latin for "The fate of a poet." Evidently another offshoot of the *Argosy* controversy, as "Jackson" in l. 9 is clearly a reference to Fred Jackson.

The Spirit of Summer: FP: *National Enquirer* 6, No. 13 (27 June 1918): 10; rpt. *Conservative* 4, No. 1 (July 1918): 1.

Spring: FP: *Tryout* 5, No. 4 (April 1919): [15–16]. The piece by Raymond (1875–1950) may be one of his "Tribune's Weekly Almanack" columns, which appear to have run from 1915 to early 1919. How HPL obtained this item is unclear.

[Stanzas on Samarkand]: The first stanza comes from a letter to Frank Belknap Long (25 February 1924; AHT); the second from an undated letter to Frank Belknap Long (c. late February 1924; AHT); the third from a letter to Frank Belknap Long (21 March 1924; AHT); the fourth from a letter to James Ferdinand Morton (8 November 1929; *JFM* 178). The stanzas are all pastiches or parodies of James Elroy Flecker's *Hassan* (1922): toward the end of that play various characters recite quatrains, all ending with the line ". . . take the Golden Road to Samarkand."

The State of Poetry: FP: *Conservative* 1, No. 3 (October 1915): 1–3. The epigraph from Ovid is from the *Metamorphoses* 1.9 ("The discordant seeds of things not well joined"), referring to the state of the universe at the beginning of time, before "Nature and a God" brought order to chaos. See HPL's juvenile translation, "Ovid's Metamorphoses," where he renders the line "Of ill-join'd seeds, congested in one place." "Mac Flecknoe" (l. 2) refers to John Dryden's celebrated satire, *Mac Flecknoe* (1682), in which Mac Flecknoe is characterised as the epitome of dulness. For Codrus (l. 8), see note on "To the Arcadian." HPL subsequently invents poets using Latin adjectives as proper names: "Raucus" (l. 11) means "harsh-sounding"; "Agrestis" (15) means "rustic"; "Durus" (l. 23) means "rough-hewn"; "Hodiernus" (l. 31) means "contemporary"; "Mundanus" (l. 47) means "mundane."

A Summer Sunset and Evening: FP: *O-Wash-Ta-Nong* 2, No. 3 (December 1937): [12] (as part of "Perverted Poesie or Modern Metre"). Probably written in 1917, when the other poems in "Perverted Poesie" were either written or assembled in this group. Michael Drayton (1563–1631) was an Elizabethan poet and prose writer. The *Poly-Olbion* is an immense poem written between 1598 and 1622 relating the beauties of the English countryside. In l. 34, HPL refers to James Thomson (1700–1748), author of *The Seasons* (1726–30), one of HPL's favourite poems.

Sunset: FP: *Tryout* 4, No. 1 (December 1917): [8]; rpt. *Presbyterian Advance* 7, No. 7 (18 April 1918): 6; *United Amateur* 17, No. 5 (May 1918): 90; *Californian* 5, No. 1 (Summer 1937): 24; *Tryout* 19, No. 3 (May 1938): [15]. One of the most successful of HPL's poems of this type. The first stanza is possibly an unconscious recollection of the first stanza of Gray's *Elegy Written in a Country Church-yard* (1751): "The Curfew tolls the knell of parting day, / The lowing herd wind slowly o'er the lea, / The plowman homeward plods his weary way, / And leaves the world to darkness and to me."

Temperance Song: FP: *Dixie Booster* 4, No. 4 (Spring 1916): 9. For HPL and temperance see note on "Monody on the Late King Alcohol" (1919). "The Bonnie Blue Flag" (1861) was a Confederate war song named after a flag adopted in 1810 for the short-lived Republic of Florida. HPL has imitated the refrain of the song in his own refrain: "Hurrah! Hurrah! / For Southern Rights, Hurrah! / Hurrah for the Bonnie Blue Flag / That bears a Single Star!"

The Teuton's Battle-Song: FP: *United Amateur* 15, No. 7 (February 1916): 85. In a letter to Maurice W. Moe (17 December 1914; AHT) HPL mentions the poem, so presumably it had been composed shortly before this date. For the epigraph see "Regner Lodbrog's Epicedium" (1914). In the first appearance HPL has added an "Author's Note" (85–86):

> The writer here endeavours to trace the ruthless ferocity and incredible bravery of the modern Teutonic soldier to the hereditary influence of the

ancient Northern Gods and Heroes. Despite the cant of the peace-advocate, we must realise that our present Christian civilisation, the product of an alien people, rests but lightly upon the Teuton when he is deeply aroused, and that in the heat of combat he is quite prone to revert to the mental type of his own Woden-worshipping progenitors, losing himself in that superb fighting zeal which baffled the conquering cohorts of a Caesar, and humbled the proud aspirations of a Varus. Though appearing most openly in the Prussian, whose recent acts of violence are so generally condemned, this native martial ardour is by no means peculiar to him, but is instead the common heritage of every branch of our indomitable Xanthochroic race, British and Continental alike, whose remote forefathers were for countless generations reared in the stern precepts of the virile religion of the North. Whilst we may with justice deplore the excessive militarism of the Kaiser Wilhelm and his followers, we cannot rightly agree with those effeminate preachers of universal brotherhood who deny the virtue of that manly strength which maintains our great North European family in its position of undisputed superiority over the rest of mankind, and which in its purest form is today the bulwark of Old England. It is needless to say to an educated audience that the term "Teuton" is in no way connected with the modern German Empire, but embraces the whole Northern stock, including English and Belgians.

In the Northern religion, Alfadur, or the All-Father, was a vague though supreme deity. Beneath him were among others Woden, or Odin, practically the supreme deity, and Woden's eldest son Thor, the God of War. Asgard, or heaven, was the dwelling-place of the Gods, whilst Midgard was the earth, or abode of man. The rainbow, or bridge of Bifrost, which connected the two regions, was guarded by the faithful watchman Heimdall. Woden lived in the palace of Valhalla, near the grove of Glasir, and had as messengers to earth the Valkyries, armed, mailed, and mounted virgins who conveyed from the earth to Asgard such men as had fallen bravely in battle. Only those who fell thus could taste to the full the joys of paradise. These joys consisted of alternate feasting and fighting. At Woden's feasts in Valhalla was served the flesh of the boar Schrimnir, which, though cooked and eaten at every meal, would regain its original condition the next day. The wounds of the warriors in each celestial combat were miraculously healed at the end of the fighting.

But this heaven was not to last forever. Some day would come Ragnarok, or the Twilight of the Gods, when all creation would be destroyed, and all the Gods and men save Alfadur perish. Surtur, after killing the last of these Gods, would burn up the world. Afterward the supreme Alfadur would make a new earth or paradise, creating again the Gods and men, and suffering them ever after to dwell in Peace and Plenty.

In DPC (June 1916) HPL notes: "'The Teuton's Battle-Song' is an attempt of the present critic to view the principles of human warfare without the hypocritical spectacles of sentimentality" (*CE* 1.117).

Theobaldian Aestivation: TMS (JHL), as by "Ludovicus Theobaldus Secundus"; FP: *M*. Another poem (like "Ex-Poet's Reply") commemorating the Boston amateur journalism convention held at 20 Webster Street in Allston in July 1920. The title means "The Summering of [Lewis] Theobald." The individuals cited are as follows: "St. John" (l. 12), Rheinhart Kleiner; "Houtain" (l. 12), "George" (l. 18), and "St. Julian" (l. 24), George Julian Houtain; "Alcalde" (l. 67), W. Paul Cook; "Conserver" (l. 72), George Julian Houtain; "Planchette" (l. 73), Edith Miniter; "Ouija" (l. 73), Laurie A. Sawyer; "Berkeley" (l. 76), Winifred Virginia Jordan; "Michael Oscar" (l. 79), Michael Oscar White; "J. Bernard" (l. 85), Joseph Bernard Lynch; "Madame La Mere" (l. 91), unknown; "The Parkers" (l. 92), Charles A. A. Parker [and wife?]; "Mistress Fairbanks" (l. 95), unknown; "Hamlet" (l. 96), Alice M. Hamlet; "Thompson" (l. 100), Eva H. Thompson; "Morton" (l. 107), James F. Morton; "Dennis" (l. 107), Mrs. Harriet Caryl Cox Dennis; "Wagner" (l. 109), Charles Wagner; "Cummings" (l. 109), Harold Cummings; "Ellis" (l. 109), H. Cox Ellis. In l. 24, "something analogous" is HPL's euphemism for "lie." In l. 78 HPL refers to the amateur journal the *Linnet*. In l. 84 HPL alludes to the Persian poet Omar Khayyám (1048–1131), whose *Rubáiyát* was translated into English in 1859 by Edward FitzGerald.

Theodore Roosevelt: 1858–1919: FP: *United Amateur* 18, No. 3 (January 1919): 52. Roosevelt died on 6 January 1919. HPL manifestly preferred ex-President Roosevelt (who vigorously urged US involvement in World War I) to the pacifist Woodrow Wilson. In "Lucubrations Lovecraftian" (*United Co-operative*, April 1921) HPL defends himself against W. Paul Cook's accusation of anti-Wilsonism when he had referred to Roosevelt as "America's greatest man": "True, the anti- Wilsonism might have been there; yet when I wrote that passage I was thinking not of the smallness of any man, but of the greatness of Theodore Roosevelt—and what American of the present age can be classed with him? . . . Of course Colonel Roosevelt was against the late Wilson administration—as the truest patriots were—but general praise of an anti-administrationist does not necessarily imply a special condemnation of the opposite party" (*CE* 1.282). See also "To Alan Seeger." "Quentin" (l. 40) refers to Roosevelt's son Quentin (1897–1918), a pilot in World War I who died in France on 14 July 1918.

[To a Cat]: AMS (JHL). An ode to an unspecified cat.

To a Dreamer: AMS (JHL), dated 25 April 1920; FP: *Coyote* No. 16 (January 1921): 4; rpt. *Weird Tales* 4, No. 3 (November 1924): 54. HPL notes in a letter (HPL to Frank Belknap Long, 4 June 1921; AHT) that the poem was founded on an idea occurring among Baudelaire's notes and jottings—as contained, presumably, in *Baudelaire: His Prose and Poetry*, ed. T. R. Smith (New York: Boni & Liveright/ Modern Library [1919]; *LL* #71). (It was from this same book that HPL derived the epigraph from Baudelaire for "Hypnos" [1922].) The name Pnath had first been invented in "The Doom That Came to Sarnath" (1919); Thok and Zin are original to this poem. All three are used again in *The Dream-Quest of Unknown Kadath* (1926–27), and they occasionally appear in other works.

To a Sophisticated Young Gentleman: AMS (JHL), dated 15 December 1928; text also found (with variant title, "An Epistle to Francis, Ld. Belknap . . .") in a letter to Maurice W. Moe, [January 1929] (*SL* 2.255–57) (original not seen). FP: *SL* 2.255–57. HPL had given a volume of Proust (*Swann's Way*, the first volume of *Remembrance of Things Past*) to Frank Belknap Long as a Christmas present. For "Cham" (l. 16), see note on "To Rheinhart Kleiner, Esq." For "Waste Land" (l. 19), see note on "My Favourite Character." "*Benda* or *Luleu*" (l. 20) refers to Lilith Benda, an author frequently published in H. L. Mencken and George Jean Nathan's cutting-edge periodical, the *Smart Set;* "Luleu" is unidentified. The reference in l. 28 is to one of many self-service cafeterias scattered throughout New York City, where various food items could be purchased for a nickel. "McCrory's" (l. 29) was a chain of nickel-and-dime stories in New York and adjacent states. The reference in l. 47 is to James Joyce's *Ulysses* (1922); in l. 49, to Ben Hecht (1894–1964), American author whose novel *Erik Dorn* (1921) HPL considered the epitome of Modernism; in l. 52, to the final line of Eliot's *Waste Land* ("Shantih Shantih Shantih"—a Buddhist word meaning tranquillity); in l. 53, to e. e. cummings (1894–1962), who refused to use capital letters in his poetry; in l. 54, to Vachel Lindsay (1879–1931), American poet; in l. 55, to American novelist James Branch Cabell (1879–1958), whose name does not in fact rhyme with "stable," but rather with "rabble"; in l. 57, to Gertrude Stein (1874–1946), American author and poet; in l. 58, to Michael Arlen (1895–1956), Armenian-born writer (also the author of a volume of *Ghost Stories* [1927], although HPL did not care for them); in l. 60, to American writer Alfred Kreymborg (1883–1966) and French writer Jean Cocteau (1889–1963); in l. 61, to Joris-Karl Huysmans (1848–1907), whose quasi-weird novels *À Rebours* (1884; *Against the Grain*) and *Là-Bas* (1891; *Down There*) HPL enjoyed; in l. 62, to American novelist and critic Kenneth Burke (1897–1993) and American writer Maxwell Bodenheim (1892–1954).

To a Young Poet in Dunedin: Text derived from a letter to Lillian D. Clark, 30 May 1931 (AMS, JHL); the poem also exists in a letter to August Derleth, 29 May 1931 (*ES* 1.345), under the title "To a Young Poet"; also in a TMS (JHL), but this was prepared by R. H. Barlow, presumably from the letter to Clark. The poem was written for Allan Brownell Grayson, a young friend of Henry S. Whitehead whom HPL met when visiting Whitehead in Dunedin, FL, in the summer of 1931.

To a Youth: AMS, TMS (JHL); FP: *Tryout* 7, No. 1 (February 1921): [18] (as by "Richard Raleigh").

To Alan Seeger: FP: *Tryout* 4, No. 7 (July 1918): [1–2]; rpt. *National Enquirer* 6, No. 20 (15 August 1918): 10; *United Amateur* 18, No. 2 (November 1918): 24. Seeger (1888–1916), an American who joined the Foreign Legion, was almost as bad a poet as HPL, but his death in the war gave his work a spurious but brief celebrity. His collected poems appeared in late 1916 and included "A Message to America" (pp. 162–66), a plea for America to enter the war. In DPC (January 1919) HPL comments that his poem "celebrat[es] the memory of a young American hero of the French Foreign Legion, who, had the fortunes of battle spared him, would have been one of our century's greatest poets. Seeger was a bard of the broadest and keenest vision, and in his verses hailed as his greatest fellow-citizen that mighty leader of men [Theodore Roosevelt] for whom the world is in recent mourning as these paragraphs are penned" (*CE* 1.220).

To Alfred Galpin, Esq.: FP: *Tryout* 6, No. 12 (December 1920): [7–8] (as by "L. Theobald"). HPL declares that he had written the poem on Galpin's seventeenth birthday (8 November 1918), but that "publication was delayed" (*JFM* 26). Galpin had become president of the UAPA at the convention in late July 1920, serving until the following July. The references in ll. 14f. are to the Greek philosopher Aristotle (384–322 B.C.E.); the Roman philosopher-poet T. Lucretius Carus (99?–55? B.C.E.), author of the *De Rerum Natura;* the Greek poet Aratus (315?–240 B.C.E.), author of the *Phaenomena,* an astronomical poem; and Roman playwright and philosopher L. Annaeus Seneca (4. B.C.E.–65 C.E.). L. 48 partially echoes the celebrated line in Virgil's *Aeneid* 6.853, *parcere subiectis et debellare superbos* ("to spare the conquered and subdue the proud").

To an Accomplished Young Gentlewoman . . .: AMS (JHL); FP: *S.* An acrostic poem. There is no indication of who "Dorrie M." is; perhaps she was involved in amateur journalism.

To an Infant: TMS (JHL), dated 26 August 1925; FP: *Brooklynite* 15, No. 4 (October 1925): 2. The poem was written for a meeting of the Blue Pencil Club for 29 August; the designated literary topic was the newborn son of amateur writer Ernest A. Dench.

To Arthur Goodenough, Esq.: FP: *Tryout* 4, No. 9 (September 1918): [1–2]; rpt. in Arthur Goodenough, "Further Recollections of Amateur Journalism," *Vagrant* [Sping 1927]: [28–29] (as "To Mr. Arthur Goodenough of New England, on His Most Meritorious Poetrie"). One manuscript of the poem (AHT) dates the poem to 20 August 1918 (HPL's 28th birthday). Goodenough had written a poem, "Lovecraft—An Appreciation" (included in Goodenough's "Further Recollections," [25–26]), which contained such fulsome praise that HPL thought it was a spoof; but W. Paul Cook convinced HPL that Goodenough was simply being naively sincere. See *In Memoriam: Howard Phillips*

Lovecraft (1941; rpt. *Lovecraft Remembered,* ed. Peter Cannon [Sauk City, WI: Arkham House, 1998], 109). HPL met Goodenough on several occasions in the late 1920s at the latter's rustic cottage in Vermont.

To Belinda . . .: See "To the Incomparable Clorinda." Unsigned.

To Charlie of the Comics: TMS (included in a letter to John T. Dunn, 25 October 1915; *Books at Brown* 38–39 [1991–92]: 175); FP: *Providence Amateur* 1, No. 2 (February 1916): 13–14. The poem is quoted in a letter to Rheinhart Kleiner, 30 September 1915 (*RK* 21), and is of course about the actor Charles Chaplin (1889–1977). Kleiner's poem "To Mary of the Movies" (about Mary Pickford) had appeared in the *Piper* No. 3 (September 1915): 12 (for the text, see Appendix 2). Chaplin and Pickford were the first true "movie stars." Of the former HPL wrote in late 1915: "Chaplin is infinitely amusing—too good for the rather vulgar films he used to appear in—and I hope he will in future be an exponent of more refined comedy" (*SL* 1.18). See also *SL* 1.50–51.

To Clark Ashton Smith . . .: AMS, TMS (JHL); FP: *Weird Tales* 31, No. 5 (April 1938): 392 (as "To Clark Ashton Smith"). The poem was written in December 1936, as it is quoted in a letter to R. H. Barlow (11 December 1936; *OFF* 382–83). It also appears in a variety of letters; one of them (to E. Hoffmann Price, [11 January 1937]; JHL) bears a variant title—"To Klarkash-Ton, Lord of Averoigne"—that has been used in some appearances. Smith (1893–1961) was, of course, a longtime associate of HPL's, having first communicated with him in 1922. "Averoigne" (l. 13) refers to Smith's invented realm in mediaeval France (probably based on the actual French province of Auvergne), used as the setting for several tales.

To Col. Linkaby Didd: AMS (JHL), dated 1 November 1918; FP: *S.* HPL comments: "'Col. Linkaby Didd', to whom the lines are inscribed, is an imaginary character figuring frequently in the local [*Providence*] *Journal*. Like Sir Roger de Coverly [*sic*] he is supposed to be an odd rural character, residing at 'Nooseneck Hill, in the town of Exeter'—the most desolate and remote spot conceivable in Rhode Island. 'Col. Didd' always takes the wrong side of public questions, arguing picturesquely and illiterately, with many comic blunders and perversions of the Malaprop variety" (HPL to Rheinhart Kleiner, 25 November 1918; *RK* 149). The poem concerns the 1918 campaign for election to the U.S. Senate from Rhode Island between the Republican LeBaron Colt (1846–1924), favoured by HPL, and the Democrat George O'Shaunessy. Colt in fact won the election and would serve until his death. In l. 54, the references are to Charles James Fox (1749–1806), British statesman who supported the Americans during the American War of Independence; Tiberius and Gaius Gracchus, Roman political figures who, in the 2nd century B.C.E., attempted to redistribute wealth from the patricians to the plebeians; Jack Cade, who led a popular revolt in England against King Henry VI; and the mythical mediaeval figure Robin Hood.

"Cato" (l. 61) refers to Cato the Younger (95–46 B.C.E.), who opposed Julius Caesar's attempt to name himself emperor. "Catiline" (l. 69) refers to L. Sergius Catilina (108–62 B.C.E.), Roman politician who attempted to lead a rebellion to overthrow the Republic; Cicero condemned him in four celebrated orations, and he eventually died in battle.

To Damon: FP: *Tryout* 8, No. 9 (August 1923): [7–9] (as by "L. Theobald"). See also HPL's poems on the joint birthday of Galpin and Margaret Galbraham ("To the Eighth of November" [1918] and "Birthday Lines to Margfred Galbraham" [1919]).

To Delia, Avoiding Damon: FP: *Tryout* 4, No. 9 (September 1918): [5–7] (as by "Edward Softly"). On Galpin's love affairs. Tityrus is a shepherd cited in the pastoral poems of Theocritus and Virgil. In l. 82, Archilochus (680?–645 b.c.e.) was a Greek poet known for his use of poetic invective.

To Edward John Moreton Drax Plunkett . . . : FP: *Tryout* 5, No. 11 (November 1919): [11–12]. Clearly written after having first read Dunsany (1878–1957) in September 1919 and having seen him lecture in Boston in October. The issue of the *Tryout* was sent to Dunsany, who responded (very charitably) by noting that the poem was "magnificent" and that "I am most grateful to the author of that poem for his warm and generous enthusiasm, crystallised in verse" (*Tryout* 5, No. 12 [December 1919]: [12]).

To Endymion: FP: *Tryout* 8, No. 10 (September 1923): [15–16] (as by "L. Theobald, Jun."). In Greek myth, Endymion was a shepherd to whom Zeus, at the behest of Selene (goddess of the moon), bestowed the gift of eternal youth. HPL had come into contact with Long (1901–1994) in early 1920; in 1922, when first meeting Long, HPL referred to him as "an exquisite boy of twenty who hardly looks fifteen" (*SL* 1.180). For an explanation as to why HPL was in error as to Long's year of birth, see Peter Cannon, "Frank Belknap Long: When Was He Born and Why Was Lovecraft Wrong?" *Studies in Weird Fiction* No. 17 (Summer 1995): 33–34.

[To Frank Belknap Long on His Birthday]: AMS (private collection); presumably dates to April 1925, when HPL (erroneously) believed Long's twenty-third birthday to be (see note on "To Endymion").

To General Villa: FP: *Blarney Stone* 2, No. 6 (November–December 1914): 8. In DPC (March 1915) HPL remarks: "'To General Villa' is a peculiar piece of verse written last summer for the purpose of defying those who had charged the author with pedantry and pomposity. . . . The changes of time and revolutions have rendered the last stanza sadly out of date" (*CE* 1.22–23). HPL means that Victoriano Huerta, who had assumed the presidency upon the assassination of Francisco I. Madero in February 1913, had been overthrown on 15 July 1914, setting up a struggle for power between Pancho Villa and Venustiano Carranza, in which the latter ultimately prevailed. "Bryan" (l. 15) is William Jennings Bryan, US Secretary of State who for a time supported Villa. See also "The Beauties of Peace."

To George Kirk, Esq.: AMS (private collection), dated 18 January 1925. Kirk (1898–1962) had just moved into quarters at 106th Street in Manhattan. Later he moved for a time into HPL's own boarding-house at 169 Clinton Street in Brooklyn.

To George Willard Kirk . . .: TMS (JHL), dated 24 November 1925; FP: *National Amateur* 49, No. 5 (May 1927): 5. Kirk had by this time moved into the boarding-house at 317 West 14th Street, on the borderline between the Chelsea and Greenwich Village districts of Manhattan; HPL's frequent visits to this residence would cause him to use it as the setting for "Cool Air" (1926). "Moore" (l. 16) refers to Clement Clarke Moore (1779–1863), author of "The Night Before Christmas," who had lived in Chelsea.

To Greece, 1917: FP: *Vagrant* No. 6 (November 1917): 15–17. The poem urges the Greeks to take action against the invading Germans. At the outset of the war Greece was very divided on its course of action, and HPL (l. 13) upbraids King Constantine I (r. 1913–17) for his pledge of neutrality. Naturally, HPL (l. 52) lauds Eleutherios Venizelos (1864–1936), prime minister of Greece (1910–20), who had sided with the Allies and in 1916 had established a separate government, forcing Constantine to flee the country on 11 June 1917. His son Alexander (r. 1917–20) took his place. The poem must have been written before June 1917, when the Greeks actually entered the war on the Allied side. "Pelides" (l. 9) means "son of Peleus," a reference to the Greek warrior Achilles, who in Homer's *Iliad* defeated the Trojans. "Hippias" (l. 14) refers to Hippias, the tyrant of Athens (525–510 B.C.E.) who fled the city and joined the Persians, leading their army at the battle of Marathon (l. 15) in 490 B.C.E., won by the Greeks. In ll. 16–18 HPL refers to two other notable battles in which the Greeks defeated the Persians: the battle of Salamis and the battle of Thermopylae, both in 480 B.C.E. In l. 22 HPL refers to Xerxes I, king of Persia (r. 486–465 B.C.E.). In l. 50 HPL refers to Cleisthenes, an Athenian nobleman who, in the late 6th and early 5th centuries B.C.E., helped to institute Athenian democracy. In l. 57 HPL refers to Pericles (495?–429 b.c.e.), leader of the Athenian democracy from 461 B.C.E. until his death, during which time Athenian culture flourished in an unprecedented fashion.

To Heliodora . . .: See "To the Incomparable Clorinda." Signed "Anacreon Microcephalos" (i.e, small-brained).

[To His Mother on Thanksgiving]: AMS (JHL), dated 30 November 1911, 3:30 a.m.; FP: *SL* 1.3. On the verso of one of the AMSs is found a note by HPL's mother, Sarah Susan Lovecraft: "Written on Thanksgiving day by HPL When I went to Lillies to dinner & he was asleep." "Lillie" is HPL's aunt Lillian D. Clark (1856–1932).

To Jonathan E. Hoag, Esq.: FP: *Eurus* 1, No. 1 (February 1918): 5–6; rpt. in *The Poetical Works of Jonathan E. Hoag*, ed. H. P. Lovecraft (New York: [Privately printed,] 1923), 61–63. For Hoag see "Prologue" to "Fragments from an Hour of Inspiration" (1917).

To Jonathan E. Hoag, Esq.: FP: *National Amateur* 49, No. 5 (May 1927): 10.

To Jonathan Hoag: FP: *Troy* [NY] *Times* (10 February 1926); rpt. *Brooklynite* 16, No. 1 (May 1926): 1. For "Dionondawa" (l. 12), see note on "Ad Scribam."

To Jonathan Hoag, Esq.: FP: *Pine Cones* 1, No. 2 (February 1919): 2–3; rpt. *The Poetical Works of Jonathan E. Hoag*, ed. H. P Lovecraft (New York: [Privately printed, 1923), 63–64. For Hoag's nickname Scriba (l. 39), see note on "Ad Scribam."

To M. W. M.: FP: *United Amateur* 16, No. 9 (July 1917): 134 (in column, "News Notes"). The poem was written to Maurice Winter Moe (1882–1940), at this time a teacher at the Appleton High School in Appleton, WI. In "News Notes" HPL comments: "Maurice W. Moe . . . is trying a novel experiment this summer for the sake of his health. He has undertaken a labourer's work on one of the new buildings of Lawrence College, lifting planks, shovelling mud, and wheeling bags of cement like a seasoned workingman. While painful at first, the regimen is proving actually beneficial, and Mr. Moe is proud of the physical prowess he is beginning to exhibit" (*CE* 1.170).

To Maj.-Gen. Omar Bundy, U.S.A.: FP: *Tryout* 5, No. 1 (January 1919): [3–5] (as by "Ames Dorrance Rowley"). Bundy (1861–1940) was commander of the 6th and 7th Army Corps from July to October 1918. The utterance attributed to him on the occasion about which HPL is writing—"Retreat? Hell, no!"—was later discovered to be apocryphal (see *New York Times* [25 May 1919]: 3). In ll. 47–48 HPL refers to England's defeat of France at Quebec (1759), the US's defeat of Spain in the Battle of Manila Bay (1898), the US's defeat of Mexico (1846) at Monterey, CA (then the capital of Mexican California), and England's defeat of France at Agincourt (1415) during the Hundred Years' War.

To Miss Beryl Hoyt: FP: *Justice* (February 1927): 3. The identity of Miss Hoyt or her parents is unknown.

To Mistress Sophia Simple, Queen of the Cinema: TMS (JHL), dated August 1917; FP: *United Amateur* 19, No. 2 (November 1919): 34 (as by "L. Theobald, Jun."). A response to Rheinhart Kleiner's "To a Movie Star," printed on the same page of the *United Amateur* (see Appendix 2). The references in l. 16 are to the celebrated actresses Margaret "Peg" Woffington (1720–1760) and Fanny Kemble (1809–1893).

To Mr. Baldwin . . .: AMS (JHL), dated 29 September 1723 [i.e., 1923]; FP: *S*. The identity of Baldwin has not been determined. HPL makes reference in 1922 to "the fatuous complacency of a [David Van] Bush or a Baldwin" (*SL* 1.178). This might refer to John Osman Baldwin, an amateur poet from Ohio whose work HPL repeatedly criticised in DPC for various technical lapses. For "Tityrus" (l. 5), see note on "To Delia, Avoiding Damon."

To Mr. Finlay . . .: AMS, TMS (JHL); FP: *Phantagraph* 6, No. 1 (May 1937); rpt. *Weird Tales* 30, No. 1 (July 1937): 17. HPL had come into contact with the artist Virgil Finlay (1914–1971) in late 1936; the poem appears to have been written in the course of HPL's letter to him of 30 November 1936. "The Faceless God" had appeared in *Weird Tales* for May 1936; Finlay's illustration for it has been called perhaps the best work of art to appear in the magazine.

To Mr. Galpin: TMS (JHL); FP: *Tryout* 7, No. 9 (December 1921): [16–17] (as by "L. Theobald, Jun.").

To Mr. Hoag: FP: *Tryout* 7, No. 1 (February 1921): [15] (as by "Ward Phillips"); rpt. *Troy* [NY] *Times* (10 February 1921) (as "On His Ninetieth Birthday: February 10, 1921: (To Jonathan Hoag of Greenwich)"); in *The Poetical Works of Jonathan E. Hoag*, ed. H. P. Lovecraft (New York: [Privately printed,] 1923), 65–66.

To Mr. Hoag: FP: *Tryout* 8, No. 11 (November 1923): [13–14] (as "To J. E. Hoag, Esq.: On His Ninetyecond [*sic*] Birthday, Feb. 10, 1293 [*sic*]"; as by "L. Theobald, Jun."); rpt. *The Poetical Works of Jonathan E. Hoag*, ed. H. P Lovecraft (New York: [Privately printed,] 1923), 67. For "Dionondawa" (l. 2), see note on "Ad Scribam." "Hoosick" (l. 39) refers to the Hoosick (now Hoosic) River, a tributary of the Hudson that runs just north of the city of Troy.

To Mr. Hoag: Text derived from a letter to Edwin Baird, 3 February 1924 (TMS, JHL); FP: *Troy* [NY] *Times* (9 February 1924) (as "His Ninety-third Birthday: To Jonathan Hoag of Greenwich—A Poem to the Poet—February 10th Anniversary"); rpt. *Pegasus* No. [3] (July 1924): 33.

To Mr. Hoag: Text derived from a letter to Annie E. Phillips Gamwell, 10 February 1925 (AMS, JHL); FP: *Troy* [NY] *Times* (10 February 1925) (as "To Jonathan Hoag of Greenwich: Upon His Ninety-fourth Birthday, February 10, 1925"); rpt. *Tryout* 9, No. 12 (March 1925): [3–4]. For the nickname "Scriba" (l. 8), see note on "Ad Scribam."

To Mr. Kleiner . . . : AMS (JHL), dated 10 April 1918; FP: *S*. The volume in question is probably *The Poetical Works of Joseph Addison; Gay's Fables; and Somerville's Chase*, ed. George Gilfillan (Edinburgh: J. Nichol, 1859 or 1866; or Edinburgh: W. P. Nimmo, 1869; or London: Cassell, Potter, & Galpin, 1875). The volume was not found in HPL's library upon his death, hence is not included in *LL*. The poets in question are Joseph Addison (1672–1719), better known for his prose contributions in the *Spectator* (1711–14), which he founded with Richard Steele; John Gay (1685–1732), best known for *The Beggar's Opera* (1728) and his *Fables* (1727–38); and William Somerville (1675–1742), best known for *The Chace* (1735), a poem about hunting. "Nicolini" (l. 40) was the stage name of Nicolo Grimaldi (1673–1732), an Italian mezzo-soprano (castrato). "The Dean" (l. 41) is Jonathan Swift (1667–1745), British satirist and Dean of St. Patrick's, Dublin. The *Guardian* (l. 41) was a periodical published in 1713 and founded by Richard Steele.

To Mr. Lockhart, on His Poetry: FP: *Tryout* 3, No. 4 (March 1917): [7–8]; rpt. *Little Budget of Knowledge and Nonsense* 1, No. 3 (June 1917): 35–36 (as "To Mr. Lockhart, of Milbank, South Dakota, U.S.A., on His Poetry"); also published in a South Dakota newspaper (presumably in Lockhart's hometown of Milbank), but only a clipping of this has been seen. Lockhart was the subject of a biographical sketch by HPL ("Little Journeys to the Homes of Prominent Amateurs: II," *United Amateur*, October 1915 [*CE* 1.78–80]; as by "El Imparcial"); see also the essay "More *Chain Lightning*" (*United Official Quarterly*, October 1915; *CE* 5.17–19), in which Lockhart's temperance efforts are praised. "Riley" (l. 40) refers to James Whitcomb Riley (1849–1916), the Indiana poet who had gained popularity for his homespun verse, much of it in dialect.

To Mr. Munroe . . .: AMS (JHL), dated 1 January 1914; FP: *Fossil* No. 2271 (July 1979): 4 (as "To My Old Friend Chester Pierce Munroe, on His Instructive and Entertaining Geographical Treatise on Switzerland"); also in *S.* Chester Pierce Munroe was one of HPL's boyhood friends, who had by this time settled in Asheville, NC. Helvetia (l. 2) was a name coined in the 17th century by the Swiss as the personification of their country, derived from the term Helvetii, which the Romans used to designate a Gaulish tribe in the Swiss Plateau. Tycho (l. 10) is a prominent crater on the moon. "Bernard's hospice" (l. 13) refers to a travellers' hospice on the St. Bernard Pass in the Western Alps, between Switzerland and Italy; it was established by Bernard of Menthon (923–1008). "Calvin" (l. 34) refers to John Calvin (1509–1564), who was born in France and died in Geneva. "Gibbon" (l. 36) refers to British historian Edward Gibbon (1737–1794), who lived in Lausanne from 1753 to 1758.

To Mr. Terhune, on His Historical Fiction: AMS (JHL); FP: *H. P Lovecraft in the Argosy*, ed. S. T. Joshi (West Warwick, RI: Necronomicon Press, 1994), 40. Undated, but probably written around 1911–13. The reference is to Albert Payson Terhune (1872–1942), later to become the creator of the fictional dog Lad (transformed in film and television as Lassie), but at this time a prolific writer of historical novels and tales being published in the *Argosy*. HPL's letter in the *Argosy* for November 1911 specifically praises Terhune: "His stories are of surpassing merit, in selection of historical period, development of plot, and purity of English." Line 14 of the poem is copied from l. 12 of "The Members of the Men's Club . . ." "The daring Smith" (l. 21) refers to Captain John Smith (1580–1631), the British explorer who helped to settle Virginia in 1607. It is not clear which work by Terhune featured Smith. The references to George Washington (l. 25) and Valley Forge (l. 34) may refer to Terhune's *The Spy of Valley Forge* (*Argosy*, October 1909–February 1910).

To Phillis: FP: *Tryout* 6, No. 1 (January 1920): [10] (as by "L. Theobald, Jun."). "Randolph St. John" is HPL's affectionate name for Rheinhart Kleiner (a take-off of Henry St John, Viscount Bolingbroke [1678–1751], a polished Georgian literary and political figure). The poem is in reply to Kleiner's "To Miriam" (see Appendix 2).

To Rheinhart Kleiner, Esq.: TMS (JHL), dated "Jany. 1723" [i.e., 1923]; FP: *Tryout* 8, No. 7 (April 1923): [11–14] (as by "Lewis Theobald, Jun."). Most of Kleiner's voluminous poetry remains uncollected, as it appeared in only a few slim volumes late in his life: *Metrical Moments* (1937), *To the Shade of Elia* (1940), *Nine Sonnets* (1940), *A Trilogy of Sonnets for Edwin B. Hill* (1943), and *Pegasus in Pasture* (1943). "Zoilus" (l. 5) refers to a Greek critic in the 4th century B.C.E. who gained notoriety for criticising the Homeric poems. HPL, Alfred Galpin, and James F. Morton used "Zoilus" as a joint pseudonym for a column titled "The Vivisector," published in the *Wolverine* (1921–23). "Macer" (l. 7) is a poet cited in Ovid's *Tristia* 4.10.44. "Nash" (l. 61) refers to Richard Nash (1674–1761), referred to as "Beau Nash," a celebrated dandy who became Master of Ceremonies at the spa town of Bath. "Cham" (l. 80) is a variant spelling of *khan*, referring to the sovereign prince of Tartary. The novelist Tobias Smollett coined the phrase "Great Cham of Literature" in reference to Samuel Johnson.

To Rhodocleia . . .: See "To the Incomparable Clorinda." Signed "A. Saphead." On the variants supplied for the colour of Rhodocleia's hair HPL comments: "Note the adaptability of the above gem to all varieties of maidens. True, the[re] is no alternative for blue eyes—but in poesy all eyes are blue."

To S. S. L.—October 17, 1920: AMS (with title "Oct, 17, 1920"), TMS (JHL); FP: *WW*. Another poem to HPL's mother, presumably written to accompany a box of chocolates.

To Saccharissa . . .: See "To the Incomparable Clorinda." Signed "Edvardus Softleius" (a Latinisation of HPL's pseudonym "Edward Softly").

To Saml. Loveman, Gent.: AMS (JHL), dated 1722 [i.e. 1922]; FP: *S*. Presumably dates to the summer of 1922, when Loveman became chairman of the Bureau of Critics of the NAPA. HPL and James F. Morton had filled similar positions in the UAPA. Later in 1922 HPL himself took over the presidency of the NAPA upon the resignation of William J. Dowdell.

To Saml Loveman Esq.: AMS (JHL), signed "Grandpa Theobald"; FP: *S*. Probably written in January 1925, soon after "To Samuel Loveman, Esq., upon Adorning His Room for His Birthday," when HPL, after furnishing Loveman's apartment in Brooklyn Heights with a bookcase and other items, suggested that the Kalem Club give Loveman some *"writing materials,* which the poet sadly lacked" (*LNY* 105). The mention of "Bacchanal" (l. 15) may allude to Loveman's poem "Bacchanale" (*United Amateur*, May 1924), dedicated to HPL.

To Samuel Loveman, Esq., upon Adorning His Room for His Birthday: AMS (JHL), signed "L. Theobald, Jun." Presumably written on or before 14 January 1925, the date when HPL and the other members of the Kalem Club bought a variety of gifts for Loveman (including a bookcase) and decorated his room as a surprise on his thirty-eighth birthday. See HPL to Lillian D. Clark, 22 January 1925 (*LNY* 104–5).

To Samuel Loveman, Esquire, on His Poetry and Drama . . .: FP: *Dowdell's Bearcat* 4, No. 5 (December 1915): [7]. HPL was not personally acquainted with Loveman (1887–1976) at this time, but had encountered his poetry in a variety of old amateur journals. HPL began a correspondence with him in 1917, and they became close associates, especially during HPL's New York period (1924–26). Loveman's collected poetry and other works have now been gathered in *Out of the Immortal Night: Selected Works of Samuel Loveman* (New York: Hippocampus Press, 2004).

To the A.H.S.P.C. . . . [1]: AMS (JHL); FP: *S*. The reference is to the *Pippin*, an amateur journal produced by the Appleton High School Press Club in Appleton, WI. The poem must date to sometime after December 1918, for an issue of the *Pippin* (2, No. 1) of that date appears to be the subject of the poem. Aside from Maurice W. Moe (l. 15), who presumably advised the press club in his function as an English teacher, and Alfred Galpin (l. 18), the contributors cited by HPL are unidentified, with the exception of Eleanor Evans Wing (l. 25), who may have been one of Galpin's sweethearts.

To the A.H.S.P.C. . . . [2]: AMS (JHL); FP: *S*. See "To the A.H.S PC. . . . [1]" above. The poem must date to sometime after May 1919, for an issue of the *Pippin* (2, No. 2) of that date under the editorship of HPL's colleague Alfred Galpin appears to be the subject of the poem. Aside from Eleanor Evans Wing (l. 26) and Margaret Abraham (l. 53), the contributors cited by HPL are unidentified.

To the Arcadian: AMS (JHL), signed "L. Theobald Jun."; FP: *S*. The poem is written on a discarded draft of a letter dated 18 October 1917. It is addressed to Winifred Virginia Jordan (1876–1959), an amateur colleague of HPL's; some have conjectured that the two had a romance of sorts in the period 1918–21. HPL published several poems by her in his *Conservative*. At the bottom of the ms. is the note: "Sent to W. V. J., V. McG [Verna McGeoch], J. R. [John Russell], S. L. [Samuel Loveman]." For "Morven" (l. 10), see note on "Content." Jordan wrote a poem, "In Morven's Mead," published in HPL's *Conservative* (April 1916). Codrus (l. 17) is a poetaster cited in Virgil's *Eclogues* 5.11. The "Stagirite" (l. 18) is the philosopher Aristotle (384–322 B.C.E.), born in Stageira, Greece. For Bavius (l. 21) and Maevius (l. 23), see note on "Unda; or, The Bride of the Sea."

To the Eighth of November: AMS (JHL), as "To Nov. 8," dated 13 December 1918; FP: *Tryout* 5, No. 11 (November 1919): [13] (as by "Archibald Maynwaring"). For the pseudonym see note on "Wisdom"; for Galpin and Abraham see note on "Damon and Delia, a Pastoral" (1918).

To the Incomparable Clorinda: Text derived from a letter to Alfred Galpin, 21 August 1918 (TLS, JHL; *AG* 29). This and the following four poems are all derived from this letter, in which HPL copies a poem by Rheinhart Kleiner written in a lady's album in July 1917 and states that at that time he "dashed off" five items of the sort to prove that he could write them. They all bear comic pseudonyms; this one is signed "Kleinhart Reiner."

To the Late John H. Fowler, Esq.: FP: *Scot* No. 7 (March 1916): 25–26. HPL comments on Fowler in DPC (January 1915): "'The Haunted Forest', a poem by J. H. Fowler [in *Outward Bound*, January 1915], is almost Poe-like in its grimly fantastic quality. We can excuse rather indefinite metre when we consider the admirably created atmosphere, the weird harmony of the lines, the judicious use of alliteration, and the apt selection of words. 'Bird-shunned', as applied to the thickets of the forest, is a particularly graphic epithet. Mr. Fowler is to be congratulated upon his glowing imagination and poetical powers" (*CE* 1.19–20). There is no clue as to the illness Fowler apparently suffered. "Waller" (l. 32) refers to British poet Edmund Waller (1606–1687), best known for the smoothness and elegance of his rhyming couplets.

To the Members of the Pin-Feathers . . .: FP: *Pinfeather* 1, No. 1 (November 1914): 34. The Pinfeathers were an all-female group of amateur journalists at Rocky Mount, NC, under the aegis of Anne Vyne Tillery (later Anne Tillery Renshaw). L. 26 had been used in two previous HPL poems; see note on "To Mr. Terhune, on His Historical Fiction."

To the Members of the United Amateur Press Association . . .: FP: *Providence Amateur* 1, No. 1 (June 1915): [1–3]. HPL became associated with the Providence Amateur Press Club in late 1914, at the urging of Edward H. Cole; he remained affiliated with it until the summer of 1916, when it disbanded. The poem describes several members of the club: Victor L. Basinet, John T. Dunn, Edmond L. Shehan, Caroline Miller, Fred A. Byland. "Mistress Kern" is unidentified (although one Eugene M. Kern was listed as a member), as is "Reilly." See also "Providence Amateur Press Club (Deceased) to the Athenaeum Club of Journalism" (1916). The reference in l. 22 is to Edward H. Cole, a member of the NAPA and a friend of HPL who had urged HPL to work with the press club.

To the Nurses of the Red Cross: AMS (JHL) (as by "Lewis Theobald, Jun."). FP: *S*. HPL dates the poem to 1917 at *SL* 1.59.

To the Recipient of This Volume: FP: *To the Recipient of This Volume* (Madison, WI: Strange Co., 1988). Dated 7 December 1915. The poem, included in an unidentified book, is addressed to Ira A. Cole (1883–?), an amateur journalist living in Kansas and editor of the *Plainsman,* where HPL's poem "On the Cowboys of the West" appeared. Cole (no relation to HPL's Boston friend Edward H. Cole) participated in the Kleicomolo, a round-robin correspondence group with Rheinhart Kleiner, Maurice W. Moe, and HPL. HPL published some of Cole's poems in the *Conservative.*

To the Rev. James Pyke: FP: *United Official Quarterly* 1, No. 1 (November 1914): 1. Pyke was for a time a neighbour of HPL's, residing next door to HPL's home at 598 Angell St. HPL states that his family "had always known" Pyke and his aged mother, but upon HPL's move to 598 Angell Street in 1904 he became more closely associated with Pyke (*SL* 1.9); by January 1916, however, Pyke had moved to East Providence (see "Introducing Mr. James Pyke," *Conservative,* January 1916; *CE* 1.97). HPL published some of Pyke's poetry in his *Conservative.* In a "Note" following the poem HPL writes:

> Rev. Mr. Pyke is an elderly retired Congregational minister who possesses poetical talent of the very highest order, but who, from native modesty, declines absolutely to have his works published. He has written verse since early boyhood, and has in manuscript enough lyrics, dramas, epics, sacred poems, and the like to fill about ten good-sized volumes.

In DPC (January 1915) HPL states: "Our own masterpiece is in full Queen Anne style with carefully balanced lines and strictly measured quantities. We have succeeded in producing eighteen lines without a single original statement or truly poetical image. Rev. Mr. Pyke, the object of the verses, deserves a better encomiast" (*CE* 1.21).

To "The Scribblers": AMS (JHL); FP: *S.* The poem dates to the summer of 1915. See "Extracts from H. P. Lovecraft's Letters to G. W. Macauley" (1938): "The next letter [was] dated August 1st [1915] . . . 'I have mailed [Edward F.] Daas a 52-line poem on his 'Scribblers Club' . . ." *Lovecraft Studies* No. 3 (Fall 1980): 15–16. Daas, residing in Milwaukee, WI, was Official Editor of the UAPA in 1913–14, during which time he invited HPL to join amateur journalism. The epigraph from Horace is from *Ars Poetica* 38–41: "All ye that write, material select / That suits your powers, and see you long reflect / What weight your shoulders will refuse to bear, / What strength they have in them. Choose, then, with care, / A fitting subject well within your border, / You'll ne'er lack matter nor a lucid order" (tr. Alexander Murison).

To Two Epgephi: AMS (JHL), signed "Epgephos" (in Greek); FP: *S.* Presumably written in the fall of 1920. The two Epgephi in question are W. Paul Cook and George Julian Houtain.

To Xanthippe . . .: AMS (JHL); FP: *S.* "Xanthippe" (the wife of Socrates) was a nickname for HPL's wife, Sonia H. Greene. Sonia explains: "The nomenclature of 'Socrates and Xantippe' [*sic*] was originated by me because as time marched on and our correspondence became more intimate, I either *saw* in Howard or endowed him with a Socratic wisdom and genius, so that in a jocular vein I subscribed myself as Xantippe" (Sonia H. Davis, *The Private Life of H. P. Lovecraft* [West Warwick, RI: Necronomicon Press, 1992], 27). Unfortunately, Xanthippe was known in antiquity as a shrew.

To Zara: TMS (JHL), dated 31 August 1922, signed "L. Theobald, Jun."; FP: *SL* 1.164–65 (in a letter to Maurice W. Moe misdated January 1922 [actually probably September 1922]). The poem is also found in a letter to Lillian D. Clark, 13–16 September 1922 (AMS, JHL), where HPL says he wrote the poem as a joke on Alfred Galpin, who thought very little of HPL's poetry. HPL and Long claimed that they had found the poem in the possession of an ancient Maine man who had known Poe; Galpin, according to HPL, did not swallow this but thought the poem to have been copied from some standard author, when in fact "it was thrown together spoofingly in fifteen minutes' time by one whom Galpin deems anything but a poet!" Sarah Longhurst appears to be fictitious.

Tryout's Lament for the Vanished Spider: FP: *Tryout* 6, No. 1 (January 1920): [18–19] (as by "Edward Softly"). "Tryout" is of course Charles W. "Tryout" Smith (1851–1948) of Haverhill, MA. HPL met him for the first time in June 1921 (see *SL* 1.139–41). The references in ll. 17f. are as follows: When the prophet Muhammad was fleeing soldiers attempting to capture him, he hid in a cave; God subsequently caused a spider to weave a web across the opening of the cave, leading the soldiers to doubt that he could be inside. The legendary Scottish king Robert the Bruce, routed by the English army on six occasions, took refuge in a cave. There he saw a spider attempting to weave a web, during which she tried and failed six times to cast her thread from one side of the cave to the other; but she succeeded on the seventh try, thereby heartening Robert to try once more to defeat the English. Frederick the Great of Prussia, about to drink a cup of hot chococate, saw that a spider had fallen into the cup from the ceiling. He requested another cup. Later it was determined that the cook had poisoned the original cup of chocolate.

Unda; or, The Bride of the Sea: FP: *Providence Amateur* 1, No. 2 (February 1916): 14–16 (as "The Bride of the Sea"; as by "Lewis Theobald, Jr."); rpt. *O-Wash-Ta-Nong* 2, No. 3 (December 1937): [10–11] (with epilogue; as part of "Perverted Poesie or Modern Metre"); *Phantagraph* 9, No. 2 (August 1941): 1–3 (as "The Bride of the Sea"). Text derived from a letter to Rheinhart Kleiner, 30 September 1915 (AHT; *RK* 22–24); epilogue from *O-Wash-Ta-Nong*. The poem is a parody of the sentimental ballads of Thomas Moore and other late Romantics. The epigraph is HPL's Latin coinage ("I, a dog, sing the moon"), another parody of Virgil's *Aeneid*. "Maevius Bavianus" is HPL's invented name derived from two poetasters, Maevius and Bavius, mentioned in Virgil's *Eclogues* (3.90). The epilogue was probably written around 1917, the apparent time when three other poems were gathered into "Perverted Poesie." In DPC (April 1916) HPL remarks: "In 'The Bride of the Sea', Mr. Lewis Theobald, Jr., presents a rather weird piece of romantic sentimentality of the sort afforded by bards of the early nineteenth century. The metre is regular, and no flagrant violations of grammatical or rhetorical precepts are to be discerned, yet the whole effort lacks clearness, dignity, inspiration, and poetic spontaneity" (*CE* 1.106).

The Unknown: Text derived from a letter to Clark Ashton Smith, 30 July 1923 (AMS, private collection), published in facsimile in *LS* No. 25 (Fall 1991): 36; FP: *Conservative* 2, No. 3 (October 1916): [12] (as by "Elizabeth Berkeley" [pseud. of Winifred Virginia Jackson]). This poem (along with "The Peace Advocate") appeared under Jackson's pseudonym "in an effort to mystify the [amateur] public by having widely dissimilar work from the same nominal hand" (HPL to the Gallomo, 12 September 1923; *AG* 108). In DPC (March 1917) HPL continues the charade: "Another bit of sinister psychology in verse is 'The Unknown', by Elizabeth Berkeley. Mrs. Berkeley's style is less restrained than that of Mrs. Jordan, and presents a picture of stark, meaningless horror, the like of which is not often seen in the amateur press. It is difficult to pass upon the actual merit of so peculiar a production, but we will venture the opinion that the use of italics, or heavy-faced type, is not desirable. The author should be able to bring out all needed emphasis by words, not printer's devices" (*CE* 1.140). See also Donald R. Burleson, "Lovecraft's 'The Unknown': A Sort of Runic Rhyme," *LS* No. 26 (Spring 1992): 19–21.

Ver Rusticum: FP: [Providence] *Evening News* 52, No. 92 (1 April 1918): 4; rpt. *National Enquirer* 6, No.7 (16 May 1918): 2; *Voice from the Mountains* (July 1918): 27–29. The poem (the Latin title means "Rustic Spring") is a revision of "Rural Springtime" (AMS, JHL; dated 25 March 1918). The epigraph from Virgil is from *Georgics* 1.217–18: "When with his golden Horns, in full Carier, / The Bull beats down the Barriers of the Year, / And Argo and the Dog forsake the Northern Sphere" (tr. John Dryden), referring to the constellations Taurus and Argo Navis and the star Sirius (= Canis, the dog-star) in the constellation Canis Major. In DPC (September 1918) HPL notes: "This is what one member of our bureau calls 'Pope-try', and has little to recommend it save a certain smoothness of metre and fidelity to the classical models" (*CE* 1.208). (The term "Pope-try" was devised by Alfred Galpin, who wrote another section of DPC for September 1918 and used the term in a long discussion of HPL's "The Poe-et's Nightmare.")

Verses Designed to Be Sent . . .: AMS (JHL); FP: *S*. A quite early poem, perhaps dating to as early as 1905. "Munroe" is either Chester Pierce or Harold Bateman Munroe, two brothers who were both close boyhood friends of HPL.

Veteropinguis Redivivus: AMS, TMS (JHL); FP: *S*. A series of poems on Edith Miniter's cats and dogs. Although HPL visited Miniter and her companion Evanore Beebe in Wilbraham in the summer of 1928 (see "Mrs. Miniter— Estimates and Recollections" [1934]; *CE* 1.378–86), the poems probably date to the summer of 1930, for that is when HPL learned of the death of Old Fats, the cat cited in the first poem (see HPL to Lillian D. Clark, 12 June 1930; AMS, JHL). The title of the series is HPL's Latin coinage ("Old Fats Returns"). Pettie was Old Fats' brother, while Little Bit was his sister; Donald (or Donnie) was a "boisterous and clumsy puppy in the process of growing to Gargantuan proportions" (*CE* 1.383); the Prince of Wails and Tardee were brothers of Old Fats; Printer (a corruption of Prince of Orange) was the "dean of the felidae"; Stitchie was "an aged collie of aristocratic lineage and impeccable courtesy." In No. 5, l. 8, "oöphagous" means "snake-eating." No. 8 is found in a letter to Helm C. Spink, 13 August 1930 (AMS, JHL).

The Voice: FP: *Linnet* (August 1920): [1–2].

The Volunteer: FP: [Providence] *Evening News* 52, No. 45 (1 February 1918): 7; rpt. *National Enquirer* 5, No. 19 (7 February 1918): 6; *Tryout* 4, No. 4 (April 1918): [11–13] (as by "Ames Dorrance Rowley"). Also rpt. (according to a note in the *United Amateur* 17, No. 5 [May 1918]) in the *Appleton* [WI] *Post*, the *St. Petersburg* [FL] *Evening Independent*, and *Trench and Camp* (military paper at San Antonio, TX); these appearances have not been located. The most reprinted poem in HPL's lifetime. The *Appleton Post* appearance was probably arranged by Maurice W. Moe; that in the St. Petersburg newspaper probably by John Russell. The poem by Sergeant Hayes P. Miller is "Only a Volunteer" (see Appendix 2). In the notes to *WW* (171) Tom Collins quotes some ms. notes written by HPL on a tearsheet of the *Tryout* appearance: "An experiment in modern metre & manner by a devotee of the past. / An answer to a poem in the same metre by Serg. H. R. [*sic*] Miller, 17th Aero Squadron—published in Jan. 1918. / The original poem by Sgt. Miller—'Only a Volunteer'—complained of the fashion in which volunteers—real men—were neglected, whilst the skulking drafted herds were coddled & petted. / It is not my fault that my 'military service' was with pen rather than sword. I did my best to enlist in the R.I. Nat'l Guard in the Spring of 1917, but could not pass the physical examination. Have been in execrable health—nervous trouble—since the age of two or three." For HPL's attempted enlistment in May–June 1917 see *SL* 1.45–49.

Waste Paper: AMS (JHL), signed "Humphry Littlewit, Gent."; FP: unknown; rpt. *WW;* see also the edition in *Books at Brown* 26 (1978): 48–52, with accompanying commentary by Barton L. St. Armand and John H. Stanley. The poem is of course a tart satire on T. S. Eliot's *The Waste Land*, which HPL read in the *Dial* (November 1922). HPL had condemned the poem in the essay "Rudis Indigestaque Moles" (*Conservative*, March 1923; *CE* 2.63–65). This poem presumably dates to late 1922 or early 1923. HPL comments that it was published in "the newspaper" (*SL* 4.159), but it has not been found in any of the Providence newspapers of the period. For the Greek epigraph see note on "The Poe-et's Nightmare." The lines of the poem are derived from a bewildering variety of sources—exactly the "practically meaningless collection of phrases, learned allusions, quotations, slang, and scraps in general" that HPL in "Rudis . . ." took *The Waste Land* to be. Ll. 9–10 and 12–16 are autobiographical reflections of HPL's childhood. In ll. 11–12 HPL refers to the songs "In the Evening by the Moonlight" (1880) by James A. Bland and "Meet Me Tonight in Dreamland" (1910) by Beth Slater Whitson and Leo Friedman. In l. 17 HPL prints the title of a famous song written by Hughie Cannon in 1902. "When the Whippoorwill Sings, Marguerite" (l. 21) is a 1906 song by J. Fred Helf and C. M. Denison. For "Shantih, shantih, shantih" (l. 30), see note on "To a Sophisticated Young Gentleman." *Shanty House* (l. 30) was a serial by William Loren Curtiss published in the *All-Story Magazine* (December 1909– April 1910). "Three O'Clock in the Morning" (l. 39) was an immensely popular 1921 song by Dorothy Terriss and Julian Robledo. Ll. 46–47 are quoted from ll. 1–2 of "Invictus" (1875) by William Ernest Henley (1849–1903). L. 54 is the first line of HPL's "Nemesis." L. 57 is the first line of Alexander Pope's translation of Homer's *Iliad* (1715–20). In l. 58 HPL cites Julian Hedworth George Byng, 1st Viscount Byng of Vymy (1862–1935), Governor-General of Canada (1921–26). His ancestor, Admiral John Byng, was courtmartialed and shot on 14 March 1757. The reference in ll. 62–64 may be to an edition of Joseph Miller's *Jests* (first published in 1739), although no American edition published in 1847 has been found. In ll. 80–82 HPL quotes from the song "Only a Message from Home Sweet Home" (1905) by Edmond L. Florant and Carroll Fleming. In ll. 84–85 HPL cites the titles of the songs "In the Shade of the Old Apple Tree" (1905) by Harry Williams and Egbert Van Alstyne and "'Neath the Old Cherry Tree, Sweet Marie" (1907) by Byron G. Harlan. *The Conchologist's First Book* (l. 86) was published in 1839 as by Edgar Allan Poe, but Poe only wrote the preface and introduction and condensed a text originally written by Thomas Wyatt. In l. 92, George Creel (1876–1953) was head of the Committee on Public Education (1917–19), established by President Wilson to drum up support for America's entry into World War I. In l. 99 HPL quotes from Canto 1, l. 1 of Sir Walter Scott's *The Lady of the Lake* (1810). In l. 102, HPL refers simultaneously to the *Double Dealer* (1921–25), an avant-garde literary magazine, and a play (1694) by British playwright William Congreve (1670–1729) (see l. 103). In l. 126 HPL quotes from the first line of Poe's "Ulalume" (1847). In l. 127 HPL alludes to an inscription on the tomb of the Revolutionary War soldier John Hereford, "Stranger, pause and shed a tear." In l. 129 HPL quotes from the fourth line of the inscription on Shakespeare's tomb in Stratford-upon-Avon. The "Leonard-Tendler fight" (l. 131) refers to one of two fights by Benny Leonard and Lew Tendler, the first on 27 July 1922 (in which Leonard won on points), and the second on 23 July 1923 (which was won decisively by Leonard). If HPL is referring to the second fight, it would suggest that the poem was written almost a year after *The Waste Land* was published.

(Wet) Dream Song: FP: [Untitled note on amateur journalism], *CE* 1.422 . A parody of amateur poetry, in an attempt to criticise some amateurs' "yen for a sort of fourth-rate, bastard decadence, in which downright incoherence with maundering silliness is fatuously mistaken for some kind of God-help-us Symbolism." HPL claimed that he wrote the poem *currente Corona* ("with my Corona [i.e., typewriter] running"); i.e., composed as HPL was at his typewriter (although the text is a handwritten ms.). Probably written in the mid-1930s.

A Winter Wish: FP: [Providence] *Evening News* 52, No. 19 (2 January 1918): 3 (without subtitle); rpt. *Tryout* 4, No. 2 (February 1918): [3–5].

Wisdom: FP: *Silver Clarion* 3, No. 8 (November 1919): 1–2 (as by "Archibald Maynwaring"); rpt. *National Enquirer* 9, No. 10 (4 December 1919): 3. The pseudonym is probably derived from Arthur Mainwaring, one of the translators of "Garth's Ovid" (1717). The poem was presumably commissioned by John Milton Samples, editor of the *Silver Clarion*, which HPL in "Comment" (*Silver Clarion*, June 1918) referred to as "an able and consistent exponent of that literary mildness and wholesomeness which in the professional world are exemplified by *The Youth's Companion* and the better grade of religious publications" (*CE* 1.198). Samuel Hall Young (1847–1927) was a Presbyterian clergyman who spent much time in Alaska. He published an autobiography, *Hall Young of Alaska, "the Mushing Parson"* (1927). It does not appear as if Young's translation of Job 28 was ever published.

With a Copy of Wilde's Fairy Tales: AMS (JHL), dated July 1920. FP: *S.* The poem was written for Alice M. Hamlet, the amateur associate who had introduced Dunsany's work to HPL. HPL owned a copy of Wilde's fairy tales himself (*LL* #954) and was probably influenced by them in some of his own tales.

The Wood: FP: *Tryout* 11, No. 2 (January 1929): [16] (as by "L. Theobald, Jun."); rpt. *HPL* (Bellville, NJ: Corwin F. Stickney, 1937); *Weird Tales* 32, No. 3 (September 1938): 324. The poem was planned for publication in the *Planeteer* 2, No. 3 (September 1936): 5–6 (ed. Jim Blish), but the issue was never completed; pages containing the poem were, however, printed.

A Year Off: AMS, TMS (JHL), dated 24 July 1925; FP: *Beyond the Wall of Sleep* (1943). Written for a meeting of the Blue Pencil Club for 24 July. HPL remarks of it: "It is worthless—but one can't be other than insipid when such insipid subjects are assigned" (HPL to Lillian D. Clark, 27 July 1925; *LNY* 153). For the phrase "The Golden Road to Samarkand" (l. 31), see note on "[Stanzas on Samarkand]." "Peary" (l. 40) refers to American explorer Robert E. Peary (1856–1920), who claimed to be the first person to reach the North Pole on 6 April 1909.

Fragments

1. Text derived from a letter to John T. Dunn, 16 May 1917 (*Books at Brown* 38–39 [1991–92]: 214), where HPL declares that it is part of his attempt to compose an alliterative poem (a poem in which every word of a given line begins with the same letter). An anonymous poem, "The Siege of Belgrade," had popularised the idea. HPL writes: "My own effort had to do with Belgium's heroic defence at the beginning of the present war, and began something like this: . . . This was written before the fall of Liege [17 August 1914]; when, in my unmilitary ignorance, I fancied the puny forts of Flanders had stemmed the Hunnish tide!" The poem must therefore date to early August 1914.

2. Text derived from the essay "July Skies," [Providence] *Evening News* 47, No. 27 (30 June 1915): 8 (*CE* 3.154). A brief retelling of the myth of Arion.

3. Text derived from the essay "October Skies," [Providence] *Evening News* 47, No. 104 (1 October 1915): 8 (*CE* 3.163). The "winged steed" is presumably Pegasus.

4. AMS (JHL). The handwriting dates the poem to c. 1915.

5. Text derived from a letter to the Kleicomolo, 8 August 1916 (*RK* 37). Will's and Button's were popular London coffeehouses frequented by the literary figures of the early 18th century.

6. Text derived from a letter to Rheinhart Kleiner, 8 November 1917 (*RK* 119–20). HPL provides commentary before each couplet: "I can never think of natural beauty, but in the terms of the eighteenth century. If I see a pleasing prospect of a distant town, I think of it as [first couplet]. If I am struck with some idyllic vistas of tilled land & cottages, I see [second couplet]. If a tangled brake or cluster of trees moves my fancy, I think of [third couplet]."

7. Text derived from the story "Polaris," *Philosopher* 1, No. 1 (December 1920): 3–5. The story was written in the summer of 1918 (see *SL* 1.62–63).

8. Text derived from a letter to Rheinhart Kleiner, 14 July 1918 (*RK* 146). The opening lines of an *"absolutely conventional"* pastoral designed "as a sort of symbol of my defiance of modern criticks." No more of the poem was ever written.

9. AMS (JHL). Written on the same page as "[On Prohibition]" (1919), hence presumably dates to around that time. There is no indication of the subject of the poem.

10. Text derived from "The Nameless City" (written January 1921), first published in the *Wolverine* No. 11 (November 1921): 3–15. The celebrated couplet is identified in this story as an "unexplainable couplet" written by "Abdul Alhazred the mad poet." The couplet was also included in all printings of "The Call of Cthulhu" (written summer 1926), first published in *Weird Tales* 11, No. 2 (February 1928): 157–78, 287. There it is explicitly stated that the couplet

appeared in the *Necronomicon*. See Dan Clore, "Overdetermination and Enigma in Alhazred's Cryptic Couplet," *LS* No. 34 (Spring 1996): 11–13.

11. Text derived from "The Defence Remains Open!" (April 1921), where HPL maintains it is part of a poem he once wrote; but the lines do not derive from any known poem.

12. Text derived from a letter to Anne Tillery Renshaw (14 June 1922; AHT). The reference is to Leo Fritter, who in an article in the *Woodbee* (October 1921) had criticised HPL's editorship of the *United Amateur*. The poem appears to suggest that HPL prevailed in his feud with Fritter, but in fact he lost his bid for re-election as Official Editor of the UAPA in the election held in July 1922, Fritter himself winning the position.

13. An inscription in a copy of *The Poetical Works of Jonathan E. Hoag* (New York: Privately printed, 1923), edited by HPL. On the flyleaf, just above the poem, is written: "For / Mr. & Mrs. Clifford M. Eddy, Jr., / From / H P Lovecraft / Octr. 14, 1923."

14. Text derived from a letter to Lillian D. Clark, 17–18 November 1924 (AMS, JHL), describing the woods of the Wissahickon Valley west of Philadelphia.

15. AMS (JHL). Apparently written to accompany a gift of Walter Pater's *The Renaissance* to HPL's wife, Sonia, hence the poem presumably dates to 1922–26.

16. Text derived from a letter to James F. Morton, 27 December 1925 (*JFM* 89); a rough draft also appears on the envelope. It was sent to acknowledge Edith Miniter's Christmas gift of "a calendar of birchbark, with leaves, red berries, evergreens, fungi, moss, & miniature pine cones glued & sewed on."

17. AMS (JHL), signed "L. Theobald, Jun." Written on the same envelope as No. 16.

18. Text derived from a letter to Lillian D. Clark, 14–19 November 1925 (AMS, JHL), giving an example of the internal double rhyme used in "October" [2].

19. Text derived from a letter to Frank Belknap Long, 6 July 1927 (AHT), as part of a description of Newport, RI.

20. Text derived from a letter to James F. Morton, 28 February 1928 (AHT; *JFM* 158).

21. Text derived from a letter to Frank Belknap Long, 1 September 1929 (AMS, JHL), describing a visit to Foster, RI, the town whence many of HPL's maternal ancestors originated.

22. Text derived from a letter to James F. Morton, [31 October 1930] (AHT; *JFM* 240). In l. 5, the blanked-out word is "bitches."

23. Text derived from a letter to Fritz Leiber, [25 January 1937] (*SL* 5.387). HPL pretends that this is part of Lewis Theobald's "privately printed English

translation (1711)" of a Latin work by the fictitious poet Valerius Trevirus, *De Noctis Rebus* [On Night-Things] (c. 390 C.E.). The passage in question purports to be a translation of the Latin line *Niger informisque ut numen Averonum Sadoqua*— about Sadoqua (= Tsathoggua), a god worshipped by the ancient Averones (who lived in the province later named Averoigne). Both Tsathoggua and Averoigne were invented by Clark Ashton Smith).

24. AMS (JHL), written on a blank Western Union telegram form.

Appendix 1

A Prayer for Universal Peace. FP: Robert L. Selle, *Apples of Gold in Pictures of Silver* (Louisville, KY: Pentecostal Publishing Company, 1917), 50–53. In a letter to Rheinhart Kleiner, 31 July 1915 (AHT; *RK* 18), HPL states that he revised this poem for Selle; for a portion of the original text, see Appendix 2. Selle, a theologian in Little Rock, AK, was an amateur journalist and also "the author of innumerable popular theological books & hymns" (*RK* 17).

[On the Duke of Leeds.] Found in all publications of "A Reminiscence of Dr. Samuel Johnson," first published in the *United Amateur* 17, No. 2 (November 1917): 21–24 (as by "Humphry Littlewit, Esq."). In the story Littlewit, the first-person narrator, claims that the quatrain is his revision of a poem written "by a Servant to the Duke of *Leeds*" that Samuel Johnson had recited to him as an example of bad verse. In fact, the original lines are found in Boswell's *Life of Johnson* (see Appendix 2).

Mors Omnibus Communis. FP: *Rainbow* No. 1 (October 1921): 8. HPL writes to Rheinhart Kleiner (21 September 1921) that he had "set aside for revision a piece of verse entitled 'Mors Omnibus Communis'. I am told that you advised the inclusion of this piece in the R[ainbow]. If so, why the hell didn't you correct it? It could not stand as it was" (*RK* 216). The title translates to "Death [is] common to all." Sonia's original does not survive.

Alone. Text derived from a letter to Lillian D. Clark, 14–19 November 1925 (AMS, JHL). FP: *Tryout* 10, No. 7 (January 1926): [7]. HPL declares in the letter that "I've just revised a poem for Mr. Hoag, which goes like this: . . ."

Unity. Text derived from a letter to James F. Morton, 18 January 1931 (AHT; *JFM* 280). FP: *SL* 3.275–76. HPL states that Clark Ashton Smith had been tasked with revising a piece of verse whose first line reads "My soul has the arms of an octopus." HPL adds: "I'm helping him out with a provisional version, spun out of my sympathetick understanding of the Eastern Spirit of Universal Oom." Lima is an actual town in northwestern Ohio.

The Dweller. FP: *Fantasy Fan* 1, No. 6 (February 1934): 88. HPL's revision of the poem is inferred by internal evidence. Lumley (1880–1960) had gotten in touch with HPL in 1931, and by all accounts he was incapable of writing verse as polished as this, as gauged by his nearly illiterate original version of "The Diary of Alonzo Typer" (1935).

Dreams of Yith. FP: *Fantasy Fan* 1, No. 11 (July 1934): 170–71 (sonnets I–V); 2, No. 2 (September 1934): 8–9 (sonnets VI–X). HPL discusses the revision of the poems in a letter to Rimel (13 May 1934; AMS, JHL), stating: "Your new series of verses sounds highly interesting, & both Barlow & I went over the enclosed specimen with minute attention & sincere appreciation." Rimel had titled the series "Dreams of Yid," not aware that "yid" is an opprobrious term for a Jew. HPL suggested "Yith," going on to use the term in "The Shadow out of Time" (*DH* 401) and his segment of "The Challenge from Beyond" (1935). In a later letter (1 June 1934) HPL states: "I like these poems exceedingly, & think C A S's corrections were all in the right direction," suggesting that Clark Ashton Smith also lent a hand in the revision of the poems.

[On John Donne.] Text derived from a letter to Lee McBride White, 10 February 1936 (AMS, JHL), published in *Lovecraft Annual* No. 1 (2007): 54. McBride had expressed fondness for Donne and written a poem about him (see Appendix 2). HPL stated: "As an anti-Donnite I fear I can't be of much real help regarding your verses—but I can at least offer a few concrete suggestions . . . ." Neither version of the poem appears to have been published.

The Wanderer's Return. AMS, JHL. FP: *Literary Quarterly* 1, No. 1 (Winter 1937): 5–6 (as "Wander's Return"). HPL states in a letter to Wilson Shepherd, 5 September 1936 (AMS, JHL): "I looked over your new verses with much interest, & believe the idea in them is very clever. As before, I've done a little straightening out & added some marginal notes. Hope you'll like the new version, & that it will get into type some time. [In margin:] I've supplied a new title, & a sort of climactic ending, for the verse." For Shepherd's version, and HPL's marginal comments, see Appendix 2.

Appendix 2

Metamorphoses 1.1–88. Written by P. Ovidius Naso (43 B.C.E.–17? C.E.) and completed around 8 C.E. The poem is in 15 books. For HPL's translation see "Ovid's Metamorphoses."

Our Apology to E. M. W. FP: *Argosy* 77, No. 3 (October 1914): 718. See HPL's "The End of the Jackson War."

Florida. FP: [Providence] *Evening News* 46, No. 26 (18 December 1914): 11. See HPL's "New England."

[Regner Lodbrog's Epicedium.] Both the Latin version and the English prose version are found in Hugh Blair (1718–1800), *A Critical Dissertation on the Poems of Ossian* (London: T. Becket & P. A. De Hondt, 1763), 6–9. The full Latin version consists of 29 stanzas.

A Prayer for Universal Peace. Text derived from a letter to Rheinhart Kleiner, 31 July 1915 (AHT; *RK* 17–18).

To Mary of the Movies. FP: *Motion Picture* 8, No. 4 (May 1915): 121; rpt. *Piper* 1, No. 3 (September 1915): 12. The subject of the poem is, of course, Mary Pickford (1892–1979), who, along with Charlie Chaplin, were the first "movie stars" (see HPL's reply, "To Charlie of the Comics"). In DPC (December 1915) HPL writes: "*The Piper* closes with an original poem by Mr. Kleiner, entitled 'To Mary of the Movies', in whose tuneful lines the author shews all his accustomed sweetness of sentiment, grace of garb, and cleverness of comparison" (*CE* 1.84).

A Prayer for Peace and Justice. FP: [Providence] *Evening News* 46, No. 119 (23 June 1916).

The Modern Business Man to His Love: FP: *Tryout* 2, No. 11 (October 1916): n.p. See "The Nymph's Reply to the Modern Business Man."

His Frank Self-Expression. FP: Paul Shivell, *Stillwater Pastorals and Other Poems* (Boston: Houghton Mifflin, 1915), 67–68. The poem is the seventh of the "Sonnets to H. L. H." HPL quotes the poem in his letter to the Kleicomolo, April 1917 (*RK* 100), after which HPL remarks: "The thing somewhat fatigues me—the fellow thinks too much on himself. I could easily write a sonnet on myself—in fact, I have done so in imitation of Shivell. It is the first sonnet I have ever written, and is probably the last as well; since I am not fond of the gentle pastime of sonneteering." Shivell (1874–1968) was an American poet and author of *Ashes of Roses* (1898) and other volumes. See HPL's "Sonnet on Myself."

To a Movie Star. TMS (JHL), dated August 1917; FP: *United Amateur* 19, No. 2 (November 1919): 34. See HPL's "To Mistress Sophia Simple, Queen of the Cinema."

[On the Duke of Leeds.] Text derived from HPL's "A Reminiscence of Dr. Samuel Johnson" (1917; see Appendix 1 under "[On the Duke of Leeds]"), where the text differs slightly from HPL's source, Boswell's *Life of Johnson* (1791), under the year 1780. Boswell is quoting the recollections of Samuel Johnson's friend Bennet Langton, who noted: "It is very remarkable, that he retained in his memory very slight and trivial, as well as important things. As an instance of this, it seems that an inferiour domestick of the Duke of Leeds had attempted to celebrate his Grace's marriage in such homely rhimes as he could make; and this curious composition having been sung to Dr. Johnson he got it by heart, and used to repeat it in a very pleasant manner." Langton supplies a second stanza: "She shall have all that's fine and fair, / And the best of silk and sattin shall wear; / And ride in a coach to take the air, / And have a house in St. James's-square."

Ruth. FP: *Brooklynite* 9, No. 2 (February 1918): 5. See HPL's "Grace."

Only a Volunteer. FP: *National Enquirer* 5, No. 16 (17 January 1918): 6; rpt. [Providence] *Evening News* (1 February 1918): 7. See HPL's "The Volunteer."

John Oldham: 1653–1683. FP: *United Co-operative* 1, No. 2 (June 1919): 7. See HPL's "John Oldham: A Defence." "Dorset" (l. 2) refers to Charles Sackville, 4th Earl of Dorset (1637–1706), British poet.

To Miriam. FP: *Tryout* 6, No. 1 (January 1920): n.p. See HPL's "To Phillis."

Ethel: Cashier in a Broad Street Buffet. FP: *Tryout* 6, No. 6 (June 1920): [19]. See HPL's "Cindy: Scrub-Lady in a State Street Skyscraper."

Pastorale. FP: *Dial* 71, No. 4 (October 1921): 422; rpt. in Crane's *White Buildings* (1926).

Odes 3.9. The third book of odes by Q. Horatius Flaccus (65–27 B.C.E.) was published, along with the first and second books, around 23 B.C.E. See HPL's translation "The Odes of Horace."

[On John Donne.] Text derived from a letter by HPL to Lee McBride White, 10 February 1936 (AMS, JHL), where HPL has rewritten the poem (see Appendix 1). FP: *Lovecraft Annual* No. 1 (2007): 56–57. In the margin, around ll. 9f., HPL has written: "Don't drag in scientific jargon. Simplicity & directness are what make poetry."

Irony. AMS (JHL). HPL has added several marginal notes. Stanza 1: "*grin*—rather inappropriate." Stanza 2: "avoid repetition of rhyme." Stanza 3: "a little prosaic in wording. Rhyme of *dawn* and *spawned* is false." Stanza 4: "false rhyme—vague development." Stanza 6: "prosaic atmosphere & phraseology." Stanza 7: "prosaic." Stanza 8: "no such word as *askant*. Rhyme absent." Stanza 8: "prosaic & fragmentary—too colloquial."

BIBLIOGRAPHY

I. *Editions of Lovecraft's Poetry*

Beyond the Wall of Sleep. Compiled by August Derleth and Donald Wandrei. Sauk City, WI: Arkham House, 1943. [Contains 30 poems.]

Collected Poems. [Edited by August Derleth.] Sauk City, WI: Arkham House, 1963. New York: Ballantine, 1971 (as *Fungi from Yuggoth and Other Poems*).

The Dark Brotherhood and Other Pieces. Edited by August Derleth. Sauk City, WI: Arkham House, 1966. [Contains *Alfredo; a Tragedy* and 6 poems.]

An Epistle to Francis, Ld. Belknap. Madison, WI: Strange Co., 1987.

*An Epistle to the Rt. Hon*ble *Maurice Winter Moe* . . . Madison, WI: Strange Co., 1987.

The Fantastic Poetry. Edited by S. T. Joshi. West Warwick, RI: Necronomicon Press, 1990, 1993.

Fungi from Yuggoth. [Washington, DC?:] FAPA (Bill Evans), 1943.

HPL. [Edited by Corwin F. Stickney.] [Bellville, NJ: Corwin F. Stickney, 1937.]

Juvenilia: 1895–1905. Edited by S. T. Joshi. West Warwick, RI: Necronomicon Press, 1984. [Contains 8 poems.]

The Lovecraft Collectors Library. Edited by George T. Wetzel. North Tonawanda, NY: SSR Publicatons, 1952–55. 7 vols. [Vols. 3 and 4 contain poetry.]

Medusa: A Portrait. New York: Oliphant Press, 1975.

Medusa and Other Poems. Edited by S. T. Joshi. Mount Olive, NC: Cryptic Publications, 1986.

Saturnalia and Other Poems. Edited by S. T. Joshi. Bloomfield, NJ: Cryptic Publications, 1984.

Something about Cats and Other Pieces. Compiled by August Derleth. Sauk City, WI: Arkham House, 1949. [Contains 11 poems.]

To the Recipient of This Volume. Madison, WI: Strange Co., 1988.

Uncollected Prose and Poetry. Edited by S. T. Joshi and Marc A. Michaud. West Warwick, RI: Necronomicon Press, 1978–82. 3 vols.

A Winter Wish. Edited by Tom Collins. Chapel Hill, NC: Whispers Press, 1977.

The Young Folks' Ulysses. Toronto: Soft Books, 1982.

II. *Other Works*

Joshi, S. T. *I Am Providence: The Life and Times of H. P. Lovecraft.* New York: Hippocampus Press, 2010. 2 vols.

———. *Lovecraft's Library: A Catalogue.* 3rd rev. ed. New York: Hippocampus Press, 2012.

———. "Two Spurious Lovecraft Poems." *CoC* No. 20 (Eastertide 1984): 25–26.

Joshi, S. T., ed. *H. P. Lovecraft: Four Decades of Criticism*. Athens: Ohio University Press, 1980.

Kleiner, Rheinhart. "A Note on Howard P. Lovecraft's Verse." *United Amateur* 18, No. 4 (March 1919): 76. In *RK* 245.

Lovecraft, H. P. *At the Mountains of Madness and Other Novels*. Ed. S. T. Joshi. Sauk City, WI: Arkham House, 1985.

―――. *Collected Essays*. Ed. S. T. Joshi. New York: Hippocampus Press, 2004–06. 5 vols.

―――. *Commonplace Book*. Ed. David E. Schultz. West Warwick, RI: Necronomicon Press, 1987. 2 vols.

―――. *Dagon and Other Macabre Tales*. Ed. S. T. Joshi. Sauk City, WI: Arkham House, 1986.

―――. *The Dunwich Horror and Others*. Ed. S. T. Joshi. Sauk City, WI: Arkham House, 1984.

―――. *Essential Solitude: The Letters of H. P. Lovecraft and August Derleth*. Ed. David E. Schultz and S. T. Joshi. New York: Hippocampus Press, 2008. 2 vols.

―――. *The Horror in the Museum and Other Revisions*. Ed. S. T. Joshi. Sauk City, WI: Arkham House, 1989.

―――. *Letters from New York*. Ed. S. T. Joshi and David E. Schultz. San Francisco: Night Shade Books, 2005.

―――. *Letters to Alfred Galpin*. Ed. S. T. Joshi and David E. Schultz. New York: Hippocampus Press, 2003.

―――. *Letters to James F. Morton*. Ed. David E. Schultz and S. T. Joshi. New York: Hippocampus Press, 2011.

―――. *Letters to Rheinhart Kleiner*. Ed. S. T. Joshi and David E. Schultz. New York: Hippocampus Press, 2005.

―――. *Miscellaneous Writings*. Ed. S. T. Joshi. Sauk City, WI: Arkham House, 1995.

―――. *Mysteries of Time and Spirit: The Letters of H. P. Lovecraft and Donald Wandrei*. Ed. S. T. Joshi and David E. Schultz. San Francisco: Night Shade Books, 2002.

―――. *O Fortunate Floridian: H. P. Lovecraft's Letters to R. H. Barlow*. Ed. S. T. Joshi and David E. Schultz. Tampa, FL: University of Tampa Press, 2007.

―――. *Selected Letters*. Ed. August Derleth, Donald Wandrei, and James Turner. Sauk City, WI: Arkham House, 1965–76. 5 vols.

Scott, Winfield Townley. "Lovecraft as a Poet." In C.52. In Scott's *Exiles and Fabrications*. Garden City, NY: Doubleday, 1961, pp. 73–77 (revised; as "A Parenthesis on Lovecraft as Poet"). In *FDOC* 211–16.

A Chronology of Lovecraft's Poems

[Dates supplied in brackets. Those in *italics* indicate date of publication.]

1897–1902

The Poem of Ulysses, or The Odyssey [8 November 1897]
Ovid's Metamorphoses [1900?]
H. Lovecraft's Attempted Journey betwixt Providence & Fall River on the
    N.Y.N.H. & H.R.R. [1901]
Poemata Minora, Volume II [1902]
    Ode to Selene or Diana
    To the Old Pagan Religion
    On the Ruin of Rome
    To Pan
On the Vanity of Human Ambition
C.S.A. 1861–1865: To the Starry Cross of the SOUTH [1902]

1905–13

De Triumpho Naturae [July 1905]
The Members of the Men's Club of the First Universalist Church of
    Providence, R.I., to Its President, About to Leave for Florida on Account
    of His Health [c. 1908–12]
[To His Mother on Thanksgiving] [30 November 1911]
To Mr. Terhune, on His Historical Fiction [c. 1911–13]
Providence in 2000 A.D. [*4 March 1912*]
New-England Fallen [April 1912]
On the Creation of Niggers [1912]
Fragment on Whitman [c. 1912]
[On Robert Browning] [c. 1912]
On a New-England Village Seen by Moonlight [7 September 1913]
Quinsnicket Park [1913]

1914

To Mr. Munroe, on His Instructive and Entertaining Account of Switzerland [1
    January]
Ad Criticos [January–May?]
Frustra Praemunitus [June?]

De Scriptore Mulieroso [June?]
To General Villa [Summer]
On a Modern Lothario [*July–August*]
The End of the Jackson War [*October*]
To the Members of the Pin-Feathers on the Merits of Their Organisation, and
    of Their New Publication, *The Pinfeather* [*November*]
To the Rev. James Pyke [*November*]
To an Accomplished Young Gentlewoman on Her Birthday, Decr. 2, 1914 [2
    December?]
Regner Lodbrog's Epicedium [c. December]
The Power of Wine: A Satire [c. 8 December]
The Teuton's Battle-Song [c. 17 December]
New England [*18 December*]
Gryphus in Asinum Mutatus [1914?]

1915

To the Members of the United Amateur Press Association from the
    Providence Amateur Press Club [c. 1 January]
March [*March*]
1914 [*March*]
The Simple Speller's Tale [*April*]
[On Slang] [*April*]
An Elegy on Franklin Chase Clark, M.D. [*29 April*]
The Bay-Stater's Policy [*June*]
The Crime of Crimes [19 June 1915]
To "The Scribblers" [July?]
Ye Ballade of Patrick von Flynn [c. 23 August]
The Isaacsonio-Mortoniad [c. 14 September]
On Receiving a Picture of Swans [c. 14 September]
Unda; or, The Bride of the Sea [c. 30 September]
[On "Unda; or, The Bride of the Sea"] [c. 30 September]
To Charlie of the Comics [c. 30 September]
Gems from *In a Minor Key* [*October*]
The State of Poetry [*October*]
The Magazine Poet [*October*]
A Mississippi Autumn [*December*]
On the Cowboys of the West [*December*]
To Samuel Loveman, Esquire, on His Poetry and Drama, Writ in the
    Elizabethan Style [*December*]
To the Recipient of This Volume [7 December]

1916

An American to Mother England [*January*]
The Bookstall [*January*]
A Rural Summer Eve [*January*]
To the Late John H. Fowler, Esq. [*March*]
R. Kleiner, Laureatus, in Heliconem [*April*]
Temperance Song [*Spring*]
Lines on Gen. Robert Edward Lee [c. 18 May]
Content [*June*]
My Lost Love [c. 10 June]
The Beauties of Peace [27 June]
The Smile [July]
Epitaph on yᵉ Letterr Rrr........ [29 August]
The Dead Bookworm [c. 29 August]
[On Phillips Gamwell] [*1 September*]
Inspiration [*October*]
Respite [*October*]
The Rose of England [*October*]
The Unknown [*October*]
Ad Balneum [c. October]
[On Kelso the Poet] [October?]
Providence Amateur Press Club (Deceased) to the Athenaeum Club of
    Journalism [24 November]
Brotherhood [*December*]
Brumalia [*December*]
The Poe-et's Nightmare [1916]

1917

Futurist Art [*January*]
On Receiving a Picture of the Marshes at Ipswich [*January*]
The Rutted Road [*January*]
An Elegy on Phillips Gamwell, Esq. [*5 January*]
Britannia Victura [January]
Lines on Graduation from the R.I. Hospital's School of Nurses [c. 13 January]
Fact and Fancy [*February*]
The Nymph's Reply to the Modern Business Man [*February*]
Pacifist War Song—1917 [*March*]
Percival Lowell [*March*]
To Mr. Lockhart, on His Poetry [*March*]
Spring [April]
A Garden [April]
Sonnet on Myself [April]

April [*24 April*]

Iterum Conjunctae [*May*]

The Peace Advocate [*May*]

To Greece, 1917 [May?]

On Receiving a Picture of yᵉ Towne of Templeton, in the Colonie of
    Massachusetts-Bay, with Mount Monadnock, in New-Hampshire, Shewn in
    the Distance [*June*]

The Poet of Passion [*June*]

Earth and Sky [*July*]

Ode for July Fourth, 1917 [*July*]

On the Death of a Rhyming Critic [*July*]

Prologue to "Fragments from an Hour of Inspiration" by Jonathan E. Hoag
    [*July*]

To M. W. M. [*July*]

To the Incomparable Clorinda [July]

To Saccharissa, Fairest of Her Sex [July]

To Rhodoclia—Peerless among Maidens [July]

To Belinda, Favourite of the Graces [July]

To Heliodora—Sister of Cytheraea [July]

To Mistress Sophia Simple, Queen of the Cinema [August]

Autumn [*November*]

Nemesis [1 November]

Astrophobos [c. 25 November]

An American to the British Flag [*December*]

Lines on the 25th. Anniversary of the *Providence Evening News*, 1892–1917
    [*December*]

Sunset [*December*]

Old Christmas [late 1917]

To the Arcadian [late 1917]

To the Nurses of the Red Cross [1917]

The Introduction [1917?]

A Summer Sunset and Evening [1917?]

1918

A Winter Wish [*2 January*]

Laeta; a Lament [*February*]

To Jonathan E. Hoag, Esq. [*February*]

The Volunteer [*February*]

Ad Britannos—1918 [*April*]

Ver Rusticum [*1 April*]

To Mr. Kleiner, on Receiving from Him the Poetical Works of Addison, Gay,
    and Somerville [10 April]

A Pastoral Tragedy of Appleton, Wisconsin [c. 27 May]
On a Battlefield in Picardy [*30 May*]
Psychopompos: A Tale in Rhyme [late 1917–Summer 1918]
A June Afternoon [*June*]
The Spirit of Summer [*27 June*]
Grace [*July*]
The Link [*July*]
To Alan Seeger [*July*]
August [*August*]
Damon and Delia, a Pastoral [*August*]
Phaeton [*August*]
To Arthur Goodenough, Esq. [20 August]
Hellas [*September*]
To Delia, Avoiding Damon [*September*]
Alfredo; a Tragedy [14 September]
The Eidolon [*October*]
Monos: An Ode [*October*]
Germania—1918 [*November*]
To Col. Linkaby Didd [1 November]
To Alfred Galpin, Esq. [November?]
Ambition [*December*]
A Cycle of Verse [November–December 1918]
    Oceanus
    Clouds
    Mother Earth
To the Eighth of November [13 December]
To the A.H.S.P.C., on Receipt of the Christmas *Pippin* [December?]
The Conscript [1918?]

1919

Greetings [*January*]
Theodore Roosevelt [*January*]
To Maj.-Gen. Omar Bundy, U.S.A. [*January*]
To Jonathan Hoag, Esq. [*February*]
Despair [c. 19 February]
In Memoriam: J. E. T. D. [*March*]
Revelation [*March*]
April Dawn [*10 April*]
Amissa Minerva [*May*]
Damon: A Monody [*May*]
Hylas and Myrrha: A Tale [*May*]
North and South Britons [*May*]

To the A.H.S.P.C., on Receipt of the May *Pippin* [May?]
Helene Hoffman Cole: 1893–1919 [*June*]
John Oldham: A Defence [*June*]
[On Prohibition] [30 June]
Myrrha and Strephon [*July*]
The House [c. 16 July]
Monody on the Late King Alcohol [*August*]
The Pensive Swain [*October*]
The City [*October*]
Oct. 17, 1919 [October]
On Collaboration [20 October]
To Edward John Moreton Drax Plunkett, Eighteenth Baron Dunsany
　　[*November*]
Wisdom [*November*]
Birthday Lines to Margfred Galbraham [November]
The Nightmare Lake [*December*]
Bells [11 December]

1920

January [*January*]
To Phillis [*January*]
Tryout's Lament for the Vanished Spider [*January*]
Ad Scribam [*February*]
On Reading Lord Dunsany's *Book of Wonder* [*March*]
To a Dreamer [25 April]
Cindy: Scrub Lady in a State Street Skyscraper [*June*]
The Poet's Rash Excuse [*July*]
With a Copy of Wilde's Fairy Tales [July]
Ex-Poet's Reply [July?]
To Two Epgephi [July?]
On Religion [*August*]
The Voice [*August*]
On a Grecian Colonnade in a Park [20 August]
The Dream [*September*]
October [1] [*October*]
To S. S. L.—October 17, 1920 [October]
Christmas [*November*]
Theobaldian Aestivation [11 November]
S. S. L.: Christmas 1920 [December?]
On Receiving a Portraiture of Mrs. Berkeley, y^c Poetess [25 December]

1921

The Prophecy of Capys Secundus [11 January]
To a Youth [*February*]
To Mr. Hoag [*February*]
The Pathetick History of Sir Wilful Wildrake [Spring?]
On the Return of Maurice Winter Moe, Esq., to the Pedagogical Profession
    [*June*]
Medusa: A Portrait [29 November]
To Mr. Galpin [*December*]
Sir Thomas Tryout [*December*]

1922

On a Poet's Ninety-first Birthday [*10 February*]
Simplicity: A Poem [c. 18 May]
To Saml: Loveman, Gent. [Summer?]
Plaster-All [August?]
To Zara [31 August]
To Damon [November?]
Waste Paper [late 1922? early 1923?]

1923

To Rheinhart Kleiner, Esq. [January]
Chloris and Damon [January]
To Mr. Hoag [February?]
To Endymion [April?]
The Feast [*May*]
[On Marblehead] [10 July]
To Mr. Baldwin, on Receiving a Picture of Him in a Rural Bower [29
    September]
Lines for Poets' Night at the Scribblers' Club [October?]
[On a Scene in Rural Rhode Island] [8 November]
Damon and Lycë [13 December]

1924

To Mr. Hoag [c. 3 February]
[On the Pyramids] [c. February]
[Stanzas on Samarkand I–III] [February–March]
[On Rheinhart Kleiner Being Hit by an Automobile] [c. 1 August]
Providence [26 September]
[On *The Thing in the Woods* by Harper Williams] [c. 29 November]
Solstice [25 December]

1925

To Samuel Loveman, Esq., upon Adorning His Room for His Birthday [c. 14 January]
To Saml Loveman Esq. [January]
To George Kirk, Esq. [18 January]
My Favourite Character [31 January]
[On the Double-R Coffee House] [1 February]
To Mr. Hoag [c. 10 February]
The Cats [15 February]
To Xanthippe, on Her Birthday—March 16, 1925 [March]
Primavera [*April*]
[To Frank Belknap Long on His Birthday] [April?]
A Year Off [24 July]
To an Infant [26 August]
[On a Politician] [c. 24–27 October]
[On a Room for Rent] [c. 24–27 October]
October [2] [30 October]
To George Willard Kirk, Gent., of Chelsea-Village, in New-York, upon His Birthday, Novr. 25, 1925 [24 November]
[On *Old Grimes* by Albert Gorton Greene] [December]
Festival [December]

1926

To Jonathan Hoag [*10 February*]
Hallowe'en in a Suburb [*March*]
In Memoriam: Oscar Incoul Verelst of Manhattan: 1920–1926 [c. 28 June]
The Return [*December*]
Εἰς Σφίγγην [December]

1927

Hedone [3 January]
To Miss Beryl Hoyt [*February*]
To Jonathan E. Hoag, Esq. [February?]
[On J. F. Roy Erford] [18 June]
[On Ambrose Bierce] [c. June]
[On Cheating the Post Office] [c. 14 August]
[On Newport, Rhode Island] [17 September]
The Absent Leader [12 October]
Ave atque Vale [18 October]

1928

To a Sophisticated Young Gentleman [15 December]

1929

The Wood [*January*]
An Epistle to the Rt. Honble Maurice Winter Moe, Esq. [July]
[Stanzas on Samarkand IV] [8 November]
Lines upon the Magnates of the Pulp [November]
The Outpost [26 November]
The Ancient Track [26 November]
The Messenger [30 November]
The East India Brick Row [12 December]
Fungi from Yuggoth [27 December 1929–4 January 1930] ["Recapture" written
    November 1929]

1930

Veteropinguis Redivivus [Summer 1930?]

1931

To a Young Poet in Dunedin [c. 29 May]
On an Unspoil'd Rural Prospect [30 August]

1934

Bouts Rimés [23 May]
Beyond Zimbabwe
The White Elephant
[Anthem of the Kappa Alpha Tau] [c. 7 August]
Edith Miniter [10 September]
[Little Sam Perkins] [c. 17 September]

1935

[Metrical Example] [27 February]
Dead Passion's Flame [Summer]
Arcadia [Summer]
Lullaby for the Dionne Quintuplets [Summer]

1936

The Odes of Horace: Book III, ix [22 January]
In a Sequester'd Providence Churchyard Where Once Poe Walk'd [8 August]
To Mr. Finlay, upon His Drawing for Mr. Bloch's Tale, "The Faceless God" [c.
    30 November]

To Clark Ashton Smith, Esq., upon His Phantastick Tales, Verses, Pictures,
    and Sculptures [c. 11 December]

n.d.

The Decline and Fall of a Man of the World
Dirge of the Doomed
[Epigrams]
Gaudeamus
The Greatest Law
Life's Mystery
On Mr. L. Phillips Howard's Profound Poem Entitled "Life's Mystery"
Nathicana
On an Accomplished Young Linguist
"The Poetical Punch" Pushed from His Pedestal
The Road to Ruin
Saturnalia
Sonnet Study
Sors Poetae
[To a Cat]
Verses Designed to Be Sent by a Friend of the Author to His Brother-in-Law
    on New Year's Day
(Wet) Dream Song
[Christmas Greetings]

INDEX OF TITLES

Index of First Lines

CPSIA information can be obtained
at www.ICGtesting.com
Printed in the USA
BVOW04s2035300717
490282BV00002B/9/P